AF607861

Collected Works of Christian M. I. M. Matthiessen
Volume 1

Systemic Functional Linguistics
Part 1

Christian M. I. M. Matthiessen
Edited by Kazuhiro Teruya, Canzhong Wu and Diana Slade

Collected Works of Christian M. I. M. Matthiessen

Editors

Kazuhiro Teruya
The Hong Kong Polytechnic University

Canzhong Wu
Independent scholar

Diana Slade
Australian National University

The series is about the nature, the functions and the structure of human language seen from a number of points of view within the framework of contemporary scientific thought. It covers about 35 years of work by one of the world's leading scholars in the field, Prof. Christian M. I. M. Matthiessen.

The series of volumes in the Collected Works of Christian M. I. M. Matthiessen are organized into a number of distinct topics. However, they all reinforce each other, and together constitute a coherent, body of theoretical and descriptive work.

Each volume consists of a series of chapters written by Matthiessen with few co-authored chapters that are included so as to present Matthiessen's whole intellectual enterprise. Each volume also contains at least one new article written specifically for each volume. These reinforce the insights presented in each volume and further update the cutting edge nature of the collective works.

Christian Matthiessen taught and held visiting positions at various universities and research institutes in Australia, Germany, Japan, China, the US, and Hong Kong. He is currently Chair Professor in Language Science at The Hong Kong Polytechnic University. Matthiessen has broad linguistic expertise as a theoretician, descriptivist, educationist, and multilingual practitioner of enormous scope and importance, coupled with him being a prolific writer throughout his career.

Collected Works of Christian M. I. M. Matthiessen
Volume 1

Systemic Functional Linguistics

Part 1

Christian M. I. M. Matthiessen
Edited by Kazuhiro Teruya, Canzhong Wu and Diana Slade

SHEFFIELD UK BRISTOL CT

Published by Equinox Publishing Ltd.

UK: Office 415, The Workstation, 15 Paternoster Row, Sheffield, South Yorkshire S1 2BX
USA: ISD, 70 Enterprise Drive, Bristol, CT 06010

www.equinoxpub.com

First published 2021

British Library Cataloguing-in-Publication Data

A catalogue record for this book is available from the British Library.

ISBN-13 978 1 78179 708 2 (hardback)
978 1 78179 709 9 (ePDF)

Library of Congress Cataloging-in-Publication Data
Names: Matthiessen, Christian M. I. M., author. | Teruya, Kazuhiro, editor. | Wu, Canzhong, editor. | Slade, Diana, editor.
Title: The collected works of Christian M. I. M. Matthiessen / Christian M. I. M. Matthiessen ; edited by Kazuhiro Teruya, Canzhong Wu and Diana Slade.
Description: Sheffield, UK ; Bristol, CT : Equinox Publishing Ltd, 2021- | Includes bibliographical references and index.
Identifiers: LCCN 2018049651 (print) | LCCN 2018061652 (ebook) | ISBN 9781781797099 (ePDF) | ISBN 9781781797082 (vol. 1 : hardback) | ISBN 9781781797099 (vol. 1 : ePDF)
Subjects: LCSH: Functionalism (Linguistics) | Systemic grammar. | Structural linguistics.
Classification: LCC P147 (ebook) | LCC P147 .M38 2019 (print) | DDC 410.1/833--dc23
LC record available at https://lccn.loc.gov/2018049651

Typeset by S.J.I. Services, New Delhi, India

Contents

List of figures

List of tables

Acknowledgements

We are grateful to the original publishers for permission to reprint the articles and chapters in this volume. Original publication details are provided below.

'Lexicogrammar in systemic functional linguistics: Descriptive and theoretical developments in the "IFG" tradition since the 1970s' from Hasan Ruqaiya, Christian Matthiessen and Jonathan J. Webster (eds.), *Continuing Discourse on Language: A Functional Perspective Volume 2*, London and Oakville: Equinox, 2007, pp. 765–858. Copyright © Hasan Ruqaiya, Christian Matthiessen, Jonathan Webster and contributors. Reproduced with permission of Equinox Publishing.

'The "architecture" of language according to systemic functional theory: Developments since the 1970s' from Hasan Ruqaiya, Christian Matthiessen and Jonathan Webster (eds.), *Continuing Discourse on Language: A Functional Perspective Volume 2*, London and Oakville: Equinox, 2007, pp. 505–561. Copyright © Hasan Ruqaiya, Christian Matthiessen, Jonathan J. Webster and contributors. Reproduced with permission of Equinox Publishing.

'Ideas and new directions' from M. A. K. Halliday and Jonathan Webster (eds.), *Continuum Companion to Systemic Functional Linguistics*, London: Continuum, 2009, pp. 12–58. Copyright © M. A. K. Halliday, Jonathan J. Webster and contributors. Reproduced with permission of Continuum Publishing.

'Systemic functional linguistics developing', *Annual Review of Functional Linguistics, Volume 2*, Beijing: Higher Education Press, 2010, pp. 8–63. Reprinted with permission of Higher Education Press.

'Halliday on language' from Jonathan Webster (ed.) *The Bloomsbury Companion to M.A.K. Halliday*, London and New York: Bloomsbury Academic, 2014, pp. 137–202. Copyright © Jonathan J. Webster and contributors. Reproduced with permission of Bloomsbury Academic.

Foreword

I got to know Christian Matthiessen at a conference in Toronto (Canada) in 1983, where he presented a text generation architecture for what subsequently became one of the world's leading text generation systems (PENMAN/NIGEL). I have since then heard talks by him at international conferences in Australia, Asia, Europe and the USA, in my memory approximately 50 talks, almost all of them invited plenary presentations. The depth and breadth of his thinking about language manifested in these contributions is exceptional, ranging from questions of the grammar and semantics of English and other languages, through issues in translation, in multimodal communication and in computational linguistics to fundamentals of linguistic and semiotic methodology. It is this breadth, together with a very consistent high level of quality, which constitutes one aspect of Matthiessen's scholarly achievements. Regrettably, too many of his ideas to date have been difficult to access, have not been placed in their most coherent thematic context or have remained unpublished altogether. This makes a representative collection of these works timely and highly welcome for the linguistic community.

Those of Matthiessen's publications which have been accessible previously are milestones in their fields: His 1991 *Systemic Linguistics and Text Generation: Experiences from Japanese and English* (co-authored with John Bateman) is a very rare, and possibly even unique, attempt at discussing the mutual influence of architectures of a linguistic theory and of text generation on a level which allows mapping these two areas onto each other in an interdisciplinary spirit. His monumental 1,000-page *Lexicogrammatical Cartography: English Systems* (1995) gives a comprehensive account of the grammar of English within the framework of Systemic Functional Grammar. This comprehensiveness, coupled with theoretical depth and consistency, is hardly matched by any other account that I am aware of. Matthiessen's *Working with Functional Grammar* (co-authored with Clare Painter and Jim Martin in 1997) shows his outstanding ability to translate a highly complex theoretical exposition (Halliday's Functional Grammar) into comprehensive operationalizations and with a superb level of didactic ability. His 1999 *Construing Experience through Meaning: A Language-based Approach to Cognition* (co-authored with M. A. K. Halliday) is again one of the few comprehensive accounts of a stratum of English, this time its ideational semantics – and, indeed, a methodologically comprehensive framework for modelling the semantics of any language, and quite clearly with implications for other semiotic systems. This book is also proof of his very unusual capability of linking arguments from linguistics, language typology, semiotics, and philosophy together and of giving them a degree of operationalization which makes a successful (and extremely rare) connection between a humanities-based framework on the one hand, and more technologically-based enterprises, in this case computational text generation, on the other. And more recently, his monumental revision of Halliday's *Introduction to Functional Grammar*, published by Routledge in 2014, is another rare and comprehensive account of English grammar in full breadth and depth.

I know many of Matthiessen's papers in addition to the book-length publications referred to above. Not a single one of them is superficial or otherwise lacking in quality, and many are among the intellectual highlights of the discipline: as examples I would like to mention *The structure of discourse and subordination* (co-authored with S. Thompson 1989), *The environments of translation* (in 2001), or *Register in the round: Diversity in a unified theory of register analysis* (1993), *Register in the round: Registerial cartography* 2015). His numerous papers on language typology and translation provide clear evidence for his ability to analyse languages from a range of language families with an excellent understanding, even if his emphasis may be on English as an object of description some of the time. The works collected in the present eight-volume-series bring together some of these papers, but additionally many of his publications which have fed into, or have been inspired by, the above mentioned works of excellence.

Matthiessen's achievements are outstanding in their combination of a consistent high quality with an unusual breadth of coverage, both of these based on the willingness – and more importantly the ability – for interdisciplinary work in areas across humanistic linguistics and computational linguistics. None of these achievements would be possible, I believe, without his unique and creative mastery of a comprehensive theory of language which helps him to bring all these strands together in a coherent view on language. Matthiessen, in my view, will be seen as one of the outstanding linguists of our time.

In addition to all of the above mentioned qualities, Matthiessen is a dedicated teacher and supervisor, admired by his many students and colleagues around the world. The linguistic community world-wide will be delighted to finally have the chance to access his thoughts on language and linguistics in a coherent and easily accessible way.

We have so far had too little opportunity to access the entire breadth and depth of Matthiessen's intellectual achievements – but this will now be remedied by his collected works.

If it is permitted, I'd like to end my introductory remarks on a personal note: I have had the privilege of sharing some of the world's beautiful sights and sounds with Christian, including Mullholland Drive in Los Angeles, Sydney Harbour and the Hawksbury River, Hong Kong's Victoria Peak, but also Brazil's Samba and Portugal's Fado. He has been a wonderful guide to all of these wonders, to be surpassed only by his guidance into the wonders of language and communication, freely offered to anyone interested in language.

Erich Steiner

Editorial introduction

We are very excited and honoured to present the collected works of Professor Christian M. I. M. Matthiessen. This brings to fruition a project that Michael Halliday had urged Kazuhiro Teruya to undertake in order to bring together work that he thought was scattered in many places, often somewhat inaccessible, and to present it in an accessible and thematic format. In this way, Michael overruled the objection that Christian might be too "young" to be the focus of such a project, viewing the collected work only as the first round. Tragically, Michael passed away before even the first volume had been published; but he was delighted that our old friends at Equinox had undertaken the project and that it was well underway.

The collected works of eight volumes is a representation of Christian's ground-breaking contribution to both linguistics in general and more specifically to Systemic Functional Linguistics. His prolific body of research, spanning over forty years, traces his intellectual enterprise as a world class general linguist, and systemic functional linguist, a semiotician, an appliable linguist and an educationalist. This first volume presents his works as a theoretician, descriptivist and analyst. The breadth and depth of Christian's scholarship and his original contribution are clearly evident in these works.

We have known Christian for more than 30 years – as a colleague, a PhD supervisor, research collaborator and a close friend. For each of us there is no-one who has made a stronger contribution to our intellectual development. We feel very privileged to have had Christian as a PhD supervisor not only for his wealth of knowledge but for his tireless and generous socio-semiotic and academic support that continue to this day.

Through his research, his teachings, his supervision and mentoring he has influenced thousands of people around the world. He has supervised over thirty PhD students and more than 100 masters and honours research students from different countries. Christian's intellectual influence, however, has reached far beyond those of his students and the institutional contexts where he has engaged in teaching, supervision and research. He has travelled extensively, giving invited plenaries, courses, consultations and interviews not only to those who have the resources but also to many colleagues and students who lacked the means to study abroad or to attend international seminars and conferences. He tirelessly extended his academic support intellectually and economically.

Christian's humanity, compassion and humility are integral to the influence and depth of his intellectual endeavour.

We are very grateful to Professor Erich Steiner, Professor of Linguistics and Translation Studies, Universität des Saarlandes, Saarbrucken, Germany for contributing the foreword to Christian's collected works. Erich has known Christian for nearly 40 years, has been co-plenary speaker at many conferences over the years and as he says in his foreword has been fortunate enough to have spent extended times with him in many beautiful locations around the world.

We feel very honoured to have been with Erich, Christian, Michael Halliday and Ruqaiya Hasan at some of these wonderful locations. And we all knew at the time – but even more clearly now – that we were in the presence of four great linguists who have been responsible for reshaping our understanding of language and how it shapes social and organizational life. The 8 volumes of Christian's collected works we believe will give a voice to their collective contributions to our understanding of language as well as further the paths that Christian has generously laid out over the course of his academic career.

As Michael Halliday said just before he died in April 2018 in relation to these works: *This collected works of Christian's is a truly great event in 21st century functional linguistics – and indeed to 21st century linguistics in general. I congratulate those who made this possible.*

Outline of Volume 1: *Systemic Functional Linguistics – Part 1*[1]

Volume 1 provides the foundation for the series of collected works of Christian Matthiessen. It includes chapters that serve as either an introduction of Systemic Functional Linguistics (SFL) or a summary of, or further advancement of SFL. It is concerned with the nature of SFL as (meta)theory, as a framework and as a school of linguistics.

Chapter 1 describes the development of accounts of lexicogrammar in SFL by locating all systemic functional contributions since around 1970 along the semiotic dimensions of the hierarchy of stratification, the spectrum of metafunctions and the cline of instantiation. It provides a rare insight into the descriptive and theoretical developments inside SFL in which these systemic functional accounts have evolved but also outside SFL where the influence of the description presented in IFG has influenced the landscape of the changing range of other approaches to lexicogrammar.

Chapter 2 models the systemic functional architecture of language in context holistically, characterizing further the developmental aspects of the key theoretical dimensions discussed in Chapter 1. It adds new semiotic dimensions such as semogenesis and the ordered typology of systems to give a more multifaceted view of language in context towards new directions in SFL. The organizational principles characteristic of different local and global dimensions that are presented in this chapter make it possible to locate all phenomena under investigation along a number of dimensions as language is modelled relationally and dimensionally.

Chapter 3 complements the discussions of Chapter 1 and Chapter 2 by exploring domains of investigation covered in those chapters in terms of new ideas and developments in SFL. It focuses in particular on registerial ranges within different fields of activity, viewing SFL as an open dynamic system serving as a resource for reflection – reflecting on language and also on other semiotic systems for analysing and theorizing language, and as a resource for language in action – intervening in social and semiotic processes, for developing plans of activity and for implementing models.

Chapter 4 tracks the development of SFL, its different starting points and points of diversification, and identifies its frontiers and gaps in the expansive multidimensional collective coverage of investigation into language in context. It also discusses the multidisciplinary character of SFL, analysing various developmental engagements within and outside the discipline of linguistics and applying SWOT analysis to identify the continued development of SFL. The Appendix offers a survey of a comprehensive overview of the frontiers and active research areas up till 2009.

Chapter 5 describes Halliday's remarkable contribution to our understanding of language, detailing his central theoretical concepts all of which flow from Halliday's conception of language as a resource – as meaning potential. Christian's meticulous account is partly chronological and partly as he calls it logical – describing Halliday's paradigmatic base for the modelling of language developed to bring out its organization as a meaning-making resource. This chapter documents Halliday's key ideas which are embraced in Matthiessen's overarching ideas about the science of language.

The last chapter is a new chapter written specifically for this volume. It intends to lay a foundation for other volumes to follow by presenting the architecture of phonology according to SFL that illuminates the relationship of semioticization between phonology and phonetics. The focus is theoretical rather than descriptive to address the importance of the organization of SFL as the metalanguage used in specifying such an architecture modelled as a sounding resource. The chapter offers an illustration of the distinction between theory and theoretical representation where representations are explicitly distinguished from metalanguage that serves as a resource of engaging with language.

Kazuhiro Teruya, Diana Slade and Canzhong Wu

Note

1 Special thanks to Elaine Espindola, Guo Xinyang, Kaela Zhang and Rolando Quijano, who helped compiling the articles collected in this volume.

Introduction

1 Preamble

About five years ago, Michael Halliday suggested to Kazuhiro Teruya that something should be done about collecting my work into a series of thematic volumes; one consideration he raised was that my papers were dispersed across different channels of publication and not very accessible. Kazu then raised the suggestion with me, and while it seemed to me that it was too early to think about such a project, the idea grew increasingly interesting and attractive, with further support and encouragement from Michael, so Kazu approached one of our top Systemic Functional Publishers, Equinox, and they agreed with certain additional suggestions, including the addition of one new chapter to each volume; and he assembled a wonderful editorial team with complementary talents and long experience of working together: in addition to Kazu himself, Di Slade and Wu Canzhong. I am immensely grateful to them for undertaking this project – one that, as our deputy president commented, also shows real devotion to the discipline.

As we began to discuss the details of this publication project, grouping my publications thematically, I was reminded of the many discussions that Michael and I had had over the years about the compilation of his own collected works – a plan that became a real project when Jonathan Webster took editorial charge of it, turning it into 10 thematic volumes + 1 additional volume, 'Halliday in the 21st century'. (I hope more volumes of my collected works will follow this first instalment of eight volumes, but I can promise with a fair degree of certainty that there won't be one of Matthiessen in the 22nd century.)

From Michael, I learned the huge value of looking back on one's own work, exploring continuities, expanding contexts, cumulative insights, adjustments and changes, and thematic motifs. I remember he remarked to me that he had realized how much of his writing had been in response to invitations and requests, and to a lesser extent that has also been true of my own work, starting in the late 1980s/

early 1990s. Like Michael, I like being given challenging tasks, ones that I might not have thought of myself but which will allow me to move a bit further in one direction or another, reading up on some area in the process.

But one central motif all along has been Systemic Functional Linguistics (SFL) – wherever I have ventured, SFL has been my main resource. And I was extremely fortunate to work with Michael on formal projects, on our own projects, and on publications, starting in 1980, a period spanning almost four decades. It was natural, stimulating and wonderful for me to be in a position of trying to expand SFL in general and his contributions in particular – an intellectual programme for more than one lifetime.

My first publications were concerned with the application of SFL to the computational modelling of language, in particular to text generation by computer, in a succession of projects directed by Bill Mann at ISI/USC. This will appear in Volume 2, which is a continuation of the theme begun in Volume 1, viz. the focus on Systemic Functional Linguistics. One reason for placing it here is that those of us involved in the projects also approached the computational work as an exercise not only in implementation, but also in modelling and theorizing; I still think that SFL in general can benefit greatly from engaging with the task of explicit modelling (with a view to implementation): it provides a context for working out the implications of the theory and checking whether everything hangs together. This is the kind of orientation towards engineering that Michael Halliday has mentioned on various occasions (as an alternative to an orientation towards philosophy).[1] While I would have liked to continue along these explicit modelling lines, this computational linguistic strand in my publications has been inactive for quite a while. Professor Michio Sugeno involved me in his laboratory research at the Brain Science Division of the RIKEN Institute in Tokyo, 2000–2005 – together with Michael Halliday, David Butt, Kazuhiro Teruya and Wu Canzhong from Sydney; but somehow I have not yet produced publications based on this very rich experience.

But in general, once I started working on, and publishing in, a certain area, I have kept going in this area (see Table 1), perhaps being something of a linguist of all trades and master of none. Michael told me many years ago that his was the last generation of linguists who could (aspire to) be generalists – and he himself was certainly a generalist; his contributions cover a very wide spectrum, in fact a spectrum of doing linguistics he expanded considerably through his own work. This kind of coverage is not possible any longer, not even for linguists of my generation, starting around 30 years after Michael (Michael would have had his first paper, co-authored with Jeffrey Ellis, in 1951, and my first paper appeared in 1981). But it has always been my inclination – at least to ensure that strands of research in different areas, or even subdisciplines of 'language sciences' keep in dialogic contact and impinge on one another. (Kazu, Canzhong and I produced our 2008 multlingual studies paper partly because we had observed how different communities of scholars undertaking such studies were not on the whole able to benefit from an ongoing dialogue and sharing frameworks and results.)

So while it is no longer possible to be a true generalist, we need scholars who attempt to draw overview maps at least, and I can think of no better framework than SFL for this work because it is holistic in theoretical conception and values comprehensive descriptions; and collectively the SFL community of students and scholars around the world are generalists, as can be seen from survey publications. This trait of collective generalism is, I think, absolutely essential (cf. David Bohm's points from the 1970s and 1980s, taken up by systemic functionalists, about the danger of the fragmentation of knowledge), and it can be supported now not only by a more widespread conception of network modelling in different sciences but also by the 'social' tools developed for collective scholarship.

This leaves open the question of where this scholarship is based institutionally, in universities and other institutions of research and scholarship. In the 'Introduction: a personal perspective' to the first volume of his collected works, Michael Halliday comments on disciplines:

> I have never really thriven in a discipline-based structure of knowledge. It was a feature of my century – the late and rather unlamented twentieth, perhaps mercifully short in Eric Hobsbawm's conception of it – that it began by erecting walls between the disciplines, and it is proving difficult to demolish these walls now that they have come to be constraining rather than enabling. They had been enabling to start with, at least for the newly founded social (and ever newer semiotic) sciences; sociologists, psychologists and linguists had to be able to lock each other out while sorting out and investigating their own chartered domains.
>
> So in the mid-century many linguists sturdily proclaimed the independence and autonomy of the discipline of linguistics, and one could sympathize with their anxiety, because language was everybody's business and there would always be outsiders looking over their shoulders and telling them how to do their job – or, more usually, telling them they were simply wasting their time.

In the second half of the twentieth century, the discipline of linguistics first became dominated by 'Chomskyan' linguistics in many places, with applied linguistics becoming increasingly institutionally separate from linguistics, in the sense theoretical linguistics. While SFL was in dialogue with applied linguistics and was taken up in many applied linguistic activities, it was appliable linguistics rather than applied linguistics: it included a holistic theory of language designed to be appliable. However, in theoretical linguistics, SFL tended to be marginalized, even when Chomskyan linguistics became less dominant and was challenged by linguists of a more functional orientation.

But now the situation is arguably changing, partly because technological developments are making it increasingly easy to open up access to data – in the form of corpora growing in size, but also in the form of techniques of scanning the brain and other parts of the body relevant to linguistic processing – and to manage and analyse large volumes of data. But also because the intellectual environment has changed in interesting ways.

In linguistics, there is now more acceptance of different approaches, perhaps partly in the context of 'eclecticism', and a number of Michael Halliday's pioneering ideas that were not accepted in the 1960s have now been arrived at in a number of other traditions (e.g. the grounding of linguistic accounts in authentic data – corpora of texts, the continuous relationship between grammar and lexis, the probabilistic nature of language, the centrality of intonation, and even the functional organization of language). Some of these developments have been given labels, like 'unification-based' theories of language and 'usage-based' approaches to language.

Outside linguistics, there are now many more resonances with Michael Halliday's systemic functional thinking, including the emphasis on 'big data', the growing importance in different areas of network thinking, the renewed interest in complex adaptive systems, and of course the central place given to information and knowledge, paving the way for a reminder that both are constructed out of language in the first instance. In the management of universities in many places around the world, there is now greater emphasis placed on 'impact' and also on 'translational research', both of which have been core concerns in Halliday's appliable linguistics from the start, including the value given to social accountability.

At the same time, SFL has survived, and even prospered, on the margins of 'mainstream' linguistics – not only in linguistics departments, but also in a rich range of other departments, including language departments, translation and interpreting departments, education departments, computer science departments – and this has been consistent with the outward-looking nature and transdisciplinarity of SFL all along. Still, it is very clear that Michael Halliday was ahead of his time from the start, and that his work can only now really be appreciated and grow in a new way.

Table 1 Key publications by area and decade

Volume	Area	1970s	1980s	1990s	2000s	2010s
1–2	SFL	(1979), *Hallidayan Linguistics* MS		(1992), "Interpreting the textual metafunction"	(2006b) "Systemic Probabilities", (2007a) "IFG tradition", (2007b) "SFL architecture"; Matthiessen & Halliday (2009) "First Step"	Matthiessen, Teruya & Lam (2010) "Key Terms"; (2015a) "Halliday's Conception of Language"
	Computational SFL		(1983b), (1984) (1987a), (1988a,b) etc.	Matthiessen & Bateman (1991) [book], Bateman *et al.* (1991), "Multilingual system networks", Bateman, Matthiessen & Zeng (1999), "Multilingual system networks"; Matthiessen *et al.* (1998a) Multimodal text generation		
3	Description of Akan		(1987a,b) MS			Mwinlaaru, Matthiessen & Akerejola (2018), "Mood in West Africa"
	Description of English			Matthiessen (1991a), "The grammar of semiosis" Matthiessen (1995b) [book], (1996) "Tense", (1992) "Theme", (1999) "Transitivity"	(2002a) "Clause complexing"; (2007c) "Lexicogrammar of emotion and attitude"; (2009a) "Collocation"	(2015c) "English Lexicogrammar through Text"; (2014b) "Extending the description of process type"
4	Discourse Analysis		Matthiessen & Thompson (1988)	Mann, Matthiessen & Thompson (1992)	(2002b) Lexicogrammatical logogenesis	(2014a) "Appliable Discourse Analysis"; Matthiessen & Teruya (2015) "Realization of Rhetorical Relations"

Volume	Area	1970s	1980s	1990s	2000s	2010s
	Multimodal Studies			Matthiessen *et al.* (1998b)	(2006b) "Page"; (2009c) "Register"	
5	Construing Experience			Halliday & Matthiessen (1999)	[Halliday & Matthiessen (2006)]	
6	Multilingual Studies: Systemic Representa-tion			Bateman *et al.* (1991), Bateman, Matthiessen & Zeng (1999), "Multilingual system networks"		(2018) "Multilingual Meaning Potential"
	Translation				(2001) "Environments of translation"	(2014c) "Choice"; Kim & Matthiessen (2015) "Textual Metafunction"
	Typology & Comparison				(2004a); Teruya et al. (2007) "Typology of mood"	Teruya & Matthiessen (2015) "Halliday and typology"; Mwinlaaru, Matthiessen & Akerejola (2018), "Mood in West Africa"
7	Register Studies			(1993b) "Register in the Round"		(2015b) "Registerial Cartography"; Matthiessen & Teruya (2015) "Registerial Hybridity"
	Verbal Art					
	Institutional Linguistics					
8	Educational Linguistics				(2006a)	
	Evolution of Language					

2 Overview of volumes

The eight volumes are organized thematically rather than chronologically (for an indication of the chronology of my publications, see Table 1), to wit:

- Volume 1. Systemic Functional Linguistics, Part 1
- Volume 2. Systemic Functional Linguistics, Part 2
- Volume 3. Description of English and Akan
- Volume 4. Discourse Analysis and Multisemiotic/Multimodal Studies
- Volume 5. Construing Experience and Multimodal Studies
- Volume 6. Multilingual Studies (including translation studies, language comparison and language typology)
- Volume 7. Register Studies, Verbal Art and Institutional Linguistics (including healthcare communication)
- Volume 8. Educational Linguistics and Evolution of Language

Let me describe each volume briefly in turn.

Volume 1, Systemic Functional Linguistics, Part 1, provides the foundation for the whole series of collected works, and includes chapters that serve as introduction to, and summaries of, Systemic Functional Linguistics. It is concerned with the nature of SFL as theory, as framework and as a school of linguistics. It includes overviews of the organization or 'architecture' of language according to SFL and of the lexicogrammatical subsystem of language, and of Halliday's conception of language as a resource for making meaning. It is also concerned with the history and development of SFL. The new chapter written for Volume 1 addresses the theme underpinning all the chapters in the volume: the architecture of language as seen through and manifested in the system of phonology. It thus also provides an introduction to systemic phonology, an area that is of crucial importance but remains under-represented in the systemic functional literature.

Volume 2, Systemic Functional Linguistics, Part 2, builds on the foundation developed in Volume 1, focusing on theoretically guided modelling of language in computational linguistic systems, drawing on the experience with the Penman text generation system and the development of the Nigel grammar, and on key aspects of the theory such as metafunction, rank (the conception of 'morphology'), indeterminacy and probability. This volume also includes a treatment of systemic functional meta-theory – the theory of the nature and appliability of theory. The new chapter written for Volume 2 extends the discussion of the challenge of theorizing language to the challenge of modelling language for applications, thus paying attention to the appliability of systemic functional linguistics.

Volume 3, Description of English and Akan. Volumes 1 and 2 are concerned with the theorizing and modelling of language, and they thus provide the resources for the description of particular languages – which is the topic of Volume 3. In this volume, certain systems of English that are outlined in the comprehensive overviews of Matthiessen (1995) [*Lexicogrammatical cartography: English systems*] and Halliday and Matthiessen (2014) [Halliday's *Introduction to functional grammar*] are explored in more descriptive detail, including the systems of TAXIS and LOGICO-SEMANTIC TYPE, THEME, TRANSITIVITY, TENSE, and MODAL ASSESSMENT (which includes appraisal). The volume also contains my previously unpublished sketch of Akan, a Niger-Congo language of the Kwa branch spoken in Ghana – including my work on Akan phonology, which demonstrates the descriptive power of systemic functional phonology, thus providing an illustration of the theoretical framework sketched in the final chapter of Volume 1. The new chapter written for Volume 3 is concerned precisely with the descriptive power of systemic functional theory as a way of meeting the challenge of describing languages. It continues the theme of cartography from Volume 1, and shows how the process of description is a process of mapping the recourses of particular languages.

Volume 4, Discourse Analysis and Multisemiotic/Multimodal Studies. While Volume 3 is concerned with the description of the meaning potential of a particular language, Volume 4 shifts the focus to the analysis of texts instantiating this potential with the help of the description of the potential. It also includes accounts developed specifically for the purpose of text analysis – Rhetorical Structure Theory, developed by William C. Mann, Christian Matthiessen and Sandra A. Thompson in the 1980s, and then revised and integrated by me as an account of the logico-semantic resources of English for the rhetorical-relational organization of text. The new chapter written for Volume 4 deals with the challenge of analysing language, adding an account of discursive cartography to the account of descriptive cartography in Volume 3. This involves a discussion of the relationship between the analysis of texts and of the description of the systems that texts instantiate, and of different tools and techniques used in the analysis of texts, including corpus analysis tools.

Volume 5, Construing Experience and Multimodal Studies, focuses on one of the three modes of meaning identified by Halliday's theory of metafunction – the ideational mode of meaning. This mode of meaning is that of construal: the ideational metafunction provides speakers with the resources for construing their experience of the world around them and inside them as meaning – i.e. for modelling experience as meaning. The volume offers the construal of our experience of space as meaning as a core example, and uses the framework of the construal of experience to explore and critique the discourse of cognitive science, suggesting that cognitive science has tended to take the linguistic folk model of the 'mind' as a basis for more elaborated cognitive models, also drawing on computational metaphors. The theoretical position that I have taken here is the same as that elaborated in Halliday and Matthiessen (1999/2006), *Construing experience as meaning: A language-based approach to cognition*: meaning and knowledge are complementary metaphors for the same realm of phenomena, but the meaning-based conception of these phenomena has important conceptual and methodological consequences, e.g. bringing to the fore social, intersubjective and interactive approaches to learning. In the new chapter written for this model, I will sketch the semantic model of our experience of the world, one developed to interface with, or even encompass, semiotic systems other than language. I will explore how this model serves as a resource for construing experience – a construal potential, discussing work linking the model to systems outside language like sensori-motor systems (e.g. John Bateman's work on robotics), and how this model 'stores' knowledge (i.e. ideational meaning), ranging from systemic to instantial knowledge.

Volume 6, Multilingual Studies (including translation studies, language comparison and language typology), brings together different strands of the engagement with multiple languages under the conceptual heading of multilingual studies: studies of translation, comparison of languages, typologizing of languages. This is the topic of 'Multilingual studies as a multi-dimensional space of interconnected language studies', and it is further expanded and updated in the new chapter written for this volume, 'The challenge of describing and comparing languages: typological cartography'. Taking a step back, I will review work in multilingual studies undertaken since 2008. I will then sketch the move from text-based comparison of a few languages towards generalized comparison of many languages – i.e. linguistic typology, and I will suggest how smaller-scale text-based comparison can be used together with the kind of typological investigation that has now become possible thanks to the development of linguistic typological databases such as (and in particular) the WALS (World Atlas of Language Structures) database of linguistic features.

Table 2 Volumes in collected works and related books

Volume in collected works	Related books
Volume 1. Systemic Functional Linguistics, Part 1	Matthiessen and Halliday (2009), *Systemic functional grammar: A first step into the theory*
Volume 2. Systemic Functional Linguistics, Part 2	Matthiessen (forthc. b), *The architecture of language according to Systemic Functional Linguistics*
	Matthiessen, Teruya, and Lam (2010), *Key terms in systemic functional linguistics*
Volume 3. Description of English and Akan	Halliday and Matthiessen (2014), *Halliday's introduction to functional grammar*
	Matthiessen (1995b), *Lexicogrammatical cartography*
Volume 4. Discourse Analysis and Multisemiotic / Multimodal Studies	Matthiessen (forthc. c), Rhetorical system and structure theory
Volume 5. Construing Experience and Multimodal Studies	Halliday and Matthiessen (2006), *Construing experience through meaning: A language-based approach to cognition*
Volume 6. Multilingual Studies (including translation studies, language comparison and language typology)	Caffarel, Martin, and Matthiessen (eds.) (2004) *Language typology: A functional perspective*
	Matthiessen (in prep.), *Multilingual introduction to systemic functional grammar*
Volume 7. Register Studies, Verbal Art and Institutional Linguistics (including healthcare communication)	Slade, Manidis, McGregor, Scheeres, Chandler, Stein-Parbury, Dunstan, Herke, and Matthiessen (2015), *Communication in hospital emergency departments*
Volume 8. Educational Linguistics and Evolution of Language	

Volume 7, Register Studies, Verbal Art and Institutional Linguistics (including healthcare communication), returns to the description of a language and to the analysis of texts instantiating it but now through the theoretical 'lens' of register variation. The theory of register and register variation is developed in the book, and based on this theory, a description is then developed of registers in English seen from the point of view of the context in language. This description is put to work in the characterization of discourse in medicine and of discourse about verbal art (literature) as examples of how registerial maps can be used in exploring the role of language in different institutions. Drawing on the accounts of description and analysis in Volumes 3 and 4, respectively, I will foreground the mid-range of the cline of instantiation of systemic theory (Volume 1) between system and text – the region of subsystems/text types, the region of registerial variation. I will explore how registers can be described as functional subsystems or analysed as text types as complementary ways of accounting for them, and then go on to sketch the long-term research programme of registerial cartography – of mapping out the registers of a language according to contextual parameters. I will show how this programme includes the systematic description of the selective and strategic deployment of semantic resources in different registers, making explicit the link between elements of contextual structure and the logico-semantic organization of the text passages that realize them. I will also show how registerial cartography can be used to profile aspects of different institutions such as institutions of healthcare.

Volume 8, Educational Linguistics and Evolution of Language, deals with semogenesis, the creation of meaning, within different time-frames – ontogenesis and phylogenesis. The longest time-frame is that of the evolution of language as part of human history, phylogenesis, which is the topic of 'The evolution of language: A systemic functional exploration of phylogenetic phases', and the shortest is that of the unfolding of text, logogenesis, which is discussed in 'Instantial system and logogenesis' in Volume 2 and also in 'Lexicogrammar in discourse development: Logogenetic patterns of wording' in Volume 4. Intermediate between these two is the growth of meaning in the individual, the ontogenetic time-frame. This is explored in two chapters in this volume, in the context of (instructed) foreign language education. These chapters build on the accounts of register variation in Volume 7 and on the account of the multilingual meaning potential in Volume 6. The new chapter written for Volume 8 provides a general account of semogenesis to serve as a basis for both developmental and educational and historical concerns. One contribution of this chapter is a bridge between the substantial body in SFL on the learning of and through the mother tongue language and the learning of and through foreign or second languages.

The first seven of these eight volumes relate to books that I have been involved in as author or as co-author, and to make the links explicit, I have listed them in Table 2. In the area of educational linguistics, one of the two topics of Volume 8, I feel I have been, as I have said on various occasions, a resource person rather than an active developer like the outstanding educational linguists in the SFL community who have a solid background in both education and linguistics, often coming from education and then doing a PhD in linguistics. When I started as an undergraduate student in linguistics in the mid-1970s, the investigation of the evolution of language with the focus of the origin of language was still largely off the agenda, where it had been put in the nineteenth century. But the situation has changed quite dramatically, and the study of the evolution of language is now a major area of research, with contributions from different disciplines, providing new sources of evidence or ways of constructing models. Since I feel that the growing number of contributions still do not engage with language as a resource for making meaning, more specifically as a higher-order semiotic system with its origins in a primary semiotic, a protolanguage, I have taken notes intending to write a book on the evolution of language informed by the systemic functional insights into language and other semiotic systems. But there are many writing projects on my desk to be completed ...

The material in the 8 Volumes is now also being approached dialogically thanks to an initiative taken by three former students of mine and now colleagues and collaborators – Wang Bo, Helen Ma and Isaac Mwinlaaru – to conduct an extensive series of interviews with me over a period of years, starting in 2016. The first has now appeared in *Functional Linguistics*:

> Matthiessen, Christian M. I. M., Wang Bo, Isaac Mwinlaaru and Ma Yuanyi (2018). 'The axial rethink' – making sense of language: an interview with Christian M. I. M. Matthiessen. *Functional Linguistics* 5 (8): 1–19. https://doi.org/10.1186/s40554-018-0058-8

Like the editors of my collected works, Helen, Wang Bo and Ike have helped me review and contextualize my engagement with language, languages and SFL over the last 40 years or so (some interviews they conducted took me back further to my high school days as a keen learner of foreign languages who was very dissatisfied with the grammars on offer).

Again like my three editors, they have – through their engagement with my work – reminded me of how absolutely essential such engagement is – I am very grateful to them for adding value and meaning to my efforts through this process of engagement. And when I reflect on their energizing engagement, I think of the extraordinary extended academic family that developed around and was created by Michael Halliday, Ruqaiya Hasan and their generation of pioneers, and half a generation later by Robin Fawcett and his tireless efforts to create and support an expanding community in a variety of ways. Along the way, so many students and scholars around the world have been immensely important to my own scholarship, and I think they will appear in different ways throughout the eight volumes of collected works.

Naturally, I had really hoped that Michael would live to see the volumes of my collected works – at least the first few, since it was his dialogue with Kazu that projected the project into the realm of the possible and even desirable. Tragically, he passed away earlier this year two days after his 93rd birthday; but as we read his work, and re-read it, we can get sense of his awesome meaning potential, the system behind and developing through his writings – one that can be a tremendous resource for those ready to explore it, and so also a much needed guide.

Búa, July 2018

Christian M. I. M. Matthiessen

Note

1 I remember Robert Kirsner at UCLA commenting sometime during the first half of the 1980s that the problem with linguistics at the time – he meant 'Chomskyan' linguistics – was that the bridge would never collapse. In other words, linguists did not produce the kinds of account that could be tested in engineering contexts. In contrast, SFL had always been an appliable kind of linguistics, even though Michael Halliday introduced the term less than 20 years ago.

Chapter 1

Lexicogrammar in systemic functional linguistics: Descriptive and theoretical developments in the 'IFG' tradition since the 1970s

1.1 Introduction

This chapter is concerned with the development of accounts of lexicogrammar in Systemic Functional Linguistics (SFL) since the 1970s – in particular, with accounts relating to Halliday's *Introduction to Functional Grammar* (IFG), the first edition of which was published in 1985. IFG has influenced other accounts both within SFL (see e.g. the contributions by Fawcett 2007 and Tucker 2007) and outside SFL (see e.g. Kay 1979; Lockwood 2002), in other traditions; but my focus is on the IFG tradition itself. The boundaries are, of course, quite indeterminate – the tradition is not a bounded body of dogma, but an open-ended network of ideas about lexicogrammar.

In a sense, systemic functional linguistics started with an account of the lexicogrammatical subsystem of language: in 1961, Halliday published his classic paper *Categories of the theory of grammar* (cf. Webster 2005), which can be regarded as the first account of 'proto-systemic' theory; and this was already evident in his descriptions of Chinese (Halliday 1956a, 1959). This 'phase I' of the theory came to be known as 'scale-and-category' theory: the foregrounding of 'scales' in this phase of the theory was the foundation on which rests the dimensional modelling that has become an important characteristic of systemic functional theory. In this dimensional modelling, language is interpreted relationally as constituted in relationships extending along a small number of **semiotic dimensions** such as the hierarchy of stratification, the spectrum of metafunctions and the cline of instantiation – dimensions that intersect to form a multidimensional semiotic space of relationships. This dimensional way of modelling language has provided an alternative to the modular modelling characteristic of the Chomskyan tradition that was aligned with Cartesian Analysis.

However, while systemic functional linguistics can be said to have started with the focus on lexicogrammar in Halliday (1961), this early contribution was in fact part of a greater whole: in the Firthian tradition, most work had been focused on the 'outer' strata of language in context – that is, on context and semantics on the one hand and on phonology and phonetics on the other. In other words, Halliday's focus on lexicogrammar 'filled in' an area of language in the evolutionary development of the contextual and functional approach to which he was contributing (see Hasan 2005; Butt and Wegener 2007). Consequently, lexicogrammar was interpreted in the 'environment' of other linguistic systems and of context from the start (cf. Figure 1.1), as is seen very clearly in e.g. Halliday (1961) and Halliday, McIntosh and Strevens (1964). In the development of accounts of lexicogrammar, the understanding of this system has always been contextualized by work on other subsystems – and recontextualized by new developments in accounts of these subsystems.

At the same time, the fact that lexicogrammar came into focus in Halliday's early work was very significant for the development of the general theory in the 1950s and 1960s: it made it possible to see that an approach to language has to be probabilistic, taking text as evidence (Halliday 1959), it made it possible to see that prosodies can be modelled systemically (Halliday 1963a, 1963b, 1967b), it opened the way for the move from system-structure theory (developed in work on phonology, in the first instance) to systemic theory (Halliday 1966b, used first in descriptions of phonology and lexicogrammar and then also in work on semantics and context) and it paved the way for the theory of metafunctions (Halliday 1967c,d, 1968, 1969, 1970b, 1978). And, underlying these developments, it provided a basis for engaging with language as system, thinking about it holistically.

The development of accounts of lexicogrammar as a stratal subsystem of language and of accounts of the lexicogrammars of particular languages since the 1970s can be described under four headings:

> **Metatheory (metagrammatics)**: the theory of the theory of grammar – that is, the model of the metalanguage used to theorize and describe grammar (Section 1.2);
>
> **Theory (grammatics)**: the systemic functional theory of grammar (Section 1.3);

Description (grammar: system): systemic functional descriptions of the grammars of particular languages (Section 1.4).

Analysis (grammar: instance): lexicogrammatical analyses of texts (Section 1.5).

I will start with 'metatheory' since this will make it possible to locate all systemic functional contributions since the 1970s in the overall scheme of things.

1.2 Metatheory (metagrammatics)

The exploration of our own theory of language – of its nature and organization – goes back to Firth (1957b) and Hjelmslev (1943). Firth noted that linguistics is language turned back on itself (cf. Butt 2005; Matthiessen and Nesbitt 1996); and this means that we can draw on our theory of language when we try, in turn, to theorize that theory. Halliday (2005b: 228–230) suggests that the systemic functional metalanguage is like language in certain key respects:

1. like language, the systemic functional metalanguage is a resource not only for thinking, but also for doing;
2. like language, the systemic functional metalanguage is comprehensive – it is a general-purpose resource, rather than a special-purpose one;
3. like language, the systemic functional metalanguage is extravagant rather than parsimonious;
4. like language, the systemic functional metalanguage is telescopic, viewing language historically on three different dimensions (phylogenesis, ontogenesis and logogenesis);
5. like language, the systemic functional metalanguage is non-autonomous, being located 'within a general theory of semiotic' and more generally within 'a general systems typology';
6. like language, the systemic functional metalanguage is variable;
7. like language, the systemic functional metalanguage is 'indeterminate in that its categories are typically fuzzy' (op. cit., p. 229).

The development of an explicit metatheory of systemic functional theory is discussed in Matthiessen (2007b). For work on grammar, two properties of the systemic functional **metalanguage** are particularly important: that it is stratified and that it is inherently variable. Its inherent variability derives from the fact that it is always calibrated to some context or other of research and application.

As a stratified system, the systemic functional metalanguage is **'embedded' within contexts of research and application** (see Figure 2.18, this volume). These contexts have included ones intrinsic to linguistics such as the development of descriptions of different languages and linguistic typology as well as extrinsic ones (cf. Halliday 1978:10–12) from the start. The extrinsic ones have involved engagement with contexts of research and application in other disciplines – prominently, education, sociology, anthropology, literary studies, medicine, computer science and neuroscience, but it has also involved engagement with contexts in the community outside the academic realm, as in the work at the Centre for Language in Social Life, the Department of Linguistics, Macquarie University.

As Hasan (2005) points out, the systemic functional metalanguage has thus never been developed as a special-purpose restricted metalanguage dedicated to questions in a narrowly-defined research context. Instead, it has been developed with a wide range of consumer contexts in mind (cf. Halliday 1964) and as a result it has been designed to be (like language itself) both 'extravagant' and 'elastic' (see e.g. Halliday 1980a, 2005b: 178–230). The range of these contexts has expanded significantly since the 1970s. One of these contexts is that of the computational modelling of language for the purpose of text generation (cf. Matthiessen 1988a: 138, for a characterization of the field, tenor and mode of the research context of text generation), text understanding and other tasks where meaning has to be computed. This research context made it possible to develop the metatheory of the nature of the organization of the systemic functional metalanguage.

In particular, in the course of the computational modelling of language, we developed a **stratified model** of the systemic functional metalanguage (see e.g. Matthiessen and Bateman 1991; Bateman 1996; Halliday and Matthiessen 1999; Teich 1999; Wu 2000; and Matthiessen 2007b), making it possible to relate high-level theoretical modelling of grammar to low-level implementation by means of some particular programming language. These two 'outer' strata of the metalanguage were related in two steps, through two strata of representation: the theoretical model was realized at the stratum of theoretical representation and this representational model was in turn realized at the stratum of computational representation. This second, lower-level representational model was in turn realized at the stratum of implementation.

Sorting out the stratal organization of the systemic functional metalanguage made it possible to be very clear about the different strands of research into grammatical theory, as shown in Table 1.1. One key aspect of this has been the long-term effort to develop **computational tools** for supporting higher-level modelling, description and analysis: see Wu (2000) and O'Donnell and Bateman (2005).

Another key aspect of this sorting out of the stratal organization of the metalanguage was the exploration of **representational problems** – areas of the theory that we did not know how to represent computationally (see Matthiessen 1988a; Bateman 1989; Matthiessen and Bateman 1991; Zeng 1996). This exploration revealed that the main representational problems were located outside the experiential metafunction, within the logical, interpersonal and textual ones; and it indicated that the problems were due to the experiential bias in the representation – particularly, in the constituency-like representation of structure that was part of the general linguistic tradition. (The problems that were identified would not be solved by switching to a dependency model, however.)

Related to the exploration of representational problems was research into the relationship between the level of theoretical representation and that of computational representation and between different kinds of computational representation such as PATR, LOOM and TFS: for some discussion, see O'Donnell and Bateman (2005). This research shed light on the theoretical level of representation, showing for example how very different logical systems with 'recursive loops' are from other kinds of system (see Matthiessen 1988a; Bateman 1989; and cf. Henrici 1965), since other kinds of system can be represented as classification in terms of unification (e.g. Mellish 1988). It also confirmed the importance of certain aspects of the theoretical model – a key aspect being the distinction between potential, instantiation of the potential and instances (cf. Halliday 1973): after the debate in the 1970s in computational linguistics and AI between those who favoured 'declarative' forms of representation and those who favoured 'procedural' forms of representation, a general consensus had emerged that the way to go was to use purely declarative forms of representation in specifying linguistic resources. (From this point of view, we must stay clear of hybrid forms of representation, such as those mixing flowcharts and system networks.)

This research showed in what respects SFG is part of a family of **unification-based grammars** (drawing on Kay 1979) at the levels of representation (cf. also Winograd 1983, on 'feature and function' grammars), while its family ties are somewhat different at the level of theory, where we find family resemblances with e.g. Prague School work (cf. Davidse 1986) and 'West-Coast' functionalism. The stratified model of the systemic functional metalanguage (the metamodel!) thus enables us to recognize multiplex relationships among approaches to grammar, which is important since particular research contexts tend to focus the attention of researchers on one set of relationships to the exclusion of others. (Referring to Mary Douglas's experiential analysis of taboo, one might argue that SFG is taxonomically problematic in the same way as pigs and shell-fish: it embodies properties deriving from different 'clean' categories in that it is functional at the level of theory, but unlike most functional theories, it is relatively more explicit and formalized at the levels of representation.)

In contexts of computational modelling, the systemic functional theory of lexicogrammar has been extensively **tested**, as have systemic functional descriptions of the lexicogrammars of various languages. The theory and the descriptions have to be explicit and detailed enough to support the modelling in terms of computational representation and implementation. In addition, the computational modelling makes it possible to test the predictive power of the description. For instance, by automatically generating examples, it is possible to check whether the systemic combinations predicted by a system network with simultaneous systems seem to be of a kind that would occur in a corpus of natural text. Such testing played an important role in the development of the 'Nigel grammar' (see O'Donnell and Bateman 2005).

More generally, as Hasan points out (2005), all contexts of research and application constitute **test beds** for the lexicogrammatical theory and descriptions. For instance, in language education informed by a genre-based curriculum, if the description of the lexicogrammar of a language fails to bring out its meaning-making nature, this will become very clear since the result will be an unnatural chasm in the programme between different aspects of language. (Second language teachers have often pointed to the problem with having to use traditional or structural accounts of grammar in programmes based on some form of communicative syllabus.) In text analysis, the coverage of the description of a lexicogrammar is tested on a continuous basis (as can be seen from the fairly steady stream of questions sent to the systemic mailing lists about how to analyse examples from texts): if the description of the system does not include patterns encountered in texts, the analysis comes to a screeching halt. Similarly, in language description, if the theory is not powerful enough, this will become clear as we use it to describe an increasing range of languages. This form of testing is the orientation in science towards **engineering**, where the primary question is 'does the account work?' contrasting with the orientation in science towards philosophy, where the primary question is 'is it true?' (and thus 'falsifiable' or 'verifiable'). (The linguist Robert Kirsner, of UCLA, used to say that one problem in linguistics was that 'the bridge would never collapse' – that is, the accounts developed by linguists were not tested in an engineering context. However, systemic functional linguists have built a good number of semiotic bridges. Some have no doubt collapsed, but most have remained intact and supported the semiotic load they were designed for.) Collectively all the contexts of research and application involving systemic functional grammar constitute a very demanding **test suite** because the contexts cover such a wide range of demands. The significance of this is, I think, clear from accounts of science coming

Table 1.1 A summary of development since the 1970s

Dimension	Values	Development
stratification	context	new fields of development and application, in addition to description, text analysis and education: computational modelling, aphasic studies, translation studies
	theory	grammatical metaphor, logogenesis, generation, analysis, etc.: see Section 1.3 below
	representation: theoretical	system networks: partitions (Bateman *et al.* 1991); generation and analysis models (Matthiessen and Bateman 1991; Fawcett and Tucker 1990) – see O'Donnell and Bateman (2005)
	representation: computational	re-representation in PATR (Kasper 1988b), LOOM, TFS (Bateman and Momma 1991) – see O'Donnell and Bateman (2005)
	implementation	Proteus (Davey 1978); Penman (Mann and Matthiessen 1985; Matthiessen and Bateman 1991); KPML (Bateman 1997); GENESYS (Fawcett and Tucker 1990) – see O'Donnell and Bateman (2005)
instantiation	registers	introductory grammars (e.g. Butt *et al.* 2000; Thompson 1998); educational grammars (e.g. Derewianka 1998; see Williams 2005a); computational grammars (e.g. Fawcett and Tucker 1990; Matthiessen and Bateman 1991; Teich 1999); text analysis grammars (e.g. Martin, Matthiessen and Painter 1997)

from the sociology, ethnography and history of science. The problem is that the view of science has sometimes (even often!) been coloured (even dominated!) by philosophers of science with an orientation towards prescription rather than description.)

In the next subsection, I will focus on the theoretical level of the systemic functional metalanguage in the research into grammar since the 1970s (for more discussion of the representational levels, see O'Donnell and Bateman 2005).

1.3 Theory (grammatics)

While the **basic** organization of the **grammatics** – Halliday's (e.g. 1996) term for the theory of grammar (see Williams 2005a), has not changed since the 1970s, there have been important new developments that have made it more powerful – developments such as the concept of grammatical metaphor, the metafunctional

Table 1.2 Theoretical developments of grammatics since the 1970s organized in terms of the dimensions of language

Dimension	Values	Development
Stratification	semantics↘ lexicogrammar	lexicogrammatical realization of semantic features: Hasan (1984b)
		grammatical metaphor: Halliday (1985a, chap. 10; 1998b); Halliday and Martin (1993); Halliday and Matthiessen (1999, chap. 6; 2004, chap. 10); Simon-Vandenbergen, Taverniers and Ravelli (2003)
		fractal resonance: Halliday (1981,1982a); Matthiessen (1987c); Martin (1995b)
		syndrome (conspiracy): Hasan (1984c); Halliday (1990); Martin (1988a)
Instantiation	probability of instantiation	relative frequency in text: Nesbitt and Plum (1988); Halliday (1991a); Halliday and James (1993); Matthiessen (1999, 2002a, 2006a)
	system pole: phylogenesis	emergence of registers: Halliday (1987); Nanri (1993)
	instance pole: logogenesis	instantial patterns in unfolding text; phasal analysis; text scores: Gregory (1985); Young (1990); Stillar (1992); Matthiessen (1995b, 2002b); see Cloran, Stuart-Smith and Young (2007)
	from instance pole towards system pole: ontogenesis	Painter (1984, 1999, 2003), Torr (1997, 1998), Derewianka (1995, 2003); Halliday (2003b); see Painter et al. (2007)
	generation	systemic generation in relation to systemic resources as sequential or parallel process: Matthiessen and Bateman (1991); see O'Donnell and Bateman (2005)
	analysis	systemic parsing: Fawcett and Weerasinghe (1993); O'Donnell (1994); see O'Donnell and Bateman (2005)
Metafunction	(all)	metafunctional modes of meaning metafunctional modes of expression (Halliday 1979; Matthiessen 1988a; Johnston 1992; Martin 1996b) media of expression (Matthiessen 2004a)
Axis	systemic	partitioned system networks in multilingual descriptions (Bateman, Matthiessen, Nanri and Zeng 1991; Bateman, Matthiessen and Zeng 1999) and in register descriptions (Matthiessen 1993b)
		topological and fuzzy interpretation of systems: Martin and Matthiessen (1991); Matthiessen (1995a); Martin (1996c); Halliday (1998a)

Dimension	Values	Development
	structural	consolidation of realization statements and operators: e.g. Matthiessen and Bateman (1991); metafunctional modes of expression: see under metafunction
Delicacy		the 'grammarian's dream' – the extension of the description of grammar in delicacy towards lexis: Hasan (1987b); Matthiessen (1991a); Cross (1992); Tucker (1997a, b); see Tucker (2007)

differentiation of different modes of expression, the representation of multilingual systems and the expansion of the power of the metalinguistic levels of representation; and thanks to the continued expansion of corpus resources and techniques, it has been possible to flesh out quantitative aspects of the grammatics. The developments since the 1970s can all be related to one or other of the dimensions of the theory of language, as summarized in Table 1.2.

1.3.1 The hierarchy of stratification

The hierarchy of stratification is represented diagrammatically in Figure 2.7, Chapter 2. Lexicogrammar is located between phonology (graphology, or sign in a sign language such as Auslan) and semantics. Lexicogrammar and semantics form the content plane of language (the expression plane being formed by phonology and phonetics): lexicogrammar stands in a natural relationship to semantics. (For a discussion of de-automatization in the relationship between semantics and lexicogrammar, see Lukin and Webster 2005)

1.3.1.1 Context realized by semantics; semantics realized by lexicogrammar

In terms of the dimension of stratification, a key development for our understanding of the role of lexicogrammar was Hasan's (1984b) investigation of the semantic realization of the generic stages in the contextual (generic, schematic) structure of a situation and of the lexicogrammatical realization of the semantics. Drawing on Hasan's discussion, I have illustrated the general principle in Figure 1.1. A generic stage such as Placement (or 'Orientation', as it has also been called) is realized semantically by certain characteristic **nuclear** meanings and these may be further **elaborated** by other meanings. I have represented the nuclear and elaborating meanings by means of Rhetorical Structure Theory (RST; see Cloran, Stuart-Smith and Young 2007). The nuclear meanings are themselves differentiated into

crucial and **associated** meanings (again represented here by means of RST). In the case of Placement, the nuclear meanings are 'person particularization' (crucial) and 'impersonalization', 'temporal distance' (associated) and the elaborative meanings are 'attribution' and 'habitude'. These meanings are, in turn, realized lexicogrammatically, but there is a considerable ***spread*** in the lexicogrammar among the wordings: the unity in the realization of a generic stage such as Placement is semantic rather than lexicogrammatical. For instance, in the example in Figure 1.1, 'temporal distance' is realized lexicogrammatically by an enhancing clause in a hypotactic

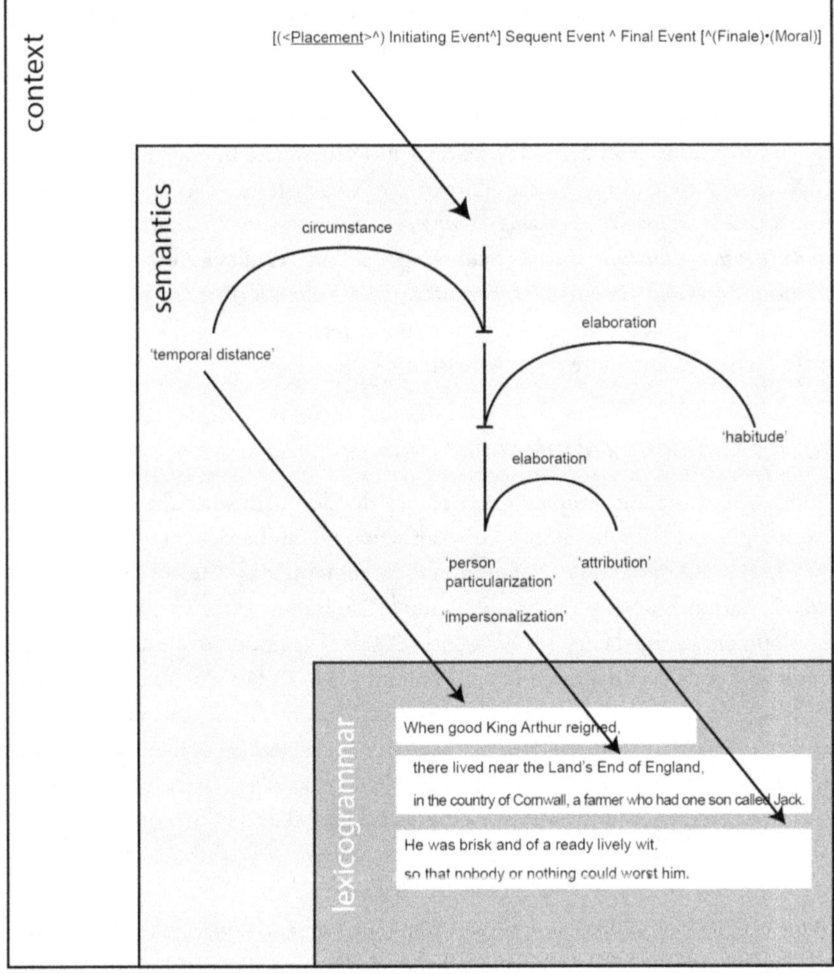

Figure 1.1 Semantic realization of the generic stage of Placement in a nursery tale and lexicogrammatical realization of semantic properties

clause nexus; but it could also be realized by an enhancing circumstance of time within the dominant clause (e.g. *During King Arthur's reign there lived near the Land's End of England...*). (As we will see below, the range of possible lexicogrammatical realizations is extended by grammatical metaphor.)

At the same time, one and the same lexicogrammatical system is typically 'deployed' in different ways within different registers (located midway along the cline of instantiation between the potential pole and the instance one) and these **registerial modes of deployment** can be represented as registerially distinct semantic systems (cf. also Hasan *et al.* 2007a for example, we could describe the semantic system of nursery tales, or even of Placement and other elements within nursery tales. The deployment of the lexicogrammar within different registers is brought out very clearly by Caffarel's (1992) account of how registerially distinct semantic systems of modelling time in French are realized by one and the same grammatical system of TENSE. (Her account theorizes and generalizes Beveniste's 1966, chap. XIX, classic study of French tense in terms of two systems – "*les temps d'un verbe Français ne s'emploient pas comme les membres d'un système unique, ils se distribuent en deux systèmes distinct et complémentaires*" (p. 238). Caffarel shows that this distribution into two systems is better interpreted semantically than grammatically. When it is interpreted semantically in terms of register variation, it becomes clear that there are in fact more than two systems.)

1.3.1.2 Grammatical metaphor

Another separate but ultimately related key development since the 1970s in the investigation of the relationship between semantics and lexicogrammar has been the elaboration of the theory of **grammatical metaphor** by reference to the interstratal relationship between semantics and lexicogrammar (for an overview of the development of the theory, see Taverniers 2003). The notion of grammatical metaphor had been foreshadowed in e.g. Halliday (1967a), but it was not spelled out in detail for both the interpersonal and ideational metafunctions until the first edition of Halliday's *Introduction to Functional Grammar* (grammatical metaphor in the interpersonal area was discussed in Halliday (1984a), based on a contribution to a conference in the 1970s). This led to a good deal of descriptive research (including Ravelli 1985, 1988; Halliday and Martin 1993, and the contributions in Martin and Veel 1998, and Simon-Vandenbergen, Taverniers and Ravelli 2003); the most detailed theoretical investigation so far is Halliday and Matthiessen (1999, chap. 6) and the most detailed discussion of computational modelling is Zeng (1996). On the significance of grammatical metaphor in translation, see Teich (2003) and Steiner (2005a).

The general theoretical principle that was worked out is that grammatical metaphor (like lexical metaphor, once it is theorized in terms of strata) involves the **decoupling** of congruent inter-stratal relationships between semantics and lexicogrammar and the **recoupling** of these to create **junctions** (cf. Figure 1.2) such as the realization of process and thing by nominalization. (Examples of the incongruent realization diagrammed in Figure 1.2 include those where the logico-semantic relation of 'cause' is realized as if it were a process: *displacement along these faults caused failure of the Baldwin Hills Reservoir in 1963, a magnitude-6 quake can cause severe damage*; by a further step, this can be realized as if it were a participant: *this implies* [[*that the temperature change is a result of ozone depletion rather than a cause of it*]].)

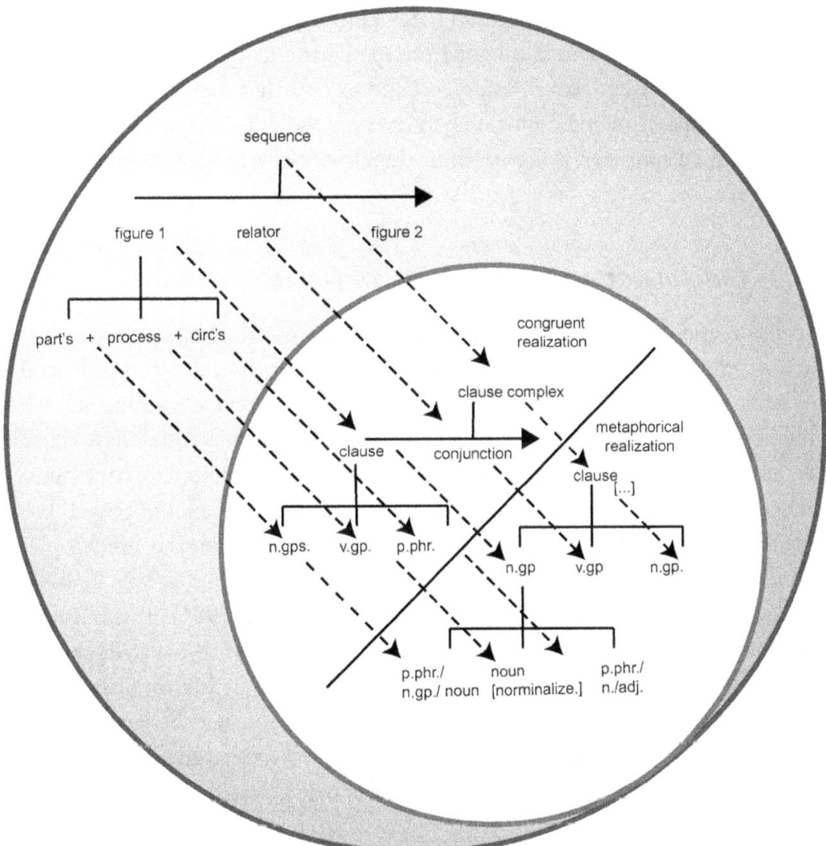

Figure 1.2 Example of grammatical metaphor (from Halliday and Matthiessen 1999, Figure 6.8)

One theoretically significant finding in the research on grammatical metaphor has been that metaphoric variants typically involve not just single features but rather **syndromes** of features (cf. Halliday and Matthiessen 2004: 632–633) – features that may themselves involve metaphor (see Halliday and Matthiessen 1999: 250–255). The metaphorical reading is thus typically 'triggered' by a combination of features.

Another theoretically significant finding has been that metaphoric realizations typically depend on the manifestation of the **fractal types** of expansion and projection within different domains of the lexicogrammatica1 system (clause nexus, clause, nominal group and so on); and metaphoric realizations make the manifestation of the fractal types more pervasive in the overall system. For instance, the differentiation of expansion into elaboration, extension and enhancement is manifested within both the clause nexus (in the system of LOGICO-SEMANTIC TYPE) and the clause (in the system of RELATION TYPE). Through metaphor, the enhancing type is extended within the clause from spatial and temporal relations to causal ones involving a causative verb as Process and by a further step this is extended to nominal groups involving nouns such as *cause*, *result* as Thing (cf. Halliday 1988, for the gradual spread of this pattern in the history of scientific English over the last 500 years or so).

1.3.2 Fractal patterns: Semantics and lexicogrammar

Expansion and projection have been found to operate within different domains of the lexicogrammar and we have theorized this phenomenon in terms of **fractals**: the same fundamental patterns are manifested in different environments, with adjustments according to the 'affordances' of these environments. These fractals have also been found to operate within the semantics in the rhetorical (conjunctive) relations by which texts are organized. Here they are part of a more general principle that there are **fractal patterns** that are manifested within the content plane in both semantics and lexicogrammar. The seminal contribution was Halliday's (1982a) paper *How is a text like a clause?* (cf. also Halliday 1981). This was developed further by Matthiessen (1987c), who suggested that a text is also like a clause complex (cf. Cloran, Stuart-Smith and Young 2007) and by Martin (1995a). The fractal patterns identified in the exploration of the 'resonance' between text and clause (complex) included centrally the account of the metafunctional modes of expression – a theoretical development that also belongs to this period: see immediately below.

1.3.3 Lexicogrammatical syndromes

The research into grammatical metaphor revealed the significance of lexicogrammatical features operating together in **syndromes**. However, the Halliday's notion of syndrome is not restricted to the domain of metaphor: it applies to any combination of features operating together in the realization of higher-level **motifs** – that is, motifs in the semantics or in the context. One area where this has been investigated in research since the 1970s is the relationship between language and culture: see Hasan (1984c), Martin (1986) and Halliday (1992e).

1.4 Metafunction

In terms of the spectrum of metafunction, the major theoretical development was Halliday's (1978: 188; 1979) theory of the relationship between metafunctional **modes of meaning** and metafunctional **modes of expression.** This contribution had a huge impact on the systemic functional theory of grammar (see e.g. Matthiessen 1988b; 1992; 2004b; Kasper 1988b; Bateman 1989; Johnston 1992), but also on the theory of semantics (see Martin 1996b) and on multimodal studies. Interpreting Pike (1959) metafunctionally, Halliday hypothesized that each metafunction constitutes a distinct mode of meaning and that each metafunctional mode of meaning is realized (in a natural rather than conventional way) by a distinct mode of expression: see Table 1.3.

The ideational mode of meaning is **construal**, but there are two modes of construal – the experiential and the logical, each with its own mode of expression, **configurations** and **series.** The interpersonal mode of meaning is **enactment** and the interpersonal mode of expression is **prosody**. The textual mode of meaning is **modulation** – the transformation of construals and enactments into information that is differentiated into different degrees of prominence and the textual mode of expression is **wave** – patterns of periodicity with alternating peaks of prominence and troughs of non-prominence.

Table 1.3 Modes of meaning, modes of expression

	Mode of meaning	**Mode of expression**
Ideational: logical	construing experience serially	serial (series of segments)
Ideational: experiential	construing experience configurationally	configurational (configuration of segments)
Interpersonal	enacting social roles and relationships	prosodic
Textual	creating information in text	periodic (wave-like)

The theory of metafunctional modes of expression is further refined in Matthiessen (2004b: 553–561), where I suggest that the different metafunctional modes of expression are manifested within different **media of expression** – segments (items), sequence and intonation. This aspect of the metafunctional modes of expression came into focus in typological research. While languages tend to use the same **modes** of expression for each metafunction, the **media** of expression may vary. For example, the prosodic realization of terms in the mood system is manifested segmentally, sequentially and/or intonationally in a given language: see Teruya *et al.* (2007).

In addition to the theoretical work on the relationship between modes of meaning and modes of expression, the nature of each metafunction has been explored in various publications since the 1970s.

(a) The **textual metafunction** has been investigated in terms of the theoretical modelling of textual statuses; this has involved the 'grounding' metaphors of abstract space (e.g. 'point of departure', 'topic' [from 'topos', place]) by means of work coming from computational linguistics, e.g. Matthiessen (1992); Bateman and Matthiessen (1993); Lavid (2000b).

(b) The **interpersonal metafunction** has been investigated with respect to the nature of exchange and the relationship between exchange and systems of various kinds of interpersonal assessment, e.g. Lemke (1992); Thibault (1993, 1995); Martin (e.g. 2000). Lemke (1992) raises the issue of 'value-orientational' prosodic patterns in text, foreshadowing the later development of the description of the systems of APPRAISAL in English (see Hood and Martin 2007).

Such systems have sometimes been seen as being different in nature from the exchange-based system of MOOD (and Fawcett 1980: 28, splits the interpersonal metafunction into four 'functional components': negativity, interactional, affective and modality). However, they are all exchange-based: exchange (or 'reciprocity') is the foundation of all human societies according to Johnson and Earle (2000) – an insight that goes back at least to the anthropological classic *The Gift*, written by Durkheim's nephew Mauss in the 1920s (Mauss 1990); and this orientation towards interaction is the foundation of human intersubjectivity (e.g. Trevarthen 1987). Thus systems of assessment such as MODALITY, EVIDENTIALITY and APPRAISAL are all based on exchange, as is very clear in dialogic texts (cf. Painter's 2003, account of the ontogenesis of appraisal in dialogue): the speaker gives or demands an assessment, assigning to the addressee the responsibility of engaging with it; interactants constantly negotiate values, calibrating their own assessments against one another and the collective norm (as Slade 1996, shows for gossip among work mates vs. gossip among friends). The exchange basis of assessment is brought out when appraisals are combined with explicitly subjective modalities in interrogative clauses, as in *Do you think that's an adequate criterion, liking? – I suppose it's not adequate*; and it is also shown by examples involving explicitly subjective appraisal, as in *Do you like librarianship as a career? – I do very much, yes.* When we extend the description of the interpersonal grammar in delicacy, we see how different mood types engender distinct forms of assessments or 'keys'; and in languages with highly grammaticalized systems of EVIDENTIALITY, we see how these systems interact with mood systems precisely because of the difference between giving and demanding as far as the assessment of evidentiality is concerned (see e.g. Aikhenvald's 2003, chap. 14, description of EVIDENTIALITY and MOOD in Tariana (Arawak)).

(c) The **ideational metafunction** has been explored as a resource for construing experience, e.g. Halliday and Martin (1993), Martin and Veel (1998), Painter (1999) and Halliday and Matthiessen (1999). Here the Whorfian, constructivist interpretation of 'construing experience' has been brought very clearly into focus, aided by Painter's (1999) investigation of the relationship between learning language and learning through language, the work on discursive 'knowledge' construction (especially in secondary school, e.g. Christie and Martin 1997; Martin and Veel 1998), the extensive work on grammatical metaphor (cf. Section 1.3.1.2) and the growing body of work on typology (cf. Teruya *et al.* 2007; and see Caffarel, Martin and Matthiessen 2004).

1.5 Instantiation

In terms of the cline of instantiation, the major theoretical development was Halliday's (1992c) clear articulation of it as a cline extending between the two poles of the potential (system) and instances (texts) and his (2000a) working out of the organization of the 'semiotic space' defined by the intersection of the cline of instantiation and the hierarchy of stratification (viewed in terms of the **instantiation-stratification matrix**, which is reproduced as Tables 1 and 2 in Matthiessen 2007b). This was important in making explicit the location of register and text type within the overall theory and of the complementarity of these two as characterizations of the region on the cline of instantiation intermediate between the two poles. Lexicogrammar, like all stratal subsystems of language, is extended along the cline of instantiation, ranging over different degrees of instantiation – from the fully systemic at the potential pole of the cline (the focus of what would traditionally be described in a dictionary or reference grammar) to the fully discursive at the instance pole via intermediate patterns discussed in terms of categories such as idioms, stock phrases, snatches, routines.

1.5.1 Probability of instantiation

Instantiation was also further illuminated by a series of papers Halliday produced in the early 1990s on a **probabilistic theory** of grammar (Halliday 1991a, 1992c, 1993b; Halliday and James 1993, collected in Halliday 2005b), drawing on the work by Nesbitt and Plum (1988). The insight that the grammatical system is inherently probabilistic and that it can be investigated through the **relative frequency** of selections of systemic terms goes back to Halliday (1959), but, since this early work, the vision of large corpora had been realized, with the corpora growing in size from around one million words to tens of millions of words and hundreds of millions of words and the computational tools for examining them becoming increasingly powerful.

Halliday had carried out manual counts of a number of systems in the 1960s and based on these he developed the hypothesis that general (indelicate) systems tend to be either **skew** (0.9/0.1 for a two-term system such as POLARITY: positive 0.9/negative 0.1) or **equiprobable** (0.5/0.5 for a two-term system such as INTERROGATIVE TYPE: yes/no 0.5/wh- 0.5). Analysing a corpus of 18 million words computationally, Halliday and James (1993) were able to confirm this contrast in probability profile for two systems: POLARITY turned out to be skew and PRIMARY TENSE turned out to be equiprobable (the past/present contrast, with future left out). I will give some additional examples from logical systems in this section and then introduce additional results for both logical and experiential systems in Section 1.9 (for more detail on ideational systems and for comparable work on interpersonal and textual systems, as well as on intersections of systems from different metafunctions, see e.g. Matthiessen 2006a; Ghadessy 1995a; Gómez-González 2001).

Nesbitt and Plum's (1988) investigation of the systems of clause complexing, TAXIS (hypotactic/paratactic) and LOGICO-SEMANTIC TYPE (projection [idea/locution]/expansion [elaborating/extending/enhancing]), revealed another aspect of the probabilistic properties of the system: the **partial association** of terms in simultaneous systems. We can see this very clearly when we 'visualize' the relative frequencies in Table 1.3 of Nesbitt and Plum's (1988: 20) study: see Figure

1.3. For example, 'idea' and 'hypotaxis' tend to be selected together, while 'locution' and 'parataxis' tend to be selected together. Such patterns are not brought out in a purely qualitative description of the system, only in a quantitative one where relative frequencies in text can be interpreted as indicative of probabilities inherent in the system. I have found similar patterns of systemic interaction for the systems of clause complexing (Matthiessen 2002a) and of the clause (Matthiessen 1999, 2006a).

Nesbitt and Plum (1988) also brought out **register variation** within their corpus of sociolinguistic interviews: they showed how phases of narratives, anecdotes, recounts, exemplifications and observation/comments vary quantitatively in their patterns of instantiation within TAXIS and LOGICO-SEMANTIC TYPE. The variation across these registers is shown for the two types of projection in Figures 1.4 and 1.5.

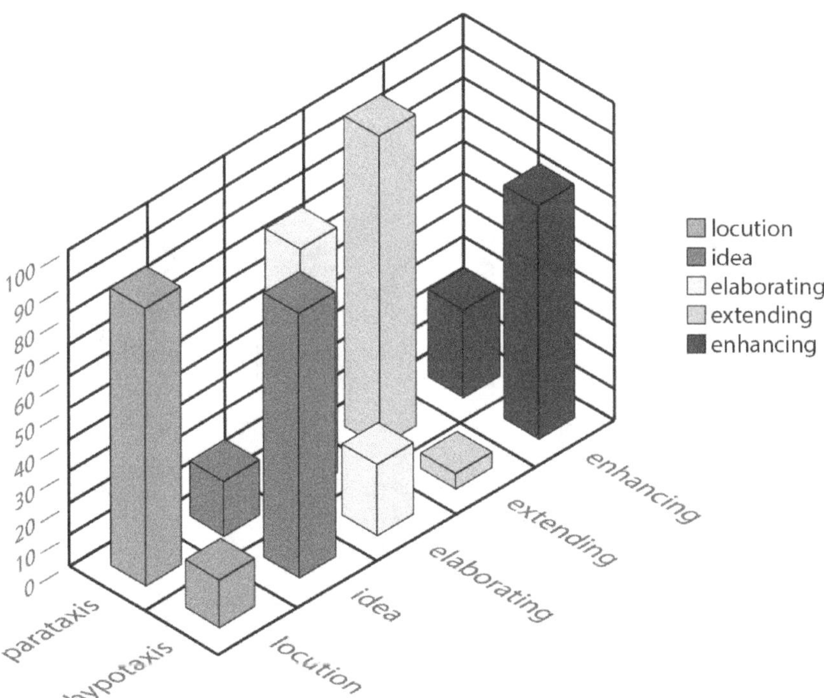

Figure 1.3 The partial association of TAXIS and LOGICO-SEMANTIC TYPE revealed by the relative frequencies in sociolinguistic interviews (Nesbitt and Plum 1988: 20 – Table 1.3)

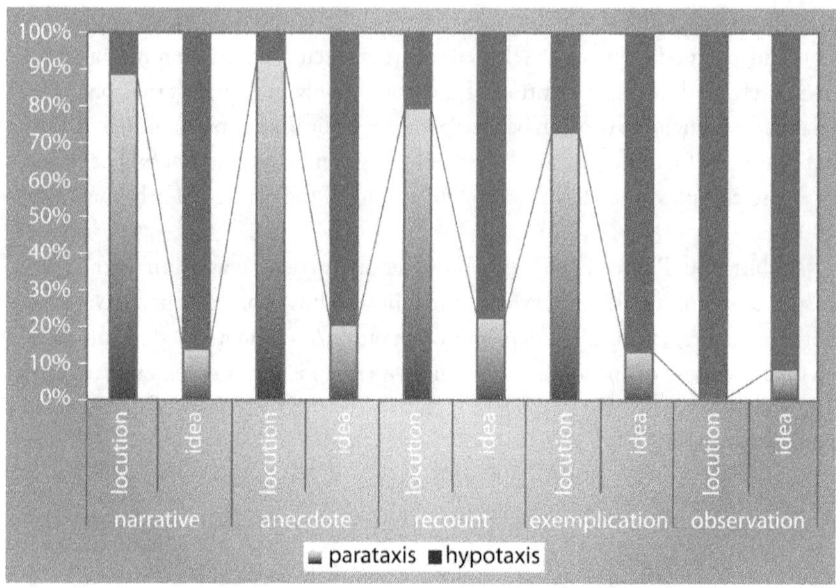

Figure 1.4 Register variation in TAXIS and LOGICO-SEMANTIC TYPE – sociolinguistic interviews (Nesbitt and Plum 1988: 30)

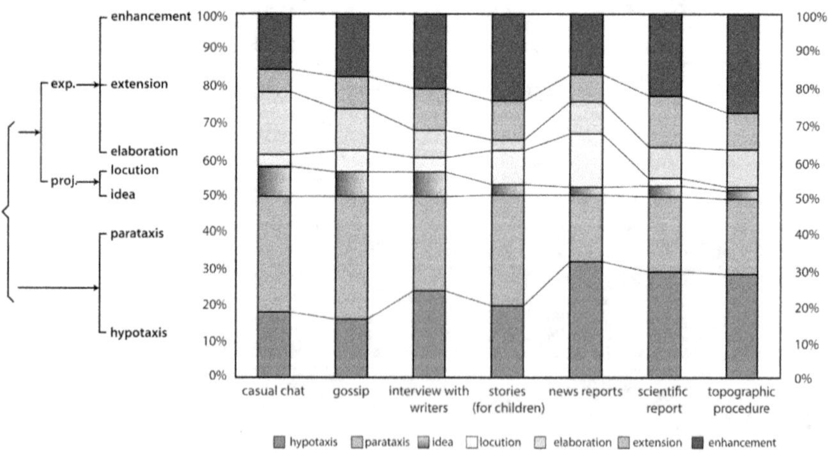

Figure 1.5 Register variation in TAXIS and LOGICO-SEMANTIC TYPE – examples from spoken and written registers

1.5.2 Semogenesis

The explicit modelling of the cline of instantiation has also made it possible to locate **semogenic processes** of (a) **phylogenesis** (b) **ontogenesis** and (c) **logogenesis** affecting the lexicogrammar of a language (e.g. Halliday and Matthiessen 1999: 18): see Table 1.4.

Table 1.4 The three forms of semogenesis

	Mode of genesis	Locus	Phases	Time scale
Phylogenesis	evolution of	meaning **potential** (human language) in species/ meaning **potentials** (human languages) in meaning groups (speech fellowships)	Phase (protolanguage) – Phase II (transition) – Phase (semiotically modern language) [Phase III:] recent past: old – middle – modern (English, etc.)	Phase I: millions of years – Phase II: c. 2 million years – Phase III: c. 150–200 K years
Ontogenesis	development of	(personalized) meaning **potential** in meaner (individual speaker)	Phase I (protolanguage) – Phase II (transition) – Phase (mother tongue), in life cycle of growth, maturation and decay	life: Phase I: c. 10 months – Phase II: c. 6 months – Phase III: remainder of life
Logogenesis	unfolding of	act of meaning in text (**instance**)	instantiation of generically determined registerial phases; purely instantial phases	text: seconds to hours

1.5.2.1 Phylogenesis

Phylogenesis came into focus with accounts of the evolution of registers within English – with Halliday's (1988) study of the evolution scientific English in the physical sciences over a period of more than 500 years (a period which included the expansion of grammatical metaphor of the ideational kind) and this was followed up by Nanri's (1993) detailed account of the emergence of the modern news report over a period of over 200 years (a period which included the transformation of news story into a kind of taxonomic news report). These studies are both text-based explorations of the evolution of a register and show the gradual emergence of 'syndromes' of features that are characteristic of that register (gradualness that can be modelled in terms of changing systemic probabilities, recorded as changing relative frequencies in text, as Ellegård (1953) did in his classic study of the emergence of the modem usage of *do* over two centuries, from 1500 to 1700). These studies also illustrate how the overall lexicogrammatical system of a language evolves through the evolution of registers, as when the standard languages of modern nation states evolved through the expansion of the registerial repertoires – including registers of science, administration and bureaucracy, the law, the media, production and commerce. The potential for this text-based kind of 'historical linguistics' is considerable, but it remains to be actualized in systematic investigations of the evolution of the overall system.

More recent work has explored the longer time-frame of the evolution of language (e.g. Halliday 1995b; Cléirigh 1998; Matthiessen 2004b), interpreting the evolution of language as a central factor in the evolution of 'Anatomically Modern Humans' and relating the account to the work by neuroscientists such as Deacon and Edelman, who see language and the brain as having co-evolved. This has shed new light on lexicogrammar as a key property of what we might call 'Semiotically Modern Humans'. The research into ontogenesis gives us a model for showing how lexicogrammar evolved gradually (cf. Steels 1998).

1.5.2.2 Ontogenesis

Ontogenesis had already been investigated in Halliday's (1975) seminal case study of how one child, Nigel, learned how to mean (see Painter, Derewianka and Torr 2007). This study showed the gradual development of the lexicogrammatical system within language in terms of both stratification and metafunction and it also showed how the wording potential is built up gradually as the child moves from protolanguage via a transitional phase into the mother tongue: systems are present from the start, but structures emerge only under the semiotic pressure of the expanding potential. Grammar emerges not with structure in the first instance but rather with the development of simultaneous systems – the ability to mean more than one thing at the same time. The research on ontogenesis also made it possible to trace the development of particular systems such as the system of MOOD (see Halliday 1984a), MODALITY (see Torr 1998), APPRAISAL (see Painter 2003) and TRANSITIVITY (see Painter 1999). Since the 1970s, additional case studies have enriched the picture, both in the development of early childhood including the transition into the mother tongue (Painter 1984, 1999; Torr 1997) and in the later development from childhood to adolescence, with a particular focus on the expansion of grammatical metaphor of the ideational kind in the course of literacy development (Derewianka 1995, 2003).

Such case studies show how individual persons – or **meaners**, since we are looking at them from a semiotic point of view (see e.g. Halliday and Matthiessen 1999) – develop **personalized meaning potentials** (cf. Section 2.2.4 of chap. 2). As a meaner keeps learning, the location of the personalized meaning potential edges further up the cline of instantiation towards the potential pole; but personalized meaning potentials will, of course, always be quite some distance away from the collective meaning potential (an insight we can trace back at least to Saussure). The growth of the personal meaning potential is a **lifelong** process that is part of the meaner's lifeline: meaners keep taking on new roles, moving into new contexts and learning the registers associated with them.[1] The notion of a meaner's personalized meaning potential is highly relevant also to studies of second/foreign language learning (see e.g. Hasan and Perrett 1994; Young 2001) and also to studies of learning in general. It is also relevant to studies of the 'decay' of the meaning potential, whether this is slow or traumatic (Armstrong *et al.* 2005).

1.5.2.3 Logogenesis

Logogenesis was explored in the 1980s with reference to lexicogrammar in studies showing how texts unfold as selections of lexicogrammatical features (e.g. Butt 1983, 1984), which included Gregorian **phrasal analysis** (e.g. Gregory 1985; Young 1990; Stillar 1992; see further Cloran, Stuart-Smith and Young 2007) and it really came into focus in the 1990s. These studies show how patterns in text emerge out of local selections in clause nexuses, clauses, groups and phrases and words.[2] These emergent patterns may be registerial and routinized in nature and correspond to conventional generic stages, or substages, in the generic (schematic) structure of the situation in which a text unfolds; but they may of course also be completely instantial, emerging within a particular text.

To make it easier to detect the logogenetic patterns, we can visualize them as a text score (to borrow Weinreich's (1972) German term *Textpartitur*, see Matthiessen 1995b; 2002b), where we indicate the number of selections of systemic features over a certain span of text (e.g. five clauses, or ten). This is illustrated in Figure 1.6, where the different types of relation used in combining clauses into clause nexuses are graphed for a gossip passage within a casual conversation. This score makes it easy to identify peaks of high numbers of selections and troughs of low numbers. The highest peaks in this example indicate a narrative passage providing evidence for evaluating a colleague in a work place pejoratively as pushy and inconsiderate.

The process of genesis in logogenesis is the **unfolding** of acts of meaning (see Figure 1.5). Since the 1970s, a good deal of work has gone into modelling this unfolding in computational projects in terms of algorithms for generation (e.g. Matthiessen and Bateman 1991) and analysis (e.g. O'Donnell 1994). This work is relevant not only computationally but also theoretically for it throws light on the relationship between the potential and the instance and between these and the process of instantiation. This area has also been illuminated in work by Ravelli (1991, 1995) with a more theoretical-descriptive (rather than computational) orientation: adopting a **dynamic perspective**, she shows how the local unfolding of

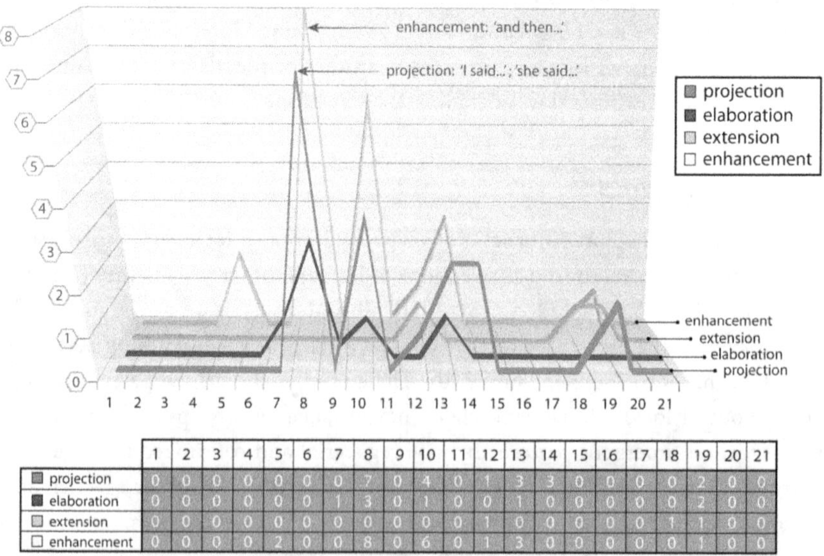

	1	2	3	4	5	6	7	8	9	10	11	12	13	14	15	16	17	18	19	20	21
projection	0	0	0	0	0	0	0	7	0	4	0	1	3	3	0	0	0	0	2	0	0
elaboration	0	0	0	0	0	0	1	3	0	1	0	0	1	0	0	0	0	0	2	0	0
extension	0	0	0	0	0	0	0	0	0	0	0	1	0	0	0	0	0	1	1	0	0
enhancement	0	0	0	0	2	0	0	8	0	6	0	1	3	0	0	0	0	0	1	0	0

Figure 1.6 Text score for LOGICO-SEMANTIC TYPE in gossip passage of a casual conversation

clauses and other grammatical units can be related to our interpretation of the system. Her work brings out the nature of grammatical structure as **patterned activity** (Halliday 1961) rather than as some kind of static construction. Discussing the clause, she notes (1995: 230): "the interplay of the metafunctional components can signal significant points of development or transfer of responsibility between metafunctions. While all three are always present, one or two can be highlighted as being more informative or pertinent at particular points in the development of the clause."

There are certainly interesting theoretical issues to be explored here. Based on advances in (computational) representation, computational linguists had arrived (by the early 1980s) at the consensus view that resources should be represented declaratively and kept distinct from (procedural) representations of processes of generation and analysis. However, as far as the modelling of lexicogrammar is concerned, this needs to be explored also 'from above', from a theoretical point of view (based on evidence from description and detailed text analysis). The challenge is not to reify the system – not to treat system and process as distinct orders of phenomena.

1.6 Axis

The theory of **axis** that is reflected in the name 'systemic theory' had been worked out by the mid-1960s (e.g. Halliday 1966b). The **paradigmatic axis** was treated as the primary axial mode of organization (see chap. 2, Section 2.1.3); and this prioritizing of the paradigmatic axis 'paid off' both theoretically and descriptively in the 1960s and 1970s. It made it possible to orient the description of the grammar towards meaning, it made it possible to develop a comprehensive description of the grammar and it led to the 'discovery' of the metafunctional organization of lexicogrammar. It also made it possible to theorize the 'resonance' between the metafunctional organization of semantics and lexicogrammar and the organization of context into systems of field, tenor and mode (Halliday 1978).

In the 1980s, the lexicogrammatical system networks that had been produced by Halliday in his description of English were implemented in the 'Nigel grammar' (see O'Donnell and Bateman 2005), starting with the 80 or so systems listed in Halliday (2005b: 268–284). This description was expanded to reflect both Halliday's description in IFG and elaborations of this description (cf. Matthiessen 1995b) and they were tested extensively. This computational modelling also meant that the realization statements relating terms in systems to 'fragments' of structure were consolidated and tested (see e.g. Matthiessen and Bateman 1991).

The extensive work on the description of paradigmatic patterns by means of system networks in the 1980s – not only in the work on lexicogrammar, but also in the work on semantics (see Section 1.3.2 and Hasan *et al.* 2007a) – gave Jim Martin and me enough experience to review the theory and representation paradigmatic organization by the early 1990s (see Martin and Matthiessen 1991). Drawing on Jay Lemke's work on genre typology, we suggested that **typology** and **topology** could be interpreted as complementary perspectives on paradigmatic organization. System networks have often been seen as representing typologies, but they can also be thought of as representing topologies. Various topological accounts of lexicogrammatical systems have been proposed (e.g. Matthiessen 1995b; Martin 1996a; Teruya 1998) and Martin (e.g. 1997) has developed topological accounts of genre agnation (illustrated in chap. 2, Table 2.1). Halliday's (1998a) description of the 'grammar of pain' shows the power of topology in bringing out patterns of agnation that are kept apart in typological descriptions.

Complementing this work and drawing on the link between systemic functional theory and fuzzy theory forged by Michio Sugeno, Ichiro Kobayashi and I have explored the possibility of representing systems in system networks in terms of **fuzzy set theory** (due to Lotfi Zadeh, see e.g. Zadeh 1987): see Matthiessen (1995a); see also Halliday (2005b, chaps. 9 and 10). One possibility is to treat systemic terms as descriptors of fuzzy sets (rather than of crisp ones), which means that they will be characterized by degrees of membership.

1.7 Delicacy

The prioritizing of the paradigmatic axis mentioned above had another fundamental consequence in the theorizing and description of lexicogrammar. It made it possible to base the notion of **delicacy** on the modelling of the paradigmatic axis. That is, delicacy could be modelled paradigmatically in the first instance; since the paradigmatic axis had been given priority, the system network could now be used to represent the **cline of delicacy** (removing the need to specify structures at secondary or higher degrees of delicacy; cf. for example Halliday [1961] 2002c: 82–83). One consequence of this was that the 'grammarian's dream' (op. cit.) could now be realized; and this happened in the 1980s, with the work by Hasan (1985a, 1987b): see Section 1.9.2 below for a brief summary of the description. Theoretically, this work was significant partly because it demonstrated that the paradigmatic foundation made the move from grammar to lexis possible and because it showed that this was not 'componential analysis' but rather 'parametric analysis' (cf. Heller and Macris 1967).[3]

1.8 Dimensional thinking

Since the 1970s, there have thus been a number of significant developments in the exploration of the semiotic dimensions that define both the internal organization of lexicogrammar and the external environment in which it is located. At the same time, systemic functional linguists have continued to gain more experience with 'dimensional thinking' – that is, with theorizing, modelling, describing, analysing, presenting and arguing – in terms of semiotic dimensions.

1.8.1 Trinocular vision in relation to stratification

These semiotic dimensions define observer perspectives and angles of approach. Halliday (1978) had made the point that any phenomenon or category can be looked at 'from above', 'from roundabout' and 'from below' in relation to the hierarchy of stratification, showing how all three views are necessary to understand the metafunctional organization of grammar (p. 131). This he later called **trinocular vision** (or perspective; e.g. Halliday [1996] 2002c: 408–409; Halliday and Matthiessen 2004: 31; Matthiessen and Halliday 2009). He characterizes it in relation to grammar as follows (2002c: 408):

> In categorizing the grammar, the grammarian works 'from above', 'from roundabout' and 'from below'; and these three perspectives are defined in terms of strata. Since the stratum under attention is the lexicogrammar, 'from roundabout' means 'from the standpoint of the lexicogrammar itself'. 'From above' means 'from the standpoint of the semantics: how the given category relates to the meaning (what it 'realizes')'. 'From below' means 'from the standpoint of morphology and phonology, how the given category relates to the expression (what it 'is realized by')'. What are taken into account are the regularities (proportionalities) at each of the three strata.

Grammatical categories are characterized from all three angles: a comprehensive characterization of a grammatical category is provided by an account of all the relationships it enters into 'from above', 'from roundabout' and 'from below' (as illustrated for 'Subject' in Halliday and Matthiessen 2004: 119): see Figure 1.7. Categories are defined 'from above' by reference to what they mean; for example, 'Subject' is defined as 'that element which is assigned modal responsibility for the proposition or proposal' and 'Theme' defined as 'that element which is assigned the status of point of departure, or local context, of the message'. Characterizing grammatical categories 'from above' is hard and Halliday (1984c) explains why: they are **ineffable.** We must therefore develop the account of semantics at least to the point where we can provide models that allow us to locate the glosses of grammatical categories (glosses which often involve metaphor), as I have shown for the category of theme (Matthiessen 1992).

Grammarians need trinocular vision; they need to be able to see the phenomena of lexicogrammar and the categories they themselves posit in the course of description, in the round, from all angles. Becoming a grammarian means learning to adopt the three different perspectives; but it also means learning to vary them independently of one another – in a sense, learning to operate with the grammar in a de-automatized way. The greatest challenge is undoubtedly learning to explore the grammar 'from roundabout' – focusing on patterns of wording and investigating them by setting up and testing, proportionalities, by identifying reactances in the system itself. Here grammarians are, of course, using the grammatics to develop some kind of awareness of patterns that are normally below the level of consciousness and to extend their ability to understand unfamiliar ways of meaning, just as phoneticians are using the theory of phonetics to become more aware of their human phonetic potential and to extend their mastery of it (cf. Catford 1977).

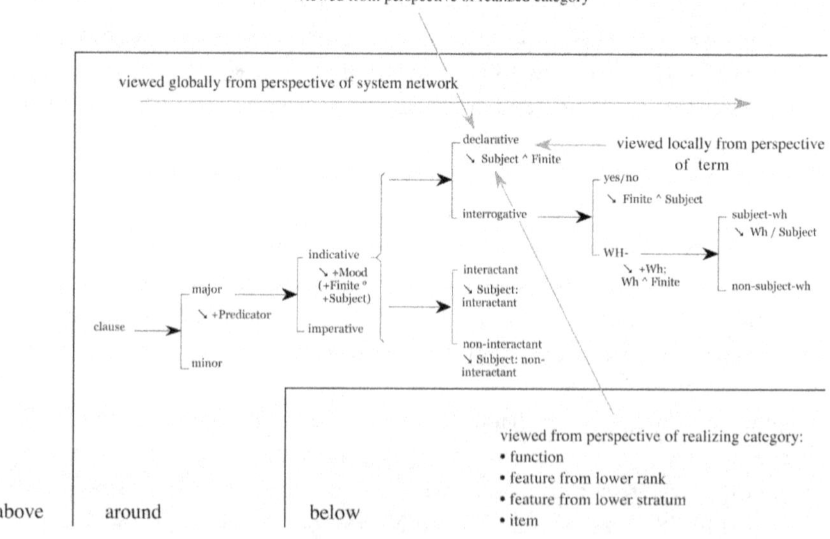

Figure 1.7 Trinocular perspective illustrated by reference to the category of 'Subject' ('from above': element held modally responsible for success of proposition/proposal; 'from around': element implicated in realization statements associated with agnate mood types; 'from below': element realized by nominal group in 'nominative' case (where relevant) agreeing with verb serving as Finite in number and person (where relevant)).

The trinocular principle we use in description also applies to the matching of patterns encountered in text analysis to grammatical categories in the description of the system: they are recognized by considering their properties 'from below', but this is checked against considerations 'from roundabout' (what are closely agnate variants of the pattern?) and considerations 'from above' (what does the pattern mean?). (Martin and Rose 2005 emphasize the significance of the trinocular principle in literacy education, showing how it makes it possible to transcend monocular thesis-antithesis debates locked into the view either 'from below' or 'from above'.)

Trinocular vision can be defined by reference not only to the dimension of stratification but more generally by reference to any of the semiotic dimensions that embody an ordering in terms of a hierarchy or a cline. Thus locally, within a given stratum, we can use the hierarchy of rank to view a phenomenon, or a category, 'from above', 'from roundabout' and 'from below' – **shunting** along the rank scale to change our perspective (see Halliday 1961).

1.8.2 Trinocular vision in relation to instantiation

As a global semiotic dimension, the cline of instantiation is methodologically important. In the development of a description of the lexicogrammar of a language, the cline of instantiation defines: (a) the **inductive** approach; (b) the **abductive** approach; and (c) the **deductive** approach (using the three approaches identified by C. S. Peirce): see Figure 1.8.

(a) The **inductive** approach starts with the view 'from below' and moves upwards to systemic generalizations: patterns are identified in authentic text instances (the 'data', as in a corpus) and as we make new generalizations based on these, we move ***upwards*** along the cline of instantiation to some higher point to describe the system at that point. This approach is what has been called **corpus-driven** description (see Section 1.10 below for references and discussion).

(b) The **abductive** approach starts with the view 'from below' and moves upwards to relate it to an existing view 'from above' (so we might say that this also involves the view 'from roundabout'): patterns are identified in authentic texts instances (the 'data', as in a corpus) and these are matched against an existing description of the system at the potential pole of the cline of instantiation (or of a registerial subsystem intermediate between instance and potential). This approach is what has been called **text** (or **discourse**) **analysis**; it has played a significant role in the development of systemic functional descriptions.

(c) The **deductive** approach starts with the view 'from above' and moves ***downwards*** to matching (types of) instances: systemic generalizations are the starting point and as we probe these generalizations, we move downwards along the cline of instantiation to some lower point, text instances being the lowest point. These instances can be patterns that we search for in a corpus to determine whether they occur as predicted by the system (for example, to differentiate between impossible systemic intersections such as 'declarative: exclamative' and 'negative' and low-frequency ones such as 'interrogative: wh-' and 'negative'); but they can also be instances constructed by a native speaker for the purpose of probing the system (either the grammarian himself/herself, or a language consultant from whom the examples are **elicited**, often mediated by translation from another language). (The process of exemplification also involves a move down the cline of instantiation, from a category in the description of the system to an instance, as in approach that has been called **corpus-based** (see Section 1.10 below): cf. Halliday [1961] 2002b: 45, on exemplificatory description.)

Induction, abduction and deduction complement one another in the process of systemic functional description. For instance, the description of the system embodies the generalizations we have made inductively and these can be tested deductively by moving down the cline of instantiation to try to match the generalization against additional text instances or abductively by moving up the cline of instantiation to match additional text instances against the generalizations.

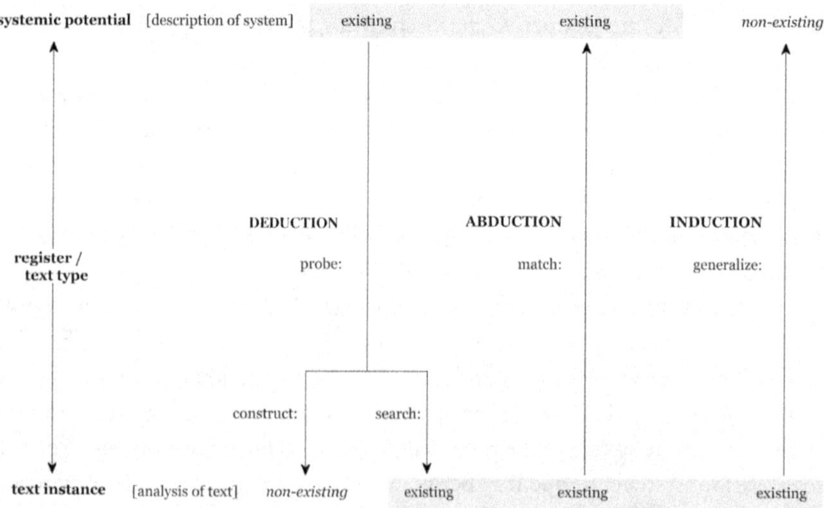

Figure 1.8 Approaches to the description of lexicogrammars defined by reference to the cline of instantiation

1.8.3 Presenting and arguing about descriptions

In presentations of lexicogrammatical descriptions, the semiotic dimensions again play a central role. Lexicogrammars are multidimensional; they are not organized linearly along some single dimension. Yet in presentations that appear in print, we have to 'linearize' the descriptions. This will involve some form of sweep across the metafunctional spectrum, starting with the highest rank and moving down to lower ranks. 'Stratal excursions' will be included wherever they are called for: comments on relevant semantic systems (e.g. speech function) and phonological systems (e.g. tone). The presentation will typically start with low delicacy and elaborate the description up to a certain point in delicacy. Generically, the document that results from these moves along the different semiotic dimensions will most likely be some form of taxonomic report (like *Lexicogrammatical cartography* – Matthiessen 1995b). The linear constraint can be overcome if we move to electronic hypertext presentations (see Nesbitt 1994; Matthiessen and Nesbitt 1996). Such a form of representation makes it possible to follow up links extending at any point along any of the dimensions; this is what the documentation facility in Bateman's KPML provides (see O'Donnell and Bateman 2005).

Presentations of lexicogrammatical descriptions organized as taxonomic reports will bring out the contours of the lexicogrammar quite clearly – even if they impose linearity where there is none. Such texts are ideational in orientation, being concerned with presenting the field of lexicogrammar to readers. However, they are generically different from arguments where alternative descriptions are compared and evaluated. Such argumentative texts are interpersonal in orientation, being concerned with changing the tenor of the relationship between writer and reader – convincing readers of some interpretation they might not otherwise deem probable. The evidence supporting a particular piece of description can be 'read off' the explicit representation of the description; for example, the description of the category of 'Subject' as an element in the interpersonal grammar of the clause is supported by the description shown in the system network in Figure 1.7: the Subject is interpersonal because realization statements in which it serves (as an operand) are located within the environment of terms in the interpersonal systems of MOOD – the presence of Subject (in 'indicative' as opposed to 'imperative' clauses), the relative sequence of Subject and Finite (Subject ^ Finite in 'declarative' clauses; Finite ^ Subject in 'interrogative: yes/no' clauses) and other aspects not shown in the system network fragment in Figure 1.7.

1.9 Description (grammar)

1.9.1 Overview

The publication in 1985 of the first edition of Halliday's *Introduction to Functional Grammar* provided the linguistic community with the first comprehensive systemic functional description of the clause and group/phrase grammar of a language. It has served as the foundation for a growing number of descriptions of English and as a model for descriptions of languages other than English (cf. Teruya *et al.* 2007): a number of these studies are listed in Table 1.5.[4] Some studies have dealt with earlier varieties of English, including Cummings (1980, 1983, 1984, 1995) on various aspects of Old English, Downing (1995) on THEME in Middle English (Chaucer) and Davies (1996) on THEME and INFORMATION until Shakespeare.

Here I will be concerned with the work on Modern English in the first instance. As can be seen from Table 1.5, the area of lexicogrammar that has received the greatest attention in systemic functional research on the grammar since the 1970s is the system of THEME, and Thompson (2007, chap. 23) is devoted to it. In the ideational area of lexicogrammar, the greatest effort has probably gone into the investigation of grammatical metaphor, while in the interpersonal area of lexicogrammar, a good deal of the effort has gone into the development of an account of interpersonal lexis, as part of the description of APPRAISAL (see Hood and Martin 2007).

1.9.2 Clause (complex)

1.9.2.1 Clause – logical: Taxis, logico-semantic type and systemic recursion

Halliday's (1985a) description of the logical systems of clause complexing – TAXIS, LOGICO-SEMANTIC TYPE, and SYSTEMIC RECURSION – provides considerably more detail than the previous references to clause complexing (e.g. Halliday 1965, 1977b), although Hudson's chapter in Huddleston *et al.* (1968) provides valuable details on clause complexes in scientific English. In Halliday (1977b), the TAXIS system is the same as now ('paratactic'/'hypotactic'), but the description of LOGICO-SEMANTIC TYPE has changed since then: the three-term system in (1977b) – 'expansion'/'identity'/'projection' – has been replaced by the systemic contrast between 'expansion' and 'projection' and the further differentiation of 'expansion' into 'elaborating', 'extending' and 'enhancing' relations. (The correspondences are roughly as follows: 1977b, 'expansion' > 'extending' and 'enhancing' types of

Table 1.5 Lexicogrammatical descriptions

Rank	Metafunction	System	English	Other languages
clause (and below)	[overview]		Halliday (1985a, 1994c); Halliday and Matthiessen (2004); Eggins (1994); Gerot and Wignell (1994); Matthiessen (1995b); Bloor and Bloor (1995); Thompson (1996)	Various: Caffarel, Martin and Matthiessen (2004) McDonald (1998); Chinese: Li (2003); Halliday and McDonald (2004) Japanese: Teruya (2004, 2007); Tagalog: Martin (2004a); Telugu: Prakasam (2004); Vietnamese: Thai (2004); Thai: Patpong (2006); Gooniyandi: McGregor (1990); Pitjantjatjara: Rose (2001b, 2004); Finnish: Shore (1992); French: Caffarel (1996, 2004, 2006); German: Steiner and Teich (2004); Danish: Andersen *et al.* (2001)
	ideational/ interpersonal	grammatical metaphor	Ravelli (1985); Halliday and Martin (1993); Halliday and Matthiessen (1999, chap. 6); Simon-Vandenbergen, Taverniers and Ravelli (2003); for work in China, see Fang *et al.* (2005)	Danish: Andersen (2003)
clause: complex	logical	TAXIS	Martin (1988b); Nesbitt and Plum (1988); Matthiessen and Thompson (1988); Matthiessen (2002a)	Chinese: Xiaoqing (1986) Japanese: Teruya (2009); Thomson (2001) Tagalog: Martin (1995a)
clause	experiential	TRANSITIVITY	Davidse (1991, 1992a,b, 1996a,b); Downing (1990); Halliday (1998a); Hasan (1987b); Matthiessen (1995b, chap. 4; 1999); Morley (1993); Steiner (1985)	Chinese: Long (1981); Japanese: Teruya (1998); Tagalog: Martin (1996b); Vietnamese: Hoang (1997); Telugu: Prakasam (1985, chap. 6); Gooniyandi: McGregor (1992, 1996); Western Desert: Rose (1996); Finnish: Shore

Rank	Metafunction	System	English	Other languages
		phase mood	Halliday (1984c); Matthiessen (1995b, chap. 5); Thibault (1995)	(1996); Danish: Smedegaard (2002); French: Caffarel (1997); Spanish: Arús (2003); Chinese: McDonald (1994); [typology:] Teruya *et al.* (2007, chap. 27) Japanese: Hori (1995) Tagalog: Martin (1990); Chinese: Zhu (1985, 1996)
	interpersonal	MODALITY	Phillips (1986); Torr (1998)	Japanese: Bateman (1988)
		POLARITY		
		MODAL	Halliday and James (1993)	
	textual	ASSESSMENT	Halliday and Matthiessen (2004: 125–32)	
		VOCATION		
		THEME	Poynton (1984)	Chinese: Peng (1993); Fang *et al.* (1995) Dari: Rashidi (1992); Japanese: Thomson (1998, 2001); Sasaki (1997); Nanri (2004) Weri: Boxwell (1995); German: Steiner and Ramm (1995); Danish: Andersen (2004); Norwegian (contrasted with English): Hasselgård (2004); Spanish: McCabe (1999)
			Bäcklund (1992); Collins (1991 a,b, 1992); Downing (1991); Fawcett and Huang (1997); Fries (1981, 1994, 1995, 2002); Francis (1989); Ghadessy (1995a); Ravelli (1995); Gosden (1993, 1996); Berry (1995, 1996); Hasan and Fries (1995); Huang (1996, 2002); Kies (1988); Martin (1992b); Thomas and Hawes (1997); Whitaker (1995); Ghadessy (1995b, 1999); Gómez-González (2001)	
group: complex (verbal)	logical	MODULATION: cause		Dutch, French: Degand (1996)

Rank	Metafunction	System	English	Other languages
group: verbal	logical	TENSE	Halliday (1980b); Matthiessen (1983a, 1984, 1996); Downing (1996a); Halliday and James (1993)	French: Caffarel (1992)
	experiential	TENSE; ASPECT EVENT TYPE		Polish: Gotteri (1996)
	Interpersonal	MODALITY, POLARITY	(see above under 'clause')	
	textual	VOICE	Downing (1996b)	
group: nominal		[general]		Indonesian: Sutjaja (1988)
	logical	MODIFICATION	Fries (1986b); Tucker (1997a,b)	
	experiential	THING TYPE EPITHESIS	Tucker (1996); Fries (1986b); Tucker (1997a,b); Halliday and Matthiessen (1999: 189–205)	
	interpersonal	ATTITUDE	Poynton (1984,1996)	
clause, group	textual	COHESION	Hasan (1984a); Ren (1993); Fine (1994); Parsons (1995, 1996); for work in China, see Fang *et al.* (2005)	Arabic: Aziz (1988) Chinese: Hu (1981)
Information unit	textual	INFORMATION	Prakasam (1985, chap.7); Davies (1996); Geluykens (1989); Bloor and Bloor (1992); Martinec (1995: 157–68); Halliday and Greaves (2008)	

'expansion'; 1977b, 'identity' > 'elaborating'.) The development of the account of the clause complex made it possible to dispense with the 'sentence' as a rank above the clause (as in Halliday 1961). The description presented in Halliday (1985b) has been the basis for further research in three areas: (a) quantitative profiles; (b) grammaticalization; and (c) discourse semantics and register variation.

1.9.2.1 Quantitative profiles of TAXIS *and* LOGICO-SEMANTIC TYPE

The quantitative profiles of TAXIS and LOGICO-SEMANTIC TYPE have been described in two research projects (cf. Section 1.5 above) – Nesbitt and Plum's (1988) study based on sociolinguistic interviews and my own long-term research project based on a range of different registers (Matthiessen 2002a; 2006a). This research has revealed the patterns of partial association between the systems of TAXIS and LOGICO-SEMANTIC TYPE, as already shown in Figure 1.2. Certain combinations are favoured – in particular, 'idea' and 'hypotaxis', 'enhancing' and 'hypotaxis'; others are disfavoured – in particular, 'idea' and 'parataxis' and 'extending' and 'hypotaxis' and yet others are neutral – 'locution' does not strongly favour either 'parataxis' or 'hypotaxis' and the same is true (to a lesser extent) of 'elaborating'. These quantitative interactions between TAXIS and LOGICO-SEMANTIC TYPE are related to other properties of the overall lexicogrammatical system having to do with the overall division of semiotic labour across grammatical environments.

The systems of TAXIS and LOGICO-SEMANTIC TYPE can also be examined in relation to the system of SYSTEMIC RECURSION within the clause complex.

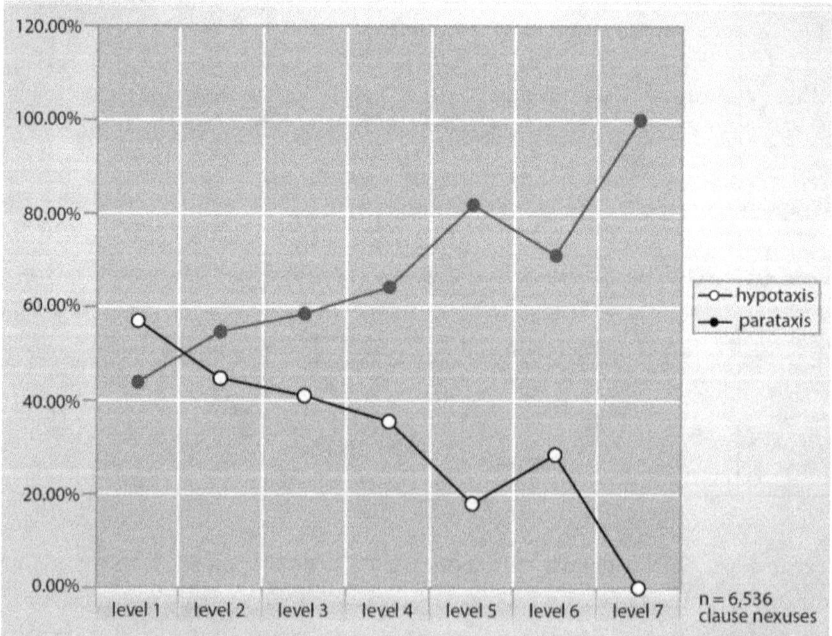

Figure 1.9 The systems of TAXIS and SYSTEMIC RECURSION SYSTEM (depth of nesting, from greatest depth = level 1) in clause complexes

Focusing on recursion involving internal nesting, shown in Figure 1.9, I found that 'hypotaxis' and 'parataxis' are close to being equiprobable at the greatest depth of nesting within the overall organization of clause complexes ('level 1') but approach the skew of 0.1/0.9 as the level of nesting decreases. In other words, 'hypotaxis' is more common in the local organization of clause complexes than in the global organization.

Based on the rhetorical-relational account of the semantic organization of text in terms of Rhetorical Structure Theory (e.g. Mann, Matthiessen and Thompson 1992; see Cloran, Stuart-Smith and Young 2007, chap. 22: Section 3), Sandy Thompson and I came to the realization in the mid-1980s that clause complexing can be interpreted as grammaticalization of rhetorical complexing in the semantic organization of text (see Matthiessen and Thompson 1988; Matthiessen 2002a; and Hopper and Traugott 1993: 169: 175–176, on this work in relation to grammaticalization). A text is organized relationally at the level of semantics by rhetorical relations of projection and expansion forming rhetorical complexes. These rhetorical complexes are nested within one another, extending from the global organization of the whole text to the local organization of units (figures/moves/messages) realized by clauses (in the congruent mode). The local rhetorical complexes may be realized by clause complexes, as illustrated in Figure 1.10. Here rhetorical relations are typically marked by structural conjunctions (binders and linkers) and this marking may be supported by non-structural, cohesive conjunctions, which typically mark less local rhetorical relations.

Clause complexes embody the same range of logico-semantic relations as rhetorical complexes – the fractal types of expansion and projection (see Sections 1.3.1.2 and 1.3.2 above). This is why they can serve as realizations of rhetorical complexes. But the fractal types are manifested in other environments as well – including the systems of CONJUNCTION and CIRCUMSTANTIATION; and these can serve to realize rhetorical complexes, as in:

> Furthermore, the occurrence of strong depletion was a year-long phenomenon south of 600S and was not confined to the spring season as in preceding years, although the greatest depletion occurred during the Southern Hemisphere spring. **Therefore** it is no longer a relatively local, isolated effect (Figure 4.3). (Cf. paratactic clause nexus: ... ~ so it is not longer a relatively local, isolated effect.)
>
> For our active duty military families, the status of military housing is a particular concern **because of** its immediate impact on quality of life. (Cf. hypotactic nexus: ... ~ because it impacts quality of life directly.)

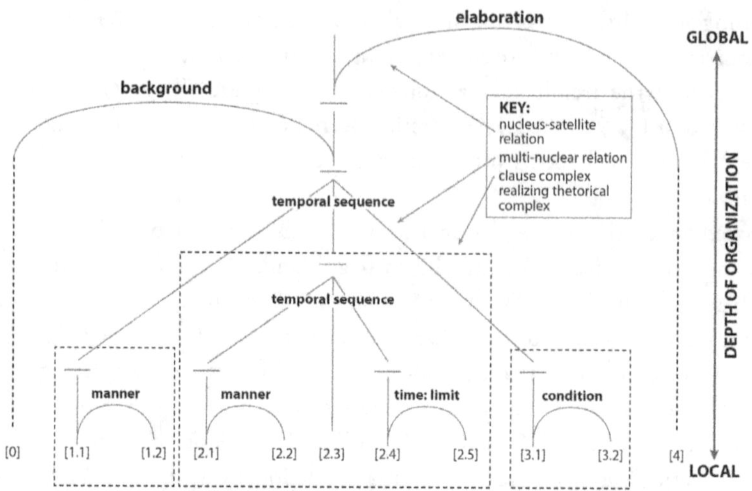

[0] [Ingredients] ||| [1.1] Cook the Brussels sprouts || [1.2] as described in the introduction. ||| [**THEN→**] [2.1] Put them in an electric blender of food processor || [2.2] (using the sharp blades); || [2.3] moisten with a little stock, milk or cream || [2.4] and process || [2.5] until the mixture is fairly smooth. ||| [**THEN→**] [3.1] Season with a little butter and << [3.2] if liked, >> a touch of freshly grated nutmeg. ||| [**ELABORATE→**] [4] Serves 4-6. |||

"Puree of Brussels Sprouts", p. 107, Margaret Fultion's "New Cookbook", Sydney: Angus & Robertson.

Figure 1.10 Rhetorical-relational organization of a text at the level of semantics; realization of local rhetorical complexes by clauses complexes (indicated by shading) at the level of lexicogrammar

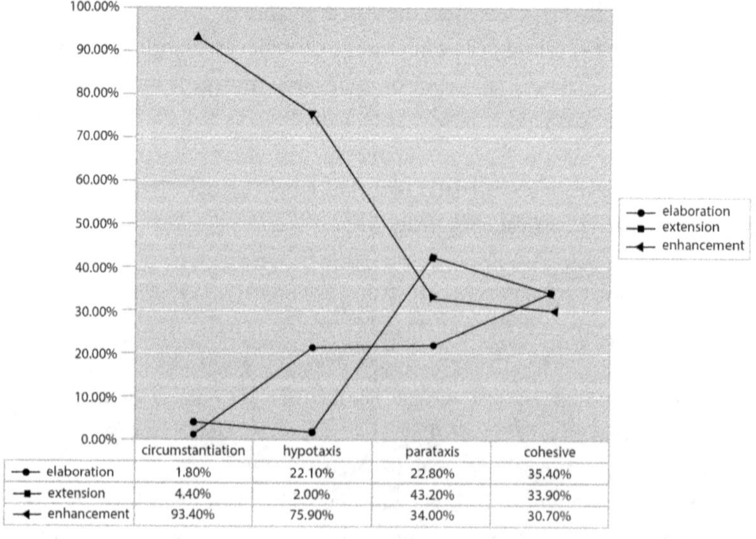

	circumstantiation	hypotaxis	parataxis	cohesive
elaboration	1.80%	22.10%	22.80%	35.40%
extension	4.40%	2.00%	43.20%	33.90%
enhancement	93.40%	75.90%	34.00%	30.70%

Figure 1.11 Relative frequencies of manifestations of expansion types in different grammatical environments – structural, clause (circumstantiation) and clause nexus (hypotaxis, parataxis); non-structural (cohesive). The cohesive counts are based on Stuart-Smith (2001)

When part of the rhetorical complex is realized circumstantially, this realization involves a grammatical metaphor as in the example above. The relative frequencies of the different types of expansion can be compared across the environments in which they are manifested (I have not included projection here, since it is not realized by cohesive conjunctions): see Figure 1.11. The frequency patterns bring out the fact that the clause complex is intermediate between cohesive conjunction and circumstantiation, with parataxis more like cohesive conjunction and hypotaxis more like circumstantiation (see Matthiessen 2002a, for further discussion).

The relationship between the rhetorical organization of texts and the grammatical organization of clause complexes explains the variation found in the relative frequencies of the terms of the systems of TAXIS, LOGICO-SEMANTIC TYPE and SYSTEMIC RECURSION across registers.

Variation in TAXIS and LOGICO-SEMANTIC TYPE has already been illustrated above. This variation reflects the fact that texts in different registers are organized according to different rhetorical relations, both globally and locally. For instance, topographic procedures depend on enhancing relations of time, which is reflected within clause complexes, where 'enhancing' relations account for about half of all the selections within LOGICO-SEMANTIC TYPE: see Figure 1.4. In contrast, 'projection' is almost absent in this register, but plays a major role in news reports, as discussed by López Folgado (2000). He draws attention to the strategy often used in the news intermediate between prototypical hypotactic reporting and prototypical paratactic quoting, as in *US-Russian relations have cooled as President Yeltsin reminded President Clinton that he still has 'a full arsenal of nuclear weapons'* (cf. Halliday and Matthiessen 2004: 465); he calls this 'blend-taxis'.

Variation in SYSTEMIC RECURSION is related to mode in the first instance. Halliday (e.g. 1985c, 1987) has shown that prototypically spoken discourse tends towards clause complexes of greater intricacy than prototypically written discourse and this is borne out by my investigation (Matthiessen 2002a). There are different ways of bringing out the difference. In Table 1.6, the difference is shown in terms of the number of clauses per clause complex (and the number of words per clause); the counts for the total set of spoken and written texts analysed are given together with counts for one prototypically spoken text (a gossip passage within casual conversation) and one prototypically written text (a scientific report on a type of rock within a geology text book). Another way of bringing out the difference is to investigate the depth of nesting in clause complexes. Figure 1.12 shows that spoken discourse tends towards greater depth than written discourse: it extends over more 'levels' of nesting and a lower proportion of nexuses are local to level 1. However, as Halliday has pointed out, when we average clause complexes over whole texts, the potential for great intricacy in the spoken mode is not revealed. To bring it out, we can compare the profiles of the unfolding of prototypically spoken and written texts. Figure 1.13 does this for a media interview and an extract from a geology text book. As the interview unfolds, it is consistent in having more clauses per clause complex than the written text; but in addition it reaches great intricacy at several points including one 'megaplex' of 17 clauses, this megaplex serves to propel a narrative episode forward within the interview.

The tendency towards more intricate clause complexes in spoken discourse than in written discourse means that clause complexes tend to cover more of the

Table 1.6 Spoken and written mode – counts for total sample and for prototypical examples

	spoken: gossip	**spoken: total**	**written: total**	**written: scientific report**
# of clauses	341	3,870	2,197	120
# of complexes (of > = 2 clauses)	64	932	653	30
# clauses/complex (of > = 2)	4.1	3.0	2.6	2.5
# words/clause	5.8	7.6	10.2	19

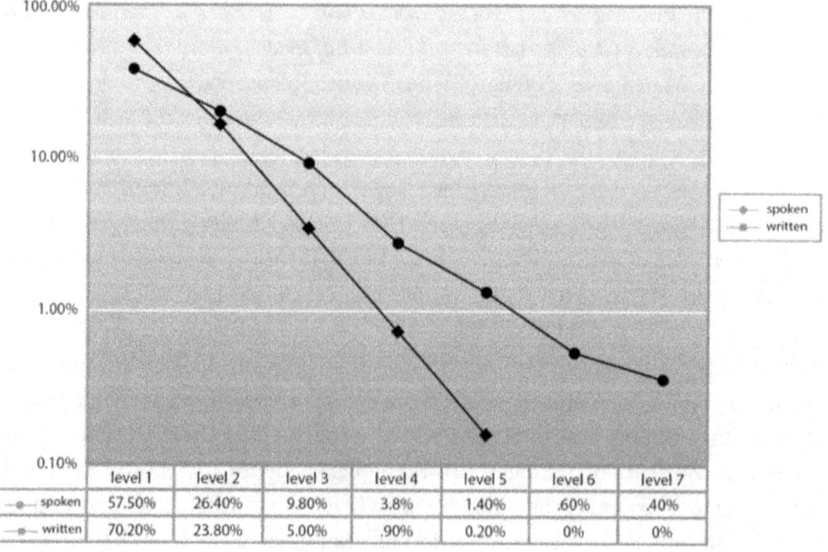

Figure 1.12 Spoken and written mode and percentage of nexuses at different levels of layering (logarithmic scale)

rhetorical relational organization of text in speech than in writing. In written discourse, rhetorical complexes are often realized incongruently by clauses rather than congruently by clause complexes (see Matthiessen 1995a; 2002a); for instance, the relation of cause is realized incongruently in the following examples from a factorial explanation in secondary school discussed in Veel (1997): [*physical weathering*] *is the cause of the breaking-up of large rocks into smaller pieces; changes in temperature cause the rock to expand and shrink*. As a result, they are compressed grammatically and the clauses are lexically denser.

High grammatical intricacy and low lexical density characterize prototypical spontaneous discourse, while low grammatical intricacy and high lexical density characterize prototypical written discourse. But this is a cline and there are points intermediate between prototypical spoken and prototypical written discourse. For example, Francis and Kramer-Dahl (1992: 68–72) show how a case history appearing in an academic journal is like prototypical writing, whereas Oliver Sacks' well-known accounts in *The man who mistook his wife for a hat* are closer to the spoken pole of the cline.

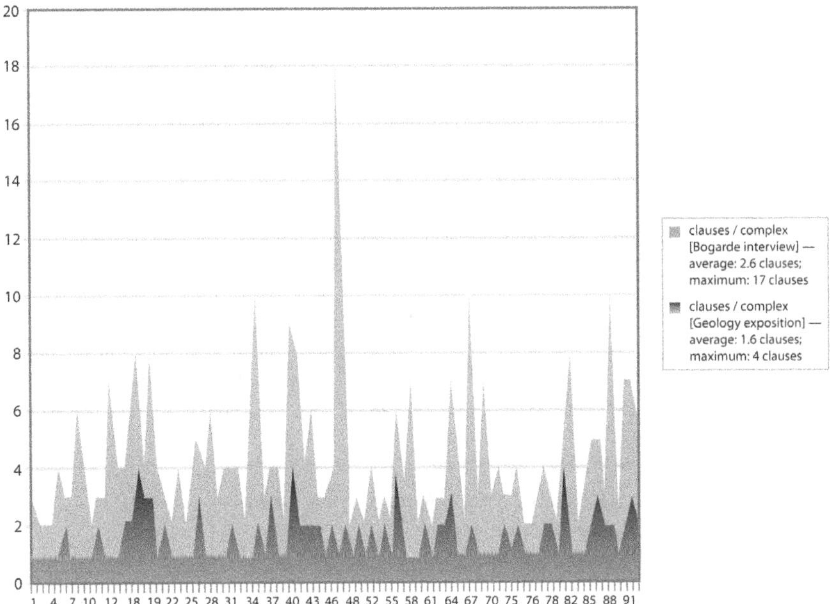

Figure 1.13 Logogenesis of prototypical spoken text (interview: light grey) and prototypically written text (scientific report: dark grey)

1.9.2.2 Clause – experiential: transitivity

Halliday's (1985a) description of the experiential system of the clause TRANSITIVITY is the result of a long-term investigation. The systemic description produced in 1964 as part of the 'Bloomington grammar' (published in Halliday 1976, and 2002c: 136) is based on the primary distinction between 'intensive' and 'extensive' clauses. 'Intensive' clauses correspond to 'relational' ones in later descriptions, while all the examples of 'extensive' clauses correspond to 'material' clauses in later work. Halliday's (e.g. 1967c,d, 1968) subsequent descriptions of the system became more explicitly comprehensive, but they also brought out more clearly the natural relation between the grammar of TRANSITIVITY and the corresponding semantic system (cf. Halliday and Matthiessen 1999, chap. 5). In IFG 1, Halliday shows very clearly that the system is a resource for construing our experience of a quantum of change in the flow of events. The IFG description is compared with other approaches to transitivity by Martin (1996a) and Matthiessen (forthcoming a: 120–156). It has been the basis for a number of further investigations dealing with: (a) the nature of the transitive and ergative models of transitivity; (b) the extension of the description of process type in delicacy; (c) the quantitative profiling of the system; and (d) discourse uses.

Halliday (1967c,d, 1968) had already shown in the 1960s that the lexicogrammar of TRANSITIVITY in English embodies two models of process and participation in the process – the transitive model and the ergative model (updated and summarized in Section 5.8 of Halliday 1985a; Halliday 1967a, refers to Dirr's 1928, work on Caucasian languages for the introduction of the term 'ergative') and

Table 1.7 'Transitive' and 'ergative' as different systemic domains of 'material' clauses in Davidse's (1992c: 130) account

	transitive	**ergative**
middle	[+ambient] *it's raining, it's snowing* [–ambient: +superventive] *he fell, he died* [–ambient: –superventive] *the children are running, the soldiers are marching*	*the glass broke, the balloon burst*
pseudo-effective	*it's raining cats and dogs, he died the death of a saint, they're running a race*	*the cooling system burst a pipe, the truck broke an axle*
effective	[goal-directed] *the teacher hit the child, the lion is chasing the tourist* [goal-achieving] *the doctor accidentally touched a nerve, the arrow hit the target*	[instigation of process] *the cat broke the glass, Lizzy burst the balloon* [instigation of action] *the general is marching the soldiers, mother sat the baby up*

he had drawn attention to the significance of these two models in the construal of experience through his analysis of passages relating to different 'world views' in Golding's *The Inheritors* (Halliday 1971). In Halliday's account, the transitive and the ergative models are interpreted as two complementary perspectives on transitivity, with both models operating throughout the entire system (Halliday and Matthiessen 1999, chap. 5, 2004: Section 5.8). In contrast, Davidse (e.g. 1992c) has reinterpreted 'transitive' and 'ergative' as different systemic domains within the overall system of transitivity, as illustrated for 'material' clauses in Table 1.7.

In my own work, I have followed Halliday, continuing to interpret the transitive and the ergative as complementary models (e.g. Matthiessen 1995b, chap. 4) and I have explored their operation in discourse. Interestingly (but not surprisingly), it seems that certain registers foreground the transitive model, whereas others foreground the ergative model (as illustrated in Section 5.8 of Halliday and Matthiessen 2004). Caffarel (1997, 2004) has found the same kind of division of labour in French. For instance, traditional narratives foreground the transitive model, whereas the discourses of physical science foreground the ergative model. If this is so, the complementarity of the two models can be understood in relation to the evolving range of registers that make up a language (cf. Rose 2001b, for discussion in relation to the Western Desert).

The work on languages other than English has thus thrown additional light on the nature of the complementarity of the transitive and ergative models, as can be seen in the contributions to Caffarel, Martin and Matthiessen (2004). This work suggests that the complementarity can vary both in terms of register (as noted above) and in terms of PROCESS TYPE (see comments on Chinese vs. English below). For example, in my exploratory work on Akan, I found that the transitive model seemed to dominate except in the area of emotive mental clauses, where there are systemic agnates that can be interpreted according to the ergative model (Medium + Process + Range vs. Phenomenon + Process + Senser), just like English pairs such as *like/please*. Martin's (1996c, 2004a) work on Tagalog has extended our knowledge of complementary transitivity models in languages: he shows that the Tagalog system of transitivity is based on the complementarity of a 'centrifugal' model and a 'centripetal' one.

The system of PROCESS TYPE is described up to a certain degree in delicacy in Halliday (1985a, chap. 5): the primary process types ('material/behavioural/mental/verbal/relational/existential') and the secondary systemic contrasts within these (e.g. 'relational: intensive/possessive/circumstantial'). There have been two complementary approaches to extending the description in delicacy, moving from the grammar to lexis.

1. Hasan (1985a, 1987b) has demonstrated how the description of certain types of 'material' clause can be extended in delicacy to the point where intersections of systemic features are realized by different lexical verbs. Part of Hasan's (1987b) system network for 'material' clauses of 'disposal' is represented in Figure 1.14 and the lexical verbs differentiated by this system network are set out in Table 1.8. (A similar example for 'verbal' clauses is given in Halliday and Matthiessen 2004: 44.) The system network models the lexical field of 'disposal' multidimensionally, the fundamental dimensions being represented by the systems of BENEFACTION, ACCESS and CHARACTER. (This is different from 'componential analysis' in that the systemic features represent paradigmatic values, not syntagmatic components.)

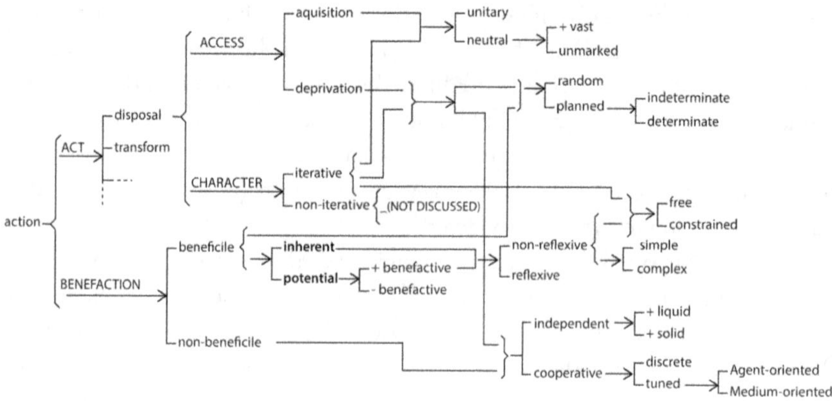

Figure 1.14 Part of Hasan's (1987b) network for processes of 'disposal'

Table 1.8 Lexical verbs realizing the Event of the verbal group serving as Process in 'material' clauses of disposal according to intersection of features in BENEFACTION, ACCESS and CHARACTER

	acquisition		**deprivation**	
non-beneficile			independent solid strew liquid *spill* cooperative *share*	
beneficile	*buy*	unitary *gather* neutral unmarked *collect* vast accumulate	random *scatter* planned indeterminate *divide* determinate *distribute*	*give*
	non-iterative	iterative		non-iterative

Table 1.9 Levin's (1993) verb classes (secondary) classified according to process type (primary)

PROCESS TYPE	Verb classes		Verbs		Verbs per verb class
	number of verb classes	percentage	number of verbs	percentage	
material	129	58.1%	2,734	62.2%	22.2
behavioural	23	10.4%	400	9.1%	17.4
mental	20	9.0%	463	10.5%	23.2
verbal	14	6.3%	350	8.0%	25
relational	30	13.6%	370	8.4%	12.3
existential	5	2.3%	79	1.8%	15.8
TOTAL	221		4,396		

2. Complementing this detailed and explicit description of certain types of process type, I have developed a rough map by classifying Levin's (1993) 'verb classes' in terms of the system of PROCESS TYPE (via subtypes within this system) and am adding classes to her description from Matthiessen (1995b) in areas that are not covered by her classification (in particular, 'mental' and 'verbal' processes). The result of this effort is stored in a database system developed together with Wu Canzhong. There are currently 221 verb classes and 4,396 verbs within these classes, distributed according to PROCESS TYPE as specified in Table 1.9.

The classification is represented diagrammatically by means of a radial graph in Figure 1.15. This gives a rough sense of the distribution of lexical resources across the process types: 'material' process clauses dominate with almost 60 per cent of all verb classes and a little over 60 per cent of all verbs (cf. Matthiessen 1999). As the radial graph shows, there are several intermediate classes between the terminal verb classes and the primary process types. In future work, these intermediate classes will no doubt be extended into additional intermediate steps in delicacy. In addition, the description will be extended in delicacy for each verb class, which currently has 19.9 member verbs on average (lower for 'relational', 'existential' and 'behavioural' processes, somewhat higher for the other process types). This work will also involve corpus evidence – to support the further differentiation of the classes in delicacy, to test the existing classes and to extend the set of 4,400 verbs in the current database. (There are of course also other sources of verb classification to be taken into account, including for example the categories established by Householder's research project in the 1960s, Dixon's 1991, verb types, and

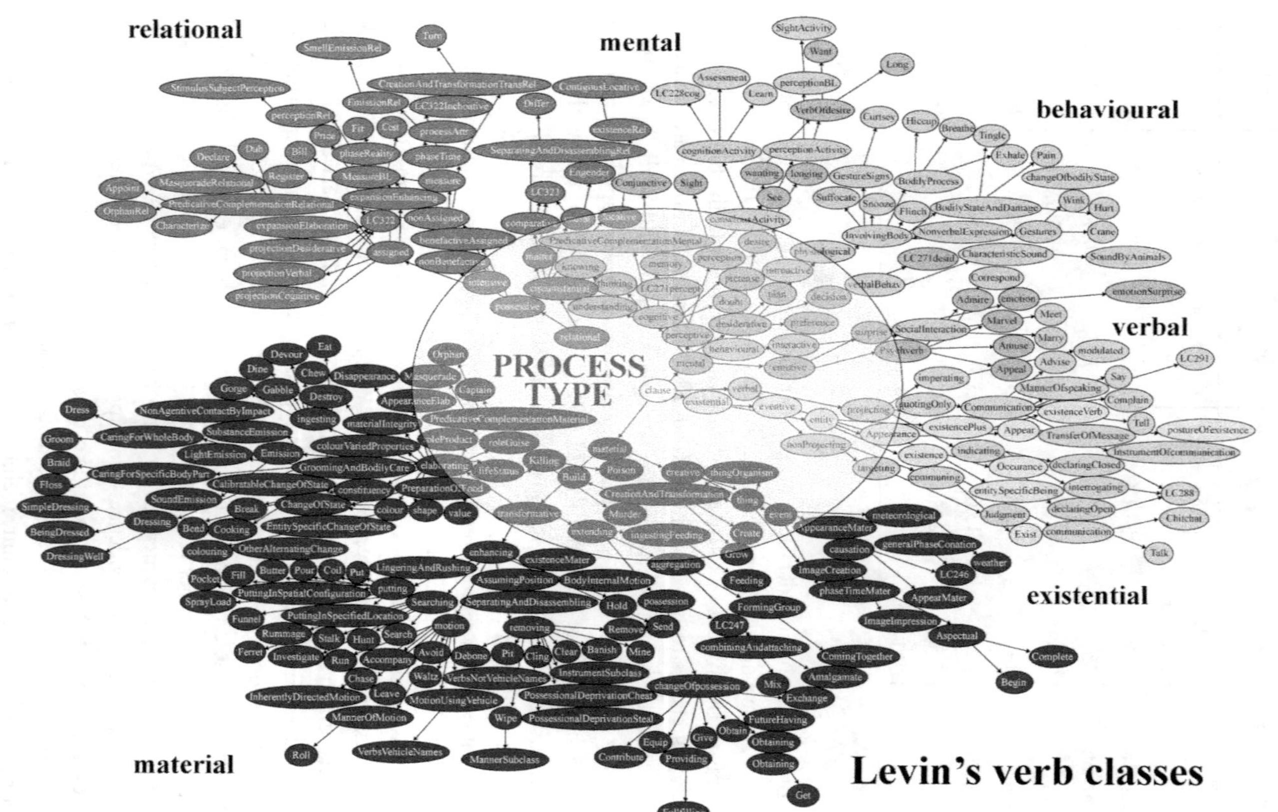

Figure 1.15 Extension of the description of process type in delicacy

Wierzbicka's 1987: 37 classes of 'speech act verbs', which can serve as a frame of reference in extending the account of 'verbal' processes in delicacy.)

While the Levinian classes are characterized as 'verb classes', it is important to keep in mind that the task in extending the description of PROCESS TYPE in delicacy is to take account of transitivity configurations – not just lexical verbs serving as (the Event in the verbal group realizing) the Process. For example, to take a contrasting pair from IFG, *break* + *heart* is a 'mental' configuration, while *break* + *bone(s)* is a 'material' one. The Levinian classes are in fact interpretable as classes of clause nuclei since they are based on syntactic transitivity properties. The most important elements in these nuclei will almost certainly turn out to be the Process and the Medium, which are also the domain of many collocational patterns (cf. Matthiessen 1995b: 251, 253–255). But other transitivity roles are also involved here – which one will depend on what kind of process type we are describing. The description will have to take account of the kinds of pattern discussed by Tucker (2007).

In addition to the research on the system of PROCESS TYPE focused on extending the description in delicacy towards lexis, there have been a number of studies concerned with particular process types. Relating the 'Cardiff grammar' description of English (see Fawcett 2007) to Halliday's description of PROCESS TYPE, Fawcett (1987) outlines a description of 'relational' clauses. He summarizes the difference between his account and Halliday's (p. 178): "the range of process types covered here is very much broader than in Halliday's (1985a) approach to relational processes, including many types that would for him probably be 'material', while he makes many fine distinctions that are not here seen as necessary – particularly in the area of the intersection, in his terms, of 'identifying' and 'attributive' processes." The question of whether clauses construing change in location and change in possession are best interpreted as 'relational' or as 'material' has been helpful in exploring the complementarity between these primary process types: see Halliday and Matthiessen (1999: 159–165: 504–505) for some discussion.

In contrast with Fawcett, Davidse (1991; 1992a; 1996b) has explored the nature of 'identifying' and 'attributive' further, extending Halliday's (1967c,d, 1968) original account of 'identifying' clauses (which is more detailed than the description in IFG) and demonstrating the status of 'identifying' and 'attributive' clauses as fundamental categories of the grammar. This includes the role of 'identifying' clauses in definitions, an area investigated by Harvey (1996, 1999) in technical discourse. She shows how such clauses serve to construe new concepts and sheds light on the continuum between 'identifying' clauses of the 'decoding' type and 'attributive' clauses. The distinctive roles played by 'attributive' and 'identifying' clauses in the construction of 'knowledge' have also been illuminated from an ontogenetic perspective by Painter (1999).

1.9.2.3 Quantitative profiling of transitivity

The quantitative profiling of TRANSITIVITY has involved not only PROCESS TYPE but also AGENCY and CIRCUMSTANTIATION – and the intersection of these simultaneous systems. This is also an ongoing project, and I have reported on it twice (Matthiessen 1999, 2006a). As in other areas of the grammar, the quantitative profiling is revealing properties of the system that are hard to see with the 'naked eye'. I will just mention three of these.

1. There is a correlation between the systemic elaboration of the system of PROCESS TYPE and the relative frequencies of the different terms in this system: see Figure 1.16. In general, the more frequent the process type, the more elaborated it will be in the system in terms of the number of verb classes and verbs belonging to it (cf. Table 1.9) and in terms of augmentation by circumstances. For the details and apparent exceptions, see Matthiessen (1999, 2006a).

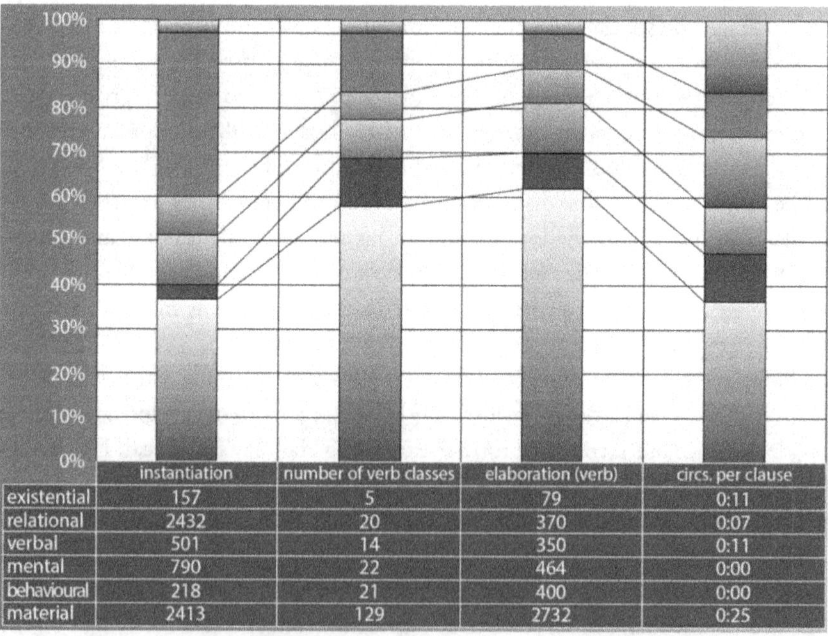

	instantiation	number of verb classes	elaboration (verb)	circs. per clause
existential	157	5	79	0:11
relational	2432	20	370	0:07
verbal	501	14	350	0:11
mental	790	22	464	0:00
behavioural	218	21	400	0:00
material	2413	129	2732	0:25

Figure 1.16 PROCESS TYPE: correlation between frequency of instantiation and systemic elaboration (number of verb classes, number of verbs and circumstances per clause)

2. The systemic contrast in agency between 'middle' and 'effective' is equiprobable for 'material' processes, but skewed fairly heavily towards 'middle' for all the other process types (though less heavily in 'relational' clauses than in 'behavioural', 'mental', 'verbal' and 'existential' ones): see Figure 1.17. This systemic interaction is an example of the general principle that probability profiles vary across languages and must be part of systemic functional typology. Thus Halliday and McDonald (2004: 376) note: 'agency as a systemic option in Chinese is largely confined to material clauses; we have classified these as either transitive or intransitive, but they could also be interpreted in ergative terms ... as either middle (with Medium, ± Range) or effective (with Medium + Agent).' So the tendencies are the same in Chinese and English, but once we have counts for Chinese comparable to those for English in Figure 1.17, they will almost certainly reveal a probabilistic difference between the two languages.

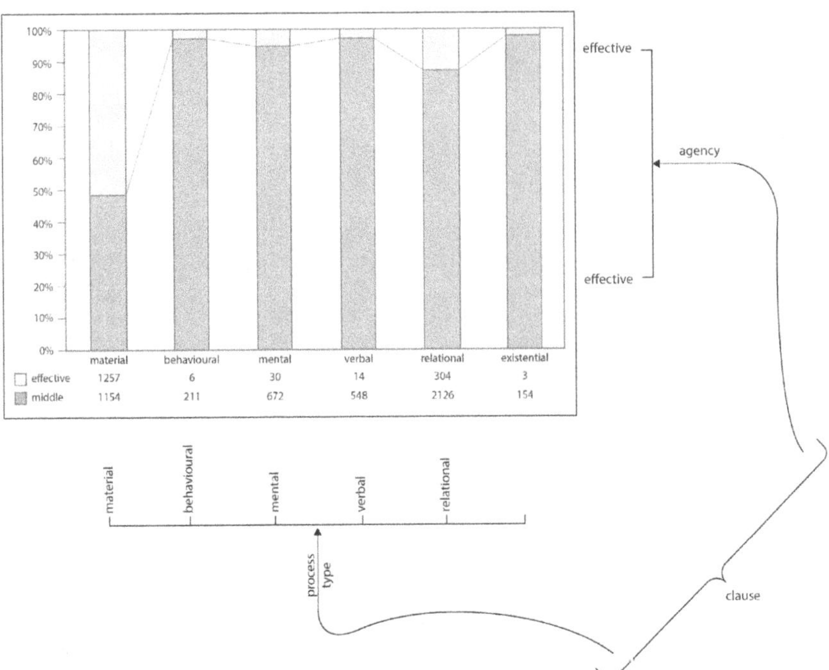

Figure 1.17 The intersection of the systems of AGENCY and PROCESS TYPE

3. Although the systems of circumstantial transitivity, CIRCUMSTANTIATION, have been represented as simultaneous with the systems of nuclear transitivity, PROCESS TYPE and AGENCY, there are paradigmatic patterns of strong 'attraction' and 'repulsion', as shown for CIRCUMSTANTIATION and PROCESS TYPE in Figure 1.18. There are many details here to take account of – for example, the 'attraction' between 'matter' and 'behavioural', 'mental' and 'verbal' processes, between 'degree' and 'behavioural' and 'mental' and between 'means' and 'material' processes; but what is important for the future research programme is to document these interactions and to describe them systemically. This task clearly goes together with the extension of the description of process type in delicacy. Many of the patterns of

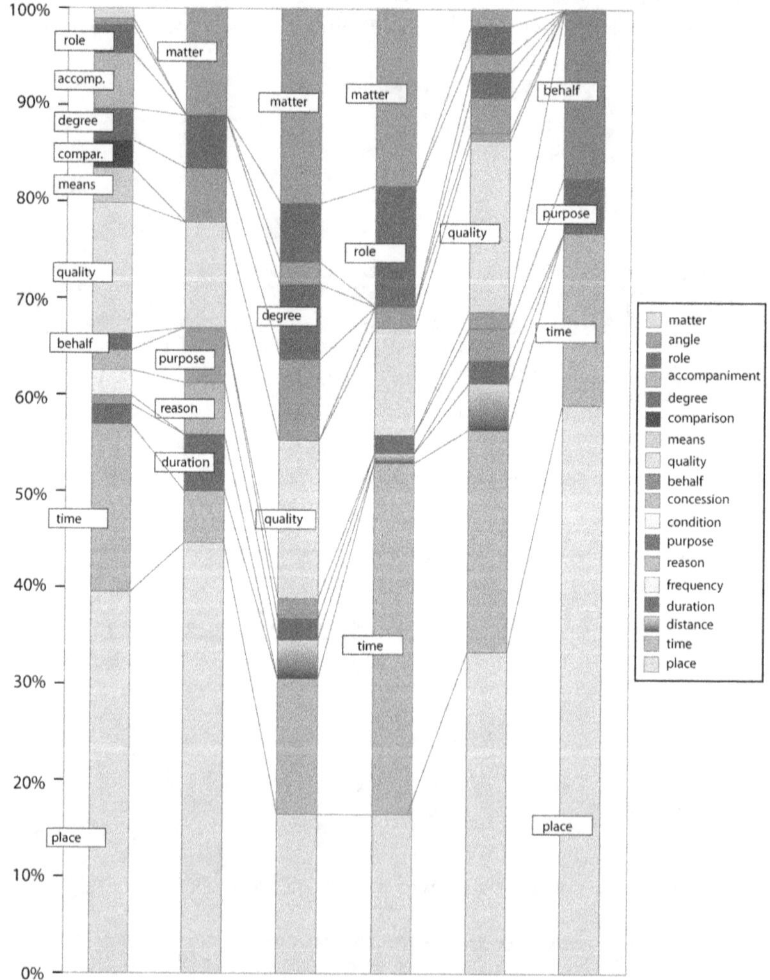

Figure 1.18 The systems of CIRCUMSTANTIATION in relation to PROCESS TYPE

interaction will be of the kind that would be described in 'construction grammar' (e.g. Kay and Fillmore 1999) or in 'pattern grammar' (Hunston and Francis 2000). The patterns of interaction shown in Figure 1.18 also indicate likely collocational domains. One such domain is Process + Degree, where we find very clear preferences for certain combinations of verb + adverb (e.g. understand + completely, want + badly, love + deeply). Some (or even most) of these can be explained by reference to lexical metaphors.

Thanks to the growing body of manually-analysed texts from a wide range of registers, a good deal has been learned in the last 25 years or so about the 'discourse uses' of different transitivity types (different process types, different combinations of process type and agency, of process type and circumstance type and so on). The connection between transitivity types and discourse uses is brought out by the kind of quantitative research discussed above.

1. There is considerable variation across texts from different registers, indicating the relative contribution made by different transitivity types to different registers. For example, in a sample of reports in science discourse, relational clauses are by far the most frequent of all the primary process types at a little over 50 per cent (compared with around 38 per cent in a cross-registerial sample of 6,490 clauses), while they only account for about 25 per cent of all process types in (hard) news reports, where 'verbal' clauses (not surprisingly!) have a much higher share (around 18 per cent) than average (around 9 per cent). If we have counts for a cross-registerial corpus of texts, we can thus characterize texts within various registers relative to these counts, as illustrated in Figure 1.19.

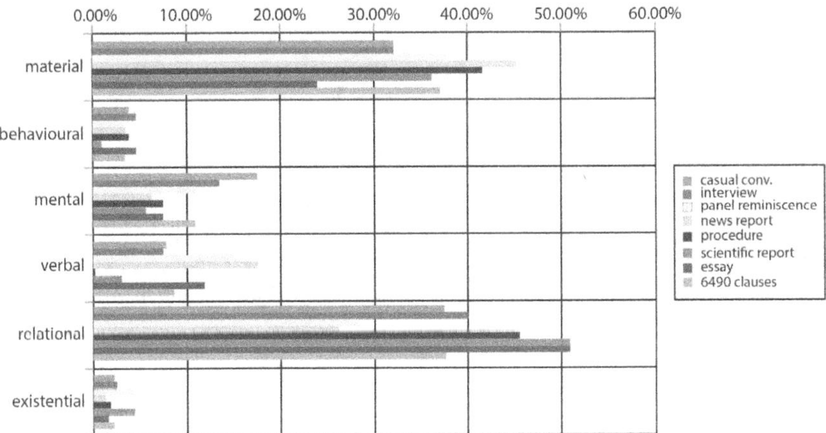

Figure 1.19 Relative frequencies of terms in the system of PROCESS TYPE in texts from seven different registers compared with a cross-registerial sample of texts (comprising 6,490 clauses). The vertical lines indicate the values for the cross-registerial sample of texts

2. Text scores representing transitivity selections in the course of the unfolding of a text give an indication of successive phases in the text, as illustrated by the graph in Figure 1.20. These phases are likely to correspond to generic stages or sub-stages in the generic (schematic) structure of the situation in which the text unfolds. For instance, the selection of 'existential' clauses at the beginning of the text is part of the Placement (cf. Hasan 1984b), illustrating the use of 'existential' clauses in introducing characters in narrative text: *Once, a very long time ago, there lived a man called Noah*. The following peak of selections of 'verbal' clauses indicate the Initiating Event of God's dialogue with Noah, illustrating the use of 'verbal' clauses in the construction of dramatic dialogue in narrative text: *One day God spoke to Noah. 'I am going to send a great flood to wash the world away,' he said*. Alternatively, one can start by identifying these stages and then count transitivity selections for each stage, as Fries (1985) and Washitake (2004) have done in studies of narrative texts. Using Rothery and Steglin's (1997) description of the generic structure of narratives, Washitake (2004: 175) shows how the selections in the system of PROCESS TYPE vary from one generic stage to another (see Figure 1.21). From example, 'existential' plays an important role in the Orientation (or 'Placement' in Hasan's 1984b, terms: *There was once a sweet little goat*), but is then not selected again in the remainder of the text. In contrast, 'relational' clauses peak in the Evaluation.

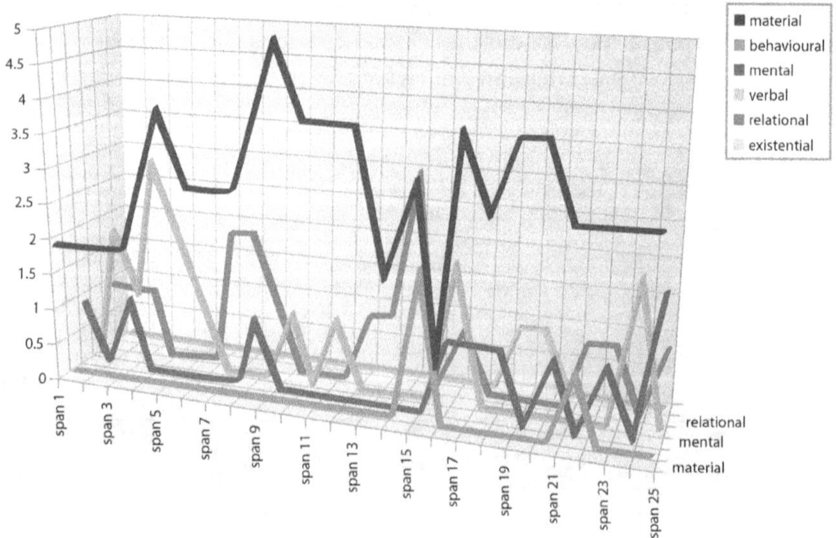

Figure 1.20 Text score showing selections in process type in spans of five clauses in the unfolding of version for children of Noah's Ark

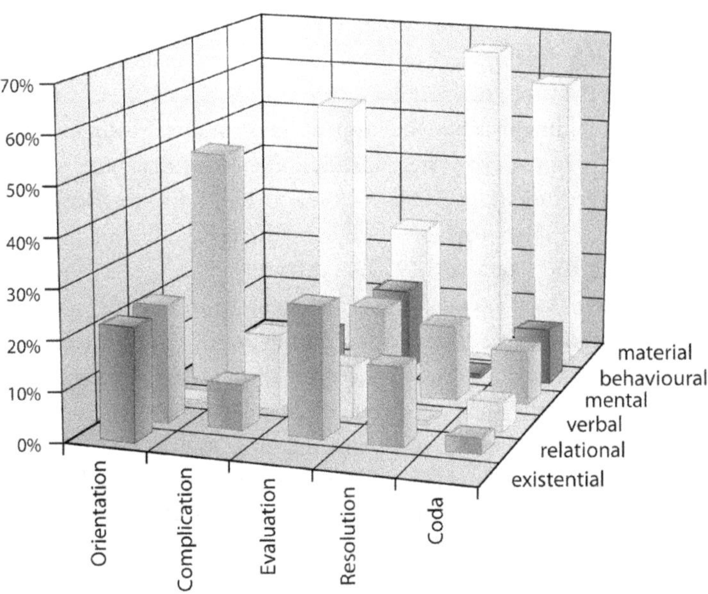

Figure 1.21 Generic staging of a narrative text – distribution of selections within PROCESS TYPE (based on Washitake 2004, Table 2: 175)

1.9.2.4 Clause – interpersonal: MOOD

Halliday had described the system of MOOD in some considerable detail already in the 'Bloomington Grammar' of 1964 (see Halliday 1976: 101–135), which was no doubt partly due to his work on tone and the 'KEY' systems realized through TONE (see Halliday 1967b). This was followed in Halliday (1970b) by his detailed account of the system of MODALITY, one key feature of which was reinterpreted in later work: modulation was first interpreted in ideational terms, but then reinterpreted in interpersonal terms as the modality of proposals. Halliday's (1985a) description of the interpersonal systems of the clause – MOOD, POLARITY, MODALITY, MODAL ASSESSMENT – showed how these systems are resources for negotiation in dialogue and constitute the grammar of exchange. The description has provided the basis for various studies of the interpersonal grammar of English (cf. Thibault 1995) and of other languages (for an overview, see Teruya *et al.* 2007, chap. 27). (For quantitative aspects of these systems comparable to those discussed with reference to TRANSITIVITY above, see Matthiessen 2005.) These include accounts of the ontogenesis of these interpersonal systems, as in Halliday (1984a) on MOOD and Torr (1998) on MODALITY. Painter (2003) shows the origins and development of the system of APPRAISAL.

However, most of the work drawing on Halliday's account of MOOD has been concerned with the development of the semantic system realized by MOOD – the system of SPEECH FUNCTION. Drawing also on Halliday (1984a), a number of systemic functional linguists have developed the account of this semantic system further, thus helping to reveal the semantic dimensions that underpin, and are grammaticalized in, mood: see Martin (1992a, chap. 2), Eggins and Slade (1997, chaps. 3, 5). Tsui (1989) provides a bridge to the Birmingham School research (based on Sinclair and Coulthard 1975) in this area.

These accounts of SPEECH FUNCTION take MOOD into account (as well as other systems of the interpersonal grammar and certain systems of the ideational grammar that are pressed into interpersonal service through the strategy of interpersonal metaphor); but they do not include explicit realization statements showing the inter-stratal relationship between semantic categories and lexicogrammatical ones: such statements are provided in Hasan's as yet largely unpublished description of the system of SPEECH FUNCTION (see Hasan 1989, 1996a: chap. 5, for work drawing on this description; and see Hasan *et al.* 2007a) – a feature which distinguishes it not only from the systemic functional accounts just mentioned but also from numerous descriptions of 'speech acts'. Since the realization statements are explicit (as illustrated in Hasan *et al.* 2007a: Table 24.4), it is possible to read off the range of meanings of the different mood types in the grammar – their 'discourse uses' and also to see how combinations of grammatical features serve to realize delicate speech-functional categories (cf. Section 1.3.1.1 above). This reveals how the systems of mood, mood person and modality work together in the realization of speech functions – particularly in incongruent realizations (see Halliday and Matthiessen 2004: 632–633; Matthiessen 1995b: 439–440); and it also shows how ideational resources are 'co-opted' to do interpersonal service in the realization of speech function.

Halliday's description of mood in English took account from the start of more delicate distinctions involving systems of key and force that are realized phonologically by terms within the system of tone (Halliday 1963b, 1967b): for references to work since the 1970s, see Greaves 2007) and for an updated, expanded account, see Halliday and Greaves (2008). In a recently completed research project at UTS and Macquarie University, we carried out a tristratal analysis of service encounters in terms of speech function, mood and tone in order to obtain quantitative information about correspondences across these systems and to extend the account in delicacy (see Matthiessen *et al.* 2005, for a progress report).

The system of modal assessment is described systemically for the first time in Halliday and Matthiessen (2004: 125–132) and related to the categories identified in the description of appraisal by Martin and others (2003); for the description of appraisal, see Hood and Martin (2007). With these developments, we can see quite clearly the significance of the system of degree of modal assessment ('high'/ 'median'/'low') within both grammar and lexis (cf. Martin 1992b).

1.9.2.5 Clause – textual: THEME

Halliday's 'Bloomington grammar' from 1964 contained a detailed account of THEME and INFORMATION, with examples from spontaneous conversation (see Halliday 1976: 137, 141–142) – for example, *aged legal gentlemen all like pipes, it's inhaling that's harmful, the metal container somehow it turns your coffee rather sour.* He gave a detailed account of the system of INFORMATION in Halliday (1967b) and of THEME in Halliday (1967c,d, 1968). Before the consolidated account in IFG (Halliday 1985c) appeared, Fries (1981) had already published his influential study of the relationship between the choice of theme and the method of development of a text. The subsequent work on THEME drawing on IFG and Fries (1981) includes quantitative profiling of theme selections in texts belonging to different registers. The development of research on the system of THEME is discussed in Thompson (2007, chap. 23). For a recent comparison of the systemic functional account with work within the Prague School and Functional Grammar, see Gómez-González (2001); for a comparison of the analysis of THEME PREDICATION in IFG and the Cardiff grammar, see Huang (2002); for a recent critical review of the description of theme and counts in texts, see also Abdullayev (2003). A number of studies have explored how the description of THEME and other textual systems can be illuminated in modelling that also draws on work in computational linguistics: see Bateman and Matthiessen (1993), Matthiessen (1992) and Lavid (2000b).

The research into THEME has been important not only because it has shed further light on the textual resources of English and other languages, but also because it has given us a deeper understanding of the relationship between text semantics and clause grammar: see Martin's work on clause Theme in relation to macro-Theme and hyper-Theme in the textual semantic organization of text, his seminal contribution being 'Life as a noun' in Halliday and Martin (1993).

In addition, investigations of the textual clause grammar have been theoretically and methodologically important because they have often served as the entry point to work on languages other than English (cf. Rose 2001a). Since the text semantic principle behind the choice of Theme in the clause is well understood, researchers have been able to explore the textual organization of the clause without making any assumptions about Theme: starting with the organization of text, they have investigated the textual grammar of the clause (thus following the meaning-based model for functional typological investigations worked out by Martin 1983b).

There has also been some work on textual systems of the clause other than THEME. The system of CONJUNCTION has been illuminated by text-based research 'from above' in terms of Martin's (1992a, chap. 4) description of the semantic system of conjunctive relations (where conjunctive relations in text are taken into account even if they are not explicitly marked by conjunctions in the grammar). This research has confirmed the significance of the distinction between 'internal' and 'external' conjunction (identified by Halliday and Hasan 1976). Internal conjunctive relations tend to play a significant role in the global organization of texts oriented towards tenor, whereas external conjunctive relations tend to play a significant role in the global organization of texts oriented towards field (cf. also Halliday 2001). Similar findings concerning the division of labour between internal and external relations have emerged in the analysis of text based on RST.

Exploring the distinction between 'internal' and 'external' 'from below', in terms of explicit conjunctions, Oshima (2004: 70–80) analysed an academic journal article in mathematics, newspaper editorials and extracts from novels. He found that external conjunctions dominate in the mathematics article (around 80 per cent, the top three being the causal *then*, *hence* and *however* in that order), internal conjunctions dominate in the editorials (around 90 per cent, the top three being the adversative *but*, *however* and *in fact* in that order) and external and internal conjunctions are about equally balanced in the novels (around 57 per cent internal, the top three being *and*, *now* and *but*, around 43 per cent external, the top three being *presently*, *then* and *but*).

In addition to THEME and CONJUNCTION, the clause is the point of origin of the system of VOICE. Halliday (e.g. 1967c,d, 1968) had shown the textual significance of this system long before the 1980s and Svartvik's (1965) classic corpus-based study on 'voice in the English verb' provided quantitative information (although not from a specifically systemic functional point of view). Contrasts in VOICE are hard to identify in a large corpus that has not been annotated (through tagging or parsing). However, Honnibal (2004) was able to obtain counts from a corpus of two million words of the *Wall Street Journal* (the Penn Treebank). He found that in major clauses with a contrast in voice between 'active' and 'passive', about 86 per cent are 'active' and 14 per cent 'passive' – a clear skew. He also found that in clauses with 'marked' topical theme, the relative frequency of the 'passive' is lower (11 per cent), which as he points out is not surprising. (Downing 1996b, presents insights into the meaning of the 'mutative' passive, where the Auxiliary is *get* rather than *be*. Based on discourse evidence, she shows that the Subject/Medium is often assessed interpersonally as being affected by adverse consequences. This may be similar to those languages where the passive has been interpreted as adversative in nature.)

1.9.3 Groups (and phrases)

Groups are located between clauses and words on the rank scale. Ontogenetically, they develop later than clauses and words, as expansions of words; and I think the same must have been the case phylogenetically (cf. Matthiessen 2004b). Around the languages of the world, the division of semiotic labour between groups and words is a significant typological variable: some languages do relatively more work at group rank, while other languages do relatively more work at word rank. In English, groups are supplemented by phrases. However, while I suspect that all languages operate with groups, I don't think all languages have phrases (prepositional or postpositional) since verbal group complexing ('serial verb constructions') or case marking may instead serve to realize circumstantial relations. As Table 1.3 indicates, groups and phrases have received considerably less descriptive attention in SFL than the clause. In research on English, most attention has probably been given to the nominal group, in descriptions of grammatical metaphor within the ideational metafunction.

1.9.3.1 Verbal group

Work on the verbal group in English has been concerned mainly with the system of TENSE; work on other languages include descriptions of PHASE and ASPECT (Chinese: Halliday and McDonald 2004; McDonald 1994, 1998) and verbal group complexing ('serial verb constructions'; Akan: Matthiessen 1995b: 380; Thai: Patpong 2006).

Halliday's description of TENSE in English in the 1964 'Bloomington grammar' (Halliday 1976: 101–135) includes complex tenses that were not part of the 'received' descriptive tradition but which occur in casual conversation. As he developed his theory of metafunctions, he was able to reveal the logical nature of this system (Halliday 1985d, Section 6.3, 1996; Halliday and Matthiessen 2004: 337–349): he shows the potential for logical recursion in the system of TENSE, making it possible to construe **serial time** (the notion of serial had been explored by the engineer J. W. Dunne in his book *An Experiment with Time*, first published in 1927; this work also influenced J. B. Priestley, who called Dunne's book 'one of the most fascinating, the most curious and perhaps the most important books of this age' and who explored non-linear time in his plays, including *An Inspector Calls*: see Halliday [1982b] 2002d: 142ff).[5] This line of interpretation is unique among contemporary accounts of tense in English. The English system is often described as a combination of tense and aspect, but Halliday, who knows both Chinese and Russian, has pointed out that the English temporal categories that have been interpreted in terms of aspect (the 'progressive', corresponding to his secondary present; the 'perfective', corresponding to his secondary past) are very different from true aspectual categories. In his view, Chinese models time in the grammar in terms of aspect, Russian models it in terms of a combination of tense and aspect (cf. Gotteri 1996, on Polish) and English in terms of tense. Caffarel's (1992) description of French, already mentioned above, shows that French embodies the same tendencies as English, but that it is more constrained than English.

As I worked through Halliday's logical description of tense in the early 1980s in order to integrate it into the computational 'Nigel grammar' (see O'Donnell and Bateman 2005), it struck me how well it accounted for tense selections in discourse – flash backs, flash forwards and so on; but it also struck me that it meant the prevailing model of tense semantics – Reichenbach (1947) – would have to be revised to bring out the modelling of serial time. Reichenbach modelled meaning of tense as it was described in traditional grammars (based on the account inherited from Latin: see Halliday 1970a); he modelled it in terms of configurations of three times, S (time of speaking), R (a reference time) and E (the time of the event denoted by the lexical verb). Using Halliday's description, I was able to show that the meaning of tense in English was better represented in terms of successive relationships between two times, expanding into series of times with successive tense selections (Matthiessen 1984, 1995b: 736–739, 1996). In this respect, Prior's (e.g. 1967) tense logic is closer to the mark than Reichenbach's model, as is Bull's (1960) model of serial time (though not his interpretation of English).

In a contrastive study of English and Spanish based on spoken discourse, Downing (1996a) shows the importance of investigating the tense categories of a language systemically – in relation to the total system in which they operate. She compares the 'past in present' in English and Spanish and notes "pastness in the present is felt to be appropriate for subjective rather than objective reasons and is grammaticalized in the spoken language to a far greater extent in Spanish than it is in English"; this is an instance of the general 'constructivist' principle that we construe our experience of the world with the ideational resources of a language (cf. Halliday and Matthiessen 1999: 17, 602). She relates this to systemic alternatives to the past in present in the two languages; for example, in the case of 'mental' clauses, the English equivalent of Spanish *me ha gustado* is more likely to be *I used to like it* rather than *I have liked it* (527–528).

1.9.3.2 Nominal group

Halliday (1961) referred to the structure of the nominal group and Halliday's 'Bloomington Grammar' of 1964 already included systems of the nominal group – with particular attention given to the systems of DETERMINATION and QUANTIFICATION. Thanks to the theory of metafunction, Halliday's (1985c) description of the nominal group in IFG reveals the metafunctional strands of meaning in the nominal group: the textual 'wave' starting with the Deictic element as a thematic peak, the interpersonally prosody of attitude, the experiential configuration of Thing + Classifier + Epithet + Qualifier and the logical series of Head + Modifiers. This description has been taken further by various researchers, as summarized in Table 1.5. Two important research contexts have been the work on discourse involving grammatical metaphor of the ideational kind and the long-term effort of extending the account of interpersonal resources.

(a) From an **ideational** point of view, the nuclear system of the nominal group is the system of THING TYPE. It is, in a sense, the nominal analogue of the clausal system of PROCESS TYPE, relating to not only the nature of the Thing itself but also to the nature of the Epithet, Classifier and Qualifier, so any account of THING TYPE will have to be based on extensive corpus investigations of combinations of Thing with other experiential elements in the structure of the nominal group. For instance, one class of Thing involves nouns of projection and nouns of fact serving as Thing and these have the potential for embedded projections serving as Qualifier (Halliday and Matthiessen 2004, Table 7(25): 469), as in *because there were neither data nor instruments nor testable theories* [[*that would let anyone go beyond the assertion* [[*that the integrated, interdisciplinary perspective might be a useful approach*]]]]. However, there is as yet no general description of the system of THING TYPE; but since the publication of the first edition of IFG, a number of contributions have been made that are steps in that direction, including Matthiessen (1995b: 671–678) with a provisional system, Tucker (1996) on the issues involved in the development of a description of the 'cultural classification of things', Halliday and Matthiessen (2004: 326–328) on general considerations involved in the classification of things, Halliday and Matthiessen (1999: 189–205) on THING TYPE from a semantic point of view, Martin (1997: 30) on 'abstractions and grammatical metaphors'.

A significant part of the challenge in developing a general description of the system of THING TYPE is that since the nominal group is a key resource in grammatical metaphor of the ideational kind (cf. Figure 1.1), such a description must take account of not only congruent things but also metaphorical ones (cf. Martin 1997:

30; Matthiessen 1995b: 678–682): metaphorical nominal groups can accommodate the clause (with the Thing standing for the Process or Attribute) or even the clause nexus (with the Thing standing for the Relator). This is brought out in the growing body of research into discourses of physical science, history, English, administration and other kinds relying heavily on grammatical metaphor (see e.g. Halliday and Martin 1993; Eggins *et al.* 1993; Christie and Martin 1997; Martin and Veel 1998); for example: *plate surface defects were probably due to brittle failure along subsurface films at columnar grain boundaries during initial stages of rolling or during early stages of slab casting* (analysed and discussed in Rose 1998). This work also contains accounts of nominal groups in the discourse of technology. These often involve a noun denoting a concrete entity as Thing; the pressure is placed on the resources of CLASSIFICATION, as in the lovely nominal group *BOS No I charger crane main hoist worm drive gearboxes* (op. cit., p. 258).

Since the first edition of IFG, advances have also been made in the description of the system of EPITHESIS (for interpersonal Epithets of attitude, see immediately below). The most comprehensive account has been provided by Tucker (1997a, b): he shows how the description of the 'quality group' of the 'Cardiff' grammar can be extended in delicacy from grammar to lexis, reporting on a system network that can handle "over 200 adjective senses" (Tucker 1997b: 233). In the course of extending the description in delicacy, Tucker shows how grammatical patterns can be accounted for in terms of semantically transparent classes of quality. In the IFG-style description, quality groups correspond to adjective or adjective complexes serving as Epithet in nominal groups and Tucker's system of QUALITY TYPE can be 'imported' to characterize these. There are four primary types, shown in Table 1.10 together with their immediate subtypes: 'relative', 'situation-oriented', 'thing-oriented' and 'environmental'. The 'relative' and 'situation-oriented' types correspond to adjectives typically serving as post-Deictic in the IFG account (see below) and one of the two subtypes of 'thing-oriented', 'classifying', corresponds to adjectives serving as Classifier; but the 'environmental' and the other subtype of 'thing-oriented', viz. 'epithetic', characterize classes of adjective serving as Epithet.

Another description of classes of quality is proposed by Halliday and Matthiessen (1999: 210–212), where we interpret qualities by reference to the 'fractal' semantic types of 'projection' and 'expansion'. Qualities of 'projection' are 'emotive', 'cognitive' or 'desiderative' (thus corresponding to three of the four types of sensing in 'mental' clauses). Qualities of 'expansion' are 'elaborating', 'extending' or 'enhancing', each with further subtypes. Like Tucker's description, ours takes account both of the inherent properties of the qualities (such as scalability) and of their properties in grammatical constructions.

Table 1.10 Tabulation of the least delicate systems in Tucker's description of the system of QUALITY TYPE (based on Tucker 1997b: 235)

Type			Examples
relative	similarity		*similar, different*
	familiarity		*familiar, well-known*
	normality		*normal, strange*
situation-oriented	usuality		*usual, general*
	likelihood		*likely, probable*
	event		*late, early*
thing-oriented	epithetic	evaluative	*good, bad*
		effect	*interesting, boring*
		dimension	*big, large*
		physical	*hard, physical*
		typically human	*happy, shy*
		age	*old, modern*
		colour	*green, red*
	classifying	substance	*wooden, plastic*
		identity	*French, Hispanic*
		human	*retired, married*
		domain	*scientific, social*
environmental			*rainy, hot*

In Halliday and Matthiessen (2004: 317), we use the same fractal types of 'projection' and 'expansion' to describe the range of adjectives that can serve as post-Deictic, in examples such as *the whole four hours*. Those of 'projection' fall into two types, 'modality' (either 'modalization' or 'modulation') and 'report' (either 'locution' or 'idea'), while those of 'expansion' fall into the three familiar types of 'elaborating', 'extending' and 'enhancing'.

(b) In her work on the **interpersonal** resources of English, Poynton (e.g. 1984, 1996) describes the interpersonal potential of the nominal group, showing how it can carry interpersonal prosodies. In the structure of the nominal group, Deictic ^ Numerative ^ Epithet ^ Classifier ^ Thing ^ Qualifier, the elements realized by lexical items, the Epithet, Classifier, Thing and Qualifier, may all include attitudinal features, as illustrated by *mummy's precious darling angel baby boy* (Poynton 1996: 318). She also notes that interpersonal prosodies may be extended through iteration, amplifying the evaluation (e.g. *you pretty pretty thing; you gorgeous darling* *cute little thing*); the film title *Dirty Rotten Scoundrels* is a nice example of a negative prosody.

The work on the interpersonal resources of English has been extended with the development of the description of APPRAISAL (see Hood and Martin 2007), but in this work the focus has shifted from grammar to lexis and the system of APPRAISAL itself is located at the stratum of (discourse) semantics. The lexicogrammatical domain of realization is not restricted to the nominal group (since it includes also the adverbial group and the verbal group – and of course the clause as the integrating domain as far as propositions and proposals are concerned), but thanks to the work on APPRAISAL there is now a good deal of material that can be used in extending the lexicogrammatical description of the nominal group.

1.9.4 Words

In the division of semiotic labour across the ranks of the grammar, languages vary considerably in the relative weight they give to the ranks of group and word: in some languages the grammar of groups is relatively more elaborated, in some languages the grammar of words is relatively more elaborated. In the work on describing a growing number of languages systemic functionally, this variation has come into focus (cf. Matthiessen 2004b). In addition to the description of languages that do relatively little work at word rank – Chinese and English and in more recent work now also Vietnamese and Thai, there is now also work (both completed and in progress) on languages that do relatively more work at word rank, including Finnish, Japanese and Arabic.

The systemic functional approach to the rank of word is the same as the approach to any of the other ranks in the grammar: 'syntax' and 'morphology' are not separated into distinct 'modules' with distinct forms of representation (see Halliday 1961). Among the approaches to morphology that had developed by the 1950s, systemic functional morphology is most like the traditional 'word-&-paradigm' approach (see Robins 1959) – one key difference being the explicit representation of the potential behind paradigms by means of system networks. This 'enhanced' word-&-paradigm approach is well suited to the description of word grammar, as has been shown by a number of studies: Hudson (1973), in his work on Beja (Afro-Asiatic: Semitic), Prakasam (1985, chap. 5), in his account of the verb in Telugu (Dravidian) and Halliday, in a talk at the International Christian University, Tokyo, in 1990, with reference to Russian. It can even handle the challenge posed by Arabic morphology with its (characteristically Semitic) model of: (a) roots realized by (typically) three radical consonants; and (b) inflectional (and also derivational) features realized by overlay patterns consisting of vowels, semivowels and certain consonants: these 'prosodic' patterns form morphological paradigms just as segmental morphemes do and can thus be handled by system networks with associated realization statements. However, few systemic functional publications on word grammar have as yet been published. Matthiessen and Halliday (in prep.) contains a systemic description of the resources of English derivational morphology, Rose (2001b) discusses Western Desert (Pama-Nyungan) and Teruya (2007) deals with Japanese.

1.9.5 Textual: COHESION

The account in IFG of COHESION is essentially a summary of the much more detailed treatment presented by Halliday and Hasan (1976). The main difference is Halliday's revision of the description of CONJUNCTION TYPE: he replaces the earlier taxonomy with the differentiation into 'elaborating', 'extending' and 'enhancing' conjunctions. (Looking at the system 'from above', from the vantage point of discourse semantics, Martin 1992a, offers another systemic account of conjunctive relations: 'additive'/'comparative'/'temporal'/'consequential'. In my own work on 'systemicizing' the rhetorical relations of RST, I have found the differentiation of expansion into 'elaborating', 'extending' and 'enhancing' relations quite helpful – partly because of their fractal nature in the overall content system of English; see Cloran, Stuart-Smith and Young 2007)

Since the publication of Halliday and Hasan (1976), a very extensive body of work using their description has appeared, including both systemic functional contributions and contributions using their description without contextualizing it in systemic functional terms. Fries (1986a) offers a helpful perspective on cohesion from the mid-1980s. One important development was Hasan's (1984a) **cohesive harmony** analysis: see Cloran, Stuart-Smith and Young (2007). Another was Hasan's refinement of the classification of the resources of cohesion (in Halliday and Hasan 1985: 82) into 'componential' and 'organic'.

Martin (1992a) complements the lexicogrammatical view of COHESION by looking at these resources 'from above', from the point of view of semantics. He presents descriptions of semantic systems and structures. As already noted, corresponding to the grammatical system of conjunction is his description of the semantic system of CONJUNCTIVE RELATIONS. Corresponding to the grammatical description of reference is the system of IDENTIFICATION ('reference as semantic choice'). Corresponding to lexical cohesion is the system of IDEATION – the account of which includes not only lexical cohesion but also Martin's semantic view of cohesive harmony, **nuclear relations.**

In the area of lexical cohesion, the work by Hasan (1984a) and Fries (1982) has revealed the significance of instantial lexical patterns. Studies of texts involving lexical cohesion have often been based on experiential features of lexis and oriented towards field and this is made explicit in Martin's (1992a, chap. 5) semantic account of lexical cohesion in terms of the system of IDEATION. However, just as conjunctive relations can be not only external (oriented towards experiential meanings) but also internal (oriented towards interpersonal meanings), so lexical cohesion can be not only external (oriented towards 'denotation') but also internal (oriented towards 'connotation'). This internal orientation is brought out very clearly in the work on APPRAISAL developed in the 1990s and 2000s: see Hood and Martin (2007). That is, appraisal analysis can be seen as revealing (among other things!) lexical cohesive patterns based on the interpersonal features of lexis and oriented towards tenor.

1.10 Analysis (text, text type)

The description of the lexicogrammatical resources in Halliday's *Introduction to Functional Grammar* has been used in the analysis of many texts from a wide range of registers (a model of lexicogrammatical text analysis is provided by Halliday 1985b). This form of analysis is **abductive** (see Figure 1.8): it moves from text instances and relates them to an existing description of the system. Table 1.11 lists a selection of studies sorted according to Jean Ure's classification of field processes in her context-based typology of texts. A number of these studies also include contextual and text-semantic analysis (typically based on Martin 1992a) and/or appraisal analysis (e.g. Martin 2000; see Hood and Martin 2007). A growing number of studies of this kind uses one of the systemic functional analysis tools (see O'Donnell and Bateman 2005).

1.10.1 Subliminal impact

Studies such as those listed in Table 1.11 reveal the power of lexicogrammatical analysis of text (always to be seen in conjunction with semantic and contextual analysis). This analysis takes account of the local selections in the text – selections that can be tracked in **text scores** (as discussed above as illustrated in Figures 1.5 and 1.20); selections that accumulate to have a 'subliminal' impact. This **subliminal impact** has been brought out in a number of studies. For example, Francis and Kramer-Dahl (1992: 72–74) show how a patient is construed experientially and presented textually in traditional medical case histories and contrast these

Table 1.11 Lexicogrammatical analyses of text types and characterizations of registers

Field: process	Register domain	Publication
expounding	scientific text	Halliday (1988); Halliday and Martin (1993); Nwogu (1990); Ventola and Mauranen (1996); Thomas and Hawes (1997); Hayakawa (2004); Banks (1991, 2005)
	text book	Martin (1985a); Wignell *et al.* (1989); Eggins *et al.* (1993); Coffin (1997, 2003); Barnard (2003); Veel (1997); D. Rose (1997)
	research article	Gosden (1993, 1996); Whitaker (1995)
	academic essay	Stuart-Smith (2001)
	popular science	Francis and Kramer-Dahl (1992); Jenkins (1992); Fuller (1995, 1998)
reporting	news reporting	Jenkins (1990) [on headlines]; Nanri (1993); Iedema *et al.* (1994); Thomas and Hawes (1997); White (1997); López (2000); Butt, Lukin and Matthiessen (2004)
	weather report	Halliday and Matthiessen (1999, chap. 8)
	financial news	Teruya (2004b)
	history	Coffin (1997, 2003); Barnard (2003); Eggins *et al.* (1993); Martin and Wodak (2003); McCabe (2004)
	interrogation	Hall (2008)
recreating	folk tale	Hasan (1984b); Thoma (2004); Patpong (2006); Zouba (2003)
	story, short story	Fries (1985); Hasan (1985b); Rothery (1990); Rothery and Stenglin (1997); Washitake (2004)
	novel	Halliday (1973); Thibault (1984); Benson and Greaves (1984, 1987); Kies (1992); Price (2003)
	drama	Gregory (1982); Halliday (1982b); Martin C. (1997)
sharing	conversation	Bäcklund (1992); Eggins and Slade (1997); Eggins (1990); Slade (1996)
	personal letter	Mortensen (2003, 2005)
doing	service encounter	Ventola (1987)
	business letter	Ghadessy (1993)
recommending	advertising	Fries (1993, 1994, 2002)
	agony aunt letter	Thibault (1988)
	fund raising letter	Halliday (1992e); Martin (1992b)
	prayer	Mar (2001)

Field: process	Register domain	Publication
enabling	technical procedure	D. Rose (1997)
	recipe	Halliday and Matthiessen (1999, chap. 8)
exploring	exposition	Veel (1997); Schleppegrell (2000)
	thesis deliberation	Halliday (1994c)

with accounts produced for the general public by Sacks in his book *The Man who Mistook his Wife for a Hat*. Similarly, Caffarel's (2004: 568) analysis of Camus' *L'Étranger* reveals "how Camus has construed the world of the absurd covertly through the de-automatization of ideational resources'. This 'world of the absurd' is construed by a **syndrome** of repeated selections involving *passé composé*, clause simplexes, logico-semantic relations of extension, middle clauses, effective clauses with inanimate agents and logical metaphors of cause". To give another example of the subliminal impact of clause by clause selections that can be brought out by lexicogrammatical text analysis, let me return to the retelling of 'Noah's Ark' diagrammed in Figure 1.20. Taking account of the participant roles in the process type selections tracked logogenetically in that diagram, we can see that the text develops a world view that is both patriarchal and centred on humans (cf. Halliday 1992e): Figure 1.22 (see p. 82) represents the **hierarchy of participant interaction** that is developed clause by clause. The point is: there is no central challengeable claim that represents this hierarchy; it is built up subliminally, clause by clause. Children are defenceless – unless they are empowered to analyse text by the kind of grammatics discussed by Williams (2005a).

1.10.2 Research contexts of text analysis: Analysis in the service of description

Lexicogrammatical text analysis has been carried out in a wide range of research contexts, including:

- educational (e.g. Christie and Martin 1997; Christie 2002; Rothery 1990; Gibbons and Markwick-Smith 1992; see also Christie and Unsworth 2005);
- administrative (e.g. Martin 1993; Iedema 1996, 1997b);

- clinical (e.g. Armstrong 1991, 1997; Mortensen 1992, 2003, 2005; Fine 1994, 1995; see also Armstrong *et al.* 2005);
- critical (e.g. Martin 1986; Martin and Wodak 2003; Barnard 2003; Butt, Lukin and Matthiessen 2004; Young and Harrison 2004);
- comparative-translational (e.g. Halliday 1993b; Teich 2003; Ventola 1995; Ghadessy and Gao 2000, 2001; Munday 2000; Zhi'an and Kuang 2002; see also Steiner 2005b);
- literary (e.g. Halliday 1971; Gregory 1982, 1995; Butt 1984; Hasan 1985b; Birch and O'Toole 1988; Ren 1993; Cranny-Francis and Martin 1994; Price 2003; Caffarel 2004; see Lukin and Webster 2005; for work on stylistics in China, see Fang *et al.* 2005).

One context in which large-scale text analysis is being carried out is of course that of extending the description of the lexicogrammatical system. In my own work, I use database tools that Wu Canzhong and I have developed (cf. Wu 2000; O'Donnell and Bateman 2005) to support the compilation of text archives and the analysis of texts. I collect 'raw' texts in the text archive (where they can be annotated according to various schemes for register typology) and 'migrate' them to SysFan, the text analysis system, when I am ready to analyse them. The archive currently contains over 1,250 texts from many different registers. SysFan contains around 400 texts in different states of lexicogrammatical analysis. They are being 'chunked' into clause complexes (currently over 15,000), which are chunked into clauses (currently over 16,000), which in turn are chunked into groups and phrases. This is a long-term analysis effort. It is part of a two-pronged effort, the other prong being corpus analysis (see below): a progress report is given in Matthiessen (2006a).

The selection of lexicogrammatical systems used in the studies in Table 1.11 and other such studies has of course been quite variable; some studies have involved a comprehensive sweep across many lexicogrammatical systems (e.g. Halliday 1992c), whereas others have focused on a smaller number of systems. However, the range and volume of lexicogrammatical analyses of texts is unprecedented in the history of linguistics: no other description of the lexicogrammar of a language has been used to process, and thus been tested against, a comparable range and volume of text. Such text analysis must also be taken into account in discussions of 'corpus-based' and 'corpus-driven' descriptions of lexicogrammar (cf. Hunston and Francis 2000; Tognini-Bonelli 2001; and Halliday's 2005b: 173–175, comments): they are complementary in that the text analysis approach is abductive, the corpus-driven approach is inductive and the corpus-based approach is deductive (see Section 1.8 and Figure 1.8). In the kind of text analysis discussed here, a text must be analysed **exhaustively** in reference to the system or systems selected for analysis. As texts are processed in this way, it becomes absolutely clear whether particular patterns encountered in them have been taken account of in the description of the system being used in the analysis or not. There are innumerable examples since the 1970s of places where the description of the lexicogrammatical system of English has been revised or extended precisely to take account of issues faced in text analysis – reflected in the successive editions of IFG, Matthiessen (1995b), Martin, Matthiessen and Painter (1997), as well as other publications.

1.10.3 Text analysis and corpus analysis

Text analysis and corpus analysis have developed as two distinct forms of analysis since the 1960s, and have remained largely distinct in the period of development since the 1970s; but as computational tools become more powerful, the gap between them will decrease (cf. Wu 2000; Matthiessen 2006a).

Text analysis has typically involved manual analysis of small samples of text with reference to contextual, semantic or higher-ranking lexicogrammatical systems. The analysis has had to be manual, because this kind of analysis has so far been hard to automate; and since the analysis has been manual, it has only been possible to process relatively small samples.

Corpus analysis has typically involved automated analysis of large samples of text (growing in size from 1 million words in the 1960s to hundreds of millions today) with reference to single lexical or grammatical items or to patterns of such items that can be defined in terms of regular expressions or the like, without recourse to any annotations added to the orthographic representation of the corpus. This means that corpus analysis has been **item-based**, with the items typically characterized in terms of orthographic strings. Consequently, it has been confined to graphology and low-ranking lexicogrammar. As Halliday (2005b) has observed, the way that corpora have been represented has been biased towards investigations of lexis: investigations of grammar have been harder (for reasons he explains on pp. 171–172) – and semantics and context have been largely out of reach. The same is true of the computational tools used in large-scale corpus analysis: they are considerably better at lexical analysis than they are at grammatical analysis or at higher-level semantic and contextual analysis. (If we operate with a comprehensive theory of language in context, we are well placed to characterize the aperture of the window on language provided by corpus analysis: we can for example see precisely how it is both enabled and constrained by current computational tools.)

In response to this kind of situation, a number of us have adopted a **two-pronged approach** involving both manual text analysis and automated corpus analysis (cf. Matthiessen 2006a, see also Hartley and Paris 1995). This is, I think, very much along the lines developed by Michael Hoey, who has demonstrated the possibility and value of combining the techniques of text analysis and corpus analysis.

However, the conditions for doing analysis in support of the development of descriptions are changing for two reasons.

1. More explicit specifications of lexicogrammatical resources are being developed and becoming available, largely thanks to research within computational SFL (see O'Donnell and Bateman 2005), including both the Penman tradition with the Nigel grammar and the KPML system and the Cardiff tradition: we are learning how to write lexicogrammatical descriptions that are explicit enough that they can be handled computationally, and this will in time also extend to descriptions of semantic systems and contextual systems. (When contextual system networks are produced without realization statements linking them to the semantics and when semantic system networks are produced without realization statements linking them to the lexicogrammar, the analysis is doomed to remain manual; it cannot be automated 'from below'.)
2. Computational tools and techniques for analysis are becoming more powerful, largely thanks to the fact that corpus analysis has developed as a field of research in computational linguistics/natural language processing (NLP) since the late 1980s: a range of techniques including ones derived from machine learning and data mining are making it possible to extract more information from corpora than has typically been done in 'corpus linguistics' as it has been pursued within linguistics and language departments. The work on corpora in NLP has produced a whole new set of techniques known as statistical NLP (see Manning and Schütze 1999). In a related development, 'probabilistic linguistics' is now emerging on the border between linguistics and computer science (see Bod, Hay and Jannedy 2003b). These developments are of course very resonant with systemic functional theory as it has been developed since the start: Halliday (1959) gave probability a central place in the theory and included counts from his text analysis. They therefore pave the way for a breakthrough in automating higher-level corpus analysis, thus reducing the gap to manual text analysis. Most likely several strategies will be involved in bringing about this breakthrough, including both second-pass systemic functional analysis of existing tagged corpora (cf. Honnibal 2004) and the further development of systemic functional parsers to handle large volumes of text (see O'Donnell and Bateman 2005).

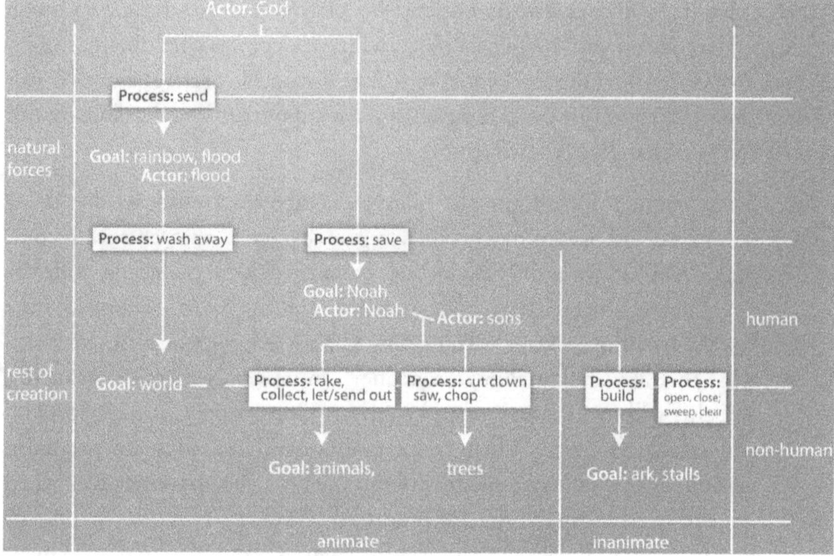

Figure 1.22 Participant role hierarchy in 'Noah's Ark'

1.11 Conclusion

The development of 'SFG' has been a process of steady evolution since Halliday (1961). The work has been additive rather than replacive: earlier descriptions may have been adjusted but they have never been discarded. For example, Halliday's account of PROCESS TYPE has been refined since Halliday (1967c,d, 1968), but the earlier account has remained relevant (as Davidse's, e.g. 1996b, extension of the description of 'identifying' clauses has shown and her comments on his original paradigm for 'identifying' clauses, 2000: 21). The development of the account of lexicogrammar in SFL has taken place in the environment of rapid progress in the development of accounts of semantics and context within SFL, but it has also been accompanied by interesting developments, outside SFL – developments relating both to the representation of grammar and to the role of texts and corpora: Table 1.12.

Within SFL, one indication of what Halliday's (1985c) first edition of IFG has achieved is the range of books on lexicogrammar it has given rise to, including translations of IFG into other languages. Around the mid-1990s, there appeared five books elaborating the account in IFG in different ways – to make it more accessible to students (Bloor and Bloor 1995; Butt *et al.* 1995; Thompson 1996),

Table 1.12 The development of 'SFG' in the environment of other developments

Time	Within SFL		Outside SFL	
	lexicogrammar	**semantics, context**	**representation**	**text, corpus**
around 1980	IFG1 being prepared for publication; 80 clause systems taken as starting point for Nigel grammar.	Beginning of development of Martin's description of (discourse) semantics above resources of cohesion.	Kay's (1979) FUG drawing on SFG just introduced. GPSG and LFG being developed.	West-Coast functionalism (WCF): interest in grammar and discourse.
1980s	Extensive lexicogrammatical text analysis (e.g. Martin and Rothery 1980). Further development of theory of grammatical metaphor. Probabilistic accounts: Nesbitt and Plum (1988). Towards lexis: Hasan (1987b).	Martin *et al.*: extensive discourse semantic analysis (in educational context); development of 'genre model' (Martin 1992a). Hasan: development of 'message semantics' (see Hasan *et al.* 2007a) Mann, Matthiessen and Thompson: development of RST	Based on FUG, development of 'unification-based' formalisms. Introduction of HPSG.	Growth of size of corpora Birmingham: COBUILD. WCF: many discourse-based studies of grammar.
Around 1990	Penman system with Nigel grammar established and being used in different research projects.	Martin's (1992a) discourse semantics and 'genre model' in place.	LFG established, GPSG gone; HPSG established as new framework in linguistics and NLP.	

Time	Within SFL		Outside SFL	
	lexicogrammar	**semantics, context**	**representation**	**text, corpus**
1990s	1994c: IFG2; 1995: LexCart (Matthiessen 1995b); Bloor and Bloor (1995); Thompson (1996); Martin, Matthiessen and Painter (1997). Development of tools for lexicogrammatical analysis (Coder; Functional Grammar Processor; Systemic; SysAm) and development (KPML). Experiments with (re-)representation of systemic functional grammars, continuing work from 1990s (see O'Donnell and Bateman 2005. Acceleration in description of different languages (see Teruya *et al.* 2007).	Martin *et al.*: extensive description of genres in schools, work places, media; development of description of appraisal (see Hood and Martin 2007). Hasan *et al.*: continued research in 'message semantics' (see Hasan *et al.* 2007a) Hasan: development of field, tenor and mode networks.	Fillmore *et al.*: development of construction grammar.	Development of statistical NLP. 1992: Linguistic Data Consortium founded. Move towards standards in annotation. Birmingham, Tuscan Word Centre: growing corpus, towards 'CDL' (Tognini-Bonelli 2001); Pattern Grammar (Hunston and Francis 2000) WCF: increasing interest in grammar and interaction (e.g. Ochs *et al.* 1996)
Around 2005	2004: IFG3			

to support discourse analysis (Martin, Matthiessen and Painter 1997) and to supplement it with system network and to provide more detail (Matthiessen 1995b). Bloor and Bloor's, Butt *et al.*'s and Thompson's books are now in their second editions and the second editions of the other two are being prepared. In addition, Eggins (1994) introduced the IFG account of the grammar of English as part of a more comprehensive picture that included introductions to Martin's (1992a) description of (discourse) semantics and context.

In another important development, the computational grammar based on the description presented in IFG (and documented in Matthiessen 1995b) – the 'Nigel grammar' – has now become publicly available as part of the KPML system thanks to the efforts of John Bateman (see http://www.fb10.uni-bremen.de/anglistik/langpro/kpml/README.html and http://www.fblO.uni-bremen.de/anglistik/langpro/kpml/genbank/R3bl2-English/Docu/; cf. also e.g. http://www.ling.helsinki.fi/~gwilcock/Tartu-2003/GW-MScThesis/node24.html; http://www.wagsoft.com/PapersHtml/IWPT93/nodel.html). Consequently, anyone can download it, examine it, use it, revise it. This is indeed a breakthrough in the development and dissemination of descriptions of lexicogrammars of different languages (KPML includes not only the original Nigel grammar of English, but also descriptions of a range of other languages).

The IFG account has also influenced other, non-systemic computational grammars, including Elhadad's influential SURGE account, implemented in FUF: see e.g. Elhadad and Robin (n.d.); and it has also been taken up in non-computational accounts of grammar, including e.g. Downing and Locke (1992), Lock (1995) and Lockwood (2002). The latter is a unique contribution drawing on stratificational linguistics, tagmemic linguistics and systemic functional linguistics – the three major theories of language 'showcased' in the first International Systemic Functional Congress held outside the UK, at Glendon College, York University (see Benson and Greaves 1985a,b). This was a historic occasion: Lamb, Pike and Halliday were all there. I can still remember Lamb's masterly deconstruction of the notion of 'mainstream' linguistics: focusing on tagmemics and systemics – the theories other than his own, he pointed out that tagmemics was 'mainstream' in having been used in the description of the largest number of languages and systemics was 'mainstream' in having been used in the most comprehensive description of any language.

Within SFL, the development of the description of the lexicogrammar of English since the 1970s has taken place in the environment of the development of descriptions of the semantics of English (see Hasan *et al.* 2007a; Hood and Martin 2007; Cloran, Stuart-Smith and Young 2007) and of the context in which English operates (see Butt and Wegener 2007). This has made it possible to recontextualize the description of lexicogrammar, relating it to the emerging descriptions of semantics. This includes the work on THEME in grammar in relation to thematic progression, method of development and macro- and hyper-theme (see Thompson 2007, chap. 23), the account of MOOD in relation to SPEECH FUNCTION (see Section 1.9.2.4 above and Hasan *et al.* 2007a), the investigation of clause complexing (TAXIS and LOGICO-SEMANTIC TYPE) in relation to rhetorical complexing (see Section 1.9.2.1 above and Cloran, Stuart-Smith and Young 2007), the modelling of TRANSITIVITY in relation to 'ideation' to account for grammatical metaphor (see Halliday and Matthiessen 1999, chap. 6). The details of the relationship between lexicogrammar and semantics are thus gradually becoming clearer and it is now possible for the grammarian to investigate 'discourse uses' systematically. New insights will emerge from the investigation of the realization of semantic patterns in lexicogrammar within the domain of what Halliday (2005b: 255) has called 'parasemes' – rhetorical paragraphs that can be analysed in terms of rhetorical complexing (RST), rhetorical units, hyper-Theme and hyper-New, episodic patterns and so on according to finely differentiated generic types described within the 'genre model' (e.g. Martin 1997).

Another aspect of the linguistic environment in which systemic functional accounts of lexicogrammar have developed since the 1970s is the changing range of other approaches to lexicogrammar. Systemic functional grammar is one of the very few current approaches to lexicogrammar with a continuous development since around 1960. But even in the quarter century since around 1980, the landscape of approaches to grammar has changed considerably: a number of them have disappeared or ceased to be developed, including GPSG (Generalized Phrase Structure Grammar) and tagmemics, while new approaches have emerged, including HPSG (Head-Driven Phrase Structure Grammar; e.g. Pollard and Sag 1993; Sag and Wasow 1999), Cognitive Grammar, Construction Grammar (e.g. Langacker 1987), Construction Grammar (e.g. Kay and Fillmore 1999) and Pattern Grammar (e.g. Hunston and Francis 2000). While there is clearly considerable variation here, we can recognize a number of themes that have been part of SFG since the 1960s:

- Lexicogrammar is semantically natural: in SFL, this is related to the metafunctional interpretation of grammar; but this principle has been articulated not only within functional approaches (see e.g. Haiman 1985) but also within approaches that are not overtly functional: it is central to Cognitive Grammar (e.g. Langacker 1987) and to HPSG (e.g. Pollard and Sag 1993).
- Grammar and lexis are different aspects of one and the same phenomenon, not different phenomena: in SFL, the relationship has been interpreted explicitly and paradigmatically in terms of delicacy; but the continuity of grammar and lexis has been recognized within other frameworks, including (in different ways) HPSG (e.g. Pollard and Sag 1993), Construction Grammar (e.g. Kay and Fillmore 1999) and Pattern Grammar (Hunston and Francis 2000); and it is given support by work on lexicosyntactic classes such as Levin (1993). The continuity of lexis and grammar has also been brought out by a range of studies of 'grammaticalization' – a process that includes the gradual change of lexical items into grammatical ones.

- The system of lexicogrammar is a potential that must be represented 'declaratively': this is a key property of the 'unification-based family' of grammars mentioned in Section 1.2 above, a family that includes not only Kay's (e.g. 1979) pioneering Functional Unification Grammar, but also LFG (e.g. Bresnan 2001) and HPSG (e.g. Pollard and Sag 1993).
- Lexicogrammar is inherently probabilistic: in SFL, this is related to the cline of instantiation (see Section 1.3.3); but this conception is now also being developed outside of SFL, in corpus linguistics (cf. Biber *et al.* 1999) and at the interface between linguistics and computational linguistics (see e.g. Manning 2003).
- Lexicogrammar is organized paradigmatically as well as syntagmatically: in SFL, the modelling of lexicogrammar has been paradigmatically based since the 1960s (e.g. Halliday 1966b); but paradigmatic organization has been given more attention in other frameworks since the 1980s in work on type hierarchies and ontologies, as in HPSG (e.g. Pollard and Sag 1993) in particular (in the form of type hierarchies, reflecting the influence on it of work on knowledge representation). This has been related to the interpretation of grammar as information and to the investigation of the nature of the organization of this information.
- Lexicogrammar includes both 'syntax' and 'morphology', without a modular boundary between the two. This notion of a unified grammar has been part of systemic functional linguistics since Halliday (1961) and linguists nowadays often use the term 'morpho-syntax' to denote 'grammar' in this unified sense.

These are, I think, promising signs of resonance across approaches and frameworks with quite different starting points. A good deal of work will clearly have to be done to bring out areas of similarity (as Kristin Davidse and her research group in Belgium have been doing for Cognitive Grammar and Systemic Functional Grammar). This extends to other frameworks not mentioned above, including Simon Dik's Functional Grammar, Robert van Valin's Role and Reference Grammar, West Coast Functionalism, Okuda's functional theory of grammar, the Prague School (cf. Davidse 1986), Ehlich and Rehbein's Functional Pragmatics, Hagège's Functionalism, Ashok Kelkar's approach (including the notion of the cognitive and communicative structure of sentences), Aravind Joshi's Tree Adjoining Grammar, and Dynamic Syntax (Kempson, Meyer-Viol and Gabbay 2001). Prakasam (1985, chap. 11) gives us additional insight into the theory of systems in systemic functional theory by showing how it is similar to the Buddhist theory of meaning – the Apoha.

Reflecting on the current state of systemic functional research into lexicogrammatical, I would say that we are on the verge – on the verge of another breakthrough. This will come about if the various current strands come together: computational grammar development work benches like KPML with support for comprehensive descriptions, computational analysis tools for supported manual analysis like Coder, Systemics and SysAm and for automated analysis like SysConc and parsers, annotated corpora that support automated higher-level analysis and semantic descriptions with explicit lexicogrammatical realization statements.

Notes

1 Arguing against the notion of a critical period for 'first language acquisition', Sampson (2001: 67–71) reports on the results of a corpus-based study of different age bands that show very clearly that grammatical 'complexity' (as defined by him) increases steadily with age.

2 The phrasal analysis done in terms of lexicogrammatical systems can of course be supplemented by local semantic analysis and local phonological analysis (taking account of selections in TONE, TONICITY and TONALITY in particular). For instance, in addition to recording selections in clausal systems, we can record selections in the semantic units realized by clauses (in the congruent case, messages, moves [propositions/proposals] and figures; see Halliday and Matthiessen 2004: 589).

3 That is, in the description of lexis, systems represented paradigmatic parameters or dimensions, just as Trubetzkoy had operated with paradigmatic dimensions in his account of phonology. These dimensions intersect to form multidimensional spaces, which can be interpreted both typologically and topologically. In contrast, Jakobson (e.g. 1949) had reinterpreted values along dimensions as 'distinctive features' – as components of phonemes and the potential for the typological/topological complementarity was lost. This approach to phonology was developed as componential analysis in later work on lexis. In systemic functional descriptions of lexis, the features are systemic terms – values along dimensions, not components of senses.

4 I regret any serious omissions: the table is not, of course, exhaustive; there is certainly work in languages other than English that has not been included (for work in Chinese, see Fang *et al.* 2005; for work in Japanese, the *JASFL Occasional Papers series* can be consulted). I have only listed work explicitly involving systemic functional grammar.

5 When we examine a wide range of languages, we find that tense can be modelled logically as serial time or experientially as taxonomized linear time (e.g. classes of past time – recent, intermediate and remote): see Matthiessen (2004b: 578–580).

Chapter 2

The 'architecture' of language according to systemic functional theory: Developments since the 1970s

2.1 Into the 1970s

2.1.1 Evolutionary development of holistic model

The development of Systemic Functional Linguistics (SFL) has always been of an evolutionary kind rather than of a revolutionary kind: Halliday (e.g. 1959, 1961) built on his immediate predecessors instead of distancing himself from them and new findings have been added in a cumulative fashion. This has been true of all aspects of SFL – theory, description, analysis, application – and it has certainly been a property of the development of the systemic functional model of the 'architecture' of language (and in more recent years of other semiotic systems as well). Here I will be concerned with the modelling of this 'architecture'. The term 'architecture' has been used quite widely in discussing the organization of language and of other systems as well (see Matthiessen, forthcoming a, for general remarks). It embodies a helpful metaphor – as long as we keep in mind that language is not rigid, it is not static and it is not designed.

The scope of the systemic functional model of the architecture of language was comprehensive from the start. The total system of language in context has always been in focus and SFL has been developed by moving from a comprehensive overview map of language in context towards more detailed maps of regions identifiable on the overview map. This move has involved not only filling in details, as in the ongoing description of the lexicogrammar of a given language (as with successive editions of Halliday's *An Introduction to Functional Grammar* and work building on this description), but it has also involved adding new semiotic dimensions to give a more multifaceted view of language in context, bringing out complementarities that were earlier hidden from view or appeared to be competing alternatives (cf. Butt 2005). With the benefit of hindsight, we can now see that the SFL approach fits in very well with holistic approaches in general and with systems thinking about complex adaptive systems (see Matthiessen and Halliday in prep.). Comparing the view of language around 1960, or around 1975, when I first began to engage with linguistics, I certainly have a very clear and powerful sense that SFL has made visible so many aspects of language that weren't visible earlier.

The comprehensive map that has guided the research into language in context and the development of the theory has been based on a set of interlocking semiotic dimensions since Halliday (1961). Halliday has increased the number of dimensions since then, allowing us to see more of language in context; but the increase has been cumulative, as when topography is added to a contour map. Key dimensions had already been established by the 1970s and much of the theoretical research since then has involved developing a deeper understanding of these dimensions and working out the implications of their intersections.

2.1.2 Stratification

One of the key dimensions is stratification, which is in a sense the defining organizational characteristic of all semiotic systems (see further below). This is a 'global' dimension that organizes language in context into an ordered series of levels or strata. It was in place from the start (e.g. Halliday 1961). The notion of levels of analysis was taken over from Firthian linguistics, but while these levels of analysis were not hierarchically ordered, Halliday (1961) modelled them as a hierarchy, as shown in the diagram in Figure 2.1, taken from Halliday, McIntosh and Strevens (1964: 18).

This model was more in tune with European structuralism, in particular with Glossematics; and it has remained remarkably robust over the years. Based on this model, the internal organization of each stratum has been explored, as have interstratal mappings; and a proposal for further levels within 'situation' in Figure 2.1 was developed by Martin and this group of educational linguists (e.g. Martin 1992a). There have also been some terminological changes. In particular, the term 'context' is now again used in its more Malinowskian and Firthian sense of the level above language (at the same level as 'situation' in Figure 2.1, 'grammar and lexis' are now referred to as lexicogrammar and 'script' is graphetics. The term 'stratum' is now often used in preference to 'level' (following Lamb's, e.g. 1966, stratificational linguistics), partly to avoid ambiguity since 'level' has been used for both stratum and rank.

The broad outlines of systemic functional linguistics can be sketched by reference to Figure 2.1. In Firthian linguistics, the focus was on the 'outer' strata – on

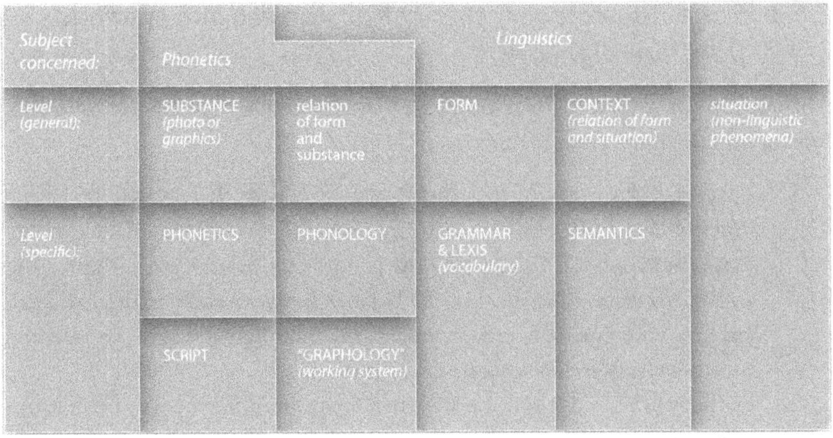

Figure 2.1 The model of levels (strata) in Halliday, McIntosh and Strevens (1964: 18)

phonetics and phonology on the one hand (e.g. Firth 1948a; Henderson 1949) and on context = 'situation' in Figure 2.1 and semantics on the other (e.g. Firth 1950; Mitchell 1957). There were some important contributions specific to the investigation of the 'inner' stratum of 'lexicogrammar' (to use the current term in SFL) – in particular the notions of collocation and colligation, but on the whole this stratum remained a gap in the account. There was clearly a need to fill this gap by developing the general theory of language to handle this stratum and by developing descriptions of the lexicogrammars of particular languages.

Halliday's work addressed this need. He developed descriptions first of the grammar of Chinese (Halliday 1956a, 1959; Halliday and McDonald 2004) and then of the grammar of English (e.g. Halliday 1964, 1967c,d, 1968, 1970b, 1976, 1984a). His descriptive work was interleaved with his development of the general theory, in an ongoing dialogue. The early description of the grammar of Chinese was followed by the first major theoretical publication, Halliday's (1961) 'Categories of the theory of grammar', which gave rise to what came to be called 'scale-and-category theory', the first phase of SFL. The development of the description of the grammar (and also intonation) of English in the 1960s provided material for and was enhanced by, the creation of systemic functional theory out of scale-and-category theory. While the examples in the theoretical discussions published during the 1960s were typically taken from the description of English, the theory was now also being used in the description of languages other than Chinese and English (e.g. Barnwell 1969 on Mbembe; Mock 1969 on Nzema; Huddleston and Uren 1969 on mood in French); see further Teruya *et al.* (2007).

2.1.3 Scale-and-category theory transformed into systemic (functional) theory

Analytically, we can identify two phases in the transformation of scale-and-category theory into systemic functional theory:

1. First Halliday transformed the system-structure theory that had been inherited from Firth into systemic theory: Halliday (1966a) made paradigmatic, or systemic, organization the primary mode of organization within a given stratum, thus shifting the balance between the paradigmatic axis and the syntagmatic axis in favour of the paradigmatic axis. The relation between the two axes was one of realization.
2. Halliday (1967c,d, 1968, 1970b) then introduced the theory of metafunctions, transforming systemic theory into systemic functional theory. He showed that the internal organization of (the content plane of) language was functional in nature, being organized into ideational, interpersonal and textual systems.

In the early scale-and-category model, axis was also present as a dimension, but the two axes, the syntagmatic axis and the paradigmatic axis (the axes of 'chain and choice', as in Halliday 1963a) carried equal weight, neither having priority over the other. This was a continuation of Firth's system-structure theory, in which systems were always 'placed' in structures (but it differed from American structuralist approaches, which gave priority to the syntagmatic axis). This approach to axis was pushed in descriptive work – in particular, in the early work on intonation (Halliday 1963b, 1963c, 1967b) and in the 'Bloomington' grammar from about the same period (e.g. Halliday 1964, 1976). In the course of this work, Halliday 'freed' systems from places in structures and transformed them into system networks with units such as the clause and the tone group as their points of origin. Specifications of structures were now located as realizations of terms in systems (the term 'realization' being a term taken over from Lamb to replace Firth's term 'exponence'; Halliday 1966b: 59). The paradigmatic axis had thus been given priority and defined the environment for syntagmatic specifications.

Prioritizing the paradigmatic mode of organization for a given stratum resonated with the general orientation of the theory and had important consequences. It resonated with the holistic approach, since it is much easier to develop a comprehensive picture of a given stratum in paradigmatic terms, using system networks (cf. Matthiessen 1995b), rather than in syntagmatic terms, using some form of syntagmatically-based rule system. It also resonated with the focus on text analysis and text based-description, since text can be conceptualized as a process of selection from system networks (cf. Halliday 1964, 1977b) and relative frequencies of selections in text can be represented in the system as systemic probabilities (as Halliday 1959, had already done).

It also resonated with prosodic analysis inherited from Firth's theory, since prosodies can be represented as terms in system networks. This was brought out very clearly in the description of intonation (Halliday 1967b, extended by Elmenoufy 1969, and now Halliday and Greaves 2008; see Greaves 2007): intonation did not have to be forced into and interpreted in terms of some form of syntagm of segments, but could instead be handled paradigmatically in the system network and represented syntagmatically as (in theory) elastic tone contours. And in the description of the grammar, Halliday was able to show how this description could be extended to cover systems realized not by grammatical syntagms but by intonation.

Finally it resonated with Firth's polysystemic theory, since systems can be simultaneous in a system network. Thus the system network of the clause turned out to be a set of simultaneous systems – those of theme, mood and transitivity (as shown in Halliday 1969). This polysystemic nature of the clause led to a 'discovery'.

One important consequence of the prioritizing of the paradigmatic mode of organization was the 'discovery' of the metafunctional organization of the content plane of language: in developing the description of the grammar, Halliday noticed that systems would 'cluster' into more interdependent systems. He asked why and the answer was his theory of metafunction (e.g. Halliday 1967c,d, 1968, 1970b, 1970c, 1969, 1976, 1978). Functional approaches to language had been around for quite a while – in particular, Malinowski's functionalism, Prague School functionalism and Bühler's organon model; but Halliday's theory was the first fully developed metafunctional theory of language modelling its intrinsic organization according to functional principles (instead of referring mainly to extrinsic uses; see Martin 1991). (Later, Halliday, e.g. 1978; Halliday and Hasan 1985; Martin 1992a, showed how the intrinsic functional organization of language related to the functional organization of context, introduced earlier, e.g. Halliday, McIntosh and Strevens 1964, as a development of Firth's contextual schema.) Metafunctions are manifested in the organization of systems along the paradigmatic axis (the systems of theme, mood and transitivity in the clause). They are also manifested in the organization of structures along the syntagmatic axis as simultaneous layers of functional configurations (Theme ^ Rheme, Mood + Residue, Process + Participants + Circumstances in the clause) and Halliday (1979) later showed that each metafunction engenders a distinct syntagmatic mode of expression.

Metafunction can be interpreted as an additional dimension in the organization of language; but (unlike stratification and rank) it is not a hierarchy, it is a spectrum of simultaneous strands within both paradigmatic and syntagmatic organization. This is brought out very clearly in the function-rank matrix introduced as an overview map of the lexicogrammatical system of English by Halliday (1970b). Such matrices show how lexicogrammatical or semantic system of a language is organized into a range of subsystems such as TAXIS, TRANSITIVITY, MOOD, THEME, TENSE, EVENT TYPE, PERSON which are distributed across the ranked units of that system.

Another important consequence of the prioritizing of the paradigmatic mode of organization was that it became possible to model grammar and lexis paradigmatically as a continuum. This had been foreshadowed by Halliday (1961), who suggested that the 'grammarian's dream' extend the description of the grammar in delicacy to include lexis. But it wasn't until the 1980s that Hasan (1987b) demonstrated the feasibility of this research programme (see Tucker 1997b, 2007).

2.1.4 Rank

In the modelling of a given stratum, the dimension of rank (the 'rank scale') was part of the theory put forward by Halliday (1961). It represents the division of semiotic labour across a hierarchy of units, ordered from the most extensive to the least extensive. According to this stratum and rank model, language is thus organized globally in terms of abstraction (stratification), but locally (within each stratum) in terms of composition (as Halliday 1966b: 66, noted: "In stratificational terms, rank defines a series of inner strata, or sub-strata, within the outer grammatical stratum, with each rank characterized by a different network of systems".).[1] Interestingly, it is the global form of organization, stratification, that is characteristic of semiotic systems in particular, whereas composition seems to be a principle of organization in systems of all kinds (cf. Steiner 1991, on action). Like stratification, rank has proved to be very robust (even though it has been discussed and challenged at various points in time, as in the early exchange between Matthews 1966 and Halliday 1966c).

In fact, the value of this local dimension of organization grew over time, as its 'cartographic power' came into focus – that is, its importance in making it possible to bring out the internal organization of lexicogrammar (or, indeed, of any other stratum): see Halliday (1970b, 1978) for early publications of the 'function-rank matrix'. Figure 2.2 presents a schematic version of a function-matrix, extended in delicacy from the grammatical zone of lexicogrammar to the lexical zone. It shows how cells in the matrix defined by rank and metafunction constitute 'semiotic addresses' (to use Butt's term) for systems, represented here by a fragment of the transitivity network within the system network of the clause. The network (taken

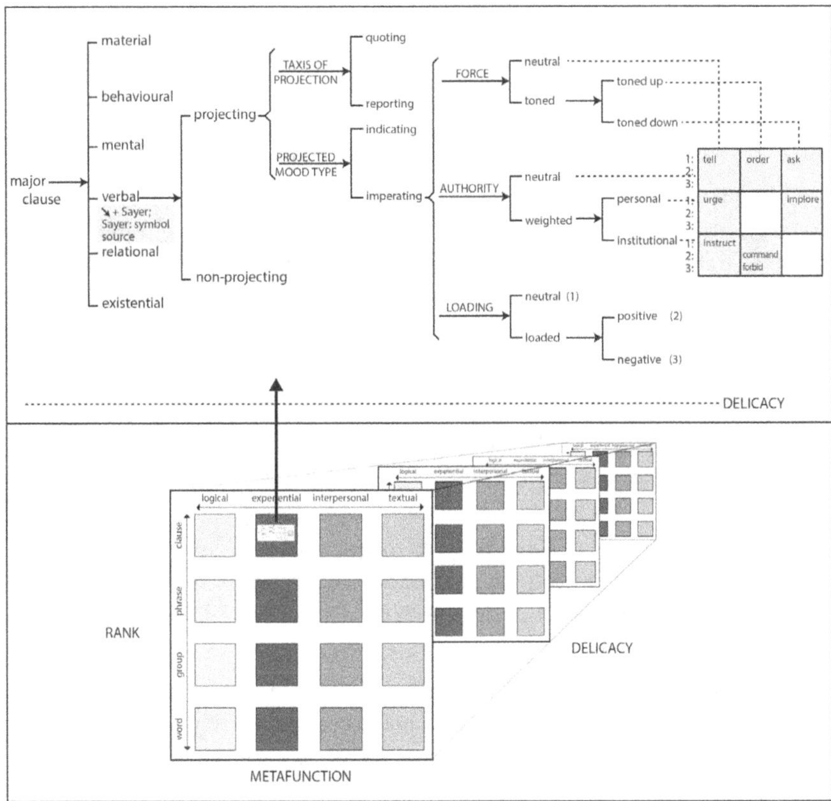

Figure 2.2 Schematic representation of function-rank matrix, showing cell in matrix defined by rank and metafunction as the 'semiotic' address for one of the simultaneous systems within the system network of the clause

from Halliday and Matthiessen 2004) has been extended in delicacy to illustrate the relation between grammar and lexis.

2.2 The 1970s

2.2.1 Areas of architectural concern in the 1970s

By the beginning of the 1970s, several key dimensions of the 'architecture' of language as modelled in systemic functional theory were in place. According to this model, language in context was organized globally into an ordered series of strata and simultaneous metafunctions and locally (within each stratal subsystem) into an ordered series of ranks, each of which constituted the point of origin for a system network. The 'grammatical gap' left by the Firthian tradition had begun to be filled by a growing number of descriptions and this descriptive research had led to new developments in the theory as well. The growth of work on grammar paved the way for studies in discourse analysis based on the description of the grammatical system (examples from the 1970s include Halliday 1971, 1977b), an area of research that accelerated in the late 1970s and 1980s; but it also made it possible to focus more on strata other than lexicogrammar. In terms of strata, phonology received some attention, semantics some and context rather more; but the combined effect was very significant in that it showed in some detail that each stratal subsystem was organized according to the same general systemic principles – a property that would later be interpreted in fractal terms (compare Halliday 1982a; and see e.g. Halliday and Matthiessen 1999; Matthiessen forthcoming a; Martin 1995b).

The 1970s was also a period when alternative systemic functional architectures were proposed and explored (mainly in the area of grammar), thanks to the contributions by Hudson (1971, 1974, 1976) and Fawcett (1973, 1974–1976, 1980). Fawcett's architecture has continued to be developed within the overall systemic functional 'flexi-model' (see Fawcett 2007, for discussion and references; see also O'Donnell and Bateman 2005 and Tucker 2007). Alongside SFL, Kay (1979) introduced his Functional Unification Grammar (FUG), which grew out of work on formalizing the systemic model and remained very close to Halliday's Systemic Functional Grammar (SFG) in many respects (cf. Kasper 1988b; see O'Donnell and Bateman 2005) and influenced the developments of both Bresnan and Kaplan's Lexical Functional Grammar (LFG) and Pollard and Sag's Head Driven Phrase Structure Grammar (HPSG). This unification-based family of grammars (SFG, FUG, LFG, HPSG and later also Joshi's TAG, Tree Adjoining Grammar) shares a number of architectural properties, including the declarative nature of descriptions and the ability to unify separate descriptive fragments.

2.2.2 Stratification: Work on different strata

2.2.2.1 Phonology and phonetics

In the development of systemic phonology, Prakasam (1972) produced a systemic description of the phonology of Telugu, thereby helping to formulate principles in systemic phonology (as a development out of Firthian prosodic analysis; cf. Tench 1992b). He followed this up in various publications (e.g. Prakasam 1977), thus establishing and maintaining research in systemic phonology. In the 1980s, other systemic functional linguists produced descriptions of (aspects of) the phonological systems of other languages (e.g. Mock 1985, on Zapotec; Matthiessen 1987a, on Akan). These various accounts demonstrated the power of the system network in the description of the phonological system of a language, deriving both from its ability to represent prosodies paradigmatically and from its ability to capture specifications at different degrees of delicacy. They also showed the value of the notion of rank in extending the coverage of the account of the phonological system of a language; systemic functional work on the phonology of intonation and rhythm has remained an active area of research since Halliday's early work noted above (see Greaves 2007). Various contributions to systemic functional phonology were collected by Tench (1992a), including an influential paper by Halliday (1992a) on the description of Peking syllable finals. Halliday (2002b) gives a retrospective overview of systemic functional phonology. Cléirigh (1998) advances the account of systemic phonology by relating it to systems thinking and evolutionary processes.

In the area of phonetics, there has not been any specifically systemic work, but the Abercrombie-Catford tradition (e.g. Abercrombie 1967; Catford 1977) represents research in phonetics that relates closely to SFL, for instance in its attention to prosodic aspects of phonetics, including the physiology of rhythm (an area where Catford 1985, has also contributed to systemic phonology). Catford's approach to phonetics is very systemic in mapping the 'total sound-producing potential of man'. Similarly, Peter Ladefoged's account of phonetic parameters is very systemic in orientation, giving us an understanding of the common bodily resources that are 'phonologized' in different ways in different languages. (The potential for systemic functional has changed, as phonetics laboratories have been miniaturized to fit into laptops: see the phonetic analyses produced by means of Praat in Halliday and Greaves 2008.)

2.2.2.2 Semantics

In the development of systemic semantics, the nature of the organization of the semantic system was still an open question (cf. Halliday 1974a); but exploratory work was undertaken to represent the semantic system as a meaning potential by means of system networks. This was done for particular situation types, as in Halliday's (1973) description of the regulatory semantic strategies open to a mother in controlling her child's behaviour (see also Turner 1987). This research 'programme' of developing register-specific semantic networks associated with particular situation types has not yet been followed up on a large scale, even though Patten (1988) demonstrated the value of such networks in text generation by computer, pointing out that register-specific semantic networks can be interpreted by reference to the technique of compiling out knowledge in AI to solve recurrent problems.

The later development of systemic semantics in the 1980s was made possible in part by work 'from below' undertaken in the 1970s – the description of the lexicogrammatical systems of cohesion by Halliday and Hasan (1976), followed up by Hasan in, for example, Hasan (1984a) with the account of cohesive harmony (see Cloran *et al.* 2007), Halliday and Hasan (1985), with a classification of cohesion into organic and componential cohesion. Here lexicogrammatical systems involved in the creation of cohesion in text were identified, described and applied in the analysis of text. This work had quite an impact also outside SFL, leading to an extensive body of work on text analysis.

2.2.2.3 Context

The later development of systemic semantics was also made possible by Hasan's (1978) model of text 'from above' from the point of view of context. She showed how the structure of a situation within context is projected onto the text unfolding in that situation (and, by implication, onto other semiotic processes, or social processes, forming part of that situation). She also showed how such contextual structures can be generalized as contextual structure schemata, or generic structure potentials, which characterize different situation types. The scene was thus set for further developments of systemic semantics – and also for investigations exploring the relationship between text semantics and clause grammar.

The work on generic structure potential was part of the advances in the 1970s in the modelling of context. The notion of context had been taken over by Firth from Malinowski and developed both in its own terms as a level of analysis and as a general 'ecological' approach to any level of analysis. His schema for the analysis of context was transformed within SFL into a model involving three general parameters – field, tenor and mode (e.g. Halliday, McIntosh and Strevens 1964 and Gregory 1967, where 'functional tenor' is identified as a distinct parameter – later reflected in Martin's 1992a, account of genre).

After Halliday's development of the theory of the metafunctional organization of the content plane of language (semantics and lexicogrammar), the account of the relationship between context and language could be taken further and made more explicit. The key publication of the 1970s was Halliday's (1978) *Language as Social Semiotic*, where he hypothesized that field resonates with ideational systems, tenor with interpersonal ones and mode with textual ones. This was illustrated by reference to a few different context-text pairs and further illustrations were given in Halliday and Hasan (1985). The hypothesis has generated a good deal of discussion and proved very productive in stimulating research and applications (e.g. Fries 1986a; Butler 1988). Based on research undertaken through the 1980s, Martin

(1992a) provides a more detailed account of the functional resonances between context and the content plane of language.

2.2.3 Instantiation: Potential and instance

In the 1970s, attention was thus given not only to lexicogrammar but also to other strata and the work on the 'outer' strata characteristic of Firthian linguistics was taken further, as indicated above. However, work on other dimensions and processes was also an important part of the contributions made in the 1970s. Beginning in the early 1970s, Halliday (e.g. 1973) began to articulate the relationship between the general system and particular texts in terms of potential and instance. (This had been covered in Firthian theory by the notion of exponence, also used in Halliday 1961; but 'exponence' tended not to differentiate between realization and instantiation: see Halliday 1992a.) The potential is what the speaker can mean; the instance is what s/he actually means (on a given occasion) – an act of meaning (see also Halliday 1993c).

There were two important points with respect to this way of theorizing the relationship between system and text. One was that they were interpreted as being part of the same 'phenomenal order': they were in fact one phenomenon, differing only in observer perspective. Instances of meaning are observed close up; the meaning potential can only be observed from a distance, through innumerable instances of meaning. (Halliday's way of theorizing the relationship between system and text thus differed from both Saussure's langue vs. parole and Chomsky's competence vs. performance – both of which had created a chasm between data observed (instances of meaning) and what is theorized based on the data (the meaning potential).)

The other was that this way of theorizing the relationship between system and text made it possible to treat them as poles on a cline rather than as a dichotomy. This possibility was already in place in the 1970s, but the notion of the cline – the cline of instantiation – was articulated in more detail in the 1990s, starting with Halliday's (1992h) explicit account of the cline of instantiation in relation to both context and language (see further below).

2.2.4 Ontogenesis

In 1975, Halliday published a case study of how one child had learned how to mean. He showed that the process started much earlier than when the first 'words' and utterances in the mother tongue began to appear – the point of departure for most 'language acquisition' studies at the time. This pioneering work put ontogenesis on the systemic functional research agenda. It has been followed up by a number of other case studies (for more detail, see Painter, Derewianka and Torr 2007), including Painter (1984, 1999), Torr (1997) and Walsh (2002); and it has been extended by Derewianka's (1995) study of the transition from childhood to adolescence. This research has important implications for a number of areas, including the development of a language-based theory of learning (see Halliday 1993d; Painter 1999). What is particularly significant here, however, is that the study of ontogenesis sheds new light on the 'architecture' of language.

Halliday (1975) reveals how as a child learns how to mean, a fairly simple semiotic system, the child's protolanguage, is gradually transformed into a complex semiotic, the child's mother tongue. He interpreted this continuous process as going through three phases. In Phase I, the young child (typically around 8 months old, allowing for considerable individual variation) begins to construct a simple semiotic system in interaction with his or her immediate caregivers. This system is based on signs consisting of content-expression pairs. The child starts with an inventory of just a few signs and expands it to well over one hundred by the time s/he starts on the transition into the mother tongue: see Figure 2.3. The content is organized into a small number of microfunctions – regulatory, instrumental, personal and interactional at the early stage (cf. Halliday 1992b). Each microfunction is a specialized meaning potential that is tightly bound to a situation type and each microfunctional meaning potential can be represented as a network of systems. The most delicate terms in this system network are realized by minimal syntagms consisting of vocal postures or gestures, as shown in Figure 2.4. The content-expression organization of protolanguage is thus simultaneously stratal and axial.[2] The dimensions of stratification and axis are not independently variable at this stage: the content stratum is organized paradigmatically, while the expression stratum is an inventory of indivisible postural or gestural syntagms. The number of systems increases in the course of Phase I (as indicated by the graph in Figure 2.3); the development of this phase can be represented as a gradual expansion of each microfunctional meaning potential, as illustrated for the interactional meaning potential in Figure 2.5.

As the Phase I system continues to expand, the child becomes able to mean more things; but the essential nature of the system remains the same until the end of Phase I and the beginning of Phase II. In Phase II (typically extending over a period of six months from about 18 to 24 months), the microfunctions are generalized into two macrofunctions, the mathetic and the pragmatic; and wordings begin to appear (see Painter, Derewianka and Torr 2007). The stratification/axis dimension is gradually split into two independently variable dimensions: stratification becomes the global organizing principle, with a split of content into meaning

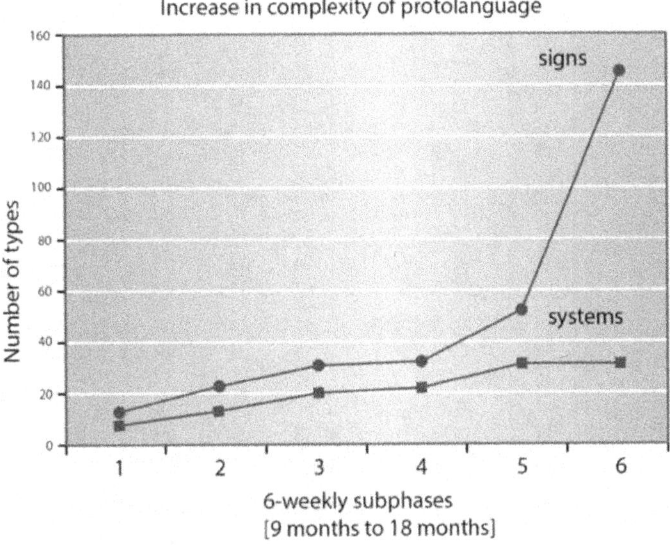

Figure 2.3 Gradual expansion of protolinguistic meaning potential (based on Halliday's 1975, case study of Nigel)

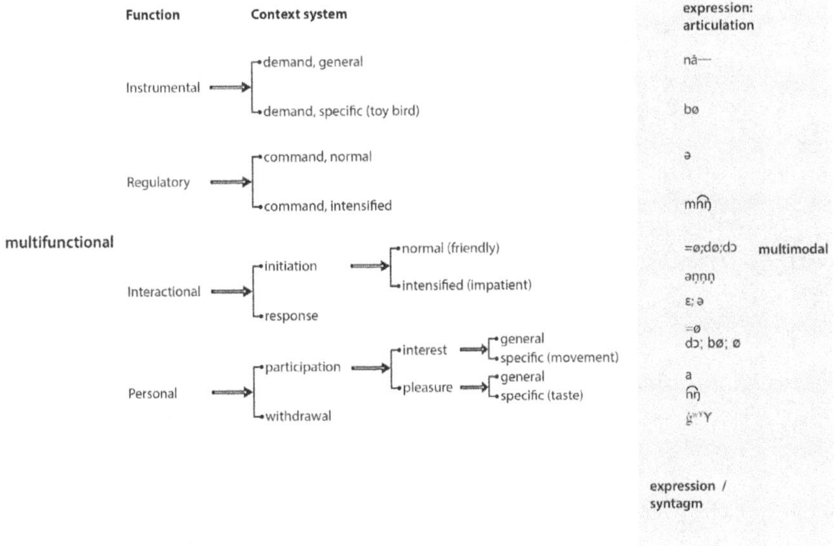

Figure 2.4 Protolinguistic organization: bi-stratal/axial

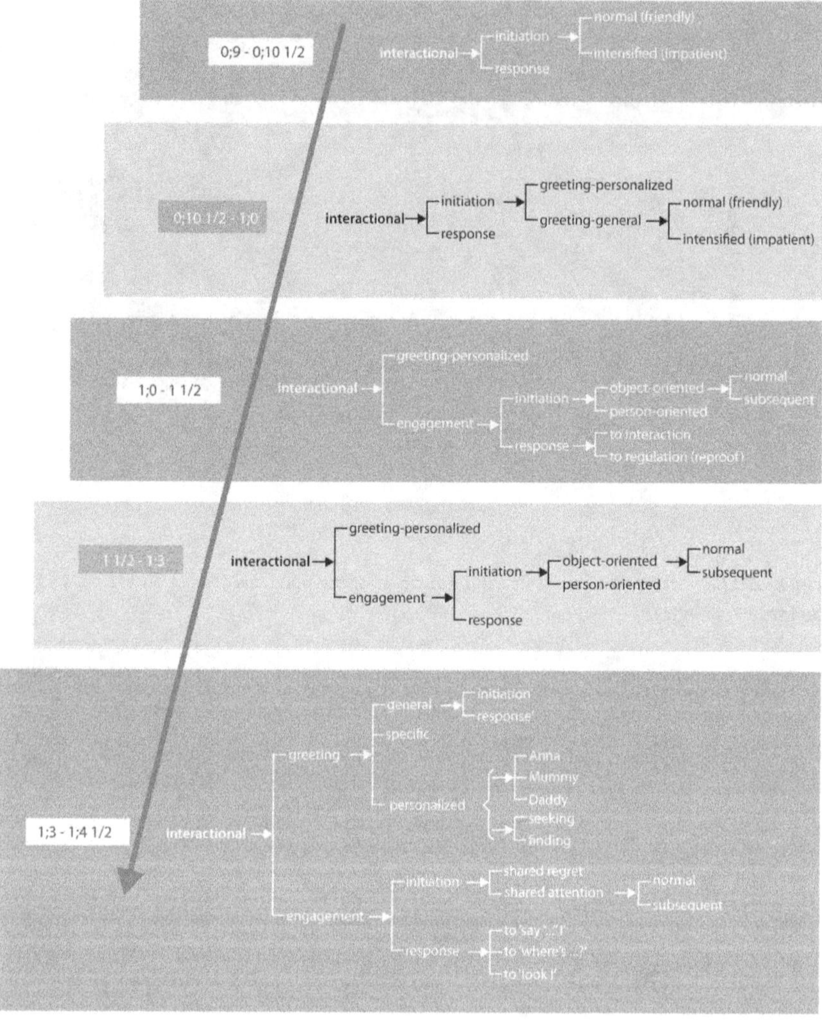

Figure 2.5 Expansion of the microfunctional potential during Phase I (interactional microfunction)

(semantics) and wording (lexicogrammar) and a split of expression into phonology and phonetics; and axis becomes the local organizing principle, manifested fractally within each emerging stratum. At the same time, rank begins to emerge. Within lexicogrammar, the first ranks to appear are clause and word (in examples such as *squeeze orange*, *man wash car*); and this two-rank scale is then expanded

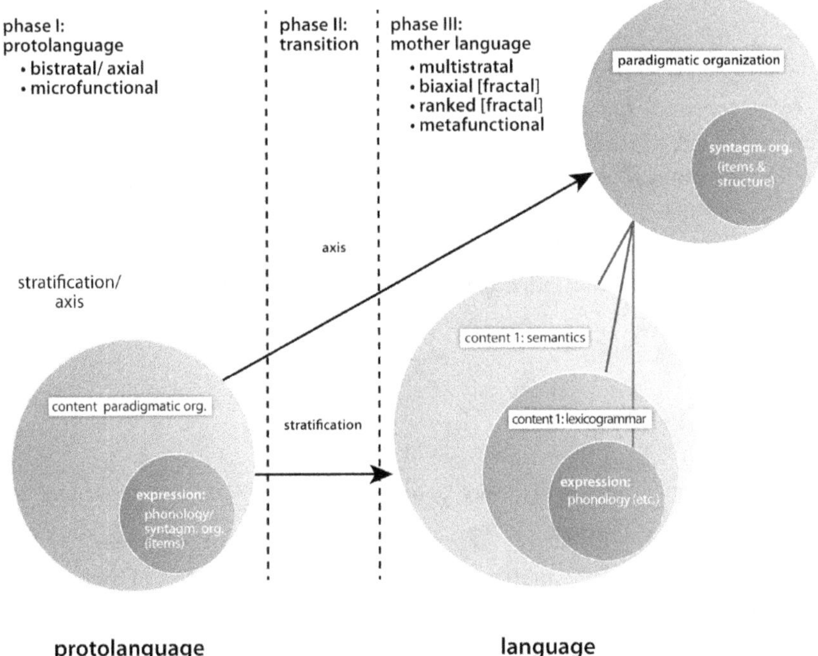

Figure 2.6 From protolanguage to language: emerging dimensions of organization

to include a rank intermediate between clause and word (group, an expansion of word and phrase, a reduction of clause) and a rank below word (morpheme). The transformation of the Phase I protolinguistic system into the Phase III adult (post-infancy) system is represented diagrammatically in Figure 2.6.

As noted above, the research into ontogenesis has been important for our understanding of the 'architecture' of language since it shows the gradual emergence of the multidimensional organization of language out of the simpler organization of protolanguage. In addition, the research into ontogenesis highlighted one kind of semogenic (meaning-creating) process – the growth of meaning along the dimension of an individual's time-scale. Later two other semogenic time-scales were also brought into research focus (see Section 1.5.2). The work on ontogenesis showed how a child constructs a personalized version of the collective meaning potential maintained by a 'speech fellowship' by accessing this meaning potential through text (see Halliday 1978, chap. 1).

The work on ontogenesis was thus also significant in another respect: it showed in considerable detail how an individual becomes a person in interaction with a social group. This focus on the person in relation to the social group and ultimately in relation to society, added another angle to the overall theoretical model of language in context. This was a theme from Firthian linguistics – Firth's (1950) interest in person, personae and personality in relation to language. The theme was expanded by Halliday's (1978) account of social man and language as social semiotic and related to role networks in sociology by Butt (1991). This social-collective perspective on a person as emerging out of interactions in different roles within social groups provides an interesting alternative to the focus in mainstream cognitive science on the individual mind (see e.g. Lemke 1995; Halliday and Matthiessen 1999).

2.3 The 1980s

The development of the 'architecture' of SFL in the 1980s was characterized by the following central concerns:

- Stratification: The interpretation of stratification in terms of metaredundancy (see Lemke 1984; Halliday 1992b).
- Stratification: The exploration of the stratal relationship between semantics and lexicogrammar in relation to interstratal realization (e.g. Mann 1983b; Matthiessen 1983a, 1988b; Matthiessen and Bateman 1991) and grammatical metaphor (see Halliday 1985c: chap. 10, 1987).
- Stratification: The exploration of a stratified model of context (see Martin 1992a 1997). Here a key context was that of educational linguistics.
- Stratification: The modelling and description of the semantic stratum (see e.g. Martin 1992a; Ventola 1987; Eggins 1990; Hasan 1984a, 1984b, 1987a; Cloran 1994).
- Instantiation: The exploration of the process of instantiation (see Matthiessen 1983b; Martin 1985a; Ventola 1987; Bateman 1989; Matthiessen and Bateman 1991). Here the key contexts were discourse analysis and text generation within computational SFL.
- Metalanguage: The development of an explicit model of the SFL metalanguage, a development which continued into the 1990s (see Matthiessen 1988a; Matthiessen and Bateman 1991; Teich 1999).

2.3.1 Stratification

2.3.1.1 Metaredundancy, denotative/connotative semiotics

In a way, the 1980s was the decade of stratification in SFL. While the hierarchy of stratification had been part of SFL since Halliday (1961) and had been central to certain other theories as well, in particular to Glossematics and Stratificational Linguistics, a great deal of work remained to be done in order to understand and model stratification better. Part of the challenge was that there were no accounts to draw on from the study of systems of other kinds since stratification is specific to semiotic systems. It was illuminated by Lemke's (1984) notion of metaredundancy, which was taken up and explored by Halliday (1992b). In this interpretation, the strata in the hierarchy of stratification are not simply related pairwise to one another by realization (that is, context to semantics, semantics to lexicogrammar, lexicogrammar to phonology, phonology to phonetics). Instead, lexicogrammar is realized by phonology, semantics is realized by the realization of lexicogrammar in phonology and context is realized by the realization of semantics in lexicogrammar. This form of stratal organization is indicated by diagrammatic representations such as those shown in Figure 2.7. (These representations also give an indication of how the size of a stratal system increases with the ascent in stratification.)

The notion of metaredundancy thus helps us understand the relationship between context and language – a relationship that Martin (e.g. 1992a) also clarified, drawing on Hjelmslev (1943). He showed that while language is a denotative semiotic system (one with its own expression plane – phonology and phonetics, or graphology and graphetics, or sign in the sign languages of deaf communities), context is a connotative semiotic system (one with another semiotic system as its expression plane).

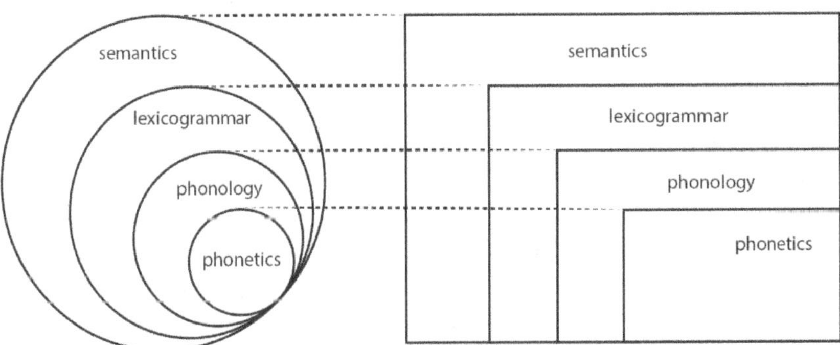

Figure 2.7 The stratal organization of language interpreted in terms of metaredundancy

2.3.1.2 Interstratal realization

Focusing on tenor and interpersonal systems, Halliday (1984a) contributed a seminal account of the stratal organization dialogue, providing both a clear statement of the theory of stratification and a description of the most general interpersonal systems located at different strata. The account identified congruent interstratal realizational relations between the semantic system of speech function and the grammatical system of mood and it showed how the overall meaning potential is expanded through incongruent mappings. The interstratal realizational relations are illustrated for a few systemic terms in Figure 2.8. Further descriptive work in the 1980s shed more light on the relationship between semantics and grammar, focusing in particular on the relationship between text and clause (cf. Halliday 1982a). In relation to the textual metafunction, the foundational study was Fries (1981); see further Thompson (2007, chap. 23).

Halliday's stratal model included the provision for incongruent realization of semantics by lexicogrammar. This was developed as his theory of grammatical metaphor, introduced in some detail first in Halliday (1985a, chap. 10) and subsequently elaborated in, for example, Halliday (1988), Halliday and Martin (1993), Halliday and Matthiessen (1999, chap. 6). It was explored from a modelling point of view by Zeng (1996).

In a complementary contribution to the modelling to interstratal realization, Hasan (1984b) focused on the relationship between context and semantics, more specifically between generic stages within a contextual structure and their realization by meanings within the semantic system. Taking Placement as an example, she showed that a generic stage is always realized by nuclear meanings (including 'person particularization', in the case of Placement) but that it may also be expanded by additional meanings (e.g. 'temporal distance', 'habitude', 'attribution', in the case of Placement). She also demonstrated that these realizations have to be 'mediated' by the semantics; they cannot be stated directly in terms of lexicogrammatical specifications. In a sense, this work can be interpreted as adding to the research programme concerned with the description of register specific semantic systems (initiated in the early 1970s; see Section 2.2.2 above); but Hasan showed the importance of narrowing the delicacy of focus from a whole situation to generic stages within that situation.

In a text generation project directed by Bill Mann at the Information Sciences Institute in Marina del Rey, California (see O'Donnell and Bateman 2005), we developed a fully explicit model of interstratal mappings between lexicogrammar and semantics. This was the chooser-and-inquiry framework (e.g. Mann 1983b; Matthiessen 1983a; 1988b; Matthiessen and Bateman 1991), designed as the interface to between a systemic functional grammar (the 'Nigel grammar') and its

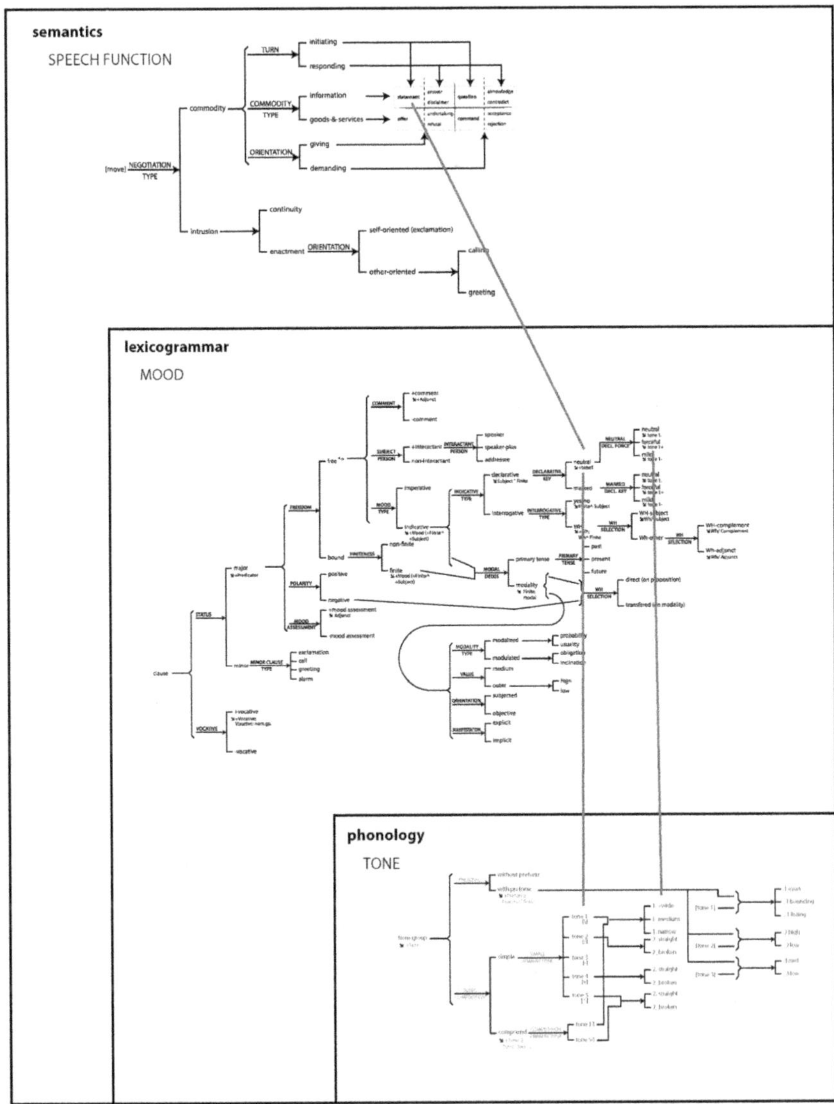

Figure 2.8 Interstratal realization (mapping) illustrated for interpersonal systems (semantics: speech function, lexicogrammar: mood, phonology: tone)

semantic environment in a text generation system (the 'Penman system'). In this framework, each system in the system network of a given grammatical unit was associated with a chooser, which consisted of a little discrimination network for making the choice according to the semantic specification for the semantic unit in question.

As far as the mapping between lexicogrammar and semantics was concerned, this interface was organized 'from below', from the vantage point of lexicogrammatical system networks. This contrasted with the approach taken by Halliday (1973) in his model of a situation-specific semantic network. In this model (adopted by Patten 1988), the mapping was done 'from above' by means of realization statements associated with terms in the semantic network. These realization statements specified preselections[3] of systemic terms within systems at the stratum of lexicogrammar. In a discussion with Bill Mann and me in 1983, Halliday suggested that the two approaches, the approach 'from below' and the approach 'from above', could be contrasted as choosers and chargers (cf. Matthiessen 1990). Theoretically the charger approach makes more sense (cf. Matthiessen and Bateman 1991), but the chooser approach proved to be a useful heuristic in exploring the demands the lexicogrammar made on the semantics – useful because the semantics of English had not yet been described. In this way, the description of the semantic system developed underpressure from below (cf. Matthiessen 1987b).

2.3.1.3 Semantics

The semantic stratum was a focus for research in the 1980s and this research continued into the 1990s. The research involved both the development of semantic theory and the development of semantic descriptions; and as had been the case with lexicogrammar in the 1960s, these two activities were interleaved. The basic unit of semantics was text, which was (as in Halliday and Hasan 1976) defined in functional terms by reference to context as language functioning in context.

In the theoretical modelling of semantics, the general tendency was to model meaning systemically along the same lines as had been done in the modelling of lexicogrammar and in the exploration of semantics in the 1970s (see Section 2.2 above). To represent the systemic organization of meaning, most researchers used system networks (cf. Hasan's 1996a, discussion of semantic system networks). However, in the work on modelling the meaning base of the Penman text generation system, we used another form of representation – a frame-based inheritance network (for discussion, see Matthiessen and Bateman 1991; Halliday and Matthiessen 1999). And in the Cardiff-based computational research later in the decade, Fawcett and his team developed a hybrid system network and flowchart representation (e.g. Fawcett 1988b).

There was more variation in the syntagmatic modelling of meaning. Semantic structures proposed and explored included the reticula introduced by Martin (1992a) to represent syntagmatic patterns of conjunction, identification and other systems realized cohesively, the interdependency structures introduced in

Rhetorical Structure Theory (e.g. Mann, Matthiessen and Thompson 1992; on its status within SFL, see Cloran *et al.* 2007) and the constituency model assumed by Cloran's (1994) account of rhetorical units.[4] In this constituency model, rhetorical units are intermediate between 'messages' (see Hasan 1984a) and the whole text (see Cloran *et al.* 2007). In this respect, it is similar to the model developed within the broad framework of tagmemics, as in Longacre's (1979) account of paragraphs; but while he treats paragraphs as grammatical, Cloran treats rhetorical units as semantic. Constituency structure was also used in the modelling of exchanges in dialogue by Martin (1992a, chap. 2) and his research group. Here the work by Berry (1981) was an important source. In addition, Halliday (1982b) had drawn attention to the different metafunctional modes of organization in the semantic structure of a text; and this was developed further in the 1990s (see Martin 1996a). The recognition of the different metafunctional modes of organization made it possible to recognize that the various proposals for semantic structure were broadly complementary modes rather than competing alternatives. Halliday had suggested that a text is analogous to a clause in organization; and I added the observation that it is also analogous to a clause complex, as shown by rhetorical structure theory analysis (Matthiessen 1987c).

The description of semantics was carried out mainly within three research contexts: a research group led by Martin at Sydney University (see e.g. Martin 1992a; Ventola 1987, on service encounters; Christie 1990a, on curriculum genres; Rothery 1990, on narratives; Eggins 1990, on casual conversation), a research group led by Hasan at Macquarie University (see e.g. Hasan 1987a; Cloran 1994) and the 'Penman' project led by Mann at the Information Sciences Institute in Marina del Rey, California (see e.g. Mann, Matthiessen and Thompson 1992; Halliday and Matthiessen 1999; Bateman *et al.* 1990). Aspects of these descriptive efforts are covered in other chapters of this book (Cloran *et al.* 2007; O'Donnell and Bateman 2005).

Halliday's account of the interpersonal semantics of speech function was taken up and extended in delicacy both by Martin and his research group at Sydney University (e.g. Martin 1992a, chap. 2; Eggins 1990) and by Hasan and her research group at Macquarie University. Hasan extended the networks in coverage and delicacy (cf. Hasan 1996a), providing explicit realization statements; and she and her research team applied them in the analysis of a large sample of conversations between mothers and their children in the home. These interactions were taken from both middle-class and working-class families (carefully defined in terms of the degree of autonomy of the salary earner) and the speech functional analysis turned up statistically significant differences in coding orientation in comparable contexts (codal variation; see Hasan 1989; Hasan and Cloran 1990). This was the first demonstration of its kind, showing the power of comprehensive and delicate semantic system networks as a resource in text analysis in general and in text analysis providing evidence for social differences in particular.

Martin (1992a) initially based the description of discourse semantics on Halliday and Hasan's (1976) account of the lexicogrammatical systems of cohesion, projecting that account up to the semantic stratum and systemicizing it in semantic terms; but he also drew on the work on discourse by Harold Gleason and other Hartford stratificationalists. His description included the semantic systems of conjunction, speech function and negotiation, ideation and identification. These descriptions were represented systemically and structurally though on the whole without explicit realization statement specifying lexicogrammatical patterns, and they were applied in a number of text analysis projects in the 1980s and 1990s.

2.3.1.4 Context: 'Internal' stratification

The development of discourse semantics by Martin and his research group was complemented by their effort to push the account further up along the hierarchy of stratification, into context. Malinowski had put context firmly on the research agenda, distinguishing between the context of situation of a text and context of culture. Firth retained the focus on context and it had remained a key area of investigation in the first two decades of SFL. In the 1960s, Firth's contextual schema was transformed into the field, tenor and mode model of context (e.g. Halliday, McIntosh and Strevens 1964). In the 1970s, these parameters were explored further. Halliday (1978) made the important distinction between first-order contextual parameters (first-order field – the social process; first-order tenor – social roles) and second-order contextual parameters (second-order field – the domain of experience or 'subject matter' created by language; second-order tenor – speech roles; and mode – the role played by language in the context). And he introduced the hypothesis about the resonance between the contextual parameters and the metafunctions of the content plane of language (see above). Further, as noted above, Hasan (1978) modelled the structure of situation and situation types in terms of Generic Structure Potential (GSP); and this was elaborated further in publications in the 1980s (Hasan 1984a; Halliday and Hasan 1985).

As he worked to extend the account of context to cover new areas (e.g. ideology, in Martin 1986) and to consolidate the various strands of the account of context, Martin used stratification as the dimension of modelling. Up to now, context had been a single stratum; but in the course of the 1980s, Martin developed a tri-stratal model of context (informed by metaredundancy and his notion of context as a connotative semiotic), represented diagrammatically in Figure 2.9: ideology, genre and register.[5] The lowest contextual stratum is 'register'; it is the domain of field, tenor and mode networks. Values in these networks resonate with meanings in language – field with ideational meanings, tenor with interpersonal meanings and mode with textual meanings (as shown in Martin 1992a, chap. 7). The next contextual stratum is genre; it represents the goal orientation co-ordinating field, tenor and mode values into recurrent genres and it is the domain of schematic structures (generic structures). The next and highest, contextual stratum in this model is ideology; it represents the (unequal) distribution of semiotic resources in society.

All three contextual strata have received attention, but the main effort so far has gone into developing the account of genre by describing a wide range of genres in different institutions, starting in the 1980s and continuing into the 1990s (see e.g. Martin 1985a, 1992a; Ventola 1987; Christie 1990b; Rothery 1990; Feez 1995; Christie and Martin 1997).

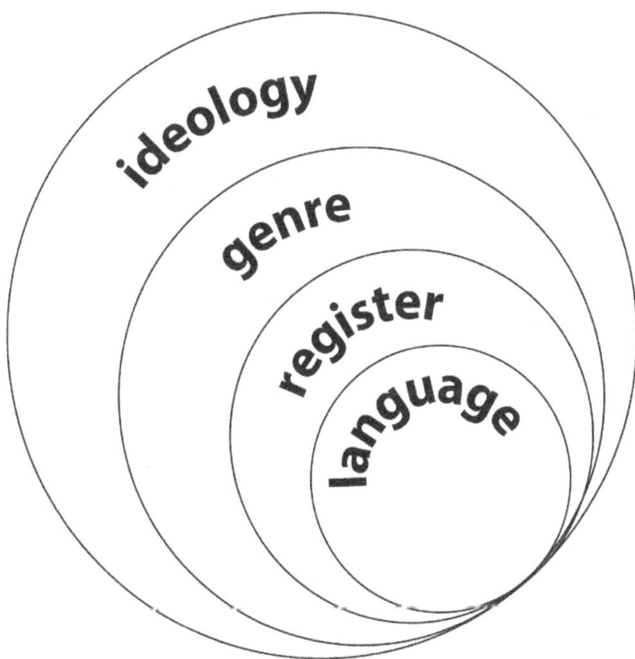

Figure 2.9 The stratified model of context developed by Martin (e.g. 1992a) and his research group

2.3.2 Instantiation

As noted above (Section 2.2.3), Halliday (e.g. 1973) identified the poles of (what is now recognized as) the cline of instantiation as potential and instance – meaning potential (what the speaker can mean) and instances of meaning (what the speaker actually means in some particular context). The relationship between the two is one of instantiation (which is of a different kind from the relationship of realization between two strata): an act of meaning instantiates the meaning potential, a text instantiates the linguistic system. It had been clear since Halliday (1961) that the system was not a 'thing' and should not be described as such; for example, he characterized structure as 'patterned activity'; and Hasan (1980) had similarly emphasized the process nature of context. But it was not until the 1980s that the process of instantiation was given significant attention. There were two research contexts; one was the work on text analysis undertaken by Martin and his research group and the other was the work on computational modelling, first in Bill Mann's Penman project at ISI and then later also in other computational research projects.

In text analysis, the challenge was how to represent text as unfolding in the course of the process of instantiation. In his contribution to the 1982 ISFC in Toronto, Martin (1985b) raised the problem of dynamic modelling and presented research at Sydney University exploring this problem. One approach was to use flowcharts to represent the sequencing of stages in the unfolding of text and this flowchart representation was adopted by Ventola (1987) in the description of service encounters (later in the decade, Fawcett 1988b, used flowcharts for 'dynamic' modelling of systems – systemic flowcharts in the representation of discourse). Other contributions to the interpretation of the unfolding text included Butt's (1983, 1984) notion of semantic drift and representations of unfolding selections and Gregory's (1985) phasal analysis.

In the computational modelling of the Penman project, the focus was initially on the more micro-scale problem of generating clauses by means of the systemic functional Nigel grammar. This had been explored already in the 1960s by Henrici (1965), who had developed a programme for generating (instantiating) selection expressions from system networks. In the Penman project, the selection expressions needed to be accompanied by function structures realizing systemic terms in the selection expressions and this process of instantiation needed to be guided semantically. This process of instantiation was modelled as an algorithm for 'traversing' system networks (discussed in Matthiessen and Bateman 1991). In this algorithm, a system network is typically traversed in the direction of increasing delicacy (from left to right in the graphic representation of networks), but if a systemic term in the network has been preselected by a realization statement, the systemic path leading to this term has to be computed first by backwards traversal in the direction of decreasing delicacy (path augmentation). Any realization statements associated with system terms selected in the course of traversal are 'activated' and they will define a function structure step by step. The process of traversal thus produces an instance of the potential represented by the system network with associated realization statements. This is the selection expression of terms from the system network and the function structure resulting from the accumulation of realization statements: see Figure 2.10.

Since algorithms in general had to be sequential, the traversal algorithm was sequential. This meant that if simultaneous systems in a system network were encountered, they had to be traversed one after the other. Similarly, if a list of simultaneous realization statements associated with a systemic term was encountered, they had to be activated one after the other. This sequentiality was thus imposed by the modelling of the process of instantiation, not by the systemic modelling of the potential in the form of the system network. In the mid-1980s, Yu-Wen Tung, Norm Sondheimer and I did a study of what the implications of parallel processing would be (Matthiessen, Sondheimer and Tung 1988a). We found that the systemic representation would support massively parallel processing. (One key reason was that there is only 'intrinsic' ordering in systemic representation, no 'extrinsic' ordering, to put this in the terms of the discussion of rule ordering in generative linguistics in the 1960s and 1970s.) Yu-Wen Tung had hoped to implement an experimental system based on our findings, using a million-dollar parallel computer (a vaguely evil-looking big black box with blinking red lights) at the Institute; but before we could start, funding for the parallel project that this would have piggy-backed on dried up and the computer disappeared.

The modelling of the process of instantiation in terms of a traversal algorithm raised various issues. One central issue was how to deal with logical systems – systems that include a 'loop' for systemic recursion. In fact, they pose a problem even in the representation of the system network itself (see Matthiessen 1988a), as noted already by Henrici (1965), since it can no longer be represented as an acyclic graph or a type hierarchy (as did Mellish 1988, for example). I visited John Bateman at Kyoto University in 1986, asking for his help in solving the problem. We discussed it for a week and he then continued working on it and later published an account of it together with a possible solution (Bateman 1989).

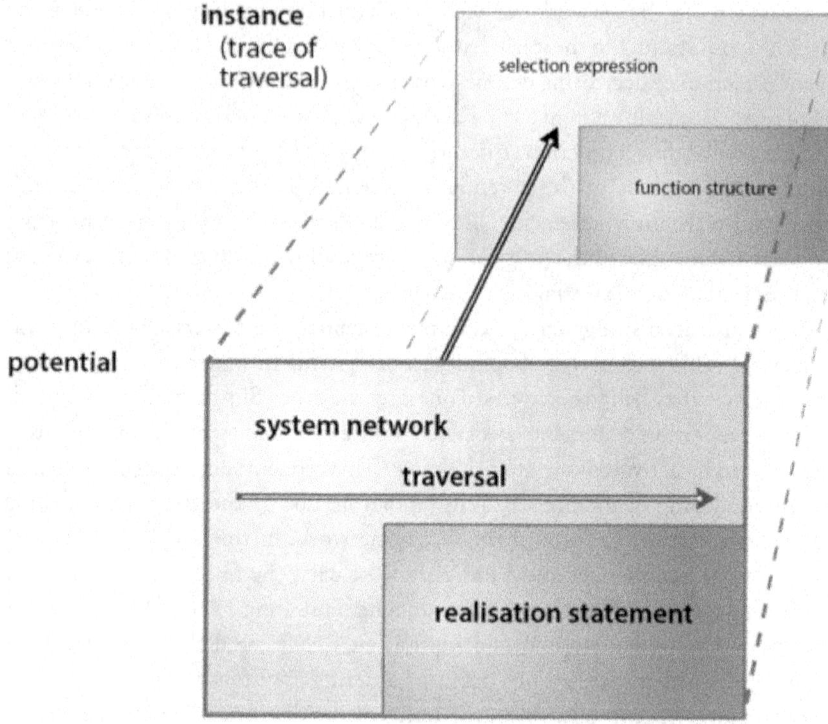

Figure 2.10 The process of instantiation modelled as system network traversal, with the instance as a trace of the traversal paths (selection expression) and realization statement activations (function structure)

2.3.3 Modelling the SFL metalanguage

The computational linguistic research just referred to was, among other things, a process of modelling the architecture of language according to systemic functional theory. The modelling task put pressure on us to think about the nature of modelling itself and this was made more urgent, but also helped, by representational challenges like the logical system challenge discussed above. I collected representational problems and sorted and interpreted them in terms of systemic functional theory (Matthiessen 1988a). This made it easier to see that modelling is stratified, just like language; and this insight was supported by Hjelmslev's (1943) observations about linguistics as a kind of (connotative) semiotic, Firth's (1957b) notion of linguistics as language turned back on itself and Halliday's (1984c) discussion of the ineffability of linguistic categories.

Another source of insight came from the 'struggle' with understanding knowledge representation in AI/computational linguistics in the second half of the 1970s. After graphic representations of semantic networks had been introduced into AI/computational linguistics in the 1960s, there was a period when this form of representation was used very 'freely'. This prompted Woods (1975) to ask 'what's in a link?' and to point out that there were inconsistencies in the use of links. Brachman (1979) dealt with the situation by differentiating different levels of representation, from epistemological and to implementational, and he pointed out that the graphic form of representation could not serve as a substitute for an explicit algebraic specification.

From a systemic functional point of view, it made sense to conceive of the modelling resource, the systemic functional metalanguage, as a (connotative) semiotic system organized into a number of strata, ranging from the stratum of theory to the stratum of implementation with two representational strata in between, one stratum of theoretically oriented representation and another of computationally oriented representation (see Matthiessen 1988a; Matthiessen and Bateman 1991; Matthiessen and Nesbitt 1996; Halliday and Matthiessen 1999; Teich 1999; Matthiessen forthcoming a). This stratification of the metalanguage is represented diagrammatically in Figure 2.11.

In Figure 2.11 the theory of systemic organization along the paradigmatic axis is used as an illustration of modelling at different metalinguistic strata. This theory is comprehensive in its coverage of the phenomena, for example including the notion that systemic contrasts are clines weighted in terms of probability of instantiation and that they are always in a state of 'flux'. This theory of systemic organization is realized at the stratum below in the form of the theoretical representation of the system network. The system network is, in a sense, a semi-formalized type of representation. It covers key aspects of the theory of systemic organization, but it does not, for example, cover the notion of probabilistically weighted clines in

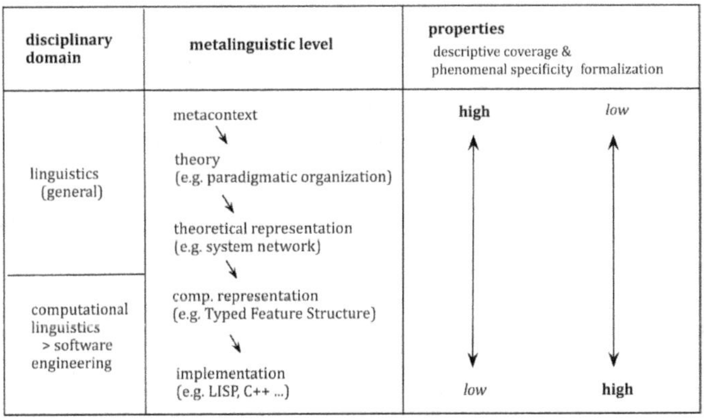

disciplinary domain	**metalinguistic level**	**properties** descriptive coverage & phenomenal specificity	 formalization
linguistics (general)	metacontext ↘	**high** ↑	*low* ↑
	theory (e.g. paradigmatic organization) ↘		
	theoretical representation (e.g. system network) ↘		
computational linguistics > software engineering	comp. representation (e.g. Typed Feature Structure) ↘		
	implementation (e.g. LISP, C++ ...)	↓ *low*	↓ **high**

Figure 2.11 Stratification of metalanguage in its metacontext

a constant state of flux. Consequently, as we descend from theory to theoretical representation, we are able to increase the degree of explicit formalization, but there is a price to pay: there are aspects of the theory we do not yet know how to represent. The same principle applies as we descend to the stratum below that of theoretical representation – to the stratum of computational representation. For example, when system networks are represented by typed feature structures, inheritance networks and similar mathematically explicit forms of computational representation (as in Bateman, Emele and Momma 1992; Henschel 1994; Mellish 1988; see also O'Donnell and Bateman 2005), the representation is fully explicit – explicit enough for implementation, but some coverage is again lost. In particular, logical systems with a recursive loop cannot be realized in the representation and marking conventions across systems (e.g. if 'exclamative' in the system 'declarative: exclamative/non-exclamative'), then 'positive' in the system 'major: positive/negative') are also likely to remain unrepresented (cf. Matthiessen 1988a). If the computational representation has already been implemented, there will not, of course, be any further loss of coverage as we descend to the stratum of implementation. However, implementational coverage often lags behind designs of computational representations.

As we move up and down the metalinguistic hierarchy of stratification, we thus find a trade-off between degree coverage and degree of formalization. In addition, there is another cline characterizing the stratification of metalanguage; this is the cline of domain specificity. At the theoretical level, the metalanguage is highly specialized in the sense that the theory is a theory of semiotic systems, not of systems of any other kind. At the other end, at the implementational level, the metalanguage is highly non-specialized in the sense that the programming languages used in the implementation have a wide range of applications across theories concerned with different kinds of phenomena. Thus as we descend the metalinguistic hierarchy of stratification, we have a range of choices open to use. For example, system networks may be represented by typed feature structures (as in Bateman, Emele and Momma 1992) or by production rules (as in Patten 1988); and different forms of representation will have different properties: typed feature structures retain the declarative aspect of the theory of systemic organization, while production rules don't.

In my view, the stratal organization is an essential property of the metalanguage, allowing researchers with different kinds of expertise to complement one another in the overall modelling effort. The fact that theory and representation have been kept distinct in the development of SFL has been enormously important. (The mistake of treating forms of representation as if they were theory has on the whole been avoided.) Similarly, it has been very productive to have a theoretical level of representation in the form of system networks and the like since this level has enabled linguists to produce and work with descriptions without having to take on the computational level of representation – and this form of high-level working environment is supported by Bateman's KPML system.

Just as language is embedded in context, metalanguage is embedded in metacontext. This is the context in which research and application are undertaken. SFL has always been multimetacontextual in the sense that it has been developed and applied within a range of different contexts. In the description of the metalanguage in this section, I have assumed the metacontext of computational modelling, since it was in this context that the pressure on formulating a metatheory of the nature of the theory first became tangible; but the metatheoretical model of metalanguage in metacontext is of general value.

By characterizing a given metacontext, we can shed light on the metalinguistic resources 'at risk' – the registerial setting of the metalanguage that will be relevant to that context. For example, in the metacontexts of discourse analysis or educational linguistics, it may not be felt to be necessary to provide system networks with explicit realization statements; but in computational modelling, these are naturally absolutely necessary. Different metacontexts will typically represent different combinations of disciplinary domains of expertise and these combinations are likely to represent different patterns complementarity across the strata of our metalanguage. For instance, in computational linguistics, there is a fairly clear line between the levels of theory and theoretical representation on the one hand and the levels of computational representation and implementation on the other (cf. Figure 2.11). However, the situation is different in metacontexts of educational and clinical work, for example. Here the complementarity has to be sorted out at the highest stratum of the metalanguage.

2.4 The 1990s

The development of the 'architecture' of SFL in the 1990s was characterized by the following central concerns:

- **Instantiation:** Developments based on a fully extended **cline of instantiation** (Halliday 1992h; 2007a), including the location along this cline of institution, situation type and context of situation within context and of text types, registers and codes within language.
- **Instantiation:** In reference to processes of instantiation, an articulation of different **'views' on and angles of access** to, the resources of language

according to the nature of the process of instantiation (O'Donnell 1994; Matthiessen and Nesbitt 1996; Zeng 1996; Matthiessen, forthcoming b).

- **Instantiation – semogenesis:** Based on the cline of instantiation, the development of a general account of processes of semogenesis (Halliday and Matthiessen 1999).
- **Axis:** Development of system networks capable of representing **multilingual specifications** (Bateman *et al.* 1991, 1999).
- **Axis:** Development of **topological interpretation** of systemic contrasts in terms of typology alongside typology (Lemke 1987; Martin and Matthiessen 1991; Matthiessen 1995b).
- **Typology of systems:** Introduction of an ordered typology of systems in different phenomenal realms (Halliday 1996; Halliday and Matthiessen 1999; Matthiessen, forthcoming a).

These 'architectural' advances took place in the context of new developments within SFL, including the emergence of an area of multilingual studies involving the description of languages and linguistic typology (see Teruya *et al.* 2007) as well as translation studies (updating the classic foundational work by Catford 1965; see Steiner 2005a), the emergence of clinical linguistics (see Armstrong *et al.* 2005), the modelling and description of semiotic systems other than language (see Bowcher 2007 and Martinec 2005) and also, of course, in the context of continuing activities, including the description of semantics (see Hood and Martin 2007; Cloran *et al.* 2007) and the work on educational processes (see Christie and Unsworth 2005; Martin and Rose 2005).

2.4.1 The cline of instantiation

2.4.1.1 The nature of the cline

If the 1980s was the decade of the hierarchy stratification, then the 1990s was arguably the decade of the cline of instantiation: early in the decade, Halliday (1992h) presented a seminal paper on this dimension, showing that potential and instance defined the outer poles of a cline, the cline of instantiation and that there were intermediate patterns: see Figure 2.12. (In one publication, Matthiessen 1993b, I had called the dimension 'potentiality'; but 'instantiation' is a preferable term.) Within context, the outer poles are defined by [context of] culture (potential) and [context of] situation (instance), the two Malinowskian concepts thus being explicitly related by a dimension of organization. The intermediate patterns are institutions (seen from the potential pole as subcultural domains within the context of culture) and situation types (seen from the instance pole as generalizations across situations). Within language, the outer poles are defined by the system of language (potential) and text (instance). The intermediate patterns are registers (seen from the potential pole as subsystems within the system of language) and text types (seen from the instance pole as generalizations across text).

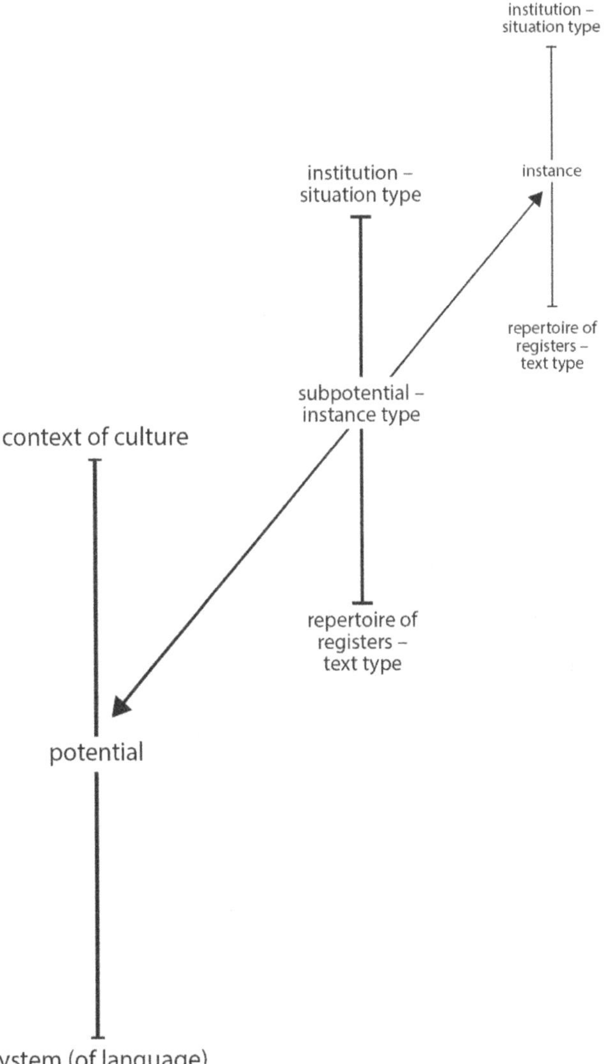

Figure 2.12 The cline of instantiation within context and language

2.4.1.2 The cline of instantiation and quantitative studies

The notion of the cline of instantiation provided the theoretical key to quantitative studies of text undertaken to illuminate features of the system: relative frequencies observed at the instance pole of the cline can be interpreted as systemic probabilities further up the cline. This kind of study had been put on the research agenda by Halliday (1959) and it was given a theoretical-descriptive boost by Nesbitt and Plum (1988). Early in the 1990s, Halliday (1991a, 1992h, 1993d) elaborated the theoretical underpinnings and as corpora and corpus tools became more widely available and were produced within SFL for systemic functional research (see Wu 2000 and O'Donnell and Bateman 2005), systemic functional researchers began producing a number of text- and corpus-based investigations exploring the probabilistic nature of the system, including Halliday and James (1993) and Matthiessen (1999, 2006a). As Tucker (2007) shows, corpus-based investigations can finally allow us to observe, study and model the region between lexis and grammar in lexicogrammar in a general way. The bottleneck in corpus-based studies is still the lack of a systemic functional parser capable of handling a flow of large volumes of text (see O'Donnell and Bateman 2005); but certain breakthroughs may be very imminent with the development of techniques for adding systemic functional value to the output produced by a mainstream parser (including parsed corpora).

2.4.1.3 The cline of instantiation and the hierarchy of stratification intersected

The cline of instantiation and the hierarchy of stratification are independently variable dimensions. While stratification is based on levels of abstraction, instantiation is based on observer perspective: the phenomena seen close up (instance pole) or from a distance (potential pole). Halliday (1992h) used an analogy with meteorological phenomena: we observe them close up as weather; but we theorize them from a distance as climate. Since stratification and instantiation are independently variable dimensions, they can be intersected and this intersection can be presented by means of an instantiation-stratification matrix, as shown in Figure 2.13 and (with glosses) in Figure 2.14 (both from Halliday 2002b).

I first learned about the full implications of this intersection in March 1995, when Halliday and I were on a flight home from Tokyo to Sydney after taking part in an international EEE and fuzzy conference in Yokohama and after exploring the modelling of language in context with the organizer, Professor Sugeno. Halliday said thoughtfully that we needed a 'Sugeno six-pack' to represent the modelling of language along both the hierarchy of stratification and the cline of instantiation. After some high-level exploration of this six-pack (approximately 33,000 feet above sea level), we concluded that it had to be a nine-pack, since lexicogrammar is also included (as shown in Figure 2.12). In fact, it can be extended to a twelve-pack to take account of phonology as well! Later that year, Halliday introduced the 'nine-pack' together with other architectural overviews in 'computing meanings', his plenary address to PACLING 95 (Pacific Rim Computational Linguistics), held at the University of Queensland, in Brisbane. Sugeno was also one of the invited plenary speakers and he arranged for Halliday's paper to be published in a Japanese translation as 'Imi no computingu' (2000a). Since the paper was a key contribution to the 'architecture' of language, I had suggested that it should be translated into Chinese and Japanese. Teruya undertook the translation into Japanese and Wu the translation into Chinese. Halliday, Teruya, Wu and I met regularly over a couple of years, discussing the translation as it progressed and compiling terms in the three languages. All three versions have now appeared in publications in China. Sugeno and his research team at the Brain Science Division of the RIKEN Institute outside Tokyo have explored the architecture of the intersection of stratification and instantiation in the last five years, treating it as the semiotic base of an everyday language computing system. In the course of this, the power of the model has been brought out and many details have been filled in.

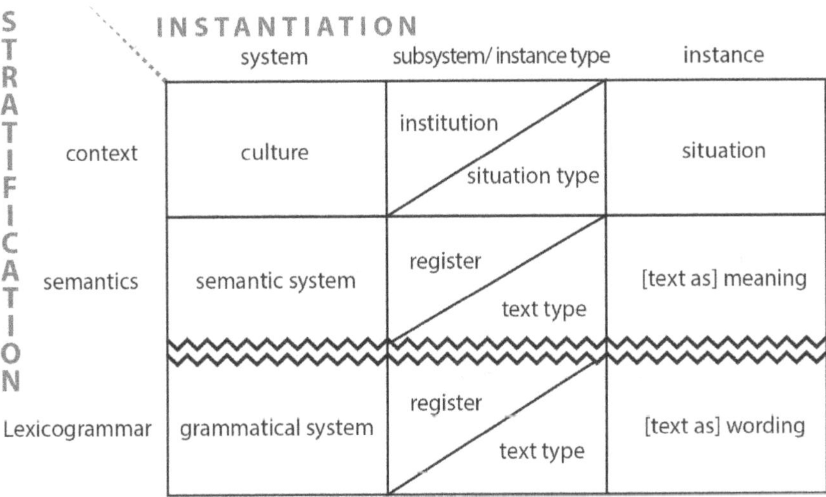

Figure 2.13 Instantiation-stratification matrix (from Halliday 2002b)

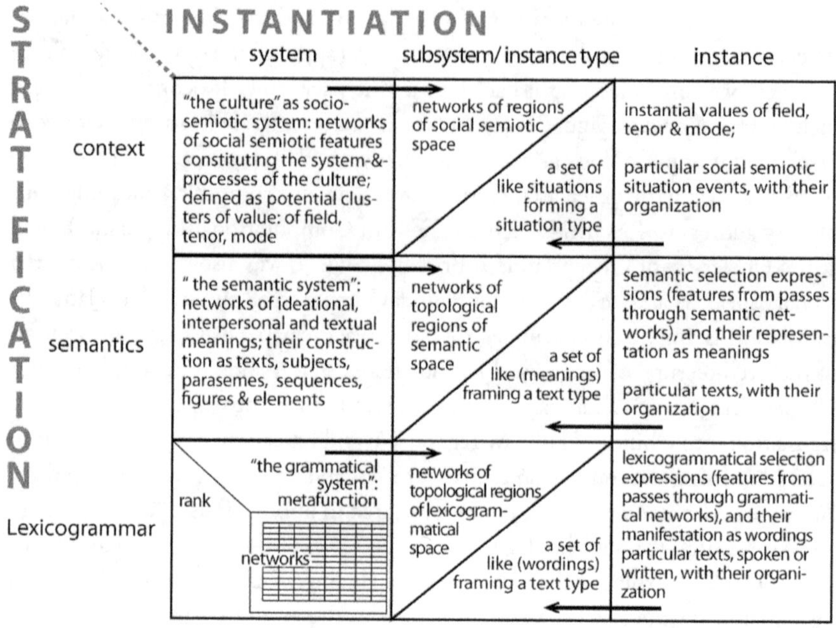

Figure 2.14 Instantiation-stratification matrix, with glosses (from Halliday 2002b)

As can be seen from Figure 2.13 the intersection of the cline of instantiation with the hierarchy of stratification opens up new possibilities of modelling language in context. In the 1980s, stratification had been explored as the primary resource for modelling context and this was of course still a valid option in the 1990s; but now situation type and register could be located relative to other contextual and linguistic domains by reference to instantiation as well as to stratification. In the theoretical model set out in Figure 2.13, context is in fact not internally stratified, but it is instead phased – that is, extended along the cline of instantiation from the overall cultural potential via regions within this potential to instantial situation.

2.4.1.4 *The cline of instantiation and variation*

Instantiation is inherently variable and different regions along the cline of instantiation are the locus for different kinds of variation (see Halliday 1994a; Matthiessen 1993b): see Figure 2.15. Variation in text at the instantial pole of the cline is just that – instantial; but this is of course where the system is maintained, renewed and changed, so consistent longer-term patterns become significant – but they are typically significant within some register or other (see immediately below). If a particular text is given value as an object in its own right (as happens with verbal art), it may be significant as an instantial model – the limiting case being what Halliday has called the 'Hamlet factor'.

Midway between instance and potential, there is variation in instantiation according to ranges of field, tenor and mode values that are characteristic of institutions and situation types within institutions. This is variation in the semantic system in the first instance – register variation (see e.g. Ghadessy 1988, 1993b). Unlike other kinds of variation located further up the cline of instantiation towards the potential pole (see below), register variation involves no higher-stratal constant: it is variation according to use and in this sense register variation also involves contextual variation. Register variation had of course been identified long before the 1990s (having been extended from Firth's notion of 'restricted languages') and discussed in, for example, Halliday, McIntosh and Strevens (1964), Gregory (1967), Hasan (1973), Halliday (1978) and Halliday and Hasan (1985); but it was now possible to give it a very explicit 'semiotic address' in the semiotic space defined by stratification and instantiation.

Somewhere between the mid-region of the cline of instantiation and the potential pole, there is semantic variation of a different kind – codal variation (see Halliday 1994b, on the location along the cline of instantiation). This is variation in semantic coding orientation ('semantic style') in comparable contexts (such as the context of controlling a young child's behaviour). Different coding orientations are associated with different classes within complex societies with hierarchic organization, so people from different classes with different coding orientations are also likely to operate with different registerial repertoires. They were first noticed and theorized by Bernstein (e.g. 1973); but it wasn't until Hasan's research project in the 1980s already referred to above that they were brought out in statistically significant ways through semantic analysis of a large corpus of texts.

Near the potential pole, there is dialectal variation. This is low-level variation affecting phonology, low-ranking lexicogrammar (morphology) and lexis in the first instance; in modern nation states, dialects tend to be reduced to accents. The semantics is constant (and thus also the context): dialects are different ways of saying the same thing (e.g. Halliday 1978).

If the outline of variation sketched here in relation to the cline of instantiation and the hierarchy of stratification is accurate, then the general principle is as follows. Variation can reflect factors 'from below' and 'from above'. Variation 'from below' is created by the dispersal of meaning over matter: the community

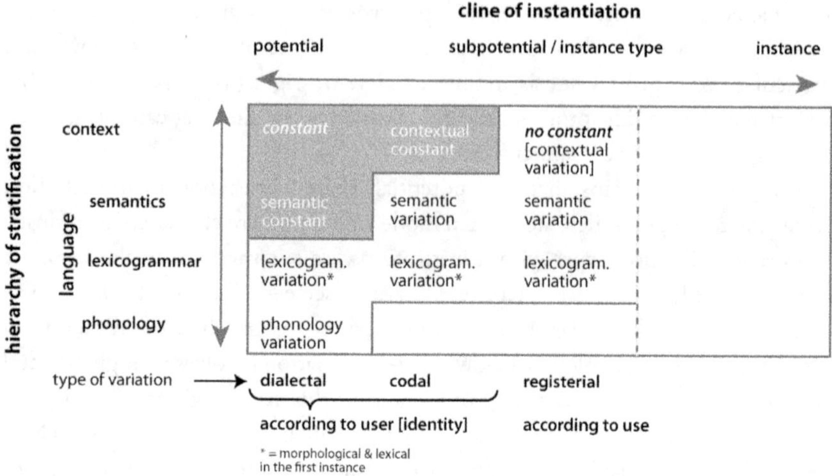

Figure 2.15 Kinds of variation in relation to the cline of instantiation and the hierarchy of stratification

of speakers of a language is extended spatially and also temporally. This variation is located towards the potential pole of the cline of instantiation and it affects the lower regions of language in the first instance – phonology and morphology and lexis within lexicogrammar (which are the features shown on dialect maps); but (as noted above) semantics is largely constant, so dialects are different ways of saying the same thing. With migration or with language contact situations, different dialects of one language may evolve into different languages. Variation 'from above' is created by the dispersal of meaning in relation to social order. This variation extends from the mid-region of the cline of instantiation (registerial variation) to a zone between the mid-region and the potential pole (codal variation) and it affects the higher regions of language – semantics in the first instance and then also lexicogrammar (since lexicogrammar stands in the natural relationship to semantics). The further up the cline of instantiation that the variation in instantiation is located, the lower down this variation is located stratally; and the further down the cline of instantiation that it is located, the higher up this variation is located stratally.

The meaning potential at the potential pole of the cline of instantiation represents a speech fellowship's collective inheritance – its reservoir of meaning (in the terms of Martin and Rose 2003). Members of the speech fellowship, meaners, are all trustees of subpotentials in this collective meaning potential (Matthiessen and Halliday, in prep.: chap. 2). As children of a speech fellowship learn how to mean, they access the collective meaning potential through texts (Halliday 1978), located at the instance pole of the cline of instantiation. This process continues through life: as meaners go through the educational system, becoming first adolescents and then young adults, they learn an increasing range of registers; and as they take on their adult roles, they continue to learn the registers that go with these roles. This is a process of developing a personalized meaning potential ('idiolect') as part of the journey along an individual **life line** (in S. Rose's 1997, sense) within a person's ontogenetic time-frame. However, access to the meaning potential, to the collective semiotic reservoir, is not equal in a society. It is determined by the division of labour in the society and, in more complex societies, by class systems; and educational systems are designed to produce meaners with different repertoires of registers to fill positions of different ranks in work places (as shown in contributions to Christie and Martin 1997).

2.4.2 Semogenesis

The cline of instantiation is thus a dimension essential in the modelling of sociosemiotic organization of a society. It also makes it possible to differentiate and locate different kinds of semogenesis (processes of creating meaning), as shown in Figure 2.16 (cf. Halliday and Matthiessen 1999: 18). At the instance pole of the cline, semogenesis takes the form of logogenesis, the unfolding of the act of meaning as text. At the potential pole of the cline, it takes the form of phylogenesis, the evolution of the meaning potential in the human species. In between these two poles, semogenesis can be interpreted either from the vantage point of logogenesis as macro-logogenesis (a text type seen as a macro-text) or from the vantage point of phylogenesis as micro-phylogenesis (a register seen as a subpotential, as in Halliday's 1988, study of the evolution of scientific English since Chaucer and in Nanri's 1993, study of the evolution of news reporting). As noted above, ontogenesis (the development of a personalized meaning potential) involves accessing the meaning potential from the instance pole of the cline of instantiation through text. In this sense, it is a move up the cline of instantiation from the instance pole towards the collective potential pole; but individual meaners never reach this collective potential and we can locate ontogenesis somewhere between the instance pole and the mid-region of the cline.

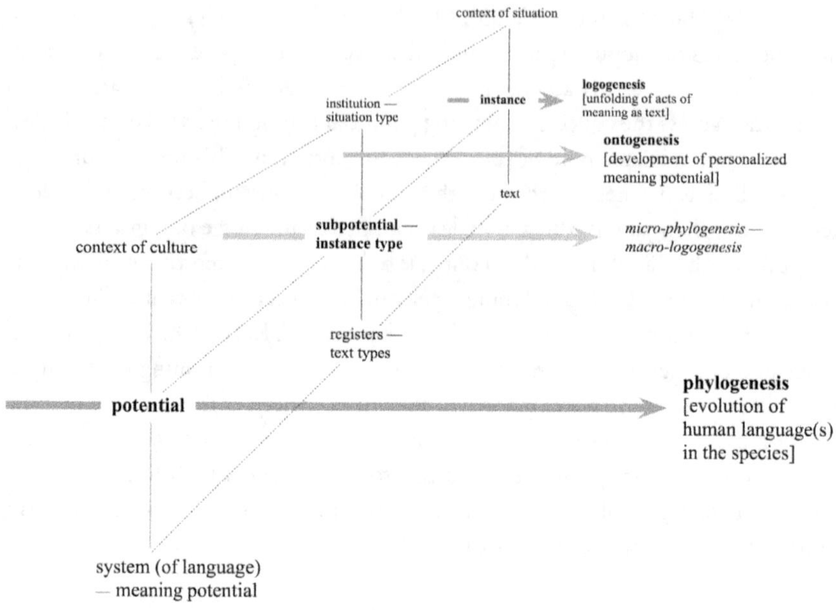

Figure 2.16 The three semogenic processes of phylogenesis, ontogenesis and logogenesis in relation to the cline of instantiation

2.4.3 *Processes of instantiation and views*

As the cline of instantiation was being explored in the 1990s, this exploration shed light on processes of instantiation and their relationship to both potential and instance. There are many semiotic processes that involve instantiation – speaking/writing, listening/reading, editing, summarizing, translating, interpreting and so on; but all these are based on the two fundamental processes of generation and analysis. Generation is the downward move along the cline of instantiation from some point located higher up than the instance pole to the instance pole, while analysis is the upward move along the cline from the instance pole to some point located higher up. In the limiting case, both processes extend all the way to the potential pole of the cline, but often they don't: a text is often processed as an instance of a register.

Generation and analysis access the resources of language, wherever they are located along the cline of instantiation, from different angles. In generation, they are accessed 'from above' in the first instance – 'from above' in terms of the hierarchy of stratification (semantics to lexicogrammar to phonology/graphology), in terms of axis (system to structure) and in terms of rank (from clause to group/ phrase and so on, in lexicogrammar). In analysis, they are accessed 'from below' in the first instance[6] – in terms of the same dimensions. The contrasting views or gateways of access came into focus in computational work within SFL in two related contexts.

1. When Kasper (e.g. 1988a; 1988b) developed an experimental systemic functional parser by 'translating' a systemic functional mini-grammar I extracted for him from the Nigel grammar into a unification-based form of representation, syntagmatic segmentation and constituency assignment emerged as the primary initial task – not surprisingly (see O'Donnell and Bateman 2005). While the gateway of access in generation was the systemic organization of the grammar, in analysis it was the specification of syntagms.
2. When I explored the organization of lexis in the context of generation, it became clear that the mainstream dictionary model was oriented towards analysis, whereas the thesaurus model was oriented towards generation (Matthiessen 1991a). This was again not surprising since the modern dictionary developed out of lists of difficult words that a reader might encounter (see e.g. Landau 1989), while the modern thesaurus was designed by Mark Roget to help writers find lexical items to construe their ideas (as he says in his 1852 foreword).

The question was how to reconcile these views of, or gateways of access to, the resources needed by different processes of instantiation. The general answer was that one view showed the canonical representation from which other views could be 'compiled' (see Matthiessen and Nesbitt 1996, Section 5; cf. also Kay 1985; Kasper 1988a). This canonical representation is the one richest in information since it can support all views needed by different processes of instantiation. The canonical representation turns out to be the systemic functional representation – a kind of thesaurus view not only on lexis but also on grammar and other linguistic resources. Thus in order to support his systemic functional parser, O'Donnell (1994) compiled different tables from the systemic functional representation (see O'Donnell and Bateman 2005).

Viewed from the instance pole of instantiation, both generation and analysis appear as an ongoing selection of features (with associated realization statements), along the lines anticipated by Halliday (1977b). But this process can also be viewed in systemic terms as an instantial system local to a given text (as had been discussed by Hasan 1984a, and Fries 1982, with reference to instantial lexical patterns in text); see Matthiessen (1993a).

Instantial systems are created as part of the process of logogenesis. This process was explored by a group of us at the University of Sydney in the early 1990s and a number of studies exploring logogenesis have been published, revealing patterns of how meaning is built up and negotiated in the unfolding of text (including Fuller 1995; O'Donnell and Sefton 1995; Matthiessen 2002b).

2.4.4 Systemic organization

By end of the 1980s, considerable experience had accumulated in describing the meaning potential in terms of systemic organization. On the one hand, semantic system networks had been developed and applied in the analysis of large samples of texts within a wide range of registers. On the other hand, lexicogrammatical system networks had been developed and applied both in text analysis and in computational modelling. This descriptive experience provided the context for two theoretical developments that started around 1990 – the interpretation of systemic contrasts in terms of topology and the development of system networks for representing multilingual resources (or more generally, multisystemic ones).

2.4.4.1 Typology/topology

Lemke (1987) had drawn attention to the possibility of modelling genre agnation not only typologically, but also topologically. Building on this insight, Jim Martin and I suggested that systemic agnation in general could be interpreted topologically and showed how this could help address a number of descriptive challenges (Martin and Matthiessen 1991). We provided illustrations from different strata and additional examples have been developed in the literature since then (e.g. lexicogrammatical topological displays in Matthiessen 1995b, and in Halliday 1998a; and semantic topological displays in Halliday and Matthiessen 1999). The exploration of the topological interpretation of systemic contrasts led, in quite a natural way, to an investigation of fuzzy representation: Ichiro Kobayashi and I discussed the possibility of interpreting terms in systems as the names of fuzzy sets in order to reflect the principle that systems construe clines where the boundaries between terms are indeterminate (fuzzy rather than crisp; see Matthiessen 1995b).

In the work on genre agnation, Martin and others in his research group have made central use of the notion of topology (see e.g. Christie and Martin 1997), as illustrated by Martin's (2003: 45) topology of history genres in Table 2.1.

2.4.4.2 Multilingual system networks

Ever since they were introduced by Halliday in the early 1960s, system networks had been used to represent the paradigmatic organization of one language at a time and one variety of one language at a time. However, the need to represent multilingual systems within one system network increased as text generation project turned to the task of multilingual generation with the Penman system: this happened at GMD/IPSI in Darmstadt Germany, where Bateman had taken up the task of developing systemic functional text generation, and at Sydney University, where I had received funding from the Australian Research Council to undertake a multilingual text generation project.

Bateman, Zeng and I worked out a way of describing multiple languages within one system network, while at the same time keeping the integrity of the description of each individual language (Bateman *et al.* 1999); an example of such a multilingual system network is given in Teruya *et al.* (2007). The main strategy was to 'partition' systemic and realizational statements according to the language they referred to (compare the notion of partitioned networks in Hendrix 1979). This was first applied to English, Chinese and Japanese (see Bateman *et al.* 1991). This approach was used in Bateman's (e.g. 1996) development of the multilingual version of the Penman-Komet systemic functional generator (KPML), which is now freely available for download, and in our own Multex system (Matthiessen *et al.* 1998b). KPML is also designed to serve as a grammar development workbench, and it has been used in the development of descriptions of a number of

Table 2.1 Topology of history genres (reproduction of Martin 2003: 45)

<table>
<tr><td colspan="2">prosodic appraisal</td><td colspan="2">periodic appraisal</td><td>thesis appraisal</td></tr>
<tr><td colspan="4">proposition</td><td>proposition/ proposal</td></tr>
<tr><td>tell</td><td>record</td><td colspan="3">explain</td></tr>
<tr><td></td><td></td><td>reveal</td><td>probe</td><td>argue</td></tr>
<tr><td>auto/ biographical recount [later]</td><td>historical recount [in/ during]</td><td>historical account [external cause/ incongruent]</td><td>factorial and consequential explanation [internal cause]</td><td>exposition/ challenge discussion</td></tr>
<tr><td>individual focus</td><td colspan="4">group (+ hero) focus</td></tr>
<tr><td colspan="3">text time = field time</td><td colspan="2">text time ≠ field time</td></tr>
<tr><td colspan="2">episodic unfolding in time</td><td>causal unfolding</td><td colspan="2">internal unfolding</td></tr>
</table>

languages, including English, German, French, Spanish, Russian, Czech, Bulgarian and Chinese (see also O'Donnell and Bateman 2005).

The multilingual network representation was designed to be used in multilingual text generation, but it is not restricted to this application. It is relevant to (machine) translation (cf. Bateman *et al.* 1999) and offers an interesting way of describing the meaning potential of multilingual speakers, making it possible to describe the resources that support both 'code switching' and 'code mixing'. However, it is relevant even more generally to the representation of different varieties of the same system, including dialectal and registerial varieties (cf. Matthiessen 1993b).

2.4.5 Typology of systems

As noted in Section 2.1.1, the approach taken to language in SFL has always been holistic, with an emphasis on comprehensive accounts; and the methodology and mode of theorizing can now be recognized as being like systems thinking about complex adaptive systems in other phenomenal realms. This was made more explicit with Halliday's proposal of an ordered typology of systems (see Halliday 1996; Halliday and Matthiessen 1999, chap. 13; Matthiessen 2004a, forthcoming a). The systems are, in order of increasing complexity: physical systems, biological systems, social systems and semiotic systems. The ordering is based on the principle that systems of a higher order are also systems of a lower order and it also reflects the order in which these systems can be assumed to have emerged since the 'big bang' – time-bound order in cosmogenesis (cf. Layzer 1990).

1. First-order systems are **physical** (or physical-chemical) **systems**. They emerged with the 'big bang' on the order of 15 billion years ago and have the widest distribution of systems of any kind, being dispersed throughout the universe. They are organized compositionally, ranging in size from the quantum world to galaxies and they are subject to the laws of physics (cause-and-effect being the classic way of modelling them); they change over time but they do not evolve (they are not subject to natural selection and have no 'memory').
2. Second-order system are **biological systems**. These are physical systems with the added property of 'life': they are self-replicating, are subject to individuation (individual organisms in biological populations, forming species) and their mode of cosmogenesis is evolution. They exist only under very special, highly constrained conditions (what James Lovelock calls the 'window of life'). As with physical systems, composition is a key

principle of organization – an organism consists of organ systems (like the nervous system, the circulatory system, the digestive system), which consist of organs (like brain, heart, stomach); an organ consists of tissue, which consists of cells; and cells are in turn organized compositionally. However, the composition is now clearly functional in nature; for example, an organ is a group of tissues serving a similar function and tissue is a group of cells serving a similar function. As far as we know at present, biological systems have emerged only once – on the planet earth, around 3.5 billion years ago.

3. Third-order systems are **social systems**. These are biological systems with the added property of social order (or value): biological populations are organized into social groups of different kinds (ranging in complexity and flexibility from insect colonies to modern human societies), with clear social division of labour among members of the group. Groups are organized as networks of roles of different kinds (institutional roles, sociometric roles, power and status roles; see e.g. Argyle *et al.* 1981) and these networks define persons or 'social subjects': persons are the assemblages of roles played by an individual in different role-relationships (see Firth 1950; Halliday 1978: 14–15; Butt 1991). A person is a social individual and so also a biological individual – that is, an organism (unless the organism is simulated by a robot); but unlike an organism, a person is (as already noted) defined relationally in terms of roles played in different social groups rather than compositionally in terms of component parts. Composition is also a principle of organization in social systems, of course: organizational units for rank scales. Social systems must have emerged under special conditions from biological systems many times in the evolution of life. How far back in time they go is hard to say; there is, not surprisingly, some indeterminacy in the distinction between a social colony of mutually adapted organisms and a single biological 'super-organism' (see Maynard Smith and Szathmáry 1999, chap. 11). In the evolution of the hominid line out of which modern *Homo sapiens* emerged, we can probably trace our own form of social organization back to the emergence of primates some 60 million years ago: Foley (1997: 173–174) emphasizes that "primates are the social order par excellence" and that "sociality is really part of the primate core adaptation". The evolution of human social organization can be interpreted as starting with family-level groups. Under certain conditions of intensification, additional social stratification has evolved – first different kinds of local groups and then, in certain contexts, regional polities, with the modern nation state as a recent adaptation (Johnson and Earle 2000).

4. Fourth-order systems are **semiotic systems**. These are social systems (so also biological and physical systems) with the added property of meaning: "meaning is socially constructed, biologically activated and exchanged through physical channels" (Halliday 2003a: 2). We can now see that the stratal organization of language is, in a sense, a replay of the ordering of systems from semiotic systems to physical systems. Semantics is an interlevel or interface (Halliday 1973); it is the resource for transforming what is not linguistic meaning into linguistic meaning – including 'meaning' in the bio-semiotic systems of perception and intention. At the other end of the hierarchy of stratification, phonetics is also an interlevel: it maps language onto the human body through the articulatory system and the auditory system.

When the four orders of system are considered from the point of view of cosmogenesis, it is important to emphasize that they do not evolve independently of one another: biological systems have co-evolved with social systems, social systems with semiotic systems and semiotic systems with biological systems (see Figure 2.17). This perspective of co-evolution has been emphasized in investigations of language and of the brain (e.g. Edelman 1992; Halliday 1995a; Deacon 1997; Matthiessen 2004a); but it also needs to be highlighted in general studies of the co-evolution of language and human societies (cf. Rose 2001b, the comparison of Western Desert and English in relation to their societies).

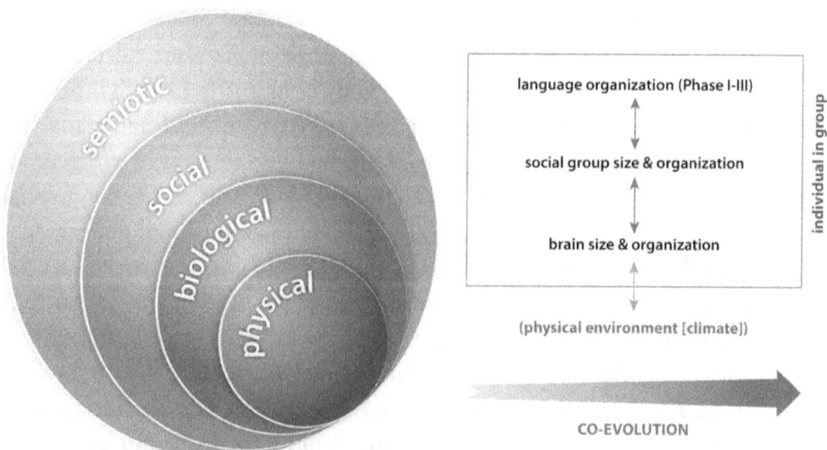

Figure 2.17 The four orders of system and co-evolution

2.5 Into the twenty-first century

The introduction of the ordered typology of systems is one of the most recent additions to the 'dimensional architecture' that has always been characteristic of SFL. Like other dimensions in the systemic functional modelling of the architecture of language, this one helps define the 'semiotic address' of different systems; here it is the semiotic address of language as a (higher-order) semiotic system. And it opens up new possibilities of research and application; for instance, patterns of organization can be located within the systems they first emerged as part of. This means for example that the dimensions of rank (composition) and instantiation pre-date semiotic systems, having emerged first in systems of a lower order of complexity. But lower-order principles of organization are always likely to be part of the organizational principles of systems of a higher order (evolution adumbrates and adapts, but does not replace and discard). What distinguishes a higher-order system from a lower-order one is the emergence of some new kind of organizational principle. In the case of semiotic systems, this was stratification (as we find it initially in protolanguage and other similar primary semiotic systems) – though organizational principles characteristic of a higher order may be 'previewed' in the organization of a lower-order system, as when a multicellular organism evolves out of a kind of role network of single cell organisms.

In the development of the systemic functional model of the architecture of language, new dimensions have been added over time. In this respect, the history of SFL is similar to the history of spatial modelling of physical systems since the late nineteenth century as described by Kaku (1994). But it also similar to the ontogenesis and the phylogenesis of language itself: language has achieved ever greater power by evolving more dimensions – gradually, in successive stages. This makes the system more complex in one sense; but at least in theorizing a system, the addition of another dimension is very likely to lead to less local complexity. The general constraint on the model is that all phenomena we try to cover should be exhaustively locatable along one or more dimensions: this follows from the fact that language is modelled relationally.

Assembling the dimensions discussed here, let me try to provide a summary diagram: see Figure 2.18. The diagram has been designed to suggest the kind of 'serial contextualization' that Firth talked about. The systemic functional metalanguage is used (by systemic functional linguists) to project a model of the phenomena under investigation. This model extends from the most global (the ordered typology of systems) to the most local (the axial organization of a rank within a given stratum). The systemic functional metalanguage is itself a semiotic system – language turned back on itself, which is what makes language ineffable (Halliday 1984c).

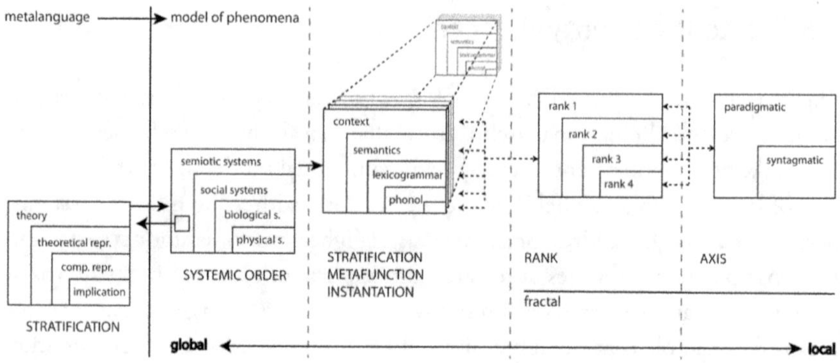

Figure 2.18 Systemic functional projecting model of the 'architecture of language'

In this model, axis is the most local dimension. This is in keeping with the principle that ranked units are the point of origin of system networks (e.g. Halliday 1966b). However, interestingly, it is possible to turn this around and interpret paradigmatic organization as the most global form of order (see Matthiessen forthcoming a, for more detailed discussion): ranks, strata and systemic orders would simply be represented as terms in successively more general systems. In fact, rank was systemicized in this way in the Nigel grammar; and in Multex strata were similarly systemicized.

Notes

1 The distinction between the two is very clear in theory, but in the development of linguistics there has been uncertainty at various points about which dimension is the relevant one in modelling a relationship: for example, is a morpheme composed of phonemes (composition) or is it realized by phonemes (stratification), is a text composed of sentences (composition) or is it realized by sentences. In SFL, stratification is the relevant dimension for both sets of relationships.

2 This interpretation is developed in Matthiessen and Halliday (in prep.); it was not foregrounded in the original account.

3 As illustrated in Figure 2.8, preselection is a purely declarative relationship between systemic terms in system networks within different domains – domains defined by stratification, but also (within a stratum) by rank.

4 In the 1970s, Sinclair and Coulthard (1975) had modelled classroom discourse in rank-based constituency terms.

5 The term 'register' is used in a different sense here from the original sense in SFL of a functional variety of language (as in Halliday, McIntosh and Strevens 1964; Hasan 1973; Halliday 1978).

6 This is an oversimplification in the sense that there are often expectations or predications 'from above'; but the access to the 'data' used in analysis is still typically 'from below'.

Chapter 3
Ideas and new directions

3.1 Sources of ideas and new directions

In this chapter, I will be concerned with ideas and new directions in systemic functional linguistics (SFL). I have designed the chapter so that it will complement the discussion of new directions in systemic functional theory in Matthiessen (2007b) and in the description of lexicogrammar in Matthiessen (2007a). Here I will foreground developments that are closely related to applications and potentially fundable research projects, which means that I will pay attention to investigations focusing on particular registers or sets of registers mid-way along the cline of instantiation.

Like language itself, SFL has always been an open dynamic system serving as a **resource** for both **reflection** and **action** (see e.g. Halliday 1985d). It is a system for reflecting on language and also on other semiotic systems – for analysing texts, for describing and comparing particular semiotic systems, and for theorizing language as a kind of semiotic system and by a further step for theorizing semiotic systems as a system of a particular kind; and it is also a resource for engaging with language in action – for intervening in social and semiotic processes, for developing plans of activity such as educational curricula and syllabi and communication networks in workplaces, for implementing models in working computational systems.

SFL is a **dynamic** system: it keeps changing in step with the environment in which it is operating. In this way, it has been remarkably stable since its beginnings in the 1960s; it has remained stable because it has kept changing. Like language, it is thus a meta-stable system. SFL is also an **open** system: as it changes, new features are added in response to new needs. In this way, the potential of SFL for reflection and action has been expanding since the 1960s; the rate of expansion has sometimes been faster, sometimes slower, but expansion has been a constant property of the development of SFL.

As SFL has expanded in new directions, into new territories, new ideas have thus tended to be added to the total resources that constitute SFL's potential for reflection and action. There have been ongoing movements within the theoretical model of language in context itself, ranging over different strata during the different phases of the development of SFL, as shown in Figure 3.1.[1] The overall effect of these movements has been to expand the domain of operation of SFL as an open dynamic system and to extend the descriptive coverage of the phenomenon under investigation, first language in context and now other semiotic systems in context. This coverage has been extended in the same way that cartographers have extended their coverage of areas around the world over the centuries – by **gradual approximation**, slowly increasing the scale. First they sketch the outlines of an area, and then they gradually fill in the details, thereby changing the scale of the map. This is a **holistic** approach to the development of maps. Of course, as they fill in the details, they may also change the overall outlines, adjusting them as they got access to new data. In the case of SFL, the approach of starting with the outlines of language and gradually filling in the details has been made possible by the **relational** and **dimensional** nature of the 'architecture' of the theoretical model of language – the 'scales' of scale-&-category theory, the first phase in the development of systemic functional theory (cf. Halliday 1961). This is illustrated by the work on filling out the details in movements up and down the dimension of stratification, as indicated in Figure 3.1. Another good illustration is the work by Tucker (e.g. 2007, cf. also 1998) and a number of other systemic functional linguists (e.g. Neale 2006) on filling in the details in the mid-region along the cline of delicacy

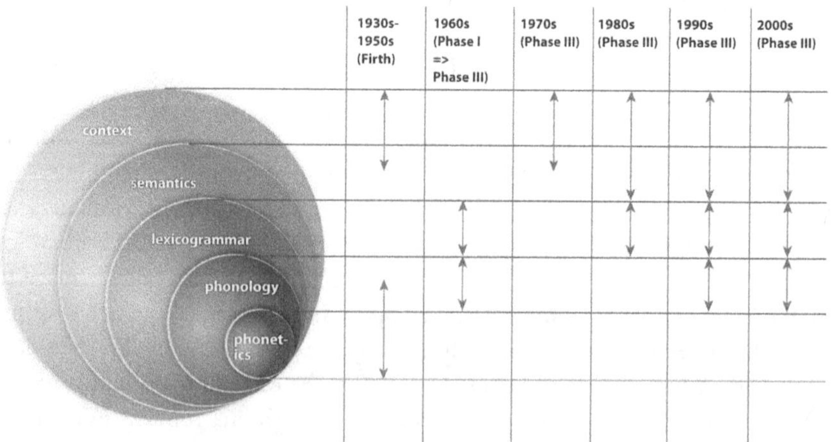

Figure 3.1 Phases in the development of SFL out of Firthian linguistics, represented as expansion of coverage of the strata of language in context

between the grammatical zone and the lexical one. As Tucker has pointed out, this work has been possible precisely because lexicogrammar is modelled 'dimensionally' as a continuum extending from low delicacy (high generality) to high delicacy (low generality).

The expansion of the stratal domain of operation of SFL represented in Figure 3.1 was partly internally driven, partly externally driven. **Internal pressures** came from within systemic functional linguistics and were due to the orientation towards systems thinking and a holistic approach to scientific exploration. High value was placed on comprehensive accounts. **External pressures** came from the environment in which researchers operated with SFL – from considerations of the contexts of research and application. For example, the development of semantics that started in the second half of the 1960s was driven by the social perspective on language and socially oriented research projects (in particular work directed by Basil Bernstein at the Sociological Research Unit), leading to what Hasan *et al.* (2007: 699) call "pressure on the semantic sciences": "it was in a climate of meeting the needs of research that functional semantics which, up to that stage, had been a neglected field in SFL, received a kick-start". This pressure resulted in early proposals for semantic system networks by Ruqaiya Hasan, M. A. K. Halliday and Geoffrey Turner. Similarly, the growing body of research since the 1990s into the expression planes of semiotic systems other than language – systems operating alongside phonology and phonetics in spoken language, and alongside graphology and graphetics in written language, and the analogous systems in signed language – has been produced in contexts where multimodality is critical (cf. Martinec 2005), including those of education, media studies, website development and information technology.

The development of the early semantic networks, discussed by Hasan *et al.* (2007: 702–709), also illustrates another principle in the expansion of the stratal coverage of language in context in SFL: experience gained in modelling and describing one stratal subsystem informs the modelling and description of new stratal subsystems. Thus system networks were originally developed by Halliday in the description of intonation (e.g. Halliday 1963b) and grammar (e.g. Halliday 1964, 1966d), so it made a good heuristic sense to apply them also to the task of mapping out the meaning potential of a language at the semantic stratum. Similarly, when I sketched a description of the phonology of Akan (mainly at the ranks of syllable and phoneme) in the mid-1980s (Matthiessen 1987a), I based my explicit representation of phonological system networks and realization statements on what we had learned from the development of the computational Nigel grammar (cf. Matthiessen 1981; Matthiessen and Bateman 1991), since I hadn't got access to any comparable descriptions of the syllabic and phonemic subsystems of the phonological system of any language (Halliday's 1992h, pioneering systemic account of 'Peking syllable finals' had not yet been written at the time).

We can treat this approach as a purely heuristic strategy. In a sense, a good deal of linguistics in general in the first half of the twentieth century can be seen as a heuristic expansion out of phonology. However, we can also reinterpret this approach as one based on a deep principle – the principle that language in context is subject to **fractal patterns**. In other words, certain patterns are manifested in different environments throughout all stratal subsystems of language in context. One such fractal pattern is the axial pattern of system networks with realizations statements specifying structural fragments underlying the stratal organization not only of phonology and lexicogrammar, where they were first explored, but also of semantics and context. In addition, this axial principle of stratal organization has also been used to explore the stratal subsystems of other semiotic systems, as in Kress and van Leeuwen (1996), with informal discursive realization statements, and Matthiessen *et al.* (1998b), with formalized realization statements in a computational system capable of generating multimodal texts (health reports with accompanying maps showing outbreaks of communicable diseases).

The fact that SFL is an open dynamic system also means that ideas and new directions in SFL have originated not only within SFL itself, but also in **metalinguistic contact situations** in the many different environments in which SFL has operated since the 1960s. These are situations where the same or similar phenomena are being explored by scholars using different metalanguages, or theoretical frameworks; for example:

- In studying and modelling supported learning, systemic functional linguists drew on Jerome Bruner's notion of scaffolding, developed within cognitive psychology since the 1950s (see e.g. Unsworth 1997; Painter 1999; Gibbons 2002; Martin and Rose 2005; cf. also Halliday 1993d).
- In investigating the probabilistic nature of language, systemic functional linguists have drawn on information theory, as developed by Claude Shannon and others since the 1940s (e.g. Halliday 1959, 1991a).
- In modelling systemic functional linguistics as a metalanguage, systemic functional linguists have drawn on Ron Brachman's work on knowledge representation in the 1970s (e.g. Matthiessen and Nesbitt 1996; Halliday and Matthiessen 1999; Teich 1999).

Numerous other examples can be given, including e.g. the sociology of Bernstein (in relation to social structure and 'codes', e.g. Hasan 1989; Halliday 1995b; in relation to the organization of knowledge, e.g. Christie and Martin 2007) and the anthropology of Malinowski (in relation to context, e.g. Hasan 1985b; and in relation to translation, e.g. Steiner 2005a).

Many systemic functional linguists have been bi- or multi-metalingual, combining the systemic functional metalanguage with other metalanguages derived from their background in fields such as education, translation, computer science, and speech pathology. In this way, systemic functional linguistics has been enriched by experts from other fields first undertaking Ph.D. research in systemic functional linguistics and then going on to supervise new areas of research.

3.2 The study of language: Areas of investigation and disciplines

3.2.1 Frame of reference: 1978

In SFL, ideas and new directions thus emerge in different areas of research on language in exchange with different fields of investigation within a wide range of disciplines. Let's take as our point of reference Halliday's (1978: 11) disciplinary map of the academic territory around language from about thirty years ago (reproduced here as Figure 3.2). He commented (10–11):

> A diagrammatic representation of the nature of linguistic studies and their relation to other fields of scholarship will serve as a point of reference for the subsequent discussion (figure 1 [Figure 3.2]). The diagram shows the domain of language study – of linguistics, to give it its subject title – by a broken line; everything within that line is an aspect or a branch of linguistic studies.
>
> In the centre is a triangle, shown by a solid line, which marks off what is the central area of language study, that of language as system. One way of saying what is meant by 'central' here is that if a student is taking linguistics as a university subject he will have to cover this area as a compulsory part of his course, whatever other aspects he may choose to take up. There are then certain projections from the triangle, representing special sub-disciplines within this central area: phonetics, historical linguistics and dialectology – the last of these are best thought of in broader terms, as the study of language varieties. These sometimes get excluded from the central region, but probably most linguists would agree in placing them within it; if one could give a three-dimensional representation they would not look like excrescences.

Then, outside this triangle, are the principal perspectives on language that take us beyond a consideration solely of language as system, and, in so doing, impinge on other disciplines. Any study of language involves some attention to other disciplines; one cannot draw a boundary round the subject and insulate it from others. The question is whether the aims go beyond the elucidation of language itself; and once one goes outside the central area, one is inquiring not only into language but into language in relation to something else. The diagram summarizes these wider fields under the three headings, 'language as knowledge', 'language as behaviour', 'language as art'.

The last of these takes us into the realm of literature, which is all too often treated as if it was something insulated from and even opposed to language: 'we concentrate mainly on literature here – we don't do much on language', as if 'concentrating on literature' made it possible to ignore the fact that literature is made of language. Similarly the undergraduate is invited to 'choose between lang. and lit.'. In fact the distinction that is being implied is a perfectly meaningful one between two different emphases or orientations, one in which the centre of attention is the linguistic system and the other having a focus elsewhere; but it is wrongly named, and therefore, perhaps, liable to misinterpretation. One can hardly take literature seriously without taking language seriously; but language is being looked at from a special point of view.

The two other headings derive from the distinction we have just been drawing between the intra-organism perspective, language as knowledge, and the inter-organism perspective, language as behaviour. These both lead us outward from language as system, the former into the region of psychological studies, the latter into sociology and related fields. So in putting language into the context of 'language and social man', we are taking up one of the options that are open for relating language study to other fields of inquiry. This, broadly, is the sociolinguistic option; and the new subject of sociolinguistics that has come into prominence lately is a recognition of the fact that language and society – or, as we prefer to think of it, language and social man – is a unified conception, and needs to be understood and investigated as a whole. Neither of these exists without the other: there can be no social man without language, and no language without social man. To recognize this is no mere academic exercise; the whole theory and practice of education depends on it, and it is no exaggeration to

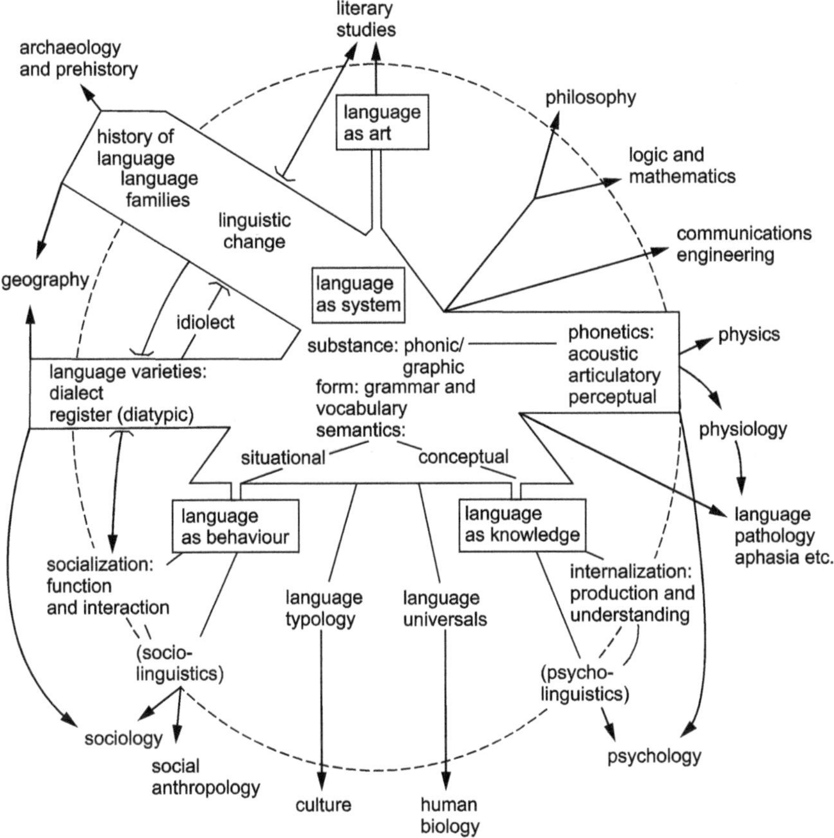

Figure 3.2 Linguistic studies in relation to other fields of scholarship around thirty years ago (Halliday 1978: 11)

suggest that much of our failure in recent years – the failure of the schools to come to grips with social pollution – can be traced to a lack of insight into the nature of the relationships between language and society: specifically of the processes, which are very largely linguistic processes, whereby a human organism turns into a social being.

3.2.2 New directions since 1978

The map of the academic territory around language in Figure 3.2 is still largely representative of today's academic landscape of engagement with different manifestations of language – as system, as behaviour, as knowledge, and as art. However, to take account of a number of new developments that have been consequential for SFL and its working environment, we can try to update the map by reviewing activities undertaken in relation to the different manifestations of language:

- in relation to 'language as knowledge': the continued expansion of cognitive science as a macro-discipline;
- in relation to 'language as behaviour' and 'language as system': the development of the field of social semiotics, and also of cultural studies;
- in relation to 'language as behaviour': the development of large-scale, systematic discourse analysis, and also of translation studies involving discourse analysis;
- in relation to 'language as system': the development of the study of complex adaptive systems (providing a new approach to a general systems science), and also the acceleration in the development of the computational modelling of language as system;

3.2.2.1 *In relation to 'language as knowledge'*

In relation to 'language as knowledge', the most significant disciplinary formation is **cognitive science**, a macro-discipline (that is, a discipline consisting of component parts of other disciplines) emerging out of developments originating in the 1950s. Since the 1970s, it has continued to expand (e.g. Hirst 1988; Posner 1989; Baumgartner and Payr 1995), with a growing number of research centres, journals and publications being devoted to it.

While systemic functional linguists in general have not worked with **mainstream** cognitive science, computational systemic functional linguists (see e.g. O'Donnell and Bateman 2005) have usually carried out their computational modelling of language in an environment where many researchers are oriented towards cognitive science. Consequently, a number of contributions to computational SFL have taken this environment into account (e.g. Matthiessen 1987b; and, with an explicitly cognitive orientation, Fawcett 1980, and the 'Cardiff Grammar' work building on this foundation).

As an alternative to the conception of knowledge in mainstream cognitive science, systemic functional linguists have offered a language-based approach, developing an account of how experience is construed as meaning in the semantic system of a language (see Halliday and Martin 1993; Martin and Veel 1998; Halliday and Matthiessen 1999; Kappagoda 2005; Christie and Martin 2007) and related this semiotic perspective (cf. Hasan 1992) to the new insights into language and the brain coming from advances in **neuroscience**, especially the work (inspired) by Gerald Edelman, Terrence Deacon and Michael Arbib (see e.g.

Halliday 1995a; Thibault 2000; Williams 2005b, and contributions to the special issue of *Linguistics and the Human Sciences* edited by Williams). This systemic functional alternative to mainstream cognitive science is a direction for further development that resonates with non-mainstream cognitive science exploring conceptions of the 'embodied mind' (e.g. Varela, Thompson and Rosch 1991), of intersubjectivity (e.g. Trevarthen 1979, 1987), of interaction (e.g. Lantolf and Thorne 2006). The orientation is towards Vygotsky rather than towards cognitive science, and the potential for new developments in this area of dialogue has been explored by scholars relating to Halliday and Vygotsky brought together by Byrnes (2006).

3.2.2.2 In relation to 'language as behaviour' and 'language as system': Social semiotics, cultural studies

In relation to 'language as behaviour' and 'language as system', Halliday's (e.g. 1978) interpretation of language as **social semiotic** has had a profound effect on the academic landscape – including the growth of social semiotics as a thematic field of activity in its own right (cf. Kress and Hodge 1988) and the launch of the *Social Semiotics* journal in the early 1990s. In Halliday's conception of language as a social semiotic system, language is seen as both system and behaviour (cf. Halliday 1984a), and this perspective complements that of cognitive science, providing an account of the social construction of meaning. Social semiotics has fed into the development of 'cultural studies', and, in its systemic functional interpretation, has also informed the development of clinical linguistics (see Armstrong 2009) and of multisemiotic studies (see Baldry and Thibault 2006), discourse analysis (see Martin 2007), and the continued development of educational linguistics.

In the 1980s, **cultural studies** emerged as a new disciplinary area relating also to 'language as art' (in English-speaking countries, sometimes combined with English but sometimes replacing, or splitting off from, traditional English literature; cf. Christie and Macken-Horarik 2007: 164–165), providing new opportunities for the analysis of texts that are highly valued by segments of the community other than the cultural elite (for SFL studies contributing to this area, see e.g. Cranny-Francis and Martin 1994, on popular films, and Veloso 2006, on comics). See further below on 'artistic linguistics'.

3.2.2.3 In relation to 'language as behaviour': Discourse analysis, translation studies

Language as 'behaviour' (cf. Halliday 1984a) takes the form of spoken, written or signed text, or discourse, and the analysis of text was central to the systemic functional research agenda from the start (see e.g. Halliday 1964; Hasan 1964). As an area of investigation, **discourse analysis** really took off in the 1980s, partly as an area within linguistics (where it has also been explored under the heading of 'text linguistics', particularly in work undertaken in continental Europe) and partly as an activity at the interfaces of different disciplines (cf. van Dijk 1985, 1997; Titscher *et al.* 2000; Schiffrin, Tannen and Hamilton 2001). Discourse analysis relates to both social semiotics and cultural studies, and it relates to developments in SFL – including the 'Birmingham School' of discourse analysis (e.g. Coulthard 1994; Coulthard and Montgomery 2001) – but also to other currents; for overviews of systemic functional approaches to discourse analysis, see e.g. Martin's (2007) on discourse studies and Cloran, Stuart-Smith and Young (2007).

One orientation within the broad area of discourse analysis is **Critical Discourse Analysis** (CDA; see e.g. van Dijk 2001, for an overview of the origins of CDA and the different strands it is made up of; see also e.g. Caldas-Coulthard and Coulthard 1996), which was influenced partly by the pioneering work in Australia and the UK in the 1970s concerned with language and power and drawing on SFL (e.g. Fowler *et al.* 1979; Kress and Hodge 1979). CDA and SFL thus overlap, and continue to develop in 'dialogue' with one another (see e.g. Martin and Wodak 2003; Young and Harrison 2004).

Within SFL, one important contribution complementing CDA has been Martin's (e.g. 2002, 2004b) programme of **Positive Discourse Analysis** (PDA), which is concerned with language and solidarity (rather than with language and power), with an emphasis of positive models for constructive socio-semiotic change such as the voices of reconciliation in South Africa.

The purposes of both CDA and PDA can be characterized in relation to the tenor variable of power (status) within context – in relation to difference in power and in relation to solidarity, respectively. However, there are of course many other purposes for undertaking discourse analysis, and we might develop an approach of appliable discourse analysis designed to be employable in a wide range of institutional settings where problems arise that can be explored through discourse analysis. Such an approach might be called Strategic Discourse Analysis (SDA, although this acronym also stands for 'soap and detergent association', 'small dead animals', and many other unrelated notions!). For example, SDA would include the methods for sampling discourse in an institution in order to shed light on problems in the operation of the institution relating to the flow of meaning through its semiotic networks ('communication networks'), the techniques for analysing the sample of discourse (including computational tools; cf. Teich 2009; Wu 2009), strategies for developing interpretations based on the analysis e.g. through visualization (cf. Matthiessen 2002b), and approaches to the development of solutions based in the analytical and interpretative findings (e.g. training materials, computer programs).

Thus SDA should support the application of discourse analysis to **translation and interpreting**, and discourse analysis has increasingly been applied to tasks associated with this area – the training of translators and interpreters, the investigation of translation and interpreting and other activities relating to the analysis of both original and translated texts. Here discourse analysis has been based on various functional traditions (cf. Munday 2001, chap. 6), including Nord's (e.g. 2005) functional approach, Hatim and Mason's (e.g. 1990) functional approach, which draws on SFL. After a long period of a fairly low level of systemic functional activity (going back to the 1960s), this is now emerging as an important area of increasing activity. I will return to it below in Section 3.4.1.

In addition to these variants of discourse analysis relating to the purpose for carrying out the analysis, we can also recognize a range of different methodologies. The most important distinction is between manual analysis and automated analysis: I will return to this distinction below in Section 3.4.1. However, it is important to note here the development of **corpus linguistics** as a growing field of investigation – going back to the 1950s (with precursors in the 1940s, as in C. C. Fries's sampling of everyday discourse for his accounts of English) but taking off in the 1980s thanks to computational developments. Corpus linguistics is a set of methods for assembling and analysing large samples of text, complementing manual discourse analysis, but it has also been treated as a separate branch of linguistics, and the contributions in Hunston and Thompson (2006) explore the connections between corpus linguistics and SFL (see also Wu's 2009, Corpus-based research). In the late 1980s, there was a parallel development in natural language processing (NLP; also computational linguistics), which has often been referred to as statistical NLP (see Manning and Schütze 1999). Here more powerful and sophisticated computational techniques than those traditionally used in corpus linguistics have been applied to large corpora to address a range of research problems in NLP. This now led to a reconceptualization of the linguistic system itself as inherently probabilistic (recalling Halliday's 1959, insights into the nature of language that have informed SFL from the start, but with a syntagmatic rather than paradigmatic orientation): see Bod, Hay and Jannedy (2003b).

3.2.2.4 In relation to 'language as system'

In relation to 'language as system', there have been important developments since the 1970s, helping create an environment conducive to dialogue with SFL. These developments include the study of complex adaptive systems, the computational engagement with language, and language typology:

- The boost to general system theory (which goes back to the 1940s) through the emergence of the study of **complex adaptive systems** as a meta-discipline – that is, a discipline based on the identification of complexity as a theme relevant to a wide range of systems of different kinds (see e.g. Gell-Mann 1994, 1995, who suggests the term 'plectics' for this 'transdisciplinary subject'), resonating with systemic holistic thinking in systemic theory (going back to Malinowski's contextualism), as shown in the work by Chris Cléirigh (e.g. 1998); see also Thibault (e.g. 2004a).
- The continued expansion of both the hard and the soft sides of **computer science**, the development of **information technology** and the continued expansion of **computational linguistics** (natural language processing, language technology), including systemic functional computational linguistics with modelling of text generation, parsing and text analysis, and translation, and of **linguistic computing** involving the development of tools and techniques aiding linguists in text analysis (for a recent overview, see O'Donnell and Bateman 2005, and Teich 2009, on linguistic computing).
- The coming of age of empirical **language typology** based on large-scale comparison of categories of linguistic systems, usually taken to have started with Joseph Greenberg's seminal work in the 1960s (but also relatable to the Prague School approach to typology from the 1920s and 1930s, in particular Trubetzkoy's work in the area of phonology), with the four volumes on universals of human language representing research at Stanford University as a landmark in the late 1970s and the subsequent explosion of research, resource development and publications in this area – a recent landmark being Haspelmath *et al.* (2005). Against the background of empirical typological work in this tradition, systemic functional work on comparison and typology has gained momentum over the last decade or decade and a half (see Caffarel, Martin and Matthiessen 2004; Teruya *et al.* 2007) as part of multilingual studies. One important aspect of this is the systemic functional conceptualization of grammaticalization (cf. Matthiessen 1995b: 49–50): see Halliday (2008).

3.2.3 Multilingual studies

The field of multilingual studies has been proposed within SFL (see Matthiessen, Teruya and Wu 2008) as an attempt to bring together multilingual concerns that have tended to be developed by distinct communities of scholars since the 1960s (in spite of the unifying efforts within SFL by Catford 1965, and Ellis 1966). It includes **description, comparison** and **typology** (e.g. Caffarel, Martin and Matthiessen 2004; Teruya *et al.* 2007; and see Teruya 2007, on cross-language survey), **translation studies** (e.g. Steiner and Yallop 2001; Steiner 2005a) and **second language education** (e.g. Byrnes 2006; 2009; Schleppegrell and Colombi 2002; Teruya 2009).

These fields have tended to be insulated from one another for various reasons, including the focus on 'language as system' (description, comparison and typology), the focus on 'language as behaviour' (translation studies), and the focus (in 'mainstream' work) on 'language as knowledge' (second language education). However, the conditions now seem right for promoting collaboration among these different multilingual strands.

3.2.4 Language as a higher-order semiotic system

In relation to the map of manifestations of language and different disciplines engaging with these set out in Figure 3.2, one important development in SFL has been the ordered typology of systems operating in different phenomenal realms proposed by Halliday, and elaborated by Halliday and by myself (e.g. Halliday and Matthiessen 1999, chap. 13; Halliday 1995a, 2005a; Matthiessen 2007b: 545–547).

These systems are, in order of increasing complexity: (a) **material** systems: (1) **physical** systems, (2) **biological** systems; (b) **immaterial** systems: (3) **social** systems, (4) **semiotic** systems. They are ordered in complexity in a number of respects, one key respect being that higher-order systems are also manifested as lower-order ones: biological systems are also physical systems, with the added property of 'life' (ability to self-replicate, with individuation and with evolution as the mode of genesis); social systems are also biological (so also physical), with the added property of 'value' (social order: networks of roles, division of labour, and so on); and semiotic systems are also social (so also biological, and also physical), with the added property of 'meaning' (stratification into content and expression). Language is interpreted as a higher-order semiotic system – one which is not only stratified into content and expression but which is also further stratified within content into semantics and lexicogrammar and within expression into phonology and phonetics, and also organized metafunctionally into a spectrum of simultaneous modes of meaning.

This ordered typology of systems is important for new directions of research because it makes it possible for us to view language in the light of other systems as part of general systems thinking (cf. above) and to reason about the complementary contributions made by representatives coming from disciplines focused on systems of different orders in solving problems that arise in the contexts of research and application. For example, in exploring medical risk jeopardizing patient safety in emergency departments of large hospitals, we have been able to differentiate different kinds of risk based on the ordered typology of systems, focusing on semiotic medical risk (see Slade *et al.* 2008). The typology also makes it possible to investigate and model correlations across systems of different orders more systematically, as when a context of situation unfolds through phases that alternate between semiotic processes and purely social processes or through phases that involve both (see Hasan 2005, on the place of context in a systemic functional model). Thus Steiner (1991) has already demonstrated recurrent patterns in the organization of semiotic action and social action.

3.3 The study of language: Areas of investigation and registers

Complementing the update given above of areas of investigation in relation to the disciplinary map in Figure 3.2, we can also explore new developments in different areas of investigation in terms of what aspects of language and other semiotic systems they have been concerned with. This can take the form of a mapping from areas of ***study*** of the phenomenon of language, or of semiotic systems in general, to the phenomenon itself. The point of this is to get a clearer picture of what aspects of language are studied in particular areas of investigation so that it becomes possible to characterize and then also to assess coverage of linguistic (and more generally, semiotic) phenomena in different areas of investigation. Such a picture would allow us to identify gaps, each gap representing a potential opportunity for new developments.

3.3.1 Ways of characterizing the focus of different areas of investigation

To produce such a picture, we could use any of the dimensions of organization embodied in language (or those embodied in any other semiotic system). If we focus on global dimensions of organization (as opposed to local ones organizing any of the stratal subsystems), we can explore and determine the phenomenal focus of areas of investigation in terms of the global dimensions of the organization of language in context: (a) the spectrum of metafunction; (b) the hierarchy of stratification; and/or (c) the cline of instantiation: see Figure 3.3.

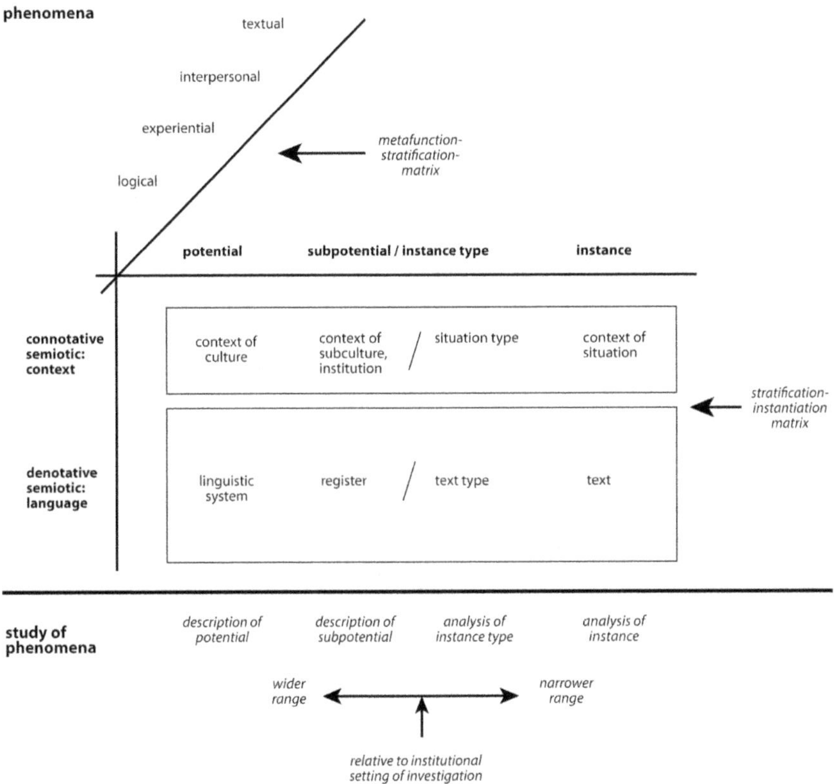

Figure 3.3 Determining the focus of the study of phenomena according to the dimensions of the organization of the phenomena

(a) Thus, we can explore and determine the phenomenal focus of areas of investigation in terms of **metafunction**, asking where the different metafunctions have been given particular attention. This would show, for example, that systemic functional translation studies have so far been more concerned with the textual metafunction than with the other metafunctions, focusing in particular on translation shifts involving the choice of theme, but that systemic functional media studies have concentrated more on the interpersonal metafunction, illuminating the significance of choices within the system of appraisal in relation to different 'media voices' (cf. Martin and White 2005: 164–184). It would also reveal imbalances of attention given to systems within a particular metafunction. For example, within the textual metafunction, theme and cohesion have been given a great deal of attention in discourse analysis, but information (in the sense of the contrast between given and new information) has received much less attention. In addition, it would show how the interpersonal metafunction has been given increasing attention over the last couple of decades, resulting in new accounts, in particular of English interpersonal resources (see e.g. Martin and White 2005). Thus a picture of showing the intersection of areas of investigation with metafunction would certainly be helpful in indicating opportunities for new research.

(b) Alternatively, we can produce a picture based on the dimension of **stratification**, asking what areas of investigation have been concerned with which strata. This would again reveal an interestingly varied picture, with significant gaps, indicating areas where future work is needed. For example, studies of any type of spoken discourse have largely focused on the content plane and on context, leaving phonology in general and the prosodic systems of intonation and rhythm in particular off the research agenda. However, the descriptive resources have long been in place to undertake prosodic analysis (see Greaves 2007), going back to the work in the 1960s by Halliday (1967b, 1970a) and, based on his work, by Elmenoufy (1969), and this tradition has been developed further by Tench (1990, 1996). Various studies have indeed dealt with prosodic features of spoken language as part of discourse analysis, and such efforts may now be given a boost for two general reasons. One is the publication of Halliday and Greaves (2008), which will serve as the key resource for new efforts to include prosodic analysis as a strand in the analysis of spoken discourse. Another is the growing body of multi-semiotic work, including the interest in 'semiotic margins'; hopefully, intonation and rhythm can also find a home here.

(c) Finally, another alternative is to base our picture on the cline of **instantiation**, asking what areas of investigation have concerned with which 'phases' of instantiation.[2] This would help us determine in what areas investigators tend to be system observers, instance observers, or some combination of both. Basing the picture on the cline of instantiation is helpful in sorting out 'multilingual studies' as a diverse yet coherent area of investigation (see Matthiessen, Teruya and Wu 2008). This is close to what Ellis (1966) called 'a general comparative linguistics' many years ago (cf. also Ellis 1987), and it includes typological and comparative linguistics, contrastive analysis, translation and interpreting studies, studies of language contact and of multilingualism (with bilingualism as a special case) in community and individual, language contact, language planning, and second/foreign language education. For example, translation and interpreting studies have tended to focus on the instance pole of the cline of instantiation, whereas typological and comparative studies have generally focused on the potential pole of the cline.

Putting together the hierarchy of stratification and the cline of instantiation, we can construct an instantiation-stratification matrix (cf. Halliday 1995b) to characterize different areas of **specialization** of linguists and the **activities** they undertake in these areas (cf. Halliday 2008: 188): see Table 3.1.

Specialization tends to be determined by stratum: semantics – semanticist, text linguist; lexicogrammar – grammarian (syntactician and morphologist), lexicographer; phonology – phonologist; and phonetics – phonetician. Within lexicogrammar, there tends to be further differentiation in terms of delicacy (grammarian, lexicographer) and rank (syntactician, morphologist); but these distinctions are a feature more of theories that do not operate with a unified system of lexicogrammar, and systemic functional lexicogrammarians shunt along both

Table 3.1 Linguist's (semiotician's) specialization and activities in relation to stratification and instantiation

<table>
<tr><th colspan="3"></th><th>specialization:</th><th>potential</th><th>sub-potential/ instance type</th><th>instance</th></tr>
<tr><td colspan="3">context</td><td>contextologist [semanticist]</td><td>cultural description</td><td>subcultural description/ institutional analysis</td><td>situational analysis</td></tr>
<tr><td rowspan="4">language</td><td rowspan="2">content</td><td>semantic</td><td>semanticist (text linguist)</td><td>semantic description</td><td rowspan="4">register description/ text type analysis</td><td>text (discourse) [including corpus] analysis</td></tr>
<tr><td>lexico-grammar</td><td>grammarian, lexicographer</td><td>lexico-grammatical description</td><td></td></tr>
<tr><td rowspan="2">expression</td><td>phonology</td><td>phonologist</td><td>phono-logical description</td><td>intonation & rhythm analysis</td></tr>
<tr><td>phonetics</td><td>phonetician</td><td>phonetic description</td><td>speech analysis</td></tr>
<tr><td colspan="3"></td><td>activity:</td><td>describe</td><td>describe/ analyse</td><td>analyse</td></tr>
</table>

the rank scale and the cline of delicacy (e.g. Tucker 1998; Neale 2006). Context is more problematic in terms of specialization; it is of course a domain explored from different vantage points by anthropologists, sociologists, social psychologists and also by AI researchers and philosophers, but in SFL, researchers working on context have naturally tended to be those who are concerned with semantics (as in the work on context by Hasan and by Butt, and by Martin), but in anticipation of an expansion of the field of description of context, we can imagine that this will be the task of contextologists.

Activity tends to be determined by instantiation: researchers **describe** systems of a language in its context of culture (at the potential pole of the cline of instantiation) and they **analyse** texts in their contexts of situation (at the instance pole of the cline). Thus we have descriptive linguists developing descriptions of (parts of) different languages (see e.g. Caffarel, Martin and Matthiessen 2004), and discourse analysts analysing (sets of) texts (see e.g. Martin and Rose 2003; Eggins and Slade 1997; Stillar 1998). Researchers concerned with the mid-region between potential and instance may adopt either a system-based approach involving description of registerial subsystems (as in descriptions of register-specific semantic systems, e.g. Halliday 1973; Patten 1988) or a text-based approach involving analysis of texts leading to generalizations about text type (as in e.g. Ghadessy 1993b).

Specialists in all stratal areas can in principle undertake activities relating to all regions of the cline of instantiation. However, in practice, certain specialists tend to focus on some regions but not on others. For example, phonologists have not on the whole worked on phonology for the purpose of characterizing a register or text type, nor based their accounts on frequency in text,[3] but there are certain important exceptions that show that at least higher-ranking phonology ('prosodic': intonation and rhythm) can be illuminated through a registerial focus: see e.g. Bowcher (2001) on intonation in sports commentary, Martinec (1995) on rhythm in news broadcasts, van Leeuwen (1985) on intonation in radio commercials, and Smith (2005) on intonation and register in general (including an overview of work on particular registers). And 'corpus linguists' have tended to define their area of work in terms of what is currently possible to extract from large corpora with the kinds of computational tools used in corpus linguistics. This has meant that they have tended to work on lexis in lexicogrammar and on the region intermediate between lexis and grammar rather than on grammar or on semantics, or on phonology, for that matter (for discussion and possible new directions, see Hunston and Thompson 2006). In general, new directions in research are likely to emerge as 'stratal specialists' increasingly engage in description and analysis along all the phases of the cline of instantiation.

3.3.2 Different fields of investigation in relation to register

Here I will try to sketch a picture showing what different areas of investigation involving some type of text analysis have been concerned with in terms of the region of registerial variation along the cline of instantiation, as shown in Figure 3.3. In other words, we are exploring the mapping between fields of investigation in the study of language and the range of registers within language, as shown in Figure 3.4.

The diagram represents a cline from fields of activity within linguistics that have a fairly narrow registerial focus to those linguistic fields that in principle engage with registers of any kind; this sorting of fields of activity is also set out in Table 3.2.

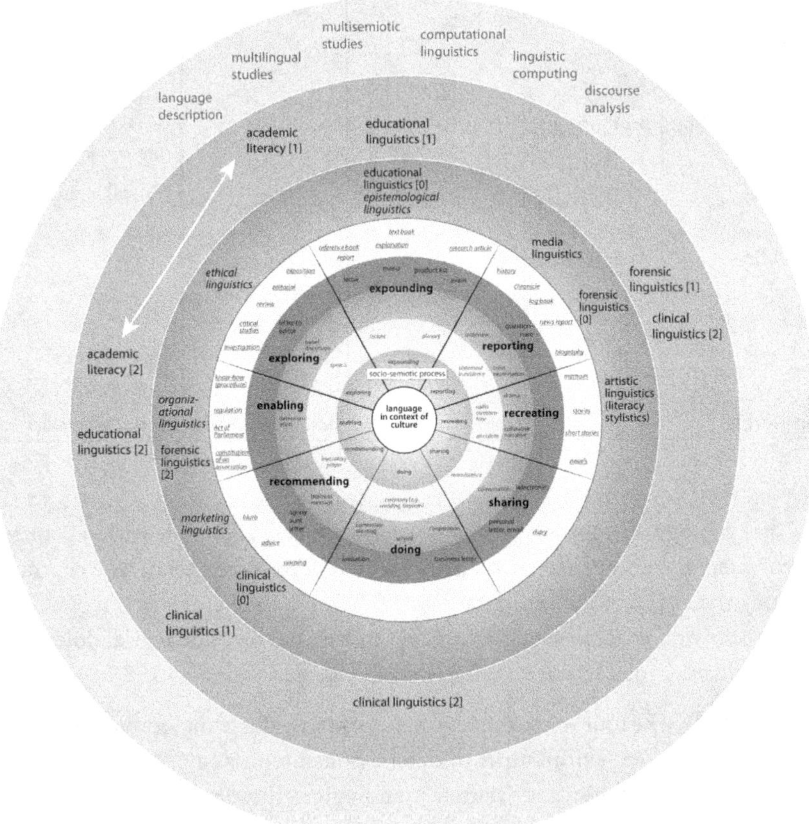

Figure 3.4 Examples of relating fields of linguistics investigation to different registers differentiated according to the contextual parameters of field and mode (see Matthiessen, Teruya, and Wu 2008, for this context-based register typology/topological, adapted from a tabular display of context-based register typology designed by Jean Ure)

Table 3.2 Fields of linguistic investigation shown in the cells of the table in relation to socio-semiotic process (row headings) and register focus (column headings)

field: socio-semiotic process **wide**		**register focus**		
		intermediate	**narrow**	
expounding		language description, multilingual studies, multisemiotic studies, computational linguistics, linguistic computing, discourse analysis	educational linguistics [1] *academic literacy*	educational linguistics [0] *epistemological linguistics*
reporting				media linguistics forensic linguistics
recreating				artistic linguistics (literary stylistics)
sharing				
doing				
recommending	**promoting**			*marketing linguistics*
	advising			clinical linguistics [0]
enabling	**empowering**		educational linguistics [2] *academic literacy*	
	regulating			organizational linguistics
exploring			*academic literacy*	*ethical linguistics*

The typology of registers is based on aspects of field and mode within context; to complete the contextual typology, we would need to add tenor as well, transforming the circles at the centre of Figure 3.4 into a sphere. (Field is represented here by activity or 'socio-semiotic process' rather than by experiential domain or 'subject matter'; for a recent investigation of field, see also Hasan 1999.)

(a) **Mode.** The four inner concentric circles of the diagram represent different mode values – from inner to outer: **spoken monologic**, **spoken dialogic**, **written dialogic**, and **written monologic**. (These are clearly prototypes; there are various further possible elaborations of the kind identified by Gregory 1967, and technologically enabled new possibilities that have appeared since then with advances in the development of new channels (cf. Martin 1992a).)

(b) **Field.** The sectors dividing the four inner circles represent different socio-semiotic processes within field. The socio-semiotic processes are (clockwise, starting at the top): expounding, reporting, recreating, sharing, doing, recommending, enabling, and exploring. They can be characterized briefly as follows:

- **first-order (social)**
  - doing: undertaking some course of action, facilitated by – but typically not constituted in – language ['language in action'].
- **second-order (semiotic [so also social])**:
  - **expounding** some general domain of experience by describing it, classifying (taxonomizing) it, explaining it and so on.
  - **reporting** some particular experiences, chronicling a flow of particular events, or surveying some particular region of space.
  - **recreating** some particular experiences – often imaginary, including the recreation of other socio-semiotic processes (sharing, doing, recommending, and so on).
  - **sharing** typically personal values and experiences as a way of 'calibrating' interpersonal relationships.
  - **recommending** some course of action, either promoting it (either benefiting the speaker [demanding]) or advising the addressee to undertake the course of action [giving]).
  - **enabling** some course of action, either empowering the addressee or regulating him/her.
  - **exploring** typically public values or hypotheses, often comparing alternative ones and arguing in favour of one.

Drawing on Halliday's (1978) distinction between first order and second order features of context, we have differentiated between the first-order social process of 'doing', where language is ancillary ('language in action'), and the second-order semiotic processes of 'expounding', 'reporting', 'recreating', 'sharing', 'recommending', 'enabling' and 'exploring', where language is constitutive.

Short texts can usually be located within a single region of the text topology in Figure 3.4, but extended **macro-texts** such as conversations in the course of a coffee break at a work place or a meal shared by family or friends (cf. Eggins and Slade 1997), newspapers and textbooks, can be analysed as rhetorical complexes formed out of rhetorical relations as modelled in Rhetorical Structure Theory (see e.g. Mann, Matthiessen and Thompson 1992); compare the work on macro-genres by Martin (e.g. 1994) and other scholars building on his work (e.g. Christie 1997). For example, the discursive nucleus of a quality newspaper lies in the written reporting region (news reports of different kinds, media interviews), but there are supporting discursive satellites in other sectors – exploring (editorials, letters to the editor, reviews), enabling (e.g. recipes), recommending (promotion: advertisements; advising: advice columns such as agony aunt letters), and recreating (e.g. cartoons).

The three outer concentric circles in Figure 3.4 represent the registerial location of different 'hyphenated' fields of investigation within, or on the borders of, linguistics – combinations of some institutional domain with 'linguistics' (e.g. 'forensic linguistics'), 'discourse' (e.g. 'professional discourse'), 'literacy' (e.g. 'academic literacy'), 'communication' (e.g. 'health communication'), 'studies' (e.g. 'multimodal studies') or 'science' (e.g. 'cognitive science'). As already noted, these three circles represent a cline of register-specificity (cf. Table 3.2), ranging from fields of investigation being focused on one particular sector in Figure 3.4 to fields of investigation ranging across all registers (at least in principle).

I will now comment on new developments in relation to the fields of activity within these three circles, starting with the one representing most register-specific activities. In terms of the cline of instantiation, we will thus move from particular (field-based) families of registers towards the potential pole of the line.

3.3.3 The first circle of investigation: Narrow register focus

The first outer circle represents those fields that have tended to focus on registers within particular sectors of Figure 3.4 – that is, fields of investigation with a narrow register focus. These include both well-established sub-disciplines and potential sub-disciplines that may emerge as areas of concentrated and coordinated work in the near future:

- **Artistic linguistics** – focus on 'recreating' texts
- **Media linguistics** – focus on 'reporting' texts
- **Organizational linguistics** – focus on 'enabling' texts
- **Marketing linguistics** – focus on 'recommending: promotional' texts

(Some of the fields of investigation in clinical, educational and forensic linguistics include a narrow register focus; however, they also range over other registers, so they will be discussed in Section 3.3.4 below.)

3.3.3.1 Artistic linguistics

Artistic linguistics is the study of verbal art – of language as art. It is concerned with the 'recreating' sector of the diagram in Figure 3.4 (the 'recreating' row in

Table 3.2) in the first instance, although poetry is a special case. Since poetry can be characterized 'from below' in terms of patterns on the expression plane of language, it is not tied to any one sector. There are different types of poetry: narrative and epic poetry belong to the recreating sector, as do ballads and verse dramas; but lyric poetry, elegies and hymns belong to the 'sharing' sector, oral history (typically in preliterate societies) belong to the 'reporting' sector, and chants, spells and incantations belong to the 'doing' sector (language as magic). The same applies to song.

In the 'recreating' sector, field-based chronology is usually the central principle for organizing texts, but this narrative principle is also used in other sectors – chiefly in the 'reporting' sector, so 'recreating' shades into 'reporting' (as in the now popular cross-over between biography and fiction in works where the lives of typically well-known people are recreated), and narrative is manifested in both the 'recreating' and the 'reporting' sector (cf. Toolan 2001).

'Artistic linguistics' is of course not a term generally used in English as the label for the linguistic study of verbal art (though there is an equivalent in Chinese, which is translated as 'artistic linguistics'). However, it would be a useful term since the term that is often used, 'stylistics', can also be seen as representing a methodology that is not restricted to verbal art.

Stylistics has been characterized as "the study of varieties of language whose properties position that language in context" (Wikipedia entry), and has been on the systemic functional research agenda from the early days (see e.g. Hasan 1964). It is in principle applicable to texts within registers of any kind in any location on the map in Figure 3.4 and could thus be seen as a branch of discourse analysis offering theory and techniques applicable to any text for revealing movements in meaning as a text unfolds (see e.g. Butt 1983), for bringing out additional layering of meaning (see e.g. Halliday 1971, 1982b), and for exploring higher-level motifs, or 'symbolic articulation' (see e.g. Hasan 1985c). However, in practice, stylistics has tended to be concerned with the study of verbal art (see Hasan 1985c): literary texts (see Lukin and Butt 2009) or highly valued texts not normally considered literature[4] – but most typically with high-valued ones of the 'high culture' variety of literature (see e.g. Lukin and Webster 2005; Birch and O'Toole 1988; Thibault 1991; Toolan 1998; Prakasam 1999). In view of this focus, we might also call this area of investigation 'aesthetic linguistics', relating it to Mukarovsky's seminal work within the Prague School on the aesthetic use of language in verbal art.[5]

One important development in artistic linguistics within SFL has been the expansion of the domain of investigation along two dimensions: (1) from the high culture variety of literature to more popular literature; and (2) from verbal art to semiotic art in general. (The first dimension we might call the cline of brows,

Table 3.3 The expanding domain of artistic SFL

	elite	**popular**
verbal art	Hasan (1985c), Lukin and Webster (2005), Lukin and Butt (2009), Birch and O'Toole (1988), Thibault (1991); Miller and Turci (2007)	Hasan (1984c), Thoma (2006)
multisemiotic art	O'Toole (1994)	Steiner (1988a); Cranny-Francis and Martin (1991, 1994); Unsworth (2006); Veloso (2006)

from high-brow via middle-brow to low-brow; but the notion of brows is arguably loaded against popular culture.) To get a sense of the future potential of artistic linguistics – or perhaps more generally 'artistic semiotics', we can represent the two dimensions in tabular form, with references to key works in SFL: see Table 3.3. The entries in the 'elite' column represent contributions that illustrate the framework and methodology of artistic linguistics in reference to elite art, but the framework and methodology can of course be applied to the investigation of popular art as well. The entries in the popular verbal art cell include work on traditional folk tales, and here we could also include work on literature for and by children (e.g. Toolan 2001: chap. 7; Williams 1995b, 2000; Rothery 1990; Unsworth 2006). However, most work on popular semiotic art in SFL seems to have been on multi-semiotic art, including folk and rock songs, e-literature, and comic books.

3.3.3.2 Media linguistics

Media linguistics (to use this as a provisional term for an emerging area of study) is concerned with discourses in the media, and has developed as an area of research activity within systemic functional linguistics in recent years. In principle, media linguistics could be concerned with texts within all registers that operate within the media, but in practice, the centre of gravity has been the 'reporting' sector in Figure 3.4: news reports of different kinds, although editorials have also been investigated within the 'exploring' sector.

While there are important examples of early work within the 'East Anglia' tradition in the 1970s, including Trew (1979) and other contributions in Fowler *et al.* (1979) and research into the 'media interview' in the 1980s and into the 1990s (including multimodal features, e.g. van Leeuwen 1985; Bell and van Leeuwen 1994), it was in the 1990s that 'media linguistics' began to gain momentum and critical mass (e.g. Nanri 1993; Iedema, Feez and White 1994; White 1997, 1998), and the first decade of the twenty-first century has seen sustained research in this area, including research projects in the Department of Linguistics at Macquarie University – like the 'Bias in the news' project at the Centre for Language in Social Life with Annabelle Lukin,[6] the research on multimodality in online news by Knox (e.g. 2007) – and the multilingual news project reported on in Thomson and White (2008), including e.g. Knox and Patpong (2008).

3.3.3.3 Organizational linguistics

Organizational (or administrative) linguistics (to use this as a provisional name) has also developed as an area of research within systemic functional linguistics in recent years. It is concerned with administrative, bureaucratic or organizational discourse, which has a centre of gravity in the 'enabling' sector of the diagram in Figure 3.4. It overlaps with the interest in language in the workplace in applied linguistics, which has been informed by various theoretical approaches, including SFL.

Iedema (1996) lays a foundation for text-based research into administrative processes in workplaces – 'organizational discourse', and has followed this up with further publications, showing for example how obligation may be construed or enacted in enabling discourse of the regulatory kind (e.g. Iedema 1996, 1997a, 1997b, 2000, 2003), with 'health communication' emerging at the intersection of clinical linguistics and organizational linguistics[7] (e.g. Iedema 2007). Harrison and Young (2004) analyse bureaucratic discourse from a critical perspective, and Lavid (2000a) compares forms designed for the public in English, German and Italian.

At the same time, there was considerable activity relating to 'language in the workplace' at UTS with contributions by Di Slade, Hermine Scheeres, and others. In joint work, Iedema and Scheeres (e.g. 2003) show how 'work' at workplaces has become increasingly semioticized, with employees having to take on roles in semiotic processes in addition to their roles in more traditional material processes.

3.3.3.4 Marketing linguistics

Marketing linguistics (to use this as a provisional name for an area of investigation that may emerge as a focus of activities) is concerned with texts marketing commodities. Such texts fall within the 'recommending' sector of the diagram in Figure 3.4, more specifically within the 'promotional' subtype (recommending for the benefit of the speaker rather than for the benefit of the addressee). They include many different kinds of advertisement, product blurbs, fund raising letters, and other types of promotional text, and also 'cross-over' registers such as infomercials (on the borderline between 'recommending' and 'reporting'). (These are texts persuading the addressee to do something, so the nucleus of such a text is typically a proposal, and the text as a whole can be interpreted as a macro-proposal, as in Martin (1992b). They contrast with texts persuading the addressee of a proposition; such texts fall within the 'exploring' sector.)

There is potential here for a systemic functional development of marketing linguistics, but while there have been a number of accounts of different aspects of recommending texts of the promotional subtype over the years (e.g. Martin 1992b; Fries 2002; McAndrew 2003; and in the context of translation, Taylor and Baldry 2001; Steiner 2004), these separate efforts have not yet come together as a field of activity within SFL. However, a research project in Mendoza by a team led by Ana Hansen demonstrates the potential through the research into the promotion of wine; and texts within the tourism industry are increasingly being analysed within SFL. Research in this area has been given a boost by the development of the description of the system of appraisal in English (see Martin and White 2005).

3.3.3.5 Other possible developments

In addition to the sectors in focus in media linguistics, administrative linguistics and marketing linguistics, it is possible to imagine that other register sectors will become the focus of dedicated fields of linguistic activity. For instance:

- **Epistemological linguistics:** while educational linguistics is concerned with 'expounding' texts within the institution of education, 'epistemological linguistics' could emerge as a field of investigation dedicated to the study of the discursive construction and dissemination of knowledge in support of a wide range of applications (e.g. within education, within information technology, within the 'knowledge industry'). It is possible to see Christie and Martin (2007) and Halliday and Matthiessen (1999) as complementary contributions towards the development of epistemological linguistics. The contributions in Christie and Martin (2007) investigate knowledge in relation to key distinctions in Bernstein's work, including centrally the distinction between vertical and horizontal organization. Halliday and Matthiessen (1999) reinterpret the cognitive notion of 'knowledge' semiotically as experience construed as meaning within the ideational semantics of language, developing an account that is detailed and explicit enough to be modelled computationally.

- **Aesthetic linguistics:** 'aesthetic linguistics' could emerge as a field of investigation dealing with 'exploring' texts concerned with the negotiation in a community of the value of works of art (and other artefacts evaluated in terms of aesthetic considerations), focusing perhaps in particular on the resources of appreciation within the system of appraisal (see Martin and White 2005). Aesthetic linguistics would include literary criticism (see Lukin 2003) and criticism of visual art (see Rada 1989; and cf. O'Toole 1994), reviews of performing arts and of film.
- **Ethical linguistics:** similarly, 'ethical linguistics' could emerge as a field of investigation focused on 'exploring' texts concerned with the exploration in a community of moral values, focusing perhaps in particular on the resources of judgement within the system of appraisal (see Martin and White 2005). One aspect of such ethical concerns would be our environment, an aspect which is now being explored in ecolinguistics.
- **Ecolinguistics:** Ecolinguistics has in fact already been established as a new area of activity, relating linguistic work to ecological concerns. The Wikipedia entry is worth quoting:

> Ecolinguistics emerged in the 1990s as a new paradigm of linguistic research which took into account not only the social context in which language is embedded, but also the ecological context in which societies arc embedded. Michael Halliday's 1990 paper 'New ways of Meaning: the challenge to applied linguistics' [Halliday 1990] is often credited as a seminal work which provided the stimulus for linguists to consider the ecological context and consequences of language.

Ecolinguistics has been pursued by a growing number of linguists, including researchers such as Andrew Goatly drawing on SFL.

Both aesthetic linguistics and ethical linguistics would investigate 'exploring' texts, trying to reveal how aesthetic and moral values are negotiated publicly in a community, typically in the media. They could also include more private contexts of people 'sharing' personal values, prototypically in casual conversations, as part of the negotiation of interpersonal relations (cf. Eggins and Slade 1997: chap. 4; Horvath and Eggins 1995). Sharing and exploring may shade into one another in technologically enabled contexts such as postings of reviews on websites (like that of the internet movie database) and exchanges in internet forums.

In addition, we can see the emergence of linguistic research centred on texts in the 'doing' sector, in particular on texts operating in service encounters. While service encounters have been an important site for systemic functional investigation for a long time (see Hasan 1978; Ventola 1987; Matthiessen *et al.* 2005), technological developments have created the conditions for a new kind of service institution – call centres. Call centres have mushroomed in a number of countries, including India, China and the Philippines. They are semiotically very interesting along a number of dimensions, and they are being explored in systemic functional terms in the Department of English language studies, the Hong Kong Polytechnic University, with links to researchers in other locations (see e.g. Forey and Lockwood 2007 and Lockwood, Forey and Elias 2009). Call centres bring together, as server and customer, interactants from potentially very different cultural and linguistic backgrounds. Their services are very often provided on an outsourced basis, which creates an additional distance between the service provider and the company whose products the services are concerned with. These factors put special pressures on interpersonal relations between server and customer (see Hood and Forey 2008), especially since customers not infrequently call up with complaints and stored-up negative affect.

3.3.4 The second circle of investigation: Intermediate register focus

The second circle of fields of investigation represents those areas of systemic functional investigation that have been concerned with certain registers in particular but which can also range across several, many or even potentially all of the different register types:

- **Educational linguistics** – focus on registers of content subjects, in particular on 'expounding' (e.g. physics, chemistry, mathematics, biology), on 'enabling' (e.g. laboratory procedures in experimental subjects), on 'reporting' (history), and on 'exploring' (e.g. literary criticism in English; argumentative and comparative expositions in any subject).
- **Clinical linguistics** – focus on 'recommending: advising' texts in clinical consultations (and on 'doing' texts in surgery and other medical procedures), but also on other types of text when these texts themselves are used for diagnosis and treatment, as in speech pathology (traditionally narratives in the 'recreating' sector, but increasingly other types as well, such as letters (see Mortensen, e.g. 2005)).
- **Forensic linguistics** – focus on 'enabling: regulating' texts (in discourses of the law) and on 'reporting' texts (in the courtroom), but also on other types of text when these texts themselves are used for investigative purposes, as in investigations of authorship.

3.3.4.1 Educational linguistics

Educational linguistics (see chaps. 9–12 in Hasan *et al.* (eds) 2005; for a recent overview of educational linguistics, see also Christie and Unsworth 2005; for a recent overview of literacy pedagogy, see Martin and Rose 2005; for recent contributions to second/foreign language education, see Byrnes 2006, 2009) deals with many aspects of language in education and has been part of the systemic functional research agenda since the very early days (see e.g. Pearce, Thornton and Mackay 1989).

Educational linguistics is, in principle, concerned with texts instantiating all registers since one key aspect of education is precisely giving pupils and students access to an ever-increasing range of registers, enabling them to expand their personal repertoires of registers so that they can master registers operating in a growing range of institutional contexts, thus removing barriers for them to access these contexts. There is an ordered registerial progression here in terms of learning and curriculum (e.g. Martin and Rothery 1981), both across the major sectors of the diagram in Figure 3.4 and within these major sections, as discussed for science education by e.g. D. Rose (1997). The principle of an ordered registerial progression also applies to second/foreign language education. Rinner and Weigert (2006) show the significance of developing and using a curriculum for second/foreign language education based on register (genre).

At the same time, educational linguistics will focus on those registers that play a central role in particular subjects (cf. Shum 2006, for recent work in the Hong Kong context) – e.g. explanations and reports (expounding) in secondary school physics (e.g. Veel 1997), historical recounts (reporting) and argumentative expositions (exploring) in secondary school history (e.g. Eggins, Wignell and Martin 1993; Martin 2003), story writing (recreating) in primary school (e.g. Rothery 1990).

The phenomena explored in educational linguistics are thus registerially composite, involving different motifs – the 'content' of a discipline, pedagogic concerns, and also the regulation of behaviour in educational institutions. Contributions in Christie and Martin (2007) shed light on the composite registerial nature of educational discourse based on Bernstein's (e.g. 2000) work.

One new area for educational research and development lies at the intersection of educational linguistics and translation studies; this is the field of translator training. This field has emerged as a new focus in academic institutions, as translation has increasingly become professionalized and the training of translators and interpreters is being given academic status in undergraduate and postgraduate programmes around the world. Taylor (1998) is an important contribution to translator training (and Baker 1992, a widely used text book in translation courses, contains key insights from SFL, particularly in the area of the textual metafunction), and a number of studies have focused on translator education, including Shore (2001) and the recent work by Mira Kim (e.g. Kim 2007; Burns, Kim and Matthiessen 2009).

3.3.4.2 *Clinical linguistics*

Clinical linguistics can be seen as an emerging formation of research and application relating to clinical and medical work, and more generally to health care. It includes speech pathology (see Armstrong, Clinical Applications 2009; for a recent overview of speech pathology, see also Armstrong *et al.* 2005, and of language breakdown in a broad sense, including autism, see also Asp and de Villiers 2010), psychotherapeutic studies (e.g. Martin and Rochester 1979; Butt *et al.* 2003; Meares *et al.* 2005; Fine 2006), patient counselling, and other areas within the institution of health care.

These forms of clinical linguistics have 'recommending' contexts as their base in the sense that a good deal of clinical linguistics has been concerned with either the register of consultation, as in the EDCOM research project investigating communication in emergency departments of hospitals (e.g. Slade *et al.* 2008),[8] or with other registers that get activated as part of consultation. Such other registers that are 'embedded' within consultations as part of diagnosis and treatment are of course not spread evenly across the registerial map in Figure 3.4, but in speech pathology the selection has expanded beyond the traditional descriptive and narrative tasks to include written letters of different kinds (see Mortensen 2003, 2005) and spoken dialogue within different contexts.

In addition, the emerging field of 'clinical' linguistics also includes 'doing' contexts such as those in which surgery is conducted in operating theatres, investigated within the 'systemic safety' project at the Centre for Language in Social Life, Linguistics, Macquarie University (cf. Butt 2008).

3.3.4.3 *Forensic linguistics*

Forensic linguistics is like clinical linguistics in that texts from any register can in principle serve as part of a 'diagnostic' phase, as when the identity of the author of a particular text becomes a legal issue (e.g. Coulthard 2004). Systemic functional linguistics has been a source of insight in forensic work, as is evident from the work by leading linguists in the field, e.g. John Gibbons (e.g., 2003, with references to registers (genres) in the legal context, including valuable work by Yon Maley) and Malcolm Coulthard.

However, at the same time, forensic linguistics has at least two institutional bases – one being geared towards goods-&-services (proposals) and the other towards information (propositions). On the one hand, it is concerned with texts instantiating registers associated with 'enabling' contexts of a regulating kind – laws and acts of parliament, constitutions, legally binding agreements and the like. Here one important concern has been with the accessibility of legal texts to people without training in this area (see e.g. Hansen-Schirra and Neumann 2004). On the other hand, it is concerned with texts instantiating registers associated with 'reporting' contexts – police interrogations (e.g. Hall 2008), statements in evidence, cross-examinations in trials, and so on.

In current research at Sydney University, restorative justice in 'Youth Justice Conferences' is being investigated from the point of view of multisemiotic systems.

3.3.5 The third circle: Wide register focus

The third circle of fields of investigation represents those areas of systemic functional investigation that could in principle be concerned with registers of any kind but which have in practice been developed through investigations focusing on certain registers. This circle includes 'multi-' studies – multilingual studies and multisemiotic studies. Both fields of investigation have benefited significantly from research projects focussed on particular registers or sets of registers.

3.3.5.1 Multilingual studies: Translation and interpreting studies

The concept of multilingual studies in general was discussed briefly above in Section 3.2.3; here I will focus on one area within multilingual studies, viz. translation and interpreting studies. Translation has been on the systemic functional research agenda for a long time (for a recent overview, see Steiner 2005a). Halliday (1956a) drew attention to the significance of choice in translation, highlighting the value of the thesaurus as a lexical resource supporting choices in machine translation, and Catford's (1965) 'linguistic theory of translation', based on the systemic functional theory of that period, has become a classic. In that sense, translation studies is not a 'new direction' in SFL. However, on the one hand, interpreting studies is now being added to translation studies (e.g. Taylor Torsello 1996, 1997), with a growing number of contributions in the last couple of years (e.g. Tebble 1999, who has contributed to our understanding of tenor relations in medical interpreting), including work on interpreting between Chinese and English at universities in China, and at Macquarie University, e.g. Wang (2008); and on the other hand, the body of work in translation studies is now expanding rapidly in many places around the world, reflected in research projects, publications and also in translation courses informed by SFL.

Translation and interpreting are semiotic processes concerned with recreating meanings derived from a source language text in a target language. The source text and the target text are of course located at the instance pole of the cline of instantiation, but translation and interpreting always operate against the background of a meaning potential higher up the cline of instantiation. This potential is typically that of a particular register: translators and interpreters translate and interpret text as text belonging to some register or other; their acts of recreating meaning are informed by registerial meaning potentials.

The distinction between translation and interpreting is of course a registerial one based on the mode variable of context: translation operates on texts in the written mode, whereas interpreting operates on texts in the spoken mode (or in the signed and spoken modes in the case of interpreters working with sign languages). There are interesting intermediate cases involving cross-over in mode: sight translation (written source text, spoken translated text) and subtitling (spoken source text, written translated text); these embody considerations pertaining to both modes. Subtitling has been investigated from a systemic functional point of view by Taylor (e.g. 2003).

In addition to this basic mode-based distinction between translators and interpreters, translators and interpreters also tend to specialize in terms of register in other respects as well (cf. Steiner 2005b) – for example, community interpreters, conference interpreters, court room interpreters, legal translators, medical translators all work with different registerial repertoires. Thus a number of studies have been concerned with the translation of texts within particular registers or with the investigation of original texts in two or more languages within the same register, e.g. Steiner (2004) on the translation of advertisements (recommending: promoting texts), Neumann (2003) on guide books in German and English, Hansen (2003) on translation of narrative text, Lavid (2000a) on instructions in bureaucratic forms in English, German and Italian, Murcia-Bielsa (2000) on directives in English and Spanish, Mason (2003) on translation of organizational discourse.

Translation and interpreting studies drawing on SFL typically involve text analysis, and attention has increasingly been given to the construction of multilingual corpora and to techniques for automated analysis of such corpora (see e.g. Teich 2003; Neumann and Hansen-Schirra 2005; Pagano, Magalhães and Alves 2004), as in the CroCo project at the Universität des Saarlandes in Saarbrücken.[9] Another important development is being pioneered by researchers led by Adriana Pagano and Fábio Alves at the Universidade Federal de Minas Gerais. This is research into the process of translation, combining methods for recording patterns in the unfolding of the translation of a text with systemic functional analysis. This approach has the potential to illuminate process-oriented accounts of texts in general, supplementing the product-oriented accounts that have come to dominate in the analysis of text (for process-oriented accounts, cf. also Martin 1985b; Ravelli 1995; Matthiessen 2002b; and in the area of text generation, Matthiessen and Bateman 1991).

3.3.5.2 Multisemiotic studies

Multisemiotic studies (for recent overviews and collections, see Martinec 2005, and Royce and Bowcher 2006; Ventola, Charles and Kaltenbacher 2004, Ventola and Guijarro 2009; see also e.g. Kress and van Leeuwen 2001) are characterized contextually in terms of mode (rather than field and tenor), so registerial focus relates to the mode-based concentric circles of the diagram in Figure 3.4 rather than to the field-based sectors: there is naturally a clear distinction between multimodality in the written mode and multimodality in the spoken mode, or of course in the signed mode (in the case of sign languages). The same principle applies to multisemiotic studies concerned with particular 'channels' such as the web, as in Djonov (2007).

As far as the field-based registerial sectors of the diagram are concerned, multisemiotic studies do in principle range over all registers. However, certain registers have attracted more attention in research than others; for example, there are natural connections between multisemiotic studies and other areas discussed here such as educational linguistics (cf. Mohan 1986, for pioneering work on 'expounding' texts; and Unsworth 2006, on the new phenomenon of 'e-literature' for children).

For general explorations of multisemiotic systems and register, see Bateman (2008b) and Matthiessen (2009c).

3.3.6 Institutional perspective

The different areas of investigation mentioned above were discussed in terms of particular registers or sets of registers. Complementing this kind of registerial map, we can also characterize areas of investigation in terms of institutional focus – in terms of institutions such as the institutions of education, healthcare and the law and in terms of the registerial ranges associated with institutions (see e.g. Christie and Martin 1997). A given institution may be focused on a particular registerial sector – e.g. media institutions will be focused on the 'reporting' sector, health care institutions on the 'recommending: advising' sector, service institutions on the 'doing' sector, and educational institutions on the 'expounding' sector; but the overall operation of a given institution will cover a wider range of complementary registers concerned with different aspects of the workings of the institution. Following Hill (1958), we could call investigations taking institutions as their frame of reference **institutional linguistics** (cf. also e.g. Ellis 1966: 17–18; Halliday 1978: 110). Since institution-based research is likely to play an increasingly important role in the future and since job opportunities may open up for systemic functional linguists within certain institutions, let me say a little bit more about institutions, relating the study of institutions to one of the key scholars informing the development of systemic functional linguistics out of Firthian linguistics – Bronislaw Malinowski (see e.g. Hasan 1985b).

Institutions are of course social constructs – that is, patterns of organization within third-order, social systems, but they are also semiotic constructs – that is, patterns of organizations within fourth-order, semiotic systems (cf. Section 3.2.4 above). Institutions were central in Malinowski's theory of society and culture, having evolved to serve certain essential human needs ('biological or derived'), and for him they thus also served as a way into the study of a culture. Malinowski (1944: 154–155) characterizes institutions as follows:

> An ethnographer taking a rapid survey of various types of human culture, from the most primitive to highly developed ones, would make an interesting discovery. He would find that the work of culture is not done by any community as a whole, nor yet by individuals, but by smaller organized groups, that is, institutions, which are organized and integrated to form the community. The significance of this discovery is due to two facts, first, that an institution always presents the same structure, and second, that institutions are of universal occurrence; thus the institution is the real isolate of culture. It is possible to indicate the structure of such a system of organized activities: they are always carried on by a group in a definite manner, using a certain type of material outfit, and obeying norms which bind the members of that group and that group only. Thus equipped with a material outfit, with specific norms of conduct, and with a social organization, including central authority, the members of the institution carry out a type of behavior through which they achieve a definite purpose and contribute in a definite manner to the work of the culture as a whole. In the family and the state, in an occupational group, a factory, a trade union, a church, or a gang, we have to study exactly the same main factors and the relations thereof.

> The study of any culture must therefore be carried out in terms of institutions. This means in other words that an object or artifact, a custom, an idea or an artistic product, is significant only when placed within the institution to which it belongs. Certain institutions are to be found in all human societies; other types of institutions, though less universal, can be found in many cultures although some of them are more characteristic of highly developed societies. As culture advances we find that various organized activities, which on the primitive level were carried out as a by-product of other institutions, become organized in their own right. First and foremost perhaps appear military groups, administrative organizations and the political state. Later on courts of law, professional leaders and judges become detached and organized. Economic institutions multiply into the various guilds of artisans and craftsmen. Since the Industrial Revolution, factories, banking systems and large mercantile enterprises have multiplied almost indefinitely.

Malinowski then goes on to list eight main types of institution (family and derived kinship organizations, municipality, tribe as the political organization based on the territorial principle, tribe as a culturally integrated unit, age-group, voluntary associations, occupational groups, status groups based on the principle of rank, caste, and economic class), and to model institutions in terms of purpose, charter, personnel, norms, material apparatus, activities, implemented action, function and results. His work on institutions is well worth reviewing further in the current context of systemic investigations with an institutional focus; for example, his 'occupational groups' can be related to current work on professional discourse. However, at this point, I will leave Malinowski and go on to locate the notion of institution in the systemic functional 'architecture' of semiotic systems since this will make it easier to identify potential new directions of research.

In terms of the different orders of system – physical, biological, social and semiotic, institutions are, as already noted, both social and semiotic: as discussed by Malinowski, and more generally in social sciences, institutions are units of social organization characterizable in terms of distinctive systems of institutional roles and distinctive patterns of behaviour (social activity). Such social institutions are also manifested in terms of lower-order, material patterns (cf. Malinowski's notion of 'material apparatus'): biologically, they may be manifested as ecosystems, and physically as habitats (including the various artefacts that accompany designed habitats). At the same time, social institutions are also interpretable at a higher order of abstraction as semiotic constructs – as patterns of meaning. Semiotically, institutions are locatable within context (as a connotative semiotic system) rather than within language and other denotative semiotic systems (cf. Martin 1992a). They can be characterized in terms of ranges of values of field, tenor and mode.

In relation to the cline of instantiation, institutions are located midway between system and instance, and they can be interpreted as a system-based view of this region of the cline – that is, they can be modelled as subsystems or subpotentials (cf. Halliday 1995b). This accords well with Malinowski's characterization of institutions. Viewed in semiotic terms, institutions are regions within the overall cultural potential of a society; they are cultural subsystems, ranging over certain field, tenor and mode values. At the same time, looking downwards towards the instance pole of the cline of instantiation, we can also characterize institutions as aggregates of situation types; that is, as situation types operate together within the 'charter' of an institution (to borrow Malinowski's terms – the 'collective purpose', the 'doctrine on which an institution is based' (Malinowski 1944: 157)).

The location of institutions in terms of the cline of instantiation and the order of systems (and stratification within semiotic systems) is represented diagrammatically in Figure 3.5. Figure 3.5 shows how we can approach the characterization of institutions by moving along the cline of instantiation and along the ordered typology of systems. Thus, moving along the ordered typology of systems and the hierarchy of stratification within semiotic systems:

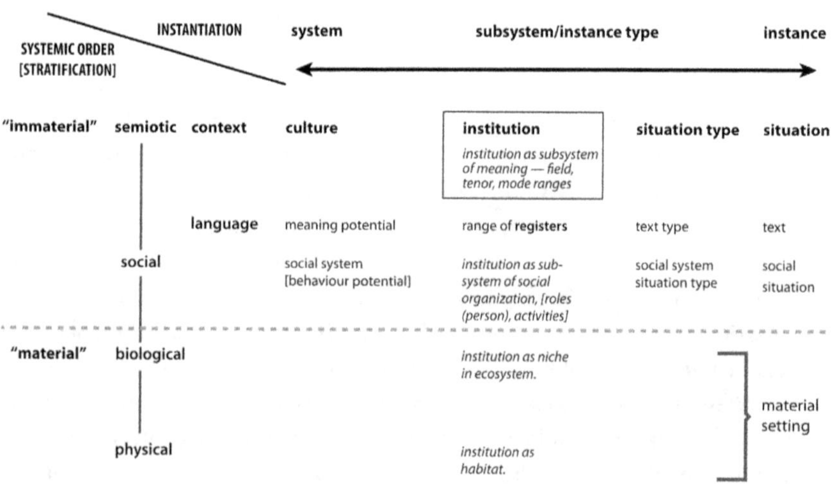

Figure 3.5 Locating institutions in terms of: (a) the cline of instantiation; and (b) the ordered typology of systems

- We can characterize institutions 'from below' in terms of their **manifestation** in social systems, drawing on research into institutional role networks, social behaviour, situations within sociology, social psychology, ethnography and anthropology and organizational studies. Interpreting characterizations of institutions from these disciplines in systemic functional terms would be a very valuable foundation for future research.
- We can characterize institutions 'from below' within the semiotic order, approaching them in terms of the **ranges of registers** that collectively define the (denotative) semiotic work being done within institutions. One example would be Gu's (e.g. 1999, 2002) 'discourse geography' (or, using my own related metaphor, 'discourse cartography') and his long-term project of mapping out Beijing in terms of a vast corpus of situated discourse. While this work is not specifically cast in terms of SFL, it serves as a very interesting compatible model. The same applies to the corpus-based 'Language in the Work Place' project directed by Janet Holmes at the University of Wellington.[10] Within SFL, Ravelli's (2006, 2007) discursive window on the institution of museums serves as a helpful model for future research with an institutional focus. She documents the registerial range of museum exhibitions – including not only the 'reporting' and 'expounding' type of socio-semiotic processes discussed above, but also the 'exploring' type, and emphasizing the multisemiotic nature of such exhibitions.

Similarly, staying within the systemic order of semiotic systems but moving along the cline of instantiation:

- We can characterize institutions 'from above' in terms of the **cultural potential** of a society – that is, in terms of the systems of field, tenor and mode that jointly define this cultural potential. This approach remains a theoretical possibility rather than a practical one at present simply because we have not yet got a 'reference description' of the cultural potential of any society. Developing such a description is the task for contextologists (cf. Table 3.2), but it is a daunting one! Nevertheless, conceiving of institutions as ranges of values within a cultural potential – as regions within the total cultural space of a community – is a helpful way of profiling them.
- We can characterize institutions 'from below' in terms of the aggregate of situation types that instantiate an institution, by focusing on the situation types themselves (systemically, in terms of their field, tenor and mode values, and/or structurally, in terms of contextual (generic, schematic) structures) or on the registers/text types that operate within them. For a number of institutions, it is now possible to compile the accounts produced over

> the years of quite a few situation types, or genres, that can be located within a given institution. The point of this kind of compilation would be to take stock of the work that has already been done, to determine what situation types still need to be investigated, and to arrive at a more comprehensive understanding of the workings of particular institutions, e.g. the institutions of the family (illuminated in particular through studies with developmental focus), of friendship, of the work place, of health care, and of education. For example, we could ask how much of the institution of a primary or secondary school has been mapped out so far in educational linguistics through the accumulation of accounts of different situation types (genres) at work in schools. We would probably find that situation types in and around the classroom and text book materials are well documented, we would need to work on situation types relating to educational work outside the classroom – both within the school (study groups, personal library work) and outside the school (personal study, study groups, pupil-parent interaction), and to processes that accompany and support educational work (negotiating social relationships, managing the school, interfacing with other agencies and with parents).

In describing institutions in semiotic terms, we must of course take all contextual variables into consideration – field, tenor and mode. A comprehensive description of an institution will include all three perspectives; but we can also describe the institution selectively in terms of only one of these perspectives. Thus we can create a map of an institution based on the social and semiotic processes (the 'activity sequences' – cf. Martin 1992a) undertaken within it, and on the domains of experience that these relate to (field), or a map based on the network of roles that the 'personnel' of the institution take on and the relationships they enter into (tenor), or a map based on the complementarity of semiotic and social systems contributing to the work achieved within the institution (mode).

A number of studies have demonstrated the value of examining institutions from the point of view of **institutional roles** and the **registerial repertoires** associated with these roles, now often discussed under the heading of 'professional discourse'. Here the basic question is: 'what repertoire of registers does a person have to master to take on a particular institutional role?'. An important example within systemic functional linguistics is Jill Kealley's (e.g. 2007) research into the language of nurses within the institution of health-care. Another is the work on different **voices** in media institutions (see e.g. Iedema, Feez and White 1994; Martin and White 2005: 164–184).

3.4 Metatheoretical, theoretical, descriptive and analytical developments

3.4.1 Analysis, description, comparison, theory and metatheory

As shown in Figure 3.2, there are many ways of exploring domains of investigation and new developments in SFL. In the preceding section, I used the cline of instantiation, focusing on registerial ranges within different fields of activity. Let me now review the location of these fields of activity relative to the different primary processes undertaken in linguistics – the analysis of particular texts, the description of the systems of particular languages, and comparison of a number of different linguistics systems, and the theorizing of language as a kind of semiotic system (or of semiotic systems in general): see Figure 3.6.

In the diagram in Figure 3.6, I have differentiated analysis, description, comparison and theory as distinct 'phases' of processing of language in linguistics (cf. Hjelmslev 1943; Halliday 1992f; Matthiessen and Nesbitt 1996).

- **Analysis** operates on instances of a language in its context: we analyse particular texts in their contexts of situation, assigning the analysis to them based on the description of the system of language.
- **Description** operates on the potential of a language in its context: we describe a particular linguistic system in its context of culture, basing the description on evidence from the investigation of instances.
- **Analysis and description** complement one another: they are concerned with different poles of the cline of instantiation (cf. Halliday 2008). When we focus on the region intermediate between the outer poles of potential and instance, we can either describe this region as sub-potentials or analyse it as instance types.
- **Comparison** operates on the potentials of two or more languages in their contexts of culture. If the sample of languages is representative of languages around the world (however we determine what constitutes a representative sample), then the comparison is highly generalized: it is typology (cf. Teruya *et al.* 2007; Matthiessen, Teruya and Wu 2008; Ellis 1966).
- **Theory** operates on language as a kind of semiotic system, or on semiotic systems in general; it serves to differentiate between higher-order semiotic systems (language) and primary semiotic systems (many other, perhaps all, semiotic systems).

As the diagram in Figure 3.6 shows, there is an increase of coverage of 'information' as we move from single instances to the general category of semiotic systems.

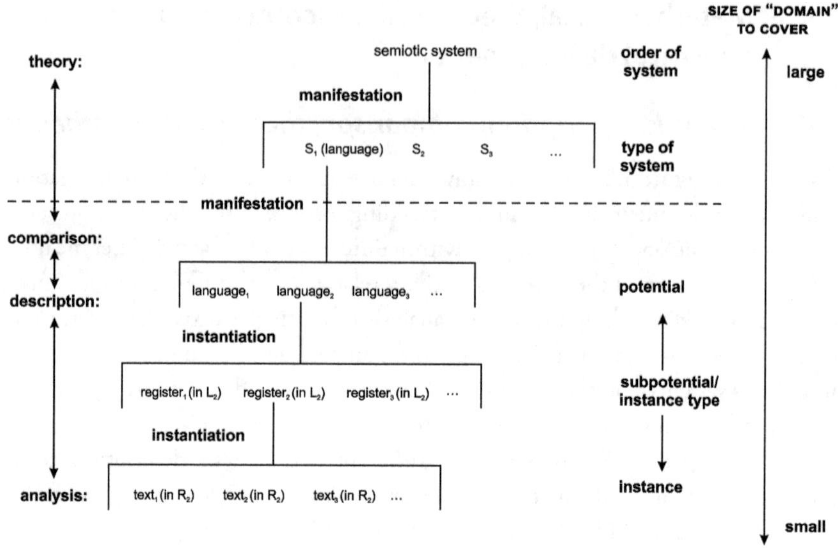

Figure 3.6 Analysis, description, comparison and theory

In analysis, we are only responsible for single instances – texts in their contexts of situation. Even if the texts are very long or we collect a considerable number of texts, they will only instantiate a small part of the total system of a language in its context of culture. In contrast, in description, we are responsible for the potential of a language in its context of culture. Such a potential is obviously quite vast, and when we try to back it up through the analysis of instances, we need huge samples – larger even than the current corpora of a few hundred million words. In comparison, we go beyond the description of particular languages in order to compare these descriptions; we are, in principle, responsible for the total potential of anything from a small handful of languages to large samples of hundreds of languages designed to be representative of the languages around the world.

Analysis, description and comparison are all concerned with the same order of abstraction – particular languages or collections of particular languages, and as the diagram shows we can locate the three processes of analysis, description and comparison at different points along the cline of instantiation. All three are thus ultimately grounded in 'data' – in observable instances; and they operate with descriptive categories that have to be justified for each language under investigation.

In contrast, theory operates at a higher level of abstraction: it is concerned not with particular languages but with language in general as a type of semiotic system and with semiotic systems in general as an order of system in an ordered typology of systems (see Halliday 1996; Halliday and Matthiessen 1999, chap. 13; Matthiessen 2007b). Theory operates with theoretical categories (rather than descriptive ones) – categories such as (the cline of) instantiation, (the hierarchy of) stratification, realization, (the cline of) delicacy, (the spectrum of) metafunction. These come together in the theoretical model of the 'architecture' of language. The theory makes it possible to characterize language as a higher-order semiotic (see Halliday 1995b) – a semiotic system embodying the metafunctional spectrum and stratified within both the content plane (semantics and lexicogrammar) and the expression plane (phonology and phonetics). Particular languages are manifestations of language as a higher-order human semiotic.

When we develop theory, we must, in principle, cover everything in the realm of semiotic systems: we are responsible for information accumulated in the move up the cline of instantiation from instance to system, and for information accumulated from descriptions of particular languages. The general theory of language must thus have a very extensive coverage – otherwise it would not be a general theory of language. Therefore we cannot construct a general theory of language – or of any part of language – based only on one particular language. There is a real sense in which analysis, description, comparison, and theory are ordered in difficulty:

analysis < description < comparison < theory

This scale is typically reflected in academic programmes where SFL is taught: students doing undergraduate programmes or masters post-graduate programmes will learn to do text analysis and if they also do an undergraduate thesis or a master's thesis, this thesis is likely to be based on a research project involving text analysis. However, while students will master text analysis, they will probably not learn how to develop descriptions of languages, let alone how to do systematic comparison or construct general theory.[11] The challenge is to develop university curricula where it is possible to learn not only text analysis but also system description – curricula where one can learn to become a descriptivist. This would be a very significant new direction in SFL in terms of the training of future generations of students.

The focus on text analysis in university programmes is of course a relatively recent development – starting around 30 years ago but becoming more prevalent in the last two decades or so. Before text analysis came into focus in university programmes, description or theory was given prominence in linguistics programmes – which of the two was given more prominence depended on the orientation of a given programme. Up through the early 1960s, many programmes focused on training 'descriptivists'. This tradition has continued, of course, in certain places; but as formal generative linguistics came to dominate in many linguistics or language studies departments, the focus shifted to theory – more specifically, to theory in the guise of theoretical representations. There was a long period when new theories, or new versions of existing theories, were developed in rapid succession.

This would seem to contradict my claim above that theory is the most challenging process of all because it presupposes comparison, description, and analysis – because it is responsible not just for a particular language but for language in general as a higher-order semiotic. However, the formal generative theory of this period was very different from the kind of theory we are concerned with in this book, systemic functional theory. On the one hand, the formal generative theory of this period was really based on one language – English (just as the missionary work in traditional grammar up through the nineteenth century was based on Latin or Greek). More specifically, it was based on relatively small fragments of English (compare Gross 1979, comments on the attempt to put together a more comprehensive description of English, the 'UCLA' grammar). On the other hand, 'theory' really meant theoretical representation (cf. Matthiessen and Nesbitt 1996; Teich 1999) – the rule systems devised at the time. Many of the findings – e.g. the principle of feeding and bleeding rule ordering – were comparable to what a programmer would deal with in developing (non-declarative) programmes in the 1960s and 1970s.

Theory in SFL is thus quite a substantial undertaking. However, there is one step beyond systemic functional theory (a step not shown in Figure 3.6). This is systemic functional metatheory: a theory of what systemic functional theory is like (cf. Halliday and Matthiessen 1999; Teich 1999; Matthiessen 2007b). Systemic functional metatheory developed first in the context of computational linguistic research because there was a pressing need to understand the distinction between theory and representation (cf. Matthiessen 1988a) and to understand the relationship between the deployment of systemic functional linguistics and the context of deployment (cf. Halliday 1964). However, it certainly has important roots in the work by Hjelmslev (in particular on connotative semiotic systems), Firth (his notion of linguistics as language turned back on itself) and Halliday (e.g. 1964, 1977a). Systemic functional metatheory has served as an important resource in work involving computational modelling, but it is relevant across all fields of systemic functional activity, and future research, application and development can hopefully be based on and supported by systemic functional metatheory as well as systemic functional theory. This would certainly be a very valuable new direction of activity.

3.4.2 Text analysis

As the diagram in Figure 3.6 indicates, the evidential or empirical basis of any work involving language is text (in context), and the fields of linguistic investigation discussed in Section 3.2 are typically grounded in the analysis of particular texts, but the research focus is usually locatable mid-way up the cline of instantiation on a register or set of registers. For instance, in the investigation of a given work place in organizational linguistics, the investigators are likely to sample a large number of texts and then to analyse them, but their focus will be on the register or registers that these texts instantiate, like the register of administrative directives. Given large enough samples of text, text analysis thus allows us to move up the cline of instantiation from instance towards potential. How far up we are able to move really depends on how large a sample the analysis can cope with. If the sample is large enough and covers an interesting range of registers, text analysis can help support the description of the systemic potential of a language. Let me comment briefly on methodology in text analysis, since this is very much part of the trajectory of current developments.

While 'text analysis' (or 'discourse analysis'[12]) is often seen as based on manual, human analysis, it can of course also be based on automated, computational analysis, or on a combination of manual and automated analysis (see Wu 2000; Matthiessen 2006b; Hoey 2006). Automated, computational analysis has been developed within corpus linguistics and linguistic computing (see Teich 2009). The complementarity of manual analysis and automated analysis can be characterized in reference to the size of the sample of texts and the 'level' (stratum, rank) of analysis (see Matthiessen 2006a: 108–113; Wu 2000): see Figure 3.7. Here the horizontal axis represents the sample size (measured in terms of words, as is customary for languages with an alphabetic writing system operating with graphological words corresponding roughly to grammatical words, as in English, and shown schematically on a logarithmic scale), ranging from small samples of single short texts via medium-size samples – register corpora of tens of thousands of words – to very large samples – reference corpora of hundreds of millions of words.

Manual analysis can range over all the 'levels' – all strata, and all ranks within a given stratum such as lexicogrammar, as long as descriptions are available, but it is severely constrained in terms of the sample size since it is very labour intensive and therefore expensive. The upper bound of the sample size is thus determined by funding: if research into language was funded at levels comparable to those of 'hard sciences', much larger samples of text could be analysed manually.

In contrast, automated analysis can range over text samples of all sizes; here the upper bound is determined by computing power and has thus constantly been

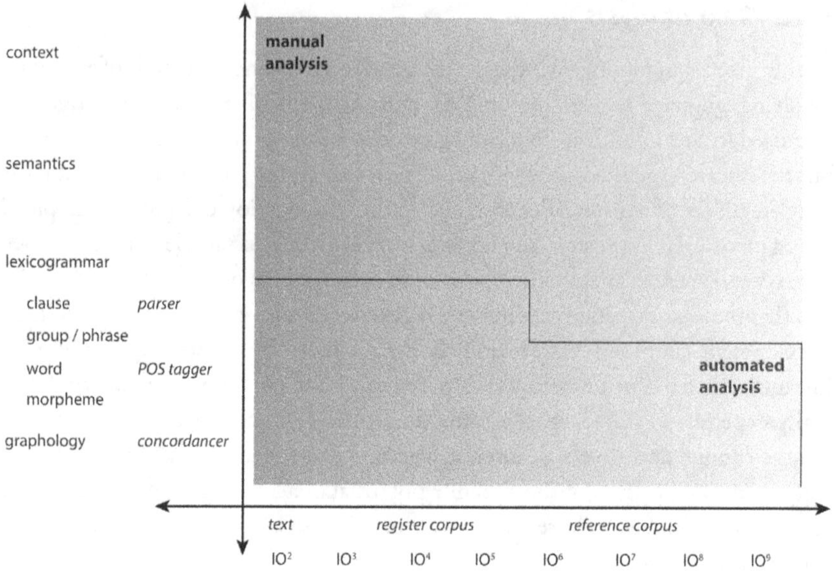

Figure 3.7 Modes of text analysis – manual and automated analysis in relation to 'level' and sample size

extended since the first systematic samples of electronically represented texts for computational processing were developed in the 1960s. Large corpora are now up to hundreds of millions of words, but even samples of this magnitude may not be extensive enough. The World Wide Web can be treated as a huge open and dynamic archive of texts, and this sample can be searched by means of search engines; but the sample is registerially quite skewed and the registerial make-up is not so easy to determine. The real constraint on automated analysis has to do with the 'level' of analysis, however; the upper bound is still located somewhere within the stratum of lexicogrammar. For smaller samples, it is possible to 'tune' parsers according to the registerial characteristics of the texts in the sample, but huge samples of registerially widely varied texts still pose a considerable challenge. Corpora that have been grammatically annotated through parsing, so-called 'tree banks', are now available for research, but they tend to be small (a couple of million words) and registerially narrow, like the annotated versions of the Brown Corpus, the LOB Corpus and the Penn Treebank of one million words of texts from the *Wall Street Journal*. The 'trees' are syntagms rather than function structures, but, in an additional cycle of parsing, such trees can themselves be analysed to produce (partial) function structures, as shown by Honnibal (2004).

3.4.3 Time-frames

Text analysis is located at the instance pole of the cline of instantiation (cf. Figure 3.6) – although it is of course always based on a prior description of a potential located further up the cline of instantiation. Let me now relate text analysis and the other processes discussed above – description, comparison, theory – to time-frames in research, application and development.

Since texts vary considerably in length (given the fact that they are defined 'from above' as language functioning in context; see Halliday and Hasan 1976), the analysis of a particular text can take anything from a few minutes to a few days or even weeks, or quite possibly months. For instance, one hour of casual conversation may take ten hours to transcribe, and 40 hours to analyse prosodically (in terms of rhythm and intonation).

Language may vary in size (although finding reliable measures of the size of a langauge is very difficult), but there is no doubt that describing a linguistic system takes orders of magnitude longer than analysing a text. Dixon (1997) suggests that it would take three years to develop the first description of a language (given a budget of around 200 K US dollars) and this is the quantum of research undertaken within a Ph.D. candidature; but his estimate is based on his notion of description based on 'basic theory', so I would multiply his estimate by three for a systemic functional description – that is, on the order of nine years for the first systemic functional description of a language (i.e. a description grounded in extensive text analysis, oriented towards meaning and designed to be a resource for the community of speakers as well as for linguists). This is equivalent to somewhere between 2–3 Ph.D. research projects (if we disregard the potential for research assistance). I think this is approximately right: researchers manage to squeeze outlines of languages into a single Ph.D. thesis – there have been a good number of systemic functional ones since the 1960s, but these are heroic efforts undertaken within a period of 4+ years and they often have to leave significant areas out (such as phonology, or at least prosodic phonology, grammar below the clause, semantics – not to mention context). So if a text takes say four weeks to analyse, a linguistic system takes on the order of 470 weeks to describe.

So much for analysis and description, but how long does it take to develop theory (setting comparison of descriptions of linguistic systems aside)? This is actually much harder to measure. One reason for this is that the development of theory is not usually the focus of research projects – neither of Ph.D. research projects nor of funded multi-person projects. Instead, systemic functional theory has been developed over a long period of time, around five decades by now, in the contexts of many projects of research, application and development and also in the contexts of many teaching programmes. Another reason why it is difficult to measure the time it takes to develop a certain quantum of theory is of course that like semiotic systems in general, theory never stands still; it is always changing. However, it is reasonable to say that the development of theory can be measured in terms of decades and generations of scholars. Here we are in the domain of scientific paradigms.

The considerations of different time-frames for the development of systemic functional linguistics are summarized schematically in Figure 3.8. Funded research projects typically last from a year to three years, or up to five years (depending on the size of the funding and the number of researchers involved); an individual Ph.D. research project lasts between three and five years. Such projects can thus deal with analysis of texts quite effectively, and there are innumerable examples of such projects. Longer projects of between three and five years may be able to produce descriptions of a particular language; above, I suggested that it would take on the order of nine years for a single senior researcher with research assistants to complete round one of a comprehensive systemic functional description of a particular language not previously described in systemic functional terms. The development of theory may fall within the scope of a research centre or laboratory

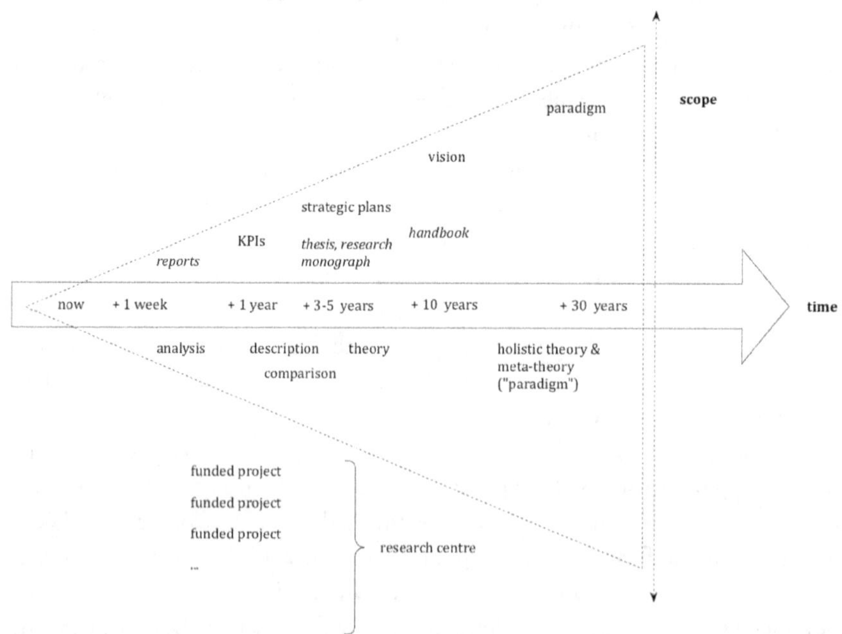

Figure 3.8 Development and time-frames

within which a number of research projects are co-ordinated.[13] Such research centres may have a life-span of five to ten years – probably of at least two cycles of funding of typical research projects. Research centres would thus be well suited to the development of theory – not only because of the time-frame but also because they involve several or even many research projects. The challenge is to build this kind of development into the vision statement for a research centre and into shorter-term strategic plans.

Above the timeline in Figure 3.8, I have included some 'buzz words' used in documents concerned with the planning and management of research. Research reports may be produced at different intervals, ranging from weekly to annual; and they will be expected at the end of a research project (maybe in the form of a Ph.D. thesis). Nowadays researchers are likely to be measured in terms of KPIs, 'key performance indicators', probably on an annual basis. Strategic plans operate over longer periods of time, probably extending beyond the duration of a single research project. They are in turn informed by vision statements, intended to give general direction to the development of research. Such vision statements are in turn informed by a research paradigm, such as the systemic functional paradigm for text-based research that began to be formulated in the early 1960s (cf. Halliday 1964a,b) and which has continued to be elaborated and inform systemic functional research.

Accounts such as the diagrammatic representation in Figure 3.8 must be treated with caution: they can sit uneasily between declarative models ('this is how research has developed according to our observations') and imperative ones ('this is how research ought to be developed according to our prescriptions'). This tension can be recognized from work within the philosophy of science – much of it has been imperative in nature, produced in arm chairs, but some of it has been declarative in nature, produced in the field; and imperative models from the philosophy of science must be reviewed in the light of declarative accounts developed within the sociology[14] of science.

The danger in today's academic world dominated by management thinking is that shorter-term research will be favoured to the detriment of longer-term research since shorter-term research is easier to manage and measure, is easier to report on, and is easier to get funding for since pay-offs are easier to articulate. However, the outlook is arguably brighter for systemic functional linguists than for many other colleagues for a number of reasons. (1) Systemic functional linguists have the skills to analyse the dominant discourses influencing the conditions for research (cf. e.g. Iedema, Feez and White 1994) to gain deeper insight into how they work, and such insight can then inform action. (2) Systemic functional linguists have a powerful multidimensional model to work with. This makes it much easier to locate fundable quanta of research within the total map of the semiotic landscape, and to use the systemic model to look ahead into the future beyond the next funding cycle. (3) Systemic functional linguists operate within many different institutional contexts and many countries around the world, so they are well placed to develop collaborative networks of mutual support.

Notes

1 This diagram only represents one aspect of the development of SFL in different phases. Complementary diagrams would show other aspects – like the development of coverage of metafunction, like the development of coverage of axis, like the development of coverage of the cline of delicacy, and like the development of coverage of the cline of instantiation. At the same time, even this stratal diagram needs to be supplemented to take into account the work in the last two decades or so on semiotic systems other than language.

2 In the diagram in Figure 3.3 and elsewhere in this chapter, I use the term 'register' in the sense established in the 1960s to refer to a functional variety of language (cf. Halliday, McIntosh and Strevens 1964; Gregory 1967; Hasan 1973; Halliday 1978; Matthiessen 1993b). A register is associated with contextual values of field, tenor and mode (cf. Hasan 1973: 272; Halliday 1978). In the work by Martin (e.g. 1992a) and scholars drawing on this work, the term 'register' has been used instead to refer to the contextual variables of field, tenor and mode (cf. also Martin 2007, for discussion).

3 For a discussion of probability in non-systemic phonology, see Pierrehumbert's (2001) overview of 'stochastic phonology' and her (2003) overview of 'probabilistic phonology'. At a special colloquium on the history of approaches to phonology organized by Goldsmith at a phonology conference at Abbaye de Royaumont outside Paris in June 1998 (Current trends in Phonology II), Halliday gave an overview of systemic phonology (see Halliday 2000b). Goldsmith presented a paper advocating revisiting the issue of probabilistic information in phonological accounts (going back to information theory). In the question period, Pierrehumbert commented that she would have thought systemic phonology was best suited to the incorporation of probabilistic information. This is an important insight and highlights the potential for future research in systemic phonology based on samples of texts at the instance pole of the cline of instantiation.

4 Cf. the award of the Nobel Prize for Literature by the Swedish Academy to Bertrand Russell in 1950 and to Winston Churchill in 1953.

5 Alternatively, we could use the term 'aesthetic linguistics' for the investigation of literary criticism (cf. Lukin 2003), which is located in the 'exploring' sector: 'recreating' texts are explored in aesthetic terms by means of the resources of appreciation within the system of appraisal (see Martin and White 2005), sometimes tending in the direction of creating a kind of 'metaliterature', echoing the aesthetic values of verbal art.

6 Website: http://www.ling.mq.edu.au/clsl/reporting_war.htm

7 See e.g. Iedema's website: http://research.hss.uts.edu.au/health-communication-research/Health%20Communication%20Research.html

8 See e.g. http://www.newsroom.uts.edu.au/news/detail.cfm?ItemId=6400

9 Website: http://fr46.uni-saarland.de/croco/index_en.html

10 See http://www.victoria.ac.nz/lals/lwp/index.aspx

11 This applies to any of the strata of the theoretical metalanguage (cf. Halliday and Matthiessen 1999; Teich 1999), including the strata of 'theoretical representation' and 'computational representation'. These areas need urgent attention, as emphasized by e.g. John Bateman and Elke Teich in recent plenary talks: for example, we need more 'powerful' representations of structure – representations suitable for computational representation in systems capable of parsing large volumes of text.

12 For discussion of 'text analysis' and 'discourse analysis', see the section on terms in Hasan, Matthiessen and Webster (2007).

13 There have been a number of these during the course of the development of SFL. A current example is the Multimodal Analysis Lab, directed by Kay O'Halloran at the National University of Singapore: http://multimodal-analysis-lab.org/. Another is the Halliday Centre for Intelligent Applications of Language Studies, directed by Jonathan Webster at Hong Kong City University: http://www. hallidaycentre.cityu.edu.hk/index.html

14 In sociology, Harold Garfinkel used to send his Ph.D. students planning to work on the sociology of science to do Ph.D.s in other disciplines so that as participant observers they would have the empirical base for developing a sociological account of how research is actually conducted.

Chapter 4
Systemic functional linguistics developing

4.1 Beginnings

Systemic Functional Linguistics (SFL) has been 'under construction' for several decades, In the development of any system of ideas, there are always various significant strands that are woven together to create the fabric of new ideas, and these strands can be traced back to different starting points.

For example, we could trace back Darwin's theory of evolution to the publication of his *On the Origin of Species*, which would make sense in terms of the public engagement with his theory. But we could also explore strands that are brought together in this book – like his fascination with collecting beetles (discussed in his autobiography), like Charles Lyell's work on the principles of geology, like the motif of evolution inherent in the Romantic movement.

Similarly, we can treat Halliday's (1961) 'Categories of the theory of grammar' as the starting point of the development of SFL – proto-SFL, or 'scale and category linguistics' as it came to be known. At the same time, we can explore the immediately preceding developments that were in a sense distilled in this article – Halliday's experience with field work on dialects of Cantonese in the Pearl River Delta, carried out under the guidance of Wang Li in the late 1940s, and Halliday's subsequent early work on Chinese (e.g. 1956a, 1959). We can go further back to identify salient features of J. R. Firth's (e.g. 1957b) system-structure theory that informed Halliday's (1961) theory of grammar; or we can go even further back to trace Firth's and later Halliday's development of Malinowski's (1923 onwards) theory of context.

The general principle is clearly that when we trace the history of any system of ideas, this will turn out to be an intellectual fabric made out of strands with very different starting points. There will thus always be many ways of representing the weaving of this fabric. In Figure 4.1, the development of SFL

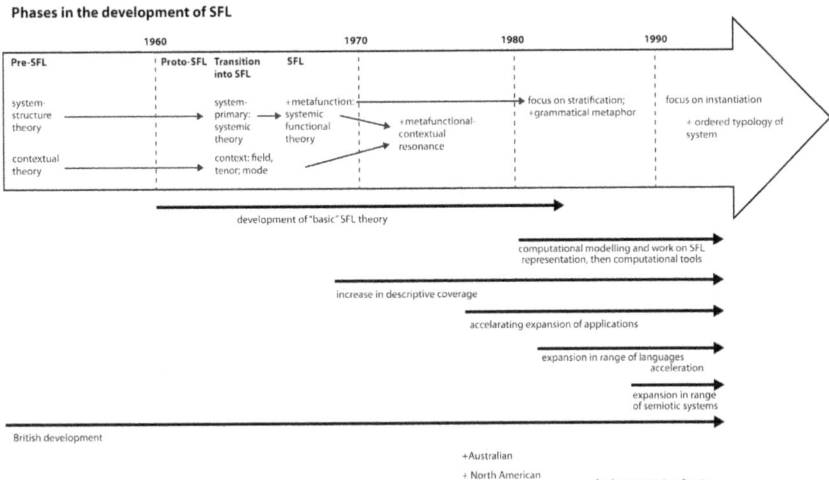

Figure 4.1 Phases in the development of SFL

is represented as a succession of phases characterized by different strands of activities and concerns.

4.2 Areas of expansion

As Figure 4.1 indicates, the mode of development in SFL has been one of continuous **expansion** of its 'territory' in terms of theory, description, application, interdisciplinary engagement, and so on.

4.2.1 Theory

Systemic functional linguists have always tried to make the theory as **comprehensive** as possible, adding new semiotic dimensions such as the spectrum of metafunctions when required; the goal has been to increase the **theoretical potential** to give it more power to model, analyse, describe and explain semiotic phenomena, As the diagram in Figure 4.1 indicates, successive semiotic dimensions came into focus, as the theory was developed from the 1960s.

Thus in the 1980s, the **hierarchy of stratification**[1] was explored and elaborated; for example, Martin (1992a) and his group, which later came to be known as the 'Sydney School' (see Martin and Rose 2008), explored the possibility of stratifying context to take account of genre and ideology as different contextual strata above the stratum of situation type (field, tenor and mode parameters), or 'register' as Martin called it.

In the 1990s, the focus shifted towards the **cline of instantiation**, and Halliday (e.g. 2002b [written in 1995]) intersected stratification and instantiation (thus elaborating on Halliday 1991b) to produce a stratification-instantiation matrix. Researchers explored processes of instantiation, in particular under the heading of logogenesis.

In this way, the **multidimensionality** of the theory has kept increasing since the 1960s (cf Matthiessen 2007b). (This would seem to be a general principle in the development of scientific theories: new dimensions are introduced to create a more powerful but simpler theory of the phenomena in focus – cf. Kaku's 1994 account of the development of physics since the nineteenth century.)

The theoretical space of SFL has thus been expanded through the addition or exploration of new semiotic dimensions. This theoretical space has also been expanded in another way – though here it would be appropriate to talk about the meta-theoretical space of SFL. Over the decades, scholars have developed **variants of SFL** or derived alternative frameworks from it. Let me use the work on the grammatical part of the theory, SFG, as an illustration since this is one area where researchers have produced explicit and clearly articulated representations of the theory (cf. Matthiessen and Nesbitt 1996) – even to the point where the theoretical models can be represented and implemented computationally. Variants of SFG and alternatives derived from it are charted for the period when researchers explored that space of grammatical theory and the versions that are still around emerged – the 1960s, 1970s and 1980s – in Figure 4.4.

By the end of this period, Halliday and his colleagues had been developing SFG for around three decades, since the early 1960s (cf. the phases in Figure 4.1). By the late 1960s, 'modern' SFG had emerged: it was both **systemic** and **metafunctional**. It is mainly this version of SFG that has served as a reference framework for the development of versions of, or alternatives to, SFG (cf Matthiessen 2007a). It is also the version used by Halliday and others to develop increasingly comprehensive descriptions, first of English and then also of other languages – descriptions that have made possible systematic text analysis at the stratum of lexicogrammar.

This version of SFG also became the foundation for extensive work in **computational modelling**, starting with the Nigel grammar of the Penman text generation project at USC/Information Sciences Institute[2] in 1980 (for an early account, see e.g. Mann 1982; for a later overview, see Matthiessen and Bateman 1991; for more recent overviews of computational SFL, see O'Donnell and Bateman 2005; Teich 2009). In this project, linguists, computational linguists and programmers worked out the computational modelling of **system networks**, **realization statements**, and **system traversal.** In the course of this work, we developed a grammar-based interface to semantics, the **chooser-&-inquiry framework** (as opposed to a semantics-based interface: see Matthiessen 1990) and used it to explore the semantic distinctions needed to control the grammar in the course of generation (see Matthiessen 1987b), we identified representational issues – areas where the theoretical representation is not explicit or detailed enough to support computational modelling without further development (e.g. Matthiessen 1988a, and see e.g. Teich 1999, for subsequent research), and Kasper (e.g. 1988a) drew on a version of Kay's **Functional Unification Grammar** (see below) to develop a systemic functional parser. The SFG computational grammar that began as the Nigel grammar of the Penman generation system is now maintained and developed as part of the KPML system by John Bateman at the University of Bremen.[3]

Towards the end of the 1960s, Richard Hudson was working on a variant of SFG in an attempt to create a non-transformational generative grammar in response to Chomsky's work (e.g. Hudson 1971). By the mid-1970s, he had produced **Daughter Dependency Grammar** (DDG, e.g. Hudson 1976), drawing on European dependency theory as well as on his earlier work on SFG. DDG was taken up by Paul Schachter (e.g. 1981) at UCLA for a while, but Hudson himself took dependency further and transformed DDG into **Word Grammar** (WG; e.g. Hudson 1984, 2007). While WG was no longer 'systemic', unlike DDG, it was closer to SFG in certain important respects (partly reflecting Hudson's work on sociolinguistics), for example in taking a more meaning-oriented approach to grammar (Hudson, p.c., around 1980).

In the early 1970s, Robin Fawcett began to develop a variant of SFG (e.g. Fawcett 1973), drawing on the work by both Halliday and Hudson. This was developed by Fawcett (e.g. 1980) and his team at Cardiff University into what came to be known as the **Cardiff Grammar** (e.g. Fawcett 2008). As a variant of SFG, it shares a number of fundamental features with Halliday's SFG. Most importantly, it is organized systemically (rather than structurally), so, as in SFG in general, lexis can be modelled as most delicate grammar, and a great deal of descriptive work on extending the grammatical description in delicacy has been done in terms of the Cardiff framework (e.g. Tucker 1997a, 2007; Neal 2006). Similarly, as in SFG in general, the systemic organization is conceived of in probabilistic terms, and terms in systems have probabilities attached to them. Systemic probabilities have been used in parsers based on the Cardiff Grammar (e.g. Fawcett and Weerasinghe 1993; Souter 1996). In addition, like Halliday's SFG, the Cardiff SFG has been modelled and implemented computationally (for an early report, see Fawcett and Tucker 1990). At the same time, the Cardiff Grammar also has unique properties.

A number of these relate to the relationship between system and structure and to the theory and representation of structure (see e.g. Fawcett 1980, 2000): the key concept is that of 'starting structure' (e.g. Fawcett 1980: 47 ff.), a kind of structural potential of a unit.

In the second half of the 1970s, Martin Kay set to work on a computational version of SFG with the goal of creating a grammar that could be used in both parsing and generation. The outcome of this project turned out to be something related but different, **Functional Unification Grammar** (FUG; e.g. Kay 1979, 1985). In a FUG representation, the systemic part of SFG is not foregrounded, but partial descriptions of the grammar, e.g. the theme, mood and transitivity structures of the clause, can be represented separately and unified into a comprehensive description of the clause. Kay's FUG influenced the development of other grammatical frameworks in the more formal tradition in the late 1970s and the 1980s – in particular, **Lexical Functional Grammar** (LFG) and **Head-Driven Phrase Structure Grammar** (HPSG, e.g. Pollard and Sag 1993). It also led to computational frameworks such as PATR (see e.g. Shieber 1986).

Interestingly, while systemic organization was not foregrounded in Kay's FUG, the general notion of **typing** has become more prominent in developments since the 1970s – in HPSG by the mid-1980s and in the application of HPSG to Construction Grammar, a framework called Sign-Based Construction Grammar, where type lattices are used to represent paradigmatic relations (see Boas and Sag 2010). Typing has also become a general concern in computational representations such as **typed feature structures** (TFs), drawing on work on knowledge representation concerned with classification hierarchies originating in the 1970s (e.g. Woods 1975; Brachman 1979); and TFs have been used in representations of SFG (Bateman, Emele and Momma 1992).

There is of course much more to be said about the development of the theory of grammar in systemic functional linguistics; but the point of this brief excursion has been to suggest how the space of systemic functional theory has been expanded over the decades through the development of SFG itself but also of variants and alternatives.

One important aspect of this expansion has been the articulation of the theory of **systemic functional metatheory**. Since the work on computational modelling in the 1980s, it has become clear that the theory must itself be modelled as a **stratified semiotic system**, as shown developmentally in Figure 4.2 (e.g. Matthiessen 1988a; Matthiessen and Nesbitt 1996; Teich 1999; Halliday and Matthiessen 1999). In this way, the theory has expanded ***stratally*** since the 1960s; the notion of theory has become 'thicker' in the last several decades.

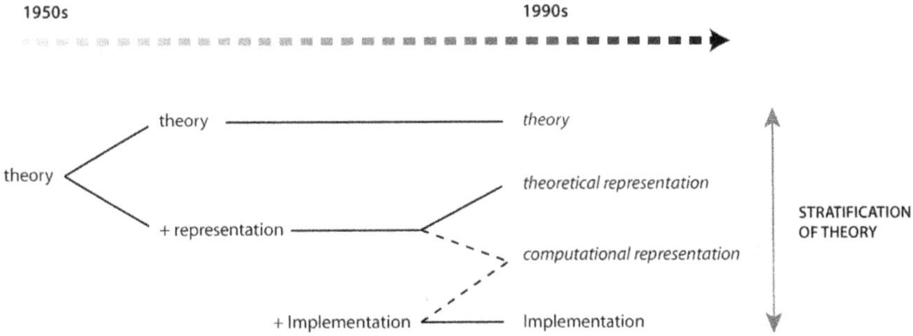

Figure 4.2 Development of the Stratification of Theory (metalanguage)

Representations were worked out in the 1960s in the form of system networks and realization statements. Early computational implementations of these representations were added already in the 1960s and 1970s, and it was thus possible to test the implementability of the representations; for example, Henrici (1965) comments on certain problems in the implementation of the representations at the time – one long-standing challenge being how to represent logical, recursive systems explicitly (see further Matthiessen 1988a; Bateman 1989). But it wasn't until the 1980s that researchers in the US, the UK and Japan began to undertake major projects involving implementation. The experience of this research led to the recognition that two levels are needed, a higher, theoretical level and a lower, computational level oriented towards computational implementations. Together these two levels mediate between theory and implementation.

The research focused on the stratification of systemic functional theory clarified the complementary contributions made by the four different strata (levels) mentioned above – **theory**, **theoretical representation**, **computational representation** and **implementation** – in terms of specificity, coverage and formalization, as illustrated for the theory of paradigmatic representation and system networks in Figure 4.3.

In terms of SPECIFICITY, theory ranks the highest and implementation the lowest: systemic functional theory is specific to the domain of language and other semiotic systems, but implementations are stated in programming languages such as LISP, Prolog and Java that are not specific to the modelling of semiotic systems.

In terms of coverage, theory is again at the highest end of a scale and implementation at the lowest: in theoretical models, it is possible to be very comprehensive or holistic precisely because theory is stated in fairly abstract terms; but in implemented models, the domain of coverage is much smaller because only those parts of the theory that can be made fully explicit first in theoretical representations and then in computational representations can be implemented.

Thus, in terms of FORMALIZATION, the scale is reversed: the highest degree of formalization is achieved at the level of implementation – the level where everything has to be spelled out and nothing can be assumed, and the level at which the 'consumer' is a computer; and the lowest degree of formalization is achieved at the level of theory – the level where models can be 'sketched' and gaps can be filled in or glossed over by human consumers.

The four strata or levels set out in Figures 4.2 and 4.3 thus complement one another; they contribute different important properties to the overall engagement with, and modelling of, language and other semiotic systems.

In the discussion above, I have distinguished variants and alternatives; but these are, of course, not clearly distinct categories; in terms of theory, they form a continuum, but variants remain within the broad community of SFL scholars whereas alternatives come to be developed within distinct communities. Variants can certainly exist and develop within the general theory of SFL; it has been designed as a **flexi theory** that gives researchers the potential to explore different versions (cf. Halliday 1980b) and the meta-theory of SFL gives value to such variation.[4]

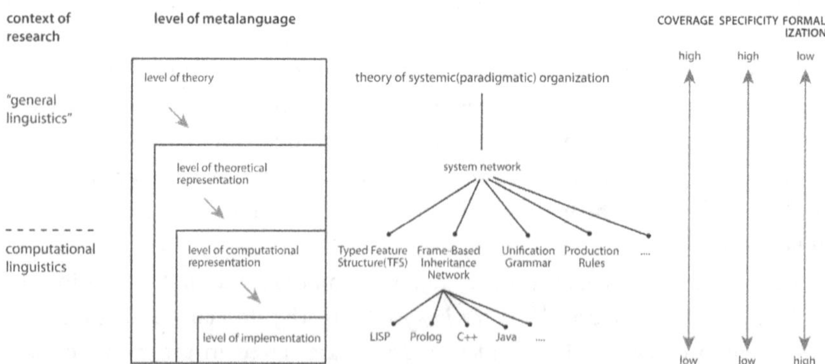

Figure 4.3 Stratification of theory in relation to the theory of paradigmatic organization and its representation by system networks

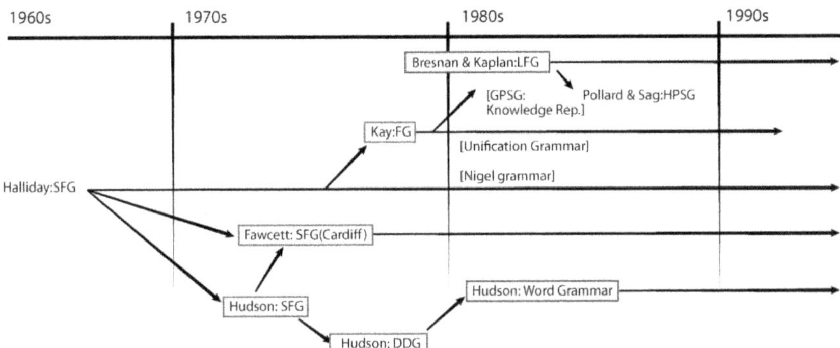

Figure 4.4 Development of systemic functional grammatical theory – expansion of metatheoretical space in terms of variants and alternatives

4.2.2 *Description*

Just as systemic functional linguists have kept increasing the theoretical coverage of SFL, they have continued to increase the coverage of the description of different languages (and also of other semiotic systems).

In work on languages being described for the first time in systemic functional terms, the initial goal has usually been to develop a low-delicacy but comprehensive account of the grammatical part of the lexicogrammar of the language being described, possibly together with some aspects of the phonology (as in the sketches presented in Caffarel, Martin and Matthiessen 2004).

In work on English, the initial descriptive focus was on the lexicogrammar, summarized first in Halliday (1985a) and later expanded in e.g. Matthiessen (1995b) and Halliday and Matthiessen (2004), and also on the prosodic systems of the phonology, first presented in Halliday (1967b) and later revised and extended in Halliday and Greaves (2008).

Since the beginning of the 1980s, the description of English has been extended from grammar to lexis and to other strata, beyond lexicogrammar:

- **towards lexis:** extension in delicacy of the description of grammar, linking it to lexis (e.g. Hasan 1996b; Tucker 1996; Neale 2006; Matthiessen 2010).
- **semantics:** the work on 'discourse semantics' (Martin 1992, simplified and updated in Martin and Rose 2003), including the description of the resources of appraisal in English (Martin and White 1995), 'message semantics' (Hasan 1996a), including the account of rhetorical units (Cloran 1994), logical-rhetorical semantics ('RST', e.g. Mann, Matthiessen and Thompson 1992), and ideational semantics (e.g. Halliday and Matthiessen 2006a).

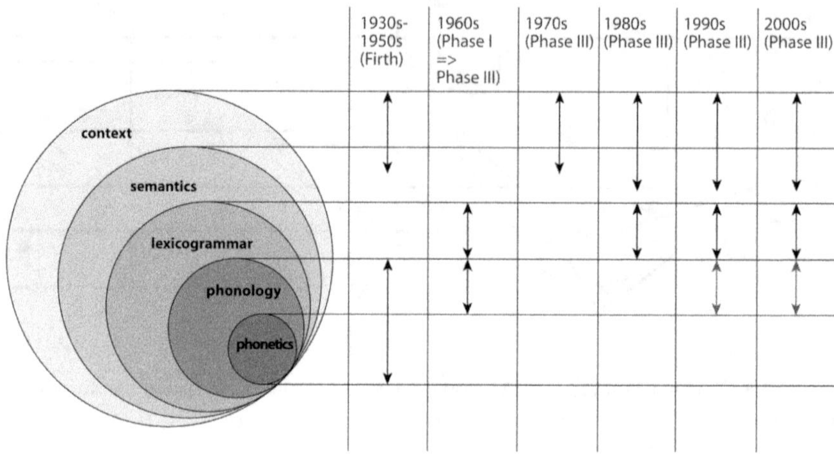

Figure 4.5 Descriptive focus in accounts of English in particular in terms of strata since the 1930s

- **context**: development of descriptions of contextual system networks in terms of field, tenor and mode (e.g. Martin 1992a, chap. 7; Hasan 1999; Butt 2003) and of contextual structures ('generic structures,' 'schematic structures;' e.g. Martin 1992a, chap. 7; Hasan 1996b; Martin and Rose 2008).

Focusing mainly on English, we can summarize the changing descriptive focus in terms of strata as follows: see Figure 4.5. During the pre-SFL phase, the main emphasis was on the outer strata – on context and on phonology/phonetics. Therefore, during the proto-SFL and early SFL phases, Halliday and others shifted the emphasis to the inner strata – in particular, to lexicogrammar. Once the basic outline of the description of lexicogrammar was in place, researchers began to describe semantics and context as well.

4.2.3 Analysis

In addition to the expansion of descriptions of languages, systemic functional linguists have kept increasing the analytical coverage of texts in different contexts, engaging with an ever-wider **range of registers**. Early descriptions are often based on a corpus of texts from a restricted range of registers (for discussion of the development of such corpora in the service of language description, see Akerejola 2005; Kumar 2009). By restricting the range of registers at the early stage of a description, researchers developing this new description can manage the complexity of the task; but the choice of registers is of course strategically important since the texts from the registers chosen will serve as the gateway into the language being described and different registers put different meanings at risk.

Once linguists have developed a basic description of a language, text analysts can analyse texts from an ever-increasing range of registers. In the analysis of English texts, the publication of Halliday (1985a) enabled researchers and students to analyse texts from different registers systematically. The expansion of the registerial sample of texts analysed has been the pattern for languages described in systemic functional terms. Thus since Halliday's (1977b) early example of the lexicogrammatical analysis of a text and since Hasan's (1978) early example of the contextual analysis of a text, analysts have tackled an ever wider range of registers; for example:

- texts in institutions of education (e.g. Christie and Martin 1997; Martin and Veel 1998) in a succession of educational linguistic projects (see Martin and Rose 2005);
- casual conversation between young children and their mothers in the home (e.g. Hasan and Cloran 1990);
- casual conversation among adults in the home and in the workplace (e.g. Eggins and Slade 2005);
- texts in the institution of the media (e.g. Nanri 1993; Iedema, Feez and White 1994; Thomson and White 2008).

More recently, researchers have turned to texts in additional institutional sites, including institutions of healthcare (e.g. Fine 2006; Kealley 2007; Henderson-Brooks 2006; Muntigl 2004) and workplaces (on workmate relations: Eggins and Slade 2005; on organizational discourse: e.g. Iedema 1995, 1997b).

The development of descriptions of appraisal (e.g. Martin and White 2005) has extended the reach of interpersonal analysis, and the development of descriptions of semiotic systems other than language and analytical tools (e.g. O'Toole 1994; Kress and van Leeuwen 1996; Baldry and Thibault 2006) has made possible the analysis of visual images, film, gesture, music and multisemiotic presentations (e.g. O'Halloran 2005; Royce and Bowcher 2006; Ventola and Guijarro 2009).

The expansion of registerial coverage has followed similar patterns in work on languages other than English. Thus the expansion of the description of the system of a given language (its meaning potential) is related to the accumulation of analysed texts from an ever-wider range of registers. This relationship can be represented in the idealized picture set out in Figure 4.6. The general principle is that as researchers accumulate analyses of texts from different registers, they can add more specifications to the description of the system.

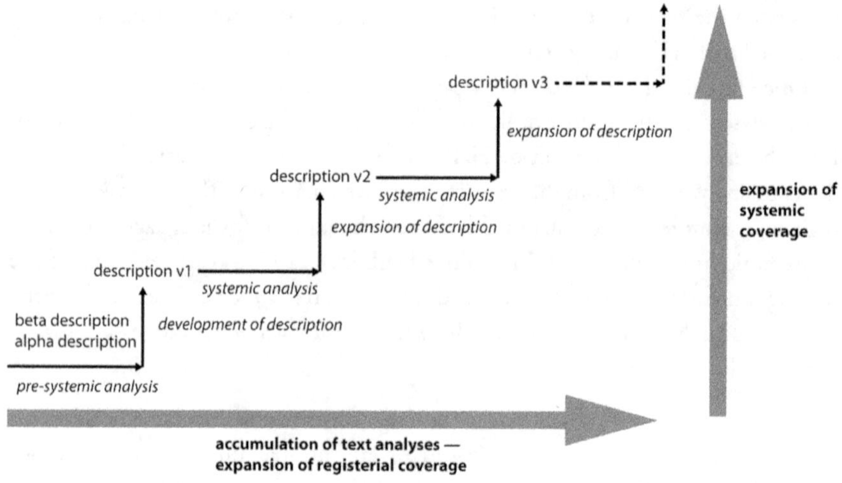

Figure 4.6 Text analysis and system description: related developments (idealized picture)

In order to develop the first version of a description of the linguistic system of a given language, researchers analyse authentic texts in context to identify recurrent patterns. (They may also use other methods, of course, such as eliciting examples from a language consultant, 'translating' an earlier description couched in a different theoretical framework, or 'transferring' aspects of the description of a different language.) This analysis is pre-systemic in the sense that it is not yet based on a description of the language; for example, if the analysis is automated, it may produce patterns involving recurrent high-frequency combinations of grammatical items such as the most frequent combinations of two items (2-grams) in a selection of corpora from ICE (the International Corpus of English; in order of descending frequency): *of the, in the, to the, it is, of knowledge, and the, on the, for the, is a.* As this pre-systemic analysis progresses, it becomes possible to begin to propose successively refined descriptions; we can think of these as alpha and beta descriptions on the model of software development. The outcome of this process is the first version of a fairly comprehensive description – the description that is likely to be published as a resource for different uses, including centrally text analysis. With access to this descriptive resource, text analysts can begin to undertake systemic analysis of texts from different registers. As such analyses accumulate, they provide material for a new, expanded version of the description – expanded, but also revised, of course. This alternation between description and analysis can, in principle, continue forever.

The picture shown in Figure 4.6 is idealized in at least two respects. (1) Since text analysis is a popular activity and can be used to address many research problems, it is easy to be tempted to use the description of a well-described language – typically English – in the analysis of texts from another language. For example, investigators have sometimes transferred the description of PROCESS TYPE, APPRAISAL and certain other systems taken from the description of English to other languages and used the descriptions of English in the analysis of texts in these other languages. This kind of transfer of the description of one language to the task of analysing text in another language can work up to a certain point, but the result is bound to be inaccurate and ultimately misleading.[5]

(2) While systemic functional linguists developing descriptions also analyse large volumes of text and draw on the results of this analysis to revise and expand their descriptions, the majority of text analysts use existing descriptions but do not themselves actively develop descriptions. Consequently, the feedback from analysis to description does not work as well as Figure 4.6 suggests. Solving this problem is one of the challenges in the development of SFL descriptions. The solution will no doubt involve a combination of strategies for sharing data and analyses within distributed research teams and communities and of computational tools that bridge the gap between analysis and description, making it easier for analysts to contribute to the process of description

4.2.4 *Application*

The extension of theoretical, descriptive and analytical coverage has developed together with the widening range of applications.

(1) Certain areas of application have been part of this range from very early on, including centrally applications to **education** (e.g. Halliday, McIntosh and Strevens 1964), **translation** (e.g. Catford 1965) and **description** of different languages, in addition to the work on Chinese and English (e.g. Barnwell 1969).

Applications to education grew into one of the major currents early on and have continued to develop in new educational contexts (e.g. Christie and Unsworth 2005).

The work on translation between, and description of, different languages was really no more than a trickle early on, but these and other aspects of multilingual studies have now become another major current (cf. Steiner and Yallop 2001; Caffarel, Martin and Matthiessen 2004; Matthiessen, Teruya and Wu 2008).

(2) Other areas of application have been added to this range over the decades: computational linguistics, multimodal studies, and healthcare linguistics.

While there were early excursions into **computational applications** (e.g. Halliday 1956b; Henrici 1965; Davey 1978), it wasn't until the beginning of the 1980s that computational modelling began to be added to range of applications (e.g. O'Donnell and Bateman 2005; Teich 2009).

About a decade and a half later, multimodal (or multisemiotic) studies began to take off, thanks to the foundational contributions by O'Toole (1994) and Kress and van Leeuwen (1990, 1996) that made it possible to undertake systematic and systemic analysis of instances of semiotic systems other than language. This field of investigation has continued to develop, engaging with additional semiotic systems (e.g. Martinec 2005).

A little later in the 1990s, research in **healthcare** contexts began to emerge as a clearly distinct field of activity within SFL, sometimes called 'clinical linguistics' (see Armstrong *et al.* 2005), including first work on 'disordered language' (e.g. Fine 1995; Armstrong 1997, with precursors such as Martin and Rochester 1979) and then also work on healthcare communication in general (e.g. Kealley 2007).

Around the same time, researchers also began to investigate different aspects of **workplaces**, including contexts of administration (e.g. Iedema 1995) and service contexts (e.g. Ventola 1987; Forey and Lockwood 2010).[6]

In the last decade or so, systemic functional linguists have begun to explore a number of areas of application that may turn into major currents in the next decade or so: language and the brain (e.g. Hailiday 1995; Thibault 2004; Williams 2005), semiosis in bonobos and in bonobo-human communities (e.g. Benson and Greaves 2009),[7] the evolution of language (e.g. Halliday 1995a; Matthiessen 2004b; Rose 2005), language as a complex system among other kinds of complex system (the work by Chris Cleirigh; Halliday and Matthiessen 2006, chap. 13; Matthiessen 2009b).

4.2.5 Inter-disciplinarity

Systemic functional linguistics has been outward looking from the start. On the one hand, systemic functional linguists have addressed questions outside their own discipline – questions arising either in other disciplines or more generally in the community outside academic institutions. This has led to the development of SFL's contributions to educational linguistics, computational linguistics, clinical – or healthcare – linguistics, forensic linguistics, translation studies and a number of other areas.

On the other hand, systemic functional linguists have turned to other disciplines for insights into language and now also other semiotic systems, thus giving SFL itself a **multidisciplinary character**. Following Firth's initiative, they have engaged with Bronislaw Malinowski's work in **anthropology** (cf. Hasan 1985c), transforming his insights into **context** developed from the 1920s to the 1940s into part of a linguistic theory of language in context, parameterizing context into field, tenor and mode (e.g. Halliday, McIntosh and Strevens 1964), relating these parameters to the metafunctions of language (e.g. Halliday 1978), and locating Malinowski's 'context of culture' and 'context of situation' along the cline of instantiation (e.g. Halliday 1991b).

Starting in the 1960s, a number of systemic functional linguists began to engage with Basil Bernstein's **sociology** because his social theories gave a central place to language, and he developed his conception of the role that language plays in social transmission and educational processes in response to systemic functional work. This dialogue has now gone through at least two very productive phases, the first concerned with Bernstein's conception of **codes** as a mode of variation in language, e.g. Turner (1973, 1987), Hasan (1973), Halliday (1994a); and the second concerned with his theories of pedagogy and the structure and transmission of knowledge, e.g. Christie and Martin (2007).

The engagement with currents within anthropology and sociology has thus been part of the development of SFL essentially from the start. The same is true of what is now called computational linguistics or natural language processing – though to a lesser extent during the early phases. Halliday's (1956b) first work in this area was a linguistic model proposed as a contribution to what later came to be known as machine translation. About a decade later, we find insights flowing from computational modelling into SFL – first Henrici (1965), providing the first clear example of the value of computational modelling, and then a bit later Winograd (1972).

Since around 1980, there has been a growing exchange between SFL and computational linguistics in the context of a number of computational linguistic research projects. As far as the development of SFL is concerned, computational linguistics has provided a framework for modelling the theory computationally, thereby testing and improving representations – compare the discussion above of the gradual development of levels or strata within the systemic functional metalanguage (see Figure 4.2). In addition, computational linguistics has provided ways of modelling linguistic processes – in particular, the logogenetic processes involved in generation and analysis. For example, a key aspect of the work on systemic functional grammars for generation was the design of algorithms for traversing system networks and activating realization statements. This research into the representation of semiotic processes is important, but it has not yet been taken up in the general theory of systemic functional linguistics.

The engagement with work in anthropology, sociology and computational linguistics has continued, and, in the last 20 to 30 years, dialogues with other disciplines have been started, either from within SFL or from within these disciplines.

In educational linguistics, systemic functional linguists have continued to draw on the work by Basil Bernstein (e.g. Christie and Martin 2007) but they have also drawn on **educational theory**, in particular the work on **scaffolding** originating with Jerome Bruner (e.g. Gibbons 2002, 2009). The approach to learning that systemic functional linguists have developed over the decades (for a seminal statement, see Halliday 1993d) is clearly resonant with the theory developed in early Soviet psychology by Lev Vygotsky in the 1920s and 1930s – his ideas about **internalization**, the **zone of proximal development**, cultural mediation (as emphasized by Wells 1994a, 1994b), and systemic functional linguists have made the connections to Vygotsky's work and to more recent contributions drawing on his work (e.g. Hasan 1992, 1995; Williams 2004; Byrnes 2006).

As systemic functional linguists have moved into new areas of application and as researchers from outside linguistics have turned to SFL as a resource in their work on language and other semiotic systems (see above), new dialogues between SFL and other disciplines have begun to open up. These include **healthcare** (e.g. Fine 2006; Kealley 2007; Henderson-Brooks 2006), **primate studies** (e.g. Benson and Greaves 2009), and **museum studies** (e.g. Ravelli 2006).

4.2.6 Geographical coverage

The early phases in the development of SFL took place in the UK, mainly Edinburgh and then London (see Figure 4.1). Ideas and influences came from various places around the world, including Czechoslovakia (Prague School functionalism), Denmark (Glossematics) and the US (anthropological linguistics); but the main developments during this period took place in the UK. Since this period, SFL has become a global collaborative undertaking with very active groups in many places around the world. International Systemic Functional Congresses usually have participants from 25 to 30 countries, the mixture of representatives changing as the Congress moves from one continent to another; and in addition, several regions have associations that hold conferences on a regular basis. The Japanese Association celebrated its 20th anniversary in 2011. The impressive development of SFL in China has been documented by Zhang, McDonald, Fang, and Huang (2005).

The expansion of the geographical coverage of SFL has been important in a number of ways; for example: (1) it has expanded the range of languages being described in systemic functional terms; (2) it has given SFL access to a range of different related frameworks; (3) it has opened up new contexts of research and application; and (4) it has enriched the systemic functional metalanguage in the sense that systemic functional work is now regularly being developed and published in languages other than English.

(1) The expansion of the geographical coverage of SFL has significantly expanded the **treasure trove of languages** that SF researchers analyse and describe, adding languages with different mixtures of typological features and thus providing new opportunities to confront the theory with new descriptive challenges, including 'serial verb constructions' (e.g. Akerejola 2005, on Oko; Patpong 2005, on Thai), 'aspect systems' (e.g. Halliday and McDonald 2004, on Mandarin), Philippine 'voice systems' (e.g. Martin 2004a, on Tagalog), 'SOV' as unmarked sequence of clausal elements (e.g. Prakasam 2004, on Telugu; Kumar 2009, on Bajjika; Teruya 2004a, on Japanese), 'verb-initial' languages ['VSO', 'VSO'j (e.g. Martin 2004a, on Tagalog; Bardi 2008, on Modern Standard Arabic), reference by 'ellipsis' (cf. 'pro-drop' in generative accounts, e.g. Boxwell 1995), elaborate nominal case (e.g. Shore 1992, on Finnish), agglutinative morphology (e.g. Teruya 2007 on Japanese), radical and overlay pattern morphology (as in Semitic languages, e.g. Bardi 2008, on Modern Standard Arabic), emergent 'polysynthetic' morphology (e.g. Caffarel 2006, on French), West African tone systems (e.g. Matthiessen 1987a, on Akan). While the value of this quite dramatic expansion of the descriptive linguistic database of SFL has perhaps not tended to be foregrounded and celebrated, it is nevertheless one of the major achievements of the last decade and a half and it is essential background for any attempts to develop the general theory of language further.

(2) The expansion of the geographical coverage of SFL has boosted the 'collective brain,' opening up dialogues with a rich range of **scholarly communities**, both past and present. For instance, Prakasam (e.g. 1985, chap. 11) deepens our understanding of systemic functional theory by drawing parallels with the Buddhist theory of meaning – the Apoha; Teruya (2007) builds a bridge between SFL and 'Okudian' functional linguistics in Japan, enriching the systemic functional description of Japanese by drawing on this indigenous tradition in Japan; and Bardi (2008) brings out striking similarities between SFL and the rich tradition of Islamic linguistics (cf. also Owens 1988), in particular during the period before Aristotle's influence began to be felt. Within computational linguistics, Michio Sugeno and members of his teams first at the Tokyo Institute of Technology and then at the Brain Science Division of the RIKEN Institute – Ichiro Kobayashi, in particular – made the connection between SFL and fuzzy theory, as Sugeno and others had developed in Japan on Lotfi Zadeh's foundation.

Another important aspect of the expansion of the range of scholarly communities is the addition of potentially complementary models of scholarship. There are, of course, culturally distinct models discussed in the literature on the development of modern science, including e.g. the contrast between the so-called Western, Islamic and Confucian models (cf. Huff 1995); but the central question here is how different traditions of scholarship can complement and enrich one another in the continued development of SFL around the world.

(3) The expansion of the geographical coverage of SFL has introduced SFL to **new contexts of research and application.**

On the one hand, fields of activity within SFL that were established a long time ago have been enriched through the addition of new strands of research in different places around the world. Within educational linguistics, work on second/foreign language education has been strengthened by researchers around the world, adding to the work on mother tongue and content areas in the Australian context that began to develop in the 1980s. The expansion of the linguistic base of researchers has also strengthened work on translation and translation studies, adding more language pairs and more research groups. In addition to research groups in Germany and Italy, there are now also groups in Australia, China (including Macau and Hong Kong), and Brazil.

On the other hand, as SFL is being taken up in a growing number of places, scholars have begun to develop new fields of activity. Examples include:

- Japan: the research on computing with meaning initiated by Michio Sugeno (cf. above);
- USA: the research on bonobo-human communication involving primatologists and systemic functional linguists (e.g. Benson and Greaves 2009);
- Brazil: the research linking the analysis of the process of translation to the analysis of the product of translation, i.e. text in context, in order to identify units of translation and translation shifts, now also in collaboration with Germany;[8]
- Argentina: the research concerned with the marketing and promotion of wine conducted by a team at the Universidad Nacional de Cuyo in Mendoza, Argentina.

There are, of course, many other examples, but the ones listed above all illustrate the principle that as SFL is used in particular places around the world, new opportunities for research will emerge because of the characteristics of these places.

(4) As SFL has been taken up in new places around the world, its **metalinguistic base** has been enriched: scholars and students are conducting work in an increasing range of languages, drawing on the resources of these languages for carrying out teaching, research and application. Publications in English by systemic functional scholars (starting with early key contributions such as Halliday and Hasan 1976; Halliday 1978) have been, and are being, translated into a growing number of languages, including Italian, French, Spanish and Portuguese; Chinese, Japanese, Vietnamese, and Indonesian. There are now a number of bilingual publications (e.g. Matthiessen and Halliday 2009, with an introduction in Chinese by Huang Guowen); Halliday's seminal paper on 'computing meaning' has been translated into Chinese by Wu Canzhong and into Japanese by Kazuhiro Teruya (see Halliday 2000a, 2002b). Original SFL publications are also increasingly appearing in languages other than English, including book-length introductions in Chinese (e.g. Hu, Zhu, and Zhang 1989), Danish (e.g. Andersen, Petersen, and Smedegaard 2001), and Swedish (Holmberg and Karlsson 2006), and journal articles in these languages as well as in several others, including German, French, Italian, Spanish and Portuguese. Translations and original works in languages other than English have also contributed to the development of multilingual glossaries. For example, Holmberg and Karlsson (2006) includes a tabular summary of technical terms in English, Danish, Norwegian and Swedish. In organizational terms, the geographic expansion has also been quite significant. It has strengthened involvement in the international organization, ISFLA, and it has led to the establishment of a growing number of national and regional organizations, each one of which nurtures activities for example by holding conferences and other academic events.[9]

4.3 Expounding – Vertical rather than horizontal construction of knowledge

As we have seen, SFL has developed primarily by ***expanding its coverage into new areas*** of theory, description, analysis, application, inter-disciplinary engagement, and so on rather than by reworking the same area through successive accounts. The SFL mode of development can thus be understood as a feature of the **holistic** nature of systemic functional theory. The systemic functional approach to science is the holistic approach characteristic of **systems thinking** in certain domains of scientific enquiry. It contrasts sharply with the approach that has dominated the development of modern science, beginning around half a millennium ago in western Eurasia (cf. Capra 1996).

The dominant approach has been that of **Cartesian analysis**; it is **componential** rather than holistic in nature. Using this approach, scientists have managed the complexity of different phenomenal realms by focusing on small and therefore manageable domains. This is the method advocated by René Descartes in his meditations, and it has been used extensively in US structuralist linguistics of the kind that Noam Chomsky built on as he developed his 'Cartesian linguistics'. One of the serious problems with Cartesian Analysis is that it leads to the **fragmentation of knowledge** (cf. Bohm 1980).

While the holistic approach has tended to be on the periphery of 'mainstream' modern science, key breakthroughs have depended on the kind of systems thinking that is characteristic of the holistic approach – in the first half of the twentieth century, the development of ecology in biological sciences and the development of contextualism in social and semiotic sciences (due to Bronislaw Malinowski). And towards the end of the twentieth century, the need for systems thinking in the study of different phenomenal realms has become increasingly urgent: holistic approaches are needed to come to terms with a range of severe environmental and social problems caused by human activities based on 'growthism' (cf. Halliday 1993d). As different forms of systems thinking (e.g. the study of complex adaptive systems, as envisaged by Gell-Mann 1994, and developed by him and colleagues at the Santa Fe Institute;[10] the study of large-scale quantitative patterns and effects, e.g. Ball 2004) become increasingly prominent, the intellectual environment in which SFL continues to develop is becoming increasingly resonant with the central characteristics of SFL (see further below). SFL is, after all, a holistic approach to language and other semiotic systems, based on systems thinking.

The way that 'knowledge' is created in SFL discourse can be characterized as 'vertical' rather than 'horizontal' (adapting these notions from Basil Bernstein's, e.g. 2000, work). Many contributions to SFL build on foundations that have already been put in place, and as the foundations are expanded, further accounts can be added on top of them. A number of central works in SFL can be interpreted as macro-reports, expounding knowledge about semiotic systems step by step (with the steps often being ordered in delicacy). In this respect, SFL is arguably more like natural science than like social sciences and the humanities (cf. the large-scale genre profiling of industrial chemistry, construction engineering, social work and psychology in Parodi 2010). In contrast, Chomskyan linguistics and linguistic developments strongly influenced by its form of rhetoric have tended to be exploring rather than expounding in orientation.

4.4 Frontiers

4.4.1 Nature of frontiers

Given the mode of development of SFL, there have always been frontier areas – extensions in stratal coverage, extensions in delicacy, extensions in metafunctional coverage; extensions in multilingual coverage, extensions in multisemiotic coverage; extensions in domains of application and implementation; and so on. Sometimes pioneering contributions will lead to the development of new areas – a fairly recent example is the development of ecolinguistics drawing centrally on Halliday (1990).[11]

In some cases, the systemic functional specialists in one area involved in territorial expansion will run into specialists from another area, as when grammarians extending the account in delicacy run into lexicographers, when linguists extending the account of language into the domain of other semiotic systems run into musicologists, and so on, or when linguists working on the linguistic resources for enacting evaluation run into social psychologists.

In other cases, systemic functional specialists in one area extending their coverage into another area will be pioneers, moving into terra nullius (in the real sense, not in the sense of the European invaders of Australia) and thus terra incognita. This type of development is probably increasingly rare since most disciplines keep expanding their coverage. But it needn't be rare. There are many languages that have never been described yet (adequately or even at all) – in fact, this is actually true of most of our rapidly disappearing 6,900+ languages: Akerejola (2005) is the first description of the grammar of Oko and Kumar (2009) is the first of Bajjika – both milestones in systemic functional linguistics. The same is true even if we focus on a single language – even one that is as well described as Chinese, Japanese or English: there are many registers and dialects that have not yet been described. And there are areas where scientists have yet to tread because the theoretical and technological conditions have only just made systematic studies possible. For example, in investigating translation as process and product, we need the right combination of technology such as key stroke logging and eye movement tracking and theory such as SFL to get on with the task – the task addressed by the joint Universidade Federal de Minas Gerais and Universitat des Saarlandes research project.

4.4.2 Current frontiers

What are the frontiers of the development of SFL and what are the areas of particularly active research? With the help of recent edited surveys, it is possible to get a fairly comprehensive overview of where we are at: Hasan, Matthiessen, and Webster (2005, 2007) and Halliday and Webster (2009). To these, we can add recent handbooks and edited thematic volumes dealing with contributions to particular areas such as media linguistics and multisemiotic studies: see the Appendix for a survey of such recent contributions. In addition, new initiatives such as this volume will help the scholarly community keep up with current developments.

Another new initiative that will hopefully make it easier to track developments is the introduction of congress proceedings – as a complement to edited volumes appearing after congresses with selections of papers, pioneered first by Benson and Greaves (1985a, 1985b) and then by Hasan in the form of thematic volumes with additional thematic contributions (Hasan and Fries 1995; Hasan, Cloran, and Butt 1996; Hasan and Williams 1996).

In 2008, we organized and hosted ISFC 35, and we published the first volume of congress proceedings in time for the congress itself (Wu, Matthiessen, and Herke 2008), and this year, the second volume from ISFC 35 and the proceedings from ISFC 36 (Fang and Wu 2010) have been published. Proceedings and edited books complement one another: proceedings appear at the time of a conference or soon after and contain short contributions from all contributors; edited books appear after some interval of time and include a limited (and probably thematic) selection of longer contributions. This complementarity is quite new in SFL, but well established in other academic fields.

4.4.3 Gaps

As noted above, SFL has continued to expand its coverage. However, this expansion has, not surprisingly, been uneven: certain areas have been covered more systematically and completely than other areas.

In terms of descriptive coverage of languages, much work remains to be done, even on English, the language that has received most attention:

- In terms of **stratification**, lexicogrammar has been better covered than the strata of the expression plane (phonology and phonetics, graphology and graphetics) and it has been better covered than the upper stratum of the content plane, semantics. Similarly, language has been described more fully than context; thus while there are systemic functional accounts that can be seen as blueprints for 'reference grammars,' there are as yet no comparable blueprints for reference descriptions of semantics and of context.
- In terms of **rank**, the higher ranks within lexicogrammar (clause and group/phrase) have been described more fully than the lower ones (word

and morpheme); and the same is true of phonology: tone group and foot have been described in more detail than syllable and phoneme (although there are accounts of both syllabic and phonemic systems in different languages in Tench 1992b).

- In terms of **delicacy**, lower delicacy systems in lexicogrammar have been described with reasonable coverage but the push to increase the delicacy to the point where systems are delicate enough to reach lexis is a major undertaking (see e.g. Hasan 1987b; Tucker 1997b, 2007; Neale 2006; Matthiessen 2014b), and will require new descriptive techniques involving the automatic analysis of very large corpora (cf. Neale 2006).

The semiotic dimensions of stratification, rank and delicacy can be intersected with **metafunction** to form matrices that we can use to probe whether the coverage of the different metafunctions – ideational (experiential and logical modes), interpersonal and textual – is even across these different dimensions. Probing the different intersections, we find for example:

- that the description of experiential systems has been extended much further in delicacy than that of interpersonal systems and textual ones. It seems likely that textual systems are systemically 'shallower' than experiential ones; this relates to the fact that textual contrasts tend to be grammaticalized – as in the case of conjunctions, whereas experiential ones are both lexicalized and grammaticalized.
- that the description of semantic systems has arguably been developed most fully so far for the interpersonal metafunction – systems of speech function and negotiation more generally, whereas researchers have not yet proposed, or agreed on, extensive semantic systems for the textual metafunction.
- that the description of interpersonal systems whose terms tend to be realized by lexical rather than grammatical items – i.e. systems of appraisal concerned with connotative meaning (see Martin and White 2005) – can in principle be located within either lexicogrammar or semantics, If it is located within lexicogrammar, one would expect it to take the form of an elaboration in delicacy of grammatical interpersonal systems in the way that has been the case in accounts of experiential lexis (see e.g. Hasan 1987b; Tucker 1997a, 2007; Neal 2006; Matthiessen 2007c). If it is located within semantics, one would expect it to be an account of semantic ***strategies*** for evaluating, judging and so on involving both grammatical and lexical realizations; it would be a **strategic semantics** in the way that descriptions of speech functional systems are strategic in orientation. In either case, one interesting question is what the nature of the complementarity between

the lexicogrammatical and semantic interpretations of interpersonal assessment is.

The gaps mentioned above are descriptive ones – gaps in the descriptions of systems of particular languages. The task of filling such gaps is often simply one of rolling up one's sleeves and working hard to develop new descriptions based on the current theoretical framework. However, certain gaps may also need additional theoretical work before systematic description can be undertaken. For example, it is possible that the expansion of descriptions of textual semantic systems concerned with the 'swell of information' in text would be greatly facilitated by theoretical developments making it possible to represent options in the creation of this flow in terms of variable ranges of ideational and interpersonal meanings (cf. Matthiessen 1988a, on representational issues, and Bateman 1989, in relation to logical systems).

The gaps mentioned above are gaps in the descriptions of particular languages. There are, of course, also many gaps in the descriptions of sets of languages – descriptions of the kind needed to account for a person's potential for code switching and mixing, translation and interpreting, second/foreign language learning, i.e., descriptions involving some kind of multilingual meaning potential (see Bateman *et al.* 1991; Bateman, Matthiessen, and Zeng 1999); and also descriptions needed in comparative and typological research (cf. Matthiessen, Teruya, and Wu 2008, on the general field of multilingual studies).

4.5 Intellectual resonances

By an accident of history, the early development of (proto-) SFL took place during an intellectual period when developments within and outside linguistics tended in a very different direction. In the 1950s and the 1960s, scholars developed a number of related paradigms and theories that can be characterized as ***mainstream* cognitive science**. Cognitive science was developed originally by scholars from computer science and AI, psychology, philosophy and linguistics in the 1950s – including George Miller, Herbert Simon, Allen Newell, Marvin Minsky, and Noam Chomsky. It led to the development of various hyphenated versions of disciplines such as **cognitive psychology, cognitive anthropology** and **cognitive linguistics.**[12]

In linguistics, Chomsky and his colleagues and students developed successive versions of a formal theory under the general heading of generative linguistics (transformational grammar; standard theory, extended standard theory, government and binding, principles and parameters, the minimalist program) designed to address certain basic concerns within the Western philosophy of knowledge, relating to the debate between empiricism and rationalism, a key goal being to identify innate and therefore universal features of language.[13]

This led, among other things, to an increasingly wider divide between 'theoretical linguistics' and 'applied linguistics', the latter being disvalued by Chomsky and his followers, and between 'theoretical linguistics' and 'descriptive linguistics' (including the emergent techniques of corpus linguistics), the latter also being disvalued.

At the same time, US political, economic and military power continued to grow after the Second World War, as did its academic power – partly energized by European scholars who had to flee Europe during the war (what Watson 2001, has called 'Hitler's gift to America'), and funded by well-equipped US funding agencies, including military ones; so US-based scholars became more visible and internationally influential than before, and during this period Chomskyan linguistics moved to many parts of the world – exported together with other aspects of US culture (China being an important exception, since this was the period of the Cultural Revolution).

It was in this context that Halliday began to develop what turned into SFL. SFL clearly did not resonate with the development of cognitive science. Many of the central aspects of systemic functional linguistics were not in phase with the kind of formal linguistics that Chomsky and others developed in the 1950s and 1960s, nor with the general framework of cognitive science, so in a number of respects SFL developed on the ***periphery*** of linguistics.[14] Halliday and Chomsky were contemporaries, but came from very different linguistic traditions and backgrounds; and unlike many linguists in the 1960s, Halliday never set out to answer Chomsky's questions about language (although Hudson 1971, 1976, did in a way, in the early stages) but instead he pursued an agenda of 'socially accountable' linguistics (cf. Halliday 1984b).

However, since the 1960s, the environment in which SFL operates has changed rather dramatically. In work outside SFL, scholars have developed frameworks and approaches that are much closer to many of the central aspects of SFL, as illustrated in Table 4.1; there has thus been a growing **convergence** among a number of frameworks and approaches. For example, in his early description of Chinese, based on the *Secret History of the Mongols*, Halliday (1959) counted relative frequencies in the text and interpreted them as systemic probabilities: the probabilistic nature of the system of language has been part of systemic functional theory from the start. However, in the 1960s, Chomsky and his colleagues did not accept the corpus as a valid source of data, nor did they develop a probabilistic theory of language. Since then, the emergence of **corpus linguistics** – beginning in the 1960s

– and of **statistical NLP** (Natural Language Processing, e.g. Manning and Schütze 1999) – beginning in the late 1980s – have changed the situation rather dramatically, and the notion of **probabilistic linguistics** is now more widely accepted and is clearly articulated by the contributors to Bod, Hay and Jannedy (2003b). They do not make the connection with Halliday's pioneering work, nor with later work on text frequencies and systemic probabilities in SFL, but this is probably hardly surprising (though still to be regretted from a scholarly point of view); it is often the case in the history of ideas in linguistics that earlier contributors coming from different traditions do not get referred to when later contributors 'rediscover' their insights.[15]

The probabilistic interpretation of language is one of many areas of research where I would suggest that linguists working outside SFL are catching up with SFL. It is certainly the case that when we compare SFL with developments outside SFL around 2010, we find many resonances where none existed in the 1960s,

Table 4.1 SFL in relation to formal linguistics in the 1960s and to current developments outside SFL

	SFL	**Formal linguistics and related work in the 1960s**	**Current developments outside SFL**
Approach	Holistic approach	Cartesian analysis	Reinvigorated systems-thinking
Orientation	Social semiotics, language and the brain	Cognitive science, language and cognition	Social-interactionism, development of neuroscience
Axial orientation	Paradigmatic	Syntagmatic	Increasing value given to paradigmatic relations
Content plane	Lexicogrammar natural in relation to semantics	Autonomous syntax	Increasing value given to paradigmatic relations
Grammar and lexis relation	Related by delicacy within lexicogrammar continuum	Separate modules	Increasingly seen as continuous resource, e.g. in variants of 'construction grammar'
Syntax and lexis relation	Ranks within lexicogrammar	Separate modules	Natural phonology, autosegmental and metrical phonology
Source of 'data'	Corpora, naturally occurring texts	Constructed examples	Increasing reliance on corpora
Probabilistic nature of language	Probabilistic	Probabilities and frequencies seen as irrelevant	'Probabilistic linguistics'

as illustrated in Table 4,1. (To these illustrations, we could add many more, for example in the area of text and context or the increasing interest in longitudinal studies of second/foreign language learning (see e.g. Ortega and Byrnes 2008)). As indicated in the table, these resonances include not only developments in linguistics in particular but also more general academic trends. For example, the breakthroughs in neuroscience have paved the way for a rather dramatic change in the understanding of the relation between language and the brain, including both the role of co-evolution (e.g. Deacon 1992, 1997) and the role of social learning (e.g. Deacon 2010).

4.6 Conclusion: Challenges and opportunities

The resonances mentioned in the previous section provide systemic functional linguists with very exciting and promising **opportunities** to collaborate with researchers in branches of linguistics and in other disciplines that may previously have been less open to exchange and collaboration. This could boost developments in a number of areas, e.g. work on second/foreign language education (including 'SLA,' Second Language Acquisition research, based on the social-interactive turn, the bilingual turn and longitudinal case studies; see e.g. Ortega and Byrnes 2008; Byrnes 2006; Ortega 2009; Lantolf and Thorne 2006) and work on language typology (based on functional, meaning-oriented approaches drawing on evidence from discourse, including studies of grammaticalization; see e.g. Martin 1983b; Caffarel, Martin and Matthiessen 2004; Matthiessen, Teruya and Wu 2008).

We can interpret such opportunities within the framework of **SWOT analysis,** used in management and planning, and represent the dimensions of this analysis systemically: see Figure 4.7. There are two simultaneous systems concerned with factors influencing the development of SFL – polarity of factors and location of factors. On the one hand, the factors influencing the development may be either 'positive' or 'negative' – either enabling the development or constraining it. On the other hand, the factors influencing the development may be located either within SFL itself or in the environment in which SFL operates – either within the system of SFL or within its context 'positive' and 'internal' are '**strengths**', 'positive' and 'external' are '**opportunities**', 'negative' and 'internal' are '**weaknesses**', and 'negative' and 'external' are '**threats**.'

Based on the systems set out in Figure 4.7, we can thus explore the factors influencing the development of SFL: see Table 4.2. The **strengths** of SFL are all the properties that have kept attracting developers and users over the last six decades, including the comprehensive coverage of language, other denotative semiotic

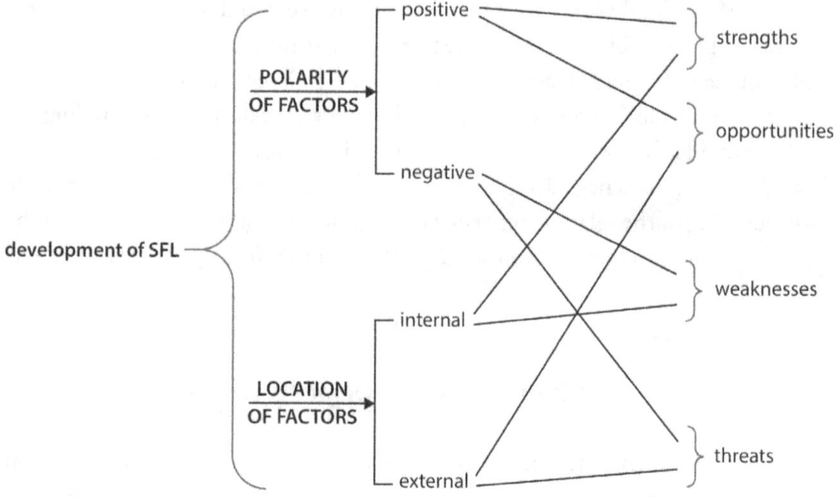

Figure 4.7 The development of SFL – SWOT analysis

systems and of the context of these denotative semiotic systems, the multidimensionality of the theory of these systems, the kind of systems-thinking about them that the multidimensional theory makes possible, the functional description and explanation of them, the growing range of often mutually relevant fields of activity and the resultant appliability of SFL combined with a strong sense of social accountability.

At the same time, there are **weaknesses.** As SFL gets deployed in a widening range of areas, there are centrifugal forces at work: researchers are likely to focus on those features of SFL that are relevant to the tasks at hand and to the colleagues from other disciplines who are concerned with the same tasks, while backgrounding other features of SFL. This is, in a sense, precisely what we would expect from what we know about register variation, except that we are now talking about register variation on a more abstract level, in the systemic functional 'metalanguage'.

There are two related dangers here. One is that increasing specialization is likely to lead to the fragmentation of knowledge, a development in science that the quantum physicist David Bohm warned about many years ago (Bohm 1980). The other is that as the areas of specialization become increasingly distinct – the relationships among them also become increasingly distant and also asymmetrical. For example, both educational linguistics and computational linguistics have been developing as areas of activity for a long time within SFL. My impression is that about a quarter of a century ago, they had a number of common concerns – e.g. the modelling of meaning or 'knowledge' in different domains, the role of grammatical metaphor in this modelling, and the representation of genre, but that since then they have moved further apart: while computational linguists in SFL keep referring to work in SFL educational linguistics, educational linguists in SFL do not engage with computational SFL, and they have moved further away from explicit concrete accounts of language towards more abstract ones relating to the sociology of knowledge (compare for example the contributions to the two seminal edited volumes in educational linguists published a decade apart, Christie and Martin 1997; Christie and Martin 2007).

Another area of weakness has to do with coverage and the relationship between description and analysis. One of the strengths of SFL is certainly its descriptive coverage – both in the sense of actual descriptions and in the sense of commitment to the value of large-scale descriptions. However, as already noted above, there are significant gaps in this coverage – perhaps particularly in the areas of semantics, context and phonology; and it is not clear that there is currently a concerted effort to fill these gaps in the way there was in the 1960s, 1970s, 1980s and into the 1990s. Instead, there has been an impressive accumulation of analyses of texts from different registers drawing on existing descriptions. This accumulation has been very valuable and has made possible many new projects in different areas of application; but the results of all these analyses have, on the whole, not informed the elaboration and extension of existing descriptions. In general, many more researchers have been involved in analytic projects than in descriptive ones. Apart from individual Ph.D. projects, there have not been many large-scale descriptive projects (with important exceptions, including the development of the Nigel and Cardiff computational grammars); and it seems that many more analysts are being trained than descriptivists.[16]

The **threats** that SFL faces are both general ones that virtually all academic disciplines are subject to at present and specific ones affecting SFL in particular. General threats include the increasing obsession with quantifying research – ranking universities, ranking journals, counting publications, counting citations, and so on. This is likely to flavour assembly line research and publication, making it harder to carry out more holistic longer-term projects. (However, at the same time, funding agencies are, ironically, also emphasizing high impact research focused on big themes.) Journal articles are already being assessed not according to the value of the research they report on but according to the ranking of the journals they appear in. This means that while SFL articles in *Functions of Language* are likely to be given reasonably high marks, SFL articles in more recently established journals which tend to publish systemic functional work such as *Linguistics and the Human Sciences* will not carry the same weight. Similarly, books and book chapters are

Table 4.2 The development of SFL – SWOT Analysis

	Positive	Negative
Internal	*Strengths* • comprehensiveness • multidimensionality • systems-thinking • functionality • range of fields of activity and multidisciplinary character • appliability • social accountability	*Weaknesses* • centrifugal forces and resultant fragmentation • uneven coverage and gaps • lack of large-scale descriptive projects • lack of automation of analysis • lack of feedback from analysis description
External	*Opportunities* • convergence towards SFL and new resonances between SFL work and non-SFL work • increasing value placed on addressing community needs • continued addition of new groups and communities around the world	*Threats* • development of standards for sharing not involving SFL • continued strengthening of centres at the expense of peripheries (e.g. associated with schemes for rating research and publications) • lack of uptake of SFL ideas and reinvention of SFL wheels • the different research agenda from that of more dominant traditions

likely to be assessed not according to the value of the research that they are concerned with but according to the status of the publisher. Citation indices are likely to favour European and North American publications, and the Web of Science is currently largely restricted to journal citations, so it gives a highly skewed – deeply flawed! – picture of SFL since many key contributions in SFL are published as book chapters or as books.

Threats of this kind affect most disciplines in one way or another, but there are also threats that affect SFL in particular. These have to do with developments in linguistics and natural language processing. On the one hand, a number of insights into language that used to be fairly unique to SFL – e.g. insights into the probabilistic nature of language, into the prosodic mode of phonological organization, into the continuity between lexis and grammar, into the natural relation between lexicogrammar and semantics, and into the centrality of text in context – have now emerged in other traditions, even within approaches with roots in formal linguistics (cf. e.g. Boas and Sag 2010). While these developments can be turned into opportunities, they can also be threats, since they may reduce the need that scholars feel to take account of SFL – even further. On the other hand, there has been a movement in linguistics and natural language processing towards the development of common standards to facilitate the sharing of large-scale resources such as corpora, tagged corpora and parsed corpora ('tree-banks'). This movement towards common standards will continue to facilitate research, but one undesirable side-effect is that approaches not using the standards will be sidelined – at least unless there is a straightforward way to convert into and out of the standard representation (see e.g. Teich, Watson and Pereira 2000, on the conversion between the 'widely used' TOBI annotation system and Halliday's systemic functional analysis).

Positive factors can, of course, be used to counter negative ones. For example, there is a movement also within SFL to provide a framework for sharing data (corpora, text archive), analyses, and computational tools (cf. O'Donnell 2009), including the new IRSFL initiative.[17] Using positive factors to counter negative ones is obviously crucially important for scholars and students around the world as they continue to develop SFL. And while one of the mega-threats to the continued development of leading ideas in science is the attempt to micro-manage research, it may still be helpful to explore the next three to thirty years using management and planning tools like SWOT analysis, harnessing them as friends rather than battling them as foes.

Notes

1 For technical terms, see e.g. Matthiessen, Teruya and Lam (2010).

2 Project overview at ISI: http://www.isi.edu/natural-language/penman/penman.html

3 KPML website: http://www.fblO.uni-bremen.de/anglistik/langpro/kpml/README.html

4 This is one of the reasons why the development of SFL has not been characterized by 'linguistic wars' of the kind that took place within generative linguistics around Chomsky in the second half of the 1960s and into the 1970s (e.g. Newmeyer 1980, chap. 5). Complementing this field-based reason are tenor-based ones, including an ethos in the systemic functional community of collaboration, support and respect for variation in approaches.

5 It is of course a variant of the approach that missionary linguists used up through the nineteenth century when they described languages spoken in areas that had been colonized by European powers based on the model of Latin (something that Tozzer 1921, warned against as late as two decades into the twentieth century) and the approach that formal linguists following Chomsky adopted using English as a model.

6 Also against the background of globalization – the research into call centre communication by Gail Forey, Jane Lockwood and their colleagues and students: http://www.engl.polyu.edu.hk/call_centre/default.html

7 Project website: http://www.glendon.yorku.ca/crlc/recherchepgindiv/Benson-projectdescription.html.

8 See e.g. http://fr46.uni-saarland de/index.php?id=probral

9 See: http://www.isfla.org/, http://www.isfla.org/Systemics/, and http://www.isfla.org/ Systemics/Associations/index.html

10 Institute website: http://www.santafe.edu/

11 From the Wikipedia (http://en.wikipedia.org/wiki/Ecolinguistics, viii/2010):

> Ecolinguistics emerged in the 1990s as a new paradigm of linguistic research which took into account not only the social context in which language is embedded, but also the ecological context in which societies are embedded. Michael Halliday's 1990 paper 'New ways of meaning: the challenge to applied linguistics' is often credited as a seminal work which provided the stimulus for linguists to consider the ecological context and consequences of language.

12 Two varieties of cognitive linguistics developed in the US. It may be helpful to associate them with the US coastlines – East Coast Cognitive Linguistics, developed by Ray Jackendoff; and West Coast Cognitive Linguistics, developed in two varieties, by George Lakoff at UC Berkeley and by Ron Langacker at UC San Diego. The latter are closer to SFL. However, there are of course also other currents in the development of cognitive linguistics.

13 Although he criticized American structuralist linguistics, Chomsky drew heavily on it. However, the concern with linguistic universals was not part of the American structuralist paradigm; it was an orientation that Roman Jakobson helped introduce into American linguistics after his arrival in the US during the war in the 1940s.

14 For an illuminating discussion of centres and peripheries in the development of 'knowledge,' see Burke (2000).

15 For comments in relation to the development of generative phonology, see Henderson (1987) – At a symposium on the history of phonology outside Paris in 1998, Halliday (2000b) presented a historical overview of systemic phonology. John Goldsmith presented a paper making the case for the incorporation of statistical statements in phonological accounts, noting that Roman Jakobson's suggestions in the middle of the twentieth century had not been followed up by generative phonologists. In the discussion session after his paper, Janet Pierrehumbert suggested that systemic phonology would be best suited to accommodate such information.

16 This is hardly surprising. In a BA or MA programme where SFL coexists with other interests and theoretical orientations, it is possible to bring students up to speed in text analysis by the end of the programme – helping them reach the point where they can use existing descriptions to analyse texts as part of an effort to solve some research problem. However, it is harder to take the next step within such a programme: to teach them to develop new descriptions based on the analysis of texts, or even to teach them to develop a new theory based on the description of languages. It would be interesting to have the opportunity to design a complete BA or MA SFL curriculum; I suspect nobody has been given this kind of exciting opportunity anywhere around the world.

17 Website: http://medien.gugw.tu-darmstadt.de/linglit/bartsch/irsfl/

Appendix: Areas of development

				SFL Companion	CDL	Handbooks	Edited overview volumes	Other reference sources
stratification	**context**			Hasan (2009): Context	Butt and Wegener (2007), Bowcher (2007)		Gladessy (1999)	
	semantics				Hasan *et al.* (2007b)	Martin and Rose (2003); Eggins and Slade (2005)		Cloran (1994); Halliday and Matthiessen (2006)
	lexicogrammar	*general*			Matthiessen (2007a)	Halliday and Matthiessen (2004)		
		grammatical metaphor					Simon-Vandenbergen, Tavermiers and Ravelli (2003); Martin and Veel (1998)	Halliday (1998); Halliday and Matthiessen (2006, chap. 6)
		grammar – lexis			Tucker (2007)			Tucker (1997b), Neale (2006)

	phonology				Greaves (2007)	Halliday and Greaves (2008); Tench (1996)	Tench (1992a); Bowcher and Smith (2014.); Matthiessen, Bowcher and Smith (in prep.)	
instantiation	**potential**				Hasan *et al.* (2007b) [semantics]			Bateman's KPML system
	subpotential/ instance type						Ghadessy (1988, 1993a); Christie and Martin (1997); Martin and Veel (1998); Halliday and Martin (1993)	
	instance			Martin (2009a); Discourse Studies; Wu (2009): Corpus Research	Cloran, Stuart-Smith and Young (2007)		Martin and Rose (2003) [semantics]; Eggins and Slade (2005)	Halliday and James (1993)

semogenesis	**phylogenesis**							Halliday (1988, 1995a); Matthiessen (2004b)
	ontogenesis			Painter (2009); Language Development	Painter, Derewianka and Torr (2007)		Williams and Lukin (2004)	Halliday (2004); Painter (1999)
	logogenesis							Matthiessen (2002a)
probability							Hunston and Thompson (2006)	
variation	**types of**					Gregory and Carroll (1978)		Gregory (1967), Hasan (1973), Halliday (1978)
	dialectal							
	codal							Hasan (1989)
	registerial				Williams (2005c)		Ghadessy (1988, 1993)	

metafunction	**logical**							Matthiessen (2002a)
	experiential							Halliday and Matthiessen (2006)
	interpersonal				Hood and Martin (2007)	Martin and White (2005)	Hunston and Thompson (2001)	
	textual				Thompson (2007)		Ghadessy (1995a); Hasan and Fries (1995)	
areas of activity	**wider registe-rial range**	**Educational linguistics**	***general***		Christie and Unsworth (2005)		Christie and Derewianka (2008); Christie and Martin (1997, 2009b); Hasan and Martin (1989)	
			literacy pedagogy		Martin and Rose (2005)			
			grammar education		Williams (2005a)			

			second/ foreign language education				Byrnes (2006, 2009); Schleppegrell and Colombi (2002)	
			content subjects			history: Coffin (2006), Schleppegrell (2004); geography: Humphrey (1996); science: Lemke (1990)		
		Clinical/ healthcare linguistics	***general***	Armstrong (2009); Clinical Applications		Asp and de Villiers (2010)		
			speech pathology		Armstrong *et al.* (2005)			
			psychiatry			Fine (2006)		
		Multilingual studies	**comparison and typology**		Teruya *et al.* (2007)			Matthiessen, Teruya and Wu (2008)

			transla-tion and interpreting		Steiner (2005)		Steiner and Yallop (2001)	
		Multisemiotic studies			Martinec (2005)	Kress and van Leeuwen (1996)	Royce and Bowcher (2006); Ventola, Charles and Kaltenbacher (2004), Ventola and Guijarro (2009)	
		Computational linguistics		Teich (2009): Computational linguistics	O'Donnell and Bateman (2005)			
		Language and other primates		Benson and Thibault (2009): Language and other primate species			Benson and Greaves (2009)	
	narrower reg-isterial range	**Artistic linguistics**	**verbal art**	Lukin and Butt (2009): Literary Stylistics	Lukin and Webster (2005)	Hasan (1985b)	Birch and O'Toole (1988)	

		Media Linguistics				Iedema, Feez and White (1994)	Thomson and White (2008)	
		Administrative Linguistics	*general*			Iedema (1995)		
			health care organization				Iedema (2007)	

Chapter 5
Halliday on language

5.1 Halliday on language: Introduction

In this third part of the Continuum Companion to M. A. K. Halliday, we are concerned with his **ideas about language** – which echoes Halliday ([1977a] 2003a), where he identifies two ideas about language that have been part of the engagement with language in Europe since Ancient Greece: language as **resource** and language as **rule**. His own engagement with language has been based on the conception of language as resource. However, before I proceed any further, let me provide a way into 'Halliday on language' drawing on my own personal experience since I think this can be a helpful way of shedding light on the fundamental nature of his contribution to our understanding of language.

While I was studying in high school (1972–1975), I started reading linguistics books because I was quite interested in language but also because I was very dissatisfied with the school grammars we were provided with for the various languages we studied: to me, they seemed unsystematic and fragmentary. Step by step I got hold of other books – for example, Jespersen's *Essentials of English Grammar*, which I found fascinating; but the two books that made the deepest impression on me were Bertil Malmberg's (1970) *Nya vägar inom språkveten-skapen* (literally, 'new paths in linguistics'; published in English as *New Trends in Linguistics*) and Alvar Ellegård's (1971) *Transformationell svensk-engelsk satslära* ('Transformational Swedish English syntax').

Malmberg's (1970) book, first published in 1959, provided a fascinating survey of different branches of linguistics before around 1960 (although later editions included an account of Chomsky's transformational grammar); but the part that intrigued me the most was his presentation of European structuralism – a theoretical development he was mainly responsible for introducing into Sweden, starting in the 1930s. The distinction between the **paradigmatic** axis and the **syntagmatic** one seemed like such a fundamental part of a theory of language.

Ellegård's (1971) book was also fascinating, and full of insight into syntactic structure: his introduction was in fact to a large extent based on generative semantics (as it had been developed in the second half of the 1960s by G. Lakoff, McCawley, Ross, Postal and others), so syntactic structures that had previously seemed purely syntactic could now be shown to be imbued with meaning – for example, the analysis of negation as a higher predicate (Ellegård 1971: 51, 55–58).

However, these two fundamental insights – the structuralist insight into the axial organization of language and the generativist insight into the semantic foundation of syntax – did not seem possible to reconcile. Malmberg's examples of axis were taken mostly from phonology (and he also discussed lexical fields), so there was no clue in his book; and Ellegård did not refer to the European structuralist tradition in his presentation. So I had found these two regions of fascinating insights into language, but they were completely disconnected: there was no bridge or tunnel to link them (at the time, the Danish and Swedish governments were still debating whether to connect the two countries by means of a bridge or a tunnel).

I had a gap year between high school and university – the year of military service all men in Sweden had to endure in those days; it was the worst year of my life so far, but luckily I had been able to sign up for a correspondence course in English at university level, and this kept me going during my dreadful year of military culture (later, I came to know men who'd gone through this kind of experience in e.g. Israel, Turkey and Singapore; I gradually realized that my experience had been like a school picnic!). One of the textbooks was John Lyons' (1968) *Theoretical Linguistics*. It wasn't exactly easy reading for someone who'd just left high school, but it was certainly very rewarding (anticipating certain later developments, like the interest in categorial grammar). However, his book didn't contain anything at all to address the troubling mystery I had been left with after reading Malmberg and Ellegård.

I can imagine that today I might have found answers to my questions very quickly by searching the World Wide Web; the breakthrough to easy access to information has been absolutely dramatic. But in those days, it took me quite a long time to find the answers. Once I had been liberated from my military service, I went on to study linguistics, English, Arabic and philosophy at Lund University. In our linguistics undergraduate programme, we were trained in the then current version of transformational grammar (the textbook was Akmajian and Henry, *An Introduction to the Principles of Transformational Syntax*) – Extended Standard Theory, which, being purely focused on syntactic form, was very disappointing to me after the insights into the semantics of syntax provided by Ellegård (1971); but we were encouraged to read widely and a number of our teachers were Ph.D. students, so we were infected with their excitement about being involved in research and discovery.[1] In the Department of English, I was introduced to work on cohesion, based on Halliday and Hasan's (1976) pioneering account of the textual resources for creating cohesive links. (And in the Department of Oriental Languages, I was told that Halliday's, 1956a, work on Chinese was very hard to understand, but definitely worthwhile!)

However, it was not until I came across Halliday's (1973) book with examples of system networks and realization statements that the puzzle that had mystified me since high school was solved – and as a bonus it also provided me with a sense of a comprehensive map of the lexicogrammatical resources of English in the form of a **function-rank matrix** (Halliday 1973: 141).

On the one hand, Halliday gave depth to the paradigmatic axis in the form of **system networks** – a totally new idea to me; and he showed how paradigmatic organization could in this way be extended far beyond the confines of phonological paradigms. On the other hand, terms in systems could have **realization statements** associated with them, and these realization statements turned out to be the bridge between the paradigmatic and syntagmatic axes that I had been looking for. I found the representation of linguistic resources by means of system networks very insightful; it revealed a form of organization that had remained hidden (later, I was able to understand this form of organization in terms of Bohm's, e.g. 1980, notion of **implicate order**), and this was reinforced when I got access to Halliday (1976) and to Halliday (1978).

In addition, of course, Halliday's work showed in a quite stunning way how grammatical structure was semantically natural (using terms that became more general by the mid-1980s): grammatical structure turned out to be **multilayered function** structure (also shown very clearly by Halliday [1970c] 2002c). This was reinforced by the work by Prague School linguists, much admired in the Linguistics Department of Lund University; one of the Ph.D. students, Milan Bílý, gave us first-hand insight into Functional Sentence Perspective.

Halliday's (1973) book thus contained the solution to a key problem that had been bothering me since high school; and more generally, this solution is one of the most fundamental contributions to our understanding of language in the last century or so – it was certainly a solution that Saussure had not been able to provide in his posthumous *Cours de Linguistique*.

Halliday's (1973) book also contained the key to another major theoretical issue in twentieth-century linguistics – the relationship between the equivalents of Saussure's *langue* and *parole* (and in another guise, between Chomsky's 'competence' and 'performance'). I don't think I had quite grasped that issue during my studies in the 1970s – although my struggle to understand the theories of Louis

Hjelmslev and (very importantly) Gustave Guillaume had prepared the ground for me; but later it became very clear to me (cf. Matthiessen 1993a).

The key, which he has spelt out in more detail since the early 1970s (e.g. Halliday [1991b] 2007a, [2002c] 2005b), was to theorize *langue* and *parole* not as different phenomena but rather as the outer poles of a cline – the **cline of instantiation.** These outer poles were conceptualized as **potential** and **instance**: language was seen as both system (meaning potential) and text (instances of meaning, i.e. acts of meaning), with texts **instantiating** the system. Intermediate between these outer poles, he located patterns of functional variation, **register variation,** and then also **codal variation,** further up the cline towards the potential pole (see Hasan 1973; Halliday [1994a] 2007b: 236–237; cf. Matthiessen 2007b, section 4.1.4). The significance of his cline of instantiation gradually became clear to me after I had become involved in a project concerned with the computational modelling of the generation of text; to model text generation, it is necessary to spell out how linguistic systems are instantiated in text (e.g. Matthiessen 1983b). However, Halliday's cline of instantiation is also very significant in another way: it is the missing link in linguistics between the domain of theory – the linguistic system – and the domain of data – texts instantiating the system; and sorting this out has become increasingly important with the development of vast sources of data in the form of corpora and methods of automated analysis in the form of corpus tools.

Up through 1979, my experience had been with Halliday on paper; but around February 1980, I had the good fortune to meet him and Ruqaiya Hasan at Stanford University, purely by chance; and later in the first half of 1980, I attended a ten-week seminar he gave at UC Irvine, at the invitation of Benjamin Colby, in anthropology. By the time I had the chance to listen to his weekly lectures, I had had the opportunity to listen to talks and lectures by a number of great linguists (Los Angeles was, of course full of them, at UCLA and USC; and in December 1979, the annual LSA meeting was held in LA), ranging from say André Martinet to Jim McCawley. What struck me so profoundly about Michael Halliday's lectures was that I was given, for the first time, a holistic deep insight into what kind of resource language is (cf. Hasan 1984d). By then, I had learned the scholarly games of doing linguistics; he cut through all that and gave me a sense of the overall organization of language – what I had been looking for since high school.

Having sketched some aspects of my own personal experience of discovering Halliday's ideas about language, let me now take a step back and discuss 'Halliday on language' more systematically.

5.2 Language as resource

When scholars develop theories of language, the nature of each theory depends on their ***conception of the nature of language*** upon which it is based. For example, if language is conceived of as an inventory of 'words', the theory is likely to be based on lexis in the first instance, and the primary source of data is likely to be corpora explored by means of standard lexis-oriented corpus tools such as concordancing programmes (cf. Halliday [2002a] 2005b). More generally, if we take a step back in order to be able to survey ideas about language and to discern the major motifs in the development of such ideas in the Western tradition, we can identify two very different conceptions of language. They have been discussed by Halliday ([1977a] 2003a) and Seuren (1998) under different headings. Halliday's earlier account is reinforced by Seuren's much longer overview of the development of Western Linguistics. I will start with Halliday's account.

Halliday ([1977a] 2003a) shows that when children begin to learn language, their conception of language is as a **resource** – a resource for making meaning. Learning language for them is thus 'learning how to mean' (e.g. Halliday 1975) – building up the resources for making meaning. However, when children enter school, they are likely to meet a different image of language, language as **rule**; in school, 'language will be not a set of resources but a set of rules' (Halliday [1977a] 2003a: 94). Halliday ([1977a] 2003a: 94) calls this the 'folk linguistics of the classroom', characterized by 'its categories and classes, its rules and regulations, its do's and, above all, its don'ts'. He goes on to show that these two ideas about language have been present in Western Linguistics since Ancient Greek, with early versions of the resource view being developed by the sophists and of the rule view by Aristotle (Halliday [1977a] 2003a: 99–100):

> We can follow these two strands throughout the subsequent history of ideas about language in the west. The one stems from Aristotle; it is 'analogist' in character, based on the conception of language as rule, and it embeds the study of language in philosophy and logic. The other has, for us today, less clearly defined origins, but it can probably be traced to Protagoras and the sophists, via Plato; it is 'anomalist' in character, and has a marked element of Stoic thought in it. It is not philosophical (the Stoics were the earliest scholars explicitly to separate linguistics from philosophy, and grammar from logic) but rather descriptive, or to use another term, ethnographic; and the organizing concept is not that of **rule** but of **resource**. [...]

> We can identify, broadly, two images of language: a philosophical logical view, and a descriptive – ethnographic view. In the former, linguistics is part of philosophy, and grammar is part of logic; in the latter, linguistics is part of anthropology, and grammar is part of culture. The former stresses analogy; is prescriptive, or normative, in orientation; and concerned with meaning in relation to truth. The latter stresses anomaly; is descriptive in orientation; and concerned with meaning in relation to rhetorical function. The former sees language as thought, the latter sees language as action. The former represents language as rules; it stresses the formal analysis of sentences, and uses for purposes of idealization (for deciding what falls within or outside its scope) the criterion of grammaticality (what is, or is not, according to the rule). The latter represents language as choices, or as a resource; it stresses the semantic interpretation of discourse, and uses for idealization purposes, the criterion of acceptability or usage (what occurs or could be envisaged to occur).

Building on Halliday's characterization of the two images of language that have run as strands through Western Linguistics, language as resource and language as rule, let me summarize and elaborate his account in tabular form: see Table 5.1. When language is conceived of as resource, theories based on this image are **functional** ones; but when language is conceived of as rule, theories are **formal** ones.

Halliday's ([1977a] 2003a) contrast between 'language as resource' and 'language as rule', investigated in functional and formal theories, respectively, is reinforced by Seuren's (1998: 25–27) very similar or even identical contrast between approaches to language that he characterizes as '**ecologism**' and '**formalism**', though without a reference to Halliday's discussion. After introducing early engagements with language in Ancient Greece, Seuren (1998: 23) takes a step back to identify these two traditions in the history of Western Linguistics:

> We thus see the outlines of two different traditions emerging in Antiquity. On the one hand, there is the tradition that developed along Heraclitean, Platonic and Stoic lines. On the other hand, there is the tradition of Aristotle and the Alexandrine philologists.

Table 5.1 Language as resource and language as rule, theorized in functional and formal theories, respectively

	functional theories	**formal theories**
(i) conception of language	***resource*** (Halliday 1977a; Hasan 1984d)	***rule***
(ii) relationship of grammar to semantics	***natural*** (Halliday 1994c; Halliday and Matthiessen 1999; cf. Haiman 1985)	***arbitrary and autonomous*** ['standard theory', but increasingly challenged today]
(iii) principle of grammatical 'modularity'	***metafunction*** – ideational [logical & experiential], interpersonal, textual], with no componential boundary between syntax and morphology (grammar = 'morpho-*syntax'*) (Halliday 1967c,d/8; 1978; 1994b)	***constituency*** – yielding at least two components: syntax and morphology
(iv) principle of linguistic organization	***paradigmatic***: system is the fundamental mode of organization (Halliday 1966b, 1969; Hasan 1996a, chap. 5; Martin 1992a; Matthiessen 1995b)	***syntagmatic***: structure is the fundamental mode of organization
(v) relationship between grammar and lexis	***continuous***: grammar and lexis are not different phenomena, but rather different perspectives on the same phenomenon (Halliday 1961; Hasan 1996b, chap. 4; Martin 1992a: 277–86)	***modular***: syntax, morphology and the lexicon are different modules, but challenged more recently in construction-based approaches
(vi) relationship between 'system' and 'text'	***one phenomenon – continuum***: system and text are conceptualized as different 'phases' of the same phenomenon, related by the cline of instantiation as potential to instance (Halliday 1991b, 2002e); the focus is on both system and text (seen as poles on a cline), with high value on naturally occurring text instances (hence corpus methods)	***distinct phenomena – dichotomy***: system and text are conceptualized as distinct phenomena, in terms of competence and performance, respectively (different from but recalling Saussure's dichotomy of langue and parole); the focus is on the system, typically with evidence from constructed examples, but now increasingly also with corpus evidence
(vii) fundamental questions for theory	large number derived from ***a wide range of contexts*** – linguistic, computational, educational, clinical, stylistic, etc., so highly powerful, ***flexible theory*** (Halliday 1980a)	small number derived ***from the context of Western philosophy*** concerning the nature and source of knowledge (the issue of innateness in the context of empiricism vs rationalism), so highly dedicated, ***constrained theory***

(viii) relationship between theory and application	***no clear distinction***, with theory and application in ongoing dialogue; both are part of ***appliable linguistics*** (Halliday 1985a, 2002e)	***sharp distinction***, with formal theory within ***theoretical linguistics*** clearly separated from ***applied linguistics***
(ix) disciplinary orientation	***social semiotics*** and ***general systems theory*** as transdisciplinary formations; sociology, ethnography, education, stylistics (Halliday 1978)	***cognitive science*** as macro-disciplinary formation and within that cognitive psychology, natural language philosophy, philosophy of mind
(x) mode of development	***evolution***, building on immediate predecessors including earlier versions of itself	***revolution***, discarding immediate predecessors or even earlier versions of itself
(xi) coverage of language in descriptions	high priority on ***comprehensiveness*** in coverage (hence value on large corpora)	tendency towards ***fragments*** selected to probe theoretical issues (as in Montague grammar)
Examples	Halliday's (1950s –) systemic functional theory;	Chomsky's (1950s –) generative theories: phrase structure grammar, transformational grammar, standard theory, extended standard theory, government and binding, principles and parameters, minimalist programme
	Other functional approaches: Prague School functionalism; Dik's functional grammar; West-Coast functionalism; Okuda's functional approach in Japan	**Formalist alternatives to Chomsky**: generative semantics, Montague grammar, lexical functional grammar (LFG), generalized phrase structure grammar (GPSG), head-driven phrase structure grammar (HPSG)

Later he emphasizes the difference between these two approaches in terms of their ***methods*** (Seuren 1998: 25):

> The point is one of method. It concerns the way in which linguistic theorists deal with the facts of language. Two main approaches can be distinguished in this respect, which we shall dub **ecologism** and **formalism.** [...] For the formalists, language is a formal system describable in terms of rule [...] In the ecological approach, on the other hand, language is primarily seen as a product of nature, and hence an object for empirical research.

Table 5.2 Seuren's (1998) characterization of ecological and formalist approaches to language

	Ecologism [i.e. functional theories]	**Formalism [i.e. formal theories]**
Early manifestation	Ancient **anomalists** ["lovers of exceptions"]	Ancient **analogists** ["lovers of regularity"]
General	"...Language is primarily seen as a **product of nature**, and hence as an object for empirical research. The expectation is that language, like nature, will manifest itself in all kinds of unexpected variations on and deviations from an as yet largely unknown rule or norm system." [p. 25]	"Language is a **formal system** describable in terms of rules for the acoustic or visual expression of meanings, and whatever appears to go against the system tends to be regarded as a nuisance, attributable to deplorable interference from outside sources. ... They prefer to approach the task of analysing language with a formal system that has been developed elsewhere, usually in logic or mathematics, and then to impose their a priori, preconceived system on what they perceive as the facts of language." [p. 25]
Merits	"The ecologists ... have the experience, the familiarity with the **data**, and the general knowledge of the terrain required for a judicious selection of a hypothesis that may have a reasonable chance of success." [p. 26]	"Formalism gives the linguist a better awareness of the **properties**, mathematical and other, of the descriptive and analytical system he is using." [p. 26]
Drawbacks	"The ecologist runs the risk of ecologism [i.e. functional theories] becoming an antitheorist, rejecting anything formal and concentrating entirely on data collecting, without any theoretical perspective. Some ecologists have been seen to reject the very notion of an underlying system, on the pretext that the use of language is 'free' and 'creative', in some ill-defined sense."	"The formalist risks becoming formalism [i.e. formal theories] blinkered by the mathematics of his system, losing sight of the reality the system should be about." [p. 26]

Ecologism corresponds to functional theories in Table 5.1, and formalism to formal theories. I have summarized his characterizations of these two approaches in Table 5.2.

With respect to the role of description in Chomsky's influential version of formal theory, Seuren (1998: 252) notes:

> The paucity of Chomsky's actual grammatical analyses and descriptions is surprising for someone who has written so much on linguistics. Ironically, the only two thorough pieces of analysis produced by Chomsky to date are in morphophonemics (his 1951 MA dissertation

> on the Morphophonemics of Modern Hebrew) and, together with Halle, in phonology (Chomsky and Halle 1968). In syntax there is not a single instance of anything approaching a thorough treatment of a construction or set of constructions in English or any other language. Hosts of general principles and constraints have seen the light in endless succession, but no actual analysis or description. All work of that nature produced within the confines of Chomsky inspired grammar came from others, who then invariably found that the principles and constraints could not be maintained. Cp. Postal in Huck and Goldsmith (1995: 142)...
>
> The significant point is then that there is an extraordinary contrast between the paucity of genuine results in Chomskyan linguistics and the forests of paper which have been, and continue to be, devoted to the linguistic ideas involved.

In the same way, in his article on the 'failure of generative grammar', Gross (1979), who had written about mathematical linguistics and worked with natural language processing (e.g. Gross 1972) and came to use corpora in linguistic research, makes a very similar point about the lack of descriptive coverage in generative grammar, suggesting that Stockwell, Schachter and Partee's (1973) (in my view) valiant and valuable effort to integrate transformational grammar descriptions[2] did not in fact constitute an integrated account comparable to traditional reference grammars. Seuren's (1998) assessment may be compared with Halliday's (1985a/1994c: xxxiv) comment on twentieth-century linguistics:

> Twentieth century linguistics has produced an abundance of new theories, but it has tended to wrap old descriptions up inside them; what are needed now are new descriptions.

And Halliday ([1992c] 2005b: 76) reinforces this point, based on his personal research experience:

> It has always seemed to me, ever since I first tried to become a grammarian, that grammar was a subject with too much theory and too little data. [...] Back in 1949, when under the guidance of my teacher Wang Li I first put together a corpus of Cantonese sentences in order to study the grammar of the dialects of the Pearl River Delta (Wang Li was then conducting a survey of their phonology), I was struck by how little was known about how people actually talked.

In this context, McEnery and Hardie's (2011: Section 1.5) comments on Chomsky (1965) are also worth noting:

> In Chomsky (1965), twenty-four invented sentences are analysed; in the parsed version of LOB, a million words are annotated with parse trees.

Clearly, a great deal has happened in formal linguistics since the 1970s; and one aspect of these developments is a far greater commitment within certain frameworks with roots in the formal tradition to comprehensive descriptions – as in work based on HPSG (particularly at the CSLI Linguistic Grammars Online Lab at Stanford University; see e.g. Copestake and Flickinger 2000). One reason for this was the increasing need for comprehensive descriptions in Natural Language Processing, starting in the late 1980s.[3]

Seuren's (1998) account of 'ecologism' and 'formalism' is balanced; he identifies 'merits' and 'drawbacks' with both approaches. Halliday's systemic functional linguistics is certainly a contribution within the ecological tradition; but it is interesting to explore where Halliday's development of SFL based on his 'ideas about language' is located in relation to these merits and drawbacks. This is actually quite revealing:

- In terms of the 'merits' of the formalist approach, it is important to note that Halliday has always been concerned with the properties of language in general, distinguishing very clearly between the theory of language as a general human semiotic system and descriptions of particular languages (e.g. Halliday [1992f] 2003a: 201–203, [1996] 2002c); and this concern has, of course, been brought out in particular in the research context of computational modelling (see e.g. Matthiessen and Bateman 1991) but also in language description, comparison and typology (see e.g. Caffarel, Martin and Matthiessen 2004).
- In terms of the 'drawbacks' of the ecologist approach, it is equally important to note that Halliday has always been concerned with theory – he has never been 'antitheorist', as is very clear from his comments throughout the last half century or so (e.g. Halliday [1961] 2002c, 2005a, [1996] 2002c, [2002e] 2005b; and cf. Matthiessen and Nesbitt 1996).

As far as the ecologist's 'risk of becoming antitheorist' is concerned, the antitheoretical stance has been a motif in certain areas of 'corpus linguistics', often associated with 'corpus-driven' as opposed to 'corpus-based methodology' – a motif that is explored and criticized by McEnery and Hardie (2011: Section 1.3 and chapter 6), who reject the distinction between 'corpus-based' and 'corpus-driven' linguistics.

Functional theories and formal ones have tended to be developed as mutually exclusive alternatives – as a thesis-&-antithesis pair; but they are, in principle, complementary rather than contradictory forms of theory, foregrounding different aspects of the vastly complex system of language. Halliday ([1992f] 2003a: 203) articulates the distinction between formal vs functional grammars in terms of his principle of **trinocularity** (e.g. Halliday 1978, [1996] 2002c; Halliday and Matthiessen 2004; Matthiessen 1995b) whereby grammatical categories are identified and characterized: (i) 'from above'; from the level of semantics; (ii) 'from roundabout', from the level of lexicogrammar in terms of patterns of agnation; and (iii) 'from below', from lower ranks within lexicogrammar and the level of phonology (as illustrated by Figure 5.1):

> In a formal grammar, perspective (iii) has priority; (i) is derived from (iii) and may not be stated at all (e.g. in some formal grammars the category corresponding to Subject in English would have no interpretation from above). In a functional grammar, such as systemic grammar, (i) has priority, and (iii) will typically be derived from it.

Since functional and formal theories are, in principle, complementary, it should be possible to develop a synthesis embodying both functional and formal insights into language. What would such a synthesis look like, and where is Halliday's systemic functional theory of language located within the overall landscape of theories of language?

Halliday's theory has certainly emerged out of the tradition of functional theories developed by 'ecologists' rather than 'formalists'. He has drawn on functional theories in linguistics (including centrally Firth's system-structure theory [see Butt 2001; Kachru 2015] and Prague School functionalism [see Halliday 1974b; Davidse 1986]) and in anthropological linguistics (the Sapir-Whorf tradition), and also on functional theories in anthropology (Malinowski's functional anthropology with its emphasis on text in context; cf. Hasan 1985c). Here Hjelmslev's (e.g. 1943) relational conception of language was important, with Lamb's (1966, 1999) work, inspired by Hjelmslev, on (what was originally called) stratificational linguistics as a key reference point.

At the same time, unlike many functional linguists, Halliday has developed representations of key aspects of his theory – system networks (representing the theory of the paradigmatic organization of language), realization statements (representing the theory of the relationship between paradigmatic organization and syntagmatic organization) and structural box diagrams (representing the theory of function structure as syntagmatic organization – e.g. Halliday ([1996] 2002c,

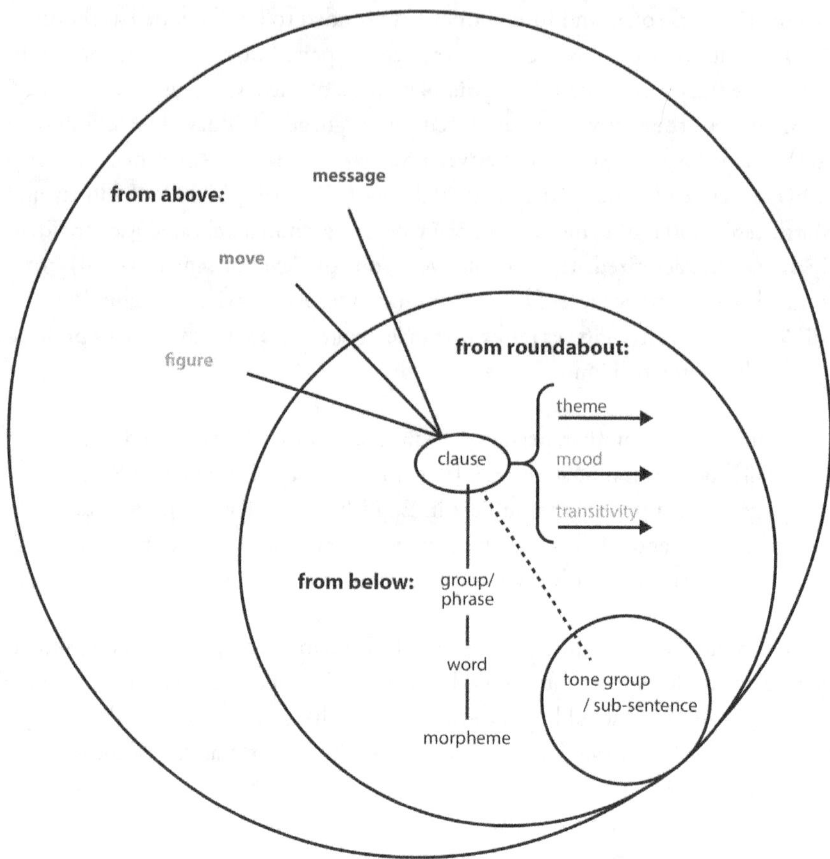

Figure 5.1 The clause viewed trinocularly – (a) 'from above' (semantics); (b) 'from roundabout' (lexicogrammatical agnation patterns); and (c) 'from below' (lower-ranking grammar, and phonology)

1976, 1978, 1985a, [2002e] 2005b), and used them in computational linguistic research that he has been involved in. Computational applications have in fact been an important area of systemic functional research involving a number of researchers from backgrounds in both linguistics and computer science (see e.g. Winograd 1983: chap. 6; Matthiessen and Bateman 1991; Teich 1999; O'Donnell and Bateman 2005; Teich 2009); and in the context of computational applications, researchers have explored system networks in more formal terms (e.g. Patten and Ritchie 1987; Mellish 1988; Bateman, Emele and Momma 1992).

Thus we can see that while systemic functional theory is a full-fledged ***functional*** theory of language, it also has characteristics normally associated with *formal* theories rather than functional ones;[4] and one could argue that this would mean that it would be treated as 'taboo' based on Mary Douglas' (e.g. 1966) experiential account of taboo as a way of dealing with taxonomic conflicts in folk taxonomies, with anomalies in classifications: the taxonomic clash inherent in a category can be resolved interpersonally by making it taboo; systemic functional theory would thus join the company of shellfish and pigs.[5]

In fact, in the area of grammar, if we view the theory 'from below', from the vantage point of types of representation that are used to formalize aspects of the theory, we can recognize a **family of grammars** with similar properties that includes systemic functional grammar (SFG), Kay's (e.g. 1979) Functional Unification Grammar (FUG), Bresnan and Kaplan's Lexical Functional Grammar (LFG), Pollard and Sag's Head-driven Phrase Structure Grammar (HPSG), Sag's Sign-Based Construction Grammar (SBCG), Categorial Grammar (CG), and also Joshi's Tree Adjoining Grammar (TAG). These have been called **unification grammars** (e.g. Sag *et al.* 1986; Shieber 1986) or **feature and function grammars** (Winograd 1983: chap. 6). Sag *et al.* (1986: 238) characterize the family of unification grammars as follows:

> In such theories the linguistic objects under study are associated with linguistic information about the objects, which information is modeled by mathematical objects called **feature structures**. Linguistic phenomena are modeled by constraints of equality over the feature structures; the fundamental operation upon the feature structures, allowing solution of such systems of equation, is a simple merging of their information content called **unification.**

The work by Kasper (e.g. 1988b) provides a bridge between formalisms used in unification grammars and SFG (for example, one manifestation of unification in SFG is 'conflation').

It would take too long to explore the location of SFG in the family of unification grammars, but let me instead locate it diagrammatically in relation to other members of this family and in relation to a selection of formal and functional theories of grammar: Figure 5.2. Halliday's theory of grammar and his description of the grammar of English influenced Martin Kay in his development of what he came to call Functional Unification Grammar (see e.g. his descriptive examples in Kay 1979), but, working with Ron Kaplan at Xerox PARC, Kay also drew on the notion of registers from Augmented Transition Networks (for part of the history, see Kay 1994). In turn, Kaplan worked with Joan Bresnan to develop what came to be known as Lexical Functional Grammar, and in this way LFG was also influenced by Halliday's SFG.[6]

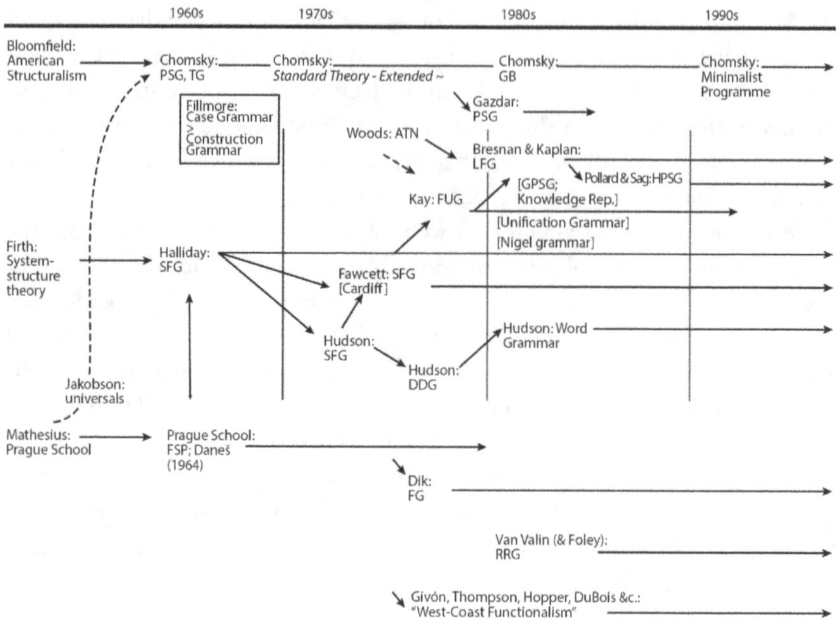

Figure 5.2 Systemic Functional Grammar in relation to the development of functional and formal theories of grammar

One difference between SFG and other members of the family is the primacy given in SFG to the paradigmatic axis, represented by means of system networks (e.g. Halliday [1966b] 2002c). This form of organization has been explored in other unification frameworks, as in Elhadad's (e.g. 1990) use of typed features. The primacy given to the paradigmatic axis in systemic functional theory is not restricted to the theory of grammar; it applies to the theory of all the subsystems of language: semantics, phonology and phonetics also have a paradigmatic 'base'. This orientation towards the paradigmatic axis differentiates systemic functional theory not only from other members of the unification grammar family but also from other functional theories. (Formal theories tend to be very strongly oriented towards the syntagmatic axis, as part of their conception of language as rule.) So let me now turn to this central feature of Halliday's theory of language.

5.3 The axial rethink

The orientation towards the paradigmatic axis that Halliday developed in the first half of the 1960s can be characterized as an **axial rethink**. In the European tradition of structuralist theories, the paradigmatic and syntagmatic axes tended to be given equal weight, balanced as the axis of choice and the axis of chain; and this was certainly the case in Firth's (e.g. 1957b) **system-structure theory**: systems were located within places in the structures of units (see e.g. Fischer-Jørgensen 1975; Dineen 1967; Catford 1969; de Beaugrande 1991: chap. 8; Butt 2001); as Catford (1969: 225) puts it:

> Firth made explicit for both grammar and phonology a useful distinction not always observed by European 'structuralists' – namely, the distinction between *structure* and *system*.
>
> Structure is a syntagmatic ordering of elements; systems are the paradigmatic sets of units which can replace each other at any place, or element, in a structure. In simpler terms, structures may be thought of as a 'horizontal' ordering of elements; systems, as a 'vertical' set of terms or units which can occur at any given place in structure. Thus, in phonology, *C1VC2* (initial consonant – vowel – final consonant) is a *structure*, exemplified in English by such words as *pit, bit, pin, pen*; whereas the sets of specific consonantal or vocalic units which may occur at *C1*, *V*, or *C2* are systems (thus in English we have a system of initial consonants: p, b, t, d, k, g, ...; a system of vowels: i, e, ae, ...).

What Halliday (e.g. [1966b] 2002c, [1969] 2005c, 1976, 2013a) did was in essence to free systems from particular places in the structure of units and give them whole units as their domains of operation.[7] As a result, systems could be organized into **system networks** – networks of simultaneous systems (like Mood type: indicative/imperative and process type: material/behavioural/mental/verbal/relational/existential) and of systems ordered in delicacy (like mood type: indicative/imperative and indicative type: declarative/interrogative, with indicative as its entry condition). In addition, **terms** in systems could have associated realization **statements** (like declarative Subject ^ Finite – the systemic term 'declarative' is realized syntagmatically by the [specification of] the sequence of Subject followed by Finite); in other words, syntagmatic patterns were specified in paradigmatic contexts as realizations of systemic terms, as shown in Figure 5.3. Here is a key passage from Halliday ([1966b] 2002c: 111–112):

> Systemic description may be thought of as complementary to structural description, the one concerned with paradigmatic and the other with syntagmatic relations. On the other hand it might be useful to consider some possible consequences of regarding systemic

> description as the underlying form of representation, if it turned out that the structural description could be shown to be derivable from it. In that case structure would be fully predictable, and the form of a structural representation could be considered in the light of this. [...] What is being considered ... is that the part of the grammar which is as it were 'closest to' the semantics may be represented in terms of systemic features.

His suggestion 'on the other hand it might be useful to consider some possible consequences of regarding systemic description as the underlying form of representation' represents a fundamental reconceptualization of the relation between the paradigmatic axis and the syntagmatic one. This axial rethink is a natural consequence of the conception of language as resource: to bring out the nature of language as resource, we can model it as choice – as paradigmatic options, treating syntagmatic patterns as realizations of one or more paradigmatic options.

System networks thus represent the overall, **global** organization of a given linguistic domain such as a unit of phonology or lexicogrammar, or a unit complex. This aspect of the axial rethink is brought out by Halliday ([1997] 2003a: 249):

> I have always felt it important to try to view a language as a whole, to get a sense of its total potential as a meaning-making resource. This is not to imply that a language is some kind of a mechanical construct all of whose parts come together in a perfect fit, any more than if you try to see a human body as a whole you are conceiving of it as an

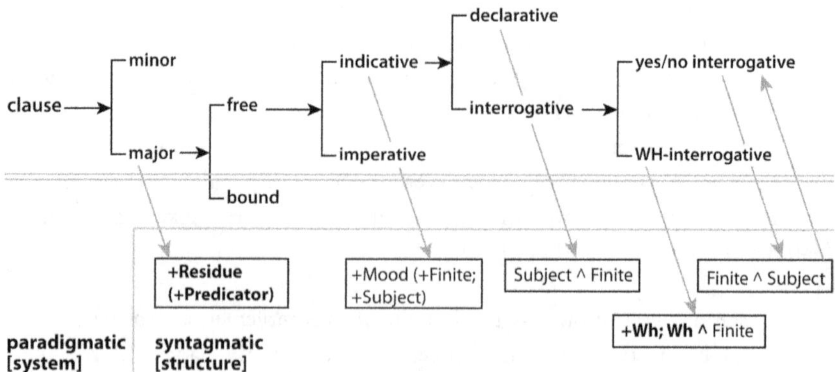

Figure 5.3 Simplified system network of mood (paradigmatic) with realization statements (syntagmatic)

> idealized machine. Indeed it is precisely because the human body is not a mechanical assemblage of parts that it is important to view it paradigmatically as well as syntagmatically (to view it panaxially, if you like); and the same consideration applies to language.

In the system network, systems have intrinsic ordering: they are either dependent on one another in delicacy (as illustrated by the system network of mood shown in Figure 5.3), or else simultaneous in delicacy (as illustrated by the system network of the tone group in Figure 5.8); there is no extrinsic ordering of systems: simultaneous systems would in principle be processed in parallel in a model of the traversal of system networks in generation or analysis (see e.g. Matthiessen and Bateman 1991: chap. 10).

Realization statements are distributed across the system network, but each individual realization statement is local to a term in a particular system; its environment is thus paradigmatic, not syntagmatic. By virtue of the fact that systems are ordered in delicacy, the systemic environments of realization statements are ordered in delicacy: a given realization statement will specify exactly what is appropriate at a given point in delicacy, no more, no less. For example, the ***presence*** of Subject and Finite in the interpersonal structure of the clause is specified in the environment of 'indicative' – +Finite, +Subject. At that point, the ***ordering*** of these two elements is not specified because it could in fact be either Subject ^ Finite or Finite ^ Subject; these relative sequences are specified in systems of greater delicacy: declarative ↘ Subject ^ Finite (in INDICATIVE type) and yes/no ↘ Finite ^ Subject (in INTERROGATIVE type). Consequently, the problem of over-specification never arises; it was a characteristic problem in generative accounts based on syntagmatic rules in the 1960s (before many generative linguists moved to more declarative forms of representation, one source of influence being Halliday's systemic functional grammar: cf. the introduction to Section 4, and Section 2, Note 5).

The same applies to phonological system networks with realization statements. Phonological units serving in the structure of a higher-ranking unit, for example phonemes serving in the structure of syllables are never overspecified; they are only specified up to the appropriate degree of delicacy. This is of course possible because all phonological units (say, tone groups – feet – syllables – phonemes) are systemicized, i.e. represented systemically by system networks. Thus a phoneme is simply the syntagmatic realization of a combination of terms in phonemic systems, and a preselection from the unit above on the phonological rank scale, the syllable, can refer to any of these terms in phonemic systems. For example, if a syllable in Akan selects for 'nasal closure' : 'velar closure' : 'vocalic', the Peak of that syllable is preselected to be a phoneme with the features 'high' and 'back', but other features are left unspecified (e.g. 'advanced' [tongue root]/'neutral'). (For the systemic description of the phonology of Akan, see Matthiessen 1987a.)

If we compare the hierarchy of axis to the hierarchy of stratification, then it seems clear that the paradigmatic axis is analogous to a higher stratum and the syntagmatic axis to a lower one.[8] Like a higher stratum in relation to a lower one, it provides the environment in which the lower patterns operate. In this sense, the paradigmatic axis of a lower stratum mediates between that stratum and the stratum next above, as is illustrated within the content plane for semantics and lexicogrammar in Figure 5.4. Lexicogrammar is of course related to semantics in terms of both system and structure – as becomes very clear when we model the relationship explicitly for the purpose of computational modelling (e.g. Matthiessen and Bateman 1991; Halliday and Matthiessen 1999). However, it is the paradigmatic axis – the systemic organization of a given stratum – that organizes the relationship to the stratum next above.

Descriptions are thus organized or shaped systemically rather than structurally: structural descriptions are, as we have seen, contextualized by systemic ones. This does not mean that structural descriptions in lexicogrammar are not related to semantic ones – they are, and they must be (as is clear from Matthiessen and Bateman 1991; Halliday and Matthiessen 1999); but it is the paradigmatic axis that *organizes* the interface between semantics and lexicogrammar (whether we approach this interface 'from above' or 'from below'; cf. Matthiessen 1990), also insofar as the syntagmatic axis is concerned. By the same token, lexicogrammatical

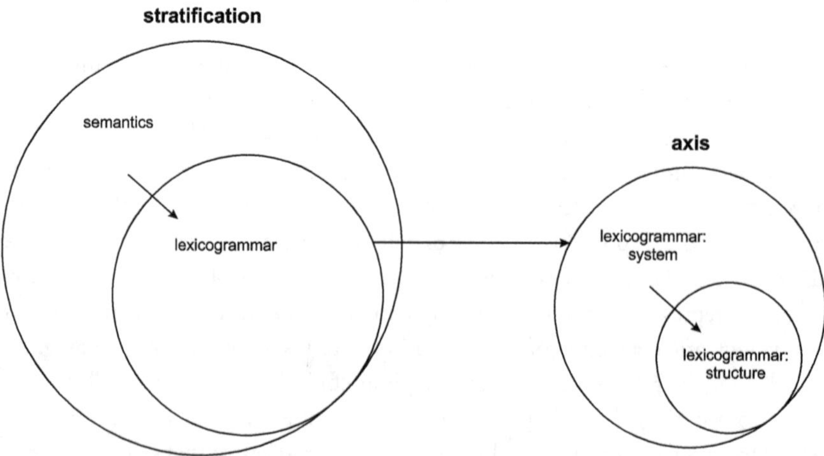

Figure 5.4 The hierarchies of stratification (global) and of axis (local)

structure interfaces with phonology; for example, the information structure of the information unit is realized by the structure of the tone group (see Halliday and Greaves 2008).

The paradigmatic axis and the syntagmatic axis are both forms of order in language – implicate order and explicate order, respectively, to draw on the distinction proposed and elaborated for physical systems by Bohm (1980) (see also Butt 1988: 75–76; Matthiessen 1994). The implicate order of the paradigmatic axis engenders the explicate order of the syntagmatic axis; systemic terms are realized by specifications of fragments of structures, as illustrated above.

5.4 Consequences of the axial rethink

The axial rethink opened up a number of important new theoretical possibilities – possibilities that weren't readily available in syntagmatically based theories, whether they were functional or formal in orientation. I will consider the following developments (see also Halliday 1996: Section 12):

- Halliday's discovery of the inherent functional organization of language in the **clustering** of systems in system networks, explained by him in the form of his theory of **metafunction** (e.g. Halliday [1969] 2005c, 2013b).
- Halliday's comprehensive overview of the resources of a language based on major systems, in the form of **function-rank matrix** (e.g. Halliday 1973: 141, 1978; Halliday and Matthiessen 2004).
- Halliday's integration of **intonation** in the description of phonology (as part of prosodic phonology) and (as a realizational resource) in the description of interpersonal and textual grammatical systems (e.g. Halliday [1963b] 2005c, [1963c] 2005c, 1967b; Halliday and Greaves 2008).
- Halliday's **probabilistic** interpretation of the system of language (anticipated in Halliday 1959), where probabilities are associated with terms in systems (e.g. Halliday [1992a] 2005d; Halliday and James [1993] 2005c).
- Halliday's modelling of the relationship between grammar and lexis as a continuum called **lexicogrammar** in terms of systems ordered in delicacy instead of as separate modules (anticipated in Halliday [1961] 2002c; Hasan 1987b; Halliday and Matthiessen 1999).
- Halliday's modelling of all stratal subsystems of language in terms of the same type of axial organization by means of system networks with realization statements (e.g. Halliday 1967b, [1969] 2005c, 1973, [1984a] 2003a, [1992a] 2005d), thereby giving the axial organization the status of a **fractal principle** manifested in different environments throughout language.

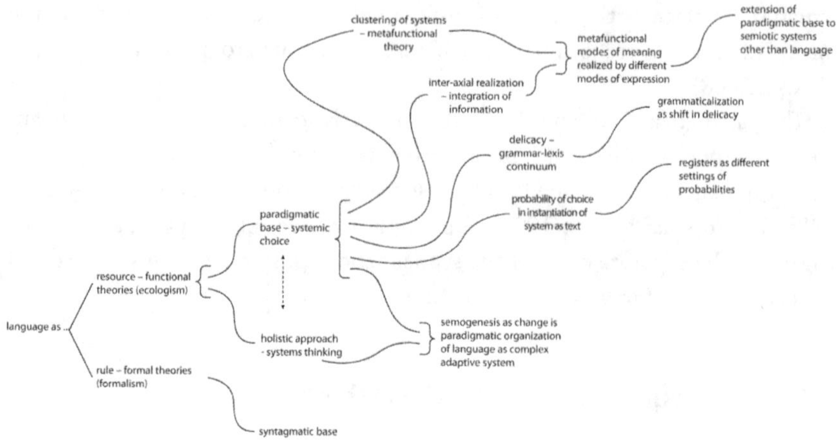

Figure 5.5 Consequences of image of language as resource

- Halliday's account of **semogenesis** as systemic changes in the meaning potential, characterized in ontogenesis as an expansion and reorganization of this meaning potential (e.g. Halliday 1975, [1984a] 2003a, 2013a).

These consequences of giving the theory of language a paradigmatic base, as an expression of the conception of language as resource, are represented diagrammatically in Figure 5.5. The diagram is designed to show how Halliday's 'stratal rethink' opened up news paths in linguistic theory and description.

Let me now discuss the consequences in Halliday's ideas about language of adopting the paradigmatic axis as the base of linguistics organization.

5.4.1 Systemic clustering: Inherent functional organization

Halliday began developing a systemic description of English in the late 1950s (intonation, in particular) and the first half of the 1960s. This (evolving) description was the basis for a series of theoretical and descriptive papers in the next decade or so, including his comprehensive account of intonation and rhythm in relation to grammar (Halliday [1963b] 2005c, [1963c] 2005c, 1967b), his brief overview of the major systems of the clause (Halliday [1969] 2005c), his description of theme and transitivity (Halliday 1967c,d; 1968), his description of modality (Halliday [1970b] 2005c) and (with a delay in publication) his description of mood (Halliday [1984a] 2003a). The 1964 version of his description, the 'Bloomington grammar', was published in Halliday (1976) and again in Volume 1 of his *Collected Works*, Halliday (2002d: 127–151).[9] As he developed the systemic description, he noticed that certain systems clustered together – that is, certain systems were more interdependent and other systems less so. This was the empirical basis of his theory of metafunction – a theory of the intrinsic functional organization of language (cf. Martin 1991). By the end of the 1960s, Halliday ([1969] 2005c: 158) wrote:

> The assignment of clause options to the three components of transitivity, mood and theme reflects their interdependence: there is a relatively high degree of interdependence within each component and a relatively low degree (though not none) between the components.

(Compare also Halliday 2013a: Section 6.) In the Penman project at the Information Sciences Institute in Los Angeles, as we began to develop a computational version of Halliday's description of the clause grammar of English in 1980,[10] we were working with 'algebraic' representations of the systems in Lisp, but it proved hard to manage the expanding and increasingly complex specification of the grammar in this format, so the project leader, Bill Mann (see Matthiessen 2005), asked one of our team members, Yasutomo Fukumochi, to develop a programme that would enable us to plot the entire grammar with a Tektronix plotter on a multi-panel display that, once assembled, covered a large wall, making it possible for us to walk along the wall to examine different parts of the overall system network. This display made it possible to discern the differing degrees of interdependency that Halliday had already detected in the 1960s. Unfortunately, I can't reproduce this display here; instead, let me provide an index to the clause systems we represented in the form of system networks in Halliday and Matthiessen (2004), see Figure 5.6.

In Figure 5.6, the rectangular boxes represent individual systems in the three sets of systems of theme, mood and transitivity. The diagram shows connections between systems, but not the details; the entry conditions and terms of systems are 'invisible'. For example, the system of mood type (free: indicative/imperative) is related to Freedom (major: free/bound) because the term 'free' in this system is its entry condition, and it is related to indicative type (indicative: declarative/interrogative) because the term 'indicative' in mood type is the entry condition to indicative type (cf. Figure 5.3). Thus the diagram is not a system network but rather an index into a system network. However, it does capture the ordering of systems in delicacy (from left to right in the display) and interdependencies of the kind just illustrated, where a term in one system serves as an entry condition in one or more other systems.

As can be seen in Figure 5.6, systems tend to cluster; and these clusters can be interpreted metafunctionally – one cluster of textual systems (theme, and also

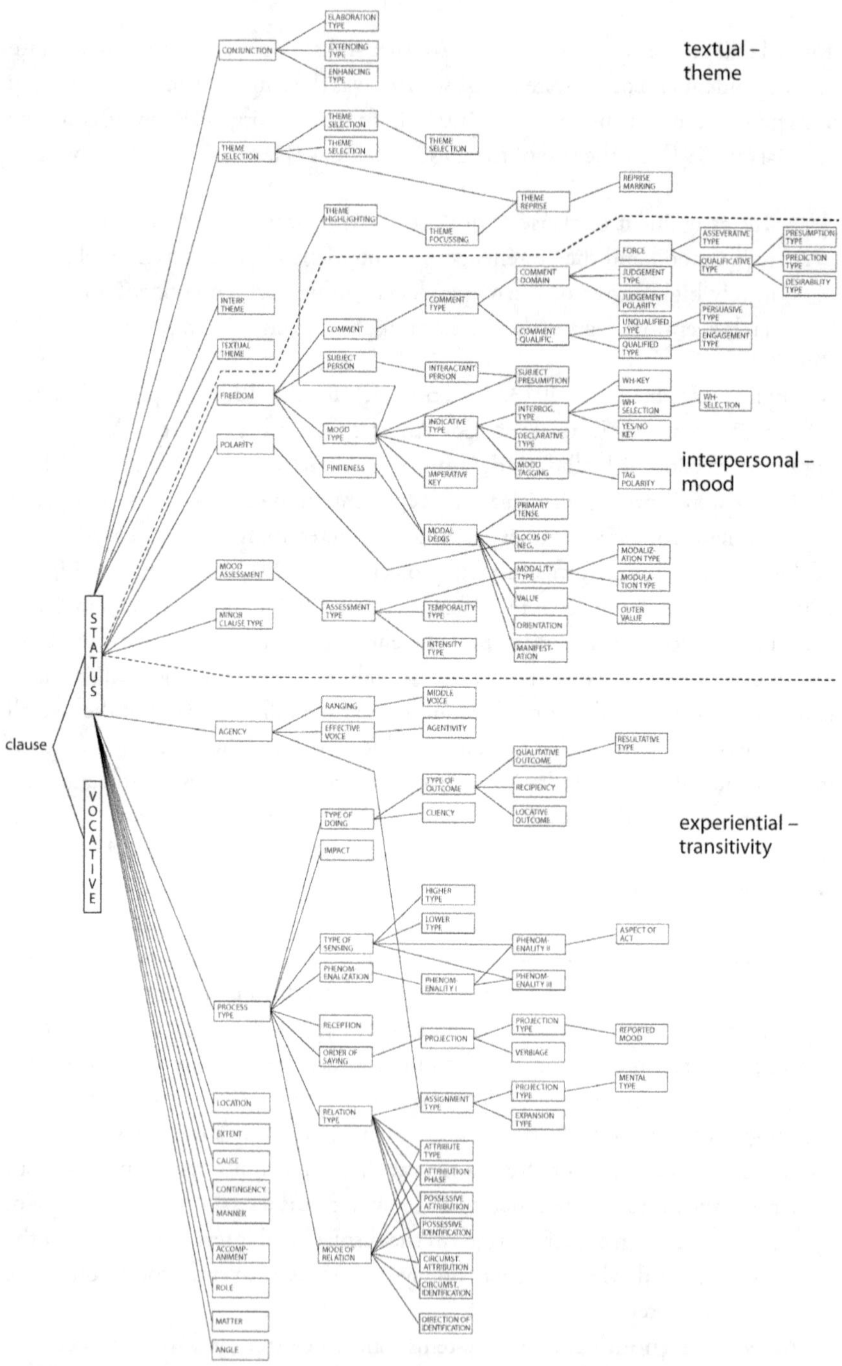

Figure 5.6 Index of clause systems in Halliday and Matthiessen (2004), with indication of metafunctional clustering

conjunction), one cluster of interpersonal systems (mood, including modal assessment) and one cluster of experiential systems (transitivity); a simplified version of these clusters is shown in the clausal system network provided by Halliday (1973: 32). There are certainly interdependencies across these three sets of systems; for example, textual systems of voice operate in the systemic environment of experiential systems of agency, range and Benefaction (cf. Matthiessen 1995b), and theme highlighting systems are only available in 'indicative' clauses, not in 'imperative' ones.

And then there are what appear to be more peripheral systems that are not part of a systemic cluster. In particular, the systems of circumstantial transitivity like location, extent, manner and cause are represented simply as simultaneous systems with 'major' (clause) as their entry conditions. However, the current description of them as simultaneous with the more nuclear transitivity systems of agency and process type may in fact reflect a need for further descriptive work. When we consider relative frequency in text, we find significant quantitative associations between circumstantial systems and the systems of agency and process type even though they are not currently shown in the qualitative description of the system network. For example, circumstances of 'matter' are much more likely to be selected in 'verbal' or 'mental' clauses than in 'material' ones: see Matthiessen (1999, 2006b). In addition, it seems very clear that additional interdependences between circumstantial and nuclear systems of transitivity will begin to emerge when we extend the account in delicacy (cf. Hasan 1987b). Such more delicate interdependencies are likely to include patterns of agnation that have been discussed extensively in the tradition of case grammar, e.g. *provide somebody with something*: *provide something to somebody*, and in descriptions of 'constructions' in different versions of construction grammar (cf. further Section 5.4.5 below).

The situation is likely to be similar in the interpersonal domain with the core system of mood and types of modal assessment. While they appear to be simply simultaneous in the system network index in Figure 5.6, interdependencies begin to emerge when we extend the description in delicacy. For example, assessments of the Subject's modal responsibility such as *rightly*, *wrongly*, *wisely*, *foolishly*, as in *he foolishly attempted to besiege the well-protected fortress of St. Malo*, can only be selected in 'indicative' clauses, not in 'imperative' ones (cf. Matthiessen 1995b: 494).

5.4.2 Systemic cartography

The diagram in Figure 5.6 provides us with an overview of the resources of the clause in English – an index to the clause systems presented in Halliday and Matthiessen

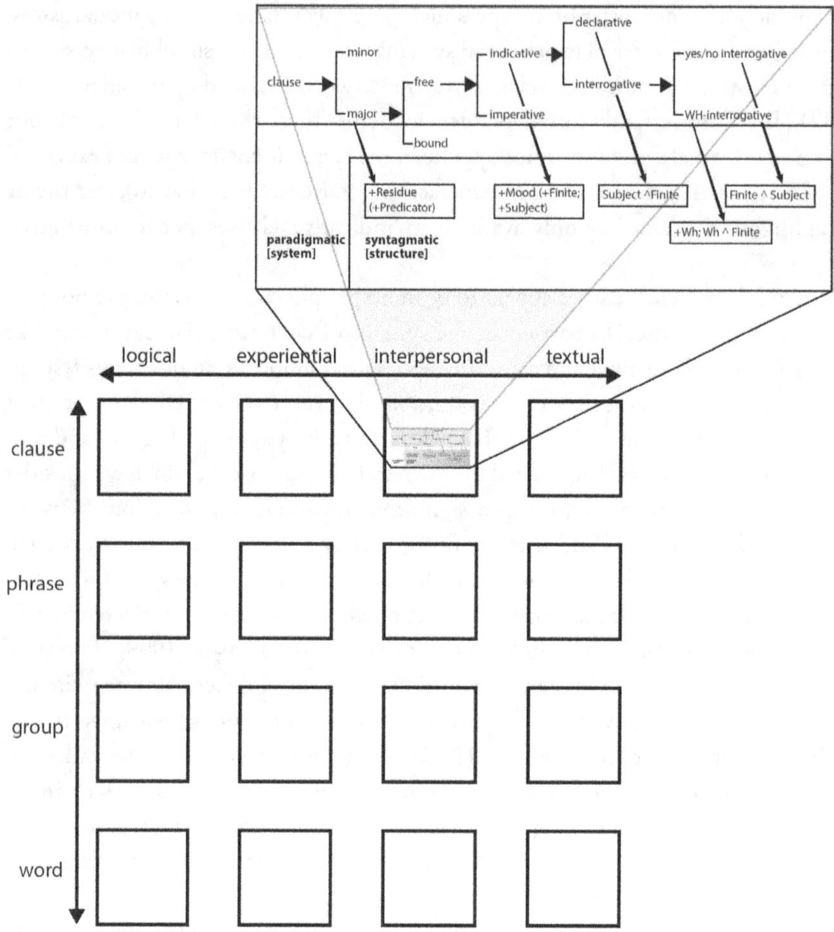

Figure 5.7 Schematic function-rank matrix (lexicogrammatical stratum), showing the location ('semiotic address') of the system of mood in terms of metafunction (interpersonal) and rank (clause)

(2004). The systems in Figure 5.6 can be located in terms of: (a) metafunction; and (b) rank: textual – theme, interpersonal – mood, and experiential – transitivity, at the rank of clause, see Figure 5.7.

Figure 5.7 shows the location of a simple version of the system of mood (cf. Figure 5.3) in terms of a matrix where metafunction and rank are intersected. Such a matrix is called a **function-rank matrix**, and was introduced by Halliday as a way of displaying an overview of the total system of a language at a particular stratum, in this case the stratum of lexicogrammar: see e.g. Halliday ([1970b] 2005c: 169,

1973: 141, 1978) on English, Halliday and McDonald (2004) on Chinese, and Teruya (2007) on Japanese.

In other words, when a language is described systemically, it becomes possible to map out its resources in the way illustrated by Figure 5.7. We can call the process of creating a map of language in this way **linguistic cartography** (cf. Matthiessen 1995b, on lexicogrammatical cartography). As in the creation of maps of the extension of material systems in space, we use the maps to identify regions, using dimensions such as the spectrum of metafunction and the hierarchy of rank as the analogues of longitude and latitude. By mapping out a language systemically, we can reason about language as a system of systems. For example, we can explore recurrent systemic patterns manifested in different 'regions' of the language – what we have called **fractal systems** (e.g. Matthiessen 1995b; Halliday and Matthiessen 1999). In this way, the paradigmatic base used in the modelling of language makes it possible to explore language as a complex adaptive system (cf. Matthiessen 2009b; Beckner *et al.* 2009, for the interpretation of language as a **complex adaptive system** along the lines of research at the Santa Fé Institute).

Function-rank matrices are maps of the lexicogrammatical resources of language; and comparing them across descriptions of different languages is very illuminating, making it possible to undertake comparison and typology based on systems (cf. Halliday [1957] 2002c). For example, the matrices providing overviews of the lexicogrammatical systems of Chinese (Halliday and McDonald 2004) and English (Halliday and Matthiessen 2004: chap. 2) make it possible to identify and then contrast the different systems for construing 'process time' grammatically, aspect and tense, respectively (cf. Halliday and Matthiessen 1999). It is also instructive to add the semiotic dimension of delicacy to the function-rank matrix for lexicogrammar: by adding this dimension, we can explore where meanings tend to be lexicogrammaticalized in different languages, and where 'constructions' (in the sense of 'construction grammars') are located somewhere midway between grammar and lexis (cf. Matthiessen 2007b: Figure 7.13).

Similar maps can be drawn for the other strata of a language, although when we survey the phonological system of a language, one of the dimensions will be different: while we can retain rank, metafunction is only reflected indirectly at the highest rank (that of the tone group) and it needs to be replaced with more phonologically motivated considerations (cf. Matthiessen 1987a).

A function-rank matrix is, of course, simply an intersection of two semiotic dimensions – the hierarchy of rank and the spectrum of metafunction. In the same way, other semiotic dimensions can be intersected – in particular, global semiotic dimensions, giving us maps of the overall resources of language in context:

- **stratification-instantiation matrix:** see Halliday ([2002e] 2005b: 254–255),
- **metafunction-stratification matrix:** see Matthiessen (forthcoming b), and cf. the cover of Halliday and Matthiessen (2004).

It is, of course, even possible to work with three-dimensional matrices, like the schematic **metafunction-stratification-instantiation matrix** on the cover of Halliday and Matthiessen (2004). These global matrices provide the locations of sets of systems like the meaning potential, the wording potential and the sounding potential of a language. The general point is that Halliday's axial rethink enables us to explore the systemic organization of a language, viewing it holistically; in other words, the axial rethink enables us to investigate language in terms of systems thinking.

5.4.3 Systemic integration: Intonation

Paradigmatic relations represented by system networks are 'freed' from the constraints of syntagmatic patterning. In theories based on structure, there will always be certain very significant non-segmental aspects of language that are very hard to accommodate theoretically and descriptively because they cannot be located within some variant of constituency structure (or dependency structure) since they are not manifested segmentally. This has certainly been true of accounts of intonation;[11] and similar considerations would apply to 'paralinguistic' features such as tembre, tempo and loudness (cf. Wan 2011). However, once the paradigmatic axis is given priority, it becomes possible to describe systemic contrasts realized intonationally without being constrained by a particular form of syntagmatic expression. Intonation contours no longer have to be accommodated as sequences of some kind of segmental 'tonemes' but can instead be treated as prosodic realizations of terms in systems (cf. Halliday [1979] 2002c).

From a systemic point of view, what is important is simply that contrasts among terms in systems are maintained through syntagmatic realizations; it does not matter what the nature of the mode of expression is (cf. again Halliday [1979] 2002c), as long as the systemic terms are realizationally distinct. This principle is really the basis of Halliday's pioneering account of intonation (e.g. Halliday [1963b] 2005c, [1963c] 2005c, 1967b; Elmenoufy 1969; Halliday and Greaves 2008). He described the resources of intonation at their own level – the level of phonology, representing them by means of a network of options in the formation of 'melodies'; and then he also described them 'from above', showing how intonation was deployed as an expressive resource in the realization of delicate terms in the system

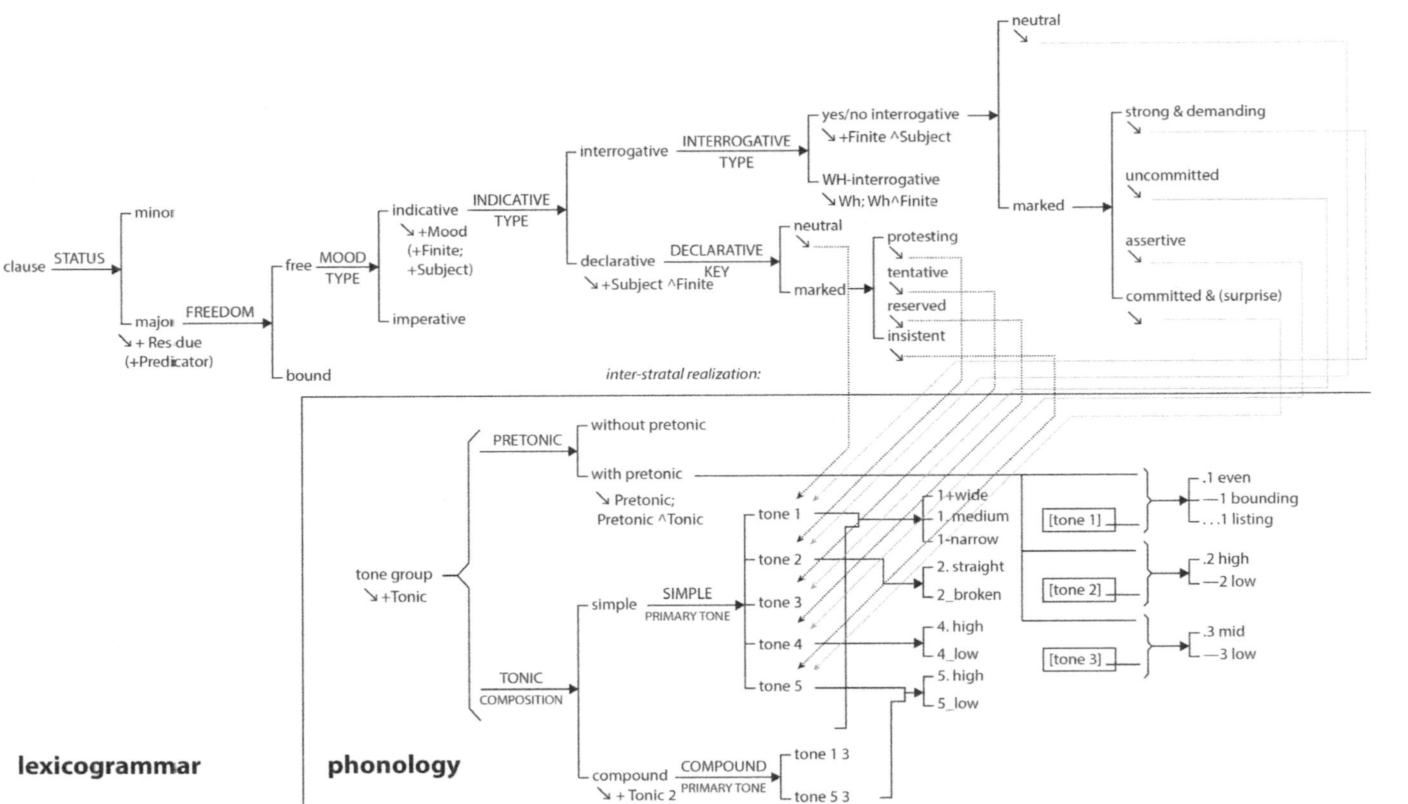

Figure 5.8 Systemic integration of intonation in the description of lexicogrammar and phonology in English

of mood, see Figure 5.8 (a simplified representation based on the detailed descriptions in Halliday 1967b; Halliday and Greaves 2008).

As Figure 5.8 shows, terms in the grammatical system of mood are realized in different ways in English. Fairly indelicate terms are realized by specifications of the modal structure of the clause (e.g. declarative ↘ Subject ^ Finite; yes/no interrogative ↘ Finite ^ Subject), but more delicate terms are realized by tonal distinctions – that is, by preselections of terms in systems forming part of the system network of intonation at the level of phonology. For example, 'neutral' yes/no interrogative key is realized by the preselection of the term 'tone 2' within the tone group realizing the clause at the stratum below, the stratum of phonology; similarly, within marked declarative key: 'protesting' ↘ 'tone 2', 'insistent' ↘ 'tone 5'. In languages other than English, we may find similar systemic distinctions within the system of mood but different syntagmatic realizations (see Teruya *et al.* 2007; and cf. Matthiessen 2004a). For example, distinctions in mood in Cantonese, ranging from more general to more delicate ones, tend to be realized by modal particles rather than by contrasts in tone in the first instance (for Cantonese, see Tam 2004; for Mandarin, see Halliday and McDonald 2004).

By separating the statements of paradigmatic relations and syntagmatic ones and by representing them by means of system networks and realization statements, respectively, we can thus deal with modes of syntagmatic expression other than constituency, integrating them as expressive resources within the total account of the system of a language. In fact, the same principle can be extended to other semiotic systems. For example, terms in pictorial systems may be realized by specifications of different aspects of images, as in Kress and van Leeuwen's (1996) informal, discursively stated, realization statements. We need to find ways of making such statements explicit in terms of some form of syntagmatic representation of images; such realization statements could be called **rendering statements** (cf. Matthiessen, Kobayashi and Zeng 1995).

5.4.4 Systemic probability

Terms in the systems of a system network contrast with one another; in the course of instantiation (whether this is in generation or analysis), one term in a given system will be selected and the other terms won't be. This invites the question of how frequently the different terms in a given system are selected (e.g. Halliday [1991c] 2005a, [1991a] 2005b, [1992a] 2005d). As Halliday ([1991c] 2006: 45) writes:

> Obviously, to interpret language in probabilistic terms, the grammar (that is, the theory of grammar, the ***grammatics***) has to be

> paradigmatic: it has to be able to represent language as **choice**, since probability is the probability of 'choosing' (not in any conscious sense, of course) one thing rather than another. Firth's concept of 'system', in the 'system/structure' framework, already modelled language as choice. Once you say 'choose for polarity: positive or negative?', or 'choose for tense: past or present or future?', then each of these options could have a probability value attached.

This was in fact a question that Halliday had explored already in the 1950s, in his text-based research on Chinese.[12] In Halliday ([1956b] 2005b), which he based on 'a small corpus of spoken material recorded by myself in Peking and elsewhere', he assigned probabilities to descriptive statements, using four degrees of probability: 'even, likely, almost certain and certain'. In Halliday ([1956a] 2005d), he gives counts of the occurrences of principal categories and items in his corpus, *The Secret History of the Mongols*. For example, in his text, there are 1,009 instances of 'perfective' aspect in free clauses and 271 instances of 'imperfective' ones (Halliday [1959] 2005d: 207), which suggests that aspect is a skew system in terms of the probability of the selection of the two terms – perfective 0.8 / imperfective 0.2. What Halliday ([1959] 2005d) had done was count occurrences, or instances, in his corpus of categories such as 'ergative', 'passive', 'perfective', 'imperfective', 'interrogative' and 'imperative' and items such as *yiu*, *duei*, *bei*, *zai*, *zuo* and other 'prepositive verbs'. Such counts can be reported as raw counts or relative frequencies. In either case, they are observations about quantitative patterns in texts, i.e. at the instance pole of the cline of instantiation. Just as qualitative patterns in texts instantiate qualitative patterns in the system – e.g. instances of 'passive' instantiate the term 'passive' in the system of voice, so quantitative patterns in texts instantiate quantitative patterns in the system: what this means is that frequencies in texts instantiate probabilities in the system, as shown in Figure 5.9.

Looked at from the potential pole of the cline of instantiation, systemic probabilities are inherent in systemic terms, or options; and the meaning of a systemic probability is 'probability of instantiation'. For example, in the system of polarity,

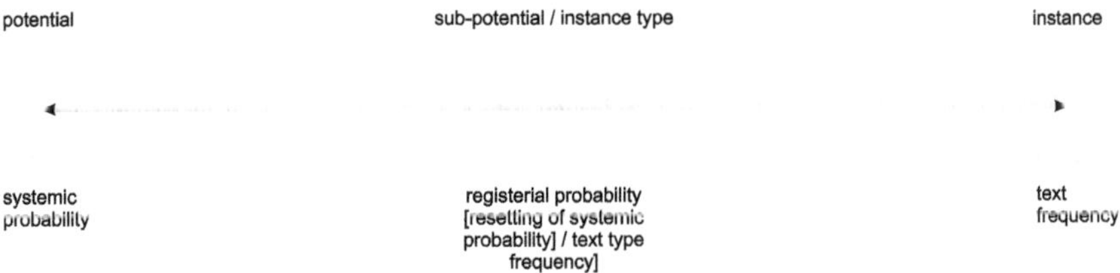

Figure 5.9 The location of probability and frequency along the cline of instantiation

the terms (with attached probabilities) are 'positive' 0.9 / 'negative' 0.1; that is, the probability that 'positive' will be instantiated (selected) is 0.9 and the probability that 'negative' will be instantiated is 0.1 (cf. Halliday and James (1993) in Halliday (2005b)). Viewed from the instance pole of the cline, texts unfold through repeated selections (instantiations) of different systemic terms (cf. Halliday [1977b] 2002d; Matthiessen 2002b). These selections form qualitative and quantitative patterns extending over the text – patterns which can be represented as **text scores** and visualized by means of graphs (see e.g. Matthiessen 1995b: 47, 824–825, 2002b, 2009b: 209–212). Such scores show the frequency of selections of different systemic terms as the text unfolds. These frequencies constitute and reconstitute systemic probabilities higher up the cline of instantiation. As new text types emerge and become established (for a detailed study of the evolution of one new text type, see Nanri 1993), they will have distinctive frequency profiles, constituted in the texts that contribute to the formation of text types. Halliday ([2010] 2013b: Section 5) comments:

> Every act of meaning perturbs, however minutely, the probabilities of the language system, and so contributes to its ongoing evolution. The meaning potential is statistically modulated; this is how it is transmitted from one generation to the next.

As noted above, Halliday's conception of language as a probabilistic system can be traced back to the 1950s (and originates in his experience as a language learner and teacher); but it only became possible to investigate it on a more extensive scale once corpora and corpus tools had come of age (but cf. Halliday [1992a] 2005d: 81, on counts in the mid-1960s). In Halliday (2005b), he summarizes a number of quantitative corpus-based studies within SFL, including the seminal work by Nesbitt and Plum (1988), and he explores a number of central theoretical issues – including different kinds of systemic probability such as transitional and conditional probabilities (cf. also Halliday [1992g] 2003a); but since this book contains a chapter devoted to Halliday on language as a probabilistic system, I won't go into further detail here.

5.4.5 Systemic elaboration: Lexicogrammar

In rule-based, modular models of language, grammar (or syntax and morphology – 'morphosyntax', to use a term that has become common) and lexicon tended to be theorized as separate modules, the grammar book and the dictionary in commonsense ideas about language. This was reinforced in Bloomfield's ([1933] 2002:

269, 274) characterization of the 'grammar' and the 'lexicon', with the lexicon as a kind of repository of items and irregularities:

> A complete description of language will list every form whose function is not determined by structure or by a marker; it will include, accordingly, a *lexicon*, or list of morphemes, which indicates the form – class of each morpheme, as well as lists all complex forms whose function is in any way irregular. (p. 269)

> The lexicon is really an appendix of the grammar, a list of basic irregularities. This is all the more evident if meanings are taken into consideration, since the meaning of each morpheme belongs to it by an arbitrary tradition. (p. 274)

This conception of the relationship between grammar and lexis, arguably grounded in the commonsense understanding, was taken over by Chomsky[13] and other generative linguists (along with other ideas from American structuralist linguistics); and it was not until the transition from the 1960s to the 1970s that relationship began to be problematized and explored, including the distinction between syntactic and lexical rules (e.g. Chomsky 1970; Wasow 1977; Hoekstra, van der Hulst and Moortgat 1980). So it was in the context of Bloomfield's conception of the relationship between grammar and lexis that Halliday ([1961] 2002c: 54) introduced the idea of 'the grammarian's dream':

> The theoretical place of the move from grammar to lexis is therefore not a feature of rank but one of delicacy. It is defined theoretically as a place where increase in delicacy yields no further systems; this means that the description is constantly shifting as delicacy increases. The grammarian's dream is (and must be, such is the nature of grammar) of constant territorial expansion. He would like to turn the whole of linguistic form into grammar, hoping to show that lexis can be defined as 'most delicate grammar'.

At the time, this way of theorizing lexis as a basis for description was very different from what was rapidly becoming the dominant rule based theory of lan guage (cf. Note 9); and lexical items (lexemes, or 'formatives') were part of the structure-based conception of language, being inserted from the lexicon into structures. In systemic functional linguistics, the relation between grammar and lexis was theorized in terms of delicacy rather than in terms of composition (i.e.

rank, in systemic functional terms), and the compositional approach was taken further in the lexical semantic models that began to be developed within certain linguistic and computational linguistic frameworks in the 1980s (for comparison of structural composition of lexical elements and systemic paradigms of lexical dimensions, see Halliday and Matthiessen 1999); but the grammarian's dream had to wait to be presented in publications: it took a quarter of a century for a substantial example of the grammarian's dream to be presented (during this quarter of a century systemic functional linguists were working very hard on theories and descriptions of grammar, semantics and context) – Hasan's (1987b) description of the extension of a field within 'material' processes in delicacy (cf. also Cross 1992; Matthiessen 1991a). However, the principle was very clear: it was the paradigmatic base of the theory of language that made it possible for the grammarian to dream about expanding into lexis. In a way, this may seem like 'componential analysis' in anthropological linguistic accounts, notably Lounsbury (1956) and Frake (1961) (cf. also Leech 1970; 1974). However, on the one hand, systemic features or terms are not syntagmatic components of (the senses of) lexical items; they are paradigmatic values defining the dimensions of the lexicogrammatical space within which lexical items can be located.[14] On the other hand, the grammarian's dream means extending the description in delicacy at the stratum of lexicogrammar, leaving space for complementary accounts one level up at the stratum of semantics.

It is difficult to illustrate the description of lexis through the extension of grammatical systems in delicacy precisely because quite a number of steps in delicacy must be taken before the description reaches the point where it is possible to distinguish even sets of lexical items by means of intersections of terms from simultaneous systems.[15] So let me use a simplified example, taken from Halliday and Matthiessen (2004: 44): see Figure 5.10. In this systemic description, there are only four steps in delicacy (i.e. systems ordered in delicacy) from the least delicate, most grammatical system, process type, to the most delicate, most lexical systems, force, authority and loading. These three systems (and their more delicate subsystems, operating in the paradigmatic environment of the non-neutral options of the three systems) define the lexical space within which lexical verbs such as tell, order and ask can be located as the realizations of (the Event function in the verbal group realizing) the Process of the clause. That is, combinations of systemic terms from these systems are realized by lexical verbs; for example, the combination of 'neutral' (authority), 'neutral' (force) and 'neutral' (loading) is realized by tell.

This description is, of course, merely illustrative; taking account of a more extensive region of lexical resources would take many more steps (cf. Hasan 1987b; Matthiessen 1995b, 2012; Neale 2002; Tucker 1998 – for an overview, see Wanner 1997: chap. 5).[16] Thus the number of verbs that may realize (the Event function in

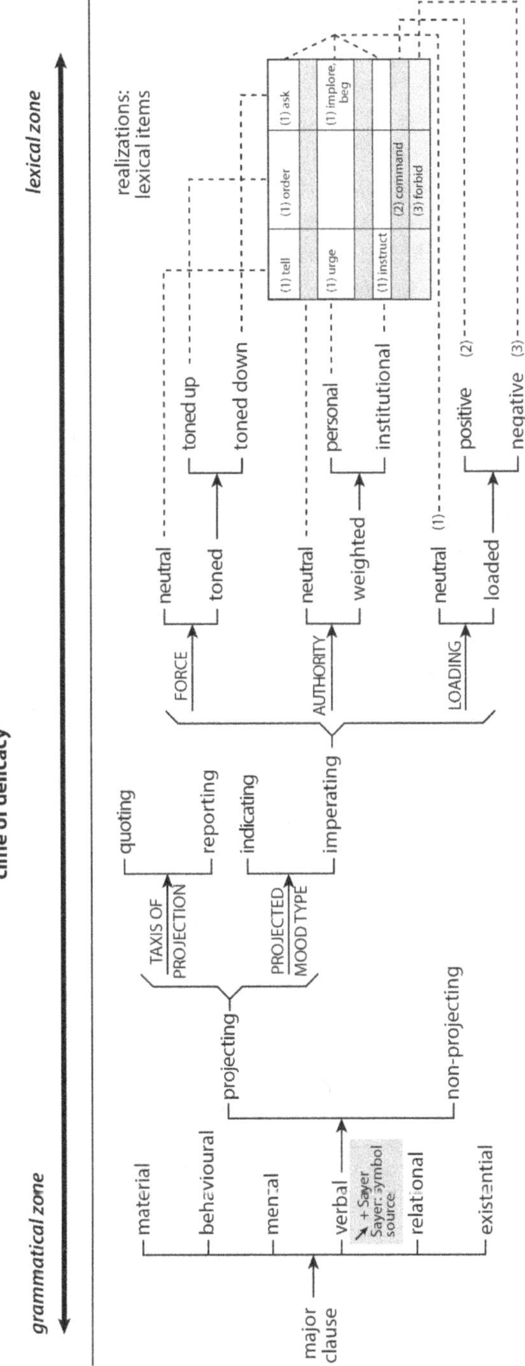

Figure 5.10 Simplified illustration of lexis as most delicate grammar

the verbal group realizing) the Process of 'verbal' clauses is around 350, based on my classification and adaptation of Levin's (1993) verb classes, and these fall into 14 verb classes (see Matthiessen 2014b), and there are surely many more: systemicizing even this 'minor' process type is a huge task. It is also important to note that within the lexical zone there is quite a range from more general lexical terms to more specific ones, recognized in studies of folk taxonomies (see Halliday and Matthiessen 1999, and references therein) and in general treatments of vocabulary (see e.g. Carter 1987); and lexical items realizing combinations of terms along this range differ in frequency, from fairly high-frequency ones (shading into the region between grammar and lexis) e.g. with verbs such as *say*, *think*, *do* and *make* to very low frequency ones.

It is the paradigmatic base that has made it possible to explore the idea that lexis can be theorized and described as most delicate grammar – that is, not as a separate module but as part of a continuum within the stratum of lexicogrammar, illuminated by Halliday (2008: chap. 2) as complementary perspectives on the resources of wording. He writes (p. 48):

> So the lexicogrammar adopts two contrasting perspectives for construing all this complexity. The one is specific and openended; hence flexible, but low in information: this is the lexical perspective, good for seeing phenomena as particular. The other is general and systemic: hence high in information, but creating closure: this is the grammatical perspective, good for seeing phenomena as generality. The two are complementary; any phenomenon can be looked at in terms of either, but they will present two different images of the whole.

When we explore the relationship between grammar and lexis along these lines, in terms of the cline of delicacy, certain generalizations about paradigmatic and

Table 5.3 The lexicogrammatical cline of delicacy in relation to the paradigmatic and syntagmatic axes

	low delicacy	**intermediate delicacy**	**high delicacy**
paradigmatic axis	systems (closed)	systems (semi-closed)	sets (open)
syntagmatic axis	structures	'constructions'	collocations
	grammatical items ('function words') low delicacy	grammatico-lexical items (e.g. comment adverbs, cohesive conjuntions, attitudinal adjectives, general nouns, phasal intermediate delicacy verbs)	lexical items ('content words') high delicacy

syntagmatic relations emerge: see Table 5.3 (cf. Halliday and Matthiessen 2004: 38–46).

Paradigmatically, the extension in delicacy from grammar to lexis is a gradual move from closed systems to open sets: lexis is more permeable than grammar; lexical items drift in and out of a language, whereas grammatical items tend to be more fixed by closed systems. In this respect, lexis provides a source of new resources for lexicogrammar; lexical items may be sucked into the vortex of grammar as expressive resources – a process that has been studied extensively in different languages in the last quarter century or so under the heading of **grammaticalization.** Based on the systemic way of modelling lexis and grammar, certain properties of grammaticalization in principle fall out automatically: terms in grammatical systems are selected much more frequently than are terms in lexical ones – so grammatical items are much more frequent than lexical ones and, as a Zipfian reflex on the expression plane, both phonologically shorter and more likely to be reduced (e.g. grammatical *the* vs lexical *supercalafragalisticexpealadocious*).

Syntagmatically, grammatical and lexical items thus differ significantly in terms of the nature of items; and whereas grammar engenders **structures** such as Theme + Rheme, Subject + Finite + Predicator + Complement, and Actor + Process + Goal, lexis engenders **collocations** (cf. Halliday [1996] 2002c; Halliday and Hasan 1976) such as *strong* + *tea*, *powerful* + *argument*, *heavy* + *traffic*, *lay* + *table* and *make* + *bed*. But if grammar and lexis shade into one another along the cline of instantiation, how do structure and collocation relate to one another? I think many collocations actually involve lexical items serving in particular configurations of grammatical functions (cf. Matthiessen 1995a); such configurations include Process + Medium (e.g. *shine* + *sun*; *twinkle* + *star*; *bark* + *dog*; *neigh* + *horse*); Process + Range (e.g. Process + Scope: *make* + *mistake*; *do* + *sum*; Process + Attribute: *turn* + *pale*; *grow* + *old*; *run* + *dry*; *go* + *crazy*), Process + Manner: degree (e.g. *understand* + *completely*; *love* + *deeply*; *want* + *badly*), Epithet: degree + Thing (e.g. *powerful* + *argument*, *strong* + *tea*, *heavy* + *traffic*). Quite a few of these involve 'lexical functions', as they have been described by Mel'chuk (e.g. 1982) and his colleagues in the Meaning Text Model (cf. Matthiessen 1995a). They seem to generalize beyond combinations of individual lexical items, which suggests that we can locate collocational patterns at different points along the cline of instantiation (see e.g. Matthiessen 2009a, on Process: emotive + Manner: degree collocations). In other words, collocations can also be located at different points along the cline of delicacy.

Intermediate between the outer poles of the cline of delicacy – between grammar and lexis, we find patterns that have come into focus more recently under the heading of 'constructions' in different varieties of Construction Grammar [CxG] such as Berkeley Construction Grammar, Sign-Based Construction Grammar and Fluid Construction Grammar (e.g. Fillmore, Kay and O'Connor 1988; Kay and Fillmore 1999; Goldberg 1995; Ruppenhofer *et al.* 2006; Sag 2010; van Trijp *et al.* 2012; Steels 2012) – but also under the heading of 'pattern grammar' in the work by Hunston and Francis (2000) in the Birmingham corpus linguistic tradition. The framework that Sag (2010) introduces is of particular interest in this context from a systemic functional point of view. It is called **Sign-Based Construction Grammar** (SBCG), and represents a merger of two distinct but related important traditions of research into lexicogrammar. Sag (2010: 29) characterizes SBCG as follows (footnotes omitted):

> a framework blending ideas developed over a quarter century of research in Head-Driven Phrase Structure Grammar (HPSG) with those presented within the tradition of Berkeley Construction Grammar (BCG) over roughly the same period. The goal is to expand the empirical coverage of HPSG, while at the same time putting BCG on a firmer theoretical footing.

The tradition of Berkeley Construction Grammar includes the work on FrameNet (e.g. Ruppenhofer *et al.* 2006), with a significant commitment to descriptive coverage of constructions; and FrameNet has been explored in systemic functional terms by Chow and Webster (2008). As noted earlier, descriptive coverage is also a priority in the HPSG tradition. Based on these two strands, SBCG also includes the notion of typing; Sag (2010: 46) observes: 'In SBCG, the more general notion of "type hierarchy" takes over the inheritance functions that **constructional inheritance** performed in some earlier traditions of CxG.' This may thus be the emergence of a paradigmatic orientation, or at least the inclusion of paradigmatic considerations, in a tradition that began with a more syntagmatic focus – cf. also above the reference to Elhadad's (e.g. 1990) use of typed features (cf. also the use of 'ontologies', as in Huang *et al.*'s, 2010, work on the lexicon referred to above).

What are constructions? They are lexicogrammatical patterns located somewhere midway between grammar and lexis along the cline of delicacy (see Table 5.3). This suggests that we can approach them either from the lexical pole of the cline or from the grammatical pole. In work outside SFL, there has been a tendency to approach them from the lexical end, and then to look for generalizations. Perhaps we could call this the 'lexicologist's dream'. This approach is certainly facilitated by the way that corpora have tended to be represented and by the lexical orientation of corpus tools (cf. Halliday [2002b] 2005b; Manning 2003, and also

McEnery and Hardie 2011). But we can also approach constructions from the grammatical end of the cline of delicacy, pursuing the 'grammarian's dream'. These two angles of approach are clearly complementary, not contradictory; but they are likely to foreground different considerations, at least in the early stages, before we arrive at a more well-rounded picture. Pursuing the grammarian's dream, we will be able to explore how the grammar engenders more delicate constructions based on more general grammatical configurations (cf. Matthiessen 2012).

The systemic functional descriptions of lexis as most delicate grammar have tended to be focused on experiential systems; but delicacy is of course a general dimension of organization that applies to all metafunctional domains. It is not surprising if the greatest extensions of lexicogrammar are found within the experiential metafunction: one key aspect of construing experience is, of course, precisely the construal of taxonomies of different fields of experience – with varying degrees of taxonomic depth depending on the degree of expertise, ranging from folk via expert to scientific (see e.g. Halliday and Matthiessen 1999; Wignell, Martin and Eggins 1989).

The logical metafunction – or rather the logical mode of construal within the ideational metafunction – is concerned instead with highly generalized logico-semantic relations, thus yielding taxonomies of grammatical items (e.g. structural conjunctions, and tenses in English) rather than of lexical items; and the textual metafunction provides a cohesive variant of these, extended further in delicacy (i.e. further from grammar towards lexis) but still not with great taxonomic depth.[17]

But what about the interpersonal metafunction? There are items that are purely interpersonal in nature; in English, these include grammatical items such as modal operators (*may*, *might*, *can*, *could*, *will*, *would*, *should*, *must*, etc.) and mood adverbs (e.g. *probably*, *surely*; *still*, *soon*, *already*; *sometimes*, *often*; *just*, *only*; *hardly*, *scarcely*, etc.), grammatico-lexical items (i.e. items realizing terms in more open systems located somewhere between grammar and lexis) such as comment adverbs (e.g. *sadly*, *honestly*, *wisely*) and attitudinal adjectives (e.g. *sweet*, *lovely*, *heavenly*; *vile*, *horrible*, *nasty*). There are also items that realize both experiential distinctions and interpersonal ones – traditionally discussed in terms of denotation and connotation, respectively; and these include general nouns with interpersonal loading (see Halliday and Hasan 1976: Section 6.1[18]), located closer to the grammatical pole of the cline between grammar and lexis. To describe interpersonal distinctions that are realized lexically, whether on their own or in combination with experiential distinctions, we probably do not need to take as many steps in delicacy as we do in descriptions of experiential lexis (cf. the networking of classes of modal assessment in Halliday and Matthiessen 2004). Halliday (2008: 49) comments:

> in the interpersonal domain, the organization of meaning into the two regions, the lexical and the grammatical, is less polarized; there is not such a clear demarcation between the general and the particular in the management of human relationships. The two contrasting perspectives are still distinct; but it becomes more apparent that the difference between them is one of depth of focus, not one of discontinuity in the phenomena themselves.

The interpersonal deployment of lexical resources has, of course, been given a major descriptive boost in systemic functional linguistics through the work on APPRAISAL by J. R. Martin (e.g. 2000) and his colleagues; there is now an extensive literature – the major overview being Martin and White (2005). The description of appraisal covers both lexical items that are purely interpersonal (like the ones characterized above as grammatico-lexical items) and lexical items that realize both experiential and interpersonal features – as noted above, traditionally, denotation and connotation, respectively.

Martin and White (2005: Section 1.3) locate the system of appraisal within the interpersonal metafunction but at the semantic stratum rather than the lexicogrammatical one (cf. their Table 1.4):

> On the basis of the complementarities introduced above we can locate appraisal as an interpersonal system at the level of discourse semantics. At this level it co-articulates interpersonal meaning with two other systems – negotiation and involvement. Negotiation complements appraisal by focusing on the interactive aspects of discourse, speech function and exchange structure (as presented in Martin 1992a). Eggins and Slade 1997 present a detailed SFL framework for analysing interactive moves in casual conversation.
>
> Involvement complements appraisal by focusing on non-gradable resources for negotiating tenor relations, especially solidarity.

This raises the interesting and important question of 'stratal address' of these systems within the content plane of language. Martin and White (2005) provide a number of informal system networks describing the potential for evaluation in English, but these networks lack 'root' features that would locate them within the overall description of either of the two content strata, semantics and lexicogrammar (e.g. Martin and White 2005: Figure 1.8). Their account of evaluation includes both examples where the evaluation is made explicit ('inscribed') and examples where it has to be inferred ('evoked'); and these may of course differ in stratal location – inference clearly being a semantic rather than a lexicogrammatical process.

If evaluation – or assessment – is taken account of exhaustively within both of the content strata of language, semantics and lexicogrammar, I think the picture would have to be adjusted (cf. Matthiessen 2007a). The semantic account would be more 'strategic' in nature – showing the strategies for assessing a range of phenomena, strategies drawing on both lexis and grammar (cf. Slade 1996; and also Matthiessen 2007a: Section 6); and the lexicogrammatical account would be 'lexis as most delicate grammar' in the interpersonal domain. If we pursue the description of interpersonal lexis systematically, treating it as extensions in delicacy of grammatical systems, I think we are likely to find that there are certain systemic prosodies: interpersonal systems that are manifested in multiple grammatical domains (cf. Matthiessen 1988a).

5.4.6 Fractality

One important finding in the development of accounts of intonation was that system networks can operate in domains with very different modes of expression. Thus even by the second half of the 1960s, Halliday's work had shown that two linguistic strata – lexicogrammar and phonology – could be represented by means of system networks accompanied by realization statements (e.g. Halliday [1966b] 2002c, [1969] 2005c, 1967b). In other words, the two formal strata of language, content form (lexicogrammar) and expression form (phonology), were organized along very similar lines.

At the time, this was very different from accounts in formal theories, as represented by Chomsky (1965) on syntax and Chomsky and Halle (1968) on phonology; and these two formal systems tended to be theorized in fairly different ways in generative linguistics, by means of different rule systems starting with different 'bases'. Later the generative theories of phonology tended to move in a more Firthian direction – from Chomsky and Halle's very abstract phonology via 'natural phonology' (as in the work by Theo Vennemann and Joan Hooper) to more prosodic conceptualizations of phonology, autosegmental and metrical phonology (as in Goldsmith 1990; on these developments in relation to Firthian prosodic analysis, cf. also Henderson 1987). The work on content form took off in another direction.

In contrast, in systemic functional work, both content form and expression form were conceived of as resources (with the term 'form' in Hjelmslev's, 1943: sense) – resources of wording and of sounding, respectively. Lexicogrammar was modelled as a **wording potential**, represented by means of lexicogrammatical system networks; and phonology was modelled as a **sounding potential**, represented by means of phonological system networks (as in Halliday 1967b; Tench 1992b; cf. also Matthiessen 1987a). In this way, both lexicogrammar and phonology were 'generative'; they were represented as what speaker 'can say' and 'can sound', respectively. Thus a phonological system network with realization statements can specify all possible sound patterns in a language, not just those that are actually in use at a given point in time and listed as entries in a lexicon.

Thus the form strata, lexicogrammar and phonology, were theorized with a paradigmatic base and represented by means of system networks with realization statements. But what about substance – **content substance (semantics)** and **expression substance (phonetics)?**[19] Is it possible to formulate semantic and phonetic system networks, with semantic and phonetic realization statements? In principle, it should be, since these strata also provide resources as part of the overall meaning-making resources of language; as Halliday (2008: 65) observes:

> The network is a theory of what the speaker can do: what he can mean, at the semantic stratum; what he can say, or 'word', at the stratum of lexicogrammar; what he can say, or 'sound' at the strata of phonology and phonetics. (cf. Matthiessen 1995b; Butt 2000)

However, the two substance strata are different in certain respects from the two form strata, one key difference being that they are **interface strata** (cf. Halliday 1973: on semantics as an 'interlevel').

Since the late 1960s, researchers have proposed a number of semantic system networks, many of which are surveyed by Hasan *et al.* (2007b); but there is no tradition of phonetic system networks – yet. While there is no comprehensive systemic description of the semantic system of any language (so far, nobody has produced the 'reference semantic' of a language comparable to the 'reference grammar' of a language), there have been a number of contributions illuminating various aspects of what the semantic system of language has evolved to deal with – including, semantics as the strategy for transforming what is not language into language in the form of meaning, in different situation types (e.g. Halliday [1972] 2003a, on the strategic semantics of maternal control; Turner 1987) and across situation types, as a general meaning potential, with particular focus on interpersonal resources (e.g. Halliday [1984a] 2003a, and the work by Hasan and her research group, summarized in Hasan *et al.* 2007b). These accounts all involve semantic system networks with fully specified realization statements referring to lexicogrammatical features (cf. Fawcett 1988a). In a partly parallel long-term research programme, J. R. Martin and his research group developed system networks for semantics, what he calls 'discourse semantics' (e.g. Martin 1992a). These range across the metafunctions (although Eggins and Slade's 1997, classic account of casual conversation focuses on interpersonal resources), but tend not to include explicit realization statements (cf. also the lack of explicit realization statement in the work on appraisal system presented in Martin and White 2005).

Alongside these accounts – contributions that tended to be geared towards the task of manual semantic text analysis, there are also accounts of semantic networks developed in the research context of computational modelling. Drawing on Halliday ([1972] 2003a), Patten (1988) shows how the notion of register-specific strategic semantic system networks resonates with ideas about planning in AI: such system networks serve as solutions that have been 'compiled' from the general semantic resources to deal with recurrent problems (cf. Matthiessen 1990).

At the same time, there has been considerable work on general semantic systems in the context of computational linguistics, both in the 'Penman' tradition, with an ideational focus (e.g. Matthiessen and Bateman 1991; Halliday and Matthiessen 1999; Bateman *et al.* 1990) and in the 'Cardiff Grammar' tradition, with work across metafunctions, where system networks within the content plane are interpreted as semantic networks (since at least Fawcett 1980): there is only one level of system networks, not two.

In the research context of computational modelling, various questions about semantic networks arise that have not tended to be addressed by those researchers who focus on applications involving manual text analysis. These questions relate both to the semantic networks themselves and to realization statements specifying fragments of semantic structure; for example:

- If reasoning and inference are theorized as semantic processes (rather than as cognitive ones[20]), how can they be supported by means of the representation of semantic resources – both systemically and instantially?
- Since semantics is the 'interface' within the content plane between language and other systems, how can semantic system networks be used to relate linguistic meaning to meaning construed or enacted in bio-semiotic systems such as perception (cf. Halliday and Matthiessen 1999; Bateman *et al.* 2010[21])?

The concern with reasoning and inference has been one motivation in computational systems for using a form of representation of semantics other than system networks – some type of frame-based inheritance network, originally proposed in the late 1970s (for foundational proposals, see Brachman 1978, 1979, in part a response to Woods' 1975, challenge to researchers working on semantic networks to develop theoretically and formally more explicit networks). Over the next couple of decades, researchers developed a family of frame-based inheritance networks such as kl-one, nikl and loom (for some discussion from a systemic functional point of view and references to the original work, see Halliday and Matthiessen 1999). These had well-understood mathematical properties, and included both paradigmatic inheritance and syntagmatic frames, the latter also represented in terms of instantial propositions supported by at least first-order predicate logic. Therefore, they support reasoning and inference both at the potential pole of the cline of instantiation and at the instance pole (cf. Halliday and Matthiessen 1999). The developments in knowledge representation involving frame-based inheritance networks also influenced new initiatives in grammatical theory in the 1980s, in particular HPSG; so this form of representation takes us back to the role of paradigmatic order in the modelling of lexicogrammar discussed above (cf. also work on 'ontology' in relation to lexis: Huang *et al.* 2010) – highly relevant to explicit representations also of systemic functional grammars; see e.g. Bateman, Emele and Momma (1992).

It turns out that adopting what we might think of as an industrial-strength representational system for semantics also opens up new possibilities for interfacing with other non-linguistic models. One key example here is the research by John Bateman and his group to link a semantic model of space (related to the 'ideation base' part of the 'meaning base' of a language presented in Halliday and Matthiessen 1999) to the kinds of models that robots need in order to engage with space as they perceive it and navigate around it: see Bateman *et al.* (2010). This is one of the crucial properties of semantics as an ***interlevel*** – to function as a resource for relating to other human systems (see Halliday [1972] 2003a), in this case systems designed for robots that are analogous to what we called biosemiotic systems in Halliday and Matthiessen (1999).

It is probably not surprising that when we turn to semantics – to the interface level within the content plane (cf. again Halliday 1973), we find 'two cultures' (to echo C. P. Snow – but cf. also the principle embodied in Halliday's, 1964, notion of 'syntax and the consumer') within systemic functional linguistics: on the one hand, the culture of researchers who are focused on manual discourse analysis and the critically important problems in human communities that can be addressed by undertaking this form of analysis; and on the other hand, the culture of researchers who engage with computational modelling to solve other classes of problems of critical importance in human communities. The dialogue between members of these two communities of researchers has tended to be conducted with a somewhat narrow channel and to be a bit one-directional: members of the second community of researchers have typically engaged with the work by the first community, but the reverse has not usually been the case.

But what does this mean for the role of system networks in the description of semantic systems of languages? In a sense, this is an open empirical question; it will be illuminated by more extensive descriptions of the semantic systems of a variety of languages, descriptions with a clear focus on semantics as the interlevel of the content plane – the level embodying the strategies for transforming what is not language into language, into meaning. At the same time, we can address it by exploring the stratal organization of systemic theory itself as a metalanguage, see Section 5.6 below.

What about expression substance – phonetics, in spoken language?[22] As far as I know, while researchers have developed a fair range of phonological system networks (including realization statements), there are as yet no phonetic ones. Building on Abercrombie's (e.g. 1967) phonetic research, Catford (1977) was probably the linguist whose work on phonetics gives the clearest indication of what the ingredients of systemic phonetics would be (for a particular example, see Catford 1985). His *Fundamental Problems in Phonetics* provides a very system-oriented – and I think systemic – view of phonetics; he says that the 'subject matter of general phonetics' is what he calls **the total sound-producing potential of man** (and in his book he includes the other phases of phonation as well), reminding us that Jan Baudouin de Courtenay had used the term 'anthropophonics'.[23]

In his review of Catford's contribution, Ladefoged (1979: 904) characterized it as 'containing more original thought on phonetics than any book since Pike (1943)'. Ladefoged himself, who had also been at Edinburgh University and learned from Abercrombie there, like Catford and Halliday, worked over the years to produce a general inventory of phonetic features – more systematic and phonetically motivated than Jakobson, Fant and Halle's (1952) pioneering contribution; and Ladefoged's feature inventory can be interpreted as a **pre-systemic** account of the human phonetic potential as it is deployed in different ways in the languages around the world (a kind of 'etic' pool, in the sense of Tagmemic linguistics). The pressure on any form of representation of the phonetic system of a language would, in principle, be the same as that exerted on the representation of the semantic system: the representation would have to be such as to make it possible to capture the interface nature of phonetics, relating it to the articulatory and auditory systems of an organism.

5.4.7 Semogenesis

By giving priority to paradigmatic organization, Halliday has been able to shed new light on **semogenesis** – the processes by which meanings are created, recreated, extended and changed **logogenetically**, **ontogenetically** and **phylogenetically** (see e.g. Halliday and Matthiessen 1999; Halliday [1997] 2003a: 250, [1992a] 2005d, [1992a] 2002d, [2002e] 2005b). In other words, by viewing the creation and maintenance of meaning paradigmatically rather than only syntagmatically, Halliday and other systemic functional linguists have been able to bring out changes in the system over time. Change is thus interpreted as change pertaining to ***choice*** in the first instance, within the three time-frames of the unfolding of meaning in the text (logogenesis), the growth of meaning in persons as they develop (ontogenesis) and the evolution of meaning in the system over generations of speech fellowships (phylogenesis).

In each of the three time-frames, particular aspects of change pertaining to choice are easier to observe; some aspects stand out – are easier to observe – logogenetically, other aspects ontogenetically and yet other aspects phylogenetically.

(i) In the **logogenetic time-frame**, we see change in choice as a flow of systemic terms, selected with different frequencies as a text unfolds (e.g. Matthiessen 2002b; cf. also Matthiessen and Bateman 1991).

In the **ontogenetic time-frame**, we see change in choice as the gradual expansion of a learner's meaning potential (e.g. Halliday 1975; Painter 1999; Painter, Derewianka and Torr 2007; Christie and Derewianka 2008; Matthiessen 2009b); learners add new terms in existing systems, they add new systems, and they dissociate systemic variables from one another.

In the **phylogenetic time-frame**, we see change in choice as the gradual evolution of the collective meaning potential of a speech fellowship. This **may** involve an expansion of the meaning potential, e.g. when a language evolves new registers of science (e.g. Halliday 1988), administration and commerce, adding them to the registerial make-up of the language, as part of becoming a standard language; but it always involves adaptation to the changing cultural environment, centrally through changes in the registerial make-up of the meaning potential. Underpinning these different manifestations of change in choice are the same systemic principles – the difference being where we observe them along the cline of instantiation.

Logogenetically, meanings are created as texts unfold over time (cf. Halliday [1992f] 2003a, on the act of meaning). This can be modelled as changing states of the system in the course of the process of instantiation (cf. Matthiessen and Bateman 1991): see Figure 5.11. The figure shows how the system of the clause is traversed in the course of instantiation. As systemic terms are chosen in the different systems that are entered (starting with 'clause', the root of all the clause systems), new systems become enterable (i.e. available for choice), and one term is chosen in each system that is currently enterable. The terms that are chosen as a unit of language emerges in the course of instantiation can be recorded as a **selection expression**, a record of the terms that have been instantiated. Some terms

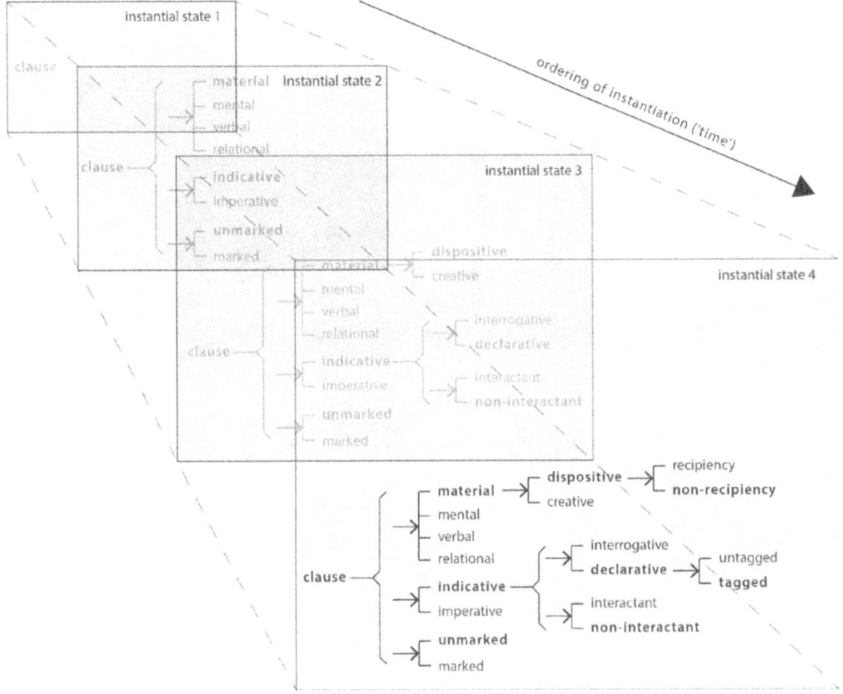

Figure 5.11 Successive instantial states of the systems of the clause

are chosen frequently, while other terms are chosen less frequently or not at all; the relative frequency of the selection of systemic terms in the course of logogenesis is an important aspect of the creation of instantial meaning (cf. discussions of foregrounding and de-automatization in verbal art, e.g. Halliday [1971] 2002d, [1982b] 2002d).

Ontogenetically, learners construct their meaning potentials out of innumerable processes of logogenesis: they engage with the instantial patterns of meaning in text, as they produce or analyse them; and out of these instantial patterns, they **distil** systemic generalizations, moving up along the cline of instantiation from the instance pole towards the potential pole (cf. Matthiessen 2009b). These systemic generalizations include systemic probabilities inferred from relative frequencies in text (as e.g. Bod, Hay, and Jannedy 2003a: 6–7, emphasize, 'unlike categorical grammars, probabilistic grammars are learnable from positive evidence alone'; 'if the language faculty is probabilistic, the learning task is considerably more achievable').[24] As learners develop, their meaning potentials **grow** – or, more specifically, follow the growth pattern characteristic of life: rapid growth through childhood

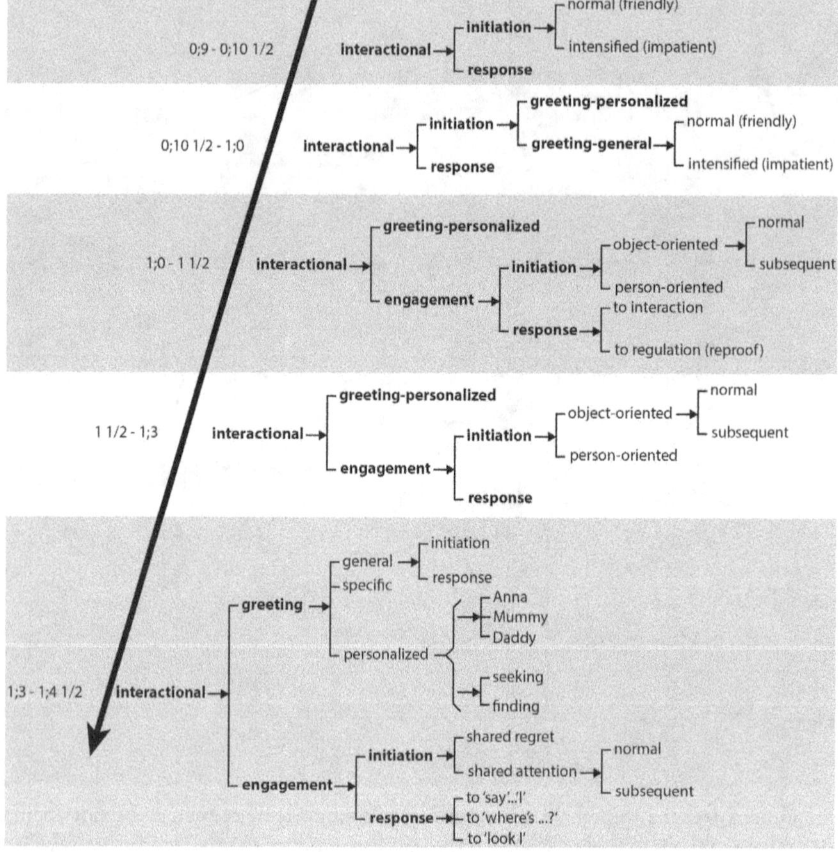

Figure 5.12 The gradual expansion of the interactional meaning potential during Nigel's protolinguistic phase, based on Halliday (1975)

(e.g. Halliday 1975) and adolescence (e.g. Christie and Derewianka 2008), steady growth through most of adult life, with the possibility of decline in late adulthood and ultimate death. It is difficult to illustrate the growth of the meaning potential, but let me give an indication of it by representing a sequence of the meaning potential for interaction (i.e. the meaning potential operating in interactional contexts) in Halliday's (1975) case study of Nigel, see Figure 5.12. The interactional meaning potential grows steadily; Nigel has more options in meaning at each interval described by Halliday. In the final version shown in Figure 5.12, there has been a qualitative change beyond the addition of new options of meaning: Nigel has deconstructed the personalized greeting into two systemic variables, the naming of the person being greeted ('Anna'/'Mummy'/'Daddy') and the orientation of the greeting ('seeking'/'finding'). This deconstruction on the content plane was helped by his deconstruction on the expression plane into articulatory sequence (naming) and prosody (orientation). For Nigel, this served as a gateway into grammar, being able to mean more than one thing at the same time (e.g. Halliday [1992e] 2002d: 363–364).

Phylogenetically, members of speech fellowships evolve the ***collective*** meaning potential over generations of meaners, through both logogenesis and ontogenesis. This collective meaning potential is an ***aggregate*** of different dialectal, diatypic (registerial) and codal varieties of a language. In particular, as new registers gradually emerge and old ones disappear when they're no longer functional, the registerial make-up of a language changes over time, as has been shown by Halliday's (e.g. 1988) account of the evolution of scientific English over the last half millennium or so. The evolution of the registers of scientific English has involved an expansion of the meaning potential of the language, a key factor being the expansion of the metaphorical mode of meaning within the ideational resources of the language.

The evolution of the meaning potential is both qualitative and quantitative in character. Quantitative changes are probabilistic in nature – observable as changes in relative frequencies in texts over extended periods of time. One classic (non-systemic) study shows this very clearly. This is Ellegård's (1953) text-based study of the gradual change in the systemic environments in which the auxiliary

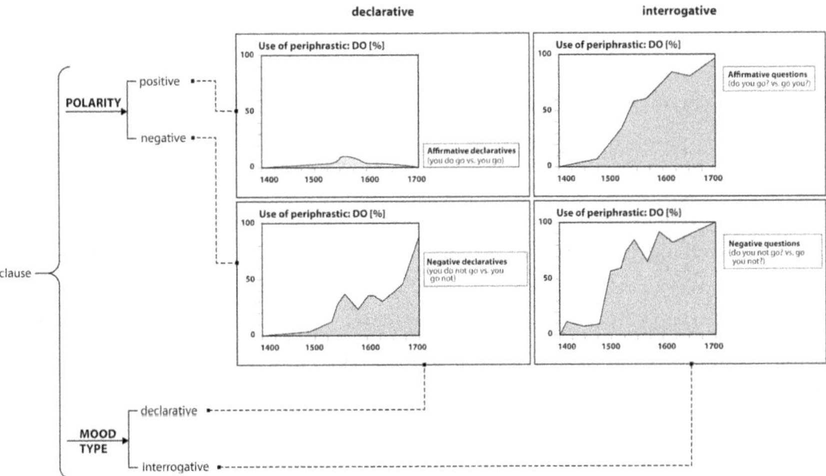

Figure 5.13 The gradual emergence of 'periphrastic *do*' since Middle English as a realization of Finite in interpersonal clause environments defined by the intersection of POLARITY and MOOD TYPE (simplified here as the contrast between 'declarative' and 'interrogative')

('supportive' or 'periphrastic') *do* appears during a period of around 250 years, from Middle English in the fifteenth century to Modern English around 1700.[25]

The environment of *do* is determined by two systemic variables, mood ('imperative'/'declarative'/'interrogative') and polarity ('positive'/'negative'), and the frequency of *do* as a realization of Finite grew in so-called non-assertive clauses, i.e. clauses that are 'interrogative' and/or 'negative', as shown schematically in Figure 5.13.[26] (For the sake of simplicity, I have left out negative imperatives; but the frequency of *do* also increased steadily in such clauses during this period, reaching 100% by the early eighteenth century.) According to Ellegård's study, negative interrogatives led the way in terms of increase in frequency, followed by positive interrogatives and then by negative declaratives. The increases in frequency were gradual; for example, by around 1500, around 50% of all negative interrogatives had *do* and by around 1700, close to 100%. At the same time, while the frequency of *do* in (non-emphatic) positive declaratives increased for a while during the mid-sixteenth century, it then decreased again and eventually became 0%. Studies of this kind show very clearly that categorical change is simply the limiting case, either 0% or 100% in terms of relative frequency in text.

The kind of gradual change brought out by Ellegård's (1953) study illustrates a general principle in semogenesis: as just noted, states of the system that appear to be categorical are simply the ***limiting cases of probability distributions***, either 0 or 1. Thus in Middle English, the probability of *do* as Finite in negative interrogatives was 0; but by the early eighteenth century, it was 1. To understand this change, we must interpret it as a gradual change in the probability of choice, as shown in Figure 5.13.

This general principle has been discussed by Halliday in various publications. In Halliday ([1992e] 2002d: 360–363), he sets out a 'model of semogenesis' where associated variables are gradually dissociated from one another, providing a number of 'postulated examples of semogenic evolution in relation to some systems of Modern English' (Halliday [1992e] 2002d: Figure 4). The gradual dissociation is based on changing probabilities; as two features as 'prised apart', they begin by being very likely to be chosen together, and then gradually become more independently variable. This can be illustrated by reference to one of Halliday's 'postulated examples', the system of projection of speech and thought. Using Halliday's model of semogenesis, we can postulate three stages: see Figure 5.14.

In Stage I, there is just one system, which we can represent as 'locution = quote'/ 'idea = report' – i.e. in traditional terms, 'direct speech'/'indirect thought'. In Stage II, his one system begins to be split into two ('locution'/'idea' and 'quote'/'report'), with 'locution' and 'quote' and 'idea' and 'report' only partially (but strongly) associated with one another: 'locution' and 'quote' are very likely to be selected

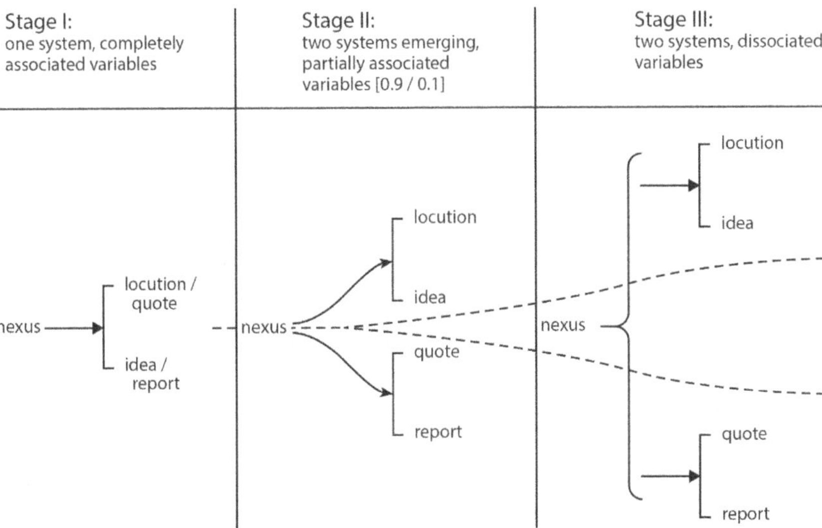

Figure 5.14 Halliday's model of semogenesis involving the gradual dissociation of associated variables (adapted from Halliday 1992b/2002c Figures 3 and 4)

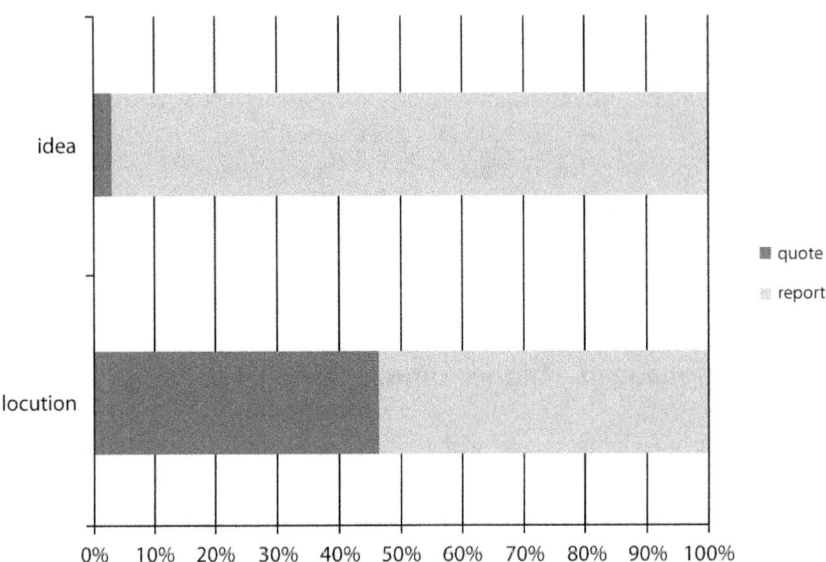

Figure 5.15 Intersection of 'locution'/'idea' and 'quote'/'report' in a registerially varied sample of texts (N = 1,393 clause nexuses)

together, and 'idea' and 'report' are similarly very likely to be selected together; in other words, there are strong conditioning probabilities. In Stage III, these associations have weakened, and there are now two simultaneous systems, 'locution'/'idea' and 'quote'/'report'. These two systems could, in principle, have reached a state of being completely independently variable. However, text-based investigations have shown that certain combinations are favoured, other ones disfavoured. Drawing on a corpus of ethnographic interviews, Nesbitt and Plum (1988) found that 'locution' favours 'quote', whereas 'idea' favours 'report' (for discussion, see also Halliday 2005b). Drawing on an opportunistic sample from a range of spoken and written registers, I arrived at a different generalization (e.g. Matthiessen 2002a): while 'idea' strongly favours 'report', 'locution' occurs approximately equally often with 'quote' as it does with 'report', see Figure 5.15.

Exploratory studies of semogenesis within the different time-frames – logogenetic, ontogenetic and phylogenetic – show very clearly that semogenesis is a systemic process in the first instance rather than a structural one. Semogenesis certainly involves changes in structure, as the now extensive literature on grammaticalization shows, but ***the pressures behind such structural changes are systemic***. Studies outside systemic functional linguistics concerned with semogenesis – in particular, either with ontogenesis or phylogenesis – have been oriented largely towards the syntagmatic axis; but there are important exceptions: in their account of 'parametric linguistics', Heller and Macris (1967) give many examples of the role of what we might call 'paradigmatic pressure' in the evolution of languages. The work on grammaticalization, particularly in the last couple of decades, is another powerful example. While grammaticalization is usually investigated in syntagmatic terms, one key issue is really how grammatical systems gradually 'import' lexical items to serve as realizations of terms in these grammatical systems: lexical items move along the cline of delicacy from the lexical zone into the grammatical zone because of 'paradigmatic pressure' – the need to realize contrasts among terms in grammatical systems.

5.5 Language as a higher-order semiotic system

Central to Halliday's engagement with language is his conception of language as a resource for making meaning. This involves, as I have noted above (see Section 5.2), viewing language ***holistically*** as a complex adaptive system, adopting the approach of **systems-thinking** rather than that of **Cartesian Analysis**, the approach that came to dominate Western science (cf. Capra 1996) in general and US American Structuralist and Generative Linguistics in particular. The holistic view of language in SFL has led to the expansion of the theory from language to semiotic systems in general. By applying systems-thinking, researchers have been able to locate language in relation to other semiotic systems – including centrally, protolanguage, making explicit how semiotic systems may differ in 'dimensionality'. For example, semiotic systems may differ in terms of the degree of stratification, in particular the bifurcation of the content plane and the expression plane into two sets of strata each (content – semantics and lexicogrammar; expression [for spoken language] – phonology and phonetics); and (related to this organizational difference) they may differ in terms of functional organization – one model being that of language development (e.g. Halliday 1975, 2003b; Painter, Derewianka and Torr 2007): micro-functional organization, macro-functional organization and metafunctional organization.

By another step, Halliday (e.g. [1996] 2002c [2005a] 2013b) has suggested that semiotic systems can be located in an ordered typology of systems operating within different phenomenal realms (see also e.g. Halliday and Matthiessen 1999): 1st-order: **physical** systems – 2nd-order: **biological** systems [= physical + life] – 3rd-order: **social** systems [= biological + value] – 4th-order: **semiotic** systems [= social + meaning]. Each new order is characterized by the emergence of new forms of organization ***superimposed*** on the organization of lower-order systems. Thus higher-order systems ***inherit*** the organizational properties of lower-order ones (cf. Matthiessen 2007b), see Figure 5.16. For example, by interpreting language as a social semiotic system (see Halliday 1978), we assign it the properties of social systems in general – including the relationship between the individual and the collective modelled as roles in role networks (cf. Firth [1950] 1957a; Butt 1991). In other words, the social properties of language – and of other social-semiotic systems – follow automatically from locating language in the ordered typology of systems; they do not have to be theorized and stated separately.

Halliday interprets language not just as a semiotic system but as a **higher-order semiotic system**, which means among other things that, in contrast with **primary semiotic systems**, it is stratified within both the content plane and the expression plane and that it is metafunctional, embodying the potential for the creation of simultaneous strands of meaning. Halliday (e.g. 1975, 2003b) has shown how language develops out of a primary semiotic system, protolanguage; and it seems plausible that his account of gradual increase in complexity is also a model of the evolution of language (see e.g. Matthiessen 2004b).

Language thus ***inherits*** the properties not only from protolanguage, but also from the social, biological and physical systems through which it is manifested. This means that as linguists we must theorize and explain language as a particular kind of 4th-order system, noting carefully the properties it has because it is also

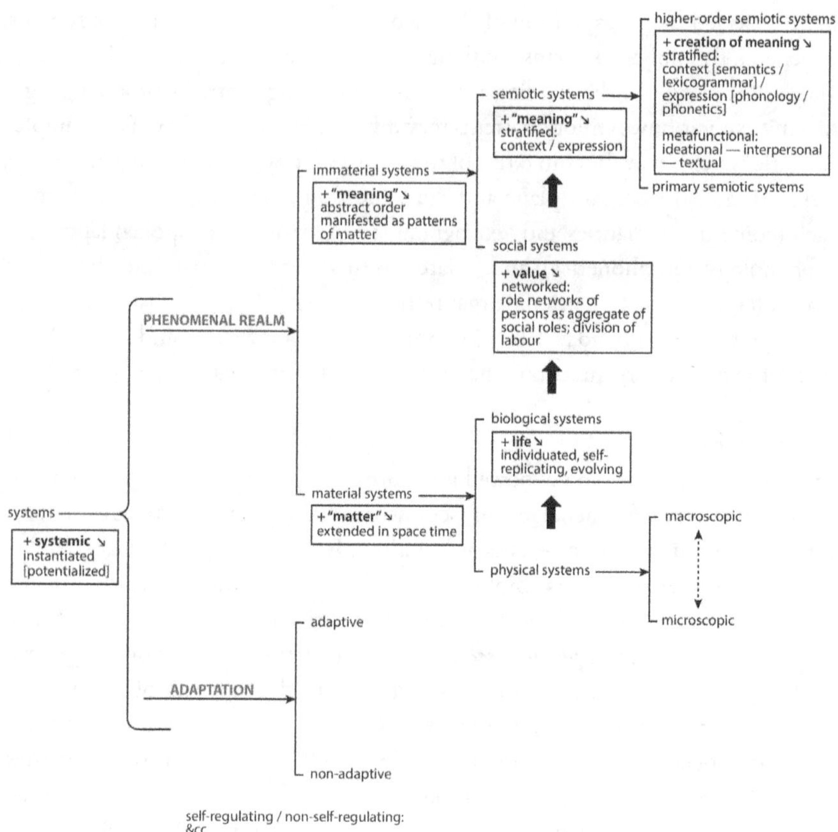

Figure 5.16 Ordered typology of systems operating in different phenomenal realms

at the same time a social, biological and physical system. In the last 30 years or so, linguists have written a great deal about the social nature of language in an attempt to reassert, in the context of the increasing dominance of cognitive science, what is of course an old insight into the nature of language. Such contributions are certainly important and valuable, but once we recognize the place of semiotic systems in the ordered typology of systems, it follows that they inherit the properties of social systems, including the enactment of individuals as persons through their participation in different social roles in different role networks (cf. Halliday 1975, 1978; Butt 1991 – both with references to Firth [1950] 1957a). Naturally, once language had emerged as a higher-order semiotic, it evolved together with the social order of modern humans, gradually paving the way for increasing social complexity (e.g. Halliday [2010] 2013b; Matthiessen 2004b). By placing language in the ordered typology of systems, Halliday has made it possible to explore it in terms of a **general theory of systems:** we can ask what properties are shared by systems of all kinds, what properties emerge in systems as they increase in complexity. For example, compositional scales are found in systems of all kinds (cf. Koestler's notion of holarchy, discussed in Sheldrake 1988); but individuation emerges only with biological systems – biological organisms, and is manifested with increasing complexity in social systems – persons (aggregates for personae, or social roles) and meaners (aggregates of meaning roles).

Let me round off the discussion of the ordered typology of systems by quoting from Halliday ([2011b] 2013b):

> I have referred elsewhere to the point made by the physicist George Williams, that as human beings we inhabit two incommensurable realms: the realm of **matter**, measurable in mass, heat, length and so on, and the realm of **information**, measured in bytes (Williams 1995a; cf. Halliday [2005a] 2013b). The realm of matter is investigated in the physical and biological sciences, and to some extent also in the social sciences; these got separated because our material world is made up of systems of different kinds. We can arrange these systems in a linear progression: first come physical systems; add **life**, then you have biological systems; add **value**, then you have social systems. At each step you are adding a new form of order: introducing more information by which the matter is becoming organized.

When we come to language, this is a system of a fourth order of complexity known as a **semiotic** system. Here what has been added is another component, that of **meaning.** In a semiotic system, information has replaced matter and taken over as the primary realm. It has been objected that all social systems are also semiotic; it is true that they have a lot of information in them, but there is still a significant distinction to be made. A hive of bees is not itself a semiotic system, although its members have evolved a system that is semiotic, the honey dance. What distinguishes the four different kinds of system is the different mix, the particular balance of matter and information that determines the properties of each.

5.6 Ideas about linguistics

Halliday's ideas about language are of course related to his ideas about the ***study*** of language, linguistics: he has developed a kind of linguistics that will enable researchers to engage with language holistically as a resource, in both theory and application. He has written about the nature of the kind of linguistic theory that he and other systemic functional linguists have been developing since the 1960s – drawing attention to various features, e.g. its orientation to 'consumers' (e.g. Halliday [1964] 2003a), its multifunctional nature (e.g. Halliday 1985a), its extravagance (e.g. Halliday 1980a), its differentiation as a theory of language as a general human system from descriptions of particular languages (e.g. Halliday [1992f] 2003a), its appliability (e.g. Halliday [2002d] 2005b), its variability (its nature as a flexi-theory; Halliday 1980a, [1997] 2003a) and its social accountability (e.g. Halliday 1984b).

In Halliday ([1997] 2003a), he explores linguistics as metaphor, suggesting five 'critical features' that linguistics shares with language: **comprehensiveness,**

Table 5.4 Halliday's (1997) five 'critical features' of language and linguistics

	phenomenon: language	**theory: linguistics**
comprehen-siveness	language construes 'all of our experience, it enacts all of our interpersonal processes'	(i) comprehensive in coverage of the different orders of manifestation of language (semiotic, social, biological and physical); (ii) 'viewing the grammar of a language (or any other stratum) in its entirety' – 'language as resource'
extravagance	complementarities (see further Halliday 2008), redundancy, metaphor	complementary ways of modelling the same phenomenon, e.g. lexicogrammar modelled either as grammar or as lexis
indeterminacy	blends, borderline cases, overlaps (cf. Halliday and Matthiessen 1999: 547–52)	the theory 'celebrates the indeterminacy in language itself', operating with 'descriptive categories that are themselves fluid and unstable'; 'the general theoretical framework offers ways of modelling indeterminacy', with probability as a central feature
non-autonomy	language is part of the human condition, and human history; it operates in context alongside other human systems	exploration of language as part of a general theory of meaning (semiotics); 'new understanding of the nature and typology of systems, and of processes of change'; applications in a growing range of institutional environments, e.g. 'in education, in medicine and in the law'
variability	language is inherently variable: dialectal variation, diatypic (functional, register) variation, codal variation	variation within the 'general model' that may be dialectal, registerial or codal in nature and which involves playing off different theoretical dimensions against one another (e.g. stratification and instantiation, stratification and axis)[27]

extravagance, indeterminacy, non-autonomy and **variability**. These five features are tabulated in Table 5.4 together with brief characterizations of their application to language and to linguistics.

Like language and other semiotic systems, systemic functional theory is thus a **resource** – a resource for making meaning about semiotic systems. Systemic functional theory is itself a kind of semiotic system – like all theories, whether they are commonsense theories (folk theories) or uncommon sense ones (scientific theories and educational versions of them). In this respect, systemic functional theory is like all other theories: all theories are constructed out of the resources of semiotic systems – language, in the first instance, but also various semiotic systems designed for the purpose of representing theory, like various branches of mathematics like trigonometric functions used to represent various kinds of wave and differential calculus used to represent rates of change as in theories of motion. However, theories of social, biological and physical systems are of a different systemic order from the systems being theorized, whereas linguistic theories are of the same systemic order as the systems that they are theories of.

Linguists have explored this relationship using different terms; J. R. Firth ([1948b] 1957b: 190) talked about linguistics as language turned back on itself, Halliday ([1957] 2002c: 30) emphasized the importance of the distinction between 'l.u.d.', language under description, and 'l.o.d.', language of description, a 'metalanguage', and Hjelmslev (1943: 105–106) had characterized linguistics as *metasprog*, metalanguage, which Weinreich (1980: 7) later characterized 'a specialized language for communication about another language (the "object language")'; see further Matthiessen and Nesbitt (1996: Section 3.2). One of the special challenges that arises in linguistics that Halliday ([1984c] 2002c) has identified and characterized is the 'ineffability of grammatical categories'.

Drawing on the insight that systemic functional linguistics is language turned back on itself, systemic functional linguists have explored the semiotic organization of this theory. Inspired by work by Brachman (e.g. 1978, [1979] 1985), by Hans Utzkoreit and by Hasan's (1985a) work on symbolic articulation and theme in verbal art (cf. Halliday's [2011c] 2013b: Section 3.2, exploration of theory and verbal science as higher-order values), we have explored the stratification of systemic functional linguistics into four strata – **theory, theoretical representation, computational representation** and **computational implementation** (e.g. Matthiessen 1988a; Matthiessen and Nesbitt 1996; Halliday and Matthiessen 1999; Teich 1999). This stratification of the metalanguage is illustrated in Figure 5.17 for the theory of paradigmatic organization.

Once we recognize that systemic functional linguistics can be modelled as a stratified metalanguage along the lines mentioned above, it becomes possible to be

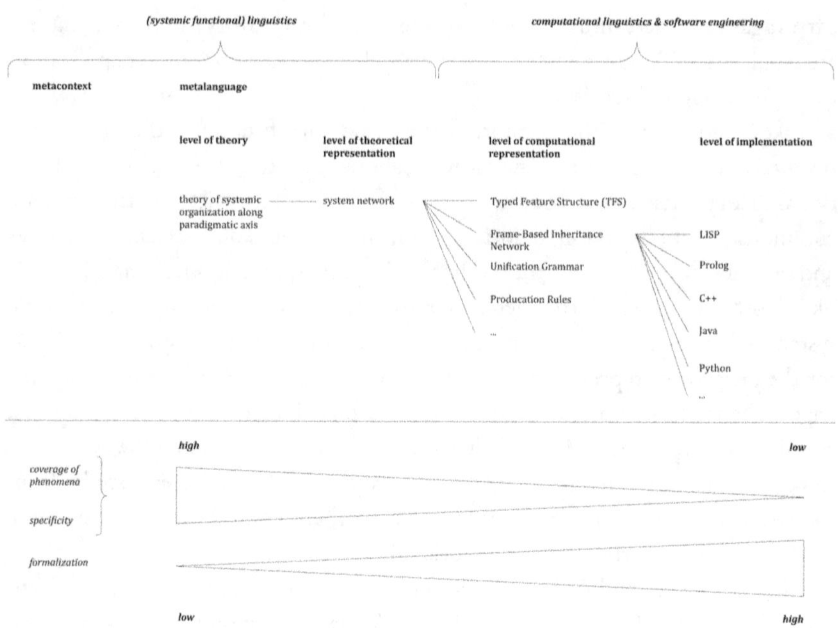

Figure 5.17 Stratification of the systemic-functional metalanguage in context exemplified by reference to paradigmatic theory and system networks

more precise about the unification-based family of grammars mentioned above in Section 5.2 and represented (in part) diagrammatically in Figure 5.2. Let me just make two observations here.

1. Some of the grammatical frameworks are **functional in a high-level theoretical sense**, relating grammar to the kind of semantics that is concerned with text in context and drawing on large volumes of natural text examples. These include the European functional traditions of the Prague School and the Firthian and Hallidayan tradition, and the US American functional tradition of anthropological linguistics (including Sapir, Whorf and Pike). Later developments in the US include what has been referred to as 'West-Coast Functionalism', where a central concern since the 1970s has been to explain features of grammar by reference to discourse.
2. Some of the grammatical frameworks are **functional in a more representational sense**, involving structural functions (also referred to as roles, relations or deep cases) as well as classes in the representation of syntagmatic organization. One early prominent example is LFG, where a distinction was made between f-structure, function structure, and c-structure, constituent structure; for example, Bresnan (1982: 4) writes:

> The lexical theory of grammar provides a formally explicit and coherent theory of how surface structures are related to representations of meaningful grammatical relations. Rules of grammar defined in the formal system of grammatical representation provide each sentence of a language with dual representations consisting of a *constituent structure* (*c-structure*) and a *functional structure* (*f-structure*). ... The constituent structure represents the superficial constituency of the sentence (which is phonologically interpreted), and the functional structure is the representation of its meaningful grammatical relations (which is semantically interpreted).

This is reminiscent of Halliday's ([1966b] 2002c) distinction between **structure** (configurations of functions) and **syntagm** (sequences of classes), even reflecting the stratal location of lexicogrammar between semantics and phonology – one significant difference of course being that Halliday incorporated this distinction within a paradigmatically based theory. I've used LFG as an example because its roots go back to the 1970s (cf. Figure 5.2), and it has influenced other later developments such as HPSG while at the same time continuing to develop in its own right as a productive grammatical framework.

Modelling the stratification of the systemic functional metalanguage makes it easier to identify complementarities in approaches to grammar, and opportunities to draw on research outside SFL to find more explicit forms of computationally oriented representation (cf. Bateman 2008a). This research programme was initiated by Kay (1979), followed up by Kasper (1988a) at the Information Sciences Institute (cf. also Matthiessen 1988b) and then by Bateman and his group of researchers in German research contexts (e.g. Bateman, Emele and Momma 1992); but it still remains to be developed further. This development is essential if there is to be a breakthrough in large-scale automated corpus analysis based on systemic functional grammar (cf. O'Donnell and Bateman 2005; Teich 2009; Wu 2009).

The concerns I have just discussed can be interpreted as falling within the ideational realm of the systemic functional metalanguage – issues relating to the construal of language within successive strata of the metalanguage. But just like language, the systemic functional metalanguage is **multifunctional**; Halliday ([1985d] 2003a: 197) emphasized the ideational and interpersonal aspects of the metalanguage:

> I have often emphasized that language, both in its nature and in its ontogenetic development, clearly reveals a dual function; it is at once, and inseparably, a means of action and a means of reflection.

> Linguistics, as metalanguage, has to serve the same twofold purpose. Systemic theory is explicitly constructed both for thinking with and for acting with.

Thus since the 1960s, systemic functional theory has been used as a means of action in many contexts – a concern that goes back to the efforts in the 1950s to develop a Marxist kind of linguistics (see Halliday [1997] 2003a: 223–224; this volume). Central to these efforts was the notion of **social accountability** (e.g. Halliday 1984b),[28] which has been manifested in a wide range of applications, including critically the work in institutions of education by J. R. Martin, Joan Rothery, Fran Christie and their group (e.g. Rose and Martin 2012; Christie 2012), Geoff Williams, Bernard Mohan, Jay Lemke and many others. Social accountability includes being critical, what Halliday ([1997] 2003a: 256) calls the 'prevailing stance';[29] but it includes so much more – in general, it is concerned with strategies for addressing problems in the community, for improving the human condition (cf. Matthiessen 2012). Describing a 'minor' language that is essential to its community but which is under threat (even if it is not yet classified as 'endangered' in the technical sense of the term) – a language such as Western Desert (Rose 2001a), Òkó (Akerejola 2005) or Bajjika (Kumar 2009), or a 'major' language whose community of speakers play a key role in world affairs – a language such as Japanese (Teruya 2007) or Arabic (Bardi 2008) – may be much more important for communities around the world than critiquing some sample of discourses of power, and it is certainly a much harder task!

5.7 Conclusion

In this chapter, I have been concerned with Halliday's ideas about language – and by extension, with his ideas about linguistics. I have tried to show how his ideas about language flow from his conception of language as a **resource** – as a meaning potential giving the speakers of a language the power to mean (cf. Figure 5.5), the power to construe all of their experience as meaning, to enact all their roles and relations as meaning, and to transform these meanings into a flow of discourse that can be exchanged between speaker and addressee. My account has been partly chronological, but perhaps more logical (without chronos) in the sense that I have tried to bring out the theoretical force of what I called Halliday's **axial rethink** – the theoretical move whereby he developed a **paradigmatic base** for the modelling of language in order to bring out its organization as a meaning-making resource.

Table 5.5 Some of Halliday's key ideas about language in non-systemic functional work, from the 1960s onwards and in current linguistics

	Halliday's SFL	**non-systemic functional linguistics**	
		1960s –	**current**
theory in relation to context of application	Halliday (1964): syntax and the consumer	no – only one 'true' theory	yes – generally accepted
relation between grammar and lexis	Halliday (1961): continuum [lexis as most delicate grammar]	no – separate modules	yes – accepted in various frameworks including those involving variants of 'construction grammar' and work based on corpus investigation
probabilistic nature of language	Halliday (1959 onwards): system inherently probabilistic	no – not seen as valuable or interesting	yes – 'probabilistic linguistics' (e.g. Bod, Hay and Jannedy 2003a)
paradigmatic base	Halliday (e.g. 1966c): systemic organization as primary, structure as derived	no – structure primary; system networks misunderstood as 'taxonomic' approach	no – structure still primary, but with interesting developments in the direction of type hierarchies
phonology: prosodic	Halliday (e.g. 1963b, 1967b; 1992c)	no – approach to phonology segmental, with phonemes being composed of features [going back to Jakobson 1949]	yes – in the development of autosegmental and metrical phonology [e.g. Goldsmith 1990; cf. Henderson 1987]
emergent complexity	Halliday (1975)	no – not yet on the agenda	yes – e.g. Steels (e.g. 1998), Larsen-Freeman, Ellis (e.g. Beckner *et al.* 2009)
language development	Halliday (1975): learning how to mean	language acquisition	maybe – powerfully by Larsen-Freeman (2011)

Like many pioneering scholars, Halliday was often ahead of his time and he has never been a scholar who adopted (or adapted to) the intellectual fashion of the day,[30] so when he presented new proposals, they were often met with indifference or even hostility (as when he presented ideas about language as a probabilistic system in the 1960s). I remember being very impressed back in Sweden in the 1970s when I came across his article 'Syntax and the consumer' (Halliday [1964] 2003a) – it was so different from the prevailing ideology at the time, and sometime after I had met him in 1980, I asked him how his contribution to the Georgetown Roundtable was received. He smiled and said (as I recall) 'I was laughed out of court! There could only be one true theory of grammar.'

Many of his other ideas about language, and about linguistics, were, as I have just noted, met with indifference or even hostility when he first presented them.[31] I've suggested that Halliday was ahead of his time; if so, what is the situation at present? Views in linguistics in general have changed quite dramatically since the 1960s. Many of Halliday's key ideas have now been accepted, either by a wide group of linguists or by powerful sectors of the community of linguists – although too often without any reference to Halliday's work. Since it would take up too much space here to document this shift in the discipline of linguistics, I can only tabulate a few key areas here where the shift has been very significant: see Table 5.5. In this table, I have set out a number of Halliday's key contributions to the development of SFL, and compared them with views in non-systemic functional linguistics in the 1960s (when he introduced many of these key ideas) and at present.[32]

Thus ideas about language in linguistics in general have, not surprisingly, changed very considerably in the last 50 years or so; and as the table indicates, in a number of critical areas, non-systemic functional ideas ('mainstream ideas') are now much closer to Halliday's ideas about language – ideas that he began articulating in the 1950s and 1960s – than they were in the 1960s. The reasons are, naturally, many and complex; but let me mention a few of them.

(a) During the last 50 years, linguists have for the first time in the history of work on language gained access to large volumes of authentic **data** thanks to the technological advances that have made corpus-studies possible as a research methodology. Consequently, linguists have now revised earlier ideas about the relationship between grammar and lexis and about the role of probability in accounts of language, arriving at views resonating with those Halliday proposed over half a century ago.

(b) During the same time, linguists have explored and tested theories and forms of representation that were very formal and segmental in orientation, and found them unworkable: transformations have (largely) disappeared, syntax is no longer treated as autonomous from semantics but is tightly aligned with it, sound structure is no longer represented only segmentally but also prosodically – and just as the stratal line between syntax and semantics is now treated as natural rather than arbitrary, so is the stratal line between phonology and phonetics.

(c) Since the 1950s, the intellectual climate outside linguistics has become more conducive to Halliday's ideas. In the 1950s, scholars from a number of fields took steps that led to the development of classical cognitive science, a kind of macro-discipline that included (the then nascent) cognitive psychology, artificial intelligence, segments of linguistics and philosophy, and also neuroscience. This version of cognitive science was conceived of as 'the science of mind', as Stillings *et al.* (1987: 1) put it, characterizing it further as follows (using common lexical and grammatical metaphors that I have discussed as part of my analysis of the discourse of cognitive science, e.g. Matthiessen 1998):

Cognitive scientists view the human mind as a complex system that receives, stores, retrieves, transforms, and transmits information.

This version of cognitive science did not produce an intellectual environment that resonated with Halliday's conception of human beings as persons and as meaners interacting with each other (see e.g. Halliday 1978) – a point that becomes particularly clear in accounts of language development (e.g. Halliday 1975). Even by the late 1980s, Stillings *et al.* (1987: chap. 9) provide a very restricted, traditional account of 'language acquisition', suggesting that the early 'milestones in acquisition' begin with pre-linguistic 'babbling' while 'the first truly linguistic stage of language acquisition seems to be the one-word stage', which 'emerges within a few months of the child's first birthday' (Stillings *et al.* 1987: 366). This view of language development is of course fundamentally different from Halliday's (1975, 2003b) account of how young children learn how to mean in interaction with their immediate caregivers, starting with protolanguage somewhere around the middle of their first year of life.

However, the views of mainstream cognitive science have now been challenged in various fundamental ways. One important challenge was the introduction of Vygotsky's work in the West,[33] and his work is much more compatible with systemic functional ideas (cf. Wells 1994b; Byrnes 2006), as has been shown by Hasan (e.g. 2002) in her research dealing with semiotic mediation. And, very importantly, the developments in neuroscience have been quite dramatic, aided by new brain scanning techniques; they have made it possible to explore and theorize the relationship between language and the brain – both now with a solid base in empirical research – without having to postulate an intermediate 'level' of cognition without a solid empirical foundation in either neuroscience or linguistics: see e.g. Deacon (1992, 1997) and Edelman (1992) and cf. Halliday ([1995a] 2003a, [1997] 2003a).[34]

Thus the second decade of the twenty-first century will certainly continue to be very conducive to Halliday's 'ideas about language'.

Notes

1 Later, the professor of linguistics who succeeded Bertil Malmberg, Bengt Sigurd, encourages me to specialize in 'Hallidayan linguistics', I remember him telling me that he thought this would also be very good for linguists in Denmark since they were still, as he put it, suffering from a 'post-Hjelmslevian hangover'.

2 In their preface, the authors write (p. iii): 'This work was originally undertaken under the title "Integration of Transformational Theories on English Syntax" in the naïve expectation that most of the information about the transformational analysis of the grammar of English available up through the summer of 1968 could be brought together and integrated in a single format.'

3 The situation was different a decade earlier; when W. C. Mann and David Webber conducted a survey in the late 1970s of potential candidates to be used in a new text generation system, they chose Halliday's systemic functional grammar for various reasons (including Davey's, 1978, use of it in the Proteus text generation system); but a key reason was the commitment to comprehensive descriptions.

4 Other cross-overs can also be noted, including computational linguistics work within the Prague School tradition by Peter Sgall, Eva Hajičová, and others, and within Simon Dik's Functional Grammar, although the latter was arguably less functional in origin, not originally being centrally concerned with text in context (unlike Discourse Functional Grammar).

5 Douglas (1979) observes: "A system of taboos covers up this weakness of the classification system. It points in advance to defects and insists that no one shall give recognition to the inconvenient facts or behave in such a way as to undermine the acceptability and clarity of the system as a whole. It stops awkward questions and prevents awkward developments."

6 I haven't been able to find a succinct reference to this in the literature; but in response to a question about the influence of SFG on LFG after her talk at AILA at Waseda University in Tokyo, 1–6 August 1999 (Bresnan 2000), Joan Bresnan drew attention to the flow of influence from Halliday via Kaplan on LFG. For a comparison of 'semantic relations' in SFG and LFG, see Steiner (1988a).

7 The important principle that had been developed in Firthian system-structure phonology (prosodic analysis) that different systems operate at different places in a structure is captured by preselection: one general system is posited but different preselections are specified for different places in a structure.

8 In terms of ontogenesis, stratification and axis arguably develop out the hierarchic ordering of content and expression (cf. Matthiessen 2007b: Section 2.4).

9 This version of his description 'was written between May and August 1964 and formed the substance of a course on the description of English at the University of Indiana' (Halliday 2002a: 127).

10 See Halliday (2005a: 268–284) for his original set of systems we started with; Matthiessen and Bateman (1991) for discussion of the computational system; and Matthiessen (1995a) for a descriptive report based on an extended version of these systems.

11 As far as the description of English is concerned, there is a difference here between US American and British approaches to intonation (cf. Teich, Watson and Pereira 2000; and also Ladd 1996). In US American accounts, intonation contours tend to be described in terms of sequences of 'pitch levels' – ranging from Pike (1945, 1948: 15–16) to the current TOBI framework for intonation analysis (e.g. Beckman, Hirschberg and Shattuck-Hufnagel 2005), where contours are essentially analysed as sequences of high (H) and low (L) tones (either pitch accents or boundary tones); in contrast, in British accounts (see e.g. Crystal 1969), intonation contours tend to be analysed as prosodies, not broken down into sequences of segments: see Halliday (1967b) and references therein. For an overview of phonetic research into intonation, see e.g. Nooteboom (1997).

12 His interest in grammatical frequencies had been stimulated as a language learner and as a language teacher (e.g. Halliday [1993b] 2005b: 131–132).

13 See e.g. Neef and Vater (2006: 35), who note that in his early work, Chomsky "adopted Bloomfield's view of the lexicon as a list of morphemes (which he later cautiously termed 'formatives')". Chomsky (1965: 84) characterized the 'lexicon' as "an unordered list of all lexical formatives", "a set of lexical entries, each lexical entry being a pair (D, C), where D is a phonological distinctive feature matrix 'spelling' a certain lexical formative and C is a collection of specified syntactic features"; and later (p. 87) he reinforces the Bloomfieldian notion of irregularities belonging to the lexicon: "In general, all properties of a formative that are essentially idiosyncratic will be specified in the lexicon."

14 Just as articulatory dimensions define the vowel space as a topology: see Halliday and Matthiessen (1999) and cf. Matthiessen (1995b).

15 Roget's (1852) Thesaurus is, of course, a model in the sense that it provides a description of lexis as a resource (cf. Halliday 1976; Matthiessen 1991a: 259–260, 275); but it is not grounded in grammar. In computational linguistic research, there is now also an extensive body of research on the taxonomic organization of lexis, explored under the heading of ontology: see Huang *et al.* (2010). This kind of taxonomic organization is implicit in traditional dictionaries in glosses, but it can be retrieved, as shown many years ago by Amsler's (1981) pioneering computational analysis of entries in Webster's Dictionary.

16 It is also important to note that the point in delicacy where lexical items realize combinations of lexicogrammatical features is not necessarily the endpoint in delicacy: see Halliday ([1996] 2002c: 23).

17 In addition, the textual metafunction provides strategies for deploying orderings in delicacy in lexis within the other metafunction to achieve lexical cohesion (see Halliday and Hasan 1976; and cf. Matthiessen 1991a, 1995a).

18 They write (p. 276): "The expression of interpersonal meaning, of a particular attitude on the part of the speaker, is an important function of general nouns. Essentially the attitude conveyed is one of familiarity, as opposed to distance, in which the speaker assumes the right to represent the thing he is referring to as it impinges on him personally; hence the attitude may be either contemptuous or sympathetic, the two being closely related as forms of personal involvement (cf. the meaning of diminutives in many languages)."

19 And the comparable pairs of form and substance for written and signed languages.

20 The cognitive and the semiotic interpretations being complementary: see Halliday and Matthiessen (1999).

21 The work by Bateman *et al.* (2010) is of enormous importance for the development of models of semantics because they 'interface' a semantic model of space with a model needed by robots to perceive space and navigate through it. See further below.

22 It is equally important to ask about the expression substance in written and signed languages; but I will focus on spoken languages here.

23 Or 'anthropophonetics'; in 'Linguistics in the Nineteenth Century', Baudouin de Courtenay characterizes it as 'a separate branch of science which deals with the investigation of the conditions of pronunciation and of the phonational-auditory production of language' (Baudouin de Courtenay 1972: 246).

24 Compare Halliday's ([1984c] 2002c: 306) emphasis of the point that "a child's semiotic experience is extraordinarily rich"; he notes that, by the age of 5, a child may have heard "anything up to a quarter of a million Subjects' and observes that children 'model the language as a probabilistic system". Halliday ([1993b] 2005b: 136) again suggests that "children seem to learn language as a probabilistic system", noting that "they are surrounded by large quantities of data, probably at least a hundred thousand clauses a year, and they are sensitive to relative frequency as a resource for ordering what they learn".

25 Since Ellegård's classic study, researchers have explored the history of 'periphrastic do' further, raising various issues such as differences during the period across registers ('genres'), as in Rissanen (1991) and Warner (2005). Registerial variation is to be expected; the evolution of the overall meaning potential of a language is simply the composite of the evolution of and within the different registers that it is composed of – often with casual spoken language leading the development (cf. Halliday [2002e] 2005b). Compare also Halliday's (1988) account of the evolution of grammatical metaphor of the ideational kind as part of the evolution of scientific English in the last half millennium.

26 The source of the graph based on Ellegård (1953: 162) is in the common domain: http://en.wikipedia.org/wiki/File:Ellegard_Periphrastic_Do.svg.

27 Cf. Halliday ([1985d] 2003a: 192): 'Systemic theory is more like language itself – a system whose stability lies in its variation. A language is a 'metastable' system; it persists because it is constantly in flux.'

28 Linguists and researchers in related fields have, not surprisingly, taken different positions. For example, as I recall the discussion in the early 1980s with respect to the use of military funding to conduct research in the US, Chomsky's position was that it was alright to accept military funding since what really mattered was how academics used their 'discretionary time'. In contrast, Terry Winograd's position was that one should not accept military funding because doing so strengthened the channels of funding through the military. Another view was that taken by my project leader, Bill Mann. He said that as long as the research was unclassified and thus publically accessible, military funding was acceptable since the military were too badly organized to make use of the results so that it was certain that the results would be in the public domain before the military got their act together. Chomsky and Halliday have, of course, taken very different positions on linguistics in relation to social accountability. Chomsky has separated his linguistics from his

political activism – related to his point that what matters is what you do with your discretionary time. His two activities seem very far apart. However, I think there is actually a deep connection, viz. the individualism of his cognitive stance in linguistics and of his anarcho-syndicalism in his political activism – and since individualism resonates nicely with mainstream US America, he is tolerated by the ruling elite; he does not actually represent the kind of threat that a Marxist scholar and activist would. In contrast, Halliday has created a kind of linguistics that relates to social accountability – that can be used in various kinds of interventions (appliable linguistics: Halliday [2002a] 2007a); systemic functional theory was never 'neutral' (cf. Halliday 2003a: 223).

29 Halliday ([1997] 2003a: 256) writes: "It is important, I think, in an age when the prevailing stance (on language, but also on other things besides) is the 'critical' – and this often means only destructively critical – to place the enabling power of language clearly in the centre of the stage; otherwise, in our own praxis, whether educational, clinical, forensic or whatever else, we will come up only with problems, and never any solutions."

30 There are many examples of this in his work; it is instructive to read his comments over the years on cognitive science, post-structuralism, postmodernism.

31 For example, Halliday ([1985d] 2003a) notes that Postal (1964) completely 'misread' Halliday ([1961] 2002c) 'as a theory of constituent structure'; this was during Postal's Chomskyan period, before he helped develop generative semantics and became a critic of both Chomsky's linguistics and his politics.

32 In the Prague School phonology developed by Nikolai Trubetzkoy, phonological features had been interpreted as values along paradigmatic dimensions, just as terms in phonological systems in systemic phonology are. Jakobson ([1949] 1962: 420) instead interpreted 'distinctive features' as components of phonemes, thereby changing their status from paradigmatic to syntagmatic: 'Meanwhile the science of language continued to treat phonemes as the most minute (further indivisible) linguistic unit. However, as the phonemes of a given language form a system of sequences, so the system of phonemes, in turn, is formed by their constituents, i.e. by distinctive features. And the breaking up of the phonemes into distinctive features follows precisely the same tested devices as the division of morphemes into phonemes.' As Fischer-Jørgensen (1975: 146) points out, this echoes Bloomfield's ([1933] 2002) statement that 'the distinctive features occur in lumps and bundles each one of which we call a phoneme'. For the drawback of Jakobson's reinterpretation, see also Halliday and Matthiessen (1999).

33 Vygotsky's *Thought and Language* appeared in an English translation in 1962 with an introduction by Jerome Bruner; but it took a long time before his ideas were picked up more generally. (There is no reference to Vygotsky in Stillings *et al.* 1987; and Bruner is only mentioned in connection with his discussion of Piaget.)

34 Available from: http://www.cl.cam.ac.uk/~aac10/papers/lrec2000.pdf; also available at: http://framenet.icsi.berkeley.edu/index.php?option=com_wrapper&-Itemid=126

Chapter 6
The architecture of phonology according to Systemic Functional Linguistics

6.1 The notion of 'architecture'

6.1.1 Interest in 'architecture'

This volume of my collected works is, to a large extent, about linguistics – about the science of language rather than directly about language, the phenomenon linguistics is concerned with. Now since linguistics is about language, it is also, of course, about language but ***indirectly***. Other volumes will deal with different aspects of languages more ***directly*** – descriptions of mostly English but also of Akan, analysis of text and of translation pairs, and language typology. But one volume will be devoted to computational modelling, more specifically the modelling of language in the service of text generation; and the papers in that volume will again to some extent be about linguistics.

In this last chapter of this volume, I will discuss the architecture of one of the subsystems that make up language, viz. the **architecture of phonology** according to SFL – both in order to shed light on phonology itself as a sounding potential, i.e. as a resource for realizing meanings through soundings, and also in order to illustrate the **fractal principle** in SFL that all the stratal subsystems of language are organized according the same basic **stratal blueprint**, most centrally axis and rank (see e.g. Matthiessen 2007b [this volume]).

The discussion of the architecture of phonology will also provide the theoretical background needed for the description of the phonology of Akan in Volume 3. In fact, I first engaged with systemic functional phonology in the mid-1980s when I tried to develop that description of the phonology of Akan. At the time, I had had to study Chomsky and Halle's SPE style generative phonology, but I had also read Fischer-Jørgensen's (1975) history of phonology; but I had very little sense of what systemic phonology might be like – beyond Halliday's (1967b) pioneering work on intonation and rhythm and references to Firth's prosodic analysis – the first anthology, Tench (1992), had not yet been published, and I had not seen the early Ph.D. theses on the grammar of two languages spoken in West Africa, Mock (1969) on Nzema and Barnwell (1969) on Mbembe. So I had to work out certain aspects of the architecture of phonology for myself, partly based on the architecture of grammar and my experience of the development of a computational model.[1] But before I turn to the architecture of phonology, I will say a few more words about linguistics as metalanguage.

We can call linguistics about linguistics **metalinguistics** to ensure that we are clear about the level of abstraction (cf. Halliday 1984c, 1996). Throughout my academic life, the metalinguistics I have used has mostly been **Systemic Functional Metalinguistics (SFM-L)** since I chose Systemic Functional Linguistics as my main resource for engaging with language many years ago (cf. the Introduction to chap. 5). Often the choice of one's metalanguage is a function of where one grew up, academically speaking: the metalanguage used in the department where one did one's first, second or third academic degree (or one of the metalanguages, in multi-metalingual departments). In my case, I had to go look for SFL; it wasn't around in my linguistics department at Lund University at all although Halliday and Hasan's (1976) *Cohesion in English*, which was published around the time I started at Lund University, was used very actively by researchers in another department where I was also an undergraduate student, the Department of English.

But in the Department of Linguistics, although generative linguistics was the dominant approach in the mid-1970s, we were actively encouraged to study different theories on our own, and the department had a fairly extensive library, where I would forage – very often alone at night, in the former villa of the Rector Magnificus of Lund University, where Linguistics was housed at the time. Thus I was lucky enough to learn from the start about different 'architectures' of language, in class (mostly Chomsky's Extended Standard Theory, but also good sample of European Structuralism in general and Hjelmslev's Glossematics in particular), in seminars (in particular, perhaps, the Prague School), and on my hunting expeditions in the library, where on my own I found intriguing accounts beyond the Chomskyan curriculum of the day: Tagmemics, Stratificational Linguistics (I remember marvelling at the aesthetic appeal of the diagrams in Lockwood 1972, which included examples from stratificational phonology) and Systemic Functional Linguistics (in addition to Halliday and Hasan 1976, I found Halliday 1973, Halliday 1976, and later Halliday 1978 – again works that appealed powerfully to my visual sense) – and, perhaps most challenging but very rewarding, accounts of Gustave Guillaume's work. My second professor of Linguistics, Bengt

Sigurd (1928–2010), who had been appointed after Bertil Malmberg (1913–1994) retired, encouraged me to produce an undergraduate thesis on what I came to call *Hallidayan Linguistics*.

During these undergraduate years, I was thus fortunate enough to become aware not of only different 'architectures' of language proposed by a wide range of linguistic theories but also of ***varied ways of doing architectural designs***. One key contrast I became aware of early on was that between: (a) boxes representing modules linked by lines or arrows – prevalent in generative architectural diagrams; and (b) relational-stratal architectures – characteristic of Stratificational Linguistics and SFL. This contrast has 'stood the test of time'; it was reinforced in my post-graduate studies at UCLA and my involvement in computational linguistic research projects at the Information Sciences Institute/USC. For example, I realized that type (a) was also the default architecture model not only in generative linguistics but also in cognitive psychology (e.g. Anderson 1983), in computational linguistics, in AI models, and in software design. And I also came to understand the fundamental distinction between **declarative** and **procedural** representations, and the need to be very clear about levels of specification in architectural representations (thanks in particular to discussions in the late 1970s and early 1980s of approaches to knowledge representation: Woods' 1975, call for much greater clarity, and Brachman's 1979, response to this call – a response that was part of a whole new strand in knowledge representation). Along the way, I learned about various forms of representation that may be helpful in showing the architecture of something – in showing how something is organized or how it works, different kinds of charts (including flow charts – used for a while in SFL in the 1980s, e.g. Martin 1985b; Ventola 1987, and pseudo-flowcharts), layouts of algorithms, type hierarchies, schemata, scripts, transition networks (of different kinds).

These insights into different kinds of architectural design are relevant to the theorizing and modelling to all subsystems of language – including, importantly in the context of this chapter, phonology. For example, when I became familiar with AI planning and with programming, I realized that various 'discoveries' in the generative work on phonology in the 1960s such as the distinction between feeding and bleeding rule ordering were simply manifestations of general principles inherent in the modelling in processes.

6.1.2 The nature of 'architecture' in and around linguistics

Thanks to O'Toole (1994, and subsequent publications), we have come to learn, as a community, about the semiotics of architecture – as part of his research programme into the semiotics of 'displayed art'. And when 'architecture' goes abstract, as in 'the architecture of language', 'the architecture of cognition', we can draw on his insights to think about the semiotics of architecture in terms of metafunction, rank, axis and delicacy, and stratification. For example, metafunctionally, we can think about architecture not only as theory but also as praxis.

I have found 'architecture' to be a helpful figure of speech in exploring language and languages – alongside 'cartography'; though I have wondered on various occasions whether 'anatomy' would be better (cf. Longacre 1976) or even 'physiology' as, in a sense, functional anatomy,[2] and I have taken note of Halliday's references to town planning and jungles.

When we examine different proposals for the architecture of language, we can identify a number of fundamental issues, including the following ones stated in terms of different architectural choices:

- NATURE: rule vs. resource – is the architecture couched in terms of language as rule or as resource?
- TYPE: modules vs. relations – is the architecture characterized in terms of modules or components linked by representations (as in generative linguistic accounts of different varieties) or in terms of relations (as in stratificational linguistics and systemic functional linguistics)?
- PHASE: states vs. system-&-processes – is the architecture concerned with all phases of language as system-&-process or only with certain states of the system (typically, potential vs. instance)? In other words, does it include an account of processes or not?
- COVERAGE: whole vs. subsystem – does the architecture focus holistically on the whole system of language (as in systemic functional linguistics) or on a particular subsystem (as in autosegmental phonology)?
- DOMAIN: local vs. global – does the architecture posit local principles of organization for different linguistic subsystems (e.g. syntax vs. phonology in generative accounts) or does it involve principles of organization that apply to all linguistic subsystems (as in stratificational linguistics and systemic functional linguistics)?
- METALINGUISTIC STRATUM: theory vs. representation – is the architecture specified in abstract terms as theory or is it couched in terms of some system of representation (like production rules, phrase structure rules, frame-based inheritance networks); or is it specified in terms of both higher-level theory and its manifestation in a system or systems of representation?
- INTERFACE to other systems: language-internal vs. interfaces to other systems – is the architecture outward-looking or inward-looking, i.e. does it or does it not relate language to other (human) systems?

- FOURTH-ORDER NATURE: semiotic vs. cognitive – if the architecture interprets language as a higher-order system (higher order than physical, biological and social systems), does it opt for a semiotic interpretation in terms of meaning or for a cognitive interpretation in terms of knowledge?

These architectural choices are, in principle, relevant to any aspect of language – including the architecture of the phonological subsystem; but some are particularly pertinent when we profile the systemic functional architecture of phonology to bring out differences from other phonological architectures. According to the systemic functional architecture of phonology:

- it is a resource rather than a rule system – a resource for making sound, a sounding potential;[3]
- being a resource, it is organized paradigmatically in the first instance (as a network of options in sounding) rather than syntagmatically, phonological structures being realizations of phonological options;
- it is organized relationally (rather than modularly) both internally (as a network of intra-stratal relations) and externally (in terms of inter-stratal realization relations);
- it is organized according to the same principles as other stratal subsystems of language (fractal principles manifested in the different stratal environments of language);
- it is modelled theoretically in the first instance but the theoretical model is related to a system of representation (system networks with realization statements);
- it is interpreted semiotically (rather than cognitively) in relation to an ordered typology of systems, with phonetics as its 'interface' to the articulatory and auditory resources of the human organism.

Here it is also important to keep in mind that just like language as a whole, phonology is both system and process, and we observe it as process (event, activity), as sounded text unfolding in time. This perspective on language has been part of SFL from the start (for emphasis on and interpretation of language as activity, see also Thibault 2004b); for example, Halliday (1961/2002c: 38) writes at the beginning of his account of the categories of the theory of grammar:

> The relevant theory consists of a scheme of interrelated categories which are set up to account for the data, and a set of scales of abstraction which relate the categories to the data and to each other. The data to be accounted for are observed language events, observed as spoken

> or as codified in writing, any corpus of which, when used as material for linguistic description, is a 'text'.

and later he emphasizes that language is **patterned activity** (1961/2002c: 42–43):

> Language is patterned activity. At the formal level, the patterns are patterns of meaningful organization: certain regularities are exhibited over certain stretches of language activity. An essential feature of the stretches over which formal patterns operate is that they are of varying extent. [...] Since language activity takes place in time, the simplest formulation of this dimension is that it is the dimension of time, or, for written language, of linear space: the two can then be generalized as 'progression' and the relation between two items in progression is one of 'sequence'.

The nature of language as 'patterned activity' is, of course, essential when we engage with the sub-systems of phonology and of phonetics. This is indeed how the study of phonetics can make patterned sound visible to us, through spectrograms or X-ray/MRI videos showing the speech organs in motion during sound production. In SFL, the study of connected speech has, in fact, been at the forefront in work on phonology, brought out in the study of its prosodic domain, intonation and rhythm (see Halliday and Greaves 2008).[4] Another example is Halliday's (1992c: 108) interpretation of the Peking syllable as a "wave", "a periodic pattern of movement characterized by a kind of 'flow-and-return'" (see further below, Section 6.7).

The patterned activity of the production of sound can be modelled as ongoing simultaneous choices within different domains (represented by means of units along the phonological rank scale), and Catford's (1977: 227) visualization of these simultaneous choices in the articulation of the word *stand* is a helpful reminder of what we must capture in our account of the phonological system of a particular language and of language in general: see Figure 6.1.[5] He characterizes this process as follows (Catford 1977: 226–228):

> we have presented the speech process as a complex event consisting of more or less constantly varying states, or 'values', of a number of parameters or ranges of conditions of co-occurring components of the speech event. [...] there are moments of rapid change, which define for us, or tend to define for us, the limits of successive segments. [...] These 'moments of rapid change' are changes occurring in any one, or more, of the co-occurrent component parameters [...] The production

of such a word as *stand* [stʰææ̃nddḍʰ] may be diagrammatically illustrated as in figure 60 [reproduced here as Figure 6.1, CMIMM]. Here, changing values are indicated for a number of parameters.

If we follow the line representing values along the parameter of *oral articulatory stricture type* we have the value 'fricative' for a time, then there is a sudden shift to *stop*, followed by a sudden switch to *resonant*, and later back to *stop* (since the oral stricture of [n] is, of course, of the stop type). As a result of the changes mentioned here, the parameter of stricture-type throughout this utterance is divided into four (numbered) parts, or four *spans*, as we shall call them, of relatively steady state, separated by three fairly rapid *transitions* from one state to the next.

For the parameter of *articulatory location* only two states are designated, namely *alveolar* (short for apicolamino-alveolar) and *palatal* (short for dorso-palatal). Each of these, of course, is a shorthand description of a tongue posture. It will be observed that in this case there are only three spans, the first stretching across to spans of stricture-type.

The parameter of state of the velic or nasal port has two values, *closed* and *open* and it can be seen that there is one short span of *open*, the start of which does not correspond to the start of any other span.

The phonation parameter again breaks down into three spans, a *voiceless* one, a *voiced* one starting almost immediately after the release of the [t], which, being preceded by [s], has minimal aspiration, and ending with a renewed short span of *voicelessness*. These spans are not quite co-extensive with any other spans.

Finally, there is a single pulse of the pulmonic initiator, a single rising-falling curve of initiator power, constituting a single span of initiator activity.

Each change in the state of one parameter is, of course, a change in the whole sound-productive event. Consequently, each such change defines the limits not only of one componential or parametric span, but also of the whole segment. On this basis, then, in *stand* we recognize eight segments, [s, t, h, æ, æ̃, n, d, ḍ], or nine, if we count the releasing [ʰ] at the end of the utterance. It is perfectly possible to perceive all the segments, auditorily or kinaesthetically, if one tries. Without giving special attention to what is going on, however, one may observe only five segments, [s, t, æ, n, d], these segments corresponding to so many minimal linear phonological units, or phonemes, of English.

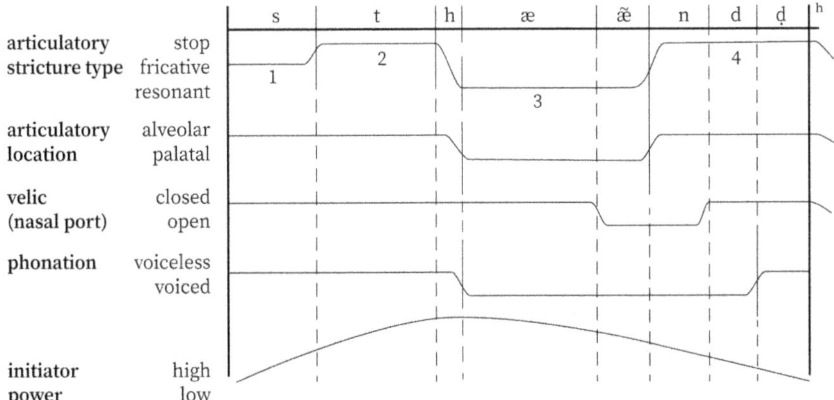

Figure 6.1 Catford's (1977: 227) segmentation of articulation of the word 'stand' – interpretable as a visualization of speaking as the unfolding of simultaneous phonological choices in articulatory stricture type, articulatory location, resonance (velic closure), phonation and initiator power

I have quoted Catford's phonetic description at some length because it indicates what a system-&-process understanding of phonology has to take into account. The phonetic parameters he mentions will be interpreted phonologically as systems, and the values as terms (features) in these systems. As speakers produce speech, they select phonological terms ongoingly in all the relevant phonological systems.[6] In the phonology, the systems will be logically simultaneous and traversed in parallel; but we also need to recognize that they will operate within different phonological domains or units, units that are arranged in a compositional hierarchy – the phonological rank scale. Thus in Catford's example, *stand* is both a syllable, and a sequence of phonemes, the syllable being characterizable as a postural wave.

6.2 The stratal location of phonology

To understand the nature of phonology, we have to locate it within language, interpreting language as a **resource for making meaning** – a **meaning potential**, as Halliday (e.g. 1973) has put it. Meaning is the key property of language and of all other semiotic systems; and, as a higher-order semiotic system, language is not only a system for *carrying* (or reflecting) meaning, but actually for *creating* meaning (cf. Halliday 1992b, 1996).

In order for a semiotic system to be able to *create* meaning, it must be **stratified** not only into two **stratal planes** – content and expression, but each stratal plane

Table 6.1 The place of phonology in the stratal organization of language

stratal plane	strata			nature of potential
content	$content_1$	substance	semantics	meaning potential
	$content_2$	form	lexicogrammar	wording potential
expression	$expression_1$		phonology	sounding potential
	$expression_2$	substance	phonetics	sounding potential[7]

must in turn be stratified into two **strata**, $content_1$ and $content_2$ and $expression_1$ and $expression_2$. These content and expression strata are, of course, well-known in accounts of the stratal organization of language: see Table 6.1. (Since the relation between lexicogrammar and phonology is one of stratification, not one of composition, it follows that morphemes are realized by syllable (or phoneme) sequences, they do not consist of them.)

In spoken language, $expression_1$ is **phonology** and $expression_2$ is **phonetics**. Given that language is a meaning potential, we can interpret phonology as a **sounding potential** in the service of this overall meaning potential. Halliday (2000b: 109) puts it as follows: "The phonology is the language's resource for making meaning with sound".

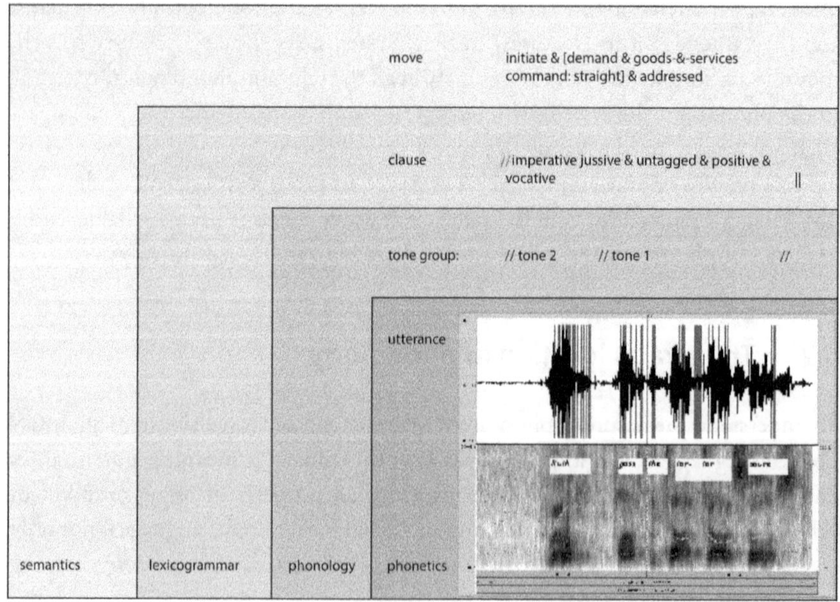

Figure 6.2 An utterance, 'Ruth, pass the tartar sauce!', analysed multi-stratally – phonetically, phonologically, lexicogrammatically and semantically

Thus any utterance that we observe in speech can be analysed multi-stratally as both expression and content, as illustrated for the utterance *Ruth, pass the tartar sauce!* in Figure 6.2. In this illustration, the phonetic analysis is acoustic (due to Praat) – pitch and amplitude, the phonological analysis is prosodic, in terms of TONE (the system controlling pitch movement), the lexicogrammatical analysis is interpersonal, in terms of the system of MOOD at clause rank (realized partially through tone), and the semantic analysis is also interpersonal, in terms of the system of SPEECH FUNCTION at the rank of move (realized through mood). To 'thicken' (or heighten!) the analysis, we could also add context, noting the tenor of the relationship between speaker and addressee: young adult brother and sister in a positional family (from a filmed play, *Spring and Port Wine*, set in the 1960s by Bill Naughton). The account of phonology is responsible for illuminating phonology in terms of its stratal location with respect to both system (the sounding potential) and instance (selections from the sounding potential in a spoken text).

The stratification of language shown in Table 6.1, including also of language in context, is often represented by means of co-tangential circles (see e.g. Halliday 1992b; Halliday and Matthiessen 2006, 2014), as shown in Figure 6.3. This brings out the fact that ***phonology is located stratally between lexicogrammar and phonetics***:

- phonology is the highest stratum within the expression plane, serving to realize lexicogrammar (the system of wording) as sounding;
- it is in turn realized by phonetics (embodied sounding, articulatory and auditory);
- since the relation between phonology and lexicogrammar is one between the two stratal planes, the relation between the two is (largely) conventional (Saussure's 'line of arbitrariness');
- since the relation between phonology and phonetics is located within the expression plane, the relation between the two is natural (rather than conventional), just as the relation between semantics and lexicogrammar is natural (rather than conventional);
- while phonology is a stratum that is internal to language just like lexicogrammar (linguistic 'form'), phonetics is a stratum that serves as an interface between language and other human systems (linguistic 'substance') within the expression plane, just as semantics does within the content plane.

To bring out the parallel stratal organization of the content plane and the expression plane into internal and interface strata, I have drawn another version of the stratal diagram: see Figure 6.4. In this figure, the main points about the

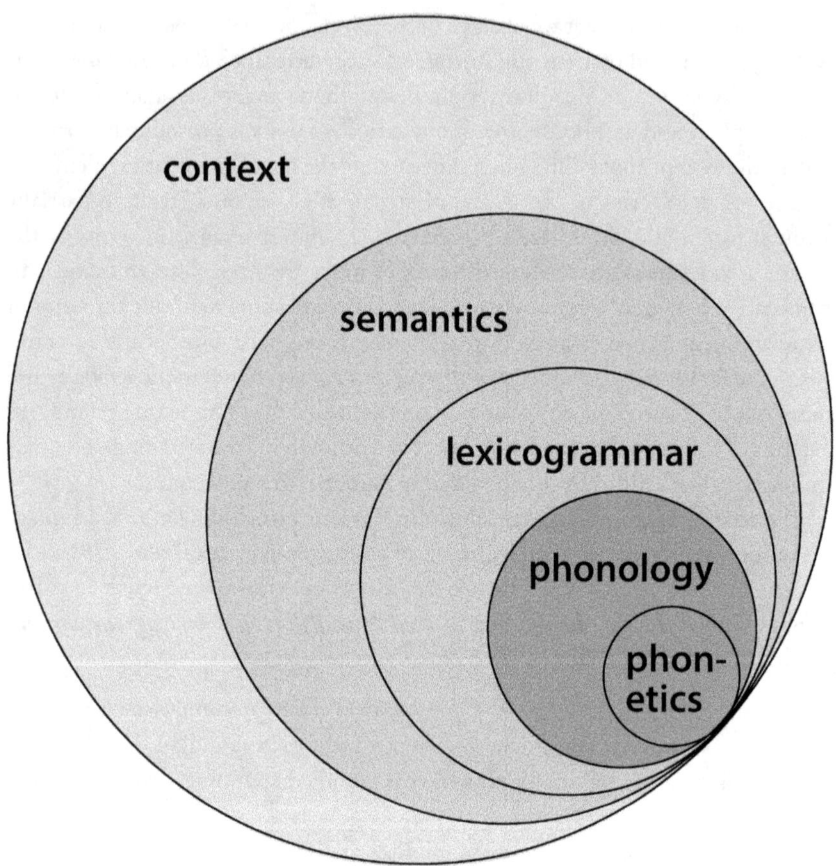

Figure 6.3 The stratal organization of language in context into the content plane (semantics and lexicogrammar) and the expression plane (phonology and phonetics, in the case of spoken language)

implications of the stratal location of phonology – in relation to lexicogrammar and phonetics – are made explicit. I have also added a specification of the nature of semantics and phonetics as stratal interfaces to what lies beyond language (cf. Section 6.5 below):

- the semantic interface to human systems beyond language is organized metafunctionally, i.e. in terms of modes of meaning: ideational – construing other systems as (linguistic) meaning, interpersonal – enacting (linguistic) meaning in other systems, with textual as internal to language in the first instance (although that needs to be somewhat modified, e.g. to take account of focus of attention);

- but the phonetic interface to human systems beyond language is organized in terms of the direction of processes of instantiation in the first instance – speaking ~ the articulatory system, and listening ~ the auditory system (potentially supplemented by the visual as in lip-reading).

Halliday and Greaves (2008: 78) make a related point about lexicogrammar and phonology being 'driven' from above and below in stratal terms, respectively:

> In grammar, the driving force comes 'from above', from the way meaning is organized on metafunctional lines: ideational elements tend to be clearly segmental, interpersonal ones much more fluid.
>
> In phonology, on the other hand, the driving force comes 'from below'. Some features, such as pitch movement, are inherently prosodic; others, such as consonantal plosion and closure, are segmental; while features like nasal/oral resonance, front/back vocalization, may be segmentally organized in one language (or one part of a language) and prosodically organized in another.

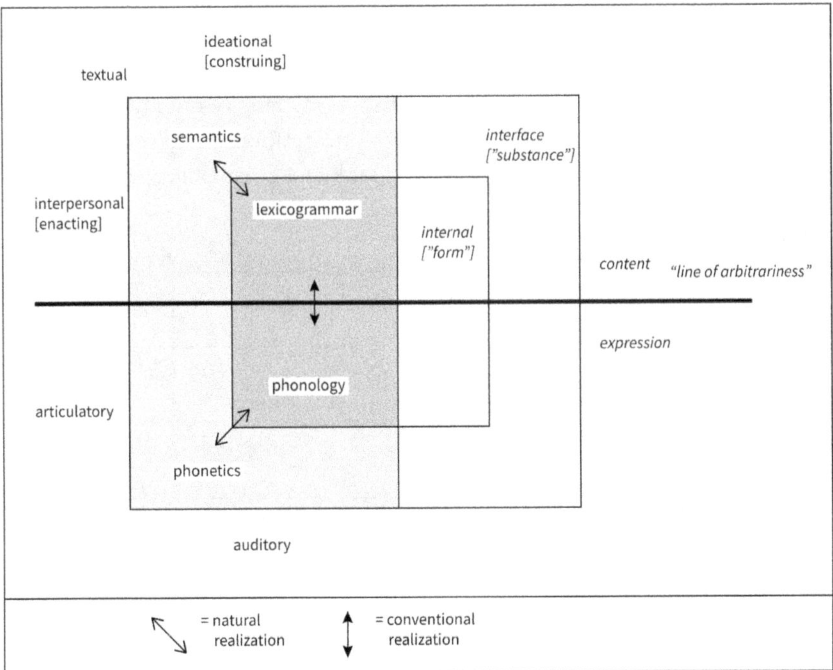

Figure 6.4 Stratification of the content and expression planes of language, with differentiation between internal strata ('form') and interface strata ('substance')

Both the conventional realizational relation between phonology and lexicogrammar and the natural one between phonology and phonetics have been the focus of a great deal of discussion and debate in linguistics since the early part of the twentieth century. Here I will only be able to comment on the two stratal relations briefly although both need considerable further elucidation.

Lexicogrammar ↘ phonology. The stratal relationship between lexicogrammar and phonology is basically conventional (rather than natural, or 'iconic'), but there has been considerable discussion in linguistics concerning the nature of the relationship. The main issue has been to what extent the relationship between lexicogrammar and phonology is conventional (or 'arbitrary' in Saussure's sense of the arbitrary relationship between the content [signified] and expression [signifier] parts of the sign).

The degree of conventionality/naturalness can be characterized by reference to two intersecting semiotic dimensions, (the spectrum of) **metafunction** and (the hierarchy of) **rank**: (a) in terms of metafunction, there is greater potential for a natural relationship within the textual, interpersonal and logical metafunctions, but at the same time greater need for a conventional relationship within the experiential metafunction, where all of our experience of the world has to be construed;[8] and (b) in terms of phonological rank, there is a greater tendency towards a natural relationship at the highest phonological rank, i.e. the rank of the tone group, and there is a greater tendency towards a conventional relationship at the rank of syllable (and phoneme, if it exists as a separate rank in a given language). These two dimensions are intersected in Figure 6.5.

	textual	interpersonal	logical	experiential
tone group	natural (tonicity)	natural (tone)	natural (tone sequence)	—
foot				
syllable				conventional *but: onomatopoeia, sound symbolism*
phoneme				

Figure 6.5 The stratal relation between phonology and lexicogrammar – tendency towards a natural or conventional ('arbitrary') realizational relationship characterized in terms metafunction and phonological rank

The tone group and the foot together constitute the domain of **prosodic systems**, while the syllable and the phoneme together constitute the domain of **articulatory systems** – with the syllable as a 'gateway' between the prosodic and articulatory domains, as illustrated further below. Prosodic systems tend to operate over longer stretches, intonation and rhythm being prototypical ones with voice quality as another candidate (on the borderline between language and paralanguage). Articulatory systems tend to operate over shorter stretches (cf. Figure 6.1 above), originating in language development as postures in protolanguage and then being reanalysed as 'phonemic' in the course of the move into the mother tongue (e.g. Halliday 1975: 171, 213).[9] Articulatory phonology has the greatest potential for possibly infinite differentiation of sound patterns, which is precisely what is needed by the experiential metafunction since in any given language it has to construe all of human experiences as meaning (realized by wording).[10]

One important aspect of the stratal relationship between lexicogrammar and phonology is the question of where units along the lexicogrammatical rank scale and units along the phonological rank scale are congruent. For example, in English, the information unit (grammar) is congruent with the tone group (phonology), as discussed at some length by Halliday and Greaves (2008).[11] However, the relationship between the two rank scales varies across languages: see Figure 6.6. For instance, in Mandarin, morphemes tend to be monosyllabic (as discussed by Halliday 2014), but this is clearly not the case in English. And there are many other details to take account of, including (word) accent in relation to rhythm, word boundaries in relation to vowel harmony or 'phonotactics'. Halliday (1992a: 120) characterizes the variation in the relationship between the grammatical and phonological rank scales as follows (cf. also Halliday 2014):

> One major variable among phonological systems that is foregrounded in a prosodic and systemic perspective is where they make contact with grammar (cf. Hill 1966). The phonological rank scale may include tonal and/or rhythmic units which may be mapped more or less consistently on to clauses or phrases; and in many languages the word is the point of origin of certain phonological systems, either with or without being fully integrated into the overall structure (Matthiessen 1987a; Prakasam 1987; and cf. the phonological hierarchy of tagmemic theory). In Chinese the word has hardly any phonological significance: none at all in many dialects, a little in Mandarin because it defines an environment within which the tonal system may be neutralized. But throughout the history of the language there has always been an overwhelming association of the syllable with the morpheme,

and this gives an added significance to the syllabary as the basis of the phonological system.

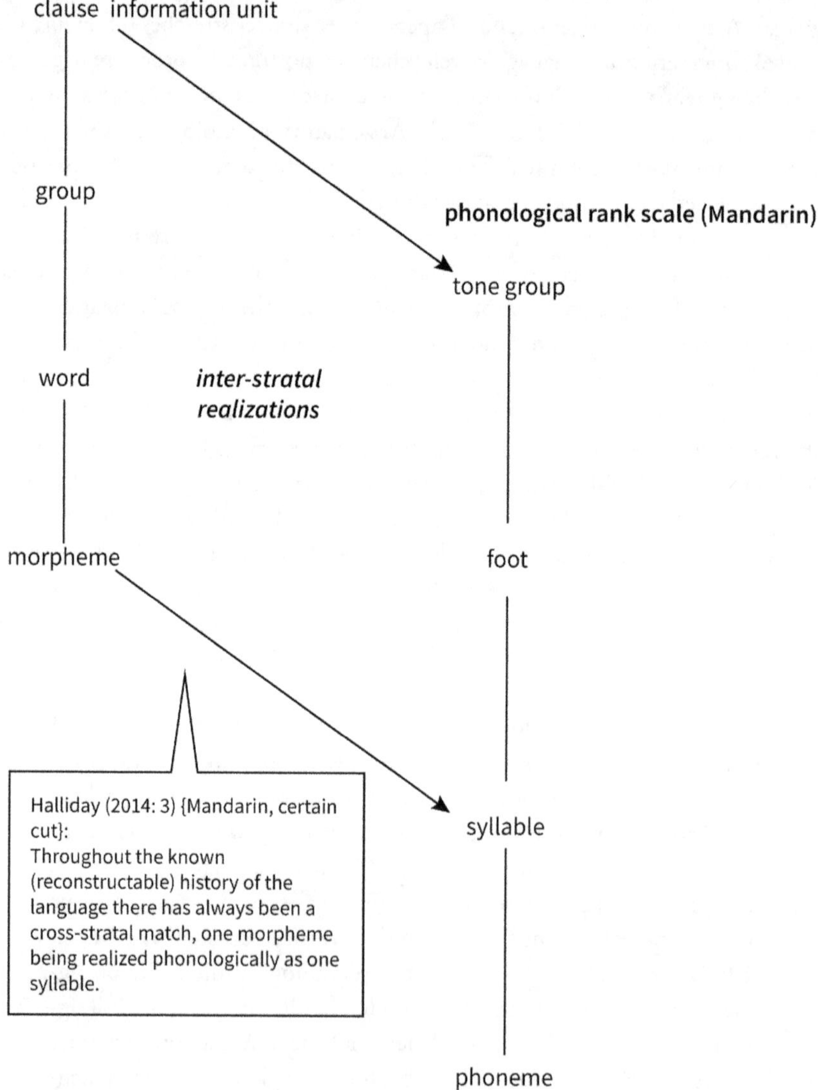

Figure 6.6 Possible correspondences between units along the grammatical and phonological rank scales

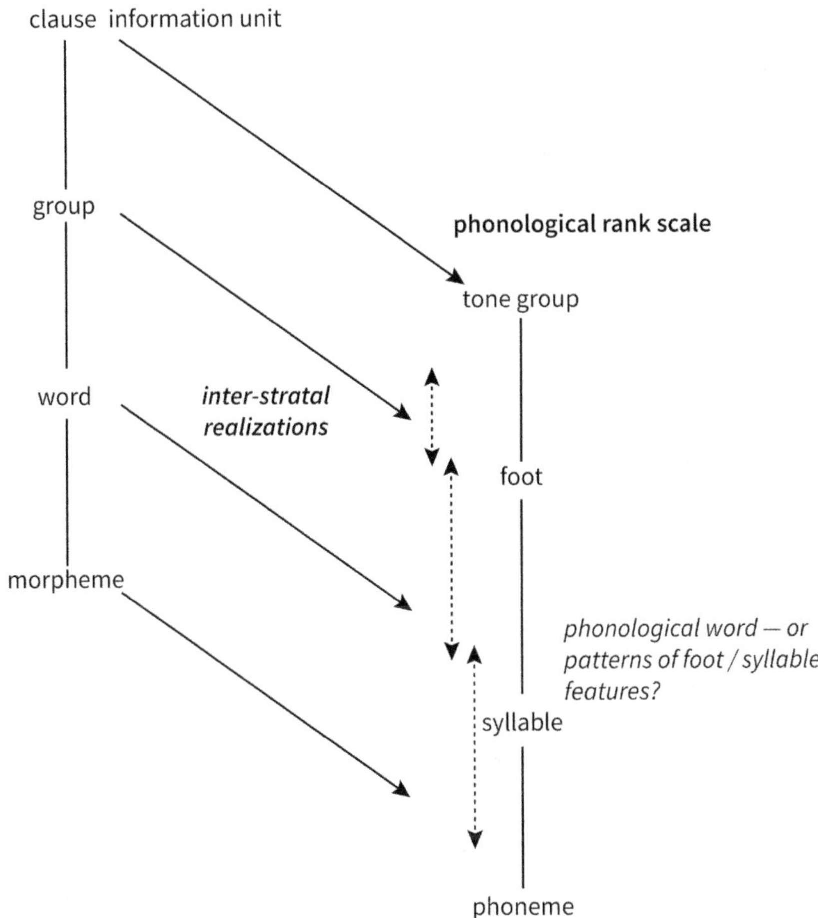

Figure 6.6 Possible correspondences between units along the grammatical and phonological rank scales ***(cont.)***

With respect to the nature of the relationship between lexicogrammar and phonology, we can also note that while in the general case it is 'automated', it can be 'de-automatized' just like the relationship between lexicogrammar and semantics (taking the notion of de-automatization Mukarovsky's, e.g. 1948, Prague School work, as interpreted systemically by Halliday 1982b). This may happen in registers where there is a high premium on creativity and thus pressure on making the phonological system work harder in the meaning making process – prototypical examples being poetry and advertising (including brand naming), as illustrated by the following two short excerpts:

> (1) Gerald Manley Hopkins' The leaden echo and the golden echo:
> HOW to kéep – is there ány any, is there none such, nowhere known some, bow or brooch or braid or brace, láce, latch or catch or key to keep
> Back beauty, keep it, beauty, beauty, beauty, ... from vanishing away?
> Ó is there no frowning of these wrinkles, rankèd rinkles deep,
> Dówn? no waving off of these most mournful messengers, still messengers, sad and stealing messengers of grey?
>
> (2) Dylan Thomas, Under Milkwood
> To begin at the beginning:
> It is spring, moonless night in the small town, starless and bible-black, the cobblestreets silent and the hunched, courters'-and-rabbits' wood limping invisible down to the sloeblack, slow, black, crowblack, fishingboat-bobbing sea. The houses are blind as moles (though moles see fine tonight in the snouting, velvet dingles) or blind as Captain Cat there in the muffled middle by the pump and the town clock, the shops in mourning, the Welfare Hall in widows' weeds. And all the people of the lulled and dumbfound town are sleeping now.

In (1), Hopkins draws on the phonological potential to create the sense of echo; and in (2), Thomas draws on it to evoke the setting – note e.g. the *sl-* and *bl-* onsets, and the evocation of repetitive movement in *fishingboat-bobbing*. (Incidentally, there is a recording of Dylan Thomas reading Hopkins' poem in a rather dramatic fashion.)

Phonology ↘ Phonetics. The stratal relationship between phonology and phonetics is a natural one, just like the relationship between lexicogrammar and semantics within the content plane of language. That is, phonology is natural in relation to phonetics, as shown in Figure 6.2 above. This means that phonology is grounded in phonetics; phonological patterns are phonetically transparent. Bringing out this natural relationship has been an important goal for both Firth's prosodic analysis and systemic functional phonology. In systemic phonology, this goal has been pursued by positing systems of features within units of different extent along the phonological rank scale, and investigating them in authentic connected speech (cf. Halliday 1967b; Catford 1985; Halliday and Greaves 2008). (In contrast, in generative phonology up through the 1960s, phonological representations tended to drift away from phonetic facts, and this led to the countermoves, natural generative phonology, in the 1970s by Joan Hooper, Theo Vennemann and others to develop more 'natural' phonological representations [e.g. Hooper 1976]; cf. also the separate strand of 'natural phonology' from the same period, e.g. Donegan and Stampe 1979.)

By characterizing the relationship between phonology and phonetics as natural, I don't mean to imply that it is simple; 'natural' must be understood in contrast with 'conventional'. There are, of course, various familiar features of the phonetics of ordinary connected speech like 'simplifications' of phonological clusters – and of variants of ordinary speech like very rapid or careful speech[12] or whispered speech. Further, phonological descriptions of vowel systems based on the phonetics of cardinal vowels are, of course, based on a fair amount of abstraction from the articulation and perception of vowels (e.g. O'Connor 1973). Here it is important to remember Halliday's (e.g. 1996) principle of trinocular vision. Phonological systems must be viewed trinocularly, like all other linguistic phenomena: (a) from above, from the vantage of lexicogrammar (and, by another stratal step, semantics); (b) from below, from the vantage point of phonetics; and (c) from roundabout, from the vantage point of phonology itself as a system of values (in Saussure's sense of *valeur*). For example, since the late nineteenth century, linguists in different traditions have tried to characterize or define the 'phoneme' (originally as a French version of German *Sprachlaut*) in different ways. These can be articulated in terms of trinocular vision, with the addition of an external view 'from outside' according to which the phoneme is a 'mental image' (along the lines of Baudouin de Courtenay): see Figure 6.7.[13] Thus approaching the phoneme 'from below' in terms of stratification, from the vantage point of phonetics, Daniel Jones explored it as a family of sounds, whereas Prague School linguists and various other linguists approached it 'from above', from the vantage point of lexicogrammar, and noted that phonemes are distinctive in the differentiation of content, e.g. morphemes. From within phonology itself, J. R. Firth (e.g. 1948a) approached phonological patterns 'from above' as prosodies, and thus did not give the phoneme a special status (except as a phonematic unit that might be useful in writing); in contrast, Roman Jakobson (e.g. 1949) reinterpreted distinctive features as components of the phoneme. Staying within phonology but switching orientation from the phonological rank scale, we can also note that phonologists have foregrounded either paradigmatic considerations, exploring phonological contrasts in terms of *valeur*

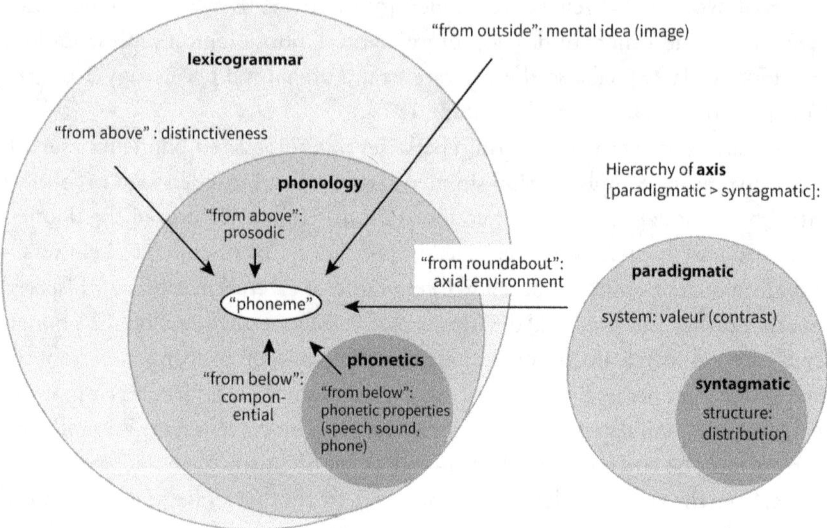

Figure 6.7 Approaches to the characterization or definition of the 'phoneme' in different phonological traditions

in a European structuralist sense, as Nikolai Trubetzkoy did, or syntagmatic considerations, exploring phonemes in terms of their distributional characteristics, as American structuralists did. Similarly, we could explore accounts of the 'syllable' trinocularly, noting attempts to come to terms with it 'from below' from the vantage point of phonetics, either articulatory or auditory, and so on.

6.3 The internal organization of phonology: Fractal organization of stratal subsystems

The interpretation of language as a **resource** in SFL is reflected in various ways in the architecture of language. Centrally, as a resource, language is theorized and modelled **paradigmatically** in the first instance, and syntagmatic patterns are stated as realizations within paradigmatic environments. In terms of the hierarchy of axis (paradigmatic – syntagmatic), the paradigmatic axis is thus given primary status over the syntagmatic axis, since it is the paradigmatic axis that makes it possible to represent language as a resource. In SFL, paradigmatic organization is represented by means of **system networks**, and syntagmatic patterns are represented as **function structures** specified by **realization statements** attached to terms in systems.[14]

This same axial principle of organization applies to all stratal subsystems of language, and, within each stratal subsystem, its resources are distributed along a **rank scale** with at least two ranks of units. Like axis, the rank scale is a hierarchy, but it is a compositional hierarchy ranging from the most inclusive units to the least inclusive, say from clause to morpheme or from tone group to syllable; and higher-ranking units provide the environment for lower-ranking ones, just as paradigmatic organization provides the environment for syntagmatic patterns. See Figure 6.8.

This **domain principle** is the same for all the stratal subsystems of language (Table 6.1). They are all organized according to axis and rank in the same general way as resources within the overall resource of language, as illustrated for axis at the highest ranks of lexicogrammar and phonology in Table 6.2. Thus, axis and rank can be characterized as **fractal dimensions**: they are dimensions of organizations that are manifested throughout language in different stratal environments.

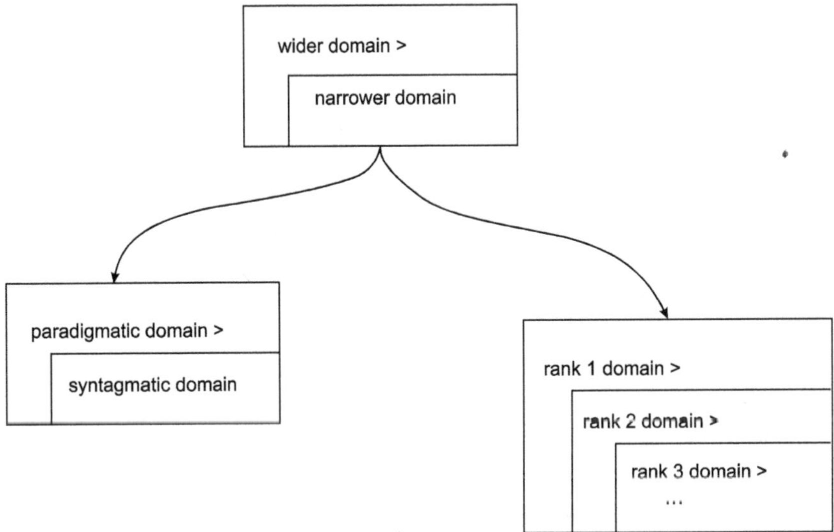

Figure 6.8 The domain principle manifested as the hierarchy of axis and the hierarchy of composition (rank scale) within a stratal subsystem of language

Table 6.2 Examples of systems, terms and realization statements from lexicogrammar and phonology in English

stratum	rank	axis		
		paradigmatic		syntagmatic
		system	term	realization
lexicogrammar	clause	MOOD	declarative	Subject ^ Finite
			interrogative	–
phonology	tone group	PRIMARY TONE	tone 1	Tonic: falling
			tone 2	Tonic: rising
			tone 3	Tonic: level
			tone 4	Tonic: falling-rising
			tone 5	Tonic: rising-falling

Like all the stratal subsystems of language, phonology must be understood as a resource for making meaning: semantics is the key system in this respect – the core meaning potential of language; but in order for language to function as a resource for making meaning, it must be organized into an ordered series of potentials – a meaning potential in the specific sense of semantics, which is realized as a wording potential, which is in turn realized as a **sounding potential**, as I put it above.

6.4 Systemicization of phonological features

Phonological features have been represented in the form of matrices or taxonomies in various accounts, ranging from say Jakobson, Fant and Halle (1952: Appendix), whose proposal was later adapted for use in generative phonology, to Ladefoged (e.g. 2001: 180); for an overview of the use of features in phonology and phonetics, and the relationship between the two see Ladefoged (2004). These forms of representation, familiar in phonology and phonetics, have different implications from representations of phonological features by means of system networks.

The fundamental reason for organizing phonological features by means of system networks in the description of the phonological system of a given language is to model its sounding potential, as I put it above: phonological system networks represent what speakers 'can sound', just as semantic system networks represent what they 'can mean' (their meaning potential; Halliday 1973). But, importantly, there are fundamental benefits internal to phonology, ones that will emerge when one sets out to develop a comprehensive description of the phonology of a particular language. For example, using system networks, (1) one can vary the degree of delicacy in phonological descriptions, so it is not necessary to over-specify or under-specify any phonological patterns – they can be specified at exactly the right degree of delicacy; (2) one can easily represent simultaneous features (which is not possible in taxonomic representations); (3) one can preselect features at a lower rank – at the right degree of delicacy, e.g. constraining a class of phonemes serving in the Onset of a syllable in one way, and the class of phonemes serving in the Coda in another.

Phonological system networks are networks of phonological systems, where:

- the terms in a phonological system are **phonological features**, as in [RESONANCE] oral/nasal; but these terms of paradigmatic values, not syntagmatic components of phonemes or other phonological units;[15]
- a system has an **entry condition**, consisting of a single term in another system, or some combination of a conjunction or disjunction of terms, as in [RESONANCE] stop: oral/nasal. Entry conditions specify the paradigmatic environment in which a given phonological system operates – in the example just given, this is stops within the consonantal part of the phoneme system network (but not fricatives or approximants, nor vowels);
- through entry conditions, systems may be ordered in **delicacy**, as in phoneme: vocalic/consonantal; consonantal: stop/fricative/approximant; stop: oral/nasal; but they may also be **simultaneous**, as in vocalic: back/central/front & high/mid/low;
- terms in simultaneous systems may be subject to systemic **conditioning**; for example, in English, if a vowel is 'central', it will also be 'mid'; there are no 'high' or 'low' central vowels.

Let me begin the exploration of the systemicization of phonology by developing a simple systemic sketch of the system network of phonemes in English step by step, drawing on Ladefoged's (e.g. 2001) widely used account. Starting with vowels, i.e. vocalic as opposed to consonantal phones, we can recognize two simultaneous systems with 'vocalic' as entry condition, BACKNESS (or POSTURE) and HEIGHT (or APERTURE), as shown in Figure 6.9. This says that the vowel sounding potential in English involves two parameters, both of which can be related in articulatory phonetics to the posture of the tongue. In a description of the vowel system of French, we would also have to include a system of APERTURE for 'front' vowels: 'rounded'/'spread' (and of RESONANCE, 'oral'/'nasal', but this would first be posited at the rank of syllable); and in a description of the vowel system of Akan, we would also have to include a system of TONGUE ROOT: 'neutral'/'advanced'. In general, when we move around the languages of the world, we will find differences in what

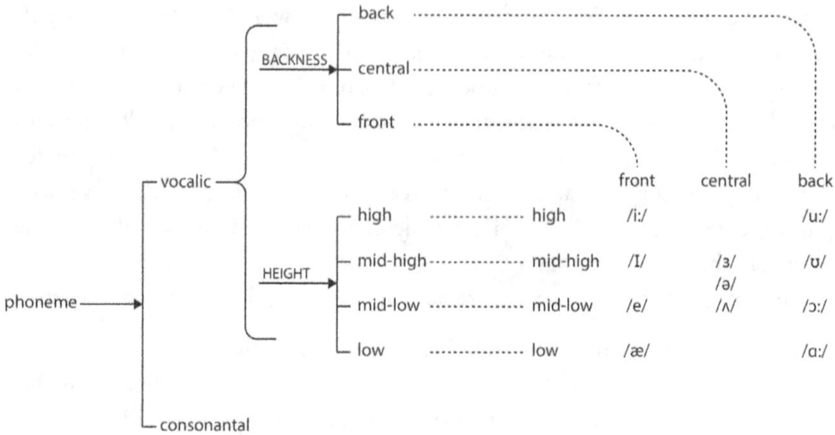

Figure 6.9 Systemicization of English vowels (based on Ladefoged's 2001: 180, "hierarchical arrangement of the features required for English"), Step 1

phonological systems we need to posit: languages differ in how they **semioticize**, or more specifically **phonologize**, our shared human articulatory and auditory potential (anthropophonics – "the study of what is common to all mankind in the sphere of vocal sound production: the study of the total sound-producing potential of man" in Catford's 1977: 2, gloss of the term introduced by Jan Baudouin de Courtenay). In English, all front vowels are 'spread', and all 'back' vowels are rounded, so there is no systemic contrast in aperture in the phonology of vowels.

The two simultaneous systems in Figure 6.9 intersect to define a vocalic paradigm, as shown in Figure 6.10; but there are gaps in this paradigm: while 'front' and 'back' combine freely with all terms in the HEIGHT system, 'central' vowels are restricted to the 'mid' values. So we need to revise the Step 1 vowel system network in Figure 6.9 to take account of and eliminate these gaps. One option is to state that if vowels are 'central', they are 'mid' – i.e. they cannot combine with 'high' or 'low': see Figure 6.10. To capture this systemic conditioning, I have introduced a graphic marking convention represented by an arrow from one systemic term to another: if 'central', then 'mid'. I have also ordered 'mid' in delicacy: first 'high/mid/low', then 'mid': 'mid-high/mid-low'. This makes it possible to capture the generalization about mid vowels, whether they are high or low within the mid-height range.

There are, of course, other possible ways of interpreting the English vowel system systemically. For example, to make explicit the fact that the vowel system of English in a sense exploits the affordances of the articulatory 'vowel space' (which we need to recognize as a theoretical construct), we can re-represent the vowel

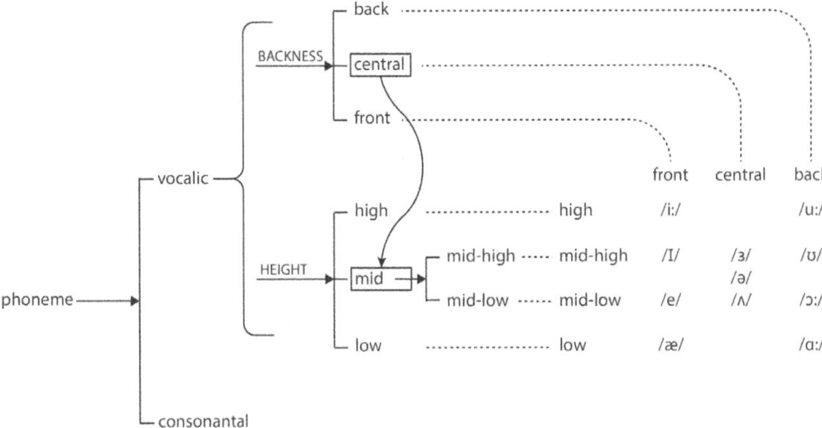

Figure 6.10 Systemicization of English vowels (based on Ladefoged's 2001: 180, "hierarchical arrangement of the features required for English"), Step 2

system as Figure 6.11. This version shows that both primary vowel systems, BACKNESS and HEIGHT, are organized according to the systemic contrast of 'outer' vs. 'middle' (just as degrees of modality in English), and that the 'outer' values combine freely.

When we are faced with different possible systemic interpretations, as in Figure Figure 6.10 vs. Figure 6.11, we may have to suspend judgement until we are in a position to consider the interpretations in relation to a more comprehensive account

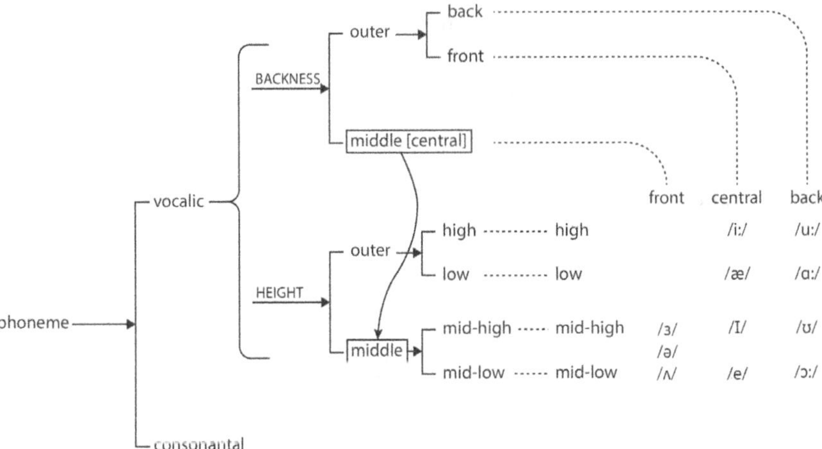

Figure 6.11 Systemicization of English vowels (based on Ladefoged's 2001: 180, "hierarchical arrangement of the features required for English"), Step 3

of the overall system. In this case, the phonological systems of syllables and feet in English are certainly relevant ('from above', in terms of the phonological rank scale), as are the phonetics of articulations ('from below', in terms of stratification).

Since I am using the phoneme system of English phonology as an ***illustration*** rather than as a descriptive goal in its own right, I will not try to choose among systemic description of the vowel system at this point, but rather I will move on to the tougher tasks of describing the English consonant system systemically. It is tougher simply because it involves more phonological and phonetic parameters, so there will be more ways of systemicizing the consonant system.

As a first step, we can simply postulate the systems of PLACE, MANNER, LATERALITY, and VOICING as simultaneous systems – all with the same entry condition: 'consonantal', as shown in Figure 6.12. As can be expected, when we examine the paradigm of intersections of systemic features – set out as a table to the right in the figure, there are many gaps, just as in Figure 6.9 – just more gaps in the case of consonants, since there are more simultaneous systems in the systemic description represented in Figure 6.12. We could continue along the same path as we did with vowels in order to differentiate all consonants while avoiding gaps. But having illustrated the tendency in consonant systems to involve quite a few parameters or systemic variables, I will stop at this point; for a tentative but complete description (up to a certain point in delicacy), see my account of the phoneme system of Akan in Figure 6.20, to be discussed below.

There are, of course, various questions that arise as we undertake the kind of exercise just illustrated. They include the following. (1) If we try to attempt to ground the description of phonological features in phonetics, how do we decide what aspects of phonetics to draw on – articulatory or auditory. I will comment on this later as I sketch my approach in the development of the systemic description of Akan phonology. (2) If we systemicize phonological features, how do we decide where to stop the account in delicacy? If we are developing a description of the phoneme system of a given language, we can in principle continue in delicacy to take account of allophonic variants – that is, variants that are phonologically conditioned in the first instance. One way of addressing this would be to refer to 'phonology and the consumer' (cf. Halliday 1964). For example, in the modelling of speech synthesis (cf. Teich, Watson, and Pereira 2000), it may turn out to be helpful to extend the delicacy for the sake of phonetic 'implementation' in the speech synthesizer; but if we orient the description of phonology towards consideration 'from above', i.e. from lexicogrammar, then we foreground considerations of what features are distinctive – 'emic' in a generalized sense (covering all phonological ranks). The latter consideration was invoked by Halliday (1967b) in his description of the systems of intonation in English.

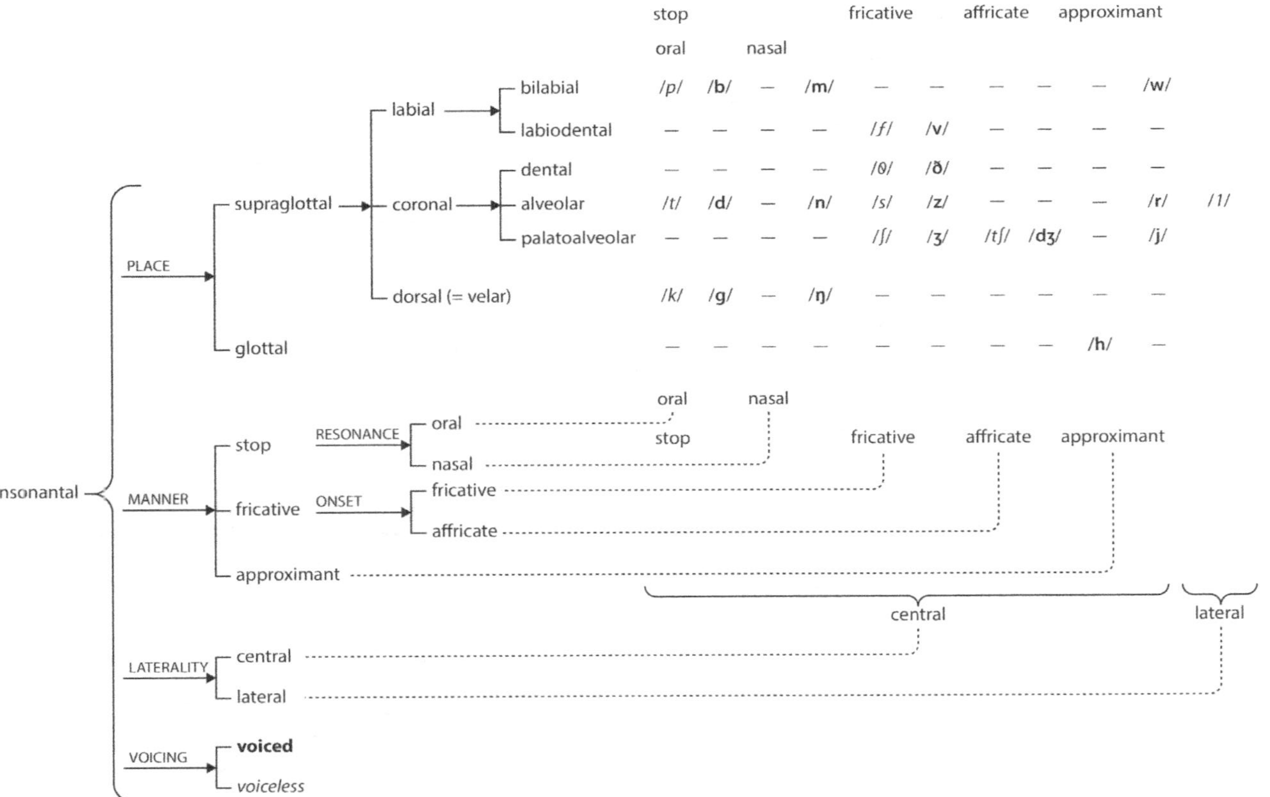

Figure 6.12 Systemicization of English consonants (based on Ladefoged's 2001: 180, "hierarchical arrangement of the features required for English")

6.5 The phonological rank scale

6.5.1 *The compositional hierarchy of phonological units and the division of phonological labour*

To illustrate the phonologization of general human phonetic features, I began with the smallest unit of the phonological rank scale in many languages (I say 'many' since for some languages we may bottom out in our description with the syllable) – the **phoneme**, since this is the domain of phonology where the notion of phonological features began to be developed in different phonological traditions (e.g. the paradigmatic values of Trubetzkoy's 1939, Prague School phonology, the distinctive features in generative phonology taken over from Jakobson). But once phonology is interpreted systemically as a resource for making sound, as a **sounding potential**, it becomes clear that ***phonological features are pervasive***: the phonological subsystem of language is simply an ***extensive network of phonological systems distributed across the phonological rank scale of units***. This distribution can be represented as a matrix of phonological domains (prosodic and articulatory) and of ranks, as illustrated for English in Table 6.3. Such matrices show the division of phonological labour in different languages;[16] for example, in a 'tone language', there would be a system of syllabic TONE in the pitch column at the rank of syllable.

As Table 6.3 illustrates, the tendency is for prosodic phonological systems to operate within higher-ranking phonological units and for articulatory ones to operate within lower-ranking phonological units. In a given language, the syllable is likely to be the 'gateway' between the two (see further below).

By intersecting the phonological rank scale and phonological domains in the matrix in Table 6.3, we can also problematize the question of where we describe

Table 6.3 The division of phonological labour in terms of the phonological rank scale in English

rank	prosodic		~	articulatory
	pitch	rhythm	salience	articulation
tone group	TONE, TONICITY, TONALITY			
foot		foot composition, ictus state		
syllable			SALIENCE	articulatory postures ("phonotactics")
phoneme				PLACE, MANNER &c

and interpret phonological phenomena. Here it is important to note that in the systemic functional architecture of phonology, features that have often been located at the rank of phoneme in other traditions may alternatively be interpreted at a higher rank to account for the fact they are 'spread' over longer stretches of speech (as in J. R. Firth's prosodic analysis; cf. Zellig Harris' notion of 'long components'). Examples include harmony phenomena such as vowel harmony (cf. Hill 1966) and juncture prosodies.[17] This also makes it possible to capture the fact that features may be manifested in different ways within and across languages (cf. Halliday and Greaves 2008: 78). For instance, if RESONANCE (nasal/oral) is recognized as a system at syllable rank, we can capture the fact that the contrast between 'nasal' and 'oral' may be spread over the 'Rhyme' of the syllable and that 'nasal' may be manifested in certain languages as a nasal vowel at the syllabic peak and in other languages as a nasal consonantal closure (e.g. Portuguese vs. Spanish).[18]

By positing the rank scale as part of the architecture of the system of phonology, we can also approach Firth's (e.g. 1957b) **polysystemic principle** in a new way. In his approach to phonology, phonological systems operate at different places in phonological structure (since Firth had not made the systemic organization along the paradigmatic axis the primary principle of organization of language). Thus in a given language, there will be a number of different consonant systems and vowel systems, each operating at a different place (for English, see Catford 1977: 218–219). This approach embodies an important insight regarding the polysystemic specialization of consonant and vowel systems according to their places in phonological structure (for example, in languages spoken largely in Africa, so-called co-articulated stops like /g͡b/ overwhelmingly occur in syllable onsets, but not in codas: see Cahill 2018); but it fails to bring out generalizations about such systems, or more generally, about the system of phonemes of as a single system (monosystem) in a given language. But with the help of the phonological rank scale, we can capture both the polysystemic insight and the monosystemic one:[19]

- Syllables are structured syntagmatically as configurations of phonological functions (elements), e.g. Onset ^ Peak ^ Coda (or Onset ^ Rhyme [Peak ^ Coda]; and we can state the phonemic possibilities for each in terms of preselections of phonemic features. For example, the Onset, if present, may be preselected to be a consonant, the Peak to be a vowel or nasal consonant, and the Coda, if present, to be a nasal consonant (as in the illustration from Akan in Figure 6.19, to be discussed below).
- Phonemes are the point of origin of a single system covering consonants and vowels, and any intermediate types (glides, semi-vowels), as illustrated for Akan below (Figure 6.20).

The same principle applies throughout the rank scale: higher-ranking units provide the **environment** in which lower-ranking ones serve, so it is at the higher ranks that we can capture adaptions of feet according to their role in tone groups, of syllables according to their role in feet, and of phonemes according to their role in syllables.

In general, in the account of the phonological system of a particular language, we should try to bring out the **'ecological' influence** of higher-ranking units on lower-ranking ones. This influence is, of course, phonetically motivated, reflecting the nature of connected speech. We might characterize it as the **rank-descendent principle** in phonology. Catford (1985: 346) articulates this principle as follows:

> Feet are logically, and physiologically, prior to syllables or segments. The foot is a unitary quantum of 'vocal effort', that is, of **initiator power**. Initiator power is the force employed to initiate airflow in the vocal tract. It is the product of initiator velocity and the pressure-load imposed by the air driven forward by the initiator, or, more simply, for voiced sounds it is the volume-velocity of transglottal airflow times subglottal pressure. (See Catford 1977: 80–84.) The power-quanta, or stress-pulses, that constitute feet characteristically start with a rapid rise to a maximum followed by a slower decline, until the moment when the power build-up for the next foot begins.
>
> We can picture the initiator-power curves of feet thus:
>
> 
>
> If a foot is realized by a single syllable, the power-curve is spread over the whole syllable. If there are several syllables in the foot, the first one, coinciding with the power peak, will be the strongest, or salient, syllable, subsequent ones being weaker.

Referring to English, he offers an example of the unfolding of an initiator-power curve, reproduced here as Figure 6.13.[20]

This rank-descendant approach to the interpretation and description of the phonological system of a language is the same approach that we adopt in the interpretation and description of the lexicogrammatical system of a language, viz. clause > group/phrase > word > morpheme. This is one manifestation of functional grammar, and we can extend this terminology to phonology: **functional phonology**.

6.5.2 Tone group and foot

As already noted, the phonological systems of different languages vary in terms of the number of ranks that their rank scales comprise. For example, in some languages, there is no pay-off in positing a rank of phoneme below that of syllable (cf. Halliday 1992a, on Chinese, referred to below); in some languages, it may be helpful to posit mora below the rank of syllable; in some languages, it may be necessary to recognize phonological words in addition to lexicogrammatical ones. This variation in phonological rank scales is related to the variation in the inter-stratal interface between lexicogrammar and phonology referred to above (see Figure 6.14).

For many languages – perhaps all, the highest-ranking unit of the phonological rank scale is a melodic one, a unit of extended pitch movement or pitch range (allowing for the possibility of pitch being exploited also at the syllable rank, as it is in tone languages). In systemic functional linguistics, this unit has been called the **tone group**; it is also known by other names, often being called the 'intonation unit'. Tone groups may be linked together in sequences and these may have particular properties in extended turns in speech such as a tendency for the pitch to drift down (cf. Halliday 1985e; Couper-Kuhlen 1986; Tench 1990; Halliday and Greaves, 2008; Couper-Kuhlen 2015). Such sequences can probably be interpreted as **complexes of tone groups** rather than as units of a higher rank. However, Halliday (1961/2002c) suggested that we would need a phonological rank above that of the tone group – a unit constituting a phonological 'paragraph', or **paraphone**:

> Statistical work on grammar may yield a further unit, above the sentence: it will then be possible to set up sentence classes, and account for sequences of them, by reference to this higher unit. Similarly, in phonology we need a unit in English above the tone group to account for sequences of different tones. The grammatical and phonological 'paragraph' (and perhaps 'paraphone'?) is probably within reach of a team of linguist, statistician, programmer and computer; cf. Firth (1957a): "Attention must be paid to the longer elements of text – such as the paragraph ..." (p. 18); Harris (1952); for Hill (1958: 406), and others, this is 'stylistics', but in the present theory it would come within exactly the same general framework of categories. (Halliday 1961/2002c: 78)

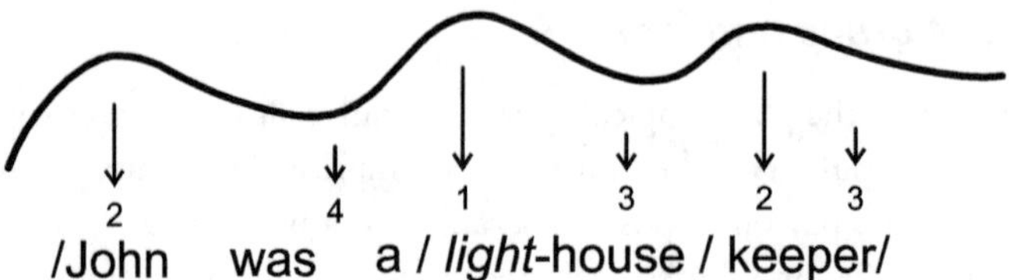

Figure 6.13 Initiator-power curve for 'John was a light-house keeper'. From Catford (1985: 347)

In many other languages, tone groups consist of units of the rank next below, i.e. of **feet**, and these consist in turn of **syllables**, as illustrated for English in Figure 6.14. The melody of the tone group or pitch contour is thus 'chunked' into feet, each of which will carry part of the pitch movement as well as their own patterning in terms of rhythm; and the feet are chunked into syllables, each of which will reflect the rhythm as well as their own patterning in terms of articulatory postures (gestures, or movements from one posture to another).

The structure of tone groups always includes the **Tonic** element, the locus of the major pitch movement of the intonation contour; and it will often include a **Pretonic** element, the pitch movement leading up to the Tonic. The Tonic is realized by one foot, the tonic foot; and (in this example) the Pretonic is realized by three feet. The structure of feet always includes the **Ictus** element, the locus of the beat; and it will often include a **Remiss** element, an element following the Ictus. The Ictus is realized by one syllable, a strong syllable; and (in this example) the Remiss is realized by two to three weak syllables.

	this	*of course de*	*pends*	*on the*	*coun*	*try where they*	***live***
tone group	tone group: with pretonic & simple tonic: tone 1						
	Pretonic						Tonic
foot	foot: compound & filled		foot: compound & filled		foot: compound & filled		foot: simple & filled
	Ictus	Remiss	Ictus	Remiss	Ictus	Remiss	Ictus
syllable	1 syllable	3 syllables	1 syllable	2 syllables	1 syllable	3 syllables	1 syllable

Figure 6.14 Tone group in English consisting of four feet, each of which consists of one to three syllables (adapted from Halliday, 1967b: 15)

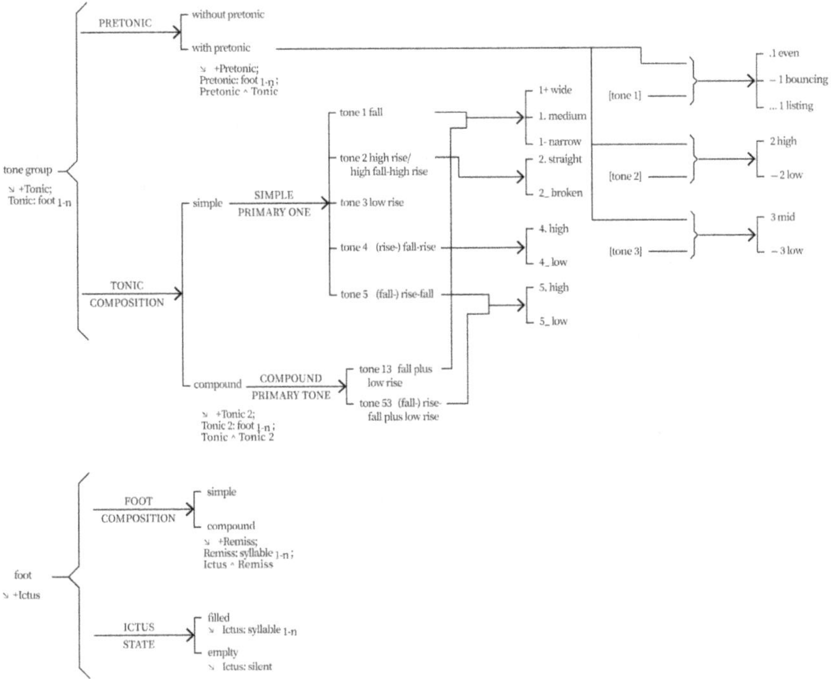

Figure 6.15 Examples of systems at the rank of tone group and foot in English (from Halliday and Matthiessen, 2014)

The system networks of the tone group (specifically, the system of TONE) and the foot in English are set out in Figure 6.15. Realization statements specifying the structure of tone groups and feet are always located in the environment of terms in phonological systems – the terms that they are structural realizations of. This means, of course, that the structural specifications given by realization statements never need to be changed; they are always specified in the appropriate systemic environment in the system network (including at the appropriate degree of delicacy).

6.5.3 *Syllable*

Just as tone group consists of the unit next below on the phonological rank scale, i.e. of feet, so feet consist of the units next below on the phonological rank scale, i.e. of **syllables**, as illustrated in Figure 6.14 above.

The syllable can be the lowest-ranking unit on the rank scale of a particular language; or, more precisely, in the ***description*** that particular language, positing the syllable as the lowest-ranking unit will provide the greatest insight into the nature of the phonology of that language, and hence enable us to explain how it works – as in the case of Halliday's (1992a) description of the Peking syllable (see below).

In the phonological and phonetic literature in general, the status of the syllable has been explored and investigated, and the possibility of identifying and characterizing it phonetically has even been questioned (e.g. Fudge 1969; Hooper 1972; van der Hulst and Ritter 1999; for a recent overview, see Cairns and Raimy 2011a, 2011b). From an articulatory point of view, the syllable can be characterized as a gesture, a move from one articulatory posture to another; and from an auditory point of view, the syllable can be characterized as a wave of sonority, with a peak of sonority (which may be the only obligatory part).

Phonologically, the syllable is a 'gateway' between the prosodic and articulatory domains of the system of phonology, as illustrated by a simplified version of the syllable system network of the phonology of Akan in Figure 6.17. Prosodically, the syllable is the domain of the system of TONE, which in Akan (as in many other languages spoken in West Africa) is based on the contrast between two level tones, 'high' and 'low' (with the option of downstep). This is characteristic of 'tone languages', but other systems may also have prosodic properties like RESONANCE (as in Akan) and PHARYNGEALIZATION (as in Modern Standard Arabic). And the syllable may also be manifested prosodically as a 'ripple' on the initiator-power curve of the foot, according to Catford (1977): see below.

As noted above, articulatorily, the syllable is an articulatory gesture, a movement through articulatory postures (which may be referred to under the heading of 'phonotactics' in phoneme-based approaches to phonology). Halliday's (1992a) description of the Peking syllable gives a good sense of how this gesture may operate in a particular language:

> The network [reproduced here as Figure 6.16, CMIMM] combines four principles of analysis. One is the Chinese phonological principle whereby all syllables are structured simply as initial plus final. The second is the Firthian prosodic principle whereby features such as posture (y/a/w) and resonance (nasal/oral) are treated non-segmentally. The third is the paradigmatic principle whereby features are interpreted as terms in systems, each system having a specified condition of entry. [Note that in Firthian system-structure theory the entry condition is specified syntagmatically, whereas in a system network it is specified paradigmatically: entry to one system depends on selecting a certain term in (at least one) other.] The fourth is the dynamic principle whereby the syllable is envisaged as a wave, a periodic pattern

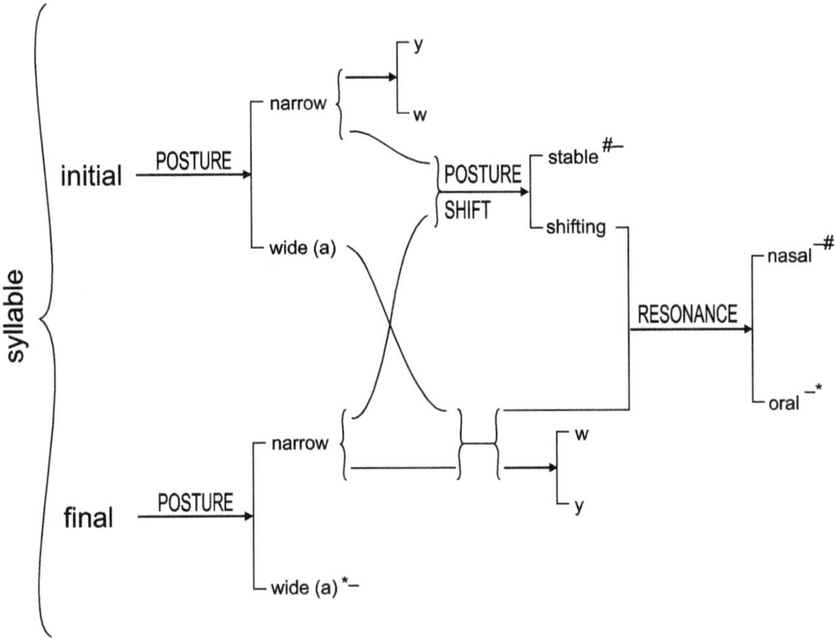

Figure 6.16 Halliday's description of the Peking syllable in terms of initial and final posture, and the shift between them (Halliday 1992a: 107); the full version of his description is reproduced as Figure 6.18

> of movement characterized by a kind of 'flow-and-return'. What this last means is that the syllable is construed as a movement from an initial state to a final state, each of these states is specified as a 'selection expression' (a cluster of features from different prosodic systems); and there is variation both temporally, in the extent to which a particular feature persists across the syllable, and spatially, in the route that is traversed from the initial to the final state. (Halliday 1992a: 107–108)

The full version of Halliday's (1992a) is reproduced here as Figure 6.18.

Picking up on Halliday's characterization of the syllable as a 'wave', let me relate this to Catford's (1985: 346) characterization of feet quoted above as "a unitary quantum of 'vocal effort', that is, of initiator power", or "stress pulse". What about initiator power in relation to the syllable? Catford (1977) suggests that in a foot-timed language like English, the syllable is 'either co-extensive with the foot, or is, at it were, a 'ripple' on the surface of the initiator-power curve'. After discussing variation across languages with respect to rhythm, he concludes:

> It seems possible, then, to sum up the discussion so far by saying that in all languages initiator power is delivered in quantum-like bursts, containing a single power peak. These correspond to English feet. If the initiator-power curve within each burst is not subject to any slight momentary diminution, or retardation, then the power curve itself (the foot) is co-extensive with what is called a syllable. If, on the contrary, there are articulatorily imposed (or, much more rarely, self-imposed) momentary retardations of the initiator-power movement, within the foot, then these are divisions between syllables within the foot. A syllable then, is a minimal 'chunk', or stretch, of initiator activity, bounded by either minor intra-foot, retardations, of by the foot divisions themselves. (Catford 1977: 89)

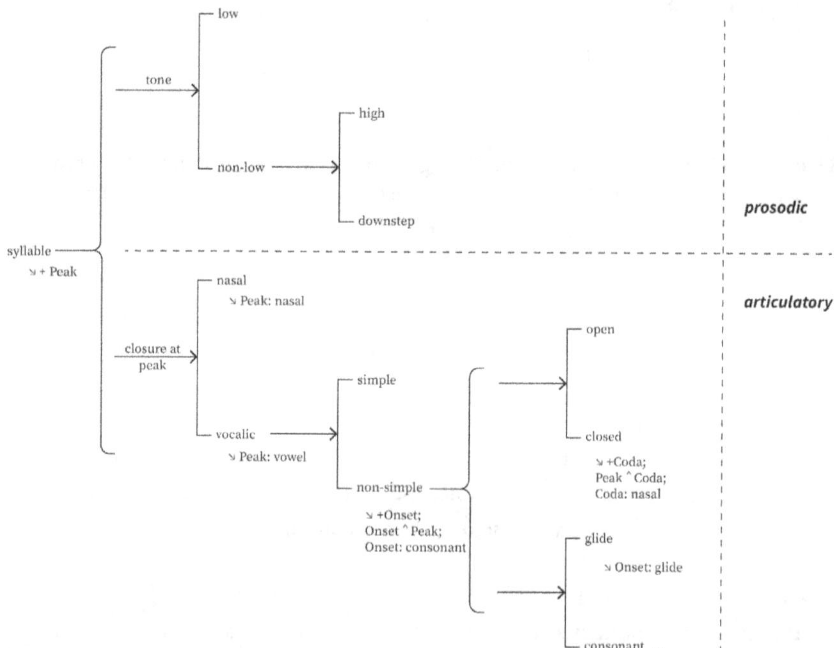

Figure 6.17 The syllable as the phonological 'gateway' between the prosodic and articulatory domains of phonology

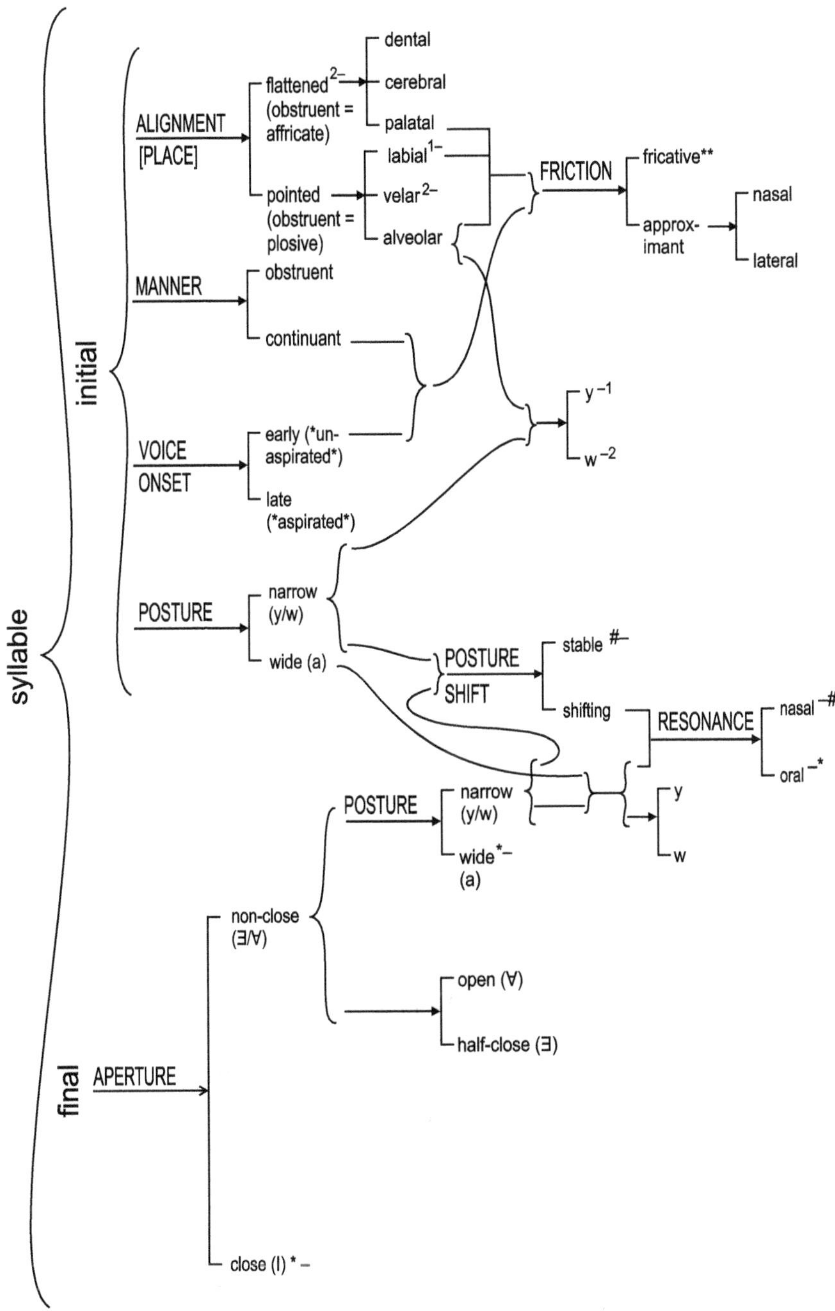

Figure 6.18 The system network of the Mandarin syllable, taken from Halliday (1992a: 118): 'Figure 6.6 Network specifying Mandarin (Pekingese) syllables'

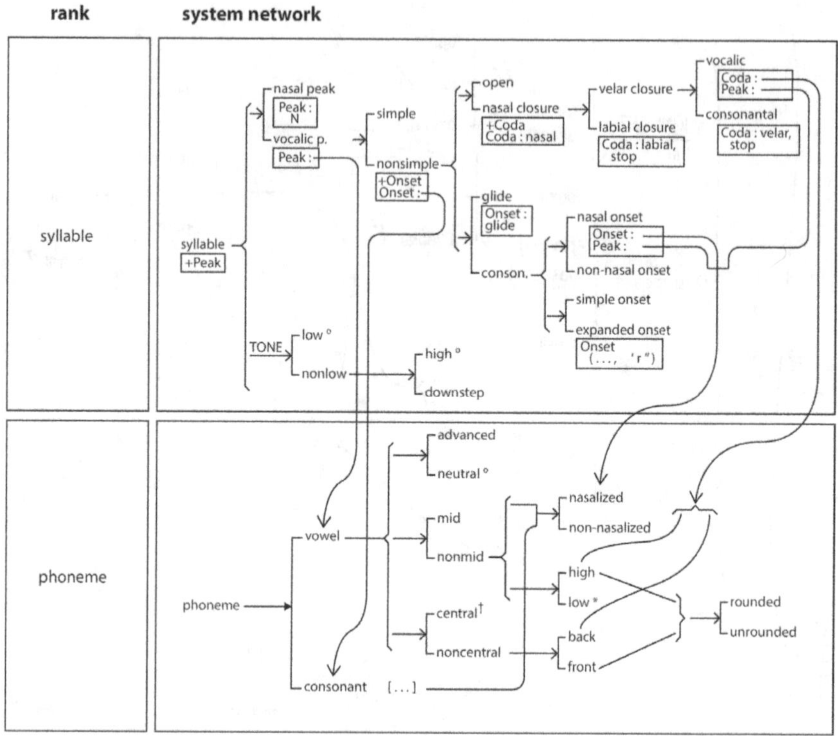

Figure 6.19 Partial description of the ranking units of syllable and phoneme in Akan, with preselections indicating realizations of elements of the structure of the syllable by phonemes (represented by arrows)

6.5.4 *Phoneme*

The relationship between syllables and phonemes varies across languages; it is one of the key typological variables in phonological systems. One aspect of the variation in this relationship is the degree to which syllables can in fact be segmented into phonemes (or in Firth's terms, phonematic units). The degree of segmentability can be illuminated by Halliday and Greave's (2008: 78–79) comparison of English and Chinese; speaking of phonological units, they write:

> Such units in phonology are often not clearly delimited – in any given language there may be some that are more and some that are less determinate. [footnote:] For example, in Chinese the syllable is a clearly defined unit; but within the syllable the constituent structure is rather

> hazy: in Mandarin the entire system is framed as a move from an initial to a terminal posture, and there are no phonematic units at all. In English, on the other hand, the syllable is rather fuzzy (are words like button, tower, police one syllable or two?), but the phoneme-like segments are relatively clear – though not perhaps as clear as in Italian or Czech.

And this difference between English and Chinese can be related to how syllables are constituted as phonological gestures; Halliday (1992a: 110) contrasts them as follows:

> But the initial and final states are what constitute the essence of the syllable. Thus, whereas in English the peak of resonance in the syllable – the vowel nucleus – is also the most 'fixed' part, so that in a set like *seen*, *soon*, *sing*, *song*, the vowel posture is projected outwards on to the initial and final consonants, in the Mandarin syllable it is the other way round: the vowel 'nucleus' is simply a degree of aperture, and the initial and final postures of the syllable are 'projected' inwards to create a movement within this broad band of phonetic space.

In languages where it makes sense in the description of their phonological systems to posit a rank of phoneme below that of the syllable (or possibly mora), this unit is the point of origin for phonemic system networks of the type that I began to illustrate in the discussion of the systemicization of phonological features above: see Figures 6.9, 6.10, 6.11 and 6.12.

Since the phoneme is the lowest-ranking unit (in languages that have this rank below that of the syllable), phonological features in phoneme systems such as PLACE and MANNER are realized inter-axially by phonological items ('phonemes'), which in turn are realized inter-stratally by phonetic specifications. These specifications have to be mapped onto articulatory and auditory specifications (or in modelling speech, by the specifications needed by a speech synthesizer); this is an important aspect of the stratum of phonetics as an interface between language and the bodily systems involved in sound production and perception. Thus features in phoneme systems are realized inter-stratally in this way rather than intra-stratally by specifications of phonological structure involving units of a lower rank. (Phonological features in systems whose domains are higher-ranking can be realized both inter-stratally, e.g. in the realization of tones referencing the vocal chords, and intra-stratally, e.g. in the realization of tones through the specification of the structure of the tone group.)

As an illustration of a systemic description of the phonemic potential of a language, let me return to my (exploratory!) description of the phonology of Akan: see Figure 6.20. This is the phoneme system that the description of the Akan syllable system refers to by means of relations of preselections, as already shown in Figure 6.19.

The features in the systems in Figure 6.20 are all grounded in the description of the general articulatory resources provided by Catford (1977). When I started to develop the description of phoneme system of Akan, I tried using the distinctive features, both articulatory and auditory, adopted in generative phonology at the time, which originated in Roman Jakobson's work (e.g. Jakobson, Fant, and Halle 1952); but I found that the description turned out to be more insightful and effective when I switched to purely articulatory features drawn from Catford (1977). This is, of course, not to claim that auditory features have no place in the description of phoneme systems. Rather, the articulatory and auditory views are complementary, and at different points in the description, one view or the other may provide greater descriptive insight – an obvious example being rhotics, which may be 'heard' as fairly similar (e.g. comparable in sonority) even when they embody clear differences in place of articulation (e.g. alveolar ridge vs. uvula; or retroflex, i.e. apico-postalveolar) or even in manner of articulation (e.g. tap, flap vs. trill). In other words, phonetically natural classes may be articulatory, auditory or both, which may be a source of variation over time or space in a language or set of genetically related languages.

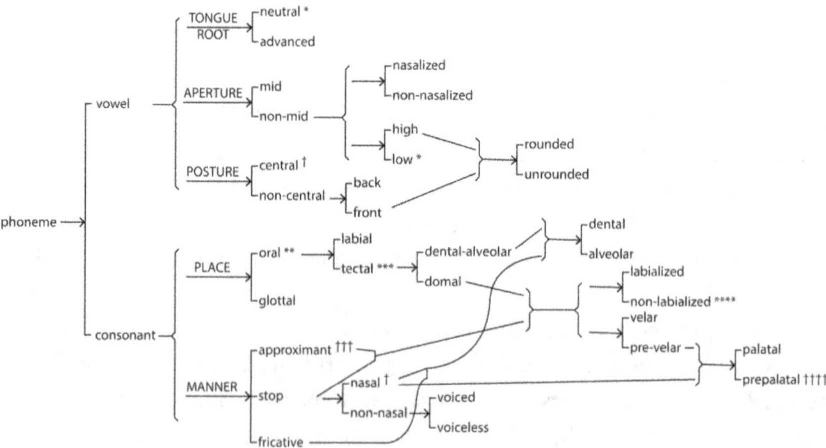

Figure 6.20 The system operating at phoneme rank in Akan

Table 6.4 Restrictions on combinations of upper and lower articulatory locations in Akan

	oral						glottal
	labial	tectal					
		dental-alveolar		domal			
		dental	alveolar	palatal		velar	
				prepal.	palatal		
labio							
apico-lamino							
dorso							

In working with Catford's (1977) account of the human articulatory potential as I was developing the systemic description of Akan consonant systems, I found one broad generalization regarding oral (in the sense of super-glottal) consonants: upper articulatory places (the upper jaw) and lower articulatory places (the lower jaw and the tongue) are not independently variable, but the specification of the upper place will determine the choice of the lower place, as shown in Table 6.4. For example, 'domal' consonants ('palatal' and 'velar') are all 'dorsal'; for instance, there are no apico-domal ('retroflex') consonants in Akan. Therefore, in naming systemic features of place, I chose names based on upper places, as can be seen in Figure 6.20. Thus the system contrasting 'dental' and 'alveolar' includes a disjunctive entry condition of 'nasal' or 'fricative', thus excluding non-nasal stops and approximants from this more delicate distinction.

Another phenomenon of systemic interaction that I had to account for in the consonant part of the phoneme system Akan shown in Figure 6.20 was that between PLACE and MANNER of articulation. While these systems are in general simultaneous, and I represented them as such in the system network in Figure 6.20, there are certain constraints; for example, fricatives articulated in the oral area are either 'dental-alveolar' or 'pre-palatal' but not 'palatal' or 'velar'. The restrictions on place and manner that I found are set out in Table 6.5. These restrictions are built into the system network in Figure 6.20 either in terms of the entry conditions of more delicate consonant systems or in terms of **systemic conditioning**. Systemic

Table 6.5 Akan consonants according to place of articulation (columns) and manner of articulation (rows); note that /w/ and /ɥ/ are both also 'labial'

MANNER:	PLACE													
	oral												sub-oral	
	labial		tectal											
			dental-alveolar		domal									
					palatal					velar				
					pre-palatal		palatal							
stop, affricate	p	b	t	d	tɕ, tɕɥ	dʑ, dʑɥ			k, k^w	g, g^w	ʔ			
nasal		m		ɱ, n		ɳ		ɲ, $ɲ^w$		ŋ, $ŋ^w$				
fricative			f, s		ç						h			
approximant		ɥ, w		r				y, [ɥ]		[w]				

Note: In each cell at the intersection of place and manner values: voiceless | voiced, e.g. p | b; sub-oral = pharyngeo-laryngeal: glottal; the approximants ɥ, w are co-articulated in terms of place: labial + palatal, and velar, respectively

conditioning is used to show e.g. that approximants are all 'tectal', excluding 'labial' and 'glottal'.

The sketch of the consonantal part of the phoneme system of Akan represents work in progress, and here it serves only as an ***illustration*** of the possibilities and issues that arise when we systemicize phonological features at the rank of phoneme.

6.6 Phonology and phonetics in relation to parallel systems

Having moved down the phonological rank scale and reached the lowest rank of unit, the phoneme, that we would posit in the description of any language,[21] let me now take a step back to locate phonology and phonetics in relation to systems external to language, both semiotic ones and non-semiotic, biological ones. Here the status of phonology and phonetics as the two strata of the expression plane (in spoken language) is essential (cf. Figure 6.4 above): see Table 6.6 and Figure 6.21.

As a system of embodied sound, phonetics is not, of course, clearly bounded from the deployment of sound as a mode of expression in other semiotic systems. Thus in the prosodic domain, linguistic prosodies shade into **paralinguistic** ones, **voice quality** being an important example. It is obvious that voice quality is used in the service of meaning-making, clearly involved in the expression of meanings that we would associate with the interpersonal metafunction (for a systemic functional study, see Wan 2010).[22] Voice quality may share expression space with the system of TONE; in English, tone 5 (rising-falling) tends to be pronounced with breathy voice quality (Halliday 1967b; Halliday and Greaves 2008); but the question is still whether voice quality is as fully systemic as the system of TONE is.

Table 6.6 Form vs. substance strata within the content and expression planes

	internal to language		**external to language**	
	form	**substance**	**immaterial: semiotic**	**material: biological**
content	lexico-grammar	semantics	context (connotative semiotic system); denotative semiotic systems other than language	bio-semiotic systems
expression	phonology	phonetics	(expression systems in 'paralanguage', including kinetics)	articulatory-auditory systems (and, secondarily, visual and kinaesthetic systems)
	core	**interface**	**extra-linguistic systems**	

The phonetic range available to speakers (and listeners) will clearly depend on the channel available to them; they may have to shout, whisper or even mouth their utterances, and the presence or absence of visual contact is clearly also crucial (cf. Martin 1992a: chap. 7). Another interesting issue relating to phonetics (and thus to phonology, approached 'from below') is what happens when spoken language is sung. This will clearly depend how stylized the singing is, since the more stylized it is, the greater the pressure on phonetic adaptation (with possible consequences for the phonology like loss of prosodic or even articulatory contrasts). In the Firthian tradition, Robins and McLeod (1956) investigated Yurok songs, and found various phonetic adaptations (e.g. p. 583, "Consonants are often articulated with less precision than is customary in normal discourse, and the phonologically voiceless consonants, when inter-vocalic, are frequently pronounced with voicing maintained throughout"). In the SFL tradition, Steiner (1988a) presents an analysis of a folk ballad, and Caldwell (2014) reports on research into rap and the sung voice.

Just as semantics is the interface stratum of the content plane ('substance'), phonetics is the interface stratum of the expression plane. In this role, it interfaces with biological systems – the articulatory and auditory systems of the human body, with respect to both of which language is 'parasitic', in the sense that it is an adaptation deploying earlier bodily systems (which may come at a cost: while chimpanzees do not have to worry about choking, we do). Since these bodily systems are not uniquely linguistic, the expression plane of language has to share the bodily resources; for example, speech has co-opted the respiratory system, so if we try to speak after running, we face difficulties because we may be out of breath. Similarly, eating and speaking compete for the same bodily resources – articulating while masticating can be challenging (so cultures may evolve constraints on 'table manners'), as do involuntary physiological behaviours combined with speaking such as sneezing, coughing and hiccupping.

At the same time, phonetics interfaces with parts of the signifying body (cf. Thibault 2004b) that are also used as the expression plane of other (denotative) semiotic systems. This applies in particular to those aspects of the articulatory system that are most readily visible: the lips, the mouth and the region around the mouth; here the articulatory system shares expression space with the system of facial expression (reflected in the fact that in many languages, speakers have a word with a spread (high) front vowel they use when they prepare to smile for photographs, like *cheese* in English, *omelett* in Swedish, *appelsin* in Danish, *qiézi* in Chinese, and *kimchi* in Korean).

While phonology is not an interface stratum but rather one internal to the stratal organization of language, it may have regular correspondences to the graphology of a language, if that writing system is based on the phonology of the language, either at the rank of phoneme (alphabets) or the rank of syllable (syllabaries): for a systemic functional account of writing systems, see Halliday (1985c).

Phonology and phonetics are likely to have connections with other semiotic systems where the channel is oral-auditory. However, taking one step further, we can ask if phonology and phonetics are related to non-oral-auditory semiotic systems – in face-to-face interaction, gesture, facial expression, gaze, posture. In general, it would seem that here the coordination is 'driven' from above, from the other interface stratum, i.e. from semantics. As young children learn how to mean, gestures and vocalizations are alternative modes of expression during the protolinguistic phase and vocalizations are really articulatory gestures, as Halliday (1975) has shown. One difference between gestures and vocal gestures is, of course, that the latter are largely hidden from view; but even in adult language it is possible (though not necessarily polite!) to use the lips or the tip of the tongue to point, as can happen with the English demonstratives. As children move from their protolanguage into the mother tongue during the second year of life, the linguistic mode of expression becomes more exclusively vocalization,[23] now being transformed into the phonology-phonetics stratification of the expression plane characteristic of post-infancy adult language. But it would appear that during this period gestures gradually become the mode of expression of a distinct semiotic system in its own right. The linguistic and the gestural systems seem to be very closely coordinated semantically, as evidence from studies of the construal of motion through space in different languages indicates (e.g. Lantolf 2010): the lexicogrammatical and gestural resources may complement one another in different ways in different languages. If we study the coordination and synchronization of speech and gesture,

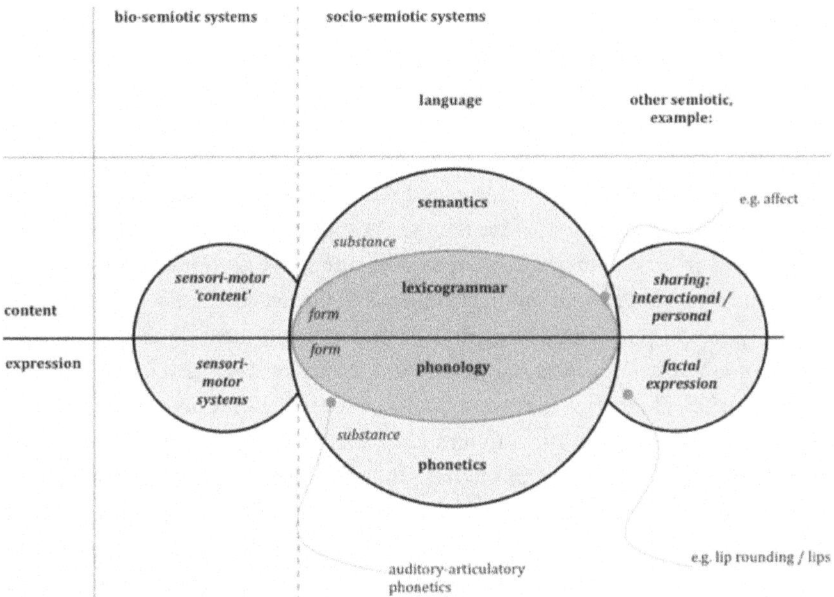

Figure 6.21 Phonology and phonetics in relation to other human systems on the expression plane

we can, of course, investigate 'from below', identifying timing links between phonetic speech production and gesture production; but the source of the complementarity is semantic, not phonetic and gestural. Indeed, it would appear that language and gesture are closely connected neurologically in the brain: see e.g. Xu *et al.* (2009).

6.7 Conclusion

In this chapter I have sketched the outline of the architecture of phonology according to systemic functional linguistics. My focus has been theoretical rather than descriptive, so descriptions of English and Akan have only served as illustrations: systemic functional descriptions and discussions of English can be found in Halliday (1967b), Elmenoufy (1969), Tench (1990, 1992a, 1996), Watt (1992, 1994), Martinec (1995), Greaves (2007), Smith (2005, 2008), Bowcher and Smith (2014), and I will return to the description of Akan in Volume 3. I have emphasized the central conception of phonology as a resource for making sound in the service of language as a resource for making meaning, and thus explored its architecture as a sounding potential. As a sounding ***potential***, its primary organization is paradigmatic rather than syntagmatic, patterns along the syntagmatic axis being derivable from realization statements associated with options in sounding. The paradigmatic organization is modelled by means of system networks with associated realization statements specifying fragments of phonological structure, and these system networks are distributed along the phonological rank scale from tone group to syllable (and phoneme), reflecting the fact that phonology encompasses both a prosodic domain and an articulatory one, the prosodic one being developmentally prior as young children learn how to sound (Halliday and Greaves 2008: 75–76).

The system of phonology must thus be understood in its role as a stratal subsystem of language as a meaning potential, located between lexicogrammar and phonetics as the higher of the two expression strata – like lexicogrammar, it is a language-internal stratum of form and like lexicogrammar, it is accompanied by its own interface stratum, i.e. phonetics. The modelling of the stratal location of phonology enables us to adopt a trinocular perspective on it, viewing it 'from above' – from the vantage point of its contribution to the realization of lexicogrammar, 'from below' – from the vantage point of its manifestation in embodied sound (sound as substance) in phonetics, and also 'from roundabout' – from its own vantage point as a system of phonological options (contrasts in value, *valeur*). Characterizing the systemic functional account of phonology, we can say that in adopting the view from above, we foreground the nature of phonology as **functional**, bringing out its organization as a resource for making distinctions in meaning (as demonstrated in a masterly way by Halliday and Greaves 2008), and in adopting the view from below, we foreground the nature of phonology as **natural**, bringing out the fact that it is grounded in phonetics, in the embodied sounding resources of the human organism.[24]

Through phonetics, phonology is realized by the bodily resources for producing and perceiving sound, and I have referred at various points to the way that phonology is grounded in phonetics. In this way, phonology is **embodied** together with the rest of language, and it can thus be interpreted in biological terms. At the same time, we can take a step back, and locate phonology as part of language within the **ordered typology of systems** operating in different phenomenal realms that a good deal of systemic functional work has been based on (see e.g. Halliday 1996, 2005a; Halliday and Matthiessen 2006; Matthiessen 2007b [this volume]):

- material systems:
  - 1st-order systems – physical systems;
  - 2nd-order systems – biological systems: physical systems + life (self-replicating individuated evolving systems);

- immaterial systems:
  - 3rd-order systems – social systems: biological systems + value (social order, including roles in social networks);
  - 4th-order systems – semiotic systems: social systems + meaning.

Some scheme like this is, of course, familiar from the study of the expression plane of spoken language: semiotic – phonology, biological – articulatory and auditory phonetics (and of course neurolinguistic considerations), physical – acoustic phonetics (and with Catford 1977, we can add aerodynamics). These orders may be set out as the phases of speech production and perception, starting with the neural phase in speech production and ending with the acoustic phase. This picture leaves out social considerations, but of course the manifestation of phonology (as part of language) as a social system has been central in sociolinguistics (and in earlier dialect studies), revealing how phonological variation among (groups of) speakers is imbued with social value (cf. discussions of dialectal variation in SFL – variation according to (identity of) language user, e.g. Halliday, McIntosh and Strevens 1964; Halliday 1978).

Let me conclude the discussion of the systemic functional architecture of phonology as a stratal subsystem of language by returning to the issue of the organization of the metalanguage itself used in specifying the architecture. I have used system networks fairly extensively in characterizing and illustrating aspects of the architecture, sketching the sounding potential as it is distributed along the phonological rank scale from tone groups to syllables and phonemes. However, phonological system networks are not themselves the theory of phonological organization but rather the ***representation*** of this theory: they are as it were at one remove from the theory itself. They can, in fact, be located within a hierarchy of the strata that make up the organization of the metalanguage we use:

- the stratum of linguistic theory: according to the theory of SFL, as it is manifested in the design of the architecture of phonology, the phonological subsystem of language is a resource for realizing wordings (and by another stratal step meanings) as sound, i.e. a resource for making sound or a sounding potential – what speakers and listeners can sound in a given language; this sounding potential is organized paradigmatically in the first instance (not syntagmatically), and the paradigmatic organization is conceptualized as options in sounding;
- the stratum of theoretical representation: the paradigmatic organization of the theory stratum is realized in the form of a particular kind of representation – system networks with accompanying realization statements specifying fragments of sound patterns along the syntagmatic axis; but in

principle we could revise the system network representation or replace it with some other form of representation in order to increase the representational coverage of the theory;

- the stratum of computational representation: as a type of representation, system networks (with accompanying) realization statements are oriented 'upwards', towards the theoretical stratum, and while they have been used in the computational modelling of language (prominently in text generation, see e.g. Matthiessen and Bateman 1991), they needed to be further specified to make them more formally explicit, e.g. with respect to traversal algorithms (cf. Matthiessen 1988a) – in the beginning, this really only meant algebraic representations in LISP, but as the work developed, more sophisticated and constrained representational systems began to be used, like typed feature structures;
- the stratum of implementation: given some type of computational representation, the next and final stratal step is the implementation of it in some programming language like LISP, Prolog, C++, Java, Python.

These stratal steps are relevant to the full specification of phonology in a computational model of language, as in the work on linking meaning-based text generation to speech synthesis undertaken by Teich, Watson and Pereira (2000). We had explored already in the mid-1980s the possibility of linking our text generation system to a speech synthesizer, but the plans remained on the drawing board, and Teich, Watson and Pereira took this work much further. It is very important in itself, but is also good for sorting out the metalinguistic strata that we need to pay attention to and develop specifications for. Of course, the 'implementation' might be a neurological one rather than a computational one, but the general point that we need to be clear about the stratification of our metalanguage remains the same (cf. Lamb 1999, and Lamb 2013: 137, on his conception of the status of system networks: "... the hypothesis [is] that relational networks are related in a rather direct way to actual brain structures. Since they are also related to system networks, they provide a bridge from the latter to the brain."). If we are relating language in general, or phonology in particular, to the brain, we need to make our theoretical model biologically implementable (which in a way has been Sidney Lamb's goal all along throughout the development of stratificational linguistics, up through relational network theory).

The examples of phonological system networks that I have presented here as illustrations are thus located within the second stratum in the stratal hierarchy of our metalanguage that I set out above. They need to be 'thickened' as accounts of phonology both in terms of the theory that they have been developed to represent and in terms of possible further lower-stratal but more explicit representations.

While this is not the place to review other approaches to phonology in comparison with the SFL account I have just sketched (cf. Halliday and Greaves 2008: 11–14), I would like to suggest that some other approaches have tended to suffer from a certain degree of confusion about the distinction between theory and theoretical representation in that representations have sometimes or even often been assumed to be theory – so we are arguably left with a kind of tension between the deep theoretical insights into phonology from the first half of the twentieth century and the pre-occupation with representational systems (often not all that explicit) in the second half of the twentieth century.

But let me end on a positive note: what I have tried to outline here is a theory of phonology (as manifested in a certain kind of theoretical representation) that interprets and models it as a sounding resource – the sounding potential available to the speakers and listeners of any language. In broad outline, this sounding potential has the same architecture as the other stratal subsystems of language; so we can treat it not only as a system in its own right but also as a metaphor for the organization of language – benefiting from the fact that even though the sounding potential of any language is vast, it is much smaller than the wording potential and (by another order of magnitude) the meaning potential. The study of the phonologization (form) of our phonetic resources (substance) can hopefully also guide us in our exploration of the lexicogrammaticalization (form) of our semantic resources (substance): it is easier to work out certain general principles on the expression plane than on the content plane. Hopefully, this study of the relationship of semioticization between phonology and phonetics can also serve as a guide in the continued investigation of the expression planes of other semiotic systems – where most work so far has arguably (and understandably) been focused on their content planes.

Notes

1 I was very fortunate to learn from the phonetic work by Peter Ladefoged, whom I met in 1979 when I arrived to study linguistics at UCLA, and by Ian Catford, whom I met at the International Systemic Functional Congress at York University in 1982 (where he gave a paper I cite here [Catford 1985]). Together with David Abercrombie, I think they give us a sense of what a systemic functional approach to phonetics would be like; and of course, the three of them all represent Edinburgh University. At the same Congress, I also heard a talk by Carol Mock on Zapotec, where she tried to relate what she'd taken prosodic analysis to the work emerging within autosegmental phonology.

2 But would the 'physiology of language' strike the right note? And as I have commented elsewhere, the 'anatomy of language' would inevitably make me think of Otto

Preminger's *Anatomy of a Murder.* The motif here is, of course, pattern or design; so other possibilities suggest themselves: the 'blueprint of language', the 'warp and woof' of language (with due recognition given to Bob Longacre: 'the warp and woof of discourse'). But we need to avoid the implication of design that comes with 'architecture': the wondrous complexity of the organization of language is due to evolution, not design; so in this respect 'anatomy' is better than 'architecture'.

3 Thus when we describe the phonological system of a language, we need to cover not only sound patterns currently used in the realization of wordings, but also sound patterns that **could** be used: this is an important aspect of the conception of phonology as a sounding potential – sounds (sound patterns) that speakers ***can*** make (and listeners can perceive) according to the system of the language.

4 This is equally important for an understanding of intonation and rhythm, but when we compare the SFL approach to rhythm with a number of other current or recent approaches it is crucially important to note that the account is grounded in connected speech, not in the pronunciation of isolated citation forms. Thus word accent is merely the latent location of the beat in connected speech. Just like syllables are 'elastic' so that they can accommodate rhythmic patterns (in English), latent accent locations can be overridden.

5 In an attempt to characterize unfolding text by reference to systemic selections within the content plane, I have used to term 'text score' (e.g. Matthiessen 2002b), which I took from Weinreich's (1972) *Textpartitur*; and this conception of text as unfolding selections (cf. Halliday 1977b) is equally appropriate to phonology.

6 Selection or choice does not imply conscious or intentional choice, of course; the default is that phonological choices are below the level of consciousness, being automated in relation to content-plane choices (cf. Halliday 2013a).

7 That is: bodily sounding potential (sound as 'substance') – articulatory potential for producing sounds by means of the speech organs and auditory potential for perceiving sounds by means of the ear and related auditory system. In addition, phonetics must also interface, by extension, with our visual system since 'lip-reading' may supplement listening, and with our kinaesthetic system since this provides feedback to us as we speak. And while the basic phonetic interface is either articulatory (motor control) or auditory (perception), the two are connected; for example, in listening to rhythm we perceive it as speakers (see e.g. Abercrombie 1967, on 'phonetic empathy').

8 The predominantly conventional relationship between lexicogrammar and phonology is not contradicted by certain areas of relative iconicity, recognized under the headings of sound symbolism (phonaesthesia) and onomatopoeia (cf. Firth 1948a; and see Halliday and Greaves 2008: 168–169). For example, Jespersen (1933: 287) discusses the tendency for [i], the unrounded high front vowel, to symbolize small size, writing: "SOUND symbolism plays a greater role in the development of languages than is admitted by most linguists. In this paper I shall attempt to show that the vowel [i], high-front-unround, especially in its narrow or thin form, serves very often to indicate what is small, slight, insignificant, or weak." Such connections may help young children as they learn how to mean and how to sound. For a discussion of the contrasting positions taken by Saussure and Jespersen, see Qu (2018). There is now a growing body of work on sound symbolism and onomatopoeia

(e.g. Else 2017), but these tendencies towards a natural or motivated relationship between content and expression are just that – limited tendencies. From a systemic functional point of view, it is helpful to differentiate experiential and interpersonal 'sound symbolism' – the latter may operate in the service of interpersonal assessment (evaluation, appraisal).

9 The distinction between prosody and articulation is real: it can be observed in the phenomenon of sounding itself, and as Halliday and Greaves (2008: 78) note (quoted above), there is variation among languages in whether they treat certain features prosodically or segmentally. But when we theorize phonological systems, we can approach either in terms of the other: phonemics pushed the segmental model of phonemes forming strings towards the prosodic domains, whereas prosodic analysis (in the work by Firth, e.g. 1948a, and his group, e.g. Henderson 1949) pushed the prosodic model towards the articulatory domain. The latter was an important corrective to the segmental tendency that prevailed in a good deal of mid-twentieth-century phonology, and avoided positing segments in an artificial way, thus paving the way for a more natural phonology (i.e. natural in relation to phonetics). See Halliday (1992a) for a prosodic analysis of syllables in Mandarin.

10 When we consider phonological structures, we find the range of modes of expression that Halliday (1979) identifies for lexicogrammar and interprets as naturally related to the metafunctional modes of meaning: logical ~ serial (chain), experiential ~ configurational (segmental, particulate), interpersonal ~ prosodic, and textual ~ periodic. For a metafunctional interpretation of phonological structure "seen from the perspective of rhythm and the foot", see Thibault (2004b: 122–125), and see also Cléirigh (1998).

11 In relation to 'arbitrariness', cf. Halliday and Greaves (2008: 79): "Intonation is the most clearly iconic of all phonological features, and hence enables us to modify the view that phonology is totally arbitrary."

12 A nice sung illustration is provided by Jacques Brel's masterful rendition of *La valse à mille temps*, where he gradually speeds up over a period of around 3 minutes and 45 seconds.

13 In an early attempt to sort out definitions of the phoneme during a period when the term was beginning to be used more frequently, Twaddell (1935: 9) identified two definitions, "definitions in terms of a mental reality, and definitions in terms of a physical reality", which he then went on to explore in detail. For a recent review of approaches, see van der Hulst (2013). (He writes about the 'discoverers' of the phoneme; it would arguably be more insightful to call them 'postulators' since the history of the phoneme concerns a theoretical construct.)

14 This is also how phonology is accounted for as a probabilistic system in the first instance: terms in phonological systems have probabilities associated with them. These probabilities can be studied by examining relative frequencies of selections in corpora of connected speech. At a special colloquium on the history of phonology organized by John Goldsmith, Michael Halliday was invited to talk about systemic functional phonology (published as Halliday 2000b). Goldsmith himself suggested that Jakobson's interest in the 1950s in information theory – and thus probabilistic models – had been dismissed too early. I remember that in the question session, Janet Pierrehumbert made the comment that she thought Halliday's systemic phonology would be best suited to probabilistic

characterizations. This is an important insight (though it did not make it into her contribution on probabilistic phonology to Bod, Hay and Jannedy 2003b).

15 Contrast Jakobson's (1949) reinterpretation of Prague School phonological parametric values (Trubetzkoy 1939) as syntagmatic feature components of phonemes.

16 Just as lexicogrammatical function-rank matrices, introduced by Halliday (1970c), do with respect to lexicogrammatical labour.

17 For example, in German, Arabic and Akan, we can find a glottal stop; but while it is clearly phonemic in Arabic (i.e. it contrasts with other phonemes), it is not in German and Akan. In both these languages, its domain seems to be more prosodic (cf. the notion of juncture prosodies, discussed in Matthiessen 1988a).

18 Cf. Halliday and Greaves (2008: 78): "Thus while phonological features, like features at other strata, can always be shown to be systemic, with a definite point of origin for each network, their phonetic reach can be very varied; a syllable prosody, for example, may be realized at syllable initial or syllable final only, or even somewhere outside the syllable altogether."

19 Other aspects of the polysystemic approach will be handled elsewhere in the description of the phonology, including (1) languages with distinct or partially distinct phonological patterns for borrowings from other languages, and (2) languages with different phonological possibilities associated with different word classes, e.g. the phonology of nouns vs. the phonology of verbs.

20 The fundamental importance of treating rhythm as a property of connected spontaneous speech has often been overlooked in accounts based on the 'rhythmic' patterns of citation forms taken in isolation. Catford's example consists of three feet: *// John was a / light-house / keeper //*, each with the structure of Ictus ^ Remiss (see Table 4.4): [Ictus:] *John* ^ [Remiss:] *was a*; [Ictus:] *light-* ^ [Remiss:] *house*; [Ictus:] *kee* ^ [Remiss:] *per*.

21 Keeping in mind that phonemes do not 'consist' of distinctive features but are rather realizations of the intersection of terms in phonological systems (values of phonological parameters).

22 Or in the indication of projected passages in spoken text, as Halliday noted in his *Introduction to functional grammar* (Halliday and Matthiessen 2014).

23 Halliday (2003b: 115) notes with respect to the child he studied: "Within four to six weeks, however, he abandoned the gestural mode almost entirely (the exception being the demand for music, expressed by 'beating time'), and settled for vocal symbols in the expression of meanings of all kinds."

24 In the case of phonology, 'functional' and 'natural' thus reflect two different stratal perspectives – from above and from below. In contrast, in the case of lexicogrammar, they reflect the same stratal perspective – from above. This is of course due to their different stratal locations, as the 'form' strata of the expression plane and of the content plane, respectively: see Figure 6.4.

References

Abdullayev, A. (2003) *Discourse analysis and theme development*. Tabriz, Iran: Akhtar Publication.

Abercrombie, D. (1967) *Elements of general phonetics*. Chicago, IL: Aldine Publishing Company and Edinburgh: Edinburgh University Press.

Aikhenvald, A. Y. (2003) *A grammar of Tariana: From northwest Amazonia*. Cambridge: Cambridge University Press.

Akerejola, E. (2005) *A systemic functional grammar of Òkó*. Ph.D. thesis, Macquarie University.

Alatis, J. (ed.) (1993) *Language, communication and social meaning*. Washington, DC: Georgetown University Press.

Amsler, R. A. (1981) A taxonomy for English nouns and verbs. In *Proceedings of the 19th Annual Meeting of the Association for Computational Linguistics*. Stanford, CA, pp. 133–138.

Andersen, T. (2003) *Spaendinger is sproget: om leksikogrammatiske metaforer i dansk*. Ph.D. thesis, University of Southern Denmark.

Andersen, T. (2004) The system of THEME in the Danish clause. In D. Banks (ed.), *Text and texture: Systemic functional viewpoints on the nature and structure of text*. Paris: L'Harmattan, pp. 191–213.

Andersen, T., Petersen, U. H. and Smedegaard, F. (2001) *Sproget som resource: dansk systemisk functionel lingvistik i teori og praksis* [Language as resource: Danish systemic functional linguistics in theory and praxis]. Odense: Odense Universitetsforlag.

Anderson, J. (1983) *The architecture of cognition*. Cambridge, MA: Harvard University Press.

Argyle, M., Furnham, A. and Graham, J. (1981) *Social situations*. Cambridge: Cambridge University Press.

Armstrong, E. (1991) The potential of cohesion analysis in the analysis and treatment of aphasic discourse. *Clinical Linguistics and Phonetics*, 5 (1): 39–51.

Armstrong, E. (1992) Clause complex relations in aphasic discourse: A longitudinal case study. *Journal of Neurolinguistics*, 7 (4): 261–275.

Armstrong, E. M. (1997) *A grammatical analysis of aphasic discourse: Changes in meaning-making over time*. Ph.D. thesis, Macquarie University.

Armstrong, E. M. (2009) Clinical applications. In M. A. K. Halliday and Webster, J. (eds), *A companion to systemic functional linguistics*. London and New York: Continuum, pp. 143–153.

Armstrong, E. M., Ferguson, A., Mortensen, L. and Togher, L. (2005) Acquired language disorders: Some functional insights. In Hasan, R., Matthiessen, C. M. I. M. and Webster, J. (eds), *Continuing discourse on language: A functional perspective*. Volume 1. London: Equinox, pp. 383–412.

Arús, J. (2003) *Hacia una especificación de la transitividad en el Español: estudio contrastivo con el Ingés* (Towards a specification of Spanish transitivity: A contrastive study with English). Ph.D. thesis, Universidad Complutense de Madrid.

Asp, E. and Villiers, J. de (2010) *When language breaks down: Analysing discourse in clinical contexts*. Cambridge: Cambridge University Press.

Aziz, Y. Y. (1988) Cohesion in spoken Arabic text. In Steiner, E. H. and Veltman, R. (eds) *Pragmatics, discourse and text: Explorations in systemic semantics*. London: Frances Pinter, pp. 148–57.

Bäcklund, I. (1992) Theme in English telephone conversation. *Language Sciences* 14(4): 545–65.

Banks, D. (1991) Some observations concerning transitivity and modality in scientific writing. *Language Sciences* 13(1): 59–78.

Banks, D. (2005) Emerging scientific discourse in the late seventeenth century: A comparison of Newton's *Opticks* and Huygens' *Traité de la lumière*. *Functions of Language* 12(1): 65–86.

Baker, M. (1992) *In other words: A coursebook in translation*. London and New York: Routledge.

Baldry, A. and Thibault, P. J. (2006) *Multimodal transcription and text analysis: A multimedia toolkit and coursebook*. London and Oakville: Equinox.

Ball, P. (2004) *Critical mass: How one thing leads to another*. New York: Farrar, Strauss and Giroux.

Bardi, M. A. (2008) *A systemic functional description of the grammar of Arabic*. Ph.D. thesis, Macquarie University.

Barnard, C. (2003) Pearl Harbor in Japanese high school history textbooks. In Martin, J. R. and Wodak, R. (eds), *Re/reading the past: Critical and functional perspectives on time and value*. Amsterdam and Philadelphia: Benjamins, pp. 247–71.

Barnwell, K. G. L. (1969) *A grammatical description of Mbembe (Adun Dialect): A cross river language*. Ph.D. thesis, University of London.

Bateman, J. A. (1988) Aspects of clause politeness in Japanese: An inquiry semantic treatment. *The 26th Annual Meeting of the Association for Computational Linguistics*, pp. 147–54.

Bateman, J. A. (1989) Dynamic systemic-functional grammar: A new frontier. *Word* 40(1–2): 263–287.

Bateman, J. A. (1996) *KPML: The KOMET-Penman (multilingual) development environment: Support for multilingual linguistic resource development and sentence generation.*

GMD/Institut für Integrierte Publikations- und Informationssysteme (IPSI), Darmstadt. (Release 1.0). {Studie der GMD}, {302}, pp. 276.

Bateman, J. A. (1997) Enabling technology for multilingual natural language generation: The KPML development environment. *Journal of Natural Language Engineering*, 3(1):15–55.

Bateman, J. A. (2008a) Systemic functional linguistics and the notion of linguistic structure: Unanswered questions, new possibilities. In Webster, J. J. (ed.), *Meaning in context: Implementing intelligent applications of language studies*. London and New York: Continuum, pp. 24–58.

Bateman, J. A. (2008b) *Multimodality and genre: A foundation for the systematic analysis of multimodal documents*. London and New York: Palgrave Macmillan.

Bateman, J. A. and Matthiessen, C. M. I. M. (1993). The text base in generation. Hao, K., Bluhme, H. and Li, R. (ed.), Proceedings of the international conference on texts and language research, Xi'an, 29–31 March 1989. Xi'an: Xi'an Jiaotong University Press. 3–45.

Bateman, J. A. and Momma, S. (1991) The nondirectional representation of systemic functional grammars and semantics as typed feature structures. Technical report, GMD/ Institut für Integrierte Publikations und Informationssysteme, Darmstadt and Institut für Maschinelle Sprachverarbeitung, Universität Stuttgart, Germany, January 1991.

Bateman, J. A., Kasper, R., Moore, J. and Whitney, R. (1990) *A general organization of knowledge for natural language processing: The Penman upper model*. Information Sciences Institute, University of Southern California.

Bateman, J., Matthiessen, C., Nanri, K. and Zeng, L. (1991) The rapid prototyping of natural language generation components: An application of functional typology. *Proceedings of the 12th international conference on artificial intelligence, Sydney, 24–30 August 1991. Sydney*. San Mateo, CA: Morgan Kaufman, pp. 966–971.

Bateman, J. A., Emele, M., and Momma, S. (1992) The nondirectional representation of systemic functional grammars and semantics as typed feature structures. *Proceedings of COLING 92*. Nantes: COLING, pp. 916–920.

Bateman, J. A., Matthiessen, C. M. I. M. and Zeng, L. (1999) Multilingual language generation for multilingual software: A functional linguistic approach. *Applied Artificial Intelligence: An International Journal* 13(6), pp. 607–639.

Bateman, J. A., Hois, J., Ross, R. and Tenbrink, T. (2010) A linguistic ontology of space for natural language processing. *Artificial Intelligence* 174: 1027–1071.

Baudouin De Courtenay, J. (1972) *A Baudouin De Courtenay anthology: The beginnings of structural linguistics*. Bloomington, Indiana: Indiana University Press.

Baumgartner, P. and Payr, S. (eds) (1995) *Speaking minds: Interviews with twenty eminent cognitive scientists*. Princeton, NJ: Princeton University Press.

Beckman, M. E., Hirschberg, J. and Shattuck-Hufnagel, S. (2005) The original ToBI system and the evolution of the ToBI framework. In Jun, S. A. (ed.), *Prosodic typology – The phonology of intonation and phrasing*. Oxford: Oxford University Press. Chapter 2, pp. 9–54.

Beckner, C., Blythe, R., Christiansen, M. H., Croft, W., Ellis, N. C., Holland, J., Ke, J., Larsen-Freeman D. and Shoenemann, T. (2009) Language is a complex adaptive system: Position paper. *Language Learning* 59: Supplement 1, *Language as a complex adaptive system*, edited by Ellis, N. C. and Larsen-Freeman, D., pp. 1–26.

Bell, P. and van Leeuwen, T. (1994) *The media interview: Confession, contest, conversation.* Sydney: University of New South Wales Press.

Benveniste, È. (1966) *Problèmes de linguistique générale*. Paris: Gallimard.

Benson, J. D. and Greaves, W. S. (1984) Ideational, interpersonal and textual meaning in Melville's 'Moby Dick'. *Forum Linguisticum* 8(2): 157–67.

Benson, J. D. and Greaves, W. S. (ed.) (1985a) *Systemic perspectives on discourse: Selected theoretical papers from the ninth international systemic workshop*. Norwood, N. J.: Ablex.

Benson, J. D. and Greaves W. S. (ed.) (1985b) *Systemic perspectives on discourse: Selected applied papers from the ninth international systemic workshop*. Norwood, N. J.: Ablex.

Benson, J. D. and Greaves, W. S. (1987) A comparison of process types in Poe and Melville. In Steele, R. and Threadgold, T. (eds) *Language topics: Essays in honour of Michael Halliday*. Amsterdam: Benjamins, pp. 131–45.

Benson, J. and Greaves, W. (eds) (2009) *Functional dimensions of ape-human discourse.* London: Equinox.

Benson, J. and Thibault, P. (2009) Language and other primate species. In Halliday, M. A. K. and J. Webster (eds), pp. 104–112.

Benson, J., Cummings, M. J. and Greaves, W. (eds) (1988) *Linguistics in a systemic perspective*. Amsterdam: Benjamins.

Benveniste, É. (1966) *Problèmes de linguistique générale*. Paris: Gallimard.

Bernstein, B. (1973) *Class, codes and control*, Volume 1. London: Routledge and Kegan Paul.

Bernstein, B. (2000) *Pedagogy, symbolic control and identity theory, research, critique.* Lanham, Boulder, New York and London: Rowman & Littlefield.

Berry, M. (1981) Systemic linguistics and discourse analysis: A multilayered approach to exchange structure. In M. Coulthard and M. Montgomery (eds), pp. 120–145.

Berry, M. (1995) Thematic options and success in writing. In M. Ghadessy (ed.) (1995b), pp. 55–94.

Berry, M. (1996) What is theme? A(nother) personal view. In M. Berry, C. Butler, R. P. Fawcett and G. Huang (eds), pp. 1–65.

Berry, M., Butler, C., Fawcett, R. P. and Huang, G. (eds) (1996) *Meaning and form: Systemic functional interpretations*. Norwood, NJ: Ablex.

Biber, D., Johansson, S., Leech, G., Conrad, S. and Finnegan, E. (1999) *The Longman grammar of spoken and written English*. London: Longman.

Birch, D. and O'Toole, M. (eds) (1988) *Functions of style*. London: Frances Pinter.

Bloomfield, L. (1933) *Language*. New York: Holt. Reprinted by Beijing: Foreign Language Teaching and Research Press (2002).

Bloor, M. and Bloor, T. (1992) Given and new information in the thematic organization of text: An application to the teaching of academic writing. *Occasional papers in Systemic Linguistics*, 6: 33–43.

Bloor, T. and Bloor, M. (1995) *The Functional analysis of English: A Hallidayan approach.* London: Edward Arnold.
Boas, H. and Sag, I. (eds) (2010) *Sign-based construction grammar*. Stanford, CA: CSLI Publications.
Bod, R., Hay, J. and Jannedy, S. (2003a) Introduction. In R. Bod, J. Hay and S. Jannedy (eds), pp. 1–10.
Bod, R., Hay, J. and Jannedy, S. (eds) (2003b) *Probabilistic linguistics*. Cambridge, MA: MIT Press.
Bohm, D. (1980) *Wholeness and the implicate order*. London: Routledge & Kegan Paul.
Bowcher, W. (2001) *Play-by-play talk on radio: An enquiry into some relations between language and context*. Ph.D. thesis, University of Liverpool.
Bowcher, W. (2007) Field and multimodal texts. In R. Hasan, C. M. I. M. Matthiessen and J. Webster (eds), pp. 619–646.
Bowcher, W. and Smith, B. (eds) (2014) *Voices around the world: Recent studies in systemic phonology*. London: Equinox.
Boxwell, M. (1995) 'Nothing' makes sense in Weri: A case of extensive ellipsis in nominals in a Papuan language. In R. Hasan and P. H. Fries (eds), pp. 123–151.
Brachman, R. (1978) *A structural paradigm for representing knowledge*. BBN Report No. 3605, Bolt Beranek and Newman, Inc. Cambridge, MA.
Brachman, R. (1979) On the epistemological status of semantic networks. In N. Findler (ed.), *Associative networks: Representation and use of knowledge by computers*. New York: Academic Press, pp. 3–50.
Brachman, R. J. and Levesque, H. J. (eds) (1985) *Readings in knowledge representation*. Los Altos, CA: Morgan Kaufman.
Bresnan, J. (1982) The passive in lexical theory. In J. Bresnan (ed.), *The mental representation of grammatical relations*. Cambridge, MA: The MIT Press, pp. 3–86.
Bresnan, J. (2000) Linguistic theory at the turn of the twentieth century. In AILA '99 Organizing Committee (eds), *Selected Papers from AILA'99 Tokyo*. Plenary Addresses, Keynote Addresses, Special Lectures, Special Symposia, Twelfth World Congress of Applied Linguistics, Waseda University Press, Tokyo, pp. 98–115.
Bresnan, J. (2001) *Lexical-functional syntax*. Oxford: Blackwell.
Bull, W. (1960) *Time, tense and the verb: A study in theoretical and applied linguistics, with particular applications to Spanish*. LA and Berkeley: University of California Press.
Burke, P. (2000) *A social history of knowledge: From Gutenberg to Diderot*. Cambridge: Polity Press.
Burns, A., Kim, M. and Matthiessen, C. M. I. M. (2009) Doctoral work in translation studies as an interdisciplinary mutual learning process: How a translator, teacher educator, and linguistic typologist worked together. *The Interpreter and Translator Trainer*, 3 (1), pp. 107–128.
Butler, C. (1988) Politeness and the semantics of modalized directives in English. In J. Benson, M. J. Cummings and W. Greaves (eds), pp. 119–154.
Butt, D. G. (1983) Semantic 'drift' in verbal art. *Australian Review of Applied Linguistics*, 6 (1), pp. 38–48.

Butt, D. G. (1984) *The relationship between theme and lexicogrammar in the poetry of Wallace Stevens*. Ph.D. thesis, Macquarie University.

Butt, D. G. (1988) Randomness, order and the latent patterning of text. In D. Birch and M. O'Toole (eds), *Functions of style*. London: Frances Pinter, pp. 74–97.

Butt, D. G. (1991) Some basic tools in a linguistic approach to personality: A Firthian concept of social process. In F. Christie (ed.), *Literacy in social processes: Papers from the Inaugural Australian Systemic Functional Linguistics Conference*, Deaking University, January 1990. Darwin: Centre for Studies in Language in Education, Northern Territory University, pp. 23–44.

Butt, D. G. (2000) The meaning of a network. In C. Matthiessen and D. G. Butt, *The meaning potential of language. Mapping meaning systematically*. Mimeo. Department of Linguistics, Macquarie University.

Butt, D. G. (2001) Firth, Halliday and the development of systemic theory. In S. Auroux, E. Koerner and K. Versteegh (eds), *History of the language sciences*, Volume 2. Berlin and New York: de Gruyter, pp. 1806–1838.

Butt, D. G. (2003) *On establishing the similarities and differences between contexts*. Mimeo: Department of Linguistics, Macquarie University.

Butt, D. G. (2005) Method and imagination in Halliday's science of linguistics. In R. Hasan, C. M. I. M. Matthiessen, and J. Webster (eds), pp. 81–116.

Butt, D. G. (2008) The robustness of realizational systems. In J. Webster (ed.), pp. 59–83.

Butt, D. G. and Wegener, R. (2007) The work of concepts: Context and metafunction in the systemic functional model. In R. Hasan, C. M. I. M. Matthiessen, and J. Webster (eds), pp. 589–618.

Butt, D. G., Fahey, R. Spinks, S. and Yallop, C. (1995) *Using functional grammar, An explorer's guide*. Sydney: Macquarie University, NCELTR (National Centre for English Language Teaching and Research).

Butt, D. G., Fahey, R. Feez, S., Spinks, S. and Yallop, C. (2000) *Using functional grammar: An explorer's guide*. 2nd edition. Sydney: Macquarie University, NCELTR (National Centre for English Language Teaching and Research).

Butt, D. G., Fahey, R. and Henderson-Brooks, C. (2003) Outer and inner weathers. In R. Meares and P. Noolan (eds), *The self in conversation*, vol. 2. Sydney: Australia and New Zealand Association of Psychotherapy, pp. 164–181.

Butt, D. G., Lukin, A. and Matthiessen, C. M. I. M. (2004) Grammar: The first covert operation of war. *Discourse and Society*, Vol. 15, No. 2–3, 267–290.

Byrnes, H. (ed.) (2006) *Advanced instructed language learning: The complementary contribution to Halliday and Vygotsky*. London and New York: Continuum.

Byrnes, H. (ed.) (2009) Instructed foreign language acquisition as meaning-making: A systemic functional approach. *Linguistics and Education*, 20 (1), pp. 1–9.

Caffarel, A. (1992) Interacting between a generalized tense semantics and register-specific semantic tense systems: A bi-stratal exploration of the semantics of French tense. *Language Sciences*, 14 (4), pp. 385–418.

Caffarel, A. (1996) *Prolegomena to a systemic-functional interpretation of French grammar*. Ph.D. thesis, University of Sydney.

Caffarel, A. (1997) Models of transitivity in French: A systemic functional interpretation. In A. Simon-Vandenbergen, K. Davidse and D. Noël (eds), pp. 249–296.

Caffarel, A. (2004a) The construal of a second-order semiosis in Camus' *L'Etranger*. In D. Banks (ed.) (2005), pp. 537–570.

Caffarel, A. (2004b) Metafunctional profile of the grammar of French. In Caffarel, A., Martin, J. R. and Matthiessen, C. M. I. M. (eds), *Language typology: A functional perspective*. Amsterdam: Benjamins, pp. 77–137.

Caffarel, A. (2006) *A systemic functional grammar of French: From grammar to discourse*. London and New York: Continuum.

Caffarel, A., Martin, J. R. and Matthiessen, C. M. I. M. (eds) (2004) *Language typology: A functional perspective*. Amsterdam: Benjamins.

Cahill, M. (2018) Labial-velars of Africa: Phonetics, phonology, and historical development. In A. Augustine and B. Adams (eds), *The Routledge Handbook of African Linguistics*. New York: Routledge. Chapter 7.

Cairns, C. E. and Raimy, E. (eds) (2011a) *The handbook of the syllable*. Leiden and Boston: Brill.

Cairns, C. E. and Raimy, E. (2011b) Introduction. In C. E. Cairns and E. Raimy (eds), pp. 1–30.

Caldas-Coulthard, C. and Coulthard, M. (eds) (1996) *Texts and practices: Readings in critical discourse analysis*. London: Routledge.

Caldwell, D. (2014) A comparative analysis of the rap and the sung voice: Perspectives from systemic phonology, social semiotics and music studies. In W. Bowcher and B. Smith (eds), pp. 235–263.

Candlin, C. (ed.) (2002) *Research and practice in professional discourse*. Hong Kong: City University of Hong Kong Press.

Capra, F. (1996) *The web of life: A new synthesis of mind and matter*. London: Harper Collins.

Carter, R. (1987) *Vocabulary: Applied linguistic perspectives*. London: Unwin Hyman.

Catford, J. C. (1965) *A linguistic theory of translation*. London: Oxford University Press.

Catford, J. C. (1969) J. R. Firth and British linguistics. In A. Hill (ed.), *Linguistics today*. New York and London: Basic Books, Inc., pp. 218–228.

Catford, J. C. (1977) *Fundamental problems in phonetics*. Indiana: Indiana University Press.

Catford, J. C. (1985) 'Rest' and 'open transition' in a systemic phonology of English. In J. Benson and W. Greaves (eds) (1985b), pp. 333–348.

Chen, Z. and Kuang, L. (2002) Theme in English and Chinese: A contrastive study. In G. Huang and Z. Wang (eds), pp. 81–90.

Chomsky, N. (1957) *Syntactic structures*. The Hague: Mouton.

Chomsky, N. (1965) *Aspects of the theory of syntax*. Cambridge, MA: MIT Press.

Chomsky, N. (1970) Remarks on nominalization. In R. Jacobs and P. Rosenbaum (eds), *Readings in English transformational grammar*. Waltham, MA: Ginn-Blaisdell, pp. 184–221.

Chomsky, N. and Halle, M. (1968) *The sound patterns of English*. New York: Harper & Row.

Chow, I. and Webster, J. (2008) Supervised clustering of the WordNet verb hierarchy for systemic functional process type identification. In *Proceedings of the 1st International Conference on Global Interoperability for Language Resources (ICGL)*, Hong Kong, PRC, 9–11 January 2008, pp. 51–58.

Christie, F. (1990a) *Curriculum genres in early childhood education: A case study in writing development*. Ph.D. thesis, University of Sydney.

Christie, F. (ed.) (1990b) *Literacy in social processes: Papers from the inaugural Australian Systemic Linguistics Conference*, held at Deakin University, January 1990. Darwin: Centre for Studies in Language in Education, Northern Territory University.

Christie, F. (1997) Curriculum macro genres as forms of initiation into a culture. In F. Christie and J. R. Martin (eds), pp. 134–160.

Christie, F. (2002) Classroom discourse analysis. London: Continuum.

Christie, F. (2012) *Language education throughout the school years: A functional perspective*. Oxford: Wiley-Blackwell.

Christie, F. and Derewianka, B. (2008) *School discourse: Learning to write across the years of schooling*. London and New York: Continuum.

Christie, F. and Macken-Horarik, M. (2007) Building verticality in subject English. In F. Christie and J. R. Martin (eds), pp. 156–183.

Christie, F. and Martin, J. R. (eds) (1997) *Genre and institutions: Social processes in the workplace and school*. London: Cassell.

Christie, F. and Martin, J. R. (eds) (2007) *Language, knowledge and pedagogy: Functional linguistic and sociological perspectives*. London and New York: Continuum.

Christie, F. and Unsworth, L. (2005) Developing dimensions of an educational linguistics. In R. Hasan, C. M. I. M. Matthiessen, and J. Webster (eds), pp. 217–250.

Christopher C. (ed.) (2002) *Theory and practice of professional discourse*. Hong Kong: CUHK Press.

Cléirigh, C. (1998) *A selectionist model of the genesis of phonic texture: Systemic phonology and universal Darwinism*. Ph.D. thesis, University of Sydney.

Cloran, C. (1994) Rhetorical units and decontextualisation: An enquiry into some relations of context, meaning and grammar. *University of Nottingham: Monographs in Systemic Linguistics*, Number 6.

Cloran, C., Butt, D. G. and Williams, G. (eds) (1996) *Ways of saying, ways of meaning: Selected papers of Ruqaiya Hasan*. London: Cassell.

Cloran, C., Stuart-Smith, V. and Young, L. (2007) Models of discourse. In R. Hasan, C. M. I. M. Matthiessen, and J. Webster (eds), pp. 647–670.

Coffin, C. (1997) Constructing and giving value to the past: An investigation into secondary school history. In F. Christie and J. R. Martin (eds), pp. 196–230.

Coffin, C. (2003) Reconstrual of the past: Settlement or invasion? In J. R. Martin and R. Wodak (eds), pp. 219–246.

Coffin, C. (2006) *Historical discourse*. London and New York: Continuum.

Collins, P. (1991a) *Cleft and pseudo-cleft constructions in English*. London and New York: Routledge.

Collins, P. (1991b) Pseudo cleft and cleft constructions: A thematic and informational interpretation. *Linguistics* 29, pp. 481–519.

Collins, P. (1992) Cleft existentials in English. *Language Sciences*, 14 (4), pp. 419–435.

Copestake, A. and Flickinger, D. (2000) An open-source grammar development environment and broad-coverage English grammar using HPSG. In *Proceedings of the Second Conference on Language Resources and Evaluation (LRECn2000)*, Athens, Greece.

Coulthard, M. (ed.) (1994) *Advances in written text analysis*. London: Routledge & Kegan Paul.

Coulthard, M. (2004) Author identification, idiolect and linguistic uniqueness. *Applied Linguistics* 25 (4), pp. 431–447.

Coulthard, M. and Montgomery, M. (eds) (2001) *Studies in discourse analysis*. London: Routledge & Kegan Paul.

Couper-Kuhlen, E. (1986) *An introduction to English prosody*. London: Edward Arnold.

Couper-Kuhlen, E. (2015) Intonation and Discourse. In D. Tannen, D. E. Hamilton and D. Schiffrin (eds), *The handbook of discourse analysis*. New York: John Wiley and Sons, pp. 82–104.

Cranny-Francis, A. and Martin, J. R. (1991) Contratextuality: The poetics of subversion. In F. Christie (ed.), *Literacy in social processes: Papers from the Inaugural Australian Systemic Functional Linguistics Conference*, Deaking University, January 1990. Darwin: Centre for Studies in Language in Education, Northern Territory University, pp. 286–344.

Cranny-Francis, A. and Martin, J. R. (1994) In/visible education: Class, gender and pedagogy in 'Educating Rita' and 'Dead Poets Society'. *Interpretations: Journal of the English Teachers Association of W.A.*, 27 (1), pp. 28–57.

Cross, M. (1992) Choice in lexis: Computer generation of lexis as most delicate grammar. *Language Sciences*, 14 (4), pp. 579–607.

Crystal, D. (1969) *Prosodic systems and intonation in English*. Cambridge: Cambridge University Press.

Cummings, M. J. (1980) Systemic analysis of Old English nominal groups. In W. McCormack and H. Izzo (eds), *The Sixth LACUS Forum (1979)* Columbia, SC: Hornbeam Press, pp. 228–242.

Cummings, M. J. (1983) A systemic functional model for Old English. In W. Gutwinski and G. Jolly (eds), *The Eighth LACUS Forum (1981)* Columbia, SC: Hornbeam Press, pp. 196–207.

Cummings, M. J. (1984) Sequence and function in the Old English nominal group. *The Eleventh LACUS Forum*. Columbia, SC: Hornbeam Press, pp. 422–431.

Cummings, M. J. (1995) A systemic functional approach to the thematic structure of the Old English clause. In R. Hasan and P. H. Fries (eds), pp. 275–317.

Davey, A. (1978) *Discourse production: A computer model of some aspects of a speaker*. Edinburgh: Edinburgh University Press.

Davidse, K. (1986) M. A. K. Halliday's functional grammar and the Prague School. In R. Dirven and V. Fried (eds), *Functionalism in linguistics*. Amsterdam: Benjamins, pp. 39–79.

Davidse, K. (1991) *Categories of experiential grammar*. Ph.D. thesis, Catholic University of Leuven.

Davidse, K. (1992a) A semiotic approach to relational clauses. *Occasional Papers in Systemic Linguistics*, 6: 99–131.

Davidse, K. (1992b) Existential constructions: A systemic perspective. *Leuvense Bijdragen (Leuven Contributions in Linguistics and Philology)*, 81 (1): 71–99.

Davidse, K. (1992c) Transitive/ergative: The Janus-headed grammar of actions and events. In M. Davies and L. Ravelli (eds), pp. 105–135.

Davidse, K. (1996a) Ditransitivity and possession. In R. Hasan, C. Cloran and D. G. Butt (eds), pp. 85–144.

Davidse, K. (1996b) Turning grammar on itself: Identifying clauses in linguistic discourse. In M. Berry, C. Butler, R. P. Fawcett and G. Huang (eds), pp. 367–393.

Davidse, K. (2000) Semiotic and possessive models in relational clauses: Thinking with grammar about grammar. *Revista Canaria de Estudios Ingleses*, 40: 13–35.

Davies, M. (1986) Literacy and intonation. In B. Couture (ed.), *Functional approaches to writing: Research perspectives*. Norwood, NJ: Ablex, pp. 199–230.

Davies, M. (1996) Theme and information until Shakespeare. In M. Berry, C. Butler, R. P. Fawcett and G. Huang (eds), pp. 113–150.

Davies, M. and Ravelli, L. (eds) (1992) *Advances in systemic linguistics: Recent theory and practice*. London: Frances Pinter.

de Beaugrande, R. (1991) *Linguistic theory: The discourse of fundamental works*. London: Longman.

Deacon, T. (1992) Brain-language coevolution. In J. Hawkins and M. Gell-Mann (eds), *The evolution of human languages*. Redwood City, CA: Addison-Wesley, pp. 49–85.

Deacon, T. (1997) *The symbolic species: The co-evolution of language and the human brain*. Harmondsworth: Penguin Books.

Deacon, T. (2010) Language and complexity: Evolution inside out. Plenary talk at ISFC 37, the University of British Columbia, 20 July 2010. Video recording available at: http://il.youtube.com/watch?v=OT-zZOPMqgI.

Degand, L. (1996) Causation in Dutch and French: Interpersonal aspects. In R. Hasan, C. Cloran and D. G. Butt (eds), pp. 207–237.

Derewianka, B. (1995) *Language development in the transition from childhood to adolescence: The role of grammatical metaphor*. Ph.D. thesis, Macquarie University.

Derewianka, B. (1998) *A grammar companion for primary teachers*. Newtown, NSW: Primary English Teaching Association.

Derewianka, B. (2003) Grammatical metaphor in the transition to adolescence. In A. Simon-Vandenbergen, M. Taverniers and L. Ravelli (eds), pp. 185–219.

Dineen, F. (1967) *An introduction to general linguistics*. New York: Holt, Rinehart & Winston.

Dirr, A. (1928) *Einführung in das Studium der kaukasischen Sprachen*. Leipzig.

Dixon, R. (1991) *A new approach to English grammar, on semantic principles*. Oxford: Clarendon Press.

Dixon, R. (1997) *The rise and fall of languages*. Cambridge: Cambridge University Press.

Djonov, E. (2007) Website hierarchy and the interaction between content organization, webpage and navigation design: A systemic functional hypermedia discourse analysis perspective. *Information Design Journal*, 15 (2), pp. 144–162.

Donegan, P. J. and Stampe, D. (1979) The study of natural phonology. In D. A. Dinnsen (ed.), *Current approaches to phonological theory*. Bloomington: Indiana University Press, pp. 126–173.

Douglas, M. (1966) *Purity and danger: An analysis of concepts of pollution and taboo*. London: Routledge & Kegan Paul.

Douglas, M. (1979) Taboo. In R. Cavendish (ed.), *Man, myth and magic*, Volume 20. London: Phoebus Publishing, pp. 2761–2771.

Downing, A. (1990) The discourse function of presentative there in existential structures in Middle English and present-day English: A systemic functional perspective. *Occasional Papers in Systemic Linguistics*, 4, pp. 103–126.

Downing, A. (1991) An alternative approach to theme: A systemic functional perspective. *Word*, 42 (2), pp. 119–144.

Downing, A. (1995) Thematic layering and focus assignment in Chaucer's 'General Prologue' to 'The Canterbury Tales'. In M. Ghadessy (ed.), pp. 147–164.

Downing, A. (1996a) Discourse-pragmatic distinctions of the past in present in English and Spanish. In M. Berry, C. Butler, R. P. Fawcett and G. Huang (eds), pp. 509–533.

Downing, A. (1996b) The semantics of get-passives. In R. Hasan, C. Cloran and D. G. Butt (eds), pp. 179–207.

Downing, A. and P. Locke. (1992) *A university course in English grammar*. New York: Prentice Hall.

Edelman, G. (1992) *Bright air, brilliant fire: On the matter of the mind*. New York: Basic Books.

Eggins, S. (1990) *Conversational structure: A systemic functional analysis of interpersonal and logical meaning in multiparty sustained talk*. Ph.D. thesis, University of Sydney.

Eggins, S. (1994) *An introduction to Systemic Functional Linguistics*. London: Frances Pinter.

Eggins, S. and Slade, D. (1997) *Analysing casual conversation*. London: Cassell.

Eggins, S. and Slade, D. (2005) *Analysing casual conversation*. London: Equinox.

Eggins, S., Wignell, P. and Martin, J. R. (1993) The discourse of history: Distancing the recoverable past. In Mohsen Ghadessy (ed.) *Register analysis: Theory and practice*. London and New York: Pinter, pp. 75–109.

Elhadad, M. (1990) Types in functional unification grammars. In *Proceedings of the 28th Annual Meeting of the Association for Computational Linguistics*, pp. 157–164.

Elhadad, M. and Robin, J. (n.d.) An overview of SURGE: A reusable comprehensive syntactic realisation component.

Ellegård, A. (1953) *The Auxiliary 'do': The establishment and regulation of its use in English*. Stockholm: Almqvist and Wiksell.

Ellegård, A. (1971) *Transformationell svensk-engelsk Satslära* ['Transformational Swedish English syntax]. Lund: Gleerup.

Ellis, J. (1966) *Towards a general comparative linguistics*. The Hague: Mouton.

Ellis, J. (1987) Some 'dia-categories'. In R. Steele and T. Threadgold (eds), pp. 81–94.

Elmenoufy, A. (1969) *A study of the role of intonation in the grammar of English*. Ph.D. thesis, University of London.

Else, H. (2017) The two meanings of sound symbolism. *Open Linguistics* 3, pp. 491–499.

Fang, Y. and Wu, C. (eds) (2010) *Challenges to systemic functional linguistics: Theory and practice*. Proceedings of the Conference ISFC 36, Beijing, July 2009 Tsinghua University and Macquarie University: The 36th ISFC Organizing Committee.

Fang, Y., McDonald, E. and Cheng, M. (1995) On theme in Chinese: From clause to discourse. In R. Hasan and P. H. Fries (eds), pp. 235–275.

Fang, Y., Zhang, D., McDonald, E. and Huang, G. (2005) The development of systemic functional linguistics in China. In R. Hasan, C. M. I. M. Matthiessen and J. Webster (eds), pp. 15–36.

Fawcett, R. P. (1973) Generating a sentence in systemic functional grammar. In M. A. K. Halliday and J. R. Martin (eds) (1981), pp. 146–183.

Fawcett, R. P. (1974) Some proposals for systemic syntax, Part 1. *MALS Journal*, 1 (2), pp. 1–15.

Fawcett, R. P. (1975) Some proposals for systemic syntax, Part 2. *MALS Journal*, 2 (1), pp. 43–68.

Fawcett, R. P. (1976) Some proposals for systemic syntax, Part 3. *MALS Journal*, 2 (2), pp. 35–68.

Fawcett, R. P. (1980) *Cognitive linguistics and social interaction*. Exeter and Heidelberg: University of Exeter and Julius Groos.

Fawcett, R. P. (1987) The semantics of clause and verb for relational processes in English. In M. A. K. Halliday, and R. P. Fawcett (eds), pp. 130–183.

Fawcett, R. P. (1988a) What makes a 'good' system network good? In D. Benson and W. Greaves (eds), pp. 1–28.

Fawcett, R. P. (1988b) Towards a systemic flowchart model for discourse analysis. In R. P. Fawcett and D. Young (eds) (1988), pp. 116–143.

Fawcett, R. P. (2000) *A theory of syntax for systemic functional linguistics*. Amsterdam: Benjamins.

Fawcett, R. P. (2007) Auxiliary Extensions: Six new elements for describing English. In R. Hasan, C. M. I. M. Matthiessen, and J. Webster (eds), pp. 921–952.

Fawcett, R. P. (2008) *Invitation to systemic functional linguistics through the Cardiff Grammar: An extension and simplification of Halliday's systemic functional grammar*, 3rd edition. London: Equinox.

Fawcett, R. P. and Huang, G. (1997) *Enhanced Theme in English: Towards a functional explanation of the 'it-cleft' construction*. London: Cassell.

Fawcett, R. P. and Tucker, G. H. (1990) Demonstration of GENESYS: A very large semantically based systemic functional grammar. In *The 13th International Conference on Computational Linguistics (COLING)*, Helsinki, pp. 47–49.

Fawcett, R. P. and Weerasinghe, A. (1993) Probabilistic incremental parsing in systemic functional grammar. In H. Bunt and M. Tomita (eds), *Proceedings of the Third Workshop on Parsing Technologies*. Tilburg: Institute for Language Technology and Artificial Intelligence, pp. 349–367.

Fawcett, R. P. and Young, D. (eds) (1988) *New developments in Systemic Linguistics: Theory and application*. London: Frances Pinter.

Feez, S. (1995) *The Write it Right research project*. MS.

Fillmore, C., Kay, P. and O'Connor, M. (1988) Regularity and idiomaticity in grammatical constructions: The case of let alone. *Language*, 64, pp. 501–538.

Fine, J. (1994) *How language works: Cohesion in normal and nonstandard communication*. Norwood, NJ: Ablex.

Fine, J. (1995) Towards understanding and studying cohesion in schizophrenic speech. *Applied Psycholinguistics*, 16, pp. 25–41.

Fine, J. (2006) *Language in psychiatry: A handbook of clinical practice*. London: Equinox.

Firth, J. R. (1948a) Sounds and prosodies. *Transactions of the Philological Society*, pp. 127–152.

Firth, J. R. (1948b) The semantics of linguistic science. *Lingua*, I, pp. 393–404.

Firth, J. R. (1950) Personality and language in society. *Sociological Review*, 42 (2), pp. 37–52.

Firth, J. R. (1957a) A synopsis of linguistic theory. In J. R. Firth, *et al.* (eds), *Studies in linguistic analysis*. Oxford: Blackwell (Special Volume of the Philological Society). Reprinted in F. R. Palmer (ed.), *Selected papers of J. R. Firth 1952–1959*. London: Longman.

Firth, J. R. (1957b) *Papers in linguistics 1934–1951*. London: Oxford University Press.

Fischer-Jørgensen, E. (1975) *Trends in phonological theory: A historical introduction*. Copenhagen: Akademisk Forlag.

Foley, R. (1997) *Humans before humanity: An evolutionary perspective*. Oxford: Blackwell.

Fontaine, L., Bartlett, T. and O'Grady, G. (eds) (2013) *Choice in language: Applications in text analysis*. London: Equinox.

Forey, G. and Lockwood, J. (2007) 'I'd love to put someone in jail for this': An initial investigation of English in the business processing outsourcing (BPO) industry. *English for Specific Purposes*, 26, pp. 308–326.

Forey, G. and Lockwood, J. (eds) (2010) *Globalization, communication and the workplace: Talking across the world*. London: Continuum.

Fowler, R., Hodge, B., Kress, G. and Trew, T. (1979) *Language and control*. London: Routledge & Kegan Paul.

Frake, C. (1961) The diagnosis of disease among the Subanum of Mindanao. *American Anthropologist*, 63, pp. 13–132.

Francis, G. (1989) Thematic selection and distribution in written discourse. *Word*, 40 (1–2), pp. 201–223.

Francis, G. (1990) Theme in the daily press. *Occasional Papers in Systemic Linguistics*, 4, pp. 51–87.

Francis, G. and Kramer-Dahl, A. (1992) Grammaticalizing the medical case history. In M. Toolan (ed.), *Language, text and context: Essays in stylistics*. London: Routledge, pp. 56–90.

Fries, P. H. (1981) On the status of theme in English: Arguments from discourse. *Forum Linguisticum*, 6 (1), pp. 1–38.
Fries, P. H. (1982) On repetition and interpretation. *Forum Linguisticum*, 7 (1), pp. 50–64.
Fries, P. H. (1985) How does a story mean what it does? A partial answer. In J. Benson and W. Greaves (eds), pp. 295–321.
Fries, P. H. (1986a) Language features, textual coherence and reading. *Word*, 37 (1–2), pp. 13–29.
Fries, P. H. (1986b) Toward a discussion of the ordering of adjectives in the English noun phrase. In B. Elson (ed.) *Language and global perspective: Papers in honor of the Summer Institute of Linguistics*, 1935–1985. Dallas, TX: Summer Institute of Linguistics, pp. 123–134.
Fries, P. H. (1993) Information flow in written advertising. In J. Alatis (ed.), pp. 336–352.
Fries, P. H. (1994) On theme, rheme and discourse goals. In M. Coulthard (ed.) *Advances in written text analysis*. London: Routledge and Kegan Paul, pp. 229–249.
Fries, P. H. (1995) Patterns of information in initial position in English. In P. H. Fries and M. Gregory (eds), pp. 47–67.
Fries, P. H. (2002) Theme and New in written advertising. In G. Huang and Z. Wang (eds), pp. 56–72.
Fries, P. H. and Gregory, M. (eds) (1995) *Discourse in society: Systemic functional perspectives*. Norwood, NJ: Ablex.
Fudge, E. C. (1969) Syllables. *Journal of Linguistics* 5, pp. 253–286.
Fuller, G. (1995) *Engaging cultures: Negotiating discourse in popular science*. Ph.D. thesis, Sydney University.
Fuller, G. (1998) Cultivating science: Negotiating discourse in the popular texts of Stephen Jay Gould. In J. R. Martin and R. Veel (eds), pp. 35–62.
Gell-Mann, M. (1994) *The quark and the jaguar: Adventures in the simple and the complex*. London: Abacus.
Gell-Mann, M. (1995) What is complexity? *Complexity*, Vol. 1, no. 1.
Geluykens, R. (1989) Information structure in English conversation – the given-new distinction revisited. *Occasional Papers in Systemic Linguistics* 3, pp. 129–147.
Gerot, L. and Wignell, P. (1994) *Making sense of functional grammar: An introductory workbook*. Cammeray, NSW: Anti-podean Educational Enterprises.
Ghadessy, M. (ed.) (1988) *Registers of written English: Situational factors and linguistic features*. London and New York: Frances Pinter.
Ghadessy, M. (1993a) On the nature of written business communication. In M. Ghadessy (ed.), pp. 149–164.
Ghadessy, M. (ed.) (1993b) *Register analysis: Theory and practice*. London and New York: Frances Pinter.
Ghadessy, M. (1995a) Thematic developments and its relationship to registers and genres. In M. Ghadessy (ed.), pp. 129–146.
Ghadessy, M. (ed.) (1995b) *Thematic developments in English texts*. London and New York: Frances Pinter.

Ghadessy, M. (1999) Textual features and contextual factors for register identification. In M. Ghadessy (ed.), *Text and context in functional linguistics*. Amsterdam: Benjamins, pp. 125–140.

Ghadessy, M. and Gao, Y. (2000) Thematic organization in parallel texts: Same and different methods of development. *Text* 20 (4): 461–488.

Ghadessy, M. and Gao, Y. (2001) Small corpora and translation: Comparing thematic organization in two languages. In M. Ghadessy, A. Henry and R. Roseberry (eds), *Small corpus studies and ELT*. Amsterdam and Philadelphia: Benjamins, pp. 335–362.

Gibbons, J. and Markwick-Smith, V. (1992) Exploring the use of a systemic semantic description. *International Journal of Applied Linguistics*, 2 (1), pp. 36–51.

Gibbons, J. (2003) *Forensic linguistics: An introduction to language in the justice system*. Oxford: Blackwell.

Gibbons, P. (2002) *Scaffolding language, scaffolding learning: Working with ESL children in the elementary mainstream classroom*. Portsmouth, NH: Heinemann.

Gibbons, P. (2009) *English learners, academic literacy and thinking: Learning in the challenge zone*. Portsmouth, NH: Heinemann.

Goldberg, A. (1995) *Constructions: A construction grammar approach to argument structure*. Chicago, IL: University of Chicago Press.

Goldsmith, J. (1990) *Autosegmental and metrical phonology*. Oxford: Blackwell.

Gómez-González, M. A. (2001) *The theme-topic interface: Evidence from English*. Amsterdam and New York: Benjamins.

Gosden, H. (1993) Discourse functions of Subject in scientific research articles. *Applied Linguistics*, 14 (1), pp. 56–75.

Gosden, H. (1996) *A genre-based investigation of theme: Product and process in scientific research articles written by NNS novice researchers*. University of Nottingham: Monographs in *Systemic Linguistics*, Number 7.

Gotteri, N. (1996) Towards a systemic approach to tense and aspect in Polish. In M. Berry, C. Butler, R. P. Fawcett and G. Huang (eds), pp. 499–507.

Greaves, W. (2007) Intonation in systemic linguistics. In R. Hasan, C. M. I. M. Matthiessen, and J. Webster (eds), pp. 979–1025.

Gregory, M. (1967) Aspects of varieties differentiation. *Journal of Linguistics*, 3, pp. 177–198.

Gregory, M. (1982) Hamlet's voice: Aspects of text formation and cohesion in a soliloquy. *Forum Linguisticum*, 7 (2), pp. 107–122.

Gregory, M. (1985) Towards 'communication' linguistics: A framework. In J. Benson, and W. Greaves (eds), pp. 119–134.

Gregory, M. (1995) Generic expectancies and discoursal surprises: John Donne's 'The Good Morrow'. In P. H. Fries and M. Gregory (eds), pp. 67–85.

Gregory, M. and Carroll, S. (1978) *Language and situation language varieties and their social contexts*. London: Routledge & Kegan Paul.

Gross, M. (1972) *Mathematical models of language*. Englewood Cliffs, NJ: Prentice Hall.

Gross, M. (1979) On the failure of generative grammar. *Language*, 55 (4), pp. 859–885.

Gu, Y. (1999) Towards a model of situated discourse. In K. Turner (ed.), *The semantics/pragmatics interface from different points of view*. Oxford: Elsevier, pp. 150–178.

Gu, Y. (2002) Towards an understanding of workplace discourse – a pilot study for compiling a spoken Chinese corpus of situated discourse. In C. Candlin (ed.), pp. 137–185.

Haiman, J. (1985) *Natural syntax*. Cambridge: Cambridge University Press.

Hall, P. (2008) Policespeak. In J. Gibbons and T. T. Teresa (eds), *Dimensions of forensic linguistics*. Amsterdam: Benjamin's, pp. 67–94.

Halliday, M. A. K. (1956a) Grammatical categories in Modern Chinese. *Transactions of the Philological Society*, pp. 177–224.

Halliday, M. A. K. (1956b) The linguistic basis of a mechanical thesaurus and its application to English preposition classification. *Mechanical Translation*, 3 (3), pp. 81–88.

Halliday, M. A. K. (1957) Some aspects of systematic description and comparison in grammatical analysis. *Studies in linguistic analysis*, 54–67. Oxford: Basil Blackwell.

Halliday, M. A. K. (1959) *The language of the Chinese 'Secret History of the Mongols'*. Oxford: Blackwell.

Halliday, M. A. K. (1961) Categories of the theory of grammar. *Word* 17 (3), pp. 242–292. Reprinted in M. A. K. Halliday (2002) *On grammar*, vol. 1 in *The collected works of M. A. K. Halliday*, edited by J. Webster. London and New York: Continuum, Chapter 2, pp. 37–94.

Halliday, M. A. K. (1963a) Class in relation to the axes of chain and choice in language. *Linguistics*, 2, pp. 5–15.

Halliday, M. A. K. (1963b) Intonation in English grammar. *Transactions of the Philological Society*, pp. 143–169.

Halliday, M. A. K. (1963c) The tones of English. *Archivum Linguisticum*, 15 (1), pp. 1–28.

Halliday, M. A. K. (1964) Syntax and the consumer. In C. I. J. M. Stuart (ed.), *Report of the Fifteenth Annual (First International) Round Table Meeting on Linguistics and Language*. Washington, DC: Georgetown University Press. 11–24. Reprinted in M. A. K. Halliday (2003) *On Language and Linguistics*, vol. 3 in *The collected works of M. A. K. Halliday*, edited by J. Webster. London and New York: Continuum, pp. 36–49.

Halliday, M. A. K. (1965) Types of structure. Working paper for the O.S.T.I. Programme in the Linguistic Properties of Scientific English. In M. A. K. Halliday and J. R. Martin (eds) (1981), pp. 29–41.

Halliday, M. A. K. (1966a) Lexis as a linguistic level. In C. Bazell, J. C. Catford, M. A. K. Halliday, and R. Robins (eds), *In memory of J. R. Firth*. Longman, pp. 148–162.

Halliday, M. A. K. (1966b) Some notes on 'deep' grammar. *Journal of Linguistics*, 2 (1), pp. 57–67.

Halliday, M. A. K. (1966c) The concept of rank: A reply. *Journal of Linguistics*, 2 (1), pp. 110–118.

Halliday, M. A. K. (1966d) Pattern in words. *The Listener* 75.

Halliday, M. A. K. (1967a) *Grammar, society and the noun*. London: H. K. Lewis for University College London.

Halliday, M. A. K. (1967b) *Intonation and grammar in British English*. The Hague: Mouton.

Halliday, M. A. K. (1967c) Notes on transitivity and theme in English, Part 1. *Journal of Linguistics*, 3 (1), pp 37–81.

Halliday, M. A. K. (1967d) Notes on transitivity and theme in English, Part 2. *Journal of Linguistics*, 3 (2), pp 199–244.

Halliday, M. A. K. (1968) Notes on transitivity and theme in English, Part 3. *Journal of Linguistics*, 4 (2), pp 179–215.

Halliday, M. A. K. (1969) Options and functions in the English clause. *Brno Studies in English*, 8, pp. 81–88.

Halliday, M. A. K. (1970a) *A course in spoken English: Intonation*. London: Oxford University Press.

Halliday, M. A. K. (1970b) Functional diversity in language, as seen from a consideration of modality and mood in English. *Foundations of Language* 6: 322–361. Reprinted in M. A. K. Halliday (2005) *Studies in English language*, vol. 7 in *The collected works of M. A. K. Halliday*, edited by J. Webster. London and New York: Continuum, pp. 164–204.

Halliday, M. A. K. (1970c) Language structure and language function. In J. Lyons (ed.), *New horizons in linguistics*. Harmondsworth: Penguin Books.

Halliday, M. A. K. (1971) Linguistic function and literary style: An enquiry into the language of William Golding's 'The Inheritors'. In S. Chatman (ed.), *Literary style: A symposium*. New York: Oxford University Press, pp. 330–368.

Halliday, M. A. K. (1972) *Towards a sociological semantics*. Università di Urbino: Centro Internazionale di Semiotica e di Linguistica.

Halliday, M. A. K. (1973) *Explorations in the functions of language*. London: Edward Arnold.

Halliday, M. A. K. (1974a) Discussion. In H. Parret (ed.), *Discussing language*. The Hague: Mouton, pp. 81–120.

Halliday, M. A. K. (1974b) The place of 'functional sentence perspective' in the system of linguistic description. In D. Daneš (ed.), *Papers on functional sentence perspective.* Prague: Academic, pp. 43–53.

Halliday, M. A. K. (1975) *Learning how to mean: Explorations in the development of language*. London: Edward Arnold.

Halliday, M. A. K. (1976) *System and function in language*. London: Oxford University Press.

Halliday, M. A. K. (1977a) Ideas about language. In M. A. K. Halliday (ed.) *Aims and perspectives in linguistics*, pp. 32–49.

Halliday, M. A. K. (1977b) Text as semantic choice in social contexts. In T. A. van Dijk and J. Petöfi (eds) *Grammars and descriptions*. Berlin: Walter de Gruyter, pp. 176–225. Reprinted in M. A. K. Halliday (2002), *Linguistic studies of text and discourse*, vol. 2 in *The collected works of M. A. K. Halliday*, edited by J. Webster. London and New York: Continuum, pp. 23–81.

Halliday, M. A. K. (1978) *Language as social semiotic: The social interpretation of language and meaning*. London: Edward Arnold.

Halliday, M. A. K. (1979) Modes of meaning and modes of expression: Types of grammatical structure and their determination by different semantic functions. In D. J.

Allerton, E. Carney, and D. Holdcroft (eds), *Function and context in linguistic analysis: A Festschrift for William Haas*. Cambridge: Cambridge University Press. 57–79. Reprinted in M. A. K. Halliday (2002) *On grammar*, vol. 1 in *The collected works of M. A. K. Halliday*. Edited by J. Webster. London and New York: Continuum, pp. 196–218.

Halliday, M. A. K. (1980a) Foreword. In A. de Joia and A. Stenton (eds), *Terms in systemic linguistics: A guide to Halliday*. London: Batsford, pp. vii–xii.

Halliday, M. A. K. (1980b) On being teaching. In S. Greenbaum, G. Leech and J. Svartvik (eds), *Studies in English linguistics for Randolph Quirk*. London: Longman, pp. 61–64.

Halliday, M. A. K. (1981) Text semantics and clause grammar: Some patterns of realisation. *Seventh LACUS Forum*. Columbia: Hornbeam Press, pp. 31–59.

Halliday, M. A. K. (1982a) How is a text like a clause? In S. Allén (ed.), *Text processing*. Stockholm: Almqvist and Wiksell, pp. 209–247.

Halliday, M. A. K. (1982b) The de-automatization of grammar: From Priestley's 'An Inspector Calls'. In J. M. Anderson (ed.), *Language form and linguistic variation: Papers dedicated to Angus McIntosh*. Amsterdam: Benjamins, pp. 129–159. Reprinted in M. A. K. Halliday (2002), *Linguistic studies of text and discourse*, vol. 2 in *The collected works of M. A. K. Halliday*, edited by Jonathan J. Webster. London and New York: Continuum, pp. 126–148.

Halliday, M. A. K. (1984a) Language as code and language as behaviour: A systemic functional interpretation of the nature and ontogenesis of dialogue. In Halliday, M. A. K., R. P. Fawcett, S. Lamb S. and A. Makkai (eds), pp. 3–35.

Halliday, M. A. K. (1984b) Linguistics in the university: The question of social accountability. In J. Copeland (ed.) *New directions in linguistics and semiotics*. Houston, TX: Rice University Studies, pp. 51–67.

Halliday, M. A. K. (1984c) On the ineffability of grammatical categories. In A. Manning, P. Martin, and K. McCalla (eds), *Tenth LACUS Forum*. Columbia, SC: Hornbeam Press, pp. 3–18. Reprinted in M. A. K. Halliday (2002) *On grammar*, vol. 1 in *The collected works of M. A. K. Halliday*, edited by J. Webster. London and New York: Continuum, pp. 291–322.

Halliday, M. A. K. (1985a) *An introduction to functional grammar*. London: Edward Arnold.

Halliday, M. A. K. (1985b) Dimensions of discourse analysis: Grammar. In T. A. van Dijk (ed.), *Handbook of discourse analysis: Discourse analysis in society*. New York: Academic Press, pp. 29–56.

Halliday, M. A. K. (1985c) *Spoken and written language*. Geelong, Vic.: Deakin University Press.

Halliday, M. A. K. (1985d) Systemic background. In J. Benson and W. Greaves (eds), pp. 1–15.

Halliday, M. A. K. (1985e) English intonation as a resource for discourse. *Beiträge zur Phonetik und Linguistik* 48, pp. 111–117. (Festschrift in Honour of Arthur Delbridge.)

Halliday, M. A. K. (1987) Spoken and written modes of meaning. In R. Horowitz and S. Samuels (eds), *Comprehending oral and written language*. New York: Academic Press, pp. 55–82.

Halliday, M. A. K. (1988) On the language of physical science. In M. Ghadessy (ed.), pp. 162–178.

Halliday, M. A. K. (1990) New ways of meaning: A challenge to applied linguistics *Journal of Applied Linguistics* (Greek Applied Linguistics Association), 6, pp. 7–36.

Halliday, M. A. K. (1991a) Corpus linguistics and probabilistic grammar. In K. Aijmer and B. Altenberg (eds), *English corpus linguistics: Studies in honour of Jan Svartvik*. London: Longman, pp. 30–43.

Halliday, M. A. K. (1991b) The notion of 'context' in language education. In T. Lean and M. McCausland (eds), *Interaction and Development Proceedings of the International Conference*, Vietnam, 30 March–1 April 1991. University of Tasmania: Language Education, pp. 1–26.

Halliday, M. A. K. (1991c) Towards probabilistic interpretations. In E. Ventola (ed.), *Trends in linguistics: Functional and systemic linguistics: Approaches and uses*. Berlin and New York: de Gruyter, pp. 39–62.

Halliday, M. A. K. (1992a) A systemic interpretation of Peking syllable finals. In P. Tench (ed.), pp. 98–121.

Halliday, M. A. K. (1992b) How do you mean? In M. Davies and L. Ravelli (eds), *Advances in systemic linguistics: Recent theory and practice*. London: Pinter, pp. 20–35. Reprinted in M. A. K. Halliday (2002) *On grammar*, vol. 1 in *The collected works of M. A. K. Halliday*. Edited by J. Webster. London and New York: Continuum, pp. 352–368.

Halliday, M. A. K. (1992c) Language as system and language as instance: The corpus as a theoretical construct. In J. Svartvik (ed.), *Directions in corpus linguistics: Proceedings of Nobel Symposium '82*. Stockholm, 4–8 August 1991. Berlin: Mouton de Gruyter, pp. 61–77.

Halliday, M. A. K. (1992d) Language theory and translation practice. In J. Dodds (ed.), *Rivista internazionale di technica della traduzione*, Numero 0. Udine: Campanotto Editore, pp. 15–25.

Halliday, M. A. K. (1992e) Some lexicogrammatical features of the zero population growth text. In S. Thompson and W. C. Mann (eds), pp. 327–358.

Halliday, M. A. K. (1992f) Systemic grammar and the concept of a 'science of language'. Waiguoyu. *Journal of Foreign Languages*, 2, pp. 1–9.

Halliday, M. A. K. (1992g) The history of a sentence: An essay in social semiotics. In V. Fortunait (ed.), *La cultura italiana e le leterature straniere moderne*. Bologna: Longo Editore (for University of Bologna), pp. 29–45.

Halliday, M. A. K. (1992h) The notion of 'context' in language education. In T. Le and M. McCausland (eds), *Interaction and development: Proceedings of the international conference*. Vietnam, 30 March 1 April 1992. University of Tasmania: Language Education, pp. 1–26.

Halliday, M. A. K. (1993a) Analysis of scientific texts in English and Chinese. In K. Hao Bluhme, H. and Li, R. (eds), pp. 90–97.

Halliday, M. A. K. (1993b) Quantitative studies and probabilities in grammar. In M. Hoey (ed.) *Data, description, discourse: Papers on the English language in honour of John McH. Sinclair*. London: Harper Collins, pp. 1–25.

Halliday, M. A. K. (1993c) The act of meaning. In J. Alatis (ed.), *Georgetown University Round Table on Language and Linguistics 1992: Language, Communication and Social Meaning*. Washington, DC: Georgetown University Press, pp. 7–21.

Halliday, M. A. K. (1993d) Towards a language-based theory of learning. *Linguistics and Education*, 5 (2), pp. 93–116.

Halliday, M. A. K. (1994a) Language and the theory of codes. In A. Sadovnik (ed.), *Knowledge and pedagogy: The sociology of Basil Bernstein*. Westport: Greenwood Publishing Group. Reprinted in M. A. K. Halliday (2007), *Language and society*, vol. 10 in *The collected works of M. A. K. Halliday*. Edited by J. Webster. London and New York: Continuum.

Halliday, M. A. K. (1994b) So you say 'pass'... thank you three muchly. In Grimshaw, A. (ed.) *What's going on here: Complementary studies of professional talk*. Norwood, NJ: Ablex, pp. 175–229.

Halliday, M. A. K. (1994c) *An introduction to functional grammar*. 2nd edition. London: Edward.

Halliday, M. A. K. (1995a) On language in relation to the evolution of human consciousness. In S. Allén (ed.), *Of thoughts and words: Proceedings of Nobel Symposium '92. The Relation between Language and Mind*. Stockholm, 8–12 August 1994. Singapore, River Edge NJ and London: Imperial College Press, pp. 45–84.

Halliday, M. A. K. (1995b) Language and the theory of codes. In A. Sadovnik (ed.), pp. 124–142.

Halliday, M. A. K. (1996) On grammar and grammatics. In R. Hasan, C. Cloran and D. G. Butt (eds), pp. 1–38.

Halliday, M. A. K. (1997) Linguistics as metaphor. In A. Simon-Vandenbergen, K. Davidse, and D. Noël (eds), pp. 3–27.

Halliday, M. A. K. (1998a) On the grammar of pain. *Functions of Language*, 5 (1), pp. 1–32.

Halliday, M. A. K. (1998b) Things and relations: Regrammaticizing experience as technical knowledge. In J. R. Martin and R. Veel (eds), pp. 185–235.

Halliday, M. A. K. (2000a) Imi no computingu: kore made no keiken to kore kara no tenbo [Computing meaning: Some reflections on past experience and present prospects]. *Nihon Faji gakkaishi (Journal of Japan Society for Fuzzy Theory and Systems)*, 12 (5), pp. 615–634.

Halliday, M. A. K. (2000b) Phonology past and present: A personal retrospect. *Folia Linguistica*, XXXIV 1–2, pp. 101–111.

Halliday, M. A. K. (2001) On the grammatical foundations of discourse. In S. Ren, W. Guthrie and I. Fong (eds), *Grammar and discourse: Proceedings of the International conference on discourse analysis*. 16–18 October 1997. University of Macau: University of Macau Publication Centre, pp. 47–58.

Halliday, M. A. K. (2002a) Applied linguistics as an evolving theme. Presented at AILA 2002, Singapore. Published in M. A. K. Halliday (2007), *Language and education*, vol. 9 in *The collected works of M. A. K. Halliday*, edited by J. Webster. London and New York: Continuum, pp. 1–19.

Halliday, M. A. K. (2002b) Computing meanings: Some reflections on past experience and present prospects. In G. Huang and Z. Wang (eds), pp. 3–25.

Halliday, M. A. K. (2002c) *The collected works of M. A. K. Halliday*, vol. 1. *On grammar*. Edited by J. Webster. London and New York: Continuum.

Halliday, M. A. K. (2002d) *The collected works of M. A. K. Halliday*, vol. 2. *Text and discourse*. Edited by J. Webster. London and New York: Continuum.

Halliday, M. A. K. (2002e) The spoken language corpus: A foundation for grammatical theory. In K. Aijmer and B. Altenberg (eds), *Proceedings of ICAME 2002: The theory and use of corpora*, Göteborg 22–26 May 2002. Amsterdam: Editions Rodopi, pp. 11–38.

Halliday, M. A. K. (2003a) *The collected works of M. A. K. Halliday*, vol. 3. *On language and linguistics*. Edited by J. Webster. London and New York: Continuum.

Halliday, M. A. K. (2003b) *The collected works of M. A. K. Halliday*, vol. 4. *The language of early childhood*. Edited by J. Webster. London and New York: Continuum.

Halliday, M. A. K. (2004) *The language of early childhood*. Volume 4 of Collected Works of M. A. K. Halliday, edited by Webster, J. J. London and New York: Continuum.

Halliday, M. A. K. (2005a) On matter and meaning: The two realms of human experience. *Linguistics and the Human Sciences*, 1 (1), pp. 59–82.

Halliday, M. A. K. (2005b) *The collected works of M. A. K. Halliday*, vol. 6. *Computational and quantitative studies*. Edited by J. Webster. London and New York: Continuum.

Halliday, M. A. K. (2005c) *The collected works of M. A. K. Halliday*, vol. 7. *Studies in English language*. Edited by J. Webster. London and New York: Continuum.

Halliday, M. A. K. (2005d) *The collected works of M. A. K. Halliday*, vol. 8. *Studies in Chinese language*. Edited by J. Webster. London and New York: Continuum.

Halliday, M. A. K. (2007a) *The collected works of M. A. K. Halliday*, vol. 9. *Language and education*. Edited by J. Webster. London and New York: Continuum.

Halliday, M. A. K. (2007b) *The collected works of M. A. K. Halliday*, vol. 10. *Language and society*. Edited by J. Webster. London and New York: Continuum.

Halliday, M. A. K. (2008) *Complementarities in language*. Beijing: The Commercial Press.

Halliday, M. A. K. (2010) Language evolving: Some systemic functional reflections on the history of meaning. Paper given at ISFC 37, University of British Columbia, Vancouver, Canada.

Halliday, M. A. K. (2011a) Some thoughts on text and discourse, information and meaning. Paper given to 'Choice and Text', Institute of Language & Communication, University of Southern Denmark.

Halliday, M. A. K. (2011b) Why do we need to understand about language? Paper given at Crossing Boundaries: The impact of language studies in academia and beyond, Queen's University, Belfast.

Halliday, M. A. K. (2011c) On text and discourse, information and meaning. In J. Webster (ed.), pp. 55–70.

Halliday, M. A. K. (2013a) Meaning as choice. In L. Fontaine, T. Bartlett and G. O'Grady, (eds), *Systemic functional linguistics: Exploring choice*. Cambridge: Cambridge University Press, pp. 15–36.

Halliday, M. A. K. (2013b) *The collected works of M. A. K. Halliday*, vol. 11, *Halliday in the 21st century*. Edited by J. Webster. London and New York: Bloomsbury Academic.

Halliday, M. A. K. (2014) 'That 'certain cut': Towards a characterology of Mandarin Chinese.' *Functional Linguistics* 1: 4–23.

Halliday, M. A. K. and Fawcett, R. P. (eds) (1987) *New developments in Systemic Linguistics: Theory and description*. London: Frances Pinter.

Halliday, M. A. K. and Greaves, W. (2008) *Intonation in the grammar of English*. London: Equinox.

Halliday, M. A. K. and Hasan, R. (1976) *Cohesion in English*. London: Longman.

Halliday, M. A. K. and Hasan, R. (1985) *Language, context and text: A social semiotic perspective*. Geelong, Vic.: Deakin University Press.

Halliday, M. A. K. and James, Z. L. (1993) A quantitative study of polarity and primary tense in the English finite clause. Sinclair, J. M., Hoey, M. and Fox, G. (ed.), *Techniques of description: Spoken and written discourse* (A festschrift for Malcolm Coulthard). London and New York: Routledge, pp. 32–66. Reprinted in Halliday, M. A. K. (2005) *Computational and quantitative studies*. Volume 6 in *The collected works of M. A. K. Halliday*, edited by Webster, J. J. London and New York: Continuum, pp. 93–129.

Halliday, M. A. K. and Martin, J. R. (eds) (1981) *Readings in systemic linguistics*. London: Batsford.

Halliday, M. A. K. and Martin, J. R. (1993) *Writing science: Literacy and discursive power*. London: Falmer.

Halliday, M. A. K. and Matthiessen, C. M. I. M. (1999) *Construing experience through meaning: A language-based approach to cognition*. London: Cassell.

Halliday, M. A. K. and Matthiessen, C. M. I. M. (2004) *An introduction to functional grammar*, 3rd edition. London: Arnold.

Halliday, M. A. K. and Matthiessen, C. M. I. M. (2006) *Construing experience through meaning: A language-based approach to cognition*. London and New York: Continuum.

Halliday, M. A. K. and Matthiessen, C. M. I. M. (2014) *Halliday's introduction to functional grammar*. 4th Edition. London: Routledge.

Halliday, M. A. K. and McDonald, E. (2004) Metafunctional profile of the grammar of Chinese. In A. Caffarel, J. R. Martin and C. M. I. M. Matthiessen (eds), pp. 305–396.

Halliday, M. A. K. and Webster, J. (eds) (2009) *Continuum companion to systemic functional linguistics*. London and New York: Continuum.

Halliday, M. A. K., McIntosh, A. and Strevens, P. (1964) *The linguistic sciences and language teaching*. London: Longman.

Halliday, M. A. K., Fawcett, R. P., Lamb, S. and Makkai, A. (eds) (1984) *The semiotics of language and culture*, vol. 1. London: Frances Pinter.

Halliday, M. A. K., Gibbons, J. and Nichols, H. (eds) (1990) *Learning, keeping and using language: Selected papers from the 8th World Congress of Applied Linguistics*. Amsterdam: Benjamins.

Hansen, S. (2003) *The nature of translated text: An interdisciplinary methodology for the investigation of the specific properties of translations* (Saarbrücken Dissertations in

Computational Linguistics and Language Technology, Volume 13) Saarbrücken: Saarland University.

Hansen-Schirra, S. and Neumann, S. (2004) Linguistische Verständlichmachung in der juristischen Realität. In K. Lerch (ed.), *Recht verstehen. Verständlichkeit, Missverständlichkeit und Unverständlichkeit von Recht.* Band 1. Schriftenreihe *Die Sprache des Rechts* der Berlin-Brandenburgischen Akademie der Wissenschaften. Berlin and New York: de Gruyter, pp. 167–184.

Hao, K., Bluhme, H. and Li, R. (eds) (1993) *Proceedings of the international conference on texts and language research*, Xi'an, 29–31 March 1989. Xi'an: Xi'an Jiaotong University Press.

Harris, Z. S. (1952) Discourse analysis. *Language* 28, pp. 1–30.

Harrison, C. and Young, L. (2004) Bureaucratic discourse: Writing in the 'comfort zone'. In L. Young and C. Harrison (eds), *Systemic functional linguistics and critical discourse analysis: Studies in social change.* London and New York: Continuum, pp. 231–246.

Hartley, A. and Paris, C. (1995) *French corpus analysis and grammatical description.* Technical Report, Project IED/4/1/5827, ITRI, University of Brighton.

Harvey, A. (1996) *Equivalence and depersonalisation in definitions: An exploration of lexicogrammatical and rhetorical patterns in English technical discourse.* Ph.D. thesis, Sydney University.

Harvey, A. (1999) Definitions in English technical discourse: A study in metafunctional dominance and interaction. *Functions of Language*, 6 (1), pp. 55–96.

Hasan, R. (1964) *A linguistic study of contrasting features in the style of two contemporary English prose writers.* Ph.D. thesis, University of Edinburgh.

Hasan, R. (1973) Code, register and social dialect. In B. Bernstein (ed.), *Class, codes and control, vol. 2, Applied studies towards a sociology of language.* London and New York: Routledge, pp. 253–292.

Hasan, R. (1978) Text in the systemic functional model. In W. Dressier (ed.), *Current trends in text linguistics.* Berlin: de Gruyter, pp. 228–246.

Hasan, R. (1980) What's going on: A dynamic view of context. In J. Copeland and R. Davis (eds), *The Seventh LACUS forum.* Columbia, SC: Hornbeam Press, pp. 106–121.

Hasan, R. (1984a) Coherence and cohesive harmony. In J. Flood (ed.) *Understanding reading comprehension.* Newark: International Reading Association, pp. 181–219.

Hasan, R. (1984b) The nursery tale as a genre. *Nottingham Linguistic Circular*, 13, pp. 71–102.

Hasan, R. (1984c) Ways of saying, ways of meaning. In M. A. K. Halliday, R. P. Fawcett, S. Lamb and A. Makkai (eds), pp. 105–162.

Hasan, R. (1984d) What kind of resource is language? *Australian Review of Applied Linguistics*, 7 (1), pp. 57–85.

Hasan, R. (1985a) Lending and borrowing: From grammar to lexis. *Beiträge zur Phonetik und Linguistik*, 48, pp. 56–67.

Hasan, R. (1985b) *Linguistics, language and verbal art.* Geelong, Vic.: Deakin University Press.

Hasan, R. (1985c) Meaning, context and text: Fifty years after Malinowski. In J. Benson and W. Greaves (eds), pp. 16–50.

Hasan, R. (1987a) Offers in the making: A systemic functional approach. MS.

Hasan, R. (1987b) The grammarian's dream: Lexis as most delicate grammar. In M. A. K. Halliday and R. P. Fawcett (eds), pp. 184–211.

Hasan, R. (1989) Semantic variation and sociolinguistics. *Australian Journal of Linguistics*, 9, pp. 221–275.

Hasan, R. (1992) Speech genre, semiotic mediation and the development of higher mental functions. *Language Sciences*, 14 (4), pp. 489–528.

Hasan, R. (1995) On social conditions for semiotic mediation: The genesis of mind in society. In A. Sadovnik (ed.), *Knowledge and pedagogy: The sociology of Basil Bernstein*. Norwood, NJ: Ablex, pp. 219–328.

Hasan, R. (1996a) Semantic networks. In Cloran, C., Butt, D. and Williams, G. (eds). (1996) *Ways of saying: Ways of meaning: Selected papers of Ruqaiya Hasan*. London: Cassell.

Hasan, R. (1996b) *Ways of saying: Ways of meaning. Selected papers of Ruqaiya Hasan*, edited by Cloran, C., Butt, D. and Williams, G. London: Cassell.

Hasan, R. (1999) Speaking with reference to context. In M. Ghadessy (ed.), *Text and context in functional linguistics*. Amsterdam: Benjamins, pp. 219–328.

Hasan, R. (2002) Semiotic mediation and mental development in pluralistic societies: Some implications for tomorrow's schooling. In G. Wells and G. Claxton (eds), *Learning for life in the 21st century*. Oxford: Blackwell, pp. 89–123.

Hasan, R. (2005). Introduction: A working model of language. In R. Hasan, C. M. I. M. Matthiessen and J. Webster (eds), pp. 37–54.

Hasan, R. (2009). The place of context in a systemic functional model. In M. A. K. Halliday and J. Webster (eds), pp. 166–189.

Hasan, R. and Cloran, C. (1990) A sociolinguistic interpretation of everyday talk between mothers and children. In M. A. K. Halliday, J. Gibbons and H. Nichols (eds), pp. 67–99.

Hasan, R. and Fries, P. H. (eds) (1995) *On subject and theme: A discourse functional perspective*. Amsterdam and Philadelphia: Benjamins.

Hasan, R. and Martin, J. R. (eds) (1989) *Language development: Learning language, learning culture, meaning and choice in language*. Norwood, NJ: Ablex.

Hasan, R. and Perrett, G. (1994) Learning to function with the other tongue: A systemic functional perspective on second language teaching. In T. Odlin (ed.) *Perspectives on pedagogic grammars*. Cambridge: Cambridge University Press, pp. 179–226.

Hasan, R. and Williams, G. (eds) (1996) *Literacy in society*. London: Longman.

Hasan, R., Cloran, C., and Butt, D. G. (eds) (1996) *Functional descriptions: Theory into practice*. Amsterdam: Benjamins.

Hasan, R., Matthiessen, C. M. I. M., and Webster, J. (eds) (2005) *Continuing discourse on language: A functional perspective*, vol. 1. London: Equinox.

Hasan, R., Matthiessen, C. M. I. M., and Webster, J. (eds) (2007a) *Continuing discourse on language: A functional perspective*, vol. 2. London: Equinox.

Hasan, R., Cloran, C., Williams, G., and Lukin, A. (2007b) Semantic networks: The description of linguistic meaning in SFL. In R. Hasan, C. M. I. M. Matthiessen and J. Webster (eds), pp. 697–738.

Haspelmath, M., Dryer, M., Gil, D., and Comrie, B. (eds) (2005) *The world atlas of language structures*. Oxford: Oxford University Press.

Hasselgård, H. (2004) Thematic choice in English and Norwegian. *Functions of Language*, 11 (2), pp. 187–212.

Hatim, B. and Mason, I. (1990) *Discourse and the translator*. London: Longman.

Hayakawa, C. (2004) Lexicogrammatical resources in spoken and written texts. *JASFL Occasional Papers*, 3 (1), pp. 5–41.

Heller, L. and Macris, J. (1967) *Parametric linguistics*. The Hague: Mouton.

Henderson, E. J. A. (1949) Prosodies in Siamese: A study in synthesis. *Asia Major* (New Series) 1, pp. 189–215. Reprinted in F. R. Palmer (ed.), (1968), *Prosodic analysis*, London: Oxford University Press, pp. 27–53.

Henderson, E. (1987) J. R. Firth in retrospect: A view from the eighties. In R. Steele and T. Threadgold (eds), pp. 57–69.

Henderson-Brooks, C. (2006) *'What Type of Person Am I, Tess?': The complex tale of self in psychotherapy*. Ph.D. thesis, Macquarie University.

Hendrix, G. (1979) Encoding knowledge in partitioned networks. In N. Finder (ed.) *Associative networks*. New York: Academic Press, pp. 51–92.

Henrici, A. (1965) Notes on the systemic generation of a paradigm of the English clause. In M. A. K. Halliday and J. R. Martin (eds), pp. 74–98.

Henschel, R. (1994) Declarative representations and processing of systemic grammars. In C. Martin-Vide (ed.), *Current issues in mathematical linguistics*. Amsterdam: Elsevier Science Publisher, pp. 363–371.

Hill, A. A. (1958) *Introduction to linguistic structures*. New York: Harcourt, Brace and World.

Hill, T. (1958) Institutional linguistics. *Orbis*, 7 (2), pp. 441–455.

Hill, T. (1966) The technique of prosodic analysis. In C. E. Bazell, J. C. C. Catford, M. A. K. Halliday, and R. H. Robins (eds), *In memory of J. R. Firth*. London: Longman, pp. 198–226.

Hirst, W. (ed.) (1988) *The making of cognitive science: Essays in honor of George A. Miller*. Cambridge: Cambridge University Press.

Hjelmslev, L. (1943) *Omkring sprogteoriens grundlaeggelse*. København: Akademisk Forlag.

Hoang, V. (1997) *An experiential grammar of the Vietnamese clause: A functional description*. Ph.D. thesis, Macquarie University.

Hoekstra, T., van der Hulst, H. and Moortgat, M. (eds) (1980) *Lexical grammar*. Dordrecht: Foris.

Hoey, M. (2006) Language as choice: What is chosen? In S. Hunston and G. Thompson (eds), pp. 37–54.

Holmberg, P. and Karlsson, A. (2006) *Grammatik med betydelse en introduktion till funktionell grammatik*. Uppsala: Hallgren & Fallgren.

Honnibal, M. (2004) *Adapting the Penn Treebank to systemic functional grammar: Design, creation and use of a metafunctionally annotated corpus*. BA Honours thesis, Macquarie University.

Hood, S. and Forey, G. (2008) The interpersonal dynamics of call-centre interactions: Co-constructing the rise and fall of emotion. *Discourse and Communication*, 2 (4), pp. 34–48.

Hood, S. and Martin, J. R. (2007) Invoking attitude: The play of graduation in appraising discourse. In R. Hasan, C. M. I. M. Matthiessen and J. Webster (eds), pp. 739–764.

Hooper, J. B. (1972) The syllable in phonological theory. *Language* 48 (3): 525–540.

Hooper, J. B. (1976) *An introduction to Natural Generative Phonology*. New York: Academic Press.

Hopper, P. and Traugott, E. (1993) *Grammaticalization*. Cambridge: Cambridge University Press.

Hori, M. (1995) Subjectlessness and honorifics in Japanese: A case of textual construal. In R. Hasan and P. H. Fries (eds), pp. 151–187.

Horvath, B. and Eggins, S. (1995) Opinion texts in conversation. In P. H. Fries and M. Gregory (eds), pp. 29–46.

Hu, Z. (1981) *Textual cohesion in Chinese*. MA Honours thesis, University of Sydney.

Hu, Z., Zhu, Y. and Zhang, D. (1989) *A survey of systemic functional grammar* [In Chinese]. Changsha: Hunan Educational Publishing House.

Huang, C., Calzolari, N., Gangemi, A., Lenci, A., Oltramari, A., and Prévot, L. (eds) (2010) *Ontology and the lexicon: A natural language processing perspective*. Cambridge: Cambridge University Press.

Huang, G. (1996) Experiential enhanced theme in English. In M. Berry, C. Butler, R. P. Fawcett and G. Huang (eds), pp. 65–113.

Huang, G. (2002) Cleft sentences as grammatical metaphors. In G. Huang and Z. Wang (eds), pp. 34–41.

Huang, G. and Wang, Z. (eds) (2002) *Discourse and language functions*. Shanghai: Foreign Language Teaching and Research Press.

Huck, G. J. and Goldsmith, J. A. (1995) *Ideology and linguistic theory: Noam Chomsky and the deep structure debate*. London and New York: Routledge.

Huddleston, R. and Uren, O. (1969) Declarative, interrogative and imperative in French. *Lingua*, 22, pp. 1–26.

Huddleston, R., Hudson, C., Winter, E., and Henrici, A. (1968) *Sentence and clause in scientific English: Final report of O.S.T.I. Programme*. University College London: Communication Research Centre.

Hudson, R. (1971) *English complex sentences*. Amsterdam: North Holland.

Hudson, R. (1973) An item-and-paradigm approach to Beja syntax and morphology. *Foundations of Language*, 9, pp. 504–508.

Hudson, R. (1974) Systemic generative grammar. *Linguistics*, 139, pp. 5–42.

Hudson, R. (1976) *Arguments for a non-transformational grammar*. Chicago, IL: Chicago University Press.

Hudson, R. (1984) *Word grammar*. Oxford: Blackwell.

Hudson, R. (2007) *Language networks: The new word grammar*. Oxford: Oxford University Press.

Huff, T. (1995) *The rise of early modern science: Islam, China and the West*. Cambridge: Cambridge University Press.

Humphrey, S. (1996) *Exploring literacy in school geography*. Sydney: Metropolitan East Disadvantaged Schools Program.

Hunston, S. and Francis, G. (2000) *Pattern grammar: A corpus-driven approach to the lexical grammar of English*. Amsterdam: Benjamins.

Hunston, S. and Thompson, G. (eds) (2001) *Evaluation in text: Authorial stance and the construction of discourse*. Oxford: Oxford University Press,

Hunston, S. and Thompson, G. (eds) (2006) *System and corpus: Exploring connections*. London: Equinox.

Iedema, R. (1995) *Administrative literacy*. Sydney: Metropolitan East Disadvantaged Schools Program.

Iedema, R. (1996) *The language of administration*. Sydney: NSW, Department of Education, Disadvantaged Schools Program Metropolitan East.

Iedema, R. (1997a) *Interactional dynamics and social change: Planning as morphogenesis*. Ph.D. thesis, Sydney University.

Iedema, R. (1997b) The language of administration: Organizing human activity in formal institutions. In F. Christie and J. R. Martin (eds), pp. 73–100.

Iedema, R. (2000) Bureaucratic planning and resemiotisation. In E. Ventola (ed.), pp. 47–69.

Iedema, R. (2003) *Discourses of post-bureaucratic organization*. Amsterdam and Philadelphia: Benjamins.

Iedema, R. (ed.) (2007) *The discourse of hospital communication: Tracing complexities in contemporary health organizations*. London and New York: Palgrave Macmillan.

Iedema, R. and Scheeres, H. (2003) From doing to talking work: Renegotiating knowing, doing and identity. *Applied Linguistics*, 24, pp. 316–317.

Iedema, R., Feez, S., and White, P. (1994) *Media literacy*. Sydney: NSW, Department of Education, Disadvantaged Schools Program Metropolitan East.

Jakobson, R. (1949) On the identification of phonemic entities. *Recherches Structurales, Travaux du Cercle Linguistique de Prague* V, pp. 205–13. Reprinted in R. Jakobson (1962) *Selected writings I: Phonological studies*. The Hague: Mouton, pp. 418–25.

Jakobson, R., Fant, G. and Halle, M. (1952) Preliminaries to speech analysis: The distinctive features and their correlates. Technical Report, Acoustics Laboratory, No. 13. MIT.

Jenkins, H. (1990) Train Sex Man Fined: Headlines and cataphoric ellipsis. In M. A. K. Halliday, J. Gibbons and H. Nichols (eds), pp. 349–362.

Jenkins, H. (1992) On being clear about time: An analysis of a chapter of Stephen Hawking's 'A Brief History of Time'. *Language Sciences*, 14 (4), pp. 529–545.

Jespersen, O. (1933) Symbolic value of the vowel i. In O. Jespersen. *Linguistica: Elected papers in English, French and German*. Copenhagen: Levin and Munksgaard, pp. 283–303. Reprinted in O. Jespersen (2010), *Selected writings of Otto Jespersen*. London: Routledge, pp. 289–300.

Johnson, A. and Earle, T. (2000) *The evolution of human societies: From foraging group to agrarian state*. Stanford, CA: Stanford University Press.

Johnston, T. (1992) The realization of the linguistic metafunctions in a sign language. *Language Sciences*, 14 (4), pp. 317–355.

Kachuru, B. B. (2015) 'Socially realistic linguistics': The Firthian tradition. In J. Webster (ed.), *The Bloomsbury companion to M. A. K. Halliday*. London: Bloomsbury Academic, pp. 72–93.

Kaku, M. (1994) *Hyperspace: A scientific odyssey through the 10th dimension*. Oxford: Oxford University Press.

Kappagoda, A. (2005) What people do to know: The construction of knowledge as a social-semiotic activity. In R. Hasan, C. M. I. M. Matthiessen and J. Webster (eds), pp. 185–216.

Kasper, R. (1988a) An experimental parser for systemic grammars. In *Proceedings of the 12th International Conference on Computational Linguistics*. Budapest, Hungary: COLING, pp. 309–312.

Kasper, R. (1988b) Systemic grammar and functional unification grammar. In D. Benson and W. Greaves (eds), pp. 176–199.

Kay, M. (1979) Functional grammar. In *Proceedings of the Fifth Annual Meeting of the Berkeley Linguistic Society*, pp. 142–158.

Kay, M. (1985) Parsing with functional unification grammar. In K. Sparck-Jones and B. Webber (eds), *Readings in natural language processing*. Los Altos, CA: Morgan Kaufman, pp. 251–278.

Kay, M. (1994) A life of language. *Computational Linguistics*, 16 (1), pp. 1–13.

Kay, P. and Fillmore, C. (1999) Grammatical construction and linguistic generalizations: What's X doing Y? construction. *Language*, 73 (1), pp. 1–33.

Kealley, D. J. (2007) *'I can't find a pulse but that's OK': Nursing in context: A systemic functional linguistic examination of nursing practice*. Ph.D. thesis, University of South Australia.

Kempson, R., Meyer-Viol, W. and Gabbay, D. (2001) *Dynamic syntax: The flow of language understanding*. Oxford: Blackwell.

Kies, D. (1988) Marked Theme with and without pronominal reinforcement: Their meaning and distribution in discourse. In E. Steiner and R. Veltman (eds), pp. 47–75.

Kies, D. (1992) The uses of passivity: Suppressing agency in 'Nineteen Eighty-Four'. In M. Davies and L. Ravelli (eds), pp. 229–251.

Kim, M. (2007) Using systemic functional text analysis for translator education: An illustration with a focus on textual meaning. *The Interpreter and Translator Trainer*, 1 (2), pp. 223–246.

Kim, M. and Matthiessen, C. M. I. M. (2015) Introduction. In J. Munday and M. Zhang (eds), *Discourse analysis in translation studies. Target* 27:3, pp. 335–350.

Knox, J. S. (2007) Visual-verbal communication on online newspaper home pages. *Visual Communication*, 6 (1): 19–53.

Knox, J. S. and Patpong, P. (2008) Reporting bloodshed in Thai newspapers: A comparative case study of English and Thai. In E. Thomson and P. R. R. White (eds) *Communicating conflict: Multilingual case studies of the rhetoric of the news media*. London: Continuum, pp. 173–202.

Kress, G. and Hodge, R. (1979) *Language as ideology*. London: Routledge and Kegan Paul.

Kress, G. and Hodge, R. (1988) *Social semiotics*. London: Polity.

Kress, G. and van Leeuwen, T. (1990) *Reading images*. Geelong, Vic.: Deakin University Press.

Kress, G. and van Leeuwen, T. (1996) *Reading images: The grammar of visual design*. London: Routledge.

Kress, G. and van Leeuwen, T. (2001) *Multimodal discourse: The modes and media of contemporary communication*. London: Arnold.

Kumar, A. (2009) *A systemic functional description of the grammar of Bajjika*. Unpublished Ph.D. thesis, Macquarie University, Australia.

Ladd, D. (1996) *Intonational phonology*. Cambridge: Cambridge University Press.

Ladefoged, P. (1979) Review of Catford (1977) Fundamental problems in phonetics. *Language*, 55 (4), pp. 904–907.

Ladefoged, P. (2001) *Vowels and consonants: An introduction to the sounds of languages*. Oxford: Blackwell.

Ladefoged, P. (2004) Phonetics and phonology in the last 50 years. Paper presented at *From Sound to Sense*: June 11–June 13, 2004 at MIT.

Lamb, S. (1966) *Outline of stratificational grammar*. Washington DC: Georgetown University Press.

Lamb, S. (1999) *Pathways of the brain: The neurocognitive basis of language*. Amsterdam: Benjamins.

Lamb, S. M. (2013) Systemic networks, relational networks and choice. In L. Fontaine, T. Bartlett and G. O'Grady (eds), pp. 137–160.

Landau, S. (1989) *Dictionaries: The art and craft of lexicography*. Cambridge: Cambridge University Press.

Langacker, R. (1987) *Foundations of cognitive grammar*. Stanford, CA: Stanford University Press.

Lantolf, J. (2010) Minding your hands: The function of gesture in L2 learning. In R. Batstone (ed.), *Sociocognitive perspectives on language use and language learning*. Oxford: Oxford University Press, pp. 131–150.

Lantolf, J. and Thorne, S. (2006) *Sociocultural theory and the genesis of second language development*. Oxford: Oxford University Press.

Larsen-Freeman, D. (2011) Saying what we mean: Making a case for 'language acquisition' to become 'language development'. Plenary at AILA 2011, Beijing.

Larsen-Freeman, D. (2015) Saying what we mean: Making a case for 'language acquisition' to become 'language development'. *Language teaching*, 48 (5), pp. 491–505.

Lavid, J. (2000a) Cross-cultural variation in multilingual instructions: A study of speech act realisation patterns. In E. Ventola (ed.), pp. 71–86.

Lavid, J. (2000b) Linguistic and computational approaches to information in discourse: Theme, focus, given and other dangerous things. *Revista Canaria de Estudios Ingleses*, 40, pp. 355–369.

Layzer, D. (1990) *Cosmogenesis: The growth of order in the universe*. New York and Oxford: Oxford University Press.

Leech, G. N. (1970) *Towards a semantic description of English*. Bloomington, IN: Indiana University Press.

Leech, G. N. (1974) *Semantics*. Harmondsworth: Penguin.

Lemke, J. L. (1984) The formal analysis of instruction. In J. L. Lemke, *Semiotics and Education*, Victoria University, Toronto: Toronto Semiotic Circle Monographs, Working Papers and Prepublication, No. 2, pp. 94–149.

Lemke, J. L. (1987) The topology of genre: Text structures and text types. MS.

Lemke, J. L. (1990) *Talking science language, learning and values*. Norwood, N.J.: Ablex.

Lemke, J. L. (1992) Interpersonal meaning in discourse: Value orientations. In M. Davies and L. Ravelli, (eds), pp. 82–105.

Lemke, J. L. (1995) *Textual politics: Discourse and social dynamics*. London and Bristol, PA: Taylor and Francis.

Levin, B. (1993) English verb classes and alternations: A preliminary investigation. Chicago and London: The University of Chicago Press.

Li, E. (2003) *A text-based study of the grammar of Chinese from a systemic functional approach*. Ph.D. thesis, Macquarie University.

Lock, G. (1995) *Functional English grammar: An introduction for second language teachers*. Cambridge: Cambridge University Press.

Lockwood, D. G. (1972) *Introduction to stratificational linguistics*. New York: Harcourt Brace Jovanovich.

Lockwood, D. (2002) *Syntactic analysis and description: A constructional approach*. London and New York: Continuum.

Lockwood, J, Forey, G., and Elias, N. (2009) Call centre communication: Measurement processes in non-English speaking contexts. In D. Belcher (ed.), *English for specific purposes in theory and practice*. Ann Arbor, MI: University of Michigan Press, pp. 143–164.

Long, R. (1981) *Transitivity in Chinese*. MA thesis, University of Sydney, Sydney.

Longacre, R. (1976) *Anatomy of speech notions*. Lisse: Peter de Ridder Press.

Longacre, R. (1979) The paragraph as a grammatical unit. In T. Givón (ed.), *Syntax and semantics: Discourse and syntax*, Volume 12. New York: Academic Press, pp. 115–134.

López F. (2000) Projection in news discourse. *Revista Canaria de Estudios Ingleses*, 40, pp. 189–207.

Lounsbury, F. (1956) Semantic analysis of the Pawnee kinship usage. *Language*, 32, pp. 159–194.

Lukin, A. (2003) *Examining poetry: A corpus-based enquiry into literary criticism*. Ph.D. thesis, Macquarie University.

Lukin, A. and Butt, D. G. (2009) Stylistic analysis: Construing aesthetic organization. In M. A. K. Halliday and J. Webster (eds), pp. 190–215.

Lukin, A. and Webster, J. (2005) SFL and the study of literature. In R. Hasan, C. M. I. M. Matthiessen and J. Webster (eds), pp. 413–456.

Lyons, J. (1968) *Theoretical linguistics*. Cambridge: Cambridge University Press.

Mahfouz, I. (2008) *Macro-textual cues and word sense disambiguation: A symantico-syntactic study to build an electronic linguistic database*. Ph.D. dissertation, 2008.

Malinowski, B. (1923) The problem of meaning in primitive languages. In C. Ogden and I. Richards (eds), *The meaning of meaning*. New York: Harcourt Brace, pp. 296–336.

Malinowski, B. (1944) *A scientific theory of culture and other essays*. Chapel Hill: University of North Carolina Press.

Malmberg, B. (1970) *Nya vägar inom Språkforskningen: En orientering i modern lingvistik*. Fjärde upplagan. Stockholm: Kungliga Boktryckeriet P.A. Nordstedt & Söner.

Manidis, M., McGregor, J., Herke, M., Matthiessen, C. M. I. M., Slade, D., McCarthy, S., Scheeres, H., Stein-Parbury, J., Dunston, R., and Iedema, R. (2008) Emergency communication: The discourse challenges facing emergency clinicians and patients in hospital emergency departments. *Discourse & Communication*, 2 (3), pp. 271–298.

Mann, W. C. (1982) *An overview of the Penman text generation system*. USC/Information Sciences Institute (RR-83–114).

Mann, W. C. (1983a) Systemic encounters with computation. *Network*, 5, pp. 27–32.

Mann, W. C. (1983b) The anatomy of systemic choices. *Discourse Processes*, 8 (1), pp. 53–74.

Mann, W. C. and Matthiessen, C. M. I. M. (1983) *Nigel: A systemic grammar for text generation*. CA: USC/Information Sciences Institute (RR-83–105).

Mann, W. C., and Matthiessen, C. M. I. M. (1985). Demonstration of the Nigel text generation grammar. In Benson, J. D. and Greaves, W. S. (eds), *Systemic perspectives on discourse*, Volume 1. Norwood: Ablex, pp. 50–83.

Mann, W. C., Matthiessen, C. M. I. M. and Thompson, S. (1992) Rhetorical structure theory and text analysis. In S. Thompson and W. C. Mann (eds), pp. 39–78.

Manning, C. D. (2003) Probabilistic syntax. In R. Bod, J. Hay and S. Jannedy (eds), pp. 289–341.

Manning, C. D. and Schütze, H. (1999) *Foundations of statistical natural language processing*. Cambridge, MA: MIT Press.

Mar, J. (2001) *The Power of prayer: Construing religious meaning through language*. Ph.D. thesis, Macquarie University.

Martin, C. (1997) *Staging the reality principle: Systemic functional linguistics and the context of theatre*. Ph.D. thesis, Macquarie University.

Martin, J. R. (1983a) Conjunction: The logic of English text. In J. Petöfi and E. Sözer (eds), *Micro and macro connexity of discourse*. Hamburg: Buske, pp. 1–72.

Martin, J. R. (1983b) Participant identification in English, Tagalog and Kâte. *Australian Journal of Linguistics*, 3 (1), pp. 45–74.

Martin, J. R. (1985a) *Factual writing: Exploring and challenging social reality*. Geelong, Victoria: Deakin University Press.

Martin, J. R. (1985b) Process and text: Two aspects of human semiosis. In J. Benson and W. Greaves (eds), pp. 248–274.

Martin, J. R. (1986) Grammaticalising ecology: The politics of baby seals and kangaroos. In T. Threadgold, E. Grosz, G. Kress, and M. A. K. Halliday (eds), *Semiotics, language, ideology*. Sydney: Pathfinder Press, pp. 225–267.

Martin, J. R. (1988a) Grammatical conspiracies in Tagalog: Family, face and fate with reference to Benjamin Lee Whorf. In J. Benson, M. J. Cummings and W. Greaves (eds), pp. 243–300.

Martin, J. R. (1988b) Hypotactic recursive systems in English: Towards a functional interpretation. In D. Benson and W. Greaves (eds), pp. 240–270.

Martin, J. R. (1990) Interpersonal grammaticalisation: Mood and modality in Tagalog. *Philippine Journal of Linguistics*, pp. 2–51.

Martin, J. R. (1991) Intrinsic functionality: Implications for contextual theory. *Social Semiotics*, 1 (1), pp. 99–162.

Martin, J. R. (1992a) *English text: System and structure*. Amsterdam: Benjamins.

Martin, J. R. (1992b) Macro-proposals: Meaning by degree. In W. C. Mann and S. Thompson (ed.), *Text description: Diverse analyses of a fundraising text*. Amsterdam: Benjamins, pp. 359–395.

Martin, J. R. (1992c) Theme, method of development and existentiality: The price of reply. *Occasional Papers in Systemic Linguistics*, 6, pp. 147–184.

Martin, J. R. (1993) Technology, bureaucracy and schooling: Discursive resources and control. *Cultural Dynamics*, 6 (1–2), pp. 84–131.

Martin, J. R. (1994) Macro-genres: The ecology of the page. *Network*, 21, pp. 29–52.

Martin, J. R. (1995a) Logical meaning, interdependency and the linking particle (-ng/na) in Tagalog. *Functions of Language*, 2 (2), pp. 189–228.

Martin, J. R. (1995b) Text and clause: Fractal resonance. *Text*, 15 (1), pp. 5–42.

Martin, J. R. (1996a) Metalinguistic diversity: The case from case. In R. Hasan, C. Cloran and D. G. Butt (eds), pp. 323–375.

Martin, J. R. (1996b) Transitivity in Tagalog: A functional interpretation of case. In M. Berry, C. Butler, R. P. Fawcett and G. Huang (eds), pp. 229–296.

Martin, J. R. (1996c) Types of structure: Deconstructing notions of constituency in clause and text. In E. Hovy and D. Scott (eds), *Burning issues in discourse: A multidisciplinary perspective*. Heidelberg: Springer.

Martin, J. R. (1997) Analysing genre: Functional parameters. In F. Christie and J. R. Martin (eds), pp. 3–39.

Martin, J. R. (2000) Beyond exchange: Appraisal systems in English. In S. Hunston and G. Thompson (eds), pp. 142–175.

Martin, J. R. (2002) Blessed are the peacemakers: Reconciliation and evaluation. In C. Candlin (ed.), pp. 187–227.

Martin, J. R. (2003) Making history: Grammar for interpretation. In J. R. Martin and R. Wodak (eds), pp. 19–57.

Martin, J. R. (2004a) Metafunctional profile of the grammar of Tagalog. In A. Caffarel, J. R. Martin, and C. M. I. M. Matthiessen (eds), pp. 255–304.

Martin, J. R. (2004b) Positive discourse analysis: Power, solidarity and change. *Revista Canaria de Estudios Ingleses*, 49, pp. 179–200.

Martin, J. R. (2007) Genre, ideology and intertextuality: A systemic functional perspective. *Linguistics and Human Sciences*, 2 (2), pp. 275–298.

Martin, J. R. (2009a) Discourse studies. In M. A. K. Halliday and J. Webster (eds), pp. 154–165.

Martin, J. R. (2009b) Genre and language learning: A social semiotic perspective. In Byrnes, H. (ed.) *Foreign/second language acquisition as meaning-making: A systemic-functional approach*. Special issue of *Linguistics and Education* 20(1): 10–21.

Martin, J. R. and Matthiessen, C. M. I. M. (1991) Systemic typology and topology. In F. Christie (ed.), *Literacy in Social Processes: Papers from the Inaugural Australian Systemic Functional Linguistics Conference*. Deakin University, January 1990 (Centre for Studies of Language in Education, Northern Territory University, 1991), pp. 345–383.

Martin, J. R. and Rochester, S. (1979) *Crazy talk: A study of the discourse of schizophrenic speakers*. New York: Plenum.

Martin, J. R. and Rose, D. (2003) *Working with discourse: Meaning beyond the clause*. London and New York: Continuum.

Martin, J. R. and Rose, D. (2005) Designing literacy pedagogy: Scaffolding democracy in the classroom. In R. Hasan, C. M. I. M. Matthiessen and J. Webster (eds), pp. 251–280.

Martin, J. R. and Rose, D. (2008) *Genre relations: Mapping culture*. London and Oakville: Equinox.

Martin, J. R. and Rothery, J. (1980) *Writing project report no. 1*. Sydney University: Linguistics Department.

Martin, J. R. and Rothery, J. (1981) The ontogenesis of written genre. *Writing project report*, no. 2: Sydney University: Linguistics Department (Working Papers).

Martin, J. R. and Veel, R. (eds) (1998) *Reading science: Critical and functional perspectives on discourses of science*. London: Routledge.

Martin, J. R. and White, P. (2005) *The language of evaluation, appraisal in English*. London and New York: Palgrave Macmillan.

Martin, J. R. and Wodak, R. (eds) (2003) *Re/reading the Past: Critical and functional perspectives on time and value*. Amsterdam and Philadelphia: Benjamins.

Martin, J. R., Matthiessen, C. M. I. M. and Painter, C. (1997) *Working with functional grammar*. London: Edward Arnold.

Martin *et al.* (2003) *Text* 23(2) (June 2003) https://www.degruyter.com/view/journals/text/23/2/text.23.issue-2.xml

Martinec, R. (1995) *Hierarchy of rhythm in English speech*. Ph.D. thesis, Sydney University.

Martinec, R. (2005) Topics in multimodality. In R. Hasan, C. M. I. M., Matthiessen and J. Webster (eds), pp. 157–181.

Mason, I. (2003) Text parameters in translation: Transitivity and institutional cultures. In E. Hajicova, P. Peter Sgall, Z. Jettmarova, A. Rothkegel, D. Rothfuß-Bastian and Heidrun Gerzymisch-Arbogast (eds), *Textologie und Translation* (Jahrbuch Übersetzen und Dolmetschen 4/2). Tübingen: Narr.

Matthews, P. (1966) The concept of rank in 'Neo-Firthian' grammar. *Journal of Linguistics*, 2, pp. 101–110.

Matthiessen, C. M. I. M. (1979) Hallidayan linguistics. MS. Lund University.

Matthiessen, C. M. I. M. (1981) A grammar and a lexicon for a text production system. *The 19th Annual Meeting of the Association for Computational Linguistics*. Stanford University. Sperry Univac, pp. 49–55.

Matthiessen, C. M. I. M. (1983a) Choosing primary tense in English. *Studies in Language*, 7 (3), pp. 369–430.

Matthiessen, C. M. I. M. (1983b) Systemic grammar in computation: The Nigel case. In *Proceedings of The First Annual Conference of the European Chapter of the Association for Computational Linguistics*. Pisa: ACL, pp. 155–164.

Matthiessen, C. M. I. M. (1984) *Choosing tense in English*. USC/ISI Report: ISI/RR, pp. 84–143.

Matthiessen, C. M. I. M. (1987a) Notes on Akan Phonology: A systemic interpretation. MS.

Matthiessen, C. M. I. M. (1987b) Notes on the organization of the environment of a text generation grammar. In G. Kempen (ed.), *Natural language generation*. Dordrecht: Martinus Nijhof, pp. 253–278.

Matthiessen, C. M. I. M. (1987c) *Rhetorical structure theory and systemic approaches to text organisation*. MS. USC/Information Sciences Institute, Marina Del Rey, CA.

Matthiessen, C. M. I. M. (1988a) Representational issues in systemic functional grammar. In J. Benson and W. Greaves (eds), pp. 136–175.

Matthiessen, C. M. I. M. (1988b) Semantics for a systemic grammar: The chooser and inquiry framework. In J. Benson, M. J. Cummings, and W. Greaves (eds), pp. 221–242.

Matthiessen, C. M. I. M. (1990) Two approaches to semantic interfaces in text generation. In COLING-90. Helsinki: COLING, pp. 322–329.

Matthiessen, C. M. I. M. (1991a) Lexico(grammatical) choice in text-generation. In C. Paris, W. R. Swartout and W. C. Mann (eds), *Natural language generation in artificial intelligence and computational linguistics*. Boston: Kluwer, pp. 249–292.

Matthiessen, C. M. I. M. (1991b) Metafunctional harmony and resonance in syntagmatic organisation. MS.

Matthiessen, C. M. I. M. (1992) Interpreting the textual metafunction. In M. Davies and L. Ravelli (eds), *Advances in systemic linguistics: Recent theory and practice*. London: Frances Pinter, pp. 37–82.

Matthiessen, C. M. I. M. (1993a) Instantial systems and logogenesis. Paper presented at Third National Chinese Systemic Symposium, Hangzhou University, Hangzhou, July 1993. MS.

Matthiessen, C. M. I. M. (1993b) Register in the round: Diversity in a unified theory of register analysis. In M. Ghadessy (ed.), pp. 221–292.

Matthiessen, C. M. I. M. (1994) Paradigmatic organization: 30 years of system networks. Paper presented at ISFC 21, Ghent, Belgium, July 1994. MS.

Matthiessen, C. M. I. M. (1995a) Fuzziness construed in language: A linguistic perspective In *Proceedings of FUZZ/IEEE*. Yokohama, pp. 1871–1878.

Matthiessen, C. M. I. M. (1995b) *Lexicogrammatical cartography: English systems*. Tokyo, Taipei, and Dallas: International Language Sciences Publishers.

Matthiessen, C. M. I. M. (1996) Tense in English seen through systemic functional theory. In M. Berry, C. Butler, R. P. Fawcett and G. Huang (eds), pp. 431–498.

Matthiessen, C. M. I. M. (1998) Construing processes of consciousness: From the commonsense model to the uncommonsense model of cognitive science. In J. R. Martin, and R. Veel (eds), pp. 327–357.

Matthiessen, C. M. I. M. (1999) The system of TRANSITIVITY: An exploratory study of text-based profiles. *Functions of Language*, 6 (1), pp. 1–51.

Matthiessen, C. M. I. M. (2001) The environments of translation in exploring translation and multilingual text production. In E. Steiner and C. Yallop (eds), *Exploring translation and multilingual text production*. Berlin: De Gruyter Mouton, pp. 41–124.

Matthiessen, C. M. I. M. (2002a) Combining clauses into clause complexes: A multifaceted view. In J. Bybee and M. Noonan (eds), *Complex sentences in grammar and discourse: Essays in honor of Sandra A. Thompson*. Amsterdam: Benjamins, pp. 237–322.

Matthiessen, C. M. I. M. (2002b) Lexicogrammar in discourse development: Logogenetic patterns of wording. In G. Huang and Z. Wang (eds), pp. 91–127.

Matthiessen, C. M. I. M. (2004a) Descriptive motifs and generalizations. In A. Caffarel, J. R. Martin and C. M. I. M. Matthiessen (eds), pp. 537–673.

Matthiessen, C. M. I. M. (2004b) The evolution of language: A systemic functional exploration of phylogenetic phases. In G. Williams and A. Lukin (eds), pp. 45–90.

Matthiessen, C. M. I. M. (2005) Remembering Bill Mann. *Journal of Computational Linguistics*, 31 (2), pp. 161–171.

Matthiessen, C. M. I. M. (2006a) Frequency profiles of some basic grammatical systems: An interim report. In S. Hunston and G. Thompson (eds), pp. 103–142.

Matthiessen, C. M. I. M. (2006b) The multimodal page: A systemic functional exploration. In T. D. Royce and W. L. Bowcher (eds), *New directions in the analysis of multimodal discourse*. Hillsdale, NJ: Lawrence Erlbaum, pp. 1–62.

Matthiessen, C. M. I. M. (2007a) Lexicogrammar in systemic functional linguistics: Descriptive and theoretical developments in the 'IFG' tradition since the 1970s. In R. Hasan, C. M. I. M. Matthiessen and J. Webster (eds), *Continuing discourse on language*, Volume 2. London: Equinox, pp. 765–858.

Matthiessen, C. M. I. M. (2007b) The 'architecture' of language according to systemic functional theory: Developments since the 1970s. In R. Hasan, C. M. I. M. Matthiessen, and J. Webster (eds), pp. 505–561.

Matthiessen, C. M. I. M. (2007c) The lexicogrammar of emotion and attitude in English. In Proceedings of the Third International Congress on English Grammar (ICEG 3), Sona College, Salem, Tamil Nadu, India, January 23–27, 2006.

Matthiessen, C. M. I. M. (2009a) Léxico-gramática y colocación lexica: Un estudio sistémico-funcional. [Lexicogrammar and collocation: A systemic functional exploration]. *Revista Signos*, 42 (71), pp. 333–383.

Matthiessen, C. M. I. M. (2009b) Meaning in the making: Meaning potential emerging from acts of meaning. *Language Learning*, 59 (Supplement 1), pp. 211–235.

Matthiessen, C. M. I. M. (2009c) Multisemiotic and context-based register typology: Registerial variation in the complementarity of semiotic systems. In E. Ventola and

A. Guijarro (eds), *The world told and the world shown: Multisemiotic issues*. Oxford: Blackwell, pp. 11–38.

Matthiessen, C. M. I. M. (2010) Systemic functional linguistics developing. *Annual Review of Functional Linguistics* 2: 8–63.

Matthiessen, C. M. I. M. (2012) Systemic functional linguistics as appliable linguistics: Social accountability and critical approaches. *DELTA*, 28, pp. 435–471.

Matthiessen, C. M. I. M. (2014a) Appliable discourse analysis. In Y. Fang and J. Webster, (eds), *Developing systemic functional linguistics: Theory and application*. Sheffield: Equinox, pp. 138–208.

Matthiessen, C. M. I. M. (2014b) Extending the description of process type in delicacy: Verb classes. *Functions of Language*, 21 (2), pp. 139–175.

Matthiessen, C. M. I. M. (2014c) Choice in translation: Metafunctional consideration. In K. Kunz, E. Teich, S. Hansen-Schirra, S. Neumann and P. Daut (eds), *Caught in the middle – language use and translation: A festschrift for Erich Steiner on the occasion of his 60th birthday*. Saarbrücken: Universaar, Saarland University Press, pp. 271–333.

Matthiessen, C. M. I. M. (2015a) Halliday's conception of language as a probabilistic system. In J. J. Webster (ed.), *The Bloomsbury companion to M.A.K. Halliday*. London and New York: Bloomsbury Academic, pp. 203–241.

Matthiessen, C. M. I. M. (2015b) Register in the round: Registerial cartography. *Functional Linguistics* 2(9), pp. 1–48.

Matthiessen, C. M. I. M. (2015c) English lexicogrammar through text: Text typology and lexicogrammatical patterns. In X. Xu and J. Chen (eds), *Language meaning: Grammar, discourse and corpus*. Shanghai: Shanghai Jiao Tong University Press, pp. 1–49.

Matthiessen, C. M. I. M. (2018) The notion of a multilingual meaning potential: A systemic exploration. In A. Baklouti and L. Fontaine (eds), *Perspectives from systemic functional linguistics*. London: Routledge, pp. 90–120.

Matthiessen, C. M. I. M. (forthcoming a) *Systemic functional theory of language: The architecture of grammar*. New Delhi: Decent Books.

Matthiessen, C. M. I. M. (forthcoming b) *The architecture of language according to systemic functional linguistics*. Book MS.

Matthiessen, C. M. I. M. (forthcoming c) *Rhetorical system and structure theory: The semantic system of RHETORICAL RELATIONS. Volume 1: Foundations*. London: Routledge.

Matthiessen, C. M. I. M. (in prep.) *Multilingual introduction to systemic functional grammar*. Book MS.

Matthiessen, C. M. I. M. and Bateman, J. A. (1991) *Systemic linguistics and text generation: Experiences from Japanese and English*. London: Frances Pinter.

Matthiessen, C. M. I. M. and Halliday, M. A. K. (2009) *Systemic functional grammar: A first step into the theory*. Beijing: Higher Education Press.

Matthiessen, C. M. I. M. and Halliday, M. A. K. (in prep.) *Outline of systemic functional linguistics*.

Matthiessen, C. M. I. M. and Nesbitt, C. N. (1996) On the idea of theory-neutral descriptions. In R. Hasan. C. Cloran and D. G. Butt (eds), pp. 39–85.

Matthiessen, C. M. I. M. and Teruya, K. (2015) Grammatical realization of rhetorical relations in different registers. *Word* 61(3), pp. 232–281.

Matthiessen, C. M. I. M. and Thompson, S. (1988) The structure of discourse and 'subordination'. In J. Haiman and S. Thompson (eds), *Clause combining in grammar and discourse*. Amsterdam: Benjamins, pp. 275–329.

Matthiessen, C. M. I. M., Kobayashi, I., and Zeng, L. (1995) Generating multimodal presentations: Resources and processes. MS.

Matthiessen, C. M. I. M., Sondheimer, N., and Tung, Y. (1998a) *On parallelism and the Penman natural language generation system*. University of Southern California/Information Sciences Institute, ISI/RR-88–195.

Matthiessen, C. M. I. M., Zeng, L., Cross, M., Kobayashi, I., Teruya, K. and Wu, C. (1998b) The Multex generator and its environment: Application and development. In *Proceedings of the International Generation Workshop '98*. Niagara-on-the-Lake, pp. 228–237.

Matthiessen, C. M. I. M., Butt, D. G., Cleirigh, C., Lukin, A. and Nesbitt, C. N. (2005) Welcome to Pizza Hut: A case study of multistratal analysis. *Australian Review of Applied Linguistics*, pp. 123–150.

Matthiessen, C. M. I. M., Teruya, K. and Wu, C. (2008) Multilingual studies as a multidimensional space of interconnected language studies. In J. Webster (ed.), pp. 146–221.

Matthiessen, C. M. I. M., Teruya, K., and Lam, M. (2010) *Key terms in systemic functional linguistics*. London and New York: Continuum.

Matthiessen, C. M. I. M., Bowcher, W. and Smith, B. (eds) (in prep.) *Voices around the world: Recent studies in systemic phonology: Languages other than English*. Sheffield: Equinox.

Mauss, M. (1990) *The Gift: The form and reason for exchange in archaic societies*. Translated by W. D. Halls. New York and London: W. W. Norton.

Maynard, S. and Szathmáry, E. (1999) *The origins of life: From the birth of life to the origin of language*. Oxford: Oxford University Press.

McAndrew, J. (2003) *Ideology, heteroglossia, and systemic functional linguistics: On analysis of a NSW Government advertisement*. Ph.D. thesis, Macquarie University.

McCabe, A. (1999) *Theme and thematic patterns in Spanish and English history texts*. Ph.D. thesis, Aston University.

McCabe, A. (2004) Thematic progression patterns and text types in history textbooks. In D. Banks (ed.), *Text and texture: Systemic functional viewpoints on the nature and structure of text*. Paris: L'Harmattan, pp. 215–237.

McDonald, E. (1994) Completive verb compounds in modem Chinese: A new look at an old problem. *Journal of Chinese Linguistics*, 22(2), pp. 317–362.

McDonald, E. (1998) *Clause and verbal group systems in Chinese: A text-based functional approach*. Ph.D. thesis, Macquarie University.

McEnery, T. and Hardie, A. (2011) *Corpus linguistics: Method, theory and practice*. Cambridge: Cambridge University Press.

McGregor, W. (1990) *A functional grammar of Gooniyandi*. Amsterdam and Philadelphia: Benjamins.

McGregor, W. (1992) Clause types in Gooniyandi. *Language Sciences*, 14 (4), pp. 355–385.

McGregor, W. (1996) Attribution and identification in Gooniyandi. In M. Berry, C. Butler, R. P. Fawcett, and G. Huang (eds), pp. 395–430.

Meares, R., Butt, D., Henderson-Brooks, C. and Samir, H. (2005) A poetics of change. *Psychoanalytic Dialogues* 15, pp. 661–680.

Mel'chuk, I. (1982) Lexical functions in lexicographic description. In *Proceedings of the Eighth Annual Meeting of the Berkeley Linguistic Society*, pp. 427–444.

Mellish, C. (1988) Implementing systemic classification by unification. *Journal of Computational Linguistics*, 14 (1), pp. 40–52.

Michael, I. (1970) *English grammatical categories and the tradition to 1800*. Cambridge: Cambridge University Press.

Miller, D. and Turci, M. (eds) (2007) *Language and verbal art revisited: Linguistic approaches to the study of literature*. London: Equinox.

Mitchell, T. (1957) The language of buying and selling in Cyrenaica: A situational statement. *Hesperis*, 26, pp. 31–71.

Mock, C. (1969) *The grammatical units of the Nzema language: A systemic analysis*. Ph.D. thesis, University of London.

Mock, C. (1985) A systemic phonology of Isthmus Zapotec prosodies. In J. Benson and W. Greaves (eds), pp. 349–373.

Mohan, B. (1986) *Language and content*. Reading, MA: Addison-Wesley.

Morley, D. (1993) On transitivity and voice in systemic grammar. *Occasional Papers in Systemic Linguistics*, 7, pp. 71–86.

Mortensen, L. (1992) A transitivity analysis of discourse in dementia of the Alzheimer's type. *Journal of Neurolinguistics*, 7 (4), pp. 309–321.

Mortensen, L. (2003) *Reconstructing the writer: Acquired brain impairment and letters of community membership*. Ph.D. thesis, Macquarie University.

Mortensen, L. (2005) Grammatical complexity in letters written by people with acquired brain impairment. *Australian Review of Applied Linguistics*, 19, pp. 87–102.

Mukařovský, J. (1948) The esthetics of language. Extract from Kapitoly z české poetiky, translated by P. Garvin (1964) *A Prague School reader on esthetics, literary structure and style*. Washington, DC: Georgetown University Press, pp. 31–69.

Munday, J. (2000) Using systemic functional linguistics as an aid to translation between Spanish and English: Maintaining the thematic development of the ST. *Revista Canaria de Estudios Ingleses*, 40, pp. 37–58.

Munday, J. (2001) *Introducing translation studies: Theories and applications*. London and New York: Routledge.

Muntigl, P. (2004) *Narrative counselling: Social and linguistic processes of change*. Amsterdam: Benjamins,

Murcia-Bielsa, S. (2000) The choice of directives expressions in English and Spanish instructions: A semantic network. In E. Ventola (ed.), pp. 117–146.

Mwinlaaru, I., Matthiessen, C. M. I. M. and Akerejola, E. (2018) A system-based typology of MOOD in African languages. In A. Agwuele, and A. Bodomo (eds), *Handbook of African languages*. London: Routledge, pp. 93–117.

Nanri, K. (1993) *An attempt to synthesize two systemic contextual theories through the investigation of the process of the evolution of the discourse semantic structure of the newspaper reporting article*. Ph.D. thesis, University of Sydney.

Nanri, K. (2004) An attempt to elucidate textual organization in Japanese. *JASFL Occasional Papers*, 3 (1), pp. 63–79.

Neale, A. (2002) *More delicate transitivity: Extending the process type system networks for English to include full semantic classifications*. Ph.D. thesis, Cardiff University.

Neale, A. (2006) Matching corpus data and system networks: Using corpora to modify and extend the system networks for TRANSITIVITY in English. In S. Hunston and G. Thompson (eds), pp. 143–163.

Neef, M. and Vater, H. (2006) Concepts of the lexicon in theoretical linguistics. In Wunderlich, D. (ed.), *Advances in the theory of the lexicon*. Berlin: de Gruyter, pp. 27–55.

Nesbitt, C. N. (1994) *Construing linguistic resources: Consumer perspectives*. Ph.D. thesis, University of Sydney.

Nesbitt, C. N. and Plum, G. (1988) Probabilities in a systemic grammar: The clause complex in English. In R. P. Fawcett and D. Young (eds), pp. 6–39.

Neumann, S. (2003) *Textsorten und Übersetzen. Eine Korpusanalyse englischer und deutscher Reiseführer*. Frankfurt u.a.: Peter Lang Verlag.

Neumann, S. and Hansen-Schirra, S. (2005) The CroCo project: Cross-linguistic corpora for the investigation of explicitation in translations. In *Proceedings from the Corpus Linguistics Conference Series*, 1 (1).

Newmeyer, F. (1980) *Linguistic theory in America: The first quarter century of transformational generative grammar*. New York: Academic Press,

Nooteboom, S. (1997) The prosody of speech: Melody and rhythm. In W. Hardcastle and J. Laver (eds), *The handbook of phonetic sciences*. Oxford: Blackwell, pp. 640–673.

Nord, C. (2005) *Text analysis in translation: Theory methodology, and didactic application of a model for translation-oriented text analysis*, 2nd edition. Amsterdam and New York: Rodopi.

Nwogu, K. (1990) *Discourse variation in medical texts: Schema, theme and cohesion*. Ph.D. thesis, Aston University.

O'Connor, J. D. (1973) *Phonetics*. Harmondsworth: Penguin.

O'Donnell, M. (1994) *Sentence analysis and generation: A systemic perspective*. Ph.D. thesis, Sydney University.

O'Donnell, M. (2009) Resources and courses. In M. A. K. Halliday and J. Webster (eds), pp. 216–228.

O'Donnell, M. and Bateman, J. A. (2005) SFL in computational contexts. In R. Hasan, C. M. I. M. Matthiessen and J. Webster (eds), pp. 343–382.

O'Donnell, M. and Sefton, P. (1995) Modelling telephonic interaction: A dynamic approach. *Journal of Applied Linguistics* 10 (1): 63–78.

O'Halloran, K. (2005) *Mathematical discourse language, symbolism and visual images*. London and New York: Continuum.

O'Toole, M. (1994) *The language of displayed art*. London: Leicester University Press.

Ochs, E., Schegloff, E. A. and Thompson, S. A. (eds) (1996) *Interaction and grammar.* Cambridge: Cambridge University Press.

Ortega, L. (2009) *Understanding second language acquisition.* London: Hodder Education.

Ortega, L. and H. Byrnes (eds) (2008) *The longitudinal study of advanced L2 capacities.* New York and London: Routledge.

Oshima, M. (2004) *Functions and meanings of the English language viewed from systemic functional grammar.* Tokyo: Eihoosha.

Ouyang, X. (1986) *Clause complex in Chinese.* MA thesis, University of Sydney.

Owens, J. (1988) *The foundations of grammar: An introduction to medieval Arabic grammatical theory.* Amsterdam: John Benjamins.

Pagano, A., Magalhães, C. and Alves, F. (2004) Towards the construction of a multilingual, multifunctional corpus: Factors in the design and application of CORDIALL. *Tradterm,* São Paulo 10, pp. 143–162.

Painter, C. (1984) *Into the mother tongue: A case study in early language development.* London: Frances Pinter.

Painter, C. (1999) *Learning through language in early childhood.* London: Cassell.

Painter, C. (2003) Developing attitude: An ontogenetic perspective on appraisal. *Text,* 23 (2), pp. 183–209.

Painter, C. (2009) Language development. In M. A. K. Halliday and J. Webster (eds), pp. 87–103.

Painter, C., Derewianka, B., and Torr, J. (2007) From microfunction to metaphor: Learning language and learning through language. In R. Hasan, C. M. I. M. Matthiessen and J. Webster (eds), pp. 563–588.

Parodi, G. (ed.) (2010) *Discourse genres in Spanish: Academic and professional connections.* Amsterdam: Benjamins.

Parsons, G. (1995) *Measuring cohesion in English texts: The relationship between cohesion and coherence.* Ph.D. thesis, Nottingham University.

Parsons, G. (1996) The development of the concept of cohesive harmony. In M. Berry, C. Butler, R. P. Fawcett, and G. Huang (eds), pp. 585–599.

Patpong, P. (2005) *A systemic functional interpretation of Thai grammar: An exploration of Thai narrative discourse.* Ph.D. thesis, Macquarie University.

Patpong, P. (2006) *A systemic functional interpretation of Thai grammar: An exploration of Thai narrative discourse.* Ph.D. thesis, Macquarie University.

Patten, T. (1988) *Systemic text generation as problem solving.* Cambridge: Cambridge University Press.

Patten, T. and Ritchie, G. (1987) A formal model of systemic grammar. In G. Kempen (ed.), *Natural language generation.* Dordrecht: Martinus Nijhof. 279–299.

Pearce, J., Thornton, G., and Mackay, D. (1989) The programme in linguistics and English teaching, University College London, 1964–1971. In R. Hasan and J. R. Martin (eds), pp. 329–383.

Peng, W. (1993) A thematic analysis of two Chinese essays. *Journal of Foreign Languages,* 2, pp. 140–157.

Phillips, J. (1986) The development of modality and hypothetical meaning: Nigel 1; 7½ – 2; 7½. *Working Papers in Linguistics* (University of Sydney), 3, pp. 3–20.

Pierrehumbert, J. (2001) Stochastic phonology. *Glot International*, 5 (6), pp. 196–207.

Pierrehumbert, J. (2003) Probabilistic phonology: Discrimination and robustness. In R. Bod, J. Hay, and S. Jannedy (eds), pp. 177–228.

Pike, K. L. (1943) *Phonetics: A critical analysis of phonetic theory and a technique for the practical description of sounds*. Michigan: University of Michigan Publications.

Pike, K. (1945) *The intonation of American English*. Ann Arbor, MI: University of Michigan Press.

Pike, K. (1948) *Tone languages: A technique for determining the number and type of pitch contrasts in a language, with studies in tonemic substitution and fusion*. Ann Arbor, MI: University of Michigan Press.

Pike, K. L. (1959) Language as particle, wave and field. *Texas Quarterly* 2(2): 37–54. Reprinted in *Kenneth L. Pike: Selected writings*, edited by Brend, R. M. The Hague: Mouton (1972), pp. 129–143.

Plum, G. and Cowling, A. (1987) Social constraints on grammatical variables: Tense choice in English. In R. Steele and T. Threadgold (eds), pp. 281–305.

Pollard, C. and Sag, I. (1993) *Head-driven phrase structure grammar*. Chicago, IL and London: The University of Chicago Press.

Posner, M. I. (ed.) (1989) *Foundations of cognitive science*. Cambridge, Mass.: The MIT Press.

Postal, P. (1964) *Constituent structure: A study of contemporary models of syntactic descriptions*. Bloomington, IN: Indiana University.

Poynton, C. (1984) Forms and functions: Names as vocatives. *Nottingham Linguistic Circular*, 13, pp. 1–34.

Poynton, C. (1996) Amplification as a grammatical prosody: Attitudinal modification in the nominal group. In M. Berry, C. Butler, R. P. Fawcett, and G. Huang (eds), pp. 211–229.

Prakasam, V. (1972) *A systemic treatment of certain aspects of Telugu phonology*. D.Phil. thesis, University of York.

Prakasam, V. (1977) An outline of the theory of systemic phonology. *International Journal of Dravidian Linguistics*, 6, pp. 24–42.

Prakasam, V. (1985) *The linguistic spectrum*. Patiala, India: Punjabi University.

Prakasam, V. (1987) Aspects of word phonology. In M. A. K. Halliday and R. P. Fawcett (eds), pp. 272–287.

Prakasam, V. (1999) *Semiotics of language, literature and culture*. New Delhi: Allied Publishers Limited.

Prakasam, V. (2004) Metafunctional profile of Telugu. In Caffarel, A., Martin, J. R. and Matthiessen, C. M. I. M. (ed.), *Language typology: A functional perspective*. Amsterdam: Benjamins, pp. 433–478.

Price, H. (2003) *Blueprints for design in verbal art. Mapping the semantics of space in The English Patient*. Ph.D. thesis, Macquarie University.

Prior, A. (1967) *Past, present and future*. Oxford: Clarendon Press.

Qu, C. (2018) Sources of Otto Jespersen's Sound Symbolism from various disciplines: A case of Linguistic Historiography. *Journal of Literature and Art Studies* 8 (4), pp. 628–634.

Rada, E. (1989) *Writing about art: A linguistic consideration of art history and related genres.* Ph.D. thesis, Sydney University.

Rashidi, L. (1992) Towards an understanding of the notion of Theme: An example from Dari. In M. Davies and L. Ravelli (eds), pp. 189–205.

Ravelli, L. (1985) *Metaphor, mode and complexity: An exploration of co-varying patterns.* BA Honours thesis, University of Sydney.

Ravelli, L. (1988) Grammatical metaphor: An initial analysis. In E. Steiner and R. Veltman (eds), pp. 133–147.

Ravelli, L. (1991) *Language from a dynamic perspective: Models in general and grammar in particular*. Ph.D. thesis, Birmingham University.

Ravelli, L. (1995) A dynamic perspective: Implications for metafunctional interaction and an understanding of Theme. In R. Hasan and P. H. Fries (eds), pp. 187–235.

Ravelli, L. (2006) *Museum texts: Communication frameworks*. London: Routledge.

Ravelli, L. (2007) Genre and the museum exhibition. *Linguistics and the Human Sciences,* 2 (2), pp. 299–317.

Reichenbach, H. (1947) *Elements of symbolic logic*. London: Macmillan.

Ren, S. (1993) The narrative structure of *The Armies of the Night*. In Y. Zhu (ed.), *Language, text, context*. Beijing: Tsinghua University Press, pp. 225–240.

Rinner, S. and Weigert, A. (2006) From sports to the EU economy: Integrating curricula through genre-based content courses. In H. Byrnes, H. Weger-Gunthrap, and J. Sprang (eds), *Educating for advanced foreign language capacities: Constructs, curriculum, instruction, assessment*. Washington, DC: Georgetown University Press, pp. 136–151.

Rissanen, M. (1991) Spoken language and the history of do-periphrasis. In D. Kastovsky (ed.), *Historical English syntax*. Berlin and New York: de Gruyter, pp. 321–342.

Robins, R. (1959) In defense of WP. *Transactions of the Philological Society*, pp. 116–144.

Robins, R. and McLeod, N. (1956) Five Yurok Songs: A Musical and Textual Analysis. *Bulletin of the School of Oriental and African Studies*, University of London, Vol. 18, No. 3 (In Honour of J. R. Firth), pp. 592–609.

Rose, D. (1996) Pitjantjatjara processes: An Australian experiential grammar. In R. Hasan, C. Cloran, and D. G. Butt (eds), pp. 287–323.

Rose, D. (1997) Science, technology and technical literacies. In F. Christie, F. and J. R. Martin (eds), pp. 40–72.

Rose, D. (1998) Science discourse and industry hierarchy. In J. R. Martin and R. Veel (eds), pp. 236–265.

Rose, D. (2001a) Some variations in theme across languages. *Functions of Language*, 8 (1), pp. 109–145.

Rose, D. (2001b) *The Western Desert Code: An Australian cryptogrammar*. Canberra: Pacific Linguistics.

Rose, D. (2004) Metafunctional profile of Pitjantjatjara. In Caffarel, A., Martin, J. R. and Matthiessen, C. M. I. M. (eds), *Language typology: A functional perspective*. Amsterdam: Benjamins, pp. 479–536.

Rose, D. (2005) Narrative and the origins of discourse: Construing experience in stories around the world. *Australian Review of Applied Linguistics*, 19, pp. 151–173.

Rose, S. (1997) *Lifelines: Biology, freedom, determinism*. Harmondsworth: Penguin.

Rose, D. and Martin, J. R. (2012) *Learning to write, reading to learn: Genre, knowledge and pedagogy in the Sydney school*. (Equinox Textbooks and Surveys in Linguistics). London: Equinox.

Rothery, J. (1990) *Story writing in primary school: Assessing narrative type genres*. Ph.D. thesis, University of Sydney.

Rothery, J. and Stenglin, M. (1997) Entertaining and instructing: Exploring experience through story. In F. Christie and J. R. Martin (eds), pp. 231–263.

Royce, T. and Bowcher, W. (eds) (2006) *New directions in the analysis of multimodal discourse*. Hillsdale, NJ: Lawrence Erlbaum.

Ruppenhofer, J., Ellsworth, M., Petruk, M., Johnson, C., and Scheffczyk, J. (2006) *FrameNet II: Extended theory and practice*. Berkeley, CA: International Computer Science Institute.

Sag, I. (2010) Sign-based construction grammar: An informal synopsis. In H. Boas and I. Sag (eds), *Sign-based construction grammar*. Stanford, CA: Center for the Study of Language and Information, pp. 69–202.

Sag, I. and Wasow, T. (1999) *Syntactic theory: A formal introduction*. Stanford, CA: CLSI Publications.

Sag, I., Kaplan, R., Karttunen, L., Kay, M., Pollard, C., Shieber, S., and Zaenen, A. (1986) Unification and grammatical theory. In *Proceedings of the Fifth Annual Meeting of the West Coast Conference on Formal Linguistics*. Stanford: SLA, CSLI Publications, pp. 238–254.

Sampson, G. (2001) *Empirical linguistics*. London and New York: Continuum.

Sasaki, M. (1997) Nihongo ni okeru theme no koozoo [Thematic structure in Japanese]. *Aichi Gakuin Tankidaigaku Kenkyu* 1, pp. 144–158.

Schachter, P. (1981) Daughter-dependency grammar. In E. Moravcsik and J. Wirth (eds), *Syntax and semantics 13: Current approaches to syntax*. New York: Academic Press, pp. 267–300.

Schiffrin, D., Tannen, D., and Hamilton, H. (2001) *The handbook of discourse analysis*. Oxford: Blackwell.

Schleppegrell, M. (2000) How can SFL inform writing instruction: The grammar of expository essays. *Revista Canaria de Estudios Ingleses*, 40, pp. 171–188.

Schleppegrell, M. (2004) *The language of schooling: A functional linguistics approach*. Mahwah, NJ: Lawrence Erlbaum.

Schleppegrell, M. and Colombi, C. (eds) (2002) *Developing advanced literacy in first and second languages: Meaning with power*. Mahwah, NJ: Lawrence Erlbaum.

Seuren, P. (1998) *Western linguistics: An historical introduction*. Oxford: Blackwell.

Sheldrake, R. (1988) *The presence of the past: Morphic resonance and the habits of nature*. London: Collins.

Shieber, S. (1986) *An introduction to unification-based approaches to grammar*. Stanford, CA: CSLI Publications.

Shore, S. (1992) *Aspects of a systemic functional grammar of Finnish*. Ph.D. thesis, Macquarie University.

Shore, S. (1996) Process types in Finnish: Implicate order, covert categories and prototypes. In R. Hasan, C. Cloran, and D. G. Butt (eds), pp. 237–265.

Shore, S. (2001) Teaching translation. In E. Steiner and C. Yallop (eds), pp. 249– 276.

Shum, M. (2006) Developing a genre-based approach for teaching subject specialisms in Chinese in post-colonial Hong Kong. *Australian Review of Applied Linguistics*, 29 (1), pp. 1–22.

Simon-Vandenbergen, A. Davidse, K., and Noël, D. (eds) (1997) *Reconnecting language: Morphology and syntax in functional perspectives*. Amsterdam: Benjamins.

Simon-Vandenbergen, A., Taverniers, M., and Ravelli, L. (eds) (2003) *Grammatical metaphor: Views from systemic functional linguistics*. Amsterdam: John Benjamins.

Sinclair, J. and Coulthard, M. (1975) *Towards an analysis of discourse: The English used by teachers and pupils*. London: Oxford University Press.

Slade, D. (1996) *The texture of casual conversation in English*. Ph.D. thesis, University of Sydney.

Slade, D., Scheeres, H., Manidis, M., Matthiessen, C. M. I. M., Iedema, R., Herke, M., McGregor, J., Dustan R. and Stein-Parbury, J. (2008) Emergency communication: The discursive challenges facing emergency clinicians and patients in hospital emergency departments. *Discourse and Communication* 2(3): 289–316.

Slade, D., Manidis, M., McGregor, J., Scheeres, H., Chandler, E., Stein-Parbury, J., Dunstan, R., Herke, M. and Matthiessen, C. M. I. M. (2015) *Communication in hospital emergency departments*. Berlin: Springer.

Smedegaard, F. (2002) *Verden i sproget: Transitivitet i dansk en systemisk funktionel beskrivelse*. Ph.D. thesis, University of Southern Denmark.

Smith, B. (2005) *Intonational systems and register: A multidimensional exploration*. Ph.D. thesis, Macquarie University.

Smith, B. (2008) Review of *Intonation in the grammar of English*, by M. A. K. Halliday and W. S. Greaves. *Linguistics and the Human Sciences*, 4 (1), pp. 91–96.

Souter, D. (1996) *A corpus-trained parser for systemic-functional syntax*, Ph.D. thesis, University of Leeds, UK.

Steele, R. and Threadgold, T. (eds) (1987) *Language topics: Essays in honour of Michael Halliday*. Amsterdam: Benjamins.

Steels, L. (1998) Synthesizing the origins of language and meaning using coevolution, self-organisation and level formation. In J. Hurford, M. Studdert-Kennedy and C. Knight (eds), *Approaches to the evolution of language: Social and cognitive bases*. Cambridge: Cambridge University Press, pp. 384–404.

Steels, L. (ed.) (2012) *Design patterns in fluid construction grammar*. Amsterdam and New York: Benjamins.

Steiner, E. (1985) Working with transitivity: System networks in semantic-grammatical descriptions. In J. Benson and W. Greaves (eds), pp. 163–184.

Steiner, E. (1988a) Language and music as semiotic systems: The example of a folk ballad. In J. Benson, M. J. Cummings, and W. Greaves (eds), pp. 393–441.

Steiner, E. (1988b) Semantic relations in EUROTRA-D and LFG – a comparison. In P. Schmidt, C. Zelinsky-Wibbelt, and E. Steiner (eds), *From syntax to semantics – insights from machine translation*. London: Frances Pinter.

Steiner, E. (1991) *A functional perspective on language, action and interpretation*. Berlin and New York: de Gruyter.

Steiner, E. (2004) *Translated texts: Properties, variants, evaluations*. Frankfurt am Main, Berlin, Bern, Bruxelles, New York, Oxford, Wien: Peter Lang.

Steiner, E. (2005a) Halliday and translation theory: Enhancing the options, broadening the range, and keeping the ground In R. Hasan, C. M. I. M. Matthiessen and J. Webster (eds), pp. 481–500.

Steiner, E. (2005b) The heterogeneity of individual languages as a translation problem. In H. Kittel, A. Frank, N. Greiner, T. Hermans, H. Koller, J. Lambert and F. Paul (eds), *Translation: An international encyclopedia of translation studies*. Berlin and New York: de Gruyter, pp. 446–454.

Steiner, E. and Ramm, W. (1995) On theme as a grammatical notion for German. *Functions of Language*, 2 (1), pp. 57–93.

Steiner, E. and Teich, E. (2004) Metafunctional profile of German. In Caffarel, A., Martin, J. R. and Matthiessen, C. M. I. M. (eds), *Language typology: A functional perspective*. Amsterdam: Benjamins, pp. 139–184.

Steiner, E. and Veltman, R. (eds) (1988) *Pragmatics, discourse and text: Explorations in systemic semantics*. London: Frances Pinter.

Steiner, E. and Yallop, C. (eds) (2001) *Exploring translation and multilingual text production: Beyond content*. Berlin and New York: de Gruyter.

Stillar, G. (1992) Phasal analysis and multiple-inheritance: An appeal for charity. *Carleton Papers in Applied Language Studies*, 9, pp. 104–128.

Stillar, G. (1998) *Analyzing everyday texts: Discourse, rhetoric and social perspective*. London: Sage.

Stillings, N., Feinstein, M., Garfield, J., Rissland, E., Rosenbaum, D., Weisler, S., and Baker-Ward, L. (1987) *Cognitive science: An introduction*. Cambridge, MA: The MIT Press.

Stockwell, R., Schachter, P., and Partee, B. (1973) *The major syntactic structures of English*. New York: Holt, Rinehart and Winston.

Stuart-Smith, V. (2001) *Rhetorical structure theory as a model of semantics: A corpus-based analysis from a systemic functional perspective*. Ph.D. thesis, Macquarie University.

Sutjaja, I. (1988) *The nominal group in Bahasa Indonesia*. Ph.D. thesis, Sydney University.

Svartvik, J. (1965) *On voice in the English verb*. The Hague: Mouton.

Tam, H. (2004) *A systemic functional interpretation of Cantonese clause grammar*. Ph.D. thesis, University of Sydney.

Taverniers, M. (2003) Grammatical metaphor in SFL: A historiography of the introduction and initial study of the concept. In A. Simon-Vandenbergen, M. Taverniers, and L. Ravelli (eds), pp. 5–33.

Taylor Torsello, C. (1996) Theme as the interpreter's path indicator through the unfolding text. *The Interpreters Newsletter*, VII, pp. 113–149.

Taylor Torsello, C. (1997) Linguistics, discourse analysis and interpretation. In Y. Gambier, D. Gile and C. Taylor (eds), *Conference interpreting: Current trends in research*. Amsterdam: John Benjamins, pp. 167–186.

Taylor, C. (1998) *Language to language: A practical and theoretical guide for Italian/English translators*. Cambridge: Cambridge University Press.

Taylor, C. (2003) Multimodal transcription in the analysis, translation and subtitling of Italian films. *The Translator*, 9 (2), pp. 191–205.

Taylor, C. and Baldry, A. (2001) Computer assisted text analysis and translation: A functional approach in the analysis and translation of advertising texts. In E. Steiner and C. Yallop (eds), pp. 277–305.

Tebble, H. (1999) The tenor of consultant physicians: Implications for medical interpreting. *The Translator*, 5 (2), pp. 179–200.

Teich, E. (1999) *Systemic functional grammar in natural language generation: Linguistic description and computational representation*. London: Cassell.

Teich, E. (2003) *Cross-linguistic variation in system and text*. Berlin and New York: de Gruyter.

Teich, E. (2009) Computational linguistics. In M. A. K. Halliday and J. Webster (eds), pp. 113–227.

Teich, E., Watson, C., and Pereira, C. (2000) Matching a tone-based and tune-based approach to English intonation for concept-to-speech generation. In *Proceedings of the 18th Conference on Computational Linguistics*, Volume 2. Morristown, NJ: Association for Computational Linguistics, pp. 829–835.

Tench, P. (1990) *The roles of intonation in English discourse*. Frankfurt: Peter Lang.

Tench, P. (1992a) From prosodic analysis to systemic phonology. In P. Tench (ed.), pp. 1–17.

Tench, P. (ed.) (1992b) *Studies in systemic phonology*. London and New York: Frances Pinter.

Tench, P. (1996) *The intonation systems of English*. London: Cassell.

Teruya, K. (1998) *An exploration into the world of experience: A systemic functional interpretation of the grammar of Japanese*. Ph.D. thesis, Macquarie University.

Teruya, K. (2004a) Metafunctional profile of Japanese. In Caffarel, A., Martin, J. R. and Matthiessen, C. M. I. M. (eds), *Language typology: A functional perspective*. Amsterdam: Benjamins, pp. 185–254.

Teruya, K. (2004b) Gaikoku kawase kiji no domein no moderuka: kinooteki bunseki [The domain modelling of foreign exchange reports: A functional analysis]. *JASFL Occasional Papers*, 3 (1), pp. 225–249.

Teruya, K. (2007) *A systemic functional grammar of Japanese*, two volumes. London and New York: Continuum.

Teruya, K. (2009) Grammar as a gateway into discourse: A systemic functional approach to SUBJECT, THEME, and logic. In special issue of *Linguistics and Education: Instructed foreign language acquisition as meaning-making: A systemic-functional approach*. In H. Byrnes (ed.) *Linguistics and Education 20*, pp. 67–79.

Teruya, K. and Matthiessen, C. M. I. M. (2015) Halliday in relation to language comparison and typology. In J. J. Webster (ed.) (2015a), pp. 427–452.

Teruya, K., Akerejoia, E., Andersen, T., Caffarel, A., Lavid, J., Matthiessen, C. M. I. M., Petersen, U. Patpong, P., and Smedegaard, F. (2007) Typology of MOOD: A text-based and system-based functional view. In R. Hasan, C. M. I. M. Matthiessen and J. Webster (eds), pp. 859–920.

Thai, M. (1998) *A systemic functional interpretation of Vietnamese grammar*. Ph.D. thesis, Macquarie University.

Thai, M. D. (2004) Metafunctional profile of the grammar of Vietnamese. *Language typology: A functional perspective*. In Caffarel, A., Martin, J. R. and Matthiessen, C. M. I. M. (eds), *Language typology: A functional perspective*. Amsterdam: Benjamins, pp. 397–431.

Thibault, P. J. (1984) *Narrative structure and narrative function in Vladimir Nabokov's Ada*. Ph.D. thesis, University of Sydney.

Thibault, P. J. (1988) Knowing what you're told by the agony aunts: Language function, gender difference and the structure of knowledge and belief in the personal columns. In D. Birch and M. O'Toole (eds), *Functions of style*. London: Frances Pinter, pp. 205–233.

Thibault, P. J. (1991) *Social semiotics as praxis: Text social meaning making and Nabokov's 'Ada'*. Minneapolis, MN: University of Minnesota Press.

Thibault, P. J. (1993) Using language to think interpersonally: Experiential meaning and the cryptogrammar of subjectivity and agency in English. *Cultural Dynamics*, 6 (1–2), pp. 131–187.

Thibault, P. J. (1995) The interpersonal grammar of mood and the ecosocial dynamics of the semiotic exchange process. In R. Hasan and P. H. Fries (eds), pp. 51–89.

Thibault, P. J. (2000) The dialogic integration of the brain in social semiosis: Edelman and the case for downward causation. *Mind, Culture and Activity*, 7 (4), pp. 291–311.

Thibault, P. J. (2004a) *Agency and consciousness in discourse: Self-other dynamics as a complex system*. London and New York: Continuum.

Thibault, P. J. (2004b) *Brain, mind and the signifying body: An ecosocial semiotic theory*. London and New York: Continuum.

Thoma, C. (2004) *The application of register theory in the translation of Cypriot folk tales into English*. Ph.D. thesis, University of Bremen.

Thoma, C. (2006) *Combining functional linguistics and Skopos theory. A case study of Greek Cypriot and British folktales*. Frankfurt am Main: Peter Lang.

Thomas, S. and Hawes, T. (1997) *Theme in academic and media discourse*. University of Nottingham: Monographs in systemic linguistics, Number 8.

Thompson, G. (1996) *Introducing functional grammar*. London: Hodder Education.

Thompson, G. (2007) Unfolding theme: The development of clausal and textual perspectives on theme. In R. Hasan, C. M. I. M. Matthiessen, and J. Webster (eds), pp. 671–696.

Thompson, S. and Mann, W. C. (eds) (1992) *Discourse description: Diverse analyses of a fund-raising text*. Amsterdam: Benjamins.

Thomson, E. (1998) Thematic development in *Noruwei no Mori*: Arguing the need to account for co-referential ellipsis. *JASFL Occasional Papers* 1 (1), pp. 5–24.

Thomson, E. (2001) Themes, T-units and method of development: An examination of the news story in Japanese. *JASFL Occasional Papers* 2, pp. 39–62.

Thomson, E. and White, P. (eds) (2008) *Communicating conflict: Multilingual case studies of the news media*. London: Continuum.

Titscher, S., Meyer, M., Wodak, R., and Vetter, E. (2000) *Methods of text and discourse analysis*. London: Sage.

Tognini-Bonelli, E. (2001) *Corpus linguistics at work*. Amsterdam: Benjamins.

Toolan, M. (1998) *Language in literature: An introduction to stylistics*. London: Hodder Arnold.

Toolan, M. (2001) *Narrative: A critical linguistic introduction*. 2nd edition. New York: Routledge.

Torr, J. (1997) *From child tongue to mother tongue: A case study of language development in the first two and a half years*. University of Nottingham: Monographs in systemic linguistics, Number 9.

Torr, J. (1998) The development of modality in the pre-school years: Language as a vehicle for understanding possibilities and obligations in everyday life. *Functions of Language*, 5 (2), pp. 157–178.

Tozzer, A. (1921) *A Maya grammar*. New York: Dover.

Trevarthen, C. (1979) Communication and cooperation in early infancy: A description of primary intersubjectivity. In M. Bullow (eds), *Before speech: The beginning of interpersonal communication*. Cambridge: Cambridge University Press, pp. 321–347.

Trevarthen, C. (1987) Sharing making sense: Intersubjectivity and the making of an infant's meaning. In R. Steele and T. Threadgold (eds), pp. 177–199.

Trew, T. (1979) Theory and ideology at work. In Fowler, R., Hodge, B., Kress, G. and Trew T. (1979) *Language and control*. London: Routledge and Kegan Paul, pp. 94–116.

Trubetzkoy, N. S. (1939) *Grundzüge der Phonologie*. (Travaux au Cercle Linguistique de Prague 7). Prague: Jednota československých matematiků a fysiků.

Tsui, A. (1989) Systemic choices and discourse processes. *Word*, 40 (1–2), pp. 163–188.

Tucker, G. H. (1996) Cultural classification and system networks: A systemic functional approach to lexical semantics. In M. Berry, C. Butler, R. P. Fawcett, and G. Huang (eds), pp. 533–566.

Tucker, G. H. (1997a) A functional lexicogrammar of adjectives. *Functions of Language*, 4 (2), pp. 215–250.

Tucker, G. H. (1997b) *The lexicogrammar of adjectives: A systemic functional approach to lexis*. London: Cassell.

Tucker, G. H. (1998) *The lexicogrammar of adjectives: A systemic functional approach to lexis*. London: Cassell.

Tucker, G. H. (2007) Between grammar and lexis: Towards a systemic functional account of phraseology. In R. Hasan, C. M. I. M. Matthiessen, and J. Webster (eds), pp. 953–977.

Turner, G. (1973) Social class and children's language of control at age five and age seven. In B. Bernstein (ed.), *Class, codes and control*, Volume 2, London: Routledge and Kegan Paul, pp. 135–201.

Turner, G. (1987) Sociosemantic networks and discourse structure. In M. A. K. Halliday and R. P. Fawcett (eds), pp. 64–93.

Twaddell, W. F. (1935) On defining the phoneme. *Language*, 11 (1), pp. 5–62.

Unsworth, L. (1997) Scaffolding reading of science explanations: Accessing the grammatical and visual forms of specialized knowledge. *Reading*, 31 (3), pp. 30–42.

Unsworth, L. (2006) *E-literature for children: Enhancing digital literacy learning*. London Routledge.

van der Hulst, H. (2013) Discoverers of the Phoneme. In K. Allen (ed.), *Oxford handbook of the history of linguistics*. Oxford: Oxford University Press, pp. 167–190.

van der Hulst, H. and Ritter, N. A. (eds) (1999) *The syllable: Views and facts*. Berlin and New York: Mouton de Gruyter.

van Dijk, T. A. (ed.) (1985) *Handbook of discourse analysis*. New York: Academic Press.

van Dijk, T. A. (ed.) (1997) *Discourse: A multidisciplinary introduction*. London: Sage.

van Dijk, T. A. (2001) Critical discourse analysis. In D. Tannen, D. Schiffrin and H. Hamilton (eds), *Handbook of discourse analysis*. Oxford: Blackwell, pp. 352–371.

van Leeuwen, T. (1985) Persuasive speech: The intonation of the live radio commercial. *Australian Journal of Communication*, 7, pp. 25–35.

van Trijp, R., Steels, L., Beuls, K. and Wellens, P. (2012) Fluid construction grammar: The new kid on the block. In *Proceedings of the 13th Conference of the European Chapter of the Association for Computational Linguistics*. pp. 63–68.

Varela, F., Thompson, E. and Rosch, E. (1991) *The embodied mind: Cognitive science and human experience*. Cambridge, MA: The MIT Press.

Veel, R. (1997) Learning how to mean – scientifically speaking: Apprenticeship into scientific discourse in the secondary school. In Christie, F. and Martin, J. R. (eds) *Genre and institutions: Social processes in the workplace and school*. London: Cassell, pp. 161–195.

Veloso, F. O. D. (2006) *'Never awake a sleeping giant ...': A multimodal analysis of post 9–11 comic books*. Ph.D. thesis, Universidade Federal de Santa, Catarina.

Ventola, E. (1987) *The structure of social interaction: A systemic approach to the semiotics of service encounters*. London: Frances Pinter.

Ventola, E. (1995) Thematic development and translation. In M. Ghadessy (ed.), pp. 85–104.

Ventola, E. (ed.) (2000) *Discourse and community: Doing functional linguistics*. Tübingen: Gunter Narr Verlag.

Ventola, E. and Guijarro, A. J. M. (eds) (2009) *The world shown and the world told*. Basingstoke: Palgrave Macmillan.

Ventola, E. and Mauranen, A. (eds) (1996) *Academic writing: Intercultural and textual issues*. Amsterdam and Philadelphia: Benjamins.

Ventola, E., Charles, C. and Kaltenbacher, M. (eds) (2004) *Perspectives on multimodality*. Amsterdam: Benjamins.

Vygotsky, L. (1962) *Language and thought*. Edited and translated by E. Hanfmann and G. Vakar. Cambridge, MA: The MIT Press.

Walsh, J. (2002) *A linguistic perspective on the development of identity*. Doctor of Education thesis, University of Technology, Sydney.

Wan Y. (2010) Call centre discourse: Graduation in relation to voice quality and attitudinal profile. In G. Forey and J. Lockwood (eds), *Globalization, communication and the workplace: Talking across the world*. London: Continuum, pp. 106–124.

Wan, Y. (2011) *Call centre communication: An analysis of interpersonal meaning*. Ph.D. thesis, Hong Kong Polytechnic University.

Wang, X. (2008) *Clause boundary shifts in interpreting: Chinese-English*. MA thesis, Macquarie University.

Wanner, L. (1997) *Exploring lexical resources for text generation in a systemic functional language model*. (Dissertation zur Erlangung des akademischen Grades eines Doktors der Philosophie der Philosophischen Fakultät der Universität des Saarlandes.) Ph.D. thesis, Universität des Saarlandes.

Warner, A. (2005) Why DO dove: Evidence for register variation in Early Modern English negatives. *Language Variation and Change*, 17, pp. 257–280.

Washitake, M. (2004) An analysis of narrative: Its generic structure and lexicogrammatical resources. *JASFL Occasional Papers*, 3 (1), pp. 173–188.

Wasow, T. (1977) Transformations and the lexicon. In P. Culicover, A. Akmajian and T. Wasow (eds), *Formal syntax*. New York: Academic Press, pp. 327–360.

Watson, P. (2001) *A terrible beauty: The people and ideas that shaped the modern mind – a history*. London: Weidenfeld & Nicolson.

Watt, D. L. E. (1992) An instrumental analysis of English nuclear tones. In P. Tench (ed.), pp. 135–160.

Watt, D. L. E. (1994) *The phonology and semology of intonation in English*. Bloomington, Indiana University Linguistics Club Publications.

Webster, J. (2005) M. A. K. Halliday: The early years, 1925–1970. In R. Hasan, C. M. I. M. Matthiessen and J. Webster (eds), pp. 3–14.

Webster, J. (ed.) (2008) *Meaning in context: Implementing intelligent applications of language studies*. London and New York: Continuum.

Weinreich, H. (1972) Die Textpartitur als heuristische Methode. *Der Deutschunterricht*, 24 (4), pp. 43–60.

Weinreich, U. (1980) *On semantics*. In W. Labov and B. S. Weinreich (eds) Philadelphia, PA: University of Pennsylvania Press.

Wells, G. (1994a) Learning and teaching 'scientific concepts: Vygotsky's ideas revisited. Paper presented at the Conference, Vygotsky and the Human Sciences, Moscow, September 1994.

Wells, G. (1994b) The complementary contributions of Halliday and Vygotsky to a 'language-based theory of learning'. *Linguistics and Learning*, 6, pp. 41–90.

Whitaker, R. (1995) Theme, processes and the realization of meanings in academic articles. In M. Ghadessy (ed.), pp. 105–128.

White, P. (1997) Death, disruption and the moral order: The narrative impulse in mass-'hard news' reporting. In F. Christie and J. R. Martin (eds), pp. 101–133.

White, P. (1998) Extended reality, proto-nouns and the vernacular: Distinguishing the technological from the scientific. In J. R. Martin, and R. Veel (eds), pp. 266–296.

Wierzbicka, A. (1987) *English speech act verbs: A semantic dictionary*. New York: Academic Press.

Wignell, P., Martin, J. R. and Eggins, S. (1989) The discourse of geography: Ordering and explaining the experiential world. *Linguistics and Education*, 1(4): 359–391.

Williams, G. (1995a) A package of information. In J. Brockman (ed.), *The third culture*. New York: Touchstone Books, pp. 38–50.

Williams, G. (1995b) *Joint book reading and literacy pedagogy: A socio-semantic examination*. Ph.D. thesis, Macquarie University.

Williams, G. (2000) Children's literature, children and uses of language description. In L. Unsworth (ed.), *Researching language in schools and communities*. London: Cassell, pp. 111–129.

Williams, G. (2004) Ontogenesis and grammatics: Functions of metalanguage in pedagogical discourse. In G. Williams and A. Lukin (eds), pp. 241–267.

Williams, G. (2005a) Grammatics in school. In R. Hasan, C. M. I. M. Matthiessen and J. Webster, (eds), pp. 281–310.

Williams, G. (2005b) Language, brain, culture. *Linguistics and the Human Sciences*, 1 (3), pp. 147–150.

Williams, G. (2005c) Semantic variation. In R. Hasan, C. M. I. M. Matthiessen and J. Webster (eds), pp. 457–480.

Williams, G. and Lukin, A. (eds) (2004) *Language development: Functional perspectives on evolution and ontogenesis*. London: Continuum.

Winograd, T. (1972) *Understanding language*. Edinburgh: Edinburgh University Press.

Winograd, T. (1983) *Language as a cognitive process: Syntax*. Reading: Addison Wesley.

Woods, W. (1975) What's in a link: Foundations for semantic networks. In D. Bobrow and A. Collins (eds), *Representation and understanding: Studies in cognitive science*. New York: Academic Press, pp. 35–82.

Wu, C. (2000) *Modelling linguistic resources*. Ph.D. thesis, Macquarie University.

Wu, C. (2009) Corpus-based research. In M. A. K. Halliday and J. Webster (eds), pp. 128–142.

Wu, C., Matthiessen, C. M. I. M. and Herke, M. (eds) (2008) *Proceedings of the 35th International Systemic Functional Linguistics Congress: Voices around the World*, Macquarie University, Sydney, 19–25 July 2008.

Xiaoqing, O. (1986) *Clause complex in Chinese*. MA thesis, University of Sydney.

Xu, J., Gannon, P. J., Emmorey, K., Smith, J. F. and Braun, A. R. (2009) Symbolic gestures and spoken language are processed by a common neural system. *PNAS* (December 8, 2009) 106 (49): 20664–20669.

Young, L. (1990) *Language as behaviour, language as code*. Amsterdam: Benjamins.

Young, L. (2001) Second language acquisition: Learning how to mean. In J. de Villiers and R. Stainton (eds), *Communication linguistics Volume 1: Papers in Honour of Michael Gregory*. Toronto: Editions Du Gref, pp. 379–395.

Young, L. and Harrison, C. (eds) (2004) *Systemic functional linguistics and critical discourse analysis: Studies in social change*. London and New York: Continuum.

Zadeh, L. (1987) *Fuzzy sets and applications: Selected papers by L. A. Zadeh*. Edited by R. R. Yager, S. Ovchinnikov, R. M. Tong and H. T. Nguyen. New York: Wiley.

Zeng, L. (1996) *Planning text in an integrated multilingual meaning space*. Ph.D. thesis, Sydney University.

Zhang D., McDonald, E., Fang, Y. and Huang, G. (2005) The development of systemic functional linguistics in China. In Hasan, R., Matthiessen, C. M. I. M. and Webster, J. J. (eds) *Continuing discourse on language: A functional perspective*, Volume 1. London: Equinox Publishing, pp. 15–36.

Zhi'an, C. and Kuang L. (2002) Theme in English and Chinese. MA Honours thesis, Department of Linguistics, Sydney University.

Zhu, Y. (1985) *Modality and modulation in English and Chinese*. MA Honours thesis, Sydney University.

Zhu, Y. (1996) Modality and modulation in Chinese. In M. Berry, C. Butler, R. P. Fawcett and G. Huang (eds), pp. 183–209.

Zouba, M. L. (2003) *Generic structure of Bissa tales: A study of placement*. Mémoire de maîtrise. Université de Ouagadougou.

Index